Convention Center Follies

AMERICAN BUSINESS, POLITICS, AND SOCIETY

Series editors: Andrew Wender Cohen, Pamela Walker Laird, Mark H. Rose, and Elizabeth Tandy Shermer

Books in the series American Business, Politics, and Society explore the relationships over time between governmental institutions and the creation and performance of markets, firms, and industries large and small. The central theme of this series is that politics, law, and public policy—understood broadly to embrace not only lawmaking but also the structuring presence of governmental institutions—has been fundamental to the evolution of American business from the colonial era to the present. The series aims to explore, in particular, developments that have enduring consequences.

A complete list of books in the series is available from the publisher.

Convention Center Follies

Politics, Power, and Public Investment in American Cities

Heywood T. Sanders

PENN

UNIVERSITY OF PENNSYLVANIA PRESS

PHILADELPHIA

Published by
University of Pennsylvania Press
Philadelphia, Pennsylvania 19104-4112
www.upenn.edu/pennpress

Printed in the United States of America on acid-free paper
10 9 8 7 6 5 4 3 2 1

Library of Congress Cataloging-in-Publication Data
Sanders, Heywood T.
Convention center follies : politics, power, and public investment in American cities / Heywood T. Sanders — 1st ed.
p. cm. (American business, politics, and society)
Includes bibliographical references and index
ISBN 978-0-8122-4577-6 (hardcover : alk. paper)
1. City promotion—Economic aspects—United States. 2. Convention facilities—Economic aspects—United States. 3. Convention facilities—Economic aspects—United States—Case studies. 4. Congresses and conventions—Economic aspects—United States. 5. Congresses and conventions—Economic aspects—United States—Case studies. I. Title. II. Series: American business, politics, and society
HT325 .S26 2014
659.2'930776 2013036503

For
Hilary and David

and for
George Wendel,
a model teacher and scholar

Contents

Preface

City governments are usually viewed as providers of basic services: police and fire protection, public works, parks and recreation, and libraries. Yet cities and a broad array of other local governments are also providers of public capital. They have long built major public buildings such as city halls, courthouses, and libraries, and in some places public auditoriums and theaters. In the 1950s and 1960s, a number of communities began the development of new convention halls—New York City's Coliseum, Cleveland's Convention Center, Atlanta's Civic Center, Baltimore's Civic Center—as part of schemes for urban renewal or downtown revitalization.

Those early convention venues were succeeded and replaced by newer, larger, and presumably more competitive centers within a decade or two. New York City's Coliseum was replaced by the new Jacob K. Javits Convention Center in 1986; Atlanta's Civic Center, opened in 1967, was superseded by the new Georgia World Congress Center in 1976. The new Baltimore Convention Center was opened in summer 1979.

During the 1980s and 1990s, the public investment in new and expanded convention centers boomed, as other cities sought to compete with New York, Chicago, and Atlanta. And that boom continues, with state and local governments spending over $13 billion on center building between 2002 and 2011. The building boom has been driven in large part by a revolution in center finance, and by a new kind of public role and promise. Expansive new convention centers increasingly became the product of state governments or special purpose public authorities, neatly avoiding the political and fiscal limits on city governments.

At the same time, a massive convention facility was no longer simply a means of accommodating an occasional national political gathering or a symbol of local pride. It was touted as a key element in local "economic development," one premised on the assumption, regularly validated by "expert" consultants, that a new or larger convention center would yield a wave of new out-of-town visitors. Those visitors, bringing "new money" to the city, would in turn spur new private development, and ultimately thousands—often tens of thousands—of new jobs. With that money, development, and jobs would come a proportional wave of new public tax revenues, revenues sufficient to provide a substantial "return" on the public investment in convention center development.

In many ways, the contemporary convention center development story is one of the unbridled successes of local government: success in overcoming political obstacles and often public opposition, success in mobilizing public revenues and dollars, success in building expansive new facilities, success in ultimately securing the ability to compete against other cities for lucrative convention business. But while communities have proven remarkably capable of building new and larger centers, they have proven remarkably unsuccessful in filling them. From Atlanta to Seattle, Boston to Las Vegas, the promises of local officials and the forecasts of consultants have come up short. State and local governments have built modern new centers, only to see half or less of the convention attendees promised by the consultants. Other cities have expanded their existing centers, yet failed to see any consistent increase in business. Indeed, there is substantial evidence that the supply of convention center space substantially exceeds demand (a "buyer's market"), with cities desperately competing by offering their center space rent free.

Why have cities and other state and local governments invested billions in convention center building when the actual results, in terms of new convention attendees, visitors, and economic impact, are quite limited or nonexistent? Why do local officials from Anaheim to Washington make convention centers, and tourism generally, such a signal public priority even as they cut back on public services and essential public facilities?

For some observers, such as economist Edward Glaeser, these investments amount to a misplaced set of public priorities on the part of elected officials, an "edifice error" exemplified by Detroit's spending on an arena and a downtown People Mover. Glaeser argues, "Too many officials in troubled cities wrongly imagine that they can lead their city back to its former glories with some massive construction project—a new stadium or light rail system, a convention center or a housing project." Correct as Glaeser's observation is, it emphasizes the question of why convention centers and stadiums, a Rock and Roll Hall of Fame, or a new aquarium routinely rise to preeminence as local policy priorities. Some observers have stressed the local interests that directly benefit from public building—architects, consulting engineers, contractors, and construction labor unions—as well as the gain for politicians who "get to cut ribbons." Others have pointed to the combination of local hospitality and tourism interests—hotels and restaurants, the convention and visitors bureau—with local policy entrepreneurs and larger national tourism interests and promoters.

The analysis that follows seeks to answer the *why* question, first by reviewing the metropolitan "arms race" that has propelled the massive expansion in convention center space around the country over the last two decades, and second by examining the genesis of this contemporary arms race through the historical experience of convention center development in three key locations: Chicago, Atlanta, and St. Louis. Unlike academic research that has focused on the visible, public side of large-scale public investment—the mayoral announcements, the newspaper headlines, the formal consultant reports—this work is focused on the interests and intent of local business and civic leaders. Those business leaders—the heads of major local banks and financial institutions, utilities, department stores, and local developers—have long played crucial roles in setting local capital investment and development priorities and in promoting convention center development. For them, the import of convention center development—and often public stadium and sports facility building—lies in the ability of public investment to shape land use and development opportunities.

These business leaders have been motivated not by promised "economic impact" but instead by concern with downtown property values, "protection from erosion," and the place of "anchors." Facing a combination of exploding suburban development and stagnant downtown cores in the 1950s, they sought—in the words of Chicago Title and Trust's Holman Pettibone—dramatic public projects that would serve the "obvious need to bolster the downtown business district." Moreover, the planners who worked for these business leaders recommended convention center development on sites that would remove "blighted conditions… detrimental to commercial development possibilities" in the downtown core, serve the necessity to "anchor the Loop securely," and provide a "healthy fringe to Downtown." The larger imperative for convention center development was thus one of land use and property value, fully focused on the downtown center.

The land use and property value focus of business leaders was not limited to just a convention center, or to one particular zone of downtown. A stadium or arena, a university campus or research center might well serve much the same goal of "anchoring" or "protecting." Indeed, the imperative to serve different downtown business and property interests, interests often divided into "factions" or "sections," divisions that demonstrated an "unhealthy rivalry," necessarily demanded multiple public development projects. Those projects, spread across "factions" and "sections," also served a broader collective purpose.

Yet even as local business leaders sought to "bolster" and "anchor" all of downtown with public projects, they faced increasingly uncooperative local electorates. Atlanta voters expressed strong reluctance to a convention center scheme in 1962, although they did approve a less costly project the following year. But by the end of the 1960s, business leaders across the country faced angry voters, as well as the related problem of "white flight." St. Louis saw a 31.7 percent decrease in its white population from 1960 to 1970. For Atlanta, it was a 20 percent drop. That population loss both reduced the market for downtown retail, and also marked the departure of the middle-income population that had long supported major public investment bond issues.

The imperative to boost downtown development and create a sense of "momentum" did not evaporate for big-city business leaders during the 1960s and 1970s. Rather, it led them to focus on new fiscal schemes that could build grand convention centers, stadiums, and arenas independent of city fiscal resources or the preferences of city voters. In this period, Atlanta, Baltimore, St. Louis, Kansas City, Philadelphia, Boston, and Seattle all turned to their state governments as a source of public investment and finance. Even as downtown department stores like Atlanta's Rich's, St. Louis's Scruggs Vandervoort and Barney, and Baltimore's Hochschild Kohn closed their doors, the business leaders in these cities pressed for new public development projects that could serve as "anchors" and "sparks" for new private investment.

In 1954, Holman Pettibone could tell Chicago's mayor and his business colleagues of the imperative for a major public project—the "obvious need to bolster the downtown business district." Almost 50 years later, his counterpart in St. Louis, Bank of America's David Darnell, would tell his colleagues that in order to "make the St. Louis region world class," it "requires that the downtown area thrives." That common quest to bolster the downtown business district, to assure that downtown thrives even as the larger city has declined or suffered, has been the central driver of convention center development in big American cities. And so even as centers fail to produce, as promised jobs, economic development, and private investment fail to appear, the calls from mayors and governors, from bankers and corporate CEOs for more public spending—and a new set of plans and consultant studies—come once again.

PART I

The Race to Build

Chapter 1

Building Boom

In 1982, Chicago's McCormick Place stood at the apex of the nation's convention centers. With 825,000 square feet of exhibit space in the main facility and another 330,000 square feet in nearby Donnelly Hall, it easily surpassed the convention halls of other cities. It routinely hosted the largest collection of major conventions and tradeshows each year, with 24 of the nation's 150 largest events in 1982 and 27 in 1983, "dominating over two-thirds of the 15 largest events."[1] The list included such blockbuster events as the International Machine Tool Show with 97,000 attendees in 1983, the National Restaurant Association Show (87,000), the National Hardware Show (84,000), and the summer Consumer Electronics Show (72,000).

But Chicago's record of tradeshow success did little to dampen the competition from other cities, and the early 1980s saw a growing list of large, new convention facilities. Las Vegas was adding a major expansion to its convention center, bringing its exhibit hall space to 759,000 square feet—not much smaller than the lakefront building of McCormick Place. New York City was in the process of constructing what would be the Jacob Javits Convention Center, with 700,000 prime square feet of exhibit space, and some 200,000 additional square feet of flexible event space. Then there were new, albeit smaller centers under construction in such historically strong visitor destinations as San Francisco, New Orleans, and Washington, D.C.

The success of McCormick Place in hosting the largest national events also came at a price. The dominance of these large events on McCormick's calendar led to a "feast or famine" impact on Chicago's hotel and restaurant business, with a surge of demand from a major show followed by a downswing, as exhibits for one event were moved out and another show moved in. The public authority owner of McCormick, the Metropolitan Fair and

Exposition Authority, sought both to accommodate growing major trade show events, and also to fill its schedule with the "mid-range exhibition market segment" that would reduce the feast or famine cycle. The authority's consultants thus recommended a new, adjacent exhibit hall with more than 600,000 square feet of exhibit space.[2]

The promise was that the new North Building would boost the annual convention and tradeshow attendance at McCormick Place from one million in 1983 to 1.5 million, with a $275 million annual increase in new visitor spending. But even with the completion of "North" in 1986, the authority was far from finished. In 1989, the reconstituted Metropolitan Pier and Exposition Authority (renamed after adding Chicago's Navy Pier to its responsibilities) proposed yet another expansion.

The "Long Range Marketing Study" consultant KPMG Peat Marwick (led by Charles H. Johnson) presented to the authority in 1990 was far bulkier than its 1982 predecessor, but it very much paralleled the assessment of the earlier analysis. Johnson and his KPMG colleagues described Chicago's "pre-eminent status in the tradeshow market," having attracted "the largest events held in the United States, resulting in extraordinary margins in attendance over its nearest competitors." But if Chicago was to remain dominant, it needed to be "aggressive." And the key element in an "aggressive" approach was "adding new exhibit space, adding meeting space, offering an enhanced environment. . . . and improving service and marketing support in order to compete more effectively."[3]

The KPMG consultants portrayed a national convention and tradeshow industry with demand for exhibit space "growing at a rate of eight percent per year," driven by "individual event growth was well as more new events." Convention attendance was consistently growing as well, averaging 6.47 percent a year from 1971 to 1988. And, KPMG predicted, "Future growth is expected to continue," supporting the need for more space at McCormick Place.[4]

The Long Range Marketing Study called for yet another major expansion, adding another one million square feet of exhibit space, more meeting rooms, and an adjacent domed stadium (then proposed for the Chicago Bears) as well. The new exhibit hall, exclusive of the stadium scheme, was forecast to solidify McCormick Place's position in hosting major tradeshow events, while increasing its appeal for "large and mid-sized conventions" that would help alleviate the fluctuations in hotel demand generated by major shows. With more space and a better planned "campus," the new McCormick Place was forecast to add some 18 annual conventions and tradeshows, boosting attendance by a total of 320,000.[5]

The Metropolitan Pier and Exposition Authority embarked on a $987 million expansion effort in 1992, completing the new South Building, with 840,000 square feet of exhibit space and a larger volume of meeting rooms than the other exhibit halls, and a companion effort to renovate the original McCormick East facility, all aimed at attracting "the medium and large convention segment of the meetings market. . . . [and] to meet the expanded need for meeting space by the trade show segment." If all went as promised, the new building would yield a steady flow of new convention delegates, yielding a 30 percent increase in the center's annual economic impact, or more than $1.1 billion.[6]

The new South Building opened in 1996. But as South added more space, the MPEA was planning on yet another major investment to boost McCormick's appeal to mid-sized events. The authority had acquired and demolished the one hotel adjacent to the McCormick Place complex in 1993, and unsuccessfully sought a private developer for a new "headquarters hotel." With its commitment to attracting medium-sized conventions, MPEA officials asserted there was a critical need for adjacent hotel rooms; in early 1996, the authority issued some $133 million in bonds for a hotel that it would finance and own. The new 800-room "Hyatt McCormick Place" opened in June 1998, with the promise from consultants Coopers & Lybrand that it would support luring three new major "Tradeshow 200" events each year (for a total of 26) and nine additional conventions and tradeshows, boosting attendance and hotel demand.[7]

The new Hyatt hotel was soon joined by another set of bond-funded projects designed to increase the competitive appeal of McCormick Place. At a cost of $100 million, the MPEA added a new six-level parking garage and a conference center to the complex, and constructed a dedicated busway from the downtown core to McCormick Place, all designed to make the center more competitive.

The Hyatt had barely opened when the MPEA leadership and Chicago city officials began another call for expansion and more exhibit hall space. A March 1999 *Chicago Tribune* article quoted MPEA CEO Scott Fawell as saying, "Some of the bigger shows that come to Chicago would like more space," and "For the future, you've got to [ask], 'Do you want to stay in the forefront of the industry?'" Mayor Richard M. Daley chimed in, "You have to look ahead." The assessment that McCormick Place should be expanded again was buttressed by a report from the PriceWaterhouseCoopers consulting firm that concluded that the convention complex would lose market share and cost the state millions in economic impact if it failed to grow.[8]

With the political backing of Mayor Daley and Illinois governor George Ryan, the state legislature ultimately approved the construction of "McCormick West" in July 2001. The authority sold the $1.1 billion bond issue that financed the addition of 460,000 square feet of exhibit hall space in June 2002.

The development of the new West Building maintained Chicago's preeminent position in convention center space. It also provided a set of lucrative contracts that Authority CEO Scott Fawell managed to manipulate. Fawell, Ryan's former chief of staff, ultimately pleaded guilty to federal charges of bid rigging in connection with the McCormick expansion, in a wide-ranging corruption investigation that ultimately convicted former governor Ryan. Expanding McCormick Place could obviously generate construction contracts that were open to political manipulation. But what was not obvious was the real economic payoff from the investment of over $2.3 million in public revenues in the continuing expansions of McCormick Place and associated facilities like the publicly financed Hyatt.[9]

In 1983, McCormick Place had hosted 27 of the convention and tradeshow industry's "150" largest events, with a total attendance of just under 645,500. The center dominated the largest events, with eight of the top fifteen. Its total convention and tradeshow attendance that year came to one million. And consultant estimates had pegged the impact of expansion—the construction of the new North Building—as yielding a 50 percent increase in business, a total annual attendance of 1.5 million. But in 1995, after the North expansion and before the opening of McCormick South, total attendance came to just 1,015,456—not much more than a decade earlier. The Chicago center's apparent dominance of the largest conventions and tradeshows also appeared less secure, with just 24 of the top "Tradeshow 200" largest events in 1995.

The development of McCormick South was also supposed to yield increases in attendance and economic impact, with an added boost from the construction of the publicly financed Hyatt. But where Coopers & Lybrand had forecast 26 of the very large events by 2000, that year's total came to just 21. It was much the same with total convention and tradeshow attendance. The expanded McCormick Place hit a peak attendance of 1.44 million in 2000. But in the wake of 9-11 and the tech bust of 2000, attendance dropped to 812,337 (with a possible additional 84,000 from meetings). And the 2007 opening of the new West Building did not have a very substantial immediate impact. Total convention and tradeshow attendance for 2008 came to 960,183. The next year, 2009, saw just 893,068 attendees. The attendance total then fell to 850,329 for 2010, and dropped farther in 2011 to just 768,685—less than half the convention and tradeshow attendance McCormick saw in 2003.

McCormick Place has also seen a continuing decline in the number and total attendance of the largest conventions and tradeshows each year, the "Tradeshow 200" events. For 2007, McCormick Place housed just 17 of the "200." It managed 18 of these big events in 2008, with attendance of 672,591—just slightly more than the large-event attendance total of 645,485 twenty five years earlier in 1983. And where McCormick Place had once captured the majority of the 15 largest events, by 2008 it managed only two, ceding its leading position to Las Vegas.

The declining attendance at McCormick Place has come in part because of the growing competition from other cities. Both Orlando and Las Vegas are now not far behind McCormick in convention center exhibit space, and a host of other cities have competed by adding more space. But Chicago also faces a dramatically different convention and tradeshow industry. Following a split between the hardware manufacturers association and show management firm Reed Exhibitions, the National Hardware Show left Chicago for Las Vegas. Another McCormick mainstay, the summer Consumer Electronics Show that brought 72,000 attendees to Chicago in 1983, folded after 1994.

Other large McCormick Place-based tradeshows have also seen substantial changes in performance. Take the case of one Chicago perennial event, the National Restaurant Association Show. That event was the second largest in attendance for McCormick Place in 1983, with 87,000 attendees. It reached a peak attendance of just under 104,000 in 1997. Since then, the Restaurant Show's attendee count has fallen to 73,664 in 2007, 71,367 in 2008, 53,319 in 2009, 57,892 in 2010, and 57,782 in 2011. Despite some recovery from the trough of the recession, attendance has remained well below the totals in 2007 and 2008.

The major tradeshow for the food machinery and packaging industry, Pack Expo, has long been among the top four or five events at McCormick in terms of exhibit space. The biennial Pack Expo (alternate years are held in Las Vegas) drew attendance of 78,321 and used 1.15 million square feet of space in 1998, its peak year during the 1990s. The show's exhibit space use has been rather flat, just 1.12 million square feet in 2012. But its attendance fell to 67,964 in 2008, a significant drop from the peak a decade earlier, and to 67,641 in 2012.

Major conventions and tradeshows like the Restaurant Show and Pack Expo have commonly grown in size as McCormick Place has added more exhibit space. But more space has not translated into more attendees, and thus greater economic impact. Their history since the late 1990s suggests a gradual but dramatic change in the "draw" and perceived value of these events, a change that has directly affected the attendance at McCormick and its economic results.

Over and over, Chicago and Illinois public officials and a roster of consultants promised that a bigger McCormick Place would yield hundreds of thousands of new convention attendees and billions in new spending and public revenues. Those repeated promises have proved to be false, the consultant projections unmet. McCormick Place and Chicago officials have tried desperate measures to respond to the brutal competition in the convention market. In August 2009, the state announced creation of a $10 million incentive fund to provide rebates to conventions and tradeshows using McCormick. But by the end of the year a number of major shows, including the International Plastics Expo, announced plans to leave Chicago for other cities, including Las Vegas and Orlando.

Faced with the loss of these major events and pressure from other event organizers, the state legislature restructured the board of the Metropolitan Pier and Exposition Authority and began hearings into McCormick's operations and finances. The result in early 2010 was a revamping of labor relations intended to reduce the cost of union labor in setting up and servicing exhibits and a massive $1.12 billion restructuring of the authority's debt, together with plans to expand the publicly financed Hyatt hotel with an added 450 rooms.[10]

The performance of the nation's largest convention center is by no means unique. The rhetoric of convention center boosters in city after city has not been matched by actual performance, and center managers and local tourism officials have ratcheted up incentive packages, free rent deals, and plans for even more space or adjacent hotel rooms.

For Atlanta and Phoenix, Boston and Philadelphia, just as for Chicago, the quest for a new or larger convention center follows a seemingly standard pattern. A local group, perhaps the city's convention and visitors bureau or the local chamber of commerce, would proclaim that the community was falling behind its competitors, the size of its convention center slipping as other cities built and expanded. There would be news stories about "lost business" and descriptions of the groups and events that could no longer come because they had outgrown the center. And, predictably, there would be a study commissioned from an experienced, "independent" consultant.

The consultant study, filled with data and charts, would describe how other cities were building new centers, presumably demonstrating the need to compete with something bigger and more up-to-date. There would be summary figures of "lost business," results from surveys of meeting planners demonstrating the attractiveness and appeal of the city, and a detailed presentation of national data indicating the consistent growth in convention and tradeshow demand and the reassuring forecast that growth would continue apace.

Armed with the consultant's estimate of future convention business and the forecast that the "economic impact" of new spending by convention attendees would grow by 50 percent, 100 percent, or more, local officials would describe the public investment in a larger convention center as the catalyst for an economic boom. More convention delegates would lead to the development of new hotels, new restaurants and retail stores, likely revitalization of part or all of the downtown core, and a new image for the city itself.

In January 2011, New York governor Andrew Cuomo proposed a development to include "the largest convention center in the nation," saying, "This will bring to New York the largest events, driving demand for hotel rooms and restaurant meals and creating tax revenues and jobs, jobs, jobs." A few months earlier, Tim Leiweke of the AEG entertainment and development firm proposed a new privately built enclosed stadium as part of the Los Angeles Convention Center, contending that "L.A. would be the greatest destination for events in the world," and that the city "could become the second or third" most sought-after convention city in the country.[11]

The promises and rhetoric have been remarkably consistent. At the same time New York, Los Angeles, San Diego, and Boston were contemplating major new centers or expansions, Cleveland and Cuyahoga County were building a $465 million Medical Mart and Convention Center, with the promise that it would attract 60 annual medical conventions bringing "300,000 visitors and $330 million in spending" after its 2013 opening. Nashville was building a $585 million convention center, slated to open in April 2013. The HVS consulting firm had forecast in early 2010 that the new Nashville venue would more than double the annual convention center hotel room nights produced in Nashville. And both Indianapolis and Philadelphia had opened major convention center expansions in 2011, each armed with consultant forecasts that they would see a sizable boost in convention attendance and resulting hotel demand.[12]

It would appear highly unlikely—indeed implausible—that each of these cities would see its convention attendance effectively double. With overall national convention and tradeshow attendance still depressed as a result of the "Great Recession" and economic restructuring, New York, Boston, Los Angeles, San Diego, Cleveland—and others like Miami Beach, Dallas, and San Francisco—would be able to increase attendance only by attracting events and people away from their competitors. And those competing cities would be unlikely to stand still and simply accept losing convention business. Communities such as Las Vegas and Orlando, Anaheim and Washington, supported by regular streams of public revenues fueled by visitors, would themselves respond by investing in more convention space and hotel rooms.

After the public promises of new spending, economic impact, job creation, and development often comes a reality that is rather different. City after city builds a big new center, only to realize little or no new convention activity and see no real job creation. The big new hotel that was *supposed* to be a direct product of the public investment in a convention center simply doesn't appear. The promised economic impact is often missing or minimal. Yet that apparent failure—the center that sees half or a third of the attendance projected by a consultant, the convention venue that is obliged to give away its space, the tradeshow mecca that largely attracts local or drive-in attendees—invariably yields a call for more space, an adjacent hotel, or a new "entertainment district" that will propel the city into the front rank of convention destinations.

The "arms race" that has propelled this massive expansion in convention center space over the last two decades has been fueled by a dramatic change in convention center financing. During the 1950s, 1960s, and into the 1970s, new convention center proposals generally had to run the gauntlet of voter review and approval. But by the 1980s state and local governments were able to adopt new financing and development mechanisms that effectively insulated center plans from local voters. The shift to public authorities or state governments from general purpose local governments, and from general taxes to dedicated visitor-based revenues, also put the choice to invest in a massive convention facility in the hands of business interests usually focused on sustaining and boosting property values and development prospects in the downtown core. The result has been to privilege convention center spending over other, alternative public investments.

At the same period as convention center finance was being reshaped and eased, the arguments and rationale for convention facilities as major sources of economic development and job creation were gaining wider visibility. The same consultant who assured Chicago and Illinois officials of the benefits from a larger McCormick Place, Charles H. Johnson, had provided much the same advice earlier to St. Louis. He would go on to offer a justification and set of forecasts for new convention centers in Charlotte, and Richmond, a bigger one in Austin, and one in Boston. The same consulting firm that advised the Georgia World Congress Center Authority on expansion in the mid-1990s would provide remarkably parallel advice and economic impact forecasts to Cincinnati, Cleveland, Indianapolis, and New York City. The consistent finding was that more space would bring more business, and more jobs.

Much as consultant forecasts of demand and center performance have proven faulty, the basic assumptions about convention and tradeshow attendees, their visitation and spending patterns, have proved unrealistic. Consultants and convention center backers have routinely assumed that convention attendees stay in a city some 3.5 days, with attendees assumed to come from out of town. Yet convention and tradeshow events often draw a substantial volume of local attendees, or those who simply visit for the day. In 2009, more than half the convention and tradeshow attendance at New York's Javits Center (excluding events like the New York Auto Show or similar public shows) was made up of "day-trippers" or other local attendees. Or take the case of one of the largest annual events at Orlando's Orange County Convention Center, the PGA Merchandise Show for the golfing industry. For the 2008 edition, 31 percent of the attendees came from Florida—many of whom likely just attended for the day. And one measure of that phenomenon is the volume of hotel room nights used by PGA show attendees. The 43,000 estimated attendees actually booked only 29,178 room nights—rather less than three, or even two, room nights per attendee. With more day-trippers and fewer out-of-town attendees, the economic impact produced by centers like these, and others, is actually far more modest than backers claim.[13]

Even as convention center building has boomed in American cities, these centers have proved remarkably unproductive as public investments, failing to provide the benefits that justify their construction. Yet even in the face of failure—a new center in Boston generating less than half the hotel room nights promised by consultants, an expanded center in downtown Atlanta yielding fewer convention attendees in fiscal year 2010 than it saw in 1989—local officials and consultants continue to argue for more space and more building. Why are center consultants not held to account for their forecast errors? How is it that these failed public projects are followed not by expressions of outrage and apology, but by calls for even more? Why is it that governors and mayors, business and civic leaders, have promoted, built, and continue to call for more convention center spending, in the face of nonperformance and an evident glut?

Though the phenomenon of the boom in convention center development has been widely recognized, there is no agreement among scholars on its roots and causes, on the interests of the elected officials who sustain it, or the interests of the business and civic leaders behind it. For some academic observers, it represents an unalloyed positive in enhancing the local economy. For others, it is a necessary adaptation to central city decline or the product of political pressures from narrow interests such as hotel owners and developers. Still others point to the existence of business-dominated coalitions or regimes or "growth machines." Yet all point to the role of *local business interests and the organized business community* as central to the initiation and promotion of these projects.[14]

If these academic analyses all point to some—perhaps the most central—role of local business in promoting and supporting convention centers and related public projects, the central *paradox* of center development remains. Why would business interests—narrowly focused ones such as hotels and restaurants, or broader ones such as department store chains, local utilities, and locally headquartered corporations—embrace public projects that appear to have such a modest and uncertain economic return? And why, when these convention centers produce far less activity than had been forecast and assumed, do supporters invariably call for more space, or a new publicly financed hotel or entertainment district next door? The answers to these questions, and to the fundamental interests and expectations that drive convention center investment, require a focus on local business and business interests, the apparently essential element in pressing and realizing the major public investment in convention centers.

For business leaders like "Cubby" Baer and Leif Sverdrup in St. Louis, the public investment in a new convention center offered the opportunity to remedy "property decay" and provide an "effective barrier against further deterioration." For Atlanta's business leaders, a convention venue on an urban renewal site could yield "protection of the Uptown area." And in these cities and others, a major public investment project would provide development "momentum," evidence of the public commitment to the downtown core, and a means to be "a big-league city."

In this context, the dual imperatives of land value reshaping and momentum creation have led many cities to replace one modern convention center with another as the frontier for development and investment opportunity shifted. Thus Washington, D.C., replaced one convention center opened at Mount Vernon Square in 1983 with a far larger one to the north in the Shaw neighborhood, completed in 2003. New Orleans replaced its 1968 Rivergate with the Morial Convention Center in 1985, then expanded the Morial in 1991 and again in 1999. Houston replaced the Albert Thomas Convention Center, opened in 1967, with the new George R. Brown Convention Center on the opposite side of downtown in 1987. Boston opened its second publicly owned center, the Boston Convention and Exhibition Center, in 2003, in an underdeveloped zone of south Boston. And New York City first replaced the 1950s-era Coliseum with the Javits Convention Center in 1986, only to see Governor Andrew Cuomo call for a new convention center at a casino in Queens in early 2012, proposing that the Javits Center be demolished and its site sold for new private development. Pressed by business leaders seeking to sustain downtown property values or boost the development fortunes of an old warehouse district or railroad yard, state and local officials have embraced one scheme after another for new or expanded convention centers.

Building Boom

The last two decades have seen a remarkable boom in convention center building across American cities. From 36.4 million square feet of exhibit hall space in 1989, the total center exhibit space reached 70.5 million square feet in 2011—an increase of 94 percent. In one sense, that building boom represents a triumph over the host of political, fiscal, and economic constraints and conflicts that routinely face state and local governments. Faced with public resistance to increased taxes, center promoters could, and did, invent alternative financing schemes. City governments often successfully shifted much of the cost of convention center development to state governments or independent authorities.

In another sense, the boom also provides ample evidence of the "me too" character of local public investment decisions. Chicago expanded to keep up with Las Vegas, Atlanta expanded to stay competitive with Chicago and New Orleans, and Boston, Philadelphia, Washington, and New York each competed to win a larger share of the convention business in the Northeast by building more space. Each and every city that successfully developed a new or expanded center appeared to believe that it was uniquely suited to win that competition and see a steady stream of new visitors. And those expectations were given a very specific and seemingly scientific justification and forecast produced by one or more of a very small group of industry consultants.

For Phoenix, convention center development efforts in the 1990s and 2000s were simply one part of a longer and continuing stream of public initiatives and investments designed to redevelop and restore the city's downtown. That effort was built on an alliance of the city's business and development interests with a succession of local officials.

Phoenix's "modern" convention facility, Civic Plaza, opened in 1972, combined exhibit hall space with a symphony hall. The facility was neatly located on the eastern edge of the downtown core, where its construction served to demolish much of "The Deuce"—the city's skid row. And despite one observation that "Civic Plaza failed miserably as a vehicle of public architecture and downtown redevelopment," the city added a host of major public projects on adjacent blocks. The new America West arena was built three blocks south in 1992, and the county-financed Bank One Ballpark (now Chase Field) opened nearby in 1988.[15]

Even with an expansion and renovation in 1985, Civic Plaza never really performed as a competitive convention venue. Local business leaders attributed that failure to the lack of a third major downtown hotel, and in 1992 the Phoenix Community Alliance, the business organization "dedicated solely to the revitalization of Central Phoenix," produced a report terming Civic Plaza "greatly underutilized" and pressing the "urgent need" for a third hotel downtown. Yet even with business backing and the promise of subsidies, no private developer appeared willing to construct a major hotel downtown. Finally, in July 1996, the city issued a formal request for developer proposals for a major downtown hotel. But even with the promise of a substantial city government subsidy, the preferred developer was unable to put together the deal, and by fall 1997 there was little prospect of the long-sought hotel.[16]

By 1998, city government leaders began shifting their focus to a major expansion of Civic Plaza, with a formal request by the city's economic development staff for a consultant study of market demand and "how to optimize the use of Civic Plaza." The justification for the study stressed the existing $112 million in annual economic impact from convention attendees. But it made particular note of the threat from competing cities expanding their own centers and building 1,000-room convention-oriented hotels. It argued that "Our competitors in Denver, Dallas, San Antonio, and San Diego all have larger facilities and are supported by a larger hotel room inventory."[17]

PriceWaterhouseCoopers delivered its Civic Plaza market study in late 1999. The consultants praised the Phoenix venue for its central location and access to the airport. But they also identified a problem with the lack of nearby hotel rooms and the age of Civic Plaza. They recommended an ambitious expansion program, including the addition of 251,000 square feet of exhibit hall space, bringing the center to a total of 500,000 square feet, as well as at least 1,050 new hotel rooms. The PWC report included a very specific forecast of how a larger Civic Plaza would perform with the added hotel rooms. It put the existing convention and tradeshow attendance for Civic Plaza at 200,000. Without an expansion, the projected annual attendance would fall to 162,500. The expansion would instead boost attendance to 325,000. Annual attendee spending would almost double, from the "existing" $282 million to $526 million, boosting city and state tax revenues and creating over 7,000 new jobs.[18]

The PWC findings and forecasts were perhaps not surprising. The firm had produced similar conclusions and predictions for Boston a couple of years earlier, as well as for San Diego. It had recommended a major expansion for Cincinnati in a series of studies. And it had supported a substantial expansion of Atlanta's Georgia World Congress Center in 1993 and 1996 analyses. It would endorse a new convention center in Cleveland in reports in 2001 and 2006.

Yet for Phoenix, the seemingly "expert" and assured conclusions seemed to provide substantial justification for a major public investment. For the director of Civic Plaza, the success of a major expansion was all but certain: "This is a serious growth industry. If you want to be in this game, you need to have the product." The real hurdle was financing a project with an estimated price tag in excess of $500 million. Mayor Skip Rimsza and the senior city staff chose a two-pronged strategy. First, the city itself would finance some $250 million, using existing hotel and restaurant taxes. While that would, under the provisions of the city charter, require a public vote for approval, the electorate could be assured that there would be no tax increase of any sort needed to pay for the expansion.[19]

The second element of the city's financing plan was a significant contribution from state government. During 2001, the city staff and consultants pitched the fiscal rewards of a Civic Plaza expansion to an ad hoc committee of the state legislature. Assistant city manager Sheryl Sculley and David Radcliffe of the Greater Phoenix Convention and Visitors Bureau stressed to the legislators how the city had fallen behind its competitors, and was regularly "losing business" because Civic Plaza was too small or other cities were offering new convention venues. At one committee meeting, a consultant from PriceWaterhouseCoopers stressed the competition with other cities: "if Arizona does nothing, there will be a loss, while other cities are still expanding their convention facilities." When questioned about the impact of the recent 9-11 events on the potential performance and benefits to the state, the consultant observed that "it is not possible to accurately predict the future, and that business travel seems to be stronger than leisure travel at the present time."[20]

The city's part of the financing scheme was resolved first. With seemingly unanimous backing from the business community (including the Phoenix Community Alliance and Downtown Partnership, which had both effectively initiated the project), the promise of no tax impact, and the PWC forecasts of a substantial increase in visitor spending, tax revenues, and jobs, Phoenix voters overwhelmingly approved the expansion project in November 2001. For the expansion backers, it was time to formalize the project design, develop detailed cost figures, and begin to sell the project to the state legislature.

In 2002 the city began an effort to win legislative support. As the city staff and area business interests sought to sell the expansion project to the state, they had both a new proposal and an added sales pitch. With a revised construction plan, the expansion had grown—from an added 280,000 square feet to the addition of 490,000. Instead of doubling the size of the center, it would in fact triple it. And with a bigger proposed center came a new consultant study. Ernst & Young produced a report on the expanded expansion in March 2003. Putting convention attendance at the existing Civic Plaza at 133,000 in 2002, the E&Y consultants argued that, while "Phoenix is the sixth largest city in the U.S., [it] ranks 60th in terms of convention center space." By tripling the size of the center, annual attendance would reach 376,861, E&Y argued, and Phoenix would be "on par with Dallas, San Diego, and San Antonio," with Dallas and San Diego having recently expanded. With the forecast threefold increase in attendance, center backers could now argue that total direct spending and state tax revenues would triple as well.

The combination of the massive business lobbying effort, led by Phoenix Suns owner Jerry Colangelo, and the seeming certitude of the consultant forecasts proved effective. The $300 million in state funding for the expansion passed both houses of the legislature, and was signed into law by Governor Janet Napolitano in June 2003.

The expanded Civic Plaza, renamed the Phoenix Convention Center, was completed in phases. The entire complex was fully opened in December 2008. City officials again promised abundant economic impact from a tide of new convention delegates, and described a city and center now poised to compete. According to center director Jay Greene, "As one of the top 20 largest convention centers in North America, this project has made history for the city, state, and the convention industry."[21]

The 1,050 new hotel rooms called for by PriceWaterhouseCoopers in 1999 proved more difficult to realize, despite the promise of the expansion and the consultant studies. The city repeatedly tried to find a private developer for a massive convention center hotel, but failed. The alternative was for the city itself to finance, build, and own the new hotel.

In July 2004, the city council approved plans to directly finance a 1,000-room, $350 million dollar hotel project, backing the hotel's bonds with a combination of net hotel revenues and city sports facility taxes. The city employed the HVS International consulting firm to evaluate the likely performance of the city-owned hotel. HVS concluded that the city financing model was "solidly financially feasible," and the city staff reported, "Conservative revenue projections show the proposed hotel would generate more than adequate revenue to cover operations and debt payments during the project stabilization period and through the life of the financing term."[22]

Phoenix ultimately sold the hotel bonds in December 2005, and the new city-owned Sheraton hotel opened in October 2008, just before the full convention center expansion was completed. Things would not work out quite the way the consultants had forecast and the city staff had promised.

The Phoenix case neatly exemplifies the dynamics and results of contemporary convention center development. A proposal for a new center or a major expansion appears to bubble up from a longstanding policy stream, often focused on downtown development and revitalization efforts. The idea comes buttressed with a seemingly compelling logic: the convention center is now old, competing cities have expanded and added more space, and expansion will bring enormous benefits in terms of spending, tax revenues, and job creation. A consultant study (or series of studies) documents the "need" for a larger convention facility, describes the expansions and additions of competing cities, and presents a highly precise forecast of expected performance and economic benefits. Local business leaders endorse the plan, and it receives an enthusiastic reception on the editorial page of the local newspaper. And, with little or no opposition, the plan receives the formal approval of the local mayor and city council.

Two central dimensions of convention center development provided the foundation for Phoenix's expansion quest. The first was the manner in which the expansion was *proposed and structured.* The expansion proposal came before the public and the city council by itself, not as part of any larger consideration or plans. It did not result from a broad analysis of downtown revitalization or even tourism development. Indeed, it seemed to result from the failure of the efforts to develop a new privately built, albeit subsidized hotel.

During the entire period that the Civic Plaza expansion was being considered, from 1998 through the November 2001 city vote to the funding decision by the state legislature in mid-2003, there was no consideration of alternative visitor-related projects or different uses for the city's $300 million investment. The city staff never offered the council or mayor an array of policy choices, or even a range of sizes and costs for the expansion itself. The proposal was literally a major investment in doubling (ultimately tripling) the size of Civic Plaza, or nothing.

The financing of the expansion was also structured in a narrow fashion, clearly designed to deal with the realities of voter sentiment while observing the formal, legal constraints on city spending. Both city staff and elected officials would no doubt have preferred to avoid any direct public vote on the project. But a 1989 amendment to the city charter required a vote on any sports or convention-related facility project costing more than $3 million. The city faced no alternative, and so structured the expansion proposal to make it salable to a tax-concerned electorate.

The vote authorization stressed that "The ballot proposition does not ask voters to authorize any new tax or funding sources," and "under no circumstances will the project result in an increase in any city tax rate." The proposition also stressed that the city government would only be responsible for half the cost—with "an additional $300 million from state or other funding sources." And the city's case for the expansion repeatedly stressed the imperative to compete with other places: "While Phoenix is the 6th largest city in the nation, we have only the 60th largest convention center. Other cities have been more aggressive at expanding and modernizing their convention centers, and have realized the economic and community benefits."[23]

The second central element of the expansion effort in Phoenix was the reliance on outside, presumably expert consultants. The initial expansion proposal was accompanied by a study from PriceWaterhouseCoopers that appeared to endorse an expansion, with the promise that more space would allow the city to "Attract additional new and/or larger events to Phoenix," "Increase capabilities of hosting simultaneous events by multiple users," and "Increase patronage to downtown business including hotels, restaurants, retail shops, [and] entertainment and cultural venues."[24]

The 1999 PWC report concluded that an expansion paired with 1,050 new hotel rooms would double convention attendance and thus increase attendee spending by a total of 86.5 percent. And when the city enlarged the scale of the expansion, it obtained another consultant study, from Ernst & Young, that was even more certain and expansive: convention and tradeshow attendance would grow from the 133,000 of 2002 to over 375,000 after expansion.

These consultant analyses and forecasts were effectively the only substantive market or demand information provided to the city council, local media, and public. They were presented as authoritative, with no sense of a range of alternative outcomes, "best" or "worst" cases, or even detailed discussions of the assumptions upon which they were based. Nor did the city staff, or any local group or organization, commission any competing or alternative analysis. Indeed, the assumption that Phoenix *had* to see a substantial boost in its convention business was accepted and regularly reported as an article of faith. That faith was neatly summarized in an *Arizona Republic* editorial before the November 2001 vote:

> What's more, a doubling of the size would allow Civic Plaza to handle multiple events, an advantage that not only helps expand business, but helps even out the ebb and flow of conventioneers into downtown Phoenix. It would help keep downtown businesses stable. It would help downtown thrive. A "yes" on Proposition 100 will allow the Valley of the Sun to continue competing for conventions and the wealth of tourism dollars that flow from them—nearly a third of convention travelers to the city venture around the state either before or after their event. And it will allow that to happen without an increase in city taxes.[25]

Much the same thing occurred with the proposal for a 1,000-room convention center hotel. The argument for a major hotel voiced by the Phoenix Community Alliance in 1992 and the "need" established by PriceWaterhouseCoopers in 1999 were never questioned. The repeated reluctance or inability of any private developer to finance such a project was taken not as a measure of risk but as simply a short-term impediment to be overcome. As they had before, the mayor and council relied on the assessment and professionalism of the city's managerial staff. And the staff reported, "Having confirmed that a privately financed downtown hotel is not feasible through developer input, staff research, and outside consultant advice, staff's findings support the publicly financed hotel model as the most reasonable and expeditious course to achieve the City's downtown hospitality objectives."[26]

The new city-financed Sheraton hotel was thus reviewed and approved by the City Council in much the same fashion as the Civic Plaza expansion. The city relied on expert consultant advice from Warnick and Company and HVS International in establishing both the future financial performance of the hotel and its place in downtown Phoenix. HVS simply relied on the Ernst & Young estimate of 375,000 total convention attendees post-expansion, and argued that these would produce 289,282 annual added room nights to support the planned hotel, yielding a 63 percent occupancy rate by 2010 with an average rate of $164.90. Warnick, in providing a "vision statement" for the hotel, contended, "All great cities have a great urban hotel, which becomes the focal point for that city. . . . .The downtown Sheraton Hotel is to be that great urban hotel for the city of Phoenix."[27]

The Phoenix Convention Center expansion and the adjacent 1,000-room Sheraton proved to be rather more a house of cards than an economic engine and "focal point for the city." In its first full year of operation, 2009, the expanded convention center drew 309,729 convention attendees who produced 358,632 room nights of hotel demand. Those were short of the Ernst & Young and HVS estimates, but a respectable showing. But attendance faltered for fiscal 2010, hitting just 229,097, and for fiscal year 2011 (through June 30, 2011) came to just 156,126.

As the center's attendance slipped back to what the smaller Civic Plaza had been producing in 1995 and 1996, the city-owned Sheraton also stumbled. Occupancy for 2009 was just 49.4 percent, at an average daily rate of $163.90. The 2010 occupancy grew to 52.5 percent, but the rate slipped to $158.34. At the end of 2010, Moody's Investors Service downgraded the hotel's bonds. In September 2011, Moody's placed a "negative outlook" on the bonds of the city-owned Sheraton, noting the rating firm's "expectation that, over the next 12 to 18 months, the hotel will likely struggle with improving its occupancy levels and average daily rates."[28]

In 2012 and into 2013, the hotel reported it could not meet its required debt payment from its operating revenues, and had to draw on a guarantee of other city funds, an action "reflecting financial difficulties."[29]

Phoenix had bet big on a massive convention center expansion and city-owned hotel. The initial results did not bear out consultant forecasts or city expectations. Yet Phoenix's investment in tripling the size of its center proved remarkably effective ammunition for the small group of industry consultants, including PriceWaterhouseCoopers and HVS. They were now in a position to tell any number of *other cities* that the Phoenix expansion posed a direct competitive threat to them.

Impressive and expensive as the Phoenix Convention Center expansion was, it was by no means unique or unusual. Vancouver, British Columbia, opened a major center expansion just a couple of months after Phoenix, and Daytona Beach, Florida, had opened its own expanded Ocean Center shortly before. Raleigh, North Carolina, opened an entirely new center in September 2008, followed in June 2009 by the new Lancaster County Convention Center in Lancaster, Pennsylvania. The first few months of 2011 saw convention center expansions open in Indianapolis and Philadelphia, with construction under way on new centers in Cleveland and Nashville. During 2011 and 2012 plans were under way for center expansions in Boston, Miami Beach, Detroit, Anaheim, San Antonio, Oklahoma City, San Diego, Los Angeles, San Francisco, and Seattle.

PriceWaterhouseCoopers, having recommended that Phoenix expand in part to keep up with the competition, could report to San Diego officials in December 2007 that "Upon completion of its expansion, exhibit space at the Phoenix Convention Center will exceed that of the SDCC, thereby lowering San Diego's rank to seventh among the Western centers."[30]

For convention center consulting firm Conventions, Sports & Leisure, founded in 1988 by the former heads of Coopers & Lybrand's convention center practice, the bigger new Phoenix Convention Center also neatly functioned as an argument and foil. The CSL firm could argue, in a November 2010 presentation to Boston convention center managers and supporters, that Phoenix had "nearly tripled the size" of its center, complementing it with a "downtown entertainment complex that consists of the U.S. Airways Center, Chase Field, Symphony Hall, Science Center, etc."

The firm also pointed to the Phoenix expansion as a competitor for San Antonio's Henry B. Gonzalez Convention Center in a study in July 2008. CSL reported that the expansion was due to open in late 2008, and that "340,000 estimated room nights have already been booked for 2009." In an updated study for San Antonio in December 2010, CSL again pointed to the opening of the expanded Phoenix center, and an expansion of Philadelphia's

Pennsylvania Convention Center—also a CSL client—due to open in 2011, noting that the San Antonio center's "exhibit space continues to rank very low relative to the centers reviewed." The CSL firm had completed a "market demand analysis" for the New Orleans Morial Convention Center in February 2009 that noted the increased competition from the expanded Phoenix Center. It also described the more than 1.1 million square feet of new center exhibit space being planned in cities such as Boston, Miami Beach, Detroit, San Antonio, Las Vegas, and Anaheim—all also CSL clients, all advised of the growing competition from new and expanded convention centers in other cities, and all advised to add more space or improved facilities.[31]

The CSL consultants managed to tell a wide array of city clients that they were facing a growing stock of competitive convention center space. The firm also managed to tell *some* cities an additional tale—that beyond the need for more exhibit space, a new ballroom, or more meeting rooms, they needed a very large new "headquarters hotel." A series of CSL studies in 2007-2011 presented the need for a thousand-room headquarters hotel adjacent to Kansas City's convention center. A CSL analysis had argued the case for a 1,200-room hotel to serve the Washington, D.C., Convention Center in 2004. And in studies for Boston and San Diego in 2009 and 2010, CSL could point to both the Phoenix Convention Center expansion and the adjacent Sheraton and recommend that each of those cities expand and add a headquarters hotel.

The argument that growing competition requires more public spending on more convention center space—bigger, newer, enhanced with the latest technology—has helped sustain a massive boom in convention facilities. From just 193 centers with at least 25,000 square feet of exhibit space in 1986, the U.S. convention center count reached 254 by 1996 and 325 in 2010.

As the number of convention centers grew, so did the stock of exhibit hall space. That total, 32.5 million square feet in 1986, hit 49.1 million in 1996 66.8 million square feet in 2006, and 70.5 million in 2011. Thus over two and a half decades, available space in U.S. convention facilities more than doubled. And with new centers under construction in places as diverse as Cleveland, Nashville, and Cedar Rapids, Iowa, the total will inevitably continue to grow.[32]

The convention center building boom has been remarkable not just for its scale. New and expanded centers cover a wide array of urban and suburban communities, across all geographic regions and city-size categories. Major visitor destination cities have committed substantial public revenues to center development. Chicago's McCormick Place, with a total of 1.8 million square feet of space in 1986, developed a major addition in the mid-1990s that brought the complex to 2.2 million square feet; another expansion, adding 470,000 square feet, opened in July 2007. Las Vegas doubled the size of its center over these two decades, to 1.94 million square feet in early 2002. And Orlando's Orange County Convention Center, which covered just 180,000 square feet in 1986, reached 2.05 million square feet in late 2003, fueled by the growing river of revenues from a tax on the county's more than 100,000 hotel rooms.

Many growing Sunbelt cities have also chosen to invest in ever larger and more expansive convention centers, much as Phoenix did. Dallas expanded its center steadily through the 1990s, reaching over one million square feet of exhibit space in 2002. Houston added 420,000 square feet of space, almost doubling the size of the George R. Brown Convention Center, in November 2003. Two years earlier, San Antonio had opened an expansion of its Henry B. Gonzalez Convention Center that doubled its size.

While the total center space has been boosted by the growth of very large centers in places like Chicago, Las Vegas, and Orlando, a broad array of cities now also boast up-to-date convention facilities intended to lure the proverbially lucrative meeting and tradeshow business. In California, the Ontario Convention Center opened in late 1997, San Jose's new McEnery Convention Center in 1989, and Sacramento's expanded center in 1996. Denver's Colorado Convention Center opened for business in 1990 and was doubled in size in 2004. Hartford's new Connecticut Convention Center began operation in 2005, the Rhode Island Convention Center in Providence in 1993, and the new Boston Convention and Exhibition Center in 2004.

The Baltimore Convention Center was expanded to more than double its original size in 1997, and entirely new centers have opened in Ocean City, Maryland; Richmond, Hampton, and Virginia Beach, Virginia. In the Midwest, the new Greater Columbus Convention Center opened its doors in 1993, Cincinnati completed a major expansion of its Duke Energy Center in 2006, and Fort Wayne, Indiana, and Grand Rapids, Michigan, are home to newly expanded centers as of 2005. Branson, Missouri, opened its new center in 2007 and Peoria, Illinois, completed an expansion the same year. The Indiana Convention Center in Indianapolis has also seen a series of expansions—in 1993, 2001, and most recently early 2011.

The convention center building boom has not been limited to central cities. Suburban communities have also sought their share of the visitor activity and economic impact promised by convention center backers. Overland Park, Kansas, a Kansas City suburb, opened its new convention center and publicly financed hotel in 2002, and Chicago suburb Schaumburg, Illinois, opened a new convention center and an adjacent publicly owned hotel in 2006. Also in suburban Chicago, Rosemont's Donald Stephens Convention Center more than doubled in size from 1986 to 2001, to 845,000 square feet of exhibit space. The suburban Atlanta area includes the Cobb Galleria Center, the North Atlanta Trade Center, the Georgia International Convention Center (near Hartsfield-Jackson Airport), and the Gwinnett Center in Duluth.

The contemporary convention center building boom is in many ways a dual triumph of politics and finance. Convention centers and expansions are major public investments, commonly in hundreds of millions of dollars. They most often are financed with some form of long-term public borrowing. And historically, they have not necessarily been widely embraced or approved by local taxpayers and voters.

The civic auditoriums and convention centers built in the first half of the twentieth century were commonly developed by city governments, financed using general obligation bonds. In the vast majority of states, that debt required majority—in some states, two-thirds majority—approval by the local electorate. When city governments began the wave of "modern" convention facilities after World War II, often as part of new civic centers or downtown renewal schemes, those too had to be voted on and approved by the local electorate.

Los Angeles civic leaders first sought a major convention venue early in the twentieth century, but local voters failed to provide the needed two-thirds majority for a memorial auditorium bond issue in 1920. Mayor Fletcher Bowron backed another auditorium bond issue in 1939 with the argument that Cleveland's auditorium was a "great success." But his enthusiasm was not shared by the city council, which voted against putting the auditorium bond proposal to the voters. A plan for a "huge civic auditorium costing $25,000,000" was on the ballot in 1951, paired with a proposed music center and slum clearance funding. All three propositions were defeated. Auditorium backers returned with a $27 million auditorium and convention hall bond plan in May 1953. Despite the editorial plea by the *Los Angeles Times* that "national gatherings . . . . pass us by," the voters again failed to produce a two-thirds majority. Convention hall backers tried again in June 1954, with the argument that the city had lost $38 million the previous year in convention business. And once again the voters said no. Los Angeles did not open a convention center until July 1971, a feat it only managed after an extended debate over the site, and by using a special authority to issue the bonds and bypass the city's voters.[33]

The efforts to build a new civic auditorium or convention hall in San Diego were no less problematic. A plan for a new civic center and auditorium in 1947 was defeated at the polls. A bond proposal for a convention hall and theater was voted on in June 1956, and failed to get the required two-thirds majority, winning approval from just over 60 percent of the voters. City officials and civic leaders chose to place the convention center scheme on the ballot again in November; again it failed, winning just a 49.9 percent "yes" vote. San Diego only succeeded in building a new convention center in 1964 by finding a way around the voters, using a combination of a lease arrangement and the proceeds from the sale of other city property. Business leaders and the Centre City Development Corporation developed a plan for a new downtown convention center in the late 1970s. Seeking to avoid a public vote, the city council adopted a scheme financed with lease revenue bonds in October 1980. But citizen antipathy and the reaction of outlying hotel owners opposed to a downtown center that would provide them little business led to a successful petition drive that forced a public vote. In a May 1981 ballot, the proposed center received just 43 percent of the vote and was defeated.[34]

Other cities demonstrated a parallel fragility of convention center bond proposals. Cleveland voters turned down two successive funding plans in the 1950s, finally approving one on the third try. Atlanta's electorate defeated a proposed Civic Center in 1962, approving a less expensive version the following year. Raleigh voters in 1992 defeated a proposed $95 million convention center bond issue by 58 to 42 percent.

In more recent years Pittsburgh area voters turned down a proposal for a new convention center (together with new sports stadium) in 1997; Columbus voters twice defeated tax issues to fund a new convention center; San Jose voters failed to provide a sufficient majority for a center expansion in 2002; and Portland, Oregon voters nixed a convention center expansion in 1998. Yet despite the verdict of local voters, each of these cities, much like Los Angeles and San Diego, succeeded in building a new convention center or expansion. That success in the face of electoral defeat has been managed with a series of financial and political innovations. Pittsburgh turned to a sports and exhibition authority; Columbus created a countywide convention facilities authority; Portland turned to a combination of city, county, and metro area government. What these cities, and a host of others, have managed is nothing less than a reconstruction of the means of financing convention facilities and similar projects, employing a variety of fiscal vehicles that avoid the "problems" of popular democracy and voter review. This fiscal reconstruction is the focus of Chapter 2.

The convention center boom has also been built on a parallel reconstruction of urban politics. It is not just reluctant voters who have stood in the way of convention center development. For decades, center building was stymied by local conflict and opposition over issues beyond the immediate fiscal ones. Much of that conflict involved disputes over location and site. Chicago's efforts to build a major convention hall from the 1920s into the 1950s were marked by continuing disputes over *where* a new facility would go, and thus who would benefit or suffer. During the 1960s, St. Louis saw two competing convention center proposals, one from the mayor and one from local business leaders, at very different downtown sites. And in San Diego, Mayor Pete Wilson's plans for a new downtown center in 1980 were opposed by a coalition of outlying hotel owners and defeated at the polls. Yet in all these cases, and dozens of others, the apparent conflict was eventually successfully managed, the opposition eventually overcome, and a new center completed.

The fundamental conflict over center location was not about technical planning questions or issues of accessibility or land cost. Rather, it was over gaining (or potentially losing) the benefits a major public investment could have for urban space. The promise of a new or bigger convention facility was that it would draw thousands of new visitors and millions of their dollars to the city—what *Cleveland Plain Dealer* editorial writers termed "the convention pot o' gold" in 1956. That flood of visitors would spur the development of new hotels, restaurants, and shops. But while local hotel owners and newspaper publishers might all agree on the great benefits for the community at large or even for downtown, much of that boost would be narrower, limited to the immediate environs of the new convention hall. That meant that property interests or developers focused on one area of the city or the downtown would not necessarily embrace a new convention facility somewhere else.[35]

A number of geographically distinct business groups in Chicago—the West Central Association, the North Central Association, the South Side Planning Board—each sought the convention center in its own area to bolster land values and encourage new development. Boston's War Memorial (later Hynes) Auditorium, opened in early 1965, was part of the new Prudential Center development on the site of the former Boston & Albany rail yards in

Back Bay, intended to support new hotel and retail construction. The goals of convention center building also went beyond encouraging and supporting new development to altering the character and potential of land in or near downtown.[36]

When the *Los Angeles Times* editorialized about the civic benefits of a new convention hall in 1953, it noted that the proposed downtown location was "in a somewhat dilapidated state," and the buildings' "removal would improve the area and cause a sprucing up of neighboring structures." And when in 1954 the leaders of the Chicago Planning Commission and Land Clearance Commission joined a group of leading business leaders to consider the Fort Dearborn development proposal for the area north of the downtown Loop, mayoral adviser James Downs noted the possibility of building a new convention hall at the south end of the Loop, arguing that "a large scale redevelopment at this site would tend to balance Fort Dearborn and anchor the Loop securely."[37]

Writing in his pioneering volume *Principles of City Land Values* in 1924, Richard M. Hurd had concluded,

> To summarize, the effect of public buildings, if located at or near the old business centre they tend to maintain central strength in their first location, as in Boston, New York, Philadelphia and Chicago. This is the normal case. The first exception would be where public buildings are located at a moderate distance from the centre, where the tendency is to draw business in their direction.[38]

For planners and real estate experts such as James Downs, Hurd's assessment tapped the potential role of a new convention center in shaping land use and development. A new facility might serve as an "anchor" for the existing central business district. Located on the edge of the downtown core, it could serve as a bulwark against adjacent areas in decline.

For Atlanta's Metropolitan Planning Commission in 1952, the potential of a new civic center with a "large convention auditorium" was that it could eliminate "one of Atlanta's worst slums. . . . a definite menace to the future health of the downtown area." The Planning Commission two years later would suggest a "new convention auditorium" at a different site, as part of the "development of space above and immediately adjacent to the railroad gulch," where it would aid the development of new office buildings, a new department store, and an 800 to 1,000-room hotel.[39]

The two conflicting Atlanta plans pointed up the political problem of siting and building a new "convention auditorium." Built as part of a slum clearance and urban renewal project east of the downtown core, it might remove a "menace." As part of the "air rights" over the gulch on the opposite side of the core, it promised to act as "magnet" for new investment and private development. But Atlanta could not necessarily afford one convention center, let alone two.

The solution for Atlanta, as it would be for any number of other cities, was a combination of *multiple public projects* in a single deal that could serve the distinct parts of the downtown core. Many of the east side "slums" described in the 1952 plan were in fact wiped out through the federal urban renewal program, providing a site for that "convention auditorium," the Atlanta Civic Center. The railroad gulch would receive its own public project a few years later, in the form of a new coliseum/arena, promoted by one of the city's major developers as the kind of magnet that could support his planned private development.

Atlanta's voters first turned down the Civic Center bond proposal in 1962. A smaller scheme was approved the following year. But when local business leaders sought to construct an Intercontinental Congress Center in the late 1960s, they avoided city government and its voters. They turned instead to the Georgia state legislature. When the new Atlanta Coliseum was planned and developed in the late 1960s, it too was financed in a fashion that avoided any public vote.

With the fundamental deals for convention center building structured first within the local business community, only emerging into public view when set, and financing arrangements arranged to avoid or limit any direct public vote, the politics of center development has been effectively reshaped since the 1960s and 1970s. The final element in sustaining the convention center boom has been the set of promises—of visitor activity, spending, job creation, and economic impact—that have singularly privileged center development as a public investment.

Economic Impact

The fiscal reconstruction of convention center finance and politics has been accompanied by a parallel shift in the rhetoric of purpose and promise. The convention halls and civic centers of the first half of the twentieth century were commonly justified as amenities for the broad urban community, capable of hosting large community events as well as conventions, and accommodating large local gatherings as well as the occasional national political convention or major event. In 1923, St. Louis voters approved a $5 million bond issue for a "Municipal Auditorium and Community Center." Cleveland voters overwhelmingly approved the bonds for a "Public Auditorium" in 1916. Los Angeles civic and business leaders promoted a new "War Memorial Auditorium" in 1920 as a "living monument" to the city's servicemen and "large enough for any indoor spectacle."[40]

Beginning in the years after World War II, cities began to promote the idea of luring major national convention and tradeshow events, often accompanied by the imperative to lure national political conventions. By the 1980s and 1990s, the rhetoric had come to center on the notion of "economic impact." The flow of new out-of-town visitors to the conventions, accommodated by a new or larger venue, would yield a growing stream of spending, visitor dollars that would be multiplied throughout the local economy. Spending by hotel guests would be re-spent by hotel employees; wages of restaurant workers and retail employees supported by new visitors would be spent on other local goods and services, magnifying the economic impact.

The increased volume of visitor spending, over a three- or four-day average stay, would in turn boost local tax revenues. Hotel and restaurant spending would produce new hotel occupancy and sales tax revenue, and increased visitor business would ultimately support new development around the convention center, development that would produce new property tax revenues. By the early 1980s, arguments that a new or expanded center would produce economic benefits were a staple of consultant studies, with forecast amounts stated with striking specificity.

Convention centers have thus come to be justified as "loss leaders." Local convention and visitors bureaus (CVBs) and center promoters acknowledge that almost every convention center in the U.S. operates at a loss, not even counting the annual cost in debt service. Centers simply do not take in revenues equal to the cost of operation. In fiscal 2011, the operating loss of Philadelphia's Pennsylvania Convention Center was $18.1 million. Washington's Walter Washington Convention Center lost $20.7 million from operations, in addition to $34.9 million annual debt service and $14.2 million for marketing. Orlando's Orange County Convention Center saw an operating loss of $14 million.

But the regular argument of convention center backers is that these persistent operating losses, in addition to the cost of building a center, are more than counterbalanced by the "essential economic activity that [drives] new tax revenues, economic benefit and employment from other services and establishments like hotels, restaurants and retail stores."[41]

The argument for convention centers as economic drivers has come to be structured around the analyses and predictions of consultants. Where once a local government research bureau or chamber of commerce might provide an estimate of future convention center business, by the 1980s and 1990s the public rhetoric of center investment revolved around formal forecasts of visitor volume, convention delegate spending, and multiplied economic impact.

These consultant forecasts, whether by hotel consulting firms such as PKF or major national accounting firms like PriceWaterhouse (and its predecessor Laventhol & Horwath), Coopers & Lybrand, and KPMG, were presented as both more expert and far more precise than their predecessors. Laventhol's promotional materials circa 1989 boasted of its computer-based "predictive attendance model" and told local officials that its "estimates of economic impact. . . . can be used to gain community support and interest." The language of public officials and newspaper headlines changed as well, describing the benefits of convention center development in terms of an exact number of annual new spending dollars and a seemingly guaranteed flow of new local tax revenues. Thus the discourse surrounding convention center investment was altered, from choosing one public investment against another in a broad package of bond proposals to a focus on the evident and certain rewards a new or bigger center would bring.[42]

For Philadelphians, the front page of the *Philadelphia Inquirer* in January 1983 brought the headline that "Big Civic Center Is a Must, Study Says." The article reported on the conclusion of the PKF study that a new downtown convention center would bring some $700 million a year in convention delegate spending, yielding the city $1 billion in new tax revenues over thirty years. A second major *Inquirer* story two weeks later added the forecast that a new center would create as many as 5,000 new jobs. And with the boom in visitor spending and jobs would come a larger if less measurable benefit. A large new convention facility would reshape the city's image from a "drab" location to a "progressive" and "forward thinking" community.[43]

The PKF analysis did include some alternatives, including a smaller center or renovation of the existing Civic Center. But the firm emphasized a large new convention center in the Center City area as its "first recommendation."

Armed with the conclusions from the PKF consultant report described by its reporters, the *Inquirer*'s editorial writers chimed in, repeating the consultant claims of delegate spending, economic impact, job creation, and tax revenues and calling on the city to "move ahead with design and construction of a new and modern convention complex in Center City. . . . It should do so with enthusiasm and resolve." Deeming the project of the "highest priority," the stirring editorial concluded, "The need now is to get on with it—with vigor and dispatch."[44]

For the *Inquirer*'s editorialists, there was little need for additional analysis or independent review. Nor was there questioning of the logic of convention center investment at a time when competing cities like New York and Washington were also building new centers. The bulky PKF study was sufficient evidence and justification for an investment that would ultimately cost $523 million, the promise of new visitor dollars and job creation far too entrancing.

As communications scholar Phyllis Kaniss recounted in her case study of local media response to the convention center proposal, coverage of the scheme was dominated by official pronouncements and the image of pressing civic need. When some independent observers, including one professor at the University of Pennsylvania, did begin to question the PKF numbers, their views were given short shrift compared to "official" accounts and forecasts.[45]

The promises of abundant visitor spending and new city jobs did not eliminate conflict over issues such as location, cost, and political control. There was an extended public debate over the proper downtown site and then over city versus state control of construction and operation. The proposed center did manage to avoid any real *local* conflict over financing. The city would ultimately contribute some $300 million from hotel room tax revenues, while the state government agreed to provide a $185 million grant. But the state fiscal role opened the project to questioning from state legislators. Facing what the *Philadelphia Daily News* termed "gales of criticism from some politicians and community leaders who saw the center as a huge waste of money," the newly formed Pennsylvania Convention Center Authority commissioned another PKF study.[46]

The PKF firm delivered its updated analysis in May 1988. The new estimate of annual convention delegate spending was slightly lower, if remarkably precise, at $618,927,900 for 2001, with 346,000 annual convention attendees producing new hotel demand of 664,800 room nights. With that presumably assured new demand, PKF promised a total of 4,848 new hotel rooms to be built in the city over the next decade, including a thousand-room convention headquarters hotel, and sufficient "over demand for the airport and City Line hotels."[47]

The series of consultant studies in Philadelphia did not necessarily eliminate conflict or debate over the massive public investment in a new convention center. But it did shape both media coverage and public perception of the proposal—the experts had assessed the performance of a new center and offered the assurance that it would succeed in delivering a host of economic and employment benefits to a city that had seen serious job loss and decline.

Even before the center's grand opening in June 1993, arguments were being made that the new Pennsylvania Convention Center was too small. In February, the *Daily News* quoted the findings of a City Planning Commission report that the 440,000 square foot center was not large enough to compete for major conventions and tradeshows against Chicago, Las Vegas, Atlanta, and New York. The city lacked both the financial resources for a bigger facility and the new hotel rooms to support it. Calls for a larger center began quite soon after 1993. In November 1997, Mayor Ed Rendell called for a major expansion, arguing, "In order to get the very, very largest groups to come back, we need more space."[48]

Before Mayor Rendell could realize his goal of a bigger center for the largest groups, he and the Pennsylvania Convention Center Authority had to grapple with two problems. The first was finding a source of funds, presumably from outside a city government increasingly strapped for cash. The second was dealing with the impact of the center's union labor rates and work rules on event organizers and exhibitors. Newspaper accounts of the possible expansion invariably included a discussion of labor issues, exemplified by a January 2000 *Inquirer* article that ended by noting that only New York and San Francisco had higher labor costs, and quoting the head of the convention center authority as saying, "Workers here have also been criticized by tradeshow and convention producers as uncouth and insensitive to their needs."[49]

It was not until fall 2002, with union agreement on new jurisdictional and work rules, that the center authority was prepared to make the case for expansion. That came from a consultant study on the case—and forecast results—for a major expansion, commissioned and paid for by the Pennsylvania Convention Center Authority. The Conventions, Sports & Leisure International (CSL) findings were released by the authority in October 2002 and headlined by the *Daily News* as "Center Survey: If You Build It, They Will Come," emphasizing that 58 percent of convention planners would "look favorably" at an expanded center. The study also promised that more space would boost the center's annual economic impact from $215 million to $308 million, or 43 percent, and create 2,850 new permanent jobs.[50]

An *Inquirer* article the same day was somewhat more questioning, with the headline "Smaller Return Seen from Center Expansion." The story went on to report the same figures from CSL—43 percent more hotel rooms filled after an expansion, with a $93 million boost in attendee spending. But it also noted that those figures were less than had been offered by studies in 1998 and 1999. The article quoted city finance director Janice Davis as saying, "We needed validation. . . . I am extremely happy that it is in support of the expansion."[51]

The findings of the CSL study effectively made the case for more convention center space, with seeming certitude that the expansion would bring real rewards in terms of increased convention business. When the study was finally finished in late January 2003, it included some specifics that had not appeared in the newspaper coverage the previous October. Indeed, those specifics never appeared in the local media, as the CSL study was not released to the public. The 58 percent "positive response rate" garnered by Philadelphia from convention planners was noted. But so was the information that Philadelphia's figure was equal to Boston's and lower than other competing cities such as Denver (65 percent), Las Vegas (70 percent), and New Orleans (77 percent). No comparable response figures were cited for New York, Baltimore, or Washington, cities CSL described as Philadelphia's "primary competition."[52]

The CSL study did offer the prediction that an expansion would increase attendance by more than 50 percent and boost annual hotel room night demand from an average of 503,000 per year to 786,000. But the analysis contained some other potentially troubling details. The center had averaged 246,839 convention and tradeshow attendees yearly from 1999 to 2002. But those totals were well below PKF's 1998 forecast of 349,500 for those years. And the CSL consultants did not bother to note that the center's room-night production of 503,000 included two years, 2000 and 2002, that were unusually successful. The 2000 total was boosted by the city's hosting of the Republican National Convention, while 2002 had seen 27 major conventions, the highest in the center's history. A more plausible baseline would have been the 470,000 room nights in 1998 or 420,000 in 1999.

CSL's promise of more than 280,000 new room nights would be a fixture of arguments for the expansion, as the state legislature passed a 2004 slots gambling bill that allocated some $400 million for the expansion. It would be a constant in the press releases and publications of the Philadelphia Convention and Visitors Bureau. It would appear—unquestioned—with some regularity in press reports of the progress of the project as it moved to an early 2011 opening.[53]

Even as the expansion project was moving ahead in late 2006, it was evident to the Pennsylvania Convention Center Authority that it would be far less productive than CSL had predicted. The authority's November 2006 "Convention Center Operating Plan" included the information that the existing center's hotel room-night generation had fallen to 363,954 for fiscal year 2004 and 297,180 for 2005. The authority's own forecast of future room-night generation was set to grow to 650,000 by fiscal 2014, a far more modest increase than the 786,000 predicted by CSL in 2003, and one not mentioned in public.[54]

When the Pennsylvania Convention Center expansion opened for business in March 2011, it faced a market environment reshaped by expansions at competing centers and the 2008 recession. The center's room-night total dropped to 336,000 in 2007 and 303,000 in 2009. The actual performance for 2010 was 179,000. A new consultant study of the expanded center's future performance and operations put the forecast at 321,300 for fiscal 2013 and 381,523 for 2014. It was clear that the expanded Pennsylvania Convention Center would be pressed to merely equal the average 503,000 annual room nights noted by CSL in 2003. Indeed, it managed 431,000 room nights in calendar 2012, well below the CSL forecast of 786,000.[55]

From the first public discussion of a new convention facility in downtown Philadelphia in the early 1980s through the opening of a new $786 million expansion in 2011, the series of consultant studies and their forecasts, regularly cited by the press and public officials, effectively defined the content and focus of the public discourse on convention center building. Those "expert" studies admitted no uncertainty about larger market realities or future performance. It was simply taken as a given that the new center would produce the anticipated benefits. And when the expansion proposal was developed, that discussion too was suffused with consultant predictions of an economic boom, with no real effort on the part of local officials, city and state bureaucrats, or news media to determine whether earlier forecasts had really been met.

The Philadelphia story neatly exemplifies the larger political and fiscal realities (or perhaps fantasies) behind the building boom. The new Pennsylvania Convention Center was financed with a combination of state dollars and local hotel tax revenues, neatly removing the question of center development from both the public and the city government. The expansion was financed with state revenues from slots gambling, in a deal—assembled and pressed by governor and former Philadelphia mayor Ed Rendell—that also aided Pittsburgh and its convention center. In both cases, the public investment decision was focused on paying for convention center space, not on any larger goal or purpose, and with no consideration of alternative needs or public investments.

Without any direct public vote, the "deals" to finance the center were shaped by state-level politics. There, the deal-making was effectively distributive and geographic, with enough benefits for enough parts of the Commonwealth and their local legislators to succeed. The fundamental "deal" for Philadelphia's center and its subsequent expansion were thus constructed in a remarkably narrow and constrained field, with serious public discourse and debate effectively limited and avoided, built on the unquestioned assumptions and presumptions of consultants who presented no record of their earlier forecasts' accuracy and no evidence of expert knowledge beyond the contention that they had done many such studies before.[56]

The dynamic of "expert" consultant studies, promises of a boom in visitor spending, specific forecasts of "economic impact," editorial endorsements, and seemingly "invisible" financing was much the same in New York City in the 1990s. Just a decade after the 1986 opening of the Jacob K. Javits Convention Center, center officials commissioned a feasibility analysis of an expansion from Coopers & Lybrand. The *New York Times* reported the findings of the Coopers & Lybrand study on the Javits Center in April 1997, that "To maintain its competitive edge" the Javits needed to double its exhibition space or risk being hurt by new centers or expansions under way in Chicago, Las Vegas, Orlando, Atlanta, and Philadelphia. From such an expansion, "the economic benefits could be huge. . . . creation of 13,000 new jobs and $87 million in annual tax revenues for the state and the city."[57] And the expansion call was renewed the following month in the *New York Times*, pegged to the opening of a new center in Atlantic City, complete with the same argument that "an expanded center would generate 13,000 new jobs and contribute $568 million in added spending at hotels, restaurants, theaters, stores and other New York City businesses."[58]

The *Times* editorial page joined the chorus in June 1998, by noting that the city's "attraction as a site for trade shows and conventions has been one of the key elements in its economic growth" and telling Mayor Rudolph

Giuliani, "Building a world-class convention center would create jobs and assure the city's ability to attract trade shows and exhibitions into the next century. . . . The Mayor must cooperate with the state in reaching that goal."[59]

For all the seeming specificity and certainty of the Coopers & Lybrand study, the *Times* reportage succeeded in misreading its findings and substance. The report did estimate the jobs to be produced by an expansion at "12,700 full and part-time jobs." And it did put "Estimated Annual Direct Spending in a Stabilized Year of Operations" at $568,254,000. But those figures would be the *total product of the expanded center*, not the added or incremental impact.[60]

The Coopers & Lybrand study did not include figures on the spending or job creation of the existing, pre-expansion Javits. Nor did it include numbers of anticipated new events or attendees, making it impossible to calculate the added impact of expansion. Indeed, the Coopers study contained only relatively limited information on the center's actual performance, with event and attendance data for just three years, two of them shown as "estimated." Had the Coopers consultants provided a longer historical view, the study might have yielded a more accurate, if more disturbing, portrait.

While the Javits was shown as hosting 60 conventions and tradeshows with total attendance of 1.1 million in fiscal year 1995, that total was substantially less than the (not reported) 1.42 million attendees of 1991 or the 1.92 million in 1990. And perhaps most problematically, where Coopers & Lybrand calculated average convention attendee spending on the basis of estimates by the International Association of Convention and Visitors Bureaus, that each spent three days or more in the convention city, Javits attendees didn't come close to that estimate. The Coopers study of the Javits expansion noted that the 1.1 million convention and tradeshow attendees in fiscal 1995 generated just 201,600 hotel room nights. The reality was that the tradeshows at the Javits were primarily attended by New York metropolitan area residents, who visited the Javits for the day, rather than by out-of-town visitors. In order to realize the jobs or economic impact promised by the Coopers consultants, the Javits would have to successfully compete for an entirely new market of rotating conventions.

The Javits expansion proposal stalled despite the economic boom promised by Coopers & Lybrand, as the result of a fight between Mayor Giuliani and New York Governor George Pataki over Giuliani's plan for a new stadium adjacent to the center. With no real progress, the Javits Center Operating Corporation commissioned another study to move the project forward, this time from Robert Canton of PriceWaterhouseCoopers.

The March 2000 PriceWaterhouseCoopers analysis concluded (in print both italicized and bold) the "JKJCC will lose existing business if it does not expand," "JKJCC will attract new events if it is expanded," and "An expanded JKJCC will generate economic and fiscal benefits to New York City and the State of New York." The PWC report offered an even more precise picture of the results of an expansion, noting that the center's exhibit halls "are currently at practical maximum occupancy," and predicting that an expansion of some 500,000 square feet would bring the Javits 504,000 more convention and tradeshow attendees each year, for a total of 1.62 million.[61]

Canton's 2000 report concluded that those half million more convention attendees would produce precisely 417,000 new hotel room nights a year and generate an added $355 million in spending and 7,000 additional jobs to the city. But at the end of the year an entirely new dimension was added, with the initially quiet floating of a proposal for a new football stadium for the New York Jets adjacent to the Javits. The Jets stadium was linked to the city's efforts to win the 2012 Olympic Games. But a stadium with a retractable roof could also be sold as offering added exhibit hall space—"the stadium could be converted within 24 hours to exhibition space and connected to the Javits Center by a footbridge"—and a solution to the presumed deficiencies of the Javits. The convention center itself was termed by the *Times* article as "widely derided as an out-of-date, second-class building unworthy of the city."[62]

Neither the Jets stadium nor the Javits Center expansion proved easily realized in the cauldron of New York City politics. So in late 2003 the Javits Center Corporation sought yet another consultant study of the market for an expanded center, turning once again to Robert Canton of PriceWaterhouse-Coopers. In the years since the 2000 analysis, convention business and travel generally had been hard hit by a recession and the aftermath of 9-11. Convention and tradeshow attendance at the Javits had fallen from 1.3 million in 1998 to just 955,000 in 2003. Canton attributed the drop to "an industry wide trend of decreased event attendance." Yet the forecast of new convention and tradeshow attendee spending in his 2004 report proved even greater than in 2000.[63]

The *New York Times* article reporting on the PriceWaterhouseCooper findings noted that "doubling the center's size. . . would attract half a million more visitors, 18 to 20 new trade shows and conventions, and nearly $700 million in additional business a year." The article also noted the reassurance provided by PriceWaterhouseCoopers that "The center does well despite its size, high labor costs and the city's high hotel rates. . . . because New York is a highly attractive international city in a region with a shortage of exhibition space."[64]

The 2004 PWC report provided the formal, seemingly expert, economic justification for New York's political leaders to endorse and press for the Javits expansion. In a joint press release on March 25, 2004, Mayor Michael Bloomberg and Governor George Pataki announced "a historic plan to transform and modernize New York City's convention industry," including a major expansion of the Javits, a new adjacent 1,500-room hotel, and a 75,000-seat stadium. Their vision and rhetoric were grandiose: "This is a smart City-State investment in New York's future and one that leverages private investment to grow our convention industry and help realize New York's Olympic dreams." Their claims that "the expansion will have a profound impact on New York's economy, increasing the existing $97 million annual tax revenue generated by Javits by an additional $53 million and 415,000 hotel nights a year. . . . [and] will create 10,830 additional jobs" were drawn directly and exactly from the 2004 PriceWaterhouseCoopers report. The seemingly expert consultant study provided ample political cover and economic rationale.

While the analysis by PriceWaterhouseCoopers provided a public justification for the expansion, the report itself had some serious deficiencies. Rob Canton of PWC argued for the success of the expanded center, despite being "mindful of the fact that overall national demand for exhibit and meeting space and overall attendance at trade shows and conventions had declined since 2001," because "the Center did not suffer substantial declines in business or attendance during this period and that it continues to turn away business because of lack of available dates."[65]

The issue of the convention and tradeshow attendance at the Javits—historic, current, and likely future—was crucial to PWC's forecasts of spending, public revenue, and job creation. It was also the vital link in understanding the reasonableness of the consultant's forecasts. But in 182 pages of the January 2004 PWC report, analysis of attendance occupied less than a single page, largely devoted to a bar chart of attendance from 1993 to 2002. The report noted that "convention/trade show attendance is estimated to have ranged from 1.0 million to 1.4 million from 1993 to 2002 and to have averaged 1.2 million annually."[66]

In the accompanying chart (Table 8), the attendance figures for 1999, 2000, 2001, and 2002 are all shown as "estimated." The PWC consultants offered no explanation for their use of "estimated" values for three or four years earlier. The actual figures, distributed by NYC & Company, the city's visitor bureau, in its monthly "Barometer," would suggest significant change in the Javits's performance. The Javits saw 1,277,800 convention and tradeshow attendees in 1999, and 1,253,400 in 2000. Yet attendance fell to 977,600 in 2001, followed by 931,850 in 2002, and 955,150 in 2003.[67]

Canton would surely have had the exact attendance numbers for 2001 and 2002 available for his analysis in late 2003. Indeed, he *should have had* at least partial year-to-date numbers through September or October. Those numbers would have shown a substantial and persistent drop in convention attendance. Yet that drop does not really appear in the report. Instead, it estimates a "No Expansion" scenario of 1,113,000 annual convention and tradeshow attendees, and a projected "Expansion" total of 1,532,000.

The proposed Javits expansion would first grow in size, as new Governor Eliot Spitzer and Senator Charles Schumer embraced a plan for a more ambitious expansion with a total cost on the order of $3 to $4 billion. Then, by 2008, it would shrink back to a renovation accompanied by a quite modest expansion—all that could be financed with the $700 million in hotel fee revenue bonds sold in November 2005. And as the expansion shrank, so did the Javits's actual convention and tradeshow attendance, to 817,200 in 2007, 708,200 in 2008, and then 533,700 in 2012.[68]

From the first announcement of the Javits expansion plan in March 2004 to the adoption of the final "General Project Plan" in March 2009, the PWC forecasts were repeated over and over by public officials and in public documents. They were treated as "real" in the project's environmental impact statement. Indeed, the final 2009 project plan neatly repeated the PWC "No Expansion" figure of 1,113,000 annual convention and tradeshow attendees at 73 events, despite the fact that the center hosted just 67 conventions and tradeshows in 2008, with an attendance of 708,200.[69]

There were no independent studies or reports in the New York City media of the remarkably parallel studies with similar estimates of economic impact completed by PriceWaterhouseCoopers for other cities at about the same time. Cleveland garnered a PWC report on a new center in 2001 with the promise of $181.7 million in annual direct spending, followed by another PWC analysis in April 2005 that forecast a larger center would boost annual convention attendance from 25,000 to 175,000, generating direct spending of $213,584,000 annually in Cleveland and Cuyahoga County.

Canton and the PriceWaterhouseCoopers consultants produced a market demand and economic analysis of a planned expansion of the Indiana Convention Center in early 2004, offering the assessment that the center's "past success is largely explained by the strong destination package it offers (numerous proximate and connected hotels, dining, and attractions)" and promising that a bigger center would bring 18 to 23 additional conventions and tradeshows, attracting at least 108,000 new attendees and producing $108,810,000 in new visitor spending each year.[70]

PriceWaterhouseCoopers, like many of the other convention center consultants, appeared fully capable of finding that more space would generate more convention business for a wide array of cities. The absence of any real questioning or re-analysis of its forecasts was, in the case of New York's Javits Center, a product of the local political environment. With a "deal" set by both Mayor Bloomberg and Governor Pataki, there was no organized or formal opposition. Local hotel owners had long pressed for a bigger Javits. With their commitment to a new hotel tax to pay a part of the cost (albeit less than the mayor had hoped), and a reliance on a broad array of seemingly "free" state and city funds, including $350 million from the Battery Park City Authority, the expansion (at least in its initial form and cost) did not appear to come at a particularly high price, or at the cost of another public investment project. And with the location of the Javits already fixed, there was no extended debate or conflict—as there had been at the Javits's birth—over site and locational benefit.[71]

From Civic Improvement to Economic Boon

The arguments for public convention center investment and the case for development have changed dramatically over the past few decades. Where cities once promoted civic memorials or public amenities, convention facilities have come to be portrayed as economic boons, sources of new dollars from visitors and spurs to private investment and development. Those arguments—and the media coverage built around them—have come to be defined by the studies and analyses of ostensibly independent, "expert" consultants.

Armed with forecasts that a new or larger convention center will surely yield a predictable stream of new attendees and visitors, the public is told this investment will produce millions of dollars in "economic impact" and a substantial boost in new local jobs. Repeated by public officials and the local media, the promise of dollars and jobs appears to be absolutely assured. Only rarely are the foundations of those consultant conclusions fully investigated, the assumptions subjected to serious review and questioning. Nor are the consultants pressed to demonstrate the success or accuracy of their predictions, or held to account for their work.

The authority and expertise behind consultant conclusions has made convention center projects more appealing to local officials, and far easier to "sell" to the general public. But the political path to convention center development has also been reshaped from the years when Los Angeles or Cleveland voters would regularly say "no" to center investment. By the 1990s, it had simply become unnecessary to ask them.

Chapter 2

Paying for the Box

The grand public convention halls of the 1920s and 1930s—Cleveland's Public Auditorium, Kansas City's Municipal Auditorium, St. Louis's Kiel Auditorium—were built by city governments and financed by city governments with general obligation debt. Those debts were backed by the "full faith and credit" of a city government, effectively the full stock of property and other tax revenues available to the city. And under state laws in these states and the vast majority of others, general obligation debt had to be approved by a majority of the local electorate.

Cleveland's Public Auditorium was approved by the city's voters in 1916 and finally completed in 1922. But when voters were presented with a scheme for financing and developing a new convention center in 1957 and 1958, they turned it down both times. Finally, in 1960, a smaller, restructured convention center scheme won voter approval. That center was supposed to vault Cleveland to the front rank of convention cities. As of 1981, it was still ninth largest in the United States.

When, after some twenty years of use, the center required improvements and refurbishing, in 1985 Mayor George Voinovich chose to invest some $28 million without asking the voters to decide. The city issued notes, largely financed by the Greater Cleveland Convention and Visitors Bureau through the bureau's receipt of countywide hotel taxes, that avoided both a public vote and the limits of the city's fiscal circumstances.

Cleveland's business and political leaders repeatedly sought to develop an entirely new downtown convention center, beginning in the late 1990s. They ultimately chose a scheme in 2007 that neatly avoided the city government and its ongoing financial problems. Instead, the initiative for the convention center and a "Medical Mart" trade mart came from the overlying Cuyahoga

County government. And in financing the $450 million project, the county's three commissioners (by a vote of two to one) avoided the need for any public vote by committing the revenues from a special countywide quarter-cent sales tax.

Cleveland's fiscal evolution neatly illustrates the changes over the twentieth century in convention finance. Where city governments once dominated development of public assembly facilities, the public role has increasingly shifted to other government entities, a diverse group ranging from county governments, as in Cleveland, to public authorities (such as the New Orleans Morial Convention Center Authority), regional entities (like the Greater Richmond Convention Center Authority), and state governments. And where the initiative to finance and build a convention facility once commonly required a majority vote of the local electorate, the new financing and organizational arrangements now regularly avoid the need for voter review and approval.

The restructuring of convention center finance away from direct voter approval was not happenstance. It reflected the increasing willingness of the national bond market to accept revenue bonds—debt issues backed solely by a limited tax or revenue source, such as a hotel or car rental—and the imagination of investment bankers seeking to serve local officials. But far more important, it was a choice, imitated and repeated across scores of cities, that served the political and development ends of both elected officials and local business leaders, as the changed social and political environment of major cities after 1970 made voter approval increasingly unlikely.

Kansas City's business leaders had long viewed their community as a natural locale for major national conventions, as it is a major Midwest rail hub. The city's Convention Bureau regularly boasted dozens of major meetings, including some 24 national conventions, 54 regional meetings, and 36 state conventions in fiscal year 1929. The city had erected a new convention hall in 1900, just in time to host the Democratic National Convention. But by the 1920s this was increasingly viewed as outdated and too small. The minutes of the convention committee of the Chamber of Commerce said, "We are gradually being eliminated from consideration through the lack of two important civic facilities now possessed by virtually all of the larger cities in the country. . . . One is dining and meeting space in hotels . . . and the other is of course the lack of a convention hall with which to care for the larger gatherings." In language that would be repeated decade after decade in Kansas City and beyond, the group argued, "Until they are realized, Kansas City must accept the fact that it is no longer a convention competitor with the larger cities of the country."[1]

Yet if the convention committee and the larger Chamber of Commerce earnestly desired a bigger convention hall, financing required voter approval of a city bond issue by a two-thirds majority. An initial modest bond proposal for $800,000 to acquire land for a new "Municipal Auditorium" had failed to receive the needed majority in November 1925. A second attempt, to secure $3.5 million to construct a new assembly hall in 1928, also went down to defeat.

The succession of bond issue defeats during the 1920s, including eight separate proposals in 1928, led the chamber leadership to propose a very different political strategy that would encompass not only the proposed Municipal Auditorium but a host of other needed public investments. In his November 1929 address to the Chamber of Commerce annual meeting, chamber head Conrad Mann argued, "We are going after this [bond issue] thing piecemeal. . . . It is just a makeshift program and the very nature of this program creates hostility among our citizens." Mann called on his colleagues to back a "non-partisan 'Kansas City Spirit' movement that will put this thing over."[2]

Mann's view of a comprehensive bond program was remarkable in fiscal terms. The failed 1928 bond program had involved some $18.5 million. Now Mann said the business leadership should "center your efforts upon a major program and submit to the citizens of Kansas City a bond issue of not less than 75 million dollars." He concluded,

> We must give visible evidence of our confidence in Kansas City to people, regardless of where they may reside, that as Kansas Citians, we have faith in our own city; that we are willing to carry the burden in order to make our city a place of happy homes as well as an abiding place for industry and business in general. There is no way in which we can do these things in a more substantial, a more convincing way than by voting a bond issue and by so doing make funds available to meet the expenditures for improvements which are so much needed for our town.

In early 1930, city manager H. F. McElroy proposed that the chamber's Conrad Mann chair a Committee of 100, charged with crafting a ten-year "plan of improvements" that would be the basis of a comprehensive package of bond proposals. While Mann and city officials sought a broad base of citizen involvement, they were not about to leave a proposal as critical to the city's economic future as the proposed auditorium to chance. The subcommittee charged with reviewing the plans for the auditorium was headed by the president of the firm operating the Muehlebach, the city's leading hotel; the secretary was the manager of the convention bureau.[3]

Citing an annual loss of millions of dollars of "convention business . . . directly attributed to the lack of an adequate public auditorium," the subcommittee recommended a $5 million bond proposal for the new convention facility. Business interests united behind a site adjacent to the existing convention hall, preserving the advantage for nearby hotels such as the Muehlebach. And despite the fact that most such recommendations were seriously trimmed to fit city financial resources, the final recommendation of the overall committee was for a $4.5 million auditorium bond—the second largest of 16 proposed city bond issues.

Mann's political calculus proved quite correct. With solid business backing and support of the Pendergast political machine, all 16 bond issues on the March 1931 ballot were approved, with the Municipal Auditorium winning a 79.2 percent "yes" vote. The Auditorium was able to take advantage of a $1.29 million federal public works grant, and some $750,000 from the sale of the existing convention hall, and opened in October 1935.[4]

Kansas City's successful 1931 bond program neatly illustrated both the potential and the constraints of voter-approved general obligation bonds for major public building projects. With Missouri's requirement for a two-thirds majority for each bond proposal, minorities of the electorate had a substantial impact on individual projects. A broad package, calculated to win the support of a broad popular coalition, could deliver what a single scheme for a new auditorium or civic center could not. That pattern of broad electoral coalition-building through a collection of public investment projects—projects that could be distributed across the community—was also exemplified by Missouri's other major urban center, St. Louis.

St. Louis in the 1920s faced a political and fiscal situation parallel to Kansas City's. While the business leadership had embraced a series of major development schemes for a new complex of public buildings and parkways, the required bond issues had often failed to pass. The city's first attempt at a grand, comprehensive package came in 1920 with a bond program including 18 individual items, with a total cost of $24 million. For the downtown interests, the 1920 package included $1.25 million for the central parkways and $900,000 for a new Municipal Auditorium.

The May 1920 effort saw six of the proposed 18 bond projects receive the required majority. The proposed auditorium garnered a 62 percent "yes" vote, and thus failed to pass. Its failure was part of a larger pattern described by historian James Primm: "For decades, small and middle-class property owners, especially in the heavily German wards, not trusting the big-business leadership and feeling that increased taxes would fall most heavily on themselves, had maintained a conservative stance that amounted to civic neglect."[5] But the failure of the auditorium and other proposals did not deter the commitment by some to a broad program of public investment. Less than two weeks after the vote, the city's chief planner, Harland Bartholomew, argued, "That plan, though it has not yet been approved by the necessary majority of voters, is practicable and necessary, and *it is only a matter of time when people will recognize its necessity and it will be adopted*."[6]

The *St. Louis Post-Dispatch* joined the call for a new bond effort, noting in December 1921 that the city needed $25 million to put local sewers in safe condition. The Chamber of Commerce also added its weight behind a broad program of improvements, including the failed public auditorium plan. As the notion of a broad package of public investments gained support, it also began to grow in size and scope. In early 1922 a General Council on Civic Needs, comprising more than 200 members, met to assess the full scope of required public spending. Their recommendation to the city government came to more than $75 million. The city's official fiscal watchdog, the Board of Estimate, reviewed and altered the plans, adding a $4 million proposal for a new courthouse. The final package came to $78.1 million. At each step in the development of the capital program, new groups and interests successfully pressed to include their own "needs" and spending priorities. And in order to win African American votes, Mayor Henry Kiel and Council President Louis Aloe agreed to finance a new city-owned hospital serving the black community.

The grand product was a February 1923 bond program including 21 separate issues, with a total cost of about $88 million. The broad, comprehensive program proved a political success, with 20 of the proposals winning the required two-thirds majority, including the new auditorium with a $5 million price tag. St. Louis's new Kiel Auditorium opened in 1934, combining an auditorium seating 3,600 and a massive exhibition hall, enabling the city to host major national events.[7]

For St. Louis, Kansas City, and a host of other cities in the first half of the twentieth century, the route to building a new convention hall was politically and fiscally difficult. The need to win majority or super-majority voter approval in most states limited the scale of public investment and often resulted in outright defeat. The electorate often proved less convinced than the city's business and political leaders of the virtues in hosting conventions. The common political response was an effort to create a broad, indeed all-embracing, political coalition through a comprehensive package of public improvements. Kansas City and St. Louis succeeded by tying the public buildings and parkways sought by downtown interests to neighborhood-level improvements and basic facilities such as sewers and local parks, carefully distributed across the city and to specific voter groups.

The political pressures to marry proposed new convention halls and auditoriums to a host of other public improvements, however, did not necessarily assure electoral success. Both Kansas City and St. Louis were obliged to repeatedly put their auditorium plans to the electorate. And other cities, such as Chicago, saw local voters regularly defeat convention hall proposals. The history of public auditorium and convention hall votes was one of electoral fragility and uncertainty rather than public enthusiasm.

Public Improvement and Downtown Revitalization

The Depression and World War II severely limited the ability of city governments to finance major public buildings and improvements. By 1945, the end of the war and the prospect of boosting new private development led a number of cities to propose major public investment initiatives. Those initiatives often reflected plans that had been developed during the Depression, and commonly were focused on efforts led by the local business community to support the downtown core and remedy slum housing problems in adjacent neighborhoods.

Dallas, pressed by both the Chamber of Commerce and the "powerful Dallas Citizens' Council," had commissioned planning consultant Harland Bartholomew to develop a new master plan in 1943. While the plan covered a range of subjects across the metropolitan area, it included a specific effort to encourage the "development of a compact and stable central business district, wherein high property values can be maintained over a long period of time." Bartholomew's vision for supporting the downtown core focused on building a new complex of public buildings, sited where it could deal with the blight of nearby slums. And he specifically added, "One of the early needs is that of a Convention Hall," located in "proximity to the downtown district."[8]

Dallas's plan for a new civic center, including a new city hall and public auditorium/convention hall, were joined with local street, sewer, and park improvements as part of a $40 million bond package in late 1945. The idea of a comprehensive package of public investments was very much parallel to the models of St. Louis and Kansas City, as was the premise that these improvements would enable Dallas to keep up with other cities of the Southwest. The civic center scheme that joined the city hall, library, and auditorium in one downtown location was the product of city planning consultant Harland Bartholomew, who viewed the proposed civic complex as a means of "exerting a stabilizing influence on the downtown district."[9] The new Municipal Auditorium, in particular, was described as a means of bringing new visitors to the downtown and supporting area hotels and retail stores.

Dallas's entire $40 million bond package was approved by the voters in December 1945. But that electoral success did reveal a continuing problem in gaining public support. Of the seventeen individual bond proposals, the auditorium came in almost at the bottom of "yes" votes, just slightly better than the proposed city hall and a livestock arena. The Dallas electorate that could readily support sewers, fire stations, and street paving was much less enthusiastic about the benefits of a new municipal auditorium.[10]

Dallas was not the only city that viewed a new public convention facility, perhaps as one part of a new civic center complex, as a means of refashioning the landscape of downtown development. Seattle business leaders too saw a new civic center as a means of both enhancing the city's visibility and boosting the development potential of the downtown core. The planned "Seattle Center" development would both provide a site for a planned 1962 World's Fair ("Century 21") and "bolster the central business district, to enable it to hold its own against the rapid growth of suburban areas."[11]

But in order to build the facilities for the civic center and fair, Seattle was obliged to turn to the local electorate for approval of general obligation bonds. The $7.5 million bond issue for acquisition of the site north of downtown, a new concert and convention hall, and a multipurpose auditorium was passed in November 1956. That success provided the impetus for a matching $7.5 million appropriation from the state that secured the development of Seattle Center and the World's Fair complex.

The focus of Seattle and Dallas on efforts to boost private investment and development in the downtown area was common to many large cities in the 1950s and 1960s. The availability of federal urban renewal funds for clearing and rebuilding slums, from the Housing Acts of 1949 and 1954, and the prospect for redeveloping deteriorated zones in and around the core, served as an impetus to a host of convention center development proposals in the decades after World War II. But where these cities succeeded in gaining sufficient voter approval for new meeting facilities, the outcome in other cities was far more problematic. Other cities tried, and often failed, to pass the necessary bond issues.

In mid-1957, Cleveland Mayor Anthony Celebrezze joined the city's business leaders in promoting a scheme by New York developer William Zeckendorf for a downtown complex of hotel, office buildings, and apartment buildings on the city's lakefront. But the cornerstone of Zeckendorf's plan was the construction of a new convention hall, one long sought by downtown business and hospitality interests. And the financing of a new convention center necessarily meant gaining voter approval for general obligation bonds. With great fanfare, the $15 million convention center bond proposal appeared on the city ballot in November 1957. The bonds managed a 52 percent "yes" vote, but fell short of the required 55 percent majority. Mayor Celebrezze and developer Zeckendorf tried again with the same scheme the following year. The "yes" vote slipped slightly, and once again the plan failed.[12]

With two successive defeats, Zeckendorf gave up on Cleveland and moved on to other cities. But Celebrezze, and more importantly the business leaders of the Greater Cleveland Chamber of Commerce and Cleveland Development Foundation, were unwilling to give up on the promise of a big new convention center and the prospect of anchoring downtown revival with it and the new hotel it would surely draw. The result was a political compromise with the leadership of the city council that involved a less costly convention facility at a different site. With that compromise, a new $10 million convention center plan was put on the ballot in November 1960, and finally succeeded in winning voter approval.[13]

The route to electoral success was no less rough for 1960s Atlanta. Newly elected mayor Ivan Allen, Jr., and the Chamber of Commerce he had just led as president proposed a new auditorium/convention hall in early 1962. A $10 million civic center bond issue was packaged with other spending proposals for street and sewer improvements and a major new cultural and arts center in Piedmont Park. Despite the unanimity of the city's white civic leadership and the promise of a broad set of community improvements, the entire bond package of $80 million failed to win voter approval.[14]

Mayor Allen and the chamber leadership were not willing to give up on the planned auditorium/convention hall, despite the fact that a post-election survey showed only 58 percent of voters willing to support it, compared to 84 percent backing for schools and 79 percent for street or sewer improvements. Allen chose to try again with a convention hall reduced in scale and cost, dropping the bond issue amount from $10 million to $9 million. Submitted to the voters again in May 1963, the convention hall issue passed. But Atlanta was left with an undersized convention facility, with business leaders complaining of its inadequacy shortly after it opened.

The cases of Cleveland and Atlanta suggested that voter support for convention center bonds was not necessarily certain, even with broad backing from business and political leaders including a seemingly popular mayor, the promise of new jobs and development, and the packaging as part of a larger bond program. That fact was certainly evident in 1960s St. Louis. A modest bond proposal for renovating city buildings, including the Kiel Auditorium, on the ballot in January 1962, was defeated. A second attempt later that year met defeat as well. And a 1966 bond issue for expanding the Kiel and adding more exhibit space was also defeated, managing the lowest "yes" vote (54 percent) of the 18 issues on the ballot.

St. Louis faced the unusual problem of having to secure a two-thirds majority under Missouri state law. But it also faced a new set of political and electoral realities during the 1960s, as the coalition of upper-income whites and African American votes that had historically provided the votes to pass major bond issues began to collapse. That change, in turn, reflected a new level of political involvement by the African American community, linked to the civil rights movement, and the increasing white outmigration from the central city. The new electoral politics of bond issues were fully evident when St. Louis business and political leaders succeeded in putting a proposal for building an entirely new convention center on the ballot in March 1971. The result was an abject defeat, termed by the *St. Louis Post-Dispatch* "the worst defeat of a local capital improvement plan here in many years," with the bonds managing just 36 percent of the vote. Even the predominantly African American wards, long the source of 75 and 80 percent margins for previous bond proposals, delivered just a 45 percent "yes" vote—far below the needed two-thirds.[15]

Plans for a new convention center in downtown Kansas City followed a very similar trajectory to those in St. Louis, with much the same outcome. By the 1960s, the Municipal Auditorium that was the great political triumph of the 1930s was showing its age, and as in Cleveland and Atlanta, local boosters were looking to compete with newer, bigger centers in other major cities. At a meeting of the board of directors in March 1964, the Kansas City Chamber of Commerce took up the question of the need for more exhibit space at the auditorium, noting "The increased competition for convention business."[16] That May, the chamber leaders moved that "a complete study be made of the possibility of new and expanded auditorium facilities in Kansas City . . . [with] suggestions for methods of financing the project."[17]

The new convention center had to wait for passage of a county government priority, a new stadium, in mid-1967. But with passage of the stadium bond proposal, the chamber leaders again took up the question of more convention space. At the chamber board's July 1967 meeting, president Robert Ingram said "that it would be necessary for revitalization of effort for the establishment of an Exhibition Hall," noting that "Mayor [Ilus] Davis advised him that the cost today would be approximately twelve million dollars" and that "hotel interests are quite concerned with building new hotel facilities until they are assured that we can have more conventions."[18] Two months later, Ingram reported to the board that he had been in touch with the city council and "that they were attempting to work it into a capital program."[19] After the city manager and staff crafted a broad capital improvement effort, Mayor Davis reported to the chamber in January 1969 that a planned bond program would join the new convention center with bonds for street lighting, swimming pools, airport improvements, and remodeling of City Hall. The Mayor concluded by saying, "We will call on you when the time arises that we need your support on these various projects."[20]

What the mayor and city council finally crafted was a package of 17 individual bond issues, for a total of more than $143 million, in keeping with the city's historical pattern of comprehensive packages of bond proposals. The largest single item on the list was proposition number 3—$23.5 million for a new exhibition hall. The campaign for the December 16, 1969, bond election was bankrolled by the chamber, promoted as a "Program for Progress," and sold vigorously by local media. The *Kansas City Star* ran a front page editorial on December 15, arguing that "The prime consideration at the polls tomorrow is whether Kansas City is to grow or retrench in the 1970s."[21] The campaign mirrored a host of past efforts. This time it did not work.

Each of the 17 bond issues was defeated, failing to win a two-thirds majority. Two, for police and fire, actually managed to top the 50 percent mark. But most did far worse, including the $23.5 million exhibition hall proposal. It managed just a 32.6 percent "yes" vote, placing it next to last in public appeal. The defeat was a stunning failure for both the city administration and the business leadership. Meeting with the chamber two weeks after the vote, Mayor Davis "explained that the Program was caught in the upgraft [sic] of feelings against taxes nation wide."[22] It was also clear that the mayor had little interest in returning to the voters quickly, as the city had in the past. The mayor said he had "no magic words or direction," and that "all issues have to be passed and it is only a matter of when," posing the question, "How do we do it?"[23]

By about 1970, the business and political leaders of both Kansas City and St. Louis faced the larger demographic and political realities that had confronted their counterparts in Cleveland, Atlanta, and a number of other cities. The bond programs that had so consistently garnered public support in the past were now far more problematic. And no single project demonstrated the public's indifference or disdain more than the investment in a new convention center or exhibition hall. However appealing these major investments might be to hotel owners, downtown firms, and local business leaders, their appeal to an electorate concerned about things like property taxes, (often dwindling) basic city services, and neighborhood change was remarkably limited.

The answer to the question posed by Kansas City mayor Ilus Davis of "How do we do it" clearly had to be *differently*—with some fiscal or political change that held the promise of reversing (or avoiding) the public's disinterest.

A Fiscal and Political Reformation

Kansas City

The plaint of Kansas City's mayor was largely irrelevant to the city's Chamber of Commerce leadership. The chamber had planned and bargained for a new convention facility for over half of the previous decade, and the group was unwilling to accept the December 1969 vote as the final verdict. Just four months after the defeat, in April 1970, Lester Siegel of the chamber's Convention and Tourism Department reported on a series of meetings to consider financing alternatives. Siegel "advised they were going to approach the people who would reap direct benefits from a new facility to participate in at least partial financing of a large facility to supplement the present space."[24] Beyond the possibility of private backing, they were also "checking with other cities on how they were able to finance their facilities."[25] Behind the scenes, business leaders were pressing the city council to move ahead on some arrangement for a new convention center. But it was not until late June 1971 that council member Sal Capra was able to publicly announce a city study of financial alternatives.[26]

The decade of the 1960s had not been kind to the Kansas City central business district. New office construction in the suburbs had matched downtown development, and in the early 1970s would substantially exceed it. In terms of constant dollars, downtown retail sales had slipped from $157 million in 1963 to $137 million in 1967 and then $95 million in 1972. And the situation was getting worse, with one 1976 study reporting, "The Kansas City CBD experienced significant declines in all indices of economic vitality in the 1970–1975 period despite regional growth over the same time frame." The city's business leaders were desperate to boost downtown's fortunes.[27]

Whatever the fiscal preferences of the city council, the chamber was insistent on a convention center *soon*. The group voted on June 28, 1971, to reaffirm its commitment to a new hall "at the earliest possible date," calling for the expansion to "be in the close proximity or adjacent to the present facilities as far as possible and that it be in a downtown location."[28] Although the chamber clearly wanted a new convention hall, the financing alternatives of a business tax or a lease-purchase deal were less enticing. The group also "urged that the need for Convention and Exhibition Hall expansion be brought before the voters at the earliest possible date."[29]

Mayor Charles Wheeler embraced the chamber position and called for a November vote on the convention center proposition alone. But council members wanted to either defer a vote, or provide for repaying the bonds with taxes on hotels, restaurants, and ultimately visitors, as a means of making the project more appealing to the voters. After one member proposed building the new center adjacent to the city's old airport rather than downtown, the council leadership and the chamber met in September 1971 to reach a politically acceptable solution.

That solution was made public on September 22. The council agreed to finance the new facility with revenue bonds issued by a nonprofit corporation, in a variation on the lease-purchase scheme.[30] They could thus avoid a public vote on the center proposal. Leaders from the hotel and restaurant business in turn agreed to a set of new taxes, and the chamber Board of Directors approved both the financing arrangement and the commitment to a downtown site. Indeed, the chamber went on to craft a plan under which it would obtain $1.25 million in private loans to finance architectural work on the center, and then promised that "if a reasonable amount of money is needed to complete the convention center, it will further undertake to obtain these funds through contributions from the business community of the Kansas City metropolitan area."[31]

The deal to finance and build the new convention center was a political masterpiece. It enabled the chamber and the hospitality industry to achieve their goal of a quick start on the structure, while avoiding the potential for defeat and public embarrassment that might well have accompanied another vote. The council members were able to argue that business and visitors would pay, rather than local property owners. And they were thus able to free up part of the city's property tax to support additional debt planned for a vote in 1972.

The political success of the convention center deal was nonetheless subject to a legal question, and in June 1972 a suit was filed that raised that question. The legal vulnerability of the planned center was mirrored by its fiscal problems. In July 1973, the *Kansas City Star* headlined "Convention Center Price Tag Rises Sharply."[32] The $19 million convention center was now estimated to cost $35 million, about the outer limits of the revenues from the hotel and restaurant taxes. But the legal problems won out—the Missouri Supreme Court in September decided against the city's financing scheme, concluding that any commitment of city tax revenues required a public vote.[33]

If the 1971 deal for the new convention center was voided by the court decision, the timing was nonetheless fortuitous. Quite independently, the city had been developing a broad gauge capital improvement program scheduled to go before the voters on December 18, 1973. The city council quickly moved to add the convention center as the fourteenth separate bond proposal, with a total cost of $30 million. Thirteen of the bond proposals, including $22 million for street improvements and $10 million for urban renewal, were to be paid for by the city's general revenues. But the new convention center was different—it could be sold as paid for by visitors, through the new hotel and restaurant taxes.

The chamber leadership did not simply trust to the public's civic spirit in winning approval for the center bonds. In late March, the leaders behind the bond program had reported on a meeting "with principals of the KANSAS CITY STAR and they have pledged full support."[34] The *Star* provided substantial backing, both on its editorial pages and in news coverage. An extensive article on the Sunday before the vote announced, "Convention Center Dividends Paid in Business, Jobs" and described the competition the city faced for convention business, noting the successful results of new centers in Dallas, Atlanta, and Denver.[35]

The Chamber of Commerce, together with the city's hospitality community, provided the bulk of campaign funds. And the campaign effort extended beyond traditional advertising and public relations. Mayor aide and political consultant Jerry Jette noted the need to bring ward political organizations into the bond campaign:

> The existing effective political organizations in certain sections of the City must be pulled into the campaign in favor of the Bond Package . . . . The areas to which I refer are wards 1, 2, 11, 12, 13, 14, 15, 16, 17 and 18. These are among the least affluent in the City and if we are to expect positive support at the precinct and on election day, certain monies must be made available. . . . Each precinct within each ward will be assigned a quota of 150 "yes" votes.[36]

The fiscal commitment of the Chamber of Commerce to an effective campaign, perhaps including "certain monies" as well as appeals to community improvement, proved vital.

Ten of the 14 bond issues on the December 1973 ballot failed to receive the required two-thirds majority. The proposals for police and fire protection passed, but urban renewal, street improvement, and parks bonds all failed. The $30 million convention center bond literally squeaked through, with a margin of 22 "yes" votes out of more than 46,000 cast.

The successful 1973 convention center vote gave Kansas City a brand-new convention center, which opened for business in 1976. It also marked the beginning of a new era in convention center financing. The commitment of new hotel and restaurant taxes to pay off the general obligation bonds sold for the center fundamentally changed the fiscal and political environment for convention center investment. The new H. Roe Bartle Exhibition Hall was built across the street from the Municipal Auditorium, where it would support the existing concentration of hotels and anchor the southwestern core of the central business district. The new center would be expanded and improved at substantial cost in subsequent years. But Kansas City voters would never again face a convention center bond issue proposal that required two-thirds majority support.

In 1988, when St. Louis business and political leaders turned to the Missouri state government for help in financing a new domed stadium for a potential National Football League team, Kansas City chamber leaders successfully lobbied to pair a state commitment for Bartle Hall expansion with the St. Louis proposal. In July 1989, Governor John Ashcroft signed legislation that both created a regional sports complex authority for St. Louis and offered Kansas City $2 million a year to help pay for expansion of the Bartle Hall facility.[37]

The commitment of state financing helped move the expansion effort ahead. Yet the state dollars could not pay the full cost of a major expansion, estimated at over $100 million. For that, Kansas City needed more local money. City leaders had imposed a set of hotel and restaurant taxes to pay for the bonds used to build Bartle in the 1970s. By raising those tax rates, it could provide a steady stream of revenue to retire new bonds for the expansion. At the same time, the tax increases would require voter approval, but only a simple majority.

By shifting to financing with a tax increase rather than a bond issue, Kansas City political leaders neatly reduced the size and scale of the electoral coalition needed to approve the expansion project. There was no need to propose a broad, all-inclusive package of public improvements for the entire city. But there was still a need to ensure the support of critical groups of voters. The result was a series of "side deals" to win council and community backing for the Bartle expansion. For the African American community, there was a commitment to neighborhood tourism projects that could include funding for a jazz hall of fame. Union leaders won a new contract for city employees.[38]

The hotel and restaurant tax increase was backed by the "Kansas City Jobs Committee" with a $337,000 campaign effort and the strong editorial backing of the city's two daily newspapers. The result was a 61 percent "yes" vote, securing some $6 million in annual revenues that could both pay for the expansion, now pegged at $120 million, and support a "tourism development fund" for projects like the Jazz Museum. The city neatly avoided the state requirement for voter approval of bond issues by crafting a lease arrangement, with the debt actually issued by the "Kansas City Municipal Assistance Corporation," a nonprofit entity created in 1984 to get around state debt restrictions, and overseen by a board that included the city manager, the city attorney, and the city's director of finance.[39]

The expanded Bartle Convention Center formally opened in late September 1994, adding some 200,000 square feet of exhibit hall space to the earlier facility, at a cost of $144 million. Kansas City mayor Emanuel Cleaver termed the larger edifice a "majestic convention center that will set the standard for convention centers around the world." The mayor added, "It makes a statement nationally that Kansas City is a big-league player when it comes to conventions." The city's convention and visitors' bureau promised that 40 new conventions had already been booked for the expanded center through 2002. And there were promises of a boom in private hotel and restaurant development in the surrounding area.[40]

Yet, much as with its original completion in 1976, the expanded Bartle almost immediately faced growing competition from other cities. And in 2000, the consultant hired by the city council and the convention and visitors bureau, John Kaatz of CSL, delivered a withering assessment of what the city had bought for its $144 million. He concluded, "Bartle Hall's meeting rooms are substandard in decor and technologically outdated, and its undersized ballroom is costing Kansas City lost convention business and tax dollars." "You have to spend some money," he added, telling a council committee, "Kansas City ranked near the bottom of several comparison lists of the nation's top 25 convention cities and risked falling even further without a Bartle Hall upgrade."[41]

Kaatz's analysis provided the justification for yet another call for investment in improving and expanding Bartle. And just as with the first expansion effort, the $74 million price tag of the new ballroom and additional upgrades would be on the ballot as an increase in city hotel and restaurant taxes, requiring only a majority vote for approval. And rather than a broad program of public improvements, the tax increases were paired on the ballot with a proposal for a $35 million revenue bond issue, much of it earmarked for downtown improvements. According to the city's economic development director, "When we can, we want to invest our dollars to create a catalytic effect, to leverage private investments and create market opportunities."[42]

The November 2002 ballot gave the Bartle upgrade tax increase a 52.8 percent "yes" vote, the lowest margin since the two-thirds majority garnered by the original bond proposal in 1973. But by changing the fiscal and political structure of convention center finance, Kansas City's business and political leaders had literally "reformed" the capacity for convention center investment. By 2002, the business community could reassuringly assert that "business travelers" would pay the higher hotel taxes, and that the burden of the increased restaurant tax, "adding a nickel to every $20 restaurant tab," was comparatively mild. The result, just as promised in every previous vote, was that Kansas City would remain a competitive convention destination, fully capable of competing with every other major city and luring tens of thousands of new convention attendees to the city each year.

The shift to revenue bonds and a vote solely on increases in the hotel and restaurant taxes did not remove the need to work out deals and compromises, both with the city's hospitality interests and with important voter blocs. But it eased the political problem of securing electoral support, while being manageable in an environment of local fiscal limits. Convention center and downtown backers could regularly assert that these taxes could only properly be used for boosting tourism. And they could reassuringly portray the convention center investment as one that would both boost visitor spending and secure the fortunes of downtown.

San Antonio

The fiscal and political reformation managed by Kansas City business leaders and elected officials was not unique. Faced with growing voter resistance to both increased taxes and downtown development projects, a broad array of other cities succeeded in creating new fiscal schemes that assured public dollars for expanded centers without a vote on long-term debt.

San Antonio's first post-World War II convention center efforts began with the plan for clearing and rebuilding much of the fringe of downtown as the site for a world's fair, Hemisfair '68. The fair plans included a new "Community and Convention Center," to be financed with city general obligation bonds. That in turn required a referendum vote, and the center proposal with a $10.9 million price tag was packaged as part of a broader seven-item, $30 million bond program, including funds for parks, libraries, and street improvements, in January 1964.

Less than a decade after the new center opened in 1968, city officials called for an expansion. This time there was no attempt to put it on the ballot for voter approval. And there would be no further votes on center expansion or financing in future years. The expanded and renamed Henry B. Gonzalez Convention Center opened in 1977, financed by the revenues from the city-owned City Public Service gas and electric utility.

By early 1983, Mayor Henry Cisneros was promoting the idea of yet another expansion, arguing that it would allow for larger conventions and draw more visitors to the city. Even before it commissioned a feasibility study of the expansion, the city council committed to an increase in the hotel-motel tax. That hotel tax increase would pay for the "certificates of obligation" issued to pay for the expansion, neatly avoiding the need for a public vote on a bond issue proposal.[43]

The expansion of the HBG Convention Center was completed in late 1986, bringing it to 240,000 square feet of exhibit space. Yet once again, only a few years passed before downtown business interests and local hoteliers were pressing for another major expansion. Arguing that the center "is at absolute full capacity during months of high traffic," consulting firm Gladstone Associates recommended in November 1990 adding up to 230,000 square feet of exhibit space, effectively doubling the center's size. The consultants recommended that the expansion be paid for with an increase in the citywide hotel tax, then at 7 percent.[44]

City leaders secured approval for the 2 percent "Expansion Hotel Occupancy Tax" from the state legislature in 1993, and three years later sold the bonds to finance the $215 million expansion effort. By using the dedicated hotel tax, San Antonio could tap the revenues generated by some 23,000 city hotel rooms, regardless of whether they were occupied by convention attendees or by families visiting the Alamo and Riverwalk. And as the city and its stock of hotel rooms grew, the 2 percent tax provided a stream of funds committed to the expansion—and future expansions—almost exclusively.[45]

The HBG Center expansion was completed in early 2001. But even before the larger center had demonstrated its success (or failure) in luring convention business, the city government was planning yet another expansion. City finance officials told bond rating agencies in 2006 of their plans, well before actually receiving a consultant market or feasibility study in July 2008. With a committed stream of hotel tax revenues, the city had effectively created a permanent convention center expansion annuity, one that operated perpetually without voter review. Unfortunately, even that annuity was subject to the vagaries of local hotel occupancy and the national economy, reducing the city's stream of hotel tax revenues. It was not until the summer of 2012 that the city was in a position to arrange financing for yet another center expansion and renovation effort, this time with a $325 million price tag, fully employing the 2 percent expansion tax with the added backing of a pledge of "any lawfully available resources of the City."[46]

After the success of the initial voter-approved bond issue in 1964, San Antonio managed a fiscal regime that has supported successive center expansions and renovations, and all without recourse to the voters. And the city appears fully capable, fiscally and politically, of continuing major convention center investment for decades to come, without the risk or need for deal-making attendant to a public vote.

Cincinnati

A new auditorium or convention hall had long been a goal for Cincinnati business and political leaders through the first half of the twentieth century. Two successive bond proposals for a new auditorium were defeated by the voters, in 1939 and 1940. The city's 1948 Metropolitan Master Plan included an "Exposition Hall-Arena," along with a merchandise mart and new stadium, as part of a proposed civic center on the city's redeveloped riverfront. But as city business leaders increasingly focused on the decline of the downtown core during the 1950s, the location and priority of a new convention center proved a point of some contention. City planners continued to envision the convention facility and auditorium as the anchors of a new civic center complex on the riverfront. Democratic city council member John Gilligan had his own proposal, for a new convention hall anchoring the west side of the downtown core area, a location embraced by the City Planning Commission in a December 1957 land use plan.[47]

For Gilligan, recalling the events after more than 30 years, a broad package of downtown investments, combined with federal urban renewal aid, offered the ultimate political solution—"It became evident that attempting to do one project at a time wasn't going to get anywhere; projects and plans began to get inclusive. . . . [We] had to put together packages that all the downtown interests saw some benefit to their situation, were not being left out."[48]

The conclusion was little different for the council's Republicans. Eugene Ruehlmann recalled, "the restaurant and hotel people were interested in the convention center, the big supporters of riverfront were the Cincinnatus Association [a local civic organization]; by putting them together we could get diverse groups together on both projects."[49]

For the city's business leaders, the central goal was revitalization of the downtown core, not the riverfront or even a new convention center. Those leaders, organized as the Citizens Development Committee, were thoroughly unwilling to see their central focus—the core area urban renewal effort—run the risk of possible defeat by the voters. Discussing the politics of the package in March 1962, the business group's conclusion was direct: "It was unanimously agreed that CDC favors the issuance of councilmanic [nonvoted] bonds for financing the City's share of the Core Area project due to the prospect that a referendum would be unsuccessful. Such a failure would naturally inhibit Council from issuing councilmanic bonds following an opposing expression from the voters."[50]

The CDC was willing to embrace the riverfront and convention hall proposals, as long as the city's focus was kept on the central business district. And while the business group was willing to back and finance an expansive bond campaign, it did so with the dual provisos that the downtown renewal be the first priority and that downtown funding not be subject to a public vote.

The decision to put the convention hall and the riverfront renewal together as a single $16.6 million proposal was almost unheard of. It reflected a clear political calculus that the convention center would be a tough "sell" to the public. According to John Gilligan, the center "in most people's eyes was not that great a thing, just of benefit to a few downtown interests."[51] Packaging it together with the riverfront, for former planning director Herbert Stevens, recognized that "you have to link them together . . . the convention center had interest with the business community, the riverfront was pizzazz."[52]

The political wisdom of packaging the riverfront renewal and convention hall plans together on the November 1962 ballot was validated by the vote results. The convention center bonds won a 56.58 percent "yes" vote—just slightly over the required 55 percent majority. And much of the voting support had come not from the city's better-off neighborhoods, but rather from lower-income, largely African American areas.

Perhaps the most salient result of the thin electoral margin for the convention center bonds was the fragility of public support for large-scale downtown public investment. The city would systematically avoid placing these kinds of proposals on the ballot in subsequent years and decades.

The new Cincinnati Convention Center officially opened in August 1967, with 95,000 square feet of exhibit space. Even by the standards of the time, it was a relatively small facility. But any potential expansion effort would have to await a suitable political and fiscal environment. Finally in early 1981, the city commissioned the Laventhol & Horwath consulting firm to examine the feasibility of an expansion and the means to pay for it. The Laventhol report argued that the center was in need of both refurbishment and expansion, at a cost of between $40 and $50 million. And the Laventhol consultants recommended a combination of a variety of financing mechanisms, including a new city bond issue, "excess" income tax revenues, and $10 million in "philanthropic contributions." The Laventhol analysis did not suggest asking the city's voters.[53]

With growing local discord over the issue of downtown versus neighborhood public investment, the city council sought to avoid a public vote: "Because there was a chance voters wouldn't approve it," according to city council member Guy Guckenberger. The council member went on, "We felt the city couldn't afford to take that chance." City director of development Nell Surber echoed Guckenberger: "But you never know what the public will do and we just plain had our backs to the wall."[54]

The final financing scheme for the expansion had the city paying $27 million, the Hamilton County government adding $16 million, $5 million from the Greater Cincinnati Convention and Visitors Bureau, and additional funds from the state and federal governments. The expanded center, renamed in honor of Cincinnatian Dr. Albert Sabin, was dedicated in June 1986 and fully opened in 1987. The expansion boosted the Sabin Center to a total of 162,000 square feet of exhibit space. A host of cost overruns brought the final to $61.9 million, with serious conflict between the city and county governments over bearing the increased cost. But by joining with Hamilton County and adding state and federal dollars, the city succeeded in getting a larger center without recourse to the voters.

It had taken more than a dozen years from the original opening of Cincinnati's convention center before there was serious consideration of an expansion. The pace proved more rapid in the wake of the 1986 unveiling of the Sabin Center. As the committee charged with reviewing the city's downtown development plans finalized its report in late 1990, a headline in the *Cincinnati Enquirer* on November 15 brought the news that "Bigger Convention Hall Urged But City Skeptical of Adding More Debt." Yet financing a major expansion, particularly while avoiding a public vote, was not a simple or easy process.[55]

When the city's chosen consultants, PriceWaterhouse, delivered their report in June 1995, it predictably called on the city to expand the center, arguing that Cincinnati would see "continuing decline in center city retail and restaurant sales if it does not expand its convention center." Their recommendation was to double the center exhibit hall space, to some 600,000 square feet, at a cost of $290 million. But the city did not have the resources to support some $300 million in new debt itself.[56]

By late 1998, with no real progress on the expansion effort, city officials brought the PriceWaterhouseCoopers consultants, led by David Petersen, back. Their February 1999 report again endorsed more space, albeit not as much as the earlier analysis. But the proposed expansion now carried a price tag estimated at $315 million. Despite an effort by city manager John Shirey to craft a package of new revenue streams from an increased city hotel tax, a boost in the county hotel tax, a restaurant tax, and a new sales tax increment scheme, it was simply impossible to finance an expansion of that scale and price. Finally, in late 2001, a special mayoral task force embraced a far smaller expansion, one that could be realized at a cost estimated at $171 million.[57]

Even a dramatically reduced expansion plan would cost far more than the city itself could afford, and that demanded an exercise in imaginative intergovernmental finance. Cincinnati Mayor Charlie Luken and Hamilton County commissioner Todd Portune were able to craft a financing deal "breakthrough" in January 2002 that joined together city and county hotel tax revenues, a $10 million contribution from the Greater Cincinnati Convention and Visitors Bureau, a annual contribution from the city, and some $15 million in naming rights, for an expansion that carried a $198 million cost. The deal continued to evolve through the year, with a significant change in May that boosted the revenue from naming rights and promised a portion of the county hotel tax revenue to suburban communities, while putting the financing of the expansion in the hands of a new public authority, the Hamilton County Convention Facilities Authority.[58]

The final deal for Cincinnati's $160 million renamed Duke Energy Convention Center neatly combined funds from the city and county hotel tax revenues with contributions from the local convention bureau, the business community's Equity Fund, and Duke Energy's naming rights. With the expanded center's grand opening in June 2006, the *Cincinnati Enquirer* touted "Convention Center Upgrade Breeds Confidence," with the observation that "Business and tourism officials hope an improved and expanded convention center will boost the local economy downtown and beyond."[59]

The story of the expansion of Cincinnati's convention center has all of the elements of a "Perils of Pauline" saga that extended over more than 15 years. The effort would regularly appear to be stalled or dead, with financing impossible to secure, only to rise again, perhaps in a different form, with yet another increasingly intricate financial arrangement. The one political and fiscal constant was that local voters were never given the choice of investing in a larger center. If Cincinnati's business leaders ended up with a far smaller expansion than they had sought, they nonetheless finally got an expansion without a public vote.

Reformation and Result

The 1970s marked a turning point in the fiscal politics of convention center investment. Faced with growing voter disenchantment or outright revolt, symbolized by the passage of California's Proposition 13 in 1978, city after city reshaped the historic pattern of building broad voter coalitions for comprehensive packages of bond projects. For some cities, like Kansas City, the initial shift reflected the defeat of a convention center bond proposal. In Cincinnati, the unwillingness of the city's business leaders and elected officials to put a proposal before the voters reflected a clear calculation that it would likely fail. For San Antonio, the shift to hotel taxes and revenue debt took somewhat longer but ultimately reflected precisely the same political calculus—the need to insulate convention center investment from direct voter review.

Other cities were no less imaginative. After decades of plans and proposals, San Jose, California, finally opened a new downtown convention center in 1989, financing it with "certificates of obligation" that did not require a public vote, and would ostensibly be repaid by tax revenues from local redevelopment projects. When the city sought to expand and renovate its McEnery Convention Center in the late 1990s, it ultimately chose to use the revenue stream from an increase in the local hotel tax (Transient Occupancy Tax). But under California law, even that tax increase required voter approval. And the voters did not approve, providing the tax increase with a 65 percent "yes" vote that fell just short of the required two-thirds. The verdict of the electorate did not end the quest for a bigger convention center for San Jose. It simply shifted the focus of local business and political leaders to a fiscal scheme that could avoid voter review. The solution proved to be a "convention center facilities district," created by the city council in August 2008, that could impose an additional hotel tax to finance the expansion. But the great virtue of the district was that its taxation only had to be approved by a vote of the city's hotel owners, based on the size of their hotels. With "yes" votes representing 78 percent of local hotel rooms, San Jose could move ahead on a $120 million expansion project, with a guaranteed steady stream of future revenues dedicated to the convention center. And with the San Jose special district model approved by a state court, San Diego and San Francisco began to move ahead to finance their own center expansions with tourism district schemes that required only a (weighted) vote of local hotel owners.[60]

The fiscal reformation of these cities and a host of others was achieved in a piecemeal fashion. Yet it evidenced a remarkable level of imagination and innovation. Cities committed to center development or expansion were willing to find revenue streams in a great many places. And, as the Cincinnati case so well demonstrates, they were often willing to "bet" on uncertain revenues or commitments in the hope of securing a politically viable deal. City boundaries were not necessarily a limitation either. Kansas City managed to piggyback on St. Louis's quest for state dollars for a domed stadium, gaining it own share of state government dollars. And Cincinnati's politicians proved amenable to sharing the responsibility for convention center expansion with the county government when the city lacked both the fiscal resources and the political capacity.

Formal legal limits were no hurdle either. State laws could be amended or changed to allow new taxes, or in the case of San Antonio, a higher tax dedicated solely to convention center expansion. State legislatures could also be persuaded to allow the creation of new governmental entities, such as the convention center districts in San Jose and San Diego, that exist solely to finance more convention center development without a public vote. The state government also represented an attractive political ally for convention center proponents, one with substantial fiscal resources where the promise of new distant visitors yielding increased tax revenues might well produce political success.

Bringing the State In

For convention center proponents, the search for financing—and a political opening—need not stop at a city or county boundary. Much as Willie Sutton observed about banks, state governments and state-created public authorities offer attractive vehicles for convention center building, often without the political or fiscal constraints and the requirement for voter approval faced by city or county governments. Consulting firms such as PriceWaterhouse have regularly argued that state governments reap a fiscal windfall, through the state sales tax, from the out-of-state attendees attracted to major centers. Yet, aside from potential fiscal benefits, business and hospitality groups already organized to lobby for their interests at the state capital find the appeal to a different level of government an easy shift to manage. State governments have come to play an increasingly important role in convention center development, one merely suggested by convention center names—the Connecticut Convention Center in Hartford, the Pennsylvania Convention Center in Philadelphia, the Georgia World Congress Center in Atlanta, the Washington State Convention and Trade Center in Seattle. That role, not entirely new, represents yet another form of the fiscal and political adaptation that has supported the enormous growth in convention center space across the U.S. over the last five decades.

New York City

New York's business leaders regularly bemoaned the lack of a major convention hall through the 1920s, 1930s, and 1940s, particularly as other cities developed new venues. A *New York Times* editorial in December 1947, headlined "A Convention Hall Needed," outlined that history from 1923, described the new auditoriums in Cleveland, Kansas City, St. Louis, and Atlantic City, and then noted the city's loss of millions of dollars in convention business.[61]

The New York Merchants Association and its convention bureau had pressed the idea of a new auditorium/convention hall for Manhattan in conjunction with the planned 1939 World's Fair, an idea endorsed by Mayor Fiorello LaGuardia. But with no prospect of federal funds, the city was not in a position to deliver a major new building. The city's convention and visitors bureau, and its longtime chair merchant Bernard Gimbel, regularly pressed for a new public convention venue, albeit with no success. The first real plan for a convention center emerged in November 1946 with the announcement by the Madison Square Garden Corporation of a scheme for a "New Madison Square Garden," combining a sports arena and a convention hall, to be built at Columbus Circle. The private corporation also announced the involvement of a public entity, the Triborough Bridge and Tunnel Authority, in financing and developing the new "Garden" and an associated garage.[62]

The role of the Triborough Authority in the proposal was particularly significant. Triborough was the seat of the empire of Robert Moses, who had crafted a reputation as a stellar public official and "master builder" through the Depression years. New York Mayor William O'Dwyer had appointed Moses New York City Construction Coordinator in January 1946, charged with expediting and building a host of public projects outlined in a postwar public works program. An alliance with Moses could make the long-planned convention hall a reality, while avoiding the problems—fiscal and political—posed by direct city involvement in a private project.

The initial plans for the "New Madison Square Garden" had the Triborough Authority providing the financing for what would be a privately operated facility. That financing role in turn required securing approval of the state legislature for an increase in the authority's debt limit and its new role. The first response in Albany was a firm "no," with proposed legislation killed in the Assembly's Ways and Means Committee. New York business leaders and Moses pressed the issue again the following year, and with the backing of Governor Thomas Dewey, won approval for the debt increase. The governor said it would make Mayor O'Dwyer "happy" and predicted "it would make New York again the pre-eminent convention city of the world," and the city Convention and Visitors Bureau pegged its yield in new visitor spending at $25 million a year.[63]

The involvement of the Triborough Bridge and Tunnel Authority in financing a new arena and convention center complex was at first glance odd. The authority had no particular mandate for such a facility—its purview was transportation. But Moses had gotten a host of public projects built, and had a strong relationship with city business leaders such as Bernard F. Gimbel of Gimbel's Department Store and Saks Fifth Avenue, as well as bankers and financiers. Indeed, Moses would later recall in his autobiography that "The business community approached the Triborough Bridge and Tunnel Authority to meet this need [for a convention hall] as a matter of public service." A new complex at Columbus Circle offered the prospect of meeting the city's convention needs and of spurring the redevelopment of the West Side.[64]

The Madison Square Garden Corporation eventually pulled out of the project, and the sports arena portion was eliminated. An effort announced by Moses in 1951 to bring both the Metropolitan Opera and the Philharmonic to a new music hall on the site also failed. Moses and Triborough were faced with two problems in developing the convention facility at the site backed by the business leaders. The built-up Columbus Circle location would be expensive to acquire and clear. And the convention hall itself was a money-losing investment. Moses needed some other activity to generate a revenue stream.[65]

Moses, as head of the city's Title I slum clearance program, chose to use the new federal urban redevelopment program to acquire the site and "write down" the cost for a new use. But federal restrictions ruled out building a home for the Opera and Philharmonic. The Triborough Authority moved ahead with the "Coliseum" as a new auditorium and convention hall on the Columbus Circle site, pairing it with a 26-story office building that would help subsidize the convention facility. The New York Coliseum opened in April 1956, giving the city some 273,000 square feet of exhibit space and filling the need for a modern convention facility that business leaders had long sought.

By turning to Moses and Triborough, the city managed to secure a new convention center and achieve a major redevelopment goal that neatly avoided any serious conflict over public investment priorities or the kinds of fiscal limits that had stymied earlier initiatives. There was no formal rationale for involving a bridge and tunnel authority in the business of building a coliseum/convention hall. But the authority route offered the opportunity to gain financing outside the city's debt limit or tax demands, while capitalizing on Robert Moses's public reputation. It made the new Coliseum appear both "free" and outside the realm of local politics. It also neatly served the interests of a businessman like department store magnate Bernard Gimbel, who served nine terms as head of the city's Convention and Visitors Bureau, while garnering political support for Moses himself.

The role of the Triborough Bridge and Tunnel Authority in getting New York a convention hall also set a strong precedent. When, in March 1970, Mayor John Lindsay announced a plan for the "nation's largest exhibition center" to be built on Manhattan's West Side with more than twice the space of the Coliseum, he made it clear that a state public authority would be responsible for financing the $100 million cost. The project's chief planner noted, "The city itself can't swallow that cost with its present debt limit."[66]

What would ultimately emerge in 1986 as the Jacob K. Javits Convention Center, after a series of conflicts over location, design, and financing, would indeed by developed by a new public authority, the New York Convention Center Development Authority, with its bonds issued by the Triborough Bridge and Tunnel Authority and backed by the promise of annual state appropriations. The new Javits Convention Center ended up costing far more—$486 million in total—than the $100 million estimated by Mayor Lindsay in 1970. And the promise that the new convention center would set off a "transformation" of the West Side area has still been unrealized.[67]

Chicago

When Chicago's new McCormick Place convention center opened in November 1960, it marked both a major step forward in the city's competitive position and a striking innovation in terms of governance and finance. The big new convention center was financed by a state tax on horseracing, rather than a local tax or as a general obligation. And the center was owned by a new public entity, the Metropolitan Fair and Exposition Authority. The new authority was created by state legislation and overseen by a 14-member board of directors jointly appointed by the Illinois governor and the mayor of Chicago, with both the mayor and the governor as ex officio members.

The financing and structure of McCormick Place were not happenstance. They represented a means of getting Chicago a new convention hall after decades of political failure, effectively crafted by the leadership of the *Chicago Tribune* to generate funding outside the political and fiscal limits on Chicago and Cook County, while effectively insulating (at least in theory) the project from the depths of Chicago politics.

Edward Banfield provided a history of the origins of McCormick Place in his 1961 study, *Political Influence*. He describes the initiative of *Tribune* publisher Col. Robert McCormick to provide for a permanent lakefront fair, replacing the temporary Railroad Fairs that had taken place in 1948 and 1949: "The Colonel, however, was determined. He told W. Don Maxwell, his managing editor, to work the problem out one way or another." Maxwell's choice of a tax that involved state government is seamless in Banfield's telling: "Maxwell had no doubt about where the needed subsidy should come from . . . [a tax] on parimutuel betting at horse races."[68]

Maxwell and the *Tribune* might well have sought some alternative revenue source, perhaps from city or county governments, for their fair plans. But the *Tribune* had, in George Tagge, its state house reporter at the capital in Springfield, someone with a broad set of connections in the legislature and a political environment where the newspaper had significant clout. Tagge recalled in a 1984 oral history interview how the horse track taxes had come to serve Col. McCormick's goal of a lakefront fair, and the eventual larger purpose of a permanent convention and trade hall, from a conversation he had in May 1951:

> So one day the place wasn't in session and I stopped at the desk of Paul Powell, then the Democratic majority leader and a fairly good news source. . . . So I said, "Well, you know, Cook County doesn't get a damn thing out of that [racing tax revenue]. . . . And he, partly because he was so happy at the time, I think—I said, "Well, we've got this problem up in Chicago. We had this lakefront fair and Maxwell has been out with his hat in his hand . . . collecting money. . . . Why couldn't something—couldn't there be a bill that would put on—I don't want to touch your dole or the county fairs, but the parallel of that for Cook County which would be used for lakefront fair building?" And Paul, a man of action, said, "Well, what the hell. That sounds square to me."[69]

George Tagge's connection of the racing taxes that supported downstate county fairs with the potential to support a permanent fair in Chicago was in large part serendipity. But it also reflected a clear political calculation. Chicago and Cook County received none of the benefits of a tax that aided county fairs, and could make a plausible case for a share. At the same time, Tagge's idea of relying on an existing *state* tax had a far larger appeal for a Republican-oriented newspaper in Chicago.

Tagge went on in his 1984 interview,

> Well, my next step was to get on the phone to Maxwell and of course he was gung ho for it. "Wonderful, Wonderful. . . . And he said, "Well, who's going to run the thing?" I said, "My notion is that it cannot be the damn Chicago City Council and it can't be the damn Cook County Board because there are just too many burglars with their hands out all the time, if not for cash then for other things. And the nearest thing we can come to a power that has a pretty good sense of decency is the Chicago Park Board." And he agreed with that.

Tagge, and likely Don Maxwell as well, had little regard for the politicians of Chicago or Cook County. The Railroad Fairs had been run by Major Lenox Lohr, a retired Army officer with an impeccable reputation, and the *Tribune* sought to keep a more permanent fair efficiently run outside local politics. When additional legislation was introduced in the 1953 legislative session to broaden the revenues to provide for a convention hall rather than a fair, the formal ownership of the convention facility was put in the hands of a new Fair and Exposition Authority.

The new authority was to have its members appointed in equal numbers by the mayor and governor. But Don Maxwell and the *Tribune* were unwilling to see the new entity come under the direction of some who lacked "civic virtue." As Tagge recalled,

> Maxwell decided to begin by choosing every member of the exposition authority and he didn't talk to the mayor, the governor. He had me do it. He wouldn't like to be turned down or argued with so I went to these people and told them what we wanted and quite properly they went along with it because we were completely and entirely responsible for getting the money.

The intent of Maxwell and Tagge, both in securing the state revenues for what would become McCormick Place, and putting it under the control of a public authority run by an appointed board, was to insulate the project from the petty politics of the city and county, while assuring a grand civic benefit run in an appropriately businesslike way. The subsequent history of McCormick Place and the Metropolitan Pier and Exposition Authority suggests that they did not fully achieve their aim. Building and then regularly expanding a major convention center was (and is) an inherently political activity in a variety of ways, with deals to be made and contracts and benefits to dole out.

The $252 million expansion, authorized by the state legislature in 1984 and financed with statewide sales and hotel tax revenues, provided an opportunity for what the *Chicago Tribune* termed "cronyism in contracts," with the foundation subcontractor owned by the Democratic state representative who sponsored the expansion legislation. The security firm awarded a no-bid contract was owned by the brother of the chair of the Cook County Democratic Party.[70]

The 1991 expansion, with its price estimated at $987 million and with backing from new taxes on car rentals, downtown Chicago restaurant meals, and airport buses, provided the opportunity for a last-minute budget deal in the state legislature, tying votes for the McCormick Place expansion to support for the continuing use of high-sulfur southern Illinois coal by Chicago utility companies. The final deal provided "'McPlace,' the $1 billion expansion of Chicago's McCormick Place convention center, for Chicago Democrats . . . property tax caps for suburban Republicans . . . a balanced budget and caps for [Governor] Edgar . . . [and] coal for downstate."[71]

Politics and deal-making has thus pervaded the business of McCormick Place. But it is a kind of politics that is fully removed from the direct influence and oversight of the mass of Chicago area citizens and voters. And when the questions of financing and implementing successive expansions with price tags on the order of one billion dollars arose, they were questions that were entirely the purview of the state legislature and the governor.

Philadelphia

Philadelphia, too, had an existing convention center in the 1970s and 1980s. The city-owned Philadelphia Civic Center boasted some 382,000 square feet of exhibit space, and had hosted a number of national political party conventions in the decades past. Its last major addition had come in 1978. But the center was old, and in the wrong place, in West Philadelphia some distance from downtown and its concentration of hotel rooms. For newly elected

Mayor Bill Green and his aides, taking office in January 1980, the focus was on downtown and the need to boost both the city's tourism industry and the larger downtown area. The city's formal business organizations, the Greater Philadelphia First Corporation and the Chamber of Commerce, were both enthusiastic promoters of a new convention center in Center City.[72]

The prospects of a new convention center were given a serious boost by the creation of a convention center steering committee in May 1982 that in turn commissioned a feasibility analysis from Houston-based Pannell Kerr Forster (PKF). The PKF findings, made public in January 1983, said the city needed a new facility with 300,000 square feet of exhibit space "to remain competitive in the conventions and meetings business." PKF considered an upgrade for the existing Civic Center, but deemed a new center on the eastern side of the center city area as the most viable, at an estimated construction cost of $114 million.[73]

City officials pressed for a center with some 400,000 square feet of space in order to beat the scale of the existing Civic Center. And construction and land acquisition costs began to soar, first to $275 million in the summer of 1983, then to some $400 million at the end of the year. With the cost regularly escalating, Mayor Green and local business and development officials chose to turn to the state government for financial assistance.

The city's quest for convention center funds from the state began in August 1983 with an effort to change state rules to enable the financing, and an initial request for $43.9 million, even as the mayor was still negotiating with the Philadelphia city council for its approval of the convention center project. The agreement with the council was finally reached in March 1984. In April, the city hired S. R. Wojdak and Associates, and Joseph McLauglin, a former deputy mayor, as lobbyists for the city in Harrisburg, and they set about seeking to expand the state's commitment well beyond $44 million.[74]

The city's convention center effort won the support of Republican Governor Richard Thornburgh. But Republican legislators had a set of specific demands, intended to limit what Philadelphia's largely Democratic politicians could do with a state-funded convention center project. First, they insisted that the new center be owned and managed by a public authority, with a board equally divided between gubernatorial appointees and appointees from Philadelphia (in turn divided between mayoral appointees and city council appointees). Second, they capped the state's fiscal commitment at $185 million. And finally, they insisted on a strict ethical code for the board and authority employees, as well as limits on contracts and employment.

State legislators and business interests outside Philadelphia also perceived the proposed state financing as an opportunity for serving their own local concerns and engaging in classic horsetrading. In the words of Democratic Senator Barry Stout of southwestern Pennsylvania,

> I kind of liken this . . . to making whole hog sausage. I do not want to see all the loin go to Philadelphia and all the hams go to Allegheny County [Pittsburgh] and those surrounding counties like Washington, Beaver, Fayette, Greene, Westmoreland and a lot of the counties that are contiguous to metropolitan areas end up with the sow belly. I want to know . . . if in the next three weeks . . . we will fatten up the hog a little bit and have a little sausage for the rest . . . of Pennsylvania?[75]

Governor Thornburgh responded to Pittsburgh legislators and business interests by promising state funding for the new midfield terminal at Pittsburgh's airport for a total of $100 to $150 million. By the time he signed the act creating the Pennsylvania Convention Center Authority and committing $185 million in state funding, the legislative deal had broadened beyond the aid for Pittsburgh's airport to include funds for small towns in upstate Pennsylvania, and the release of flood control funding for the northeastern area of the state. The final cost of the center, estimated at $114 million by PKF in 1983, came to $523.4 million when it opened in June 1993.[76]

State Deals, Local Goodies

The deal that sealed millions in state funding for Philadelphia's new convention center proved both a model and a harbinger. When Pittsburgh and Allegheny County officials began the search for financing an expanded center to replace what one consultant termed "worn and dated," they turned—as had Philadelphia—to the state. Governor Tom Ridge came through with a commitment of $150 million in April 1998 for what would be a final cost of more than $370 million. When Philadelphia leaders concluded that the existing Pennsylvania Convention Center needed to be expanded, to keep up with the competition from other cities and accommodate "lost business," they won a state commitment to finance the expansion debt service over 30 years, using the proceeds from newly authorized slot gambling at racetracks and casinos. The same new slots revenue source also provided funding for Pittsburgh as part of the deal, with funds to pay off the debt of the city's convention center and build a new arena for the Pittsburgh Penguins. And Pennsylvania governors have been equally accommodating and distributive with smaller communities, providing state funds for new convention centers in both Lancaster and Erie in recent years.

State governments have come to be central players in convention center development and expansion in recent decades. The state of Maryland provided the bulk of financing for the Baltimore Convention Center, opened in 1979. When the center was expanded in the late 1990s, the state provided $101 million of the $151 million total cost. And the state also helped finance both a new convention center in Ocean City and a conference center in Montgomery County. Hartford's new Connecticut Convention Center, opened in mid-2005 at a cost of $271 million, was entirely financed by the state government. The Arizona state government picked up $300 million of the roughly $600 million cost of a major expansion of the Phoenix Convention Center. Nebraska supports the Qwest Center convention center and arena complex in Omaha through an arrangement in which state sales tax revenues generated from the facility are "turned back" to the city of Omaha. Washington state enacted legislation in 1999 providing for the creation of "public facility districts" which can capture a portion of the sales tax revenue that would otherwise flow to the state, all without a vote at the local level. The public facility district scheme has supported new convention centers in Tacoma, Kennewick, Vancouver, Lynwood, Spokane, and Yakima. And in 2009, the state of Michigan passed legislation providing for the transfer of Detroit's Cobo Convention Center to a new regional authority (with a board made up of representatives of the state and Wayne, Oakland, and Macomb counties as well as Detroit) and a $279 million expansion financed by a state liquor tax and hotel tax.

The "deals" that create and sustain these state initiatives vary. In some cases, like Pennsylvania's, the state legislature's "price" for funding a major project in one city or region is a companion project—or multiple projects—in other places. In other cases, like Detroit's Cobo or again Philadelphia's Pennsylvania Convention Center, the price of broad political and legislative support is a shift in control from the central city to a broader regional or state authority. And what appears to be a single instance of state involvement can easily become a "model" for a far larger set of facilities and investments. Washington state's multiplying convention centers, built through public facility districts, employ the same financing vehicle the state provided a few years earlier to build Seattle's Safeco Field baseball stadium.

The state-level politics of creating logrolling legislative coalitions and providing governors with "goodies" to distribute around their states thus tends to shape convention center building rather more than the realistic prospects of economic return or market feasibility. It leads to the proliferation of new convention centers in untested visitor destinations like Erie, Pennsylvania, or Vancouver, Washington. But it does offer local business leaders seeking a way to revitalize a downtown core, or local elected officials promoting a major new public project, a means of getting those things done—and claiming the credit—without relying entirely on local revenues or selling the community electorate on a bond issue. Perhaps most important, "taking it to the state" neatly avoids any serious debate over local, *city* priorities, ensuring that those interests that want a new or larger convention center succeed.

Riding a Visitor Wave

For most cities, financing and building a new or expanded convention center requires a substantial—albeit manageable—stock of political initiative and fiscal ingenuity. Local governments often need to overcome a combination of legal and fiscal constraints, as well as the possible opposition of the local electorate. For some communities, however, convention center financing and building is a far easier task. Those places are able to capitalize on effectively dedicated streams of public revenue that are legally linked to center finance and tend to grow over time.

Las Vegas

The Las Vegas Convention Center today boasts 1.94 million square feet of exhibit space, a far cry from the 40,000 square foot hall at its opening in 1959. Much like those in Orange County, Florida, the expansions of the Las Vegas Convention Center have been powered by the stream of revenues generated by a tax on Clark County hotel rooms. As the city and county have prospered as a gambling center and visitor mecca, the river of annual visitors has provided an enormous fiscal boon to the Las Vegas Convention and Visitors Authority.

The contemporary Las Vegas Convention Center began with an effort by a small group of local businessmen to build up the volume of visitors in off-peak periods. Led by electrical contracting firm owner and county commissioner George "Bud" Albright, the city and county jointly named a convention hall subcommittee in January 1955. The subcommittee of Horseshoe Club executive Joe Brown, Last Frontier owner William Moore, and Edmund Converse recommended building a new convention facility on an undeveloped site (the former Las Vegas Racetrack), owned by Brown, adjacent to the "Strip" of Las Vegas Boulevard.[77]

The choice of the Strip, rather than downtown, as the center site was an enormously important one. It provided an abundant stock of relatively inexpensive land on which to expand, and it reinforced (and in turn was supported by) the explosion in development of casino hotels on the Strip, outside the limits of the city of Las Vegas.

Albright and the county commissioners faced another central question in choosing how to finance the planned $4.5 million convention center. Fearing opposition from local voters to a tax hike, Albright came up with the idea of financing with a dedicated five percent room tax on resort hotels and a more modest three percent tax on motels. That differential tax rate neatly accommodated the small motel owners, while providing a steady revenue stream. Albright's son recalled seeing his father at an adding machine, trying to calculate the yield from varying tax rates, and "The numbers he produced were enormous." Indeed, Kenny Albright remembered, "He thought he had put the decimal in the wrong place."[78]

Albright and the county commissioners had secured approval from the state legislature to develop the convention center through a new entity, the Clark County Fair and Recreation Board. The county commission approved the project in November 1955, and it was enthusiastically endorsed by both the *Las Vegas Sun* and the *Review-Journal*. The one final piece in securing the funds for the proposed center was approval by the voters of a county general obligation bond issue. With the argument that hotel taxes rather than their property taxes would pay, the county's voters approved the bonds at a special election in March 1956. The grand opening of the new Las Vegas Convention Center came in 1959.[79]

The argument that hotel taxes, not property taxes, would repay the bonds for convention center construction was a powerful one. As both Las Vegas and the casino hotels along the "Strip" grew, the hotel tax would provide an expanding stream of public revenues to finance the convention center and its expansions. But both the county commission and county voters had to approve the Fair Board's expansion plans and the needed county general obligation bonds. They were not necessarily always supportive, and there were other political interests involved as well.

By 1964, the Fair and Recreation Board was planning for a major expansion of the center. The first step was to secure enough adjacent land to accommodate future growth, a total of 411 acres. The board's plans also included a host of new civic facilities, including a concert hall and a stadium. But in order to win the support of the casino hotels, the board promised not to lease any of the land for a new casino for the next ten years. The promise once again was that the ever-growing stream of hotel tax revenues would pay off the bonds, with no impact on local property taxpayers. However, the *Review-Journal* mounted a spirited attack on the bond proposal, including an editorial that argued that the land deal amounted to "giving a group of politicians control over some of the most valuable property in the county, opening the door for all kinds of transactions, handing them a blank check to do anything they want with it." County voters overwhelmingly opposed the $18 million bond proposal.[80]

Four years later, the renamed Convention Authority returned to the county's voters with a proposal for a $22 million bond issue to fund center expansion, a stadium near downtown Las Vegas, and a museum for Henderson. This time the *Review-Journal* backed the bond issue, terming center expansion "an inevitable step in our effort to remain competitive in the convention market." Yet once again, the county's voters proved unwilling to endorse funds for convention center expansion.[81]

Convention Authority board members blamed the 1968 defeat on a "lack of understanding" by the voters, with some concern expressed over the decision to include facilities beyond just the convention center. Still, both local business leaders and authority board members were unwilling to give up on the prospect of a bigger convention center. Promoting a new albeit far more modest $7.5 million bond issue in August 1970, businessmen created a $50,000 fund to back the claim that "The Convention Center has been open and operated for 11 years and not one cent of its cost has ever been assessed against property taxes." The *Review-Journal* described the Greater Las Vegas Chamber of Commerce as "going all out to get their message across" and pass the bond issue. The September 1970 vote proved—finally—successful, with a three to one margin in favor of the bonds.[82]

The Convention and Visitors Authority followed the modest success in 1970 with a larger, $12 million bond proposal in late 1974. Again promising, "Not one penny out of your pocket," the November 1974 bond proposal was passed by county voters. That electoral success was followed by a $20 million bond proposal in May 1980. This included funding for convention center expansion ($12 million), new parking ($5.5 million), and convention and recreation facilities for the cities of North Las Vegas, Henderson, and Boulder City. The county's voters approved the general obligation bonds on May 27.[83]

The succession of electoral defeats and successes made evident the reality that Clark County voters were not consistently supportive of investment in an expanded convention center, despite the repeated arguments that the bonds would be repaid solely with hotel tax revenues. As a result, the Convention and Visitors Authority had been forced to scale back its expansion plans to bond issue amounts that could win voter approval. That had the effect of slowing up the convention center's growth, even as the total number of hotel rooms in the county grew, from 25,430 in 1970 to 45,815 in 1980 and 73,730 in 1990.

The Convention and Visitors Authority also faced another political problem. Its stream of hotel tax revenues was a tempting target for city officials, who had long seen the downtown area and its casinos suffer as the "Strip" casino hotels near the convention center expanded. The downtown business interests, represented by the Downtown Progress Association, sought their own convention complex. The resulting deal, completed in 1977, led to the Convention and Visitors Authority financing the development of a "mini-convention center" and sports complex, the Cashman Center, adjacent to the downtown core. In subsequent years there would be other interests, notably at the state level, that also sought their own pieces of the authority's stream of tax revenues.

Faced with the history of bond issue defeats at the polls and the need to craft convention center plans to gain voter support, the Las Vegas Convention Authority board sought some fiscal alternatives that avoided voter review. The first such effort came in 1983, with a deal the authority struck with local tradeshow owner Sheldon Adelson. Adelson, who put on the annual Comdex show for the computer industry, sought to gain more space by paying for an expansion of the center in return for guaranteed rent of just $1 per day. The Adelson deal enabled the authority to expand the center once again, but without having to sell local voters. By the middle of the 1980s, the organization and casino hotel owners sought a more permanent means of avoiding voter review. The result was a change in state law that allowed the county commissioners to authorize bonds backed by pledged revenue—in this case, the dedicated hotel tax—by a two-thirds vote, bypassing the need for public vote on a bond issue.[84]

The exact timing and substance of the change in bond procedures is not documented, but when the Convention and Visitors Authority began to consider a $35 million expansion and renovation effort in early 1988, the bonds did not go before the county's voters. The 1988 bond issue was followed by a regular—and regularly growing—stream of new bond issues to pay for even more expansion and improvement of the Las Vegas center. The Convention and Visitors Authority sold a $50 million bond issue in August 1993, followed by a $78 million issue in 1996, and a $5 million issue (for athletic facilities for the University of Nevada at Las Vegas) in 1998.

The Convention and Visitors Authority opened a major new expansion with 279,000 more square feet of exhibit space, funded by those bond issues, in November 1998. But even before that latest expansion was open and operating, the authority was making plans for yet another, far grander, expansion. The LVCVA commissioned a consultant study of expansion possibilities in June 1998. And, perhaps recognizing the growing claims by other units of government on its stream of hotel tax revenues—the county public schools would succeed in getting a piece of the tax for school construction in early 1999—the Convention Authority unveiled an innovative approach to financing more convention space.[85]

The LVCVA heard from three major tradeshow organizers, including the Consumer Electronics Show and Reed Exhibitions, that they and other show managers were prepared to put up $40 million towards the expansion cost, then estimated at $79 million. Tim McGinnis of Reed Exhibitions termed Las Vegas, along with Orlando, as "the two hottest markets for conventions," and said, "A lot of shows want to come to Las Vegas but can't get dates. Without additional space, it puts a strain on generating additional revenue for a company."[86]

By relieving the hotel tax, and the Clark County government, from a large part of the burden of financing a major expansion, the Convention and Visitors Authority was attempting to both "sell" an expansion and compete head-to-head with Orlando, then planning its own major expansion. But both the expansion and the financing arrangement generated an immediate and sustained outcry from Sheldon Adelson. Adelson had gone on to build his own major *private* convention center as part of the Sands Hotel, with one million square feet of exhibit space. He opposed the financing arrangement, arguing that it would take business from his facility and imperil the authority's future income stream, threatening to sue if the authority moved ahead.[87]

Sheldon Adelson's opposition had the effect of slowing expansion plans, delaying action from April until June 1999. Yet even as he argued that the

LVCVA should bring its expansion and bond plans directly to the voters, the authority was planning on an even more effective end-run around the public review of new debt plans. The authority had sought state legislation that would enable it to issue revenue bonds itself, without the approval of Clark County commissioners. That revenue bond authority would ease the financing of this, and future, expansion efforts while stymieing any attempt by Adelson, or the convention center's neighbors, to appeal to the county commission. Nevada Governor Kenny Guinn signed the revenue bond authority for both the Las Vegas and Reno convention authorities at the end of May.[88]

The LVCVA's new revenue bond legislation also enabled the Convention Authority to tackle a far larger and more expensive project. By the end of June, the expansion's cost had grown to $150 million, and the board chose to move ahead despite Adelson's objections. Predictably, Sheldon Adelson and his Venetian Hotel filed suit against the authority the next month, alleging that the LVCVA had violated state law by seeking to issue revenue bonds backed by hotel tax revenues.[89]

The court decision in October 1999 fully upheld the Convention and Visitors Authority and its use of revenue bonds for the expansion. District Judge James Mahan wrote, "It appears that The Venetian's quarrel is with the Legislature, which authorized the issuance of revenue bonds . . . and not with the LVCVA." With the lawsuit moot, the authority moved ahead with a $150 million bond issue in November. The new South Hall of the Las Vegas Convention Center opened at the beginning of January 2002, just in time to accommodate the annual Consumer Electronics Show and its 110,000 attendees, and bringing the Las Vegas Convention Center to a total of 1.94 million square feet of exhibit space.[90]

From its beginnings as the Fair and Recreation Board, through a series of bond defeats and political machinations in the 1960s and 1970s, the Las Vegas Convention and Visitors Authority has emerged as a massive fiscal engine, effectively free of direct control by Clark County voters or even the county commission. Convention center boosters had succeeded in reconstructing the political and fiscal constraints on the LVCVA, first managing to avoid direct public votes on expansion bonds, then legislating revenue bond authority that enabled the authority to avoid the potential hurdle of the Clark County commission. The state legislature did shift some hotel taxes to the local schools, and it would also take a portion of the hotel tax revenues to pay for transportation projects. But by 2007, the 132,947 hotel and motel rooms in Clark County were pumping out almost $220 million a year for the LVCVA, dedicated almost entirely to marketing, promoting, and financing the convention center. The authority's room tax revenues were hit hard by the recession—the total for 2010 came to just $163.8 million. A planned expansion that would add more meeting room space and renovate older areas was put off. Yet the LVCVA still sits atop a stock of hotel rooms that can, as occupancies and room rates gradually improve, produce a stream of tax revenues that can and likely will support even more expansions.

In November 2011, LVCVA head Rossi Ralenkotter told the *Review-Journal* editorial board that it was time to revive the $890 million expansion project that had been put on hold during the recession. The authority's room tax revenues for 2011 had grown to $194.3 million, and the authority's vice president of sales argued, "If you look at what our competitors around the country have leading up to their convention centers, ours doesn't match up."[91]

Beyond City Limits

Beginning in the 1980s, it became increasingly common for academic analysts of urban politics and city policy to describe the constraints and limits on city governments. Paul Peterson's 1981 *City Limits* focused on the notion that "local politics is most limited," and posited the central necessity for cities to pursue "policies which contribute to the economic prosperity of the local community." Economists Helen Ladd and John Yinger documented the fiscal straits of big city governments in their 1991 volume, *America's Ailing Cities*. The fiscal problems of older cities like Detroit, Baltimore, Cleveland, and St. Louis that have seen continuing population loss since 1990 have not gotten better since they wrote.[92]

For other urban observers and commentators, the fiscal and economic plight of the nation's large older cities called for a restructuring of local government, focusing on the creation of metropolitan and regional solutions to governance and local finance. Former Albuquerque Mayor David Rusk, in *Cities Without Suburbs* and *Baltimore Unbound*, called for urban solutions such as the creation of a "Metropolitan Municipality of Greater Baltimore" with the capacity to raise and spend region-wide revenues that could resolve metropolitan scale housing, economic, and social issues.[93]

Journalist Neal Peirce has similarly embraced metropolitan and regional government initiatives—"citistates"—as a means of moving beyond narrow local government boundaries to deal with broad regional needs. Peirce and his colleagues have stressed the importance of marshaling regional economic and fiscal resources to deal with the full range of contemporary metropolitan needs.[94]

For all the seemingly broad agreement among urban analysts about the constraints on big city governments and the myriad limitations faced by cities and their leaders, those limits have represented no impediment to the proponents of convention center development. The massive public investment that a city like Baltimore, Philadelphia, or Hartford can no longer manage either fiscally or politically can instead be—and has been—readily managed by an independent public authority or a state government. What a fiscally strapped and racially divided community like St. Louis, Richmond, or Cleveland cannot achieve on its own (or with the approval of the city's electorate) can in turn be politicked, financed, and realized by a county government or through a new regional entity. Thus, the convention center in downtown St. Louis is owned by the regional Convention and Visitors Commission, the Richmond facility by the Greater Richmond Convention Center Authority, Hartford's Connecticut Convention Center by the Capital City Economic Development Authority (now Capital Region Development Authority), and the new Cleveland "Med Mart" by Cuyahoga County.

The *structure* of American local government, with an array of different agencies and multiple levels, provides ample opportunity to secure support for a convention center project from a variety of officials with varying outlooks and orientations. There was no necessity or compelling functional logic for involving New York's Triborough Bridge and Tunnel Authority in building the Coliseum and later the Javits Center. Nor was the *Chicago Tribune*'s successful use of horseracing tax revenues to construct McCormick particularly logical. But these cases, and a host of others, worked.

Even where the responsibility for convention center development has remained with a general purpose local government such as a city or a county, as in the cases of Kansas City, San Antonio, and Cincinnati, it has proven possible to restructure the politics and finances to effectively insulate proposed centers from public review and debate. These cities, and others, have long since devised means of financing convention facilities without a direct public vote. They have made use of dedicated revenues from taxes on local hotel rooms and car rentals. These funds, often combined with the commitment of private dollars for naming rights or project aid, make a convention center seem a "bargain" or affordable even where government revenues are tight. And it is possible to structure such revenue sources to contend, as center backers often do, that these dollars are the rightful purview of local hotel owners, and somehow cannot be used for any other public purpose.

The product of a local governmental system of multiple responsibilities, revenues, and political openings is an unusual kind of "political privilege" that attaches to convention center development efforts. No longer packaged as one part of a broad effort to address investment and infrastructure needs with voter-approved bonds, convention centers are promoted as unique vehicles that will assuredly generate ever more "economic impact," jobs, and new public revenues. And in those cases where a mayor, manager, or county official is less than fully enthusiastic about center building or expansion, proponents have been able to "wait out" resistant officials until the next election.

In Nashville, the city commission vote in January 2010 that officially began work on a $650 million new "Music City Convention Center" was the product of politics, deals, and consultant studies—from CSL, KPMG, Tradeshow Week, C. H. Johnson, and HVS—that extended back to April 1999, through the eight years of Bill Purcell's mayoralty, to newly elected Mayor Karl Dean. Where Purcell's finance director, David Manning, had issued a memo warning of "a serious over-supply of convention center space in recent years . . . [such that] the [Music City Center] could become a serious drain on Metro's financial resources," his successor found a way to make a more costly if no less uncertain project a reality. Nashville's financing scheme for the Music City Center ultimately combined a hotel tax, a hotel tax surcharge, an airport departure tax, a vehicle rental tax, a redirection of state and city sales taxes at the center and adjacent hotel, and the creation of a Tourism Development Zone and tax. The combination of strong local business backing and mayoral support succeeded in gaining new state legislation that allowed the Metro Nashville government to tap a whole range of new revenue streams, dedicated to a convention center and nothing else.[95]

Freed from the need to build the kind of electoral consensus required to "sell" bond issues to local voters, able to literally pick and choose the unit of government that is most fiscally flush and politically amenable, capable of outwaiting an unhelpful or unsupportive elected official, and ultimately positioned to garner the tax revenues generated by visitors and tourists rather than local taxpayers, convention center backers have managed to reconstruct local fiscal resources and politics to build even more centers. But if that political reconstruction has assured that convention center space in Orlando or San Jose, Baltimore or Omaha can grow, and will likely continue to grow, it does not assure that it works—that anyone will in fact come.

The fiscal reformation of American cities has made it possible for new and expanded centers to be developed across a wide array of places, even those like St. Louis, Cleveland, and Philadelphia that face serious economic problems and fiscal constraints. Yet just as those cities (or their county and state governments) have built and expanded their centers, so too have tourist meccas like Las Vegas and Orlando, major urban centers like Chicago, and even suburban jurisdictions such as Rosemont and Schaumburg, Illinois. Each has managed to craft its own unique fiscal and political solution. And each effort was justified by one or more consultant studies that described growing demand for convention center space and market "feasibility" for every new center. Those consultant analyses, and ultimately their inadequacies, errors, and failings, are the focus of the next two chapters.

Chapter 3

Promises and Realities

Laying out a "long range" strategic plan for Chicago's McCormick Place convention center in January 1990, consultant Charles H. Johnson described a vibrant and growing convention and tradeshow market. He noted that "facility space requirements have been growing at a rate of eight percent per year" and "Future growth is expected to continue." He illustrated that finding with two charts, one depicting sharp upward growth in both tradeshow exhibit space use from 1971 to 1987 (8.66 percent) and attendance (6.47 percent), the other showing an even more dramatic upward slope, with annual increases in the size of Tradeshow "200" events—the 200 largest conventions and tradeshows each year—continuing from 1988 though 2000.[1]

For Johnson and his client, the Metropolitan Pier and Exposition Authority, the presumption of constant and predictable future growth was vital in justifying ever more space and investment in McCormick Place, with the conclusion that "McCormick Place must be bold so that it can stake its claim to maintain the largest events and increasingly attract international delegates."[2]

The presumption of industry growth was just as vital for Johnson and convention center backers in Boston and Massachusetts in 1997. Using data from the annual Tradeshow Week *Data Book*, Johnson argued, "Over the last three years, the number of exhibitions and the amount of demand for exhibit space increased dramatically," referring to a table showing exhibit space use growing from 399 million square feet in 1994 to over 452 million for 1996, with attendance increasing from 85.3 million to 102.2 million. Under the heading "Future Growth," Johnson reported projections from the Center for Exhibition Industry Research that the convention and tradeshow industry would reach 550 million square feet of space used and 140 million annual attendees by 2000.[3]

Johnson employed the same set of data for 1990 through 2000, attributed to the Center for Exhibition Industry Research (the tradeshow industry's research and promotion arm), in a November 1998 "Boston Convention & Exhibition Center Marketability Study" published by the Boston Redevelopment Authority. His conclusion on the future market environment for a new Boston center—"Over the decade, the industry is expected to add approximately 1,000 annual exhibition events to the market and attendance will nearly double, growing from 75 million in 1990 to a projected 140 million in the year 2000."[4]

The growth argument and the numbers were just the same in Johnson's July 2000 analysis of the prospects for a new convention center in Jackson, Mississippi. Noting annual growth of exhibit space use averaging 6.9 percent from 1990 to 2000, with a table (labeled "Cumulative Exhibition Growth") showing an "estimate" of 140 million total attendees in 2000, Johnson told the Jackson Convention and Visitors Bureau that "Continuing growth in the demand for various types of conventions, tradeshows, and meetings has motivated communities across the country to develop new or expanded convention center facilities." The conclusion for Jackson—"As regional and national conventions and tradeshows continue to increase in number and size, Jackson will enjoy increasing demand from these segments as well."[5]

But the promise of convention event and attendance growth (and expansive future estimates) from Johnson and the Center for Exhibition Industry Research appeared to have run afoul of larger forces in 2000 and 2001, including an economic downturn and the events of 9-11. Individual convention centers reported sharp drops in attendance. At Chicago's McCormick Place, convention and tradeshow attendance fell from 1.44 million in 2000 to 1.33 million in 2001 and 1.16 million in 2002. At Boston's Hynes Convention Center, hotel room night generation fell from 401,367 in 2000 to 293,743 in 2002 and 253,698 in 2003. The figure reported in the annual Tradeshow Week *Data Book* fell as well, from 126 million in 2000 to 75 million in 2001 and 56 million in 2002.

If the prediction of attendance growth from Johnson and the Center for Exhibition Industry Research—140 million convention and tradeshow attendees for 2000, the forecast Johnson had given Boston and Jackson—had proven erroneous, this seemed to have little impact on Johnson's subsequent assessment of convention and tradeshow industry growth for other cities.

The overall convention industry had clearly seen a dramatic attendance drop, easily visible in the annual *Data Book* summaries. But that drop was not at all evident in Table 7-1 of Johnson Consulting's July 2003 study for Rockford, Illinois. There was a table of "Cumulative Exhibition Growth," just as in the Jackson study of three years earlier, with the same annual figures for the 1990s as in Johnson's 1997 Boston report. But the table in the Rockford report neatly ended with an "estimated" figure of 112 million total attendees in 2000. No data were reported for 2001 or 2002. That was apparently sufficient for Johnson to conclude, "While larger economic conditions will continue to impact the convention industries, there will remain an ongoing demand because manufacturers and other exhibitors typically view conventions and tradeshows as a cost effective marketing tool for highly targeted audiences."[6]

By his October 2003 analysis of the prospects for a new convention center in St. Charles, Missouri, Johnson had updated his data (from the annual *Data Book*) on "Cumulative Exhibition Demand Growth" to include 2001 and 2002. The table now portrayed a sharp drop in the number of events, from 4,637 in 2000 to just 4,342 for 2002. But while the historic counts of shows and space use were consistent with previous reports, the attendance totals had somehow changed—indeed, changed all the way back to 1990. Where the exhibition demand table in the July Rockford report had shown 75 million attendees in 1990 growing to 110 million in 1998 (as in earlier reports), the October report for St. Charles put the 1990 figure at 39 million, reaching 52.9 million for 1998. And although the St. Charles table was updated to 2002, there was no evidence of a sharp attendance decline after 2001. Instead, Johnson showed total attendance of 55.1 million in 2002—down just slightly from 56.3 million in 2000 and 58.5 million in 2001. The obvious dramatic change in total convention and tradeshow attendance—evident in the actual Tradeshow Week data and reports from individual convention centers—had somehow disappeared.[7]

The revised data, attributed to Tradeshow Week, ostensibly supported the conclusion that "While larger economic conditions will continue to impact the convention industries, there will remain an ongoing demand for events because manufacturers and other exhibitors typically view conventions and trade shows as a cost-effective marketing tool for highly targeted audiences." And with that assessment of future demand, Johnson could assert, "St. Charles, because of its growth, destination attraction, corporate presence, and other factors, is a natural location for a main convention facility to serve the region."[8]

A few months later, the same Tradeshow Week data, presented in a table labeled "Cumulative Exhibition Demand Growth," bulwarked the analysis of industry demand and growth in Johnson's February 2004 study for Bryan-College Station, Texas. Once again, the total attendance figures had shrunk from those in comparable tables in earlier reports, showing no real decline in 2002 or 2003. And again Charlie Johnson stated his conclusion that "While larger economic conditions will continue to impact the convention and meetings industries, there will remain an ongoing demand for events because manufacturers and other exhibitors typically view conventions and trade shows as a cost-effective marketing tool for highly targeted audiences." That finding about convention demand sustained his finding for the Texas A& M University community: "The area, because of its growth in population, corporate presence, and tourism is a natural location for a dedicated, high-quality convention facility to serve as the primary center for the region."[9]

Johnson Consulting returned to Rockford, with a follow-up study dated January 7, 2010, for a new downtown convention center and hotel. And despite the global economic turmoil of 2008 and 2009 and the dramatic downturn in travel and hotel demand, Johnson once again offered an upbeat account of the performance of the convention and tradeshow industry and its prospects for the future. A preamble to the formal report offering answers to "frequently asked questions" brought the finding that "there is a nationwide demand for meeting and conference space that is not being met . . . .This trend will continue as the economy rebounds and business travel increases." Johnson proffered the reassurance that "Virtually all categories of meeting activities have experienced rapid worldwide growth since the early 1970s." The body of the report contained the finding that "In recent years, the growth rate in demand for exhibition space has been exceeding the rate of increase in the supply of exhibition space." That supported Johnson's central conclusion for Rockford's leaders: "Through sustained and thoughtful initiatives and investment in projects such as a new convention/conference center and hotel, downtown Rockford can have a revitalized identity and re-emerge as an economic center and resource for the community." And a year later, in a February 2011 report for Clemson, South Carolina, Johnson could observe, "Virtually all categories of meeting activities have experienced rapid worldwide growth since the early 1970s," and offer the conclusion that "Clemson is well suited to participate in the convention, conference, and meetings sector, given that it is home to Clemson University."[10]

Other consultants also tied their recommendations that cities add more convention center space to the presumed growth of the convention industry, employing much the same arguments and just the same sources of data Johnson Consulting relied on.

Assessing the state of convention and tradeshow demand for thc city of Anaheim in 1995, the consultants at Coopers & Lybrand, including Craig Skiem and John Kaatz, also turned to Tradeshow Week's annual report on the industry's largest events, the Tradeshow Week "200." They told Anaheim officials that "Following a period of slow growth in 1991–92 brought on by a recession and the Gulf War, the growth rate in the trade show industry rebounded in 1993." The consultants concluded, "This trend is expected to continue, with industry growth ranging from three to five percent annually over the next five years." That growth, and increasing competition from expanding centers in Los Angeles, Chicago, New York, Dallas, and New Orleans, meant Anaheim's own expansion "must be seriously considered."[11]

Two years later, in 1997, the convention center consultants at Coopers & Lybrand justified an expansion of New York's Javits Center with another analysis of Tradeshow Week's "200." They argued, "Following a period of relatively slow growth in 1991 and 1992, brought on by a recession and the Gulf War, the growth rate in the trade show industry rebounded in 1993 and has been steadily increasing each year since." The Coopers consultants added, "Preliminary estimates for 1996 through 1999 indicate continued steady annual growth in attendance, exhibiting companies and space requirements of between three and five percent which are anticipated to continue into the twenty-first century." And with that assumption of growth, they concluded that an expanded Javits Center represented a "significant opportunity" for New York.[12]

With the demise of Coopers & Lybrand in 1998, the principals of the convention center consulting practice, including Craig Skiem and John Kaatz, formed a new firm, Conventions, Sports and Leisure International. The new CSL firm produced a market analysis for the New Orleans Morial Convention Center in 1999 that again turned to the Tradeshow Week "200" as an index of demand. For the CSL analysts, those data indicated that "Since 1990, the largest 200 trade shows have experienced a steady growth in terms of net square feet of paid exhibit space and attendance." With that historical pattern and "Industry projections [that] forecast future growth at two to four percent annually as the importance of face-to-face business interaction continues to position the industry as recession resistant," the CSL report called for an expansion of 500,000 to 600,000 square feet of exhibit space "needed to support the long-term demand for the space in New Orleans . . . [to] target added multiple events in the 200,000 to 600,000 gross square foot range."[13]

The CSL firm continued to rely upon Tradeshow Week data, albeit almost entirely in terms of year-to-year percent changes and index values, in describing the state of the convention center market, even as industry performance changed in 2001 and after. For the Pennsylvania Convention Center Authority in a January 2003 report, CSL argued, "Until recent trends, the square footage, number of exhibitors and attendance levels of the convention, tradeshow and meetings market have continually grown since 1984, with the exception of a brief two-year period in the early 1990s." And although "Recent events and economic conditions have resulted in significant decreases in attendance and space use in many markets throughout the country," they could confidently predict an industry "rebound over the next 12 to 24 months."[14]

The CSL consultants also provided their upbeat view of the future of the convention and tradeshow industry to a broader audience of local officials. CSL principal Bill Krueger's May 2007 presentation at the International Economic Development Council's "If You Build It, Will They Come?" conference, "Is the Convention and Conference Center Market Saturated?," answered with a series of slides titled "The Recovery of the Biggest . . ." and "Decades of Growth for the Largest . . .," illustrating a "Growth Index" of space use, exhibitors, and attendance. And a CSL analysis of the prospects for a new convention center in Jackson, Michigan, in October 2007 included the same chart that Krueger's presentation had titled "Decades of Growth for the Largest. . . ." For the Jackson report, the graph was now titled "Tradeshow 200—Convention & Tradeshow Industry Growth," clearly referring to the source of its data, Tradeshow Week's annual summary of space use, exhibitor, and attendance indices for the "200" largest convention and tradeshow events. "Exhibit IV-4" showed attendance steadily growing from 1987 (value of 100) to 2000, albeit flat in 1990–1991. Growth appeared to resume in 2003, hitting an index value of about 156 in 2005 and 162 in 2006—both above the previous peak of 155 for 2000.[15]

CSL provided an optimistic assessment of the state of the convention industry and its future for the Greater Jackson Chamber of Commerce, noting, "The most recent industry data suggests [sic] that the nationwide convention and tradeshow industry is in the midst of a renewed expansion, with demand levels generally recovering beyond pre-9/11 levels." There was still a cautionary note: "While it is believed that challenges have and will continue to exist in certain localized markets, every community and destination is unique and application of blanket industry-wide, macro assessments of supply and demand phenomena are often ill-advised." "Destination appeal" mattered, and "facilities located in destinations with weak appeal and/or deficient visitor amenities more often struggle or underperform industry averages." But Jackson apparently had sufficient appeal, as CSL stated: "A new Jackson convention center, as envisioned, would act as an economic generator and a public resource for the local community, hosting conventions, conferences, tradeshows, public/consumer shows, meetings and other events of both a non-local and local nature."[16]

When CSL reported on the market feasibility of a new convention center in Oklahoma City to the Greater Oklahoma City Chamber of Commerce in March 2009, the national economy and the convention industry had changed in dramatic fashion. But the consultants still relied on Tradeshow Week's figures on the annual performance of the "200" largest events (including exhibit space and attendance), again shown as a "growth index" to demonstrate the "short-lived" impact of 9-11, with growth having "picked up" starting in 2002 and "continuing through 2007." After noting the current conditions "negatively impacting" the convention and tradeshow business, the report argued that convention growth would parallel GNP change, and that industry change "will have to be monitored over the coming months and years." But that need to monitor convention demand did not have much impact on CSL's recommendation that Oklahoma City add 200,000 square feet of exhibit space, effectively tripling the center's size. Nor was there any evidence of uncertainty in the forecast that a larger center would boost convention attendee direct spending from the current $16,724,000 to $45,566,000 each year.[17]

It was impossible for the CSL consultants to ignore the impact of the 2007–2008 recession on the convention business when, in November 2009, they completed a "Strategic Development Plan" for the Boston Convention & Exhibition Center. As they had observed for Oklahoma City, they noted "several conditions that are negatively impacting convention and tradeshow activity nationally." But that impact was taking place in a presumed historical context of exhibit space demand tied to the state of the national economy. The historic growth index chart of the "200" from earlier reports was not part of the Boston report. Instead, it included a graph showing "Annual Changes to Large Convention & Tradeshow Demand and S&P 500 Earnings Per Share," reflecting solely space use data from the annual Tradeshow "200," rather than attendance, through 2008. CSL could thus go on to conclude, "If projections of future economic growth are generally accurate, it is likely that although the convention and tradeshow industry experienced a downturn through 2009, recovery in demand will take place towards the end of 2010 or early in 2011."

That expectation of certain demand recovery was apparently sufficient for CSL to recommend the development of a second headquarters hotel for the BCEC, more ballroom space, added meeting room space, a new auditorium, and the potential addition of up to 400,000 square feet of exhibit hall space.[18]

CSL's belief in the recovery of the convention business, and its focus on "Large Convention & Tradeshow Demand" based on the presumed historic performance of the "200" events also extended into 2010, exemplified by a March 22, 2010, study of potential convention center development for Boise, Idaho. The Boise analysis included the same graphic of demand trends and earnings per share included in the Boston report, and concluded, "if projections of future economic growth are generally accurate, it is likely that the convention and tradeshow industry will continue to experience a downturn into 2010, with a potential recovery in demand taking place sometime late in 2010." CSL could thus recommend that Boise develop 50,000 square feet of new exhibit space, while noting an attached or adjacent headquarter hotel as an "important amenity" to include in center development and funding plans.[19]

The CSL firm's optimism about the long-term future of the convention business continued through 2010. In its study of demand for an expanded and improved Henry B. Gonzalez Convention Center in San Antonio, dated December 1, 2010, the CSL consultants did note, "If projections of future economic growth are generally accurate, and given the continued viability of the convention model as a means of conducting key elements of a successful business, it is likely that while the convention industry will continue to experience a downturn into 2010, a potential recovery in demand is likely to take place sometime in 2011." But the report then added, "We continue to believe that demand for convention and tradeshow space is tied to the overall health of the economy, and that demand levels will rebound by 2011." With that outlook, CSL recommended an expansion of 100,000 square feet.[20]

The CSL firm's positive outlook on the future of the national convention and tradeshow business extended through 2011. In an analysis of the "proposed LACC [Los Angeles Convention Center] enhancement project"—actually a new football stadium to be developed as part of the city's convention center complex—CSL forecast that the city would gain a "significant increase" in major conventions and tradeshows, amounting to about five each year, boosting annual "non-local attendee days" from a five-year average of 331,190 to a forecast 522,000. And the firm did offer city officials the conclusion that "Given the stable condition of convention and tradeshow industry demand projected into the future, the large majority of additional LACC citywide events will have to result from attracting events that otherwise would have booked into centers in competitive markets such as San Diego, Anaheim, Phoenix, San Francisco and Denver." But even with that competitive reality, Los Angeles presumably stood to see more convention business.[21]

The passage of another year of limited national economic recovery apparently did little to alter CSL's outlook on future convention demand. When the CSL consultants presented their December 2010 assessment for San Antonio, they had argued, "demand levels will rebound by 2011." When a year later CSL completed a broader report on San Antonio tourism in November 2011, it concluded "If projections of future economic growth are generally accurate (even at modest levels), and given the continued viability of the convention model as a means of conducting key elements of a successful business, it is likely that while [sic] the convention industry will continue to stabilize, with slight increases through the remainder of 2011."[22]

From the 1990s to 2011, through economic growth and recession, for cities as large and well known as New York and New Orleans or as modestly sized as Jackson and Boise, the CSL International consultants (at both Coopers & Lybrand and CSL) emphasized the persistence and predictability of convention and tradeshow industry growth. Over and over, the firm relied upon data from Tradeshow Week, most commonly from the "200" largest events and expressed either as annual percentage changes or as index numbers, to make the case that there was room for more exhibit space, across a broad swath of communities, that would inevitably lead to more conventions and tradeshows, with more attendees and greater "economic impact" from visitor spending. Even in the face of dramatic economic change after the 2007–2008 recession, the firm continued to promise that recovery was just around the corner. And the persistent forecast of growth also characterized the work of other convention center consultants.[23]

From the early 1990s to about 2000, the convention center consulting practice at PriceWaterhouse (subsequently PriceWaterhouseCoopers) was directed by David C. Petersen. Petersen had effectively founded the convention center practice at Laventhol & Horwath in 1981, which he headed until the firm's bankruptcy in 1990. At PriceWaterhouse, he directed studies for a long list of communities and clients, including Boston, San Diego, Cincinnati, and Atlanta. Those cities too heard a story (much as Laventhol clients had earlier) of historical growth in convention center demand based on the Tradeshow Week "200," and the forecast that growth "is expected to continue in future years."[24]

Reviewing the market prospects for an expanded convention center for Atlanta's Georgia World Congress Center in early 1993, PriceWaterhouse focused on the historical pattern of growth for the nation's largest conventions and tradeshows, the Tradeshow "200." The PriceWaterhouse consultants noted, "Growth for the country's largest 200 trade shows, all of which require more than 225,000 gross square feet, has been similar to growth for the entire U.S. trade show industry"—a figure the consultants put at 6 to 8 percent annually. The demand assessment went on, "Research shows that growth in demand for convention center exhibition space will continue . . . there is no persuasive evidence that exhibition space demand growth for either trade shows or conventions will abate in the foreseeable future." Looking ahead, PriceWaterhouse saw growth in the future, for fiscal years 1992 to 2001, estimating demand for space increasing "at approximately 7 percent compounded annually."[25]

David Petersen and his PriceWaterhouse colleagues returned to Atlanta in 1996, with a second market analysis of an expansion of the Georgia World Congress Center. Once again, they focused on the growth of the overall industry, reviewing "the growth trends of the 200 largest trade association events in the U.S, 'The Tradeshow 200.'" They described trends in both exhibit space use and attendance as "sporadic," while going on to note that "the last three years have seen a recovery in both of these factors." They finally concluded in a "summary of key factors," "Demand, measured in terms of net exhibition space occupied, has grown at approximately 5 percent per year, on average, for the 200 largest trade association events in the U.S." They then used the assumption of 5 percent annual growth in exhibit space use to argue, "An additional 700,000 square feet of exhibition space would provide sufficient space for these events to be held alone in the Center, or simultaneously with larger events."[26]

The PriceWaterhouse consulting team (merged and renamed PriceWaterhouseCoopers and led by Robert Canton after David Petersen's retirement) delivered an analysis of the market prospects for an expanded Jacob Javits Convention Center in New York in March 2000. The Javits report set out its central findings in a series of bullet points, with headings printed in bold and italics. Much as for Atlanta, the case for a larger center was built on event growth. "JKJCC will lose existing business if it does not expand" was the first point, noting, "Several major recurring trade show users are outgrowing the facility and have stated that they will be forced to leave JKJCC if the facility is not expanded." The second major point was the Javits center would attract new events with an expansion, with the argument that events were now unable to come "due to size constraints and date availability." The final point was that "growth in demand is exceeding supply of exhibit space in major convention and trade show destinations including New York City."[27]

The Javits study included an entire section of "Tradeshow 200 Analysis," focused on the large cities with which New York competed and the pattern of attendance growth for the "200." The study's findings on overall attendance, presented in a chart of total attendance by year from 1988 to 1999, were somewhat mixed. Attendance at these large events had grown steadily from 1988 to 1996. But there was a clear and dramatic drop in 1997 and 1998. That decline was excused by Tradeshow Week with the argument that it reflected higher travel costs and "site factors such as rotational pattern and/or weather." The consultants did not dwell on the apparent inconsistency of recent attendance trends and the historical pattern. PWC went on to present a further analysis by industry group that focused on "fast growing industries" such as telecommunications and media. That apparently allowed the consultants to conclude, "Average growth in attendance for industries consistent with JKJCC orientation range [sic] from four to nine percent." It was those industries that really mattered to New York and the Javits.[28]

PriceWaterhouseCoopers also elaborated another set of growth measures in the 2000 Javits study, a set of measures unique to the firm. Since 1985, PriceWaterhouseCoopers has published an annual Convention Center Report with summary data on major convention centers that chose to provide information. For the New York study, PWC focused on the historical performance of major convention destinations, "gateway cities" with more than 20,000 metropolitan area hotel rooms. The Convention Center Report data measured both exhibit space use (largely in terms of annual average exhibit hall occupancy) and average attendance at conventions and tradeshows, much like the Tradeshow "200." But by looking at the actual performance of a group of major convention centers, PWC was tapping the *joint effects* of both supply and demand.

The 2000 Javits study showed average exhibit space occupancy for conventions and tradeshows "gateway centers" at about 50 percent in 1998, up from about 49 percent in 1995 and 45 percent in 1990. The consultants argued that as available space had increased during this period, "demand for these centers has increased at a higher rate than the increase in supply of space." Average convention attendance had gone up as well: "Between 1990 and 1998, average annual growth of attendance was seven percent for gateway . . . centers." The average attendance had hit about 620,000 in 1999, up from a little over 500,000 attendees in 1995 and about 410,000 in 1990. The consultants then concluded, "Demand growth for exhibit space is expected to continue at strong rates over the next several years, particularly in major cities . . . . Current excess demand could occupy an expanded JKJCC."[29]

The New York Convention Center Operating Corporation, the operator of the Javits Center, commissioned another expansion market analysis from PriceWaterhouseCoopers in the fall of 2003. The report the firm delivered in January 2004 lacked the bullet points of its predecessor, but emphasized that even "when the national convention and trade show markets experienced downturns or slowdowns, Javits has consistently operated at or very close to its practical maximum capacity." The PWC consultants continued to endorse a major expansion of the Javits, boosting exhibit space from 814,000 to 1.34 million square feet, together with a nine-fold increase in meeting room space and a new ballroom. But their analysis of potential demand was obliged to deal with the changed reality of the convention business after 2000 and 9-11.[30]

The demand analysis in the 2004 Javits study again employed data from the Tradeshow "200" and PWC's own Convention Center Reports. The PWC assessment of the "200" showed total annual volume of exhibit space and event attendance, rather than year-to-year percent changes. The total exhibit space use graph demonstrated that growth had begun to slow after 1998, with 2000 and 2001 about flat, followed by a clear drop in 2002, back to the level of 1998. The picture of overall attendance was rather different, with a peak in 1996, followed by two years of decline, a modest rebound in 1999 and 2000, and then a further drop. The 2002 attendance total came to just over 4.2 million—equal to the attendance in 1993, and well below the over 4.6 million in 1996. The report noted a drop of 6 percent from 2000, and attributed "Recent declines" to "economic and geopolitical conditions and associated trends in reduced travel away from home and corporate budget constraints."[31]

The PWC report also discussed the performance history of "gateway centers" (based on major centers' reports of actual performance), describing "substantial declines" in convention and tradeshow occupancy between 2001 and 2003. But the assessment attributed "these declines to failure of demand for convention/space to keep pace with supply changes, the concurrent economic downturn, and to a limited extent, event cancellations due to the events of September 11, 2001." The decline was not limited to occupancy rates. The Javits report included a graphic charting total convention and tradeshow attendance, demonstrating a fall-off beginning in 2000. That drop brought 2003 total "Gateway" attendance back to the 1997 level. Still, the analysis concluded, "Increases and declines in exhibit space demand and attendance at Gateway Centers have been consistent with periods of economic growth and decline—a trend that is expected to continue in the future." And as if to reassure Javits officials, the report ventured, "Javits occupancy rates have remained consistently high during periods of industry decline."[32]

The consultants continued to rely on their annual convention center reports to index convention center demand. An analysis of "gateway center" trends was part of the analysis of the prospective performance of an expanded Indiana Convention Center in Indianapolis in early 2004. As with the 2004 Javits analysis, the consultants promised that center performance would vary with the state of the national economy. But, their report contended, "Over the past several years, despite difficult times experienced industry-wide, ICCRD exhibit hall occupancy has remained strong, repeatedly bordering on practical maximum occupancy." The final recommendation of PWC was for an expansion of 275,000 square feet of exhibit space, as well as additional meeting and support space.[33]

PWC's Robert Canton also shared his view of the state and future of the convention center industry with the association of center managers, the International Association of Assembly Managers, in an article in the April/May 2004 issue of *Facility Manager* magazine. Titled "The Sky Is Falling! Or Is It Just a Little Rain?," Canton's piece noted, "the good news is that demand, while not keeping pace with the most recent additions to supply, is not declining as much as occupancy rates might suggest . . . the current economic recovery is expected to bring demand back up to pre-9/11 levels by 2005." And while Canton went on to describe an "oversupply of space," he posed the question of whether that meant expansions in the "haves . . . such as New York, San Diego, and Indianapolis should be halted? The simple answer is, of course not."[34]

Both the Tradeshow "200" and the performance of "gateway centers" also figured in PWC's May 2006 report on the market feasibility of a new convention center in Irving, Texas. Examining the history of "200" exhibit space usage and attendance, the consulting firm described the drops in 2001 and 2002 but concluded, "Based on 2003 and 2004 growth rates, attendance and [Gross Domestic Product] may be returning to pre-recession levels." Presenting the "gateway center" data, a series of graphs showed average convention and tradeshow attendance, as well as convention-related exhibit hall occupancy, still below the levels of 1999 and 2000. The trends summary concluded, "Growth and decline in exhibit space demand and attendance at Gateway centers have been consistent with periods of national economic growth and decline—a trend that is expected to continue in the future."[35] The firm recommended that Irving build a new "multi-purpose center" with 50,000 square feet of exhibit space.

Both the Tradeshow Week "200" data and the figures for "Gateway Centers" appeared in PWC's report on the Gwinnett County, Georgia, convention center for the Gwinnett Convention and Visitors Bureau. And once again, PWC found market "demand to support a 50,000 square-foot expansion," though the firm found a justification for a 75,000 square foot addition. With that expansion and a new 400-room hotel, the Gwinnett Center would presumably see its annual convention and tradeshow attendance grow from 16,300 to 50,500—a more than threefold increase.[36]

The demand for more convention center space that would presumably fill an expanded Javits Center, a larger Indiana Convention Center, a new center in Irving, and an expansion of the Gwinnett Center would also be sufficient to neatly accommodate an expansion of the San Diego Convention Center. PWC's December 2007 208-page "Strategic Plan Update" and expansion analysis for the San Diego Convention Center focused on a "building program . . . to accommodate the current and estimated future demand for the SDCC." As it had been for clients since the mid-1990s, the firm's assessment of demand was based in large part on both historic "200" and "Gateway Center" performance.

For the "200" large convention and tradeshow events, the PriceWaterhouseCoopers consulting team now had a few years of data beyond the immediate impact of 9-11. The charts of the total attendance and exhibit space use of the "200" events that had appeared in the two successive studies for the Javits Center were nowhere to be found. Instead there was a set of graphs, based on the annual "200" figures, showing year-to-year percentage change. And PWC's view of those data was upbeat, saying that growth of the indices "continued in 2005 and 2006, although not nearly as strong as the growth experienced in the mid-1990s."[37]

The data on "gateway centers," defined as centers in metro areas with more than 30,000 hotel rooms and including San Diego with its 53,800 rooms, also provided a view of convention and tradeshow demand. The San Diego report noted these centers saw an average of 53 conventions and tradeshows for 2007, with attendance of about 400,000. In terms of exhibit hall occupancy from those events, PWC said, "Gateway centers have nearly reached their pre-9/11 levels." Their final oft-repeated conclusion about growth: "Growth and decline in exhibit space demand and attendance at Gateway centers have been consistent with periods of national economic growth and decline—a trend that is expected to continue in the future." With that expectation, PWC recommended that San Diego add 474,000 square feet of exhibit hall space, almost doubling the center's size to one million square feet.[38]

The Logic of Growth

The repeated invocation of convention growth—in event space, attendance, and total number—has been central to the justification for ever more new or expanded convention facilities. By portraying the convention and tradeshow industry as constantly growing, it was possible to simultaneously offer the judgment that Boston, Richmond, Overland Park, Rockford, and Peoria—and Atlanta, New York, Indianapolis, and Irving—could succeed in gaining convention business and "economic impact" by building more space.

The argument that the volume of exhibit space demand was regularly growing (and would do so far into the future) underpinned the contention, repeated in study after study to a wide range of communities, that expanding events, requiring ever more exhibit hall space, would "outgrow" a particular city. That argument was made for small and medium-sized centers, just as it was employed for the biggest centers such as Las Vegas and Chicago. As Charlie Johnson put it to Chicago and Illinois officials: "Many shows in McCormick Place need more space . . . . These shows, if they can not grow, may choose to leave the City."[39]

For individual cities, the threat or reality of losing a long-time event has often been portrayed as a striking blow to civic pride and the community's sense of economic competitiveness. When the annual meeting of the Future Farmers of America decamped from Kansas City to Louisville, a *Kansas City Star* editorial was headed "An Emotional Blow," and one news article described it as "a heavy blow to Kansas City's convention industry and civic self-esteem." The *New York Times* offered the assessment, "But what has made old men here weep and younger ones wonder about loyalty was the news last month that the blue jackets [of the FFA] would be leaving town" after almost seventy years. And when, just a few years later, the Future Farmers relocated their annual gathering from Louisville to Indianapolis, the public gnashing of teeth in Louisville was just as dramatic, followed by the offer of cash or corporate sponsorships and thousands of local volunteers to lure the event back. Even Indianapolis was not immune, with the annual Performance Racing Industry Tradeshow moving its annual event from Indianapolis to Orlando in 2005.[40]

In a world of growing conventions and tradeshows, more space appeared to be a necessity simply to keep existing business. But simply staying even—keeping the Future Farmers in Kansas City, for example—would represent a very limited return on a substantial public investment in building and operating a center. The second element of the constant growth argument was that attendance was growing in parallel with the demand for space. By portraying consistently growing attendance, consultants could support and justify the forecast that more convention center space—either an expansion or an entirely new facility—would inevitably yield new attendees. More space would enable a community to go upmarket to lure larger and more lucrative events. It is the prospect of more out-of-town attendees, thereby bringing new visitor dollars and "economic impact" while stimulating new private development, that has long provided the central justification for ever more space.[41]

While an association or a tradeshow producer could profit from simply having more space to offer exhibitors for their booths and displays (thereby boosting his or her rental income), local communities and their governments only realized a return indirectly, through the attendees brought to their community. If bigger events, in terms of exhibit space, yielded no new visitors, the public investment in a new or bigger center would be unproductive. So the image of growing attendance, both at individual events and in total, has been a vital part of the consultants' analyses and the local sales pitch for convention center spending.

The growth argument rests on a third leg. It has long been a central tenet of industry promoters that the overall universe of convention and tradeshow events has been consistently growing as well. If space demand or attendance were growing, with no enlargement of the pool of events, every city would be facing an effectively "zero-sum" market environment, able to fill its new center or added space only at the expense of competing locales. The image of an expanding universe implied that there would inevitably be new events. From the 1980s through the 1990s and beyond 2000, industry consultants and observers consistently described the constant birthing of new events—to serve new industries and innovations such as the personal computer or the rise of the Internet, to provide regional offshoots of national events, or as targeted events for specialized niche markets.

David C. Petersen, long considered the "dean" of convention center consultants, first at Laventhol & Horwath and then at PriceWaterhouse and PriceWaterhouseCoopers, could tell those assembled for the Exhibit Hall Management Conference in November 1984, "The market is growing as fast as, or faster than, the buildings are growing. . . . I don't see anything that's static or declining. Everything is increasing—size, attendance, number of shows—and sponsors are demanding better and better facilities."[42]

Petersen would repeat much the same argument in his 1989 book on convention center development: "While many people are alarmed at the amount of new convention center construction and expansion, it is apparent that the dominant users of these facilities are increasing in number at a pace consistent with the expansion and supply of the facilities." And Petersen's successor at PriceWaterhouseCoopers, Robert Canton, could point in 2004 to the 4,778 trade and consumer exhibitions counted by Tradeshow Week and tell Javits Center officials that "space limitations have precluded the Center from hosting many events that would like to be in New York City . . . [giving New York City] tremendous untapped potential in the trade and consumer exhibitions market."[43]

The Center for Exhibition Industry Research, the research entity established and funded by the tradeshow industry, also published regular "Size of the Exhibition Industry" reports (based on Tradeshow Week *Data Book* data) through the 1990s that forecast consistent growth in the number of annual events. The 1996 edition, for example, estimated that the count of annual events would grow from 4,400 in 1996 to almost 4,800 by 2000, together with the contention that "Over 500 new shows will be launched by the end of the decade." And the overall argument from trade publications was that there was a growing stock of events, including new initiatives and those outgrowing hotel facilities, to fill more convention center space. Together with the forecasts from the small number of convention center consultants, the overall "pitch" was that center development was a "can't miss" public investment.

The logic of convention industry growth had one additional foundational argument during the 1990s. Industry spokespeople, as well as consultants, regularly termed it "recession-proof." Much of the case for the "recession-proof" conclusion rested on the apparent performance of the industry in 1990, during the Gulf War recession. The annual percent change figures for the Tradeshow "200" in 1991 actually showed some modest growth—1.3

percent in exhibit space use—from 1990 to 1991. Only the attendance measure failed to show positive growth, at 0 percent. What did not appear to have occurred was any real downturn. And the "200" measures quickly turned up from 1991 to 1992. The annual "200" directory summary for 1992 was headed "The Big Shows Bounce Back in 1992," with the report that the "200" had a 1.9 percent increase in exhibit space, and 3.7 percent in attendance.

It was possible for Doug Ducate, head of the Center for Exhibition Industry Research, to describe the period before 2000 as "boom times for 15 straight years in the tradeshow industry, with annual growth and fistfuls of profits." The assumption of consistent growth then ran into the realities of a changed economy with the collapse of the tech bubble, and the dramatic shift in travel behavior after 9-11.[44]

Before 2001, industry spokespeople and center consultants spoke of a long-term history of demand growth. Tradeshow Week's "200" directory for 2000 headlined "Solid Growth Reported in All Indexes," with a reported 2.8 percent increase in average attendance from 1999. The headline the following year, in the directory published in April 2002 covering the previous year, was "Shows Report Steepest Declines in Directory's History." Exhibit space use was reported to have fallen 1.3 percent from 2000, with average attendance down 4.5 percent. The 2002 edition of the "200" directory offered no better news. The summary analysis read, "U.S. Exhibit Space Drops" and reported a 6.0 percent fall in exhibit space use and a decline of 4.4 percent in attendance.[45]

Tradeshow Week presented 2003 as the year the "200" and the industry managed a dramatic turnaround. Although the exhibit space use still showed a decline from the previous year in percentage terms—0.7 percent—it was far smaller than previous drops. And attendance actually showed a year-over-year gain of 3.4 percent, putting it back into the growth category. PWC joined in soon thereafter with its 2004 "Convention Center Report," signaling "significant improvement in the performance of convention centers." The report went on to describe an increase in convention and tradeshow occupancy rates at large centers (over 500,000 square feet), and a "2003 to 2004 increase in attendance to conventions and trade shows of 14 percent!"[46]

As the convention industry appeared to be rebounding in 2003 and 2004, consultant reports began to return to the growth argument, eventually arguing that the industry had returned to a pre-2000 level of demand, and would continue to grow in future years. A "white paper" on supply and demand, produced by the CSL International firm for the International Association of

Convention and Visitors Bureaus in the fall of 2004, included a section headed "Demand Is Increasing" that argued, "there are encouraging signs for the industry." The firm's survey of 127 meeting planners found between 63 and 75 percent "foresee exhibit space growth over the next two to five years," and "Similar data is registered for growth in attendance." The demand analysis concluded, "The concept of the gathering of people works, and in a capitalist society, the private sector will exploit this fact to continually find profitable ways to utilize a growing inventory of facility space."[47]

Yet had convention demand actually recovered by 2006? Was the industry back to a pattern of consistent annual growth in exhibit space use and attendance? The PWC assessment, using data from its annual report on center performance, was largely cast in terms of occupancy and exhibit space use rather than attendance. The CSL "white paper" for the convention bureau association was built on survey data regarding expectations. And CSL's consultant reports for a host of cities displayed *index numbers* derived from annual percent change calculations, rather than actual numbers.

The "official story" of convention industry demand, repeated by consultants, convention and visitors bureaus, industry publications, and the Center for Exhibition Industry Research, was that some 15 years of consistent growth had been interrupted—briefly and not seriously—by the Gulf War recession in 1991, followed by steady and consistent growth through the 1990s. The recession and 9-11 had seriously affected convention demand, with drops in exhibit space use and attendance. But by circa 2005 and 2006, the convention industry had fully rebounded, back to pre-2000 levels, with the prospect of consistent future growth for the balance of the decade. That history and prospect could offer substantial assurance to those cities choosing to invest in new centers or expanded space that they would inevitably fill.[48]

But what if the steady growth scenario was not a full or accurate portrayal of convention demand? What if the figures the consultants quoted and relied on really provided a larger, more complex, and quite different picture of demand? And what if error and misinterpretation, built into the manner in which the demand measures were calculated, regularly led to faulty analyses and erroneous conclusions?

Demand Realities

Growth, in terms of the volume of annual conventions and tradeshows, volume of space used, and count of event attendees, has long been at the heart of the case for building ever more convention centers. Even when economic downturns and recessions have had a demonstrable impact on activity and attendance, industry representatives and consultants have contended it is a temporary situation—the convention business would inevitably return to steady, annual growth. The reality of demand, indexed by the same measures relied on by consultants, has been notably different.

Counting Events

Tradeshow Week's annual *Data Book* has commonly been used as a source for the aggregate size and growth of the convention industry, both directly and as reported in the Center for Exhibition Industry's regular "The Size of the Exhibition Industry" reports during the 1990s, regularly cited by industry consultants. The *Data Book* volume, at about three inches thick and a weight of five pounds, includes a detailed listing of every event in the U.S. and Canada using 5,000 or more square feet of exhibit space. Published in the fall *prior to* the events it includes, it serves as an index and calendar for future events. Thus, rather than counting events that have happened, it effectively provides a short-term forecast for the coming year. The *Data Book*'s summary analysis also includes information on *anticipated* exhibit space use and attendance. But those figures are available for only a fraction of the events included in the volume. Tradeshow Week typically calculates an average for the events that provide space and attendance estimates, and then multiplies the averages by the total (or subtotal) of events.

The annual *Data Book* listings include both typical association conventions, such as the annual Congress of Cities of the National League of Cities, the annual meeting of the National Education Association, and the conference of the Association of Fundraising Professionals, and tradeshow events such as the National Hardware Show and the Produce Marketing Association's Fresh Summit. These events utilize a range of venues, including hotels, trade marts, and convention centers. But the *Data Book* also includes (and counts in its totals) a wide array of public consumer shows. The book contained page after page of listings for local home and garden shows such as the Madison, Wisconsin, Home Expo, Maricopa County Home & Garden Show,

Minneapolis Home & Garden Show, and North Iowa Home & Landscaping Show. They are joined by an array of local auto shows (the Dallas Auto Show, the Portland Rod & Custom Show), boat shows (the Lehigh Valley Boat Show, the Nashville Boat & Sports Show), and sports shows (the Chicagoland Children's Expo, the Cincinnati Hunting & Fishing Show).

These public or consumer shows often use convention center space. But unlike conventions and tradeshows, they serve an almost entirely local market, drawing residents from the immediate city or metropolitan area. They thus do not generate the visitor activity or spending that most convention centers are designed to produce. By including these local events together with conventions and tradeshows, the *Data Book* annual total figures often provide a misleading impression of both the total size of the event universe, and its growth over time.

Consultant C. H. Johnson routinely employed the overall *Data Book* totals to describe demand growth during the 1990s. The HVS firm has used the same *Data Book* annual counts to describe demand growth from 1989 to 2007 in its consultant reports and its "Convention Centers: Is the Industry Overbuilt?" analysis in 2008. The "Overbuilt" article described exhibition events as growing from 3,289 in 1989 to 5,036 in 2007, "an annual average growth rate of approximately 2.4 percent . . . over the past 18 years."[49] These analyses, and others based on the *Data Book* event totals, unfortunately combine two very different kinds of events—conventions/tradeshows and local public or consumer shows—to create a misleading impression of growth. The reality is that the local public show category has provided effectively all the growth in annual event counts seen over the last decade and a half.

Tradeshow Week began publishing separate counts of local public shows in the 1994 edition of the *Data Book*. That year, the public events made up about 11 percent of the total. By 1999, public events comprised over 15 percent, and that proportion grew to 25 percent by 2007, continuing at that share through 2010. There is no indication in the *Data Books* if the growth in these public events reflected real change in numbers, or a greater effectiveness on the part of the volume's editors in listing consumer events.

Limiting an analysis of event growth to just conventions and tradeshows provides a very different image of demand change. In the first year the breakdown was available, 1994, there were 3,820 conventions and tradeshows. The total reached a peak of 4,016 in 2000—a modest level of growth. But it then fell to 3,648 in 2002 before increasing to a post-2000 peak of 3,850 in 2006. The 2009 event total came to 3,745. Then, reflecting the impact of recession, the 2010 total dropped to just 3,552—the lowest figure in the *Data Book*'s recent history.

The annual count of conventions and tradeshows has thus fluctuated with the national economy. Yet the "rebound" in convention and tradeshow demand described by consultants circa 2005 and 2006 did not match the peak year counts of the 1990s. There was certainly not the consistent growth described by C. H. Johnson or HVS. And the 2010 figure—the last year Tradeshow Week published before its demise—represented an unprecedented decline.

The "200"

Since the mid-1980s, Tradeshow Week has also compiled an annual listing of the 200 largest—in terms of exhibit space used—conventions and tradeshows in the U.S. The "200" listing is thus a changing annual group, one that by definition includes only those events that grow at a rate comparable to the largest events. The "200" listing includes both for-profit annual, biennial, and triennial tradeshows such as the now defunct COMDEX computer show, the annual Consumer Electronics Show, and the winter and summer New York International Gift Fairs, as well as annual association conventions, such as the meeting of the American Urological Association and the Chicago Dental Society annual meeting. Unlike the *Data Book*, it excludes public consumer shows. And it reflects actual event performance, unlike the *Data Book*'s pre-event estimates.

In terms of total annual exhibit space use, the "200" events grew regularly through the 1990s, from 51 million square feet in 1991 to a peak of 69.8 million in 2000. That pattern changed dramatically after 2000, with space use total falling to 61.9 million in 2003. Growth began again in 2004, with 63.6 million square feet in 2004, hitting a peak of 71.3 million in 2008. It was only in 2007 and 2008 that space usage exceeded (albeit slightly) the peak of 2000. But the recession had a dramatic impact on exhibit space use in 2009, plunging to just 58.6 million square feet—the smallest total since 1996, and a drop of 17.8 percent.

The "200" events, the largest and by definition among the most successful in the industry, would thus appear to follow the growth argument of industry consultants. But the real pattern of exhibit space use and growth has actually differed quite a bit across the "200" events. The single largest event, a changing annual example that often includes the biennial CONEXPO for construction equipment or the International Consumer Electronics Show (both in Las Vegas) has shown quite a dramatic increase in exhibit space use. In 1991, for example, the fall COMDEX spanned 1.14 million square feet. By 1999, the top event spanned 1.73 million square feet. And in 2008, the largest event (the CONEXPO) covered a total of over 2.2 million square feet.

But the dramatic growth of the single largest event was not necessarily mirrored by the more typical "200" event. The median "200" event grew much more slowly and less consistently in exhibit space use. That mid-sized event covered 195,500 square feet in 1991, hit 267,677 in 2000, dropped to 224,800 for 2002, and finally hit a post-2000 peak of 248,580 in 2007. Compared to the largest events, the mid-sized convention and tradeshows in the "200" grew only modestly during the 1990s, and had not returned to the 2000 peak by 2008.

A pattern of no consistent growth in space also marked the bottom of the "200." The single smallest "200" event in 1991 covered 113,000 square feet, reaching 125,300 by 1995. The peak year for the smallest event came in 1999, at 148,700 square feet. But the smallest event to be included among the "200" never again reached that size. For 2008, the smallest event covered 125,000 square feet—unchanged from 1995. Had the overall convention and tradeshow industry been consistently expanding in exhibit space, the smallest event among the "200" should have grown steadily as well. The fact that it did not suggests that the growth in space use for the overall "200" was a product of the largest events, not the "200" as a whole.

The most recent results, for 2009, the last year of Tradeshow Week's operation, add one final fillip to the oft-repeated claims of convention and tradeshow exhibit space growth. The largest event in 2009, the International Consumer Electronics Show (CES), spanned 1,711,403 square feet—a drop of 7.9 percent from 2008. And the impact of the recession was even more dramatic at the middle and bottom of the "200." The median-sized event fell to 218,541 square feet, a drop of 10.5 percent, and the smallest fell from 125,000 in 2008 to just 95,000 in 2009—a drop of 24 percent.

The exhibit space use of the "200" events thus differs from the consistent year-over-year growth pattern regularly shown in consultant graphics and reports. Very large events have demonstrated significant growth since the early 1990s. But that growth has not been the norm, even within this select group of the largest annual conventions and tradeshows. The more common result has been slow and inconsistent growth from 2002, followed by the sharp plunge in 2009.

The growth of the largest events also reflects their location. Every year but one since 1991, the single largest event has been held in Las Vegas. And Las Vegas offers a uniquely abundant scale of convention center space. The publicly owned Las Vegas Convention Center expanded from one million square feet of space to two million in 2002. The triennial CONEXPO large construction equipment typically spilled out to the center's surrounding parking lots and nearby hotels as well. And the Consumer Electronics Show has been able to take advantage of the million square feet of exhibit space at the privately owned Sands/Venetian Expo and exhibit space at the Hilton hotel in addition to the space at Las Vegas Convention Center. There has thus been a ready availability of new exhibit space in Las Vegas for events that could sell it.

The case for more, and newer, convention center space has not been built solely on the image of a growing demand for exhibit hall space. Industry consultants also argue that convention and tradeshow attendance has been growing as well, and thus a larger center will pay rewards in terms of more attendees and their economic impact. Indeed, if only space use was growing, cities would be seeing no added attendance—or greater visitor spending and economic impact—from building more center space. Yet for the "200" events over the past two decades, the pattern of total attendance has not been one of consistent growth. Instead, total "200" event attendance hit a peak in 1996—a peak that has not been equaled in the years since.

The "200" events grew in terms of attendance from 3.88 million in 1991 to a high of 5.08 million in 1996, propelled in large part by the growth of very large events, such as the COMDEX show. The Las Vegas-based COMDEX grew from about 127,000 attendees in 1991 to over 216,000 in 1996. But subsequent years saw the behemoth show's attendance sink to under 125,000 in 2002 and 44,000 in 2003 before finally being canceled in 2004. Other big tradeshows shared a similar fate. The Super Show for the sporting goods industry fell from 112,000 attendees in 1995 to 81,000 in 2002 and 20,000 in 2005 before being ended in 2006.

The years after the 1996 peak saw a slide in 1997 and again in 1998, with a bump up to 4.77 million total attendees for 2000. But in the wake of recession and 9-11, overall attendance fell and remained low, at just 4.18 million for 2004. Tradeshow Week reported a notable jump in attendance in 2006, up to 4.62 million from 2005's 4.16. Yet that sharp increase in 2006 was really a product of the decision to add six events put on by privately owned trade marts in Dallas, Las Vegas, and High Point, North Carolina. These trade mart events averaged 50,000 attendees, well above the average for the balance of the "200," thus boosting the overall attendance. Yet even with these added events, total attendance remained at about the level of the mid-1990s.

The "200" attendance for 2007 was 4.41 million, followed by 4.56 million in 2008—still below the 1996 peak of 5.08 million and the 4.8 million of 1997, and equal to the total for 1998. Then, for 2009, the "200" attendance total came to just 3.84 million—a drop of 15.8 percent. Major event attendance had not, by 2008, even rebounded to the peak levels of the late 1990s. The 2009 total brought the "200" events back to the total attendance they had garnered in 1989.

A Note on Measuring the "200"

Contemporary consultant analyses that employ measures of the "200" events usually show historical data in terms of year-to-year percent change or index numbers. For example, a February 2009 market analysis for the New Orleans Morial Convention Center by CSL International included a chart of "Tradeshow Week 200—Convention & Tradeshow Industry." The chart showed index number values of space use, attendance, and exhibiting companies for "200" events from 1987 through 2007. The index value for total attendance in 1991 was 110, hitting 142 in 1997 and, after a post-9-11 drop, reaching about 163 by 2007. The clear impression from this chart is that attendance steadily grew through the 1990s, fell in 2001 and 2002, and then resumed a steady upward trajectory. That image of annual attendance growth is thoroughly incorrect.[50]

The CSL chart indicates that "200" attendance grew by some 48 percent from 1991 to 2007. The actual totals for 1991—3.88 million—and 2007—4.56 million—yield a percent change of 17.5 percent. And where the CSL chart indicates that attendance for 2007 neatly exceeded the total for 1997 (about 15 percent greater), the actual total attendance figures were 4,795,872 in 1997 and 4,413,372 for 2007—a clear drop. How could CSL turn slow growth into dramatic increases and a decline into a gain?

Each year, Tradeshow Week provided a summary total of each measure of the "200," including attendance and exhibit space use. The editors also report these totals for the prior year. So, for example, the 2007 events attracted a total of 4.4 million attendees, compared to a reported total of 4.29 million for 2006—an apparent increase. Yet the report a year earlier on the 2006 events showed a total attendance of 4.62 million. In the aggregate, attendance dropped. Tradeshow Week nonetheless reported an *increase in attendance of*

1.6 percent. Tradeshow Week thus compares an event's current performance to a *revised figure* for a year earlier submitted by the event organizer. And those revised figures for individual events often differ substantially from those reported a year earlier. For example, the "200" listing for the 2007 SEMICON West show for the semiconductor industry gave an attendance figure of 14,348, together with a previous year (2006) figure of 12,740. That worked out to 12.6 percent increase in attendance. Yet a year earlier, the Tradeshow Week "200" listing showed attendance for SEMICON West's 2006 event at 19,600. By employing the revised attendance total for 2006, what should have been a *decrease of 27 percent* turned into apparent attendance growth.

Much the same thing occurred for the 2007 Outdoor Retailer Summer Market. Attendance for 2007 was shown as 7,840, compared to a revised 2006 total of 7,150—an increase of 9.6 percent. Yet the Summer Market's attendance in the 2006 edition of the "200" was shown as 7,879, for a real if modest *decrease.* And a similar revised attendance figure for a year earlier for the annual Shooting, Hunting, and Outdoor Trade show (a revised 24,366 for 2006 versus the original 26,139) reduced the event's attendance drop from 22 percent to 16 percent. This same pattern of a revised figure for the previous year occurs for exhibit space use. Not every "200" event restates its attendance and space use numbers for the previous year. But enough do so to affect the overall totals and the calculation of percent change.

Tradeshow Week's consistent use of revised figures for the previous year has led to the calculation of annual percent change values that do not accurately represent the performance of the actual events. Modest actual increases turn into large gains; small seeming declines are actually far larger. The overall result, whether reported as the calculated percent change or transformed into index numbers based on percent change, as the CSL firm has done, is to create the appearance of regular year-to-year growth when actual growth is far more modest. Even Tradeshow Week's recent "200" publications have made the gap between the annual percent change numbers and the actual performance evident, by presenting a table of cumulative annual growth rates based on the aggregate "200" totals. In the table and bar chart showing the 1997 and 2007 attendance totals, 2007 is *lower* than 1997, yielding an annual growth rate of –0.8 percent. Still, the consultant reports portray the 2007 attendance as well *above* the 1997 figure.

The gap between CSL and other consultants' index numbers and reality is even more dramatic for 2009. The chart in the 2009 edition of the "200" shows the total attendance of 4.51 million in 1999 and 3.84 for 2009, noting a cumulative annual growth rate of −1.8 percent.

The figures on annual convention and tradeshow performance produced by Tradeshow Week thus have to be evaluated and employed with real care. By employing index values or percent change measures rather than actual totals, it has been possible for almost every industry consultant, including John Kaatz and Bill Krueger of CSL, Charlie Johnson of C. H. Johnson Consulting, Tom Hazinski and Hans Detlefsen of HVS, and David Petersen and Rob Canton of PWC, to overstate demand growth and provide an inaccurate picture of the industry. Such a picture would, of course, help local officials and business leaders make the case, in city after city, that a new or larger convention center would see a substantial and growing stream of new business.

PriceWaterhouseCooper's Annual Convention Center Report

Where both the Tradeshow Week data sources, and the more recent Center for Exhibition Industry Research annual Index, sought to measure only the demand side of the convention equation, PriceWaterhouseCoopers has long tracked a series of measures of the *actual performance* of convention centers. The firm's annual "Convention Center Report," begun in 1985 by Laventhol & Horwath, covers just over 100 individual centers each year, with the most consistent reporting from larger centers in major metropolitan areas. These "Gateway Centers" are located in metropolitan areas with at least 30,000 hotel rooms and have at least 100,000 square feet in exhibit space, a group that amounts to some 30 centers each year. PWC also reports figures for two other categories of centers. "National Centers" are in metropolitan areas with between 15,000 and 30,000 area hotel rooms, or in areas with over 30,000 rooms but with less than 100,000 square feet of exhibit space. "Regional Centers" are located in smaller metropolitan areas, or are smaller or secondary facilities. The Convention Center Report only shows center performance on such things as occupancy and attendance purely as means, with no breakdown of data for individual centers. And it does rely on voluntary reporting by center managers. But it has the decided advantage of tapping real performance, separating center events between the conventions and tradeshows that generally draw out-of-town attendees and the largely local public or consumer shows, like an auto show or home show.[51]

PWC presented an analysis of the performance of Gateway Centers as part of its strategic plan for an expansion of the San Diego Convention Center, with a chart covering 1999 through 2007. In 1999, these centers averaged about 67 conventions and tradeshows, figures that excluded consumer or public shows. That total fell to some 59 for 2000 and 62 for 2001. No year from 2001 through 2007 has equaled those totals—the highest convention and tradeshow total since 2001 was 2003, at 56. The total for 2007 came to 53.[52]

PWC included more recent data in its 2008, 2009, and 2010 Convention Center Reports. The firm reported an average of 57 conventions and tradeshows at Gateway Centers in 2008, with 55 in 2009. Thus the average count of conventions and tradeshows has consistently been below the levels of 1999–2001. The 2010 report, covering performance in 2009, brought an even more striking result: the count of conventions and tradeshows at Gateway Centers averaged just 51. In 2011, the average convention and tradeshow count was at 50, falling in 2012 to just 48.

The report for San Diego also included a chart of Gateway Center exhibit hall occupancy by conventions and tradeshows from 1999, a measure directly tapping the use of exhibit hall space. The occupancy rates for 1999 and 2000 stood at about 48 percent, with an increase to 50 percent for 2001. After 2001, convention and tradeshow occupancy fell to a low of 39.3 percent in 2003. Occupancy rates then hovered in the low 40s until hitting roughly 48 percent in 2007. The more recent editions of the annual Convention Center Report show an occupancy rate of 44.1 percent for 2008, 36.6 percent for 2009, 42.3 percent in 2010, 40.6 percent for 2011, and 39.2 percent in 2012.

Convention and tradeshow occupancy after 2001 has remained at levels below that for the 1999 to 2001 period, with the single exception of a boost in 2007. The most recent years have slipped back to the levels of 2003 and 2004. Paralleling the event count figures, recent exhibit hall occupancy has remained below the peak years of the late 1990s.

The figures for convention and tradeshow attendance are more dramatic than those for occupancy, and far more relevant to cities seeking to lure visitors. The average convention and tradeshow attendance at Gateway Centers for 1999 was about 620,000, followed by some 540,000 in 2000 and roughly 480,000 in 2001. In only one post-2001 year did attendance equal these earlier figures—an average of 520,000 for 2003. The total convention and tradeshow attendance in 2007 was just under 400,000. The attendance reported in 2008 and 2009 came to 419,300 and 416,300 respectively. The 2010 report showed attendance dropping even more to just 351,400—more than 40 percent below the 1999 figure. For 2011, a modest increase brought the attendance average to 410,900, but it fell to 387,400 in 2012.

PWC included a limited presentation of data on "National Centers" as part of its April 2005 report on a proposed new convention center for Cleveland. A chart in the Cleveland report included data on exhibit hall occupancy by conventions and tradeshows at these centers covering 1992–2004. Exhibit hall occupancy grew from an average of 30 percent in the early 1990s to some 40 percent for 1996–1999 and 31.2 percent in 2000. Occupancy then fell steadily to a low of 21.5 percent in 2003. The Cleveland analysis stated, "The decline in occupancy may be attributed to several factors, including economic conditions, and a growth in supply of exhibit space that exceeds a growth in demand of [sic] exhibit space."[53]

The most recent PWC data on National Center convention and tradeshow occupancy show an increase to 32 percent for 2006, followed by 27 percent in 2007, 25.1 percent in 2007, 25.1 percent in 2008 and 21.8 percent for 2009 and then 20.1 percent for 2010, 23.1 percent in 2011, and 22.5 percent in 2012. These recent occupancy levels are thus considerably below the average of 40 achieved in the latter part of the 1990s and the peak year of 1999, with about 42 percent occupancy.

The Cleveland report did not include a historical time series on events or attendance from National Centers. But the annual Convention Center Reports indicate an average convention and tradeshow attendance at national centers of 212,000 for 2003 and 217,000 for 2004. More recent years have seen average attendance consistently well below these two years, with 163,000 in 2007, 141,000 in 2008, and 169,300 for 2009. The 2010 report gave average attendance as 149,600, dropping to just 125,400 in 2011, and then rebounding in 2012 to 165,400.

These data tell a consistent tale. For both the Gateway Centers and the smaller National Centers, the peak levels of events, occupancy, and attendance came in 1999 or 2000. There were notable drops in all of these measures after 9-11. Although center exhibit hall occupancy rebounded somewhat after 2004, it subsequently fell in 2008 and after. Those increased center occupancy figures may simply reflect the discounts on space rental and incentives centers increasingly offered after 2001 to lure new business. And convention and tradeshow attendance—the central driver of economic impact and visitor spending for cities, the phenomenon that has spurred center building—failed to rebound to pre-9-11 levels, and then plunged to a new low point in 2010 or 2011. What there manifestly was not was evidence of a growing, expanding industry filling the nation's convention halls with ever more attendees—just the opposite.

Summing Up the Growth Argument

Over and over, consultant market and feasibility studies for new or expanded convention centers have forecast a significant return in terms of new convention attendees, visitor spending, economic impact, and jobs. They regularly have tied those findings to a picture of the national convention and tradeshow market that describes a history of consistent growth in demand, with an optimistic outlook for continued future growth.

That picture was fundamentally misleading. Although some of the measures regularly employed by consultants such as Coopers & Lybrand, CSL, C. H. Johnson, SAG, HVS, and PriceWaterhouseCoopers did indeed show growth during the 1990s, that pattern shifted dramatically after 2000 and 2001. The total volume of annual convention and tradeshows for 2007 and 2008 was at or slightly below the levels of the mid- to late 1990s. The convention and tradeshow event count then plummeted in 2010.

Much the same image of an industry that remains below the peaks of the late 1990s is provided by the Tradeshow "200" data. Although overall exhibit space use has grown in recent years—perhaps due to the rampant discounting of convention center space rentals—total attendance remains below the peak years of 1990s, even as there has been an explosion in the growth of available convention center space. And the annual data series on actual convention center performance from PriceWaterhouseCoopers provides yet another set of metrics that mirror the story from the Tradeshow Week series. In terms of convention and tradeshow event counts, exhibit hall occupancy, and attendance, center performance has remained below the peak levels of the 1990s, with substantial declines after 2007 or 2008.

The growth of the national economy in the years after 2002 did not produce a parallel level of growth in convention center activity. It appears that demand had been "reset" to a lower level since 2001. Yet that conclusion is nowhere evident in the bulky consultant studies for cities from Boston and New York to Midland and Jackson. Instead, there has been a consistent invocation of the notion that convention demand is growing. Charlie Johnson could employ both Tradeshow Week and PriceWaterhouseCoopers data in his 2005 study for College Station, Texas, and offer the conclusion, "Despite the economic downturn that began in early 2000, the meetings market has remained fairly strong and a long term need for event space still exists . . . . It is up to the host community to capture that potential." For Tucson in 2007, he could proffer the assessment, "The meetings and convention industry has expanded significantly over the past ten years in both supply of events and new and/or expanded quality venues but the Tucson Convention Center has not participated in this sector to any degree." And in a 2007 presentation, CSL's Bill Krueger offered an audience of local elected and economic development officials a series of slides on "The Recovery for the Biggest . . ." and "Decades of Growth for the Largest . . ."[54]

Over and over, major industry consultants have either misread or misrepresented the data on convention and tradeshow demand. By focusing on a subset of years, using inaccurate annual percent change numbers, or basing their conclusions on an overly broad definition of events, they have succeeded in painting an upbeat and optimistic portrait of demand growth. That illusion of persistent growth could help justify "build it and they will come" recommendations for a remarkably broad array of communities, from the largest to the most modestly sized.

The reality of far more limited growth, even in the face of a continuing expansion of supply, is that the convention market appeared to be increasingly zero-sum. Las Vegas and Orlando succeeded in gaining some events and attendees with major expansions (at least prior to 2008). But their success came largely at expense of cities like New York, Chicago, and Los Angeles. Chicago, for example, saw its share of the "200" events plummet from 30 in 1993 to just 18 in 2008. And even Las Vegas and Orlando have failed to achieve the increased business they had been promised and anticipated.

The world of convention center activity changed over the years after 2001. The boom in center building had produced an oversupply of space. If the growing competition for conventions was not obvious to the consultants (or their clients) after 2001, it was evident to the industry, to both the local convention and visitor bureaus that market centers and the convention center managers themselves. In January 2006, a group of CVB heads and center managers assembled in Phoenix to begin to discuss the growing problems in selling center space. By that June, a series of presentations at the annual meeting of the Destination Marketing Association International in Austin noted the "Increased competition in marketplace" and "Price erosion." Peggy Daidakis, director of the Baltimore Convention Center, described the growing use of "Opportunity Funds," where "CVB's are paying a portion of the Center's rental; picking up transportation costs; covering the costs of ancillary charges," and Bob Hodge, head of the Austin Convention Center, described how his city was "Pricing [the] Convention Center competitively within our market and allowing for discounts when business warrants."[55]

By 2007, discounts, incentives, opportunity funds, and offers of free center rent had become commonplace in the convention center world. Tradeshow Week reported in fall 2007 that fully 60 percent of centers maintained "incentive funds" to lure business. And when the joint study committee of CVB heads and center managers issued its report on center sales and operations in August 2007, the conclusion was quite direct. The report noted "the recognition that supply of available exhibit and meeting space across the nation currently exceeds demand, resulting in a 'buyers market'" and that "The resulting 'buyers market' has exacerbated an already competitive environment, resulting in the need to discount rental rates or increase services that can create a competitive advantage." That view of a "buyer's market" and an oversupply of space was not particularly in evidence in the consultant reports.[56]

At the same time as centers and CVBs were trying to buy business with discounts, the cost and difficulties of travel had grown, making attendance at a convention or tradeshow a more problematic investment for firms and organizations. The changed technology of communication and interaction, from PCs, tablets, and cell phones to virtual meetings and the Internet, had significantly altered communication and information sharing. Even where Indianapolis might lure an event from Kansas City, or Chicago beat out Baltimore for a convention, the number of attendees they would see likely would be far smaller than in years past.

Convention Demand and the Economy after 2008

The path of convention and tradeshow demand after 2000 and 9-11 demonstrates that the industry is far from insulated from larger economic forces. For 2002, Tradeshow Week reported a drop of 6 percent in exhibit space use and a 4.4 percent decline in attendance for the "200" events. The impact of the financial meltdown and recession of 2008 and 2009 has been, by all measures, even more dramatic, albeit not fully evident until 2009 and after.

The annual count of convention and tradeshow events from the Tradeshow Week *Data Book* provides one measure of the impact of the recession. The event total was 3,742 for 2008 and 3,745 in 2009. As events are commonly planned well in advance, the 2009 count did not immediately reflect any real change on the part of event organizers. Since the *Data Book* directory is prepared during the year before the events are held, it could not reflect meeting cancellations such as the decision by the American Society of Newspaper Editors to cancel its 2009 convention, made just months before its April date.

But the 2010 event volume reflected a significant change, falling to 3,552. That amounted to a decrease of five percent, bringing the convention and tradeshow count to its lowest level since the data were first reported in 1994, clearly below the previous low of 3,648 in 2002.

Event cancellations do not directly affect the annual set of top "200" events. Instead, those events may shrink in size as exhibitors choose to reduce the size of their booths or simply not attend, and they can drop in attendance as firms, organizations, and individuals decide to reduce travel spending and cut back on event attendance. Tradeshow Week reported that in 2008 the "200" showed a 1.6 percent drop in exhibit space use and a 3 percent decrease in attendance.

The full brunt of the recession's impact on the "200" came in 2009. Exhibit space use dropped 17.8 percent and total attendance 15.8 percent, to a level equal to that of 1989. There would be no "200" listing for 2010 or after—Tradeshow Week ceased publication in April 2010.

The dramatic drops in space use and attendance from 2008 to 2009 far exceeded the greatest fall-off previously seen: a drop in exhibit space use of 6.0 percent and an attendance drop of 4.4 percent, both in 2002. These recent changes can also be seen in the attendance performance of individual events, most accurately for the small set of events that have their attendance figures audited and verified by a third party. Audited attendance for the annual Rental Show in Atlanta in 2009 was 7,007, a drop of 35 percent from the previous year in Las Vegas. The 2009 INTERPHEX pharmaceutical event in New York saw attendance fall by 19.7 percent from the 2008 event in Philadelphia, to 12,343. INTERPHEX attendance slid again in 2010 to 11,739 and 11,100 in 2011. The 2009 Motivation Show for the incentive industry (consistently held at Chicago's McCormick Place) witnessed a 26.6 percent attendance drop. Attendance dropped again in 2010 by 33.2 percent, to just 6,006—less than half the 2008 total.

The Las Vegas-based Global Gaming Expo, long a growing event, saw attendance fall 5.5 percent from 2008 to 2009, to 24,771. Attendance was again down in 2010, by 2.1 percent, and in 2011, to 23,648. And the annual convention of the American Institute of Architects had a 7.9 percent attendance drop from Boston's 2008 total of 19,520 to 17,977 the next year in San Francisco. The 2010 meeting in Miami saw attendance fall to 15,574—a 13.4 percent drop. The 2011 event in New Orleans garnered even lower attendance, just 12,366, although the 2012 edition in Washington, D.C., saw attendance increase to 15,214.

Major convention centers have also seen substantial declines in convention and tradeshow attendance. At Chicago's McCormick Place, attendance dropped 7 percent from 2008 to 2009, despite completion of a major expansion in August 2007. It fell another 4.8 percent in 2010 and 9.6 percent in 2011. The Las Vegas Convention Center saw attendance fall from 1.6 million in 2008 to 1.12 million in 2009, a drop of 30.3 percent. There was a slight rebound of 3 percent in 2010. Orlando's Orange County Convention Center had a convention and tradeshow attendance drop of 21.8 percent in 2009, to about 780,000. It managed to make up a part of that loss in 2011, seeing attendance of just under one million—still shy of 2007's 1.08 million.

Atlanta's Georgia World Congress Center saw fiscal year 2008 (through June 30) convention and tradeshow attendance fall by 21.4 percent in 2009. and another 13.7 percent in 2010. The 2010 convention and tradeshow attendance total of 473,448 was demonstrably smaller than the 601,000 attendees the GWCC had accommodated in 1989. A modest increase brought attendance almost back to the 2009 level, at 539,680.

Other major destination cities also saw dramatic declines in convention center business. New York City's Javits Center saw its convention and tradeshow attendance fall from 817,100 in 2007 to 708,200 the following year and 633,600 in 2009. The hotel room nights produced by the Walter Washington Convention Center in the nation's capital fell from 376,296 in fiscal year 2008 to 280,478 in fiscal 2009. The room-night total dropped again in fiscal 2010, to 274,951—a decline of 26.9 percent from fiscal 2008.

Whether for individual major events or for large and historically well-performing convention centers, two conclusions stand out regarding recent change. First, the drops in attendance have been remarkably pervasive, across a broad array of events and centers, including centers that have long dominated the industry. Second, the scale of attendance and hotel room night decline has been substantial, indeed remarkable. Those declines substantially exceed the fall-off in attendance in the years immediately after 9-11. Indeed, for convention centers in cities such as Atlanta and San Francisco, they represent a return to attendance levels seen a decade or two earlier, effectively wiping out the growth of the 1990s. This magnitude of attendee loss suggests a dynamic very different from what was seen after 9-11. For example, the Las Vegas Convention Center witnessed an attendance drop of 3 percent in 2002, followed by a further 6 percent in 2003. The center's attendance drop of 30 percent from 2008 to 2009 is of an entirely different order of magnitude, an experience paralleled by many other centers.

The full import of the change in convention center attendance will only become clear over future years. But compared to the impact of previous recessions, the change in 2008, 2009, 2010, and 2011 suggests a sea change in patterns of attendance and convention activity. One assessment was provided by the senior staff of New York's Javits Center, in a December 3, 2010, presentation to the center's board on "Maximizing Economic Impact." After slides noting the "Sales Challenges" faced by the Javits, the presentation included a slide titled "Relevant Industry Trends." The slide's bullet points noted "Oversupply of convention center space" and "Economic challenges to convention center customers."[57]

The Javits Center staff was fully aware of the impact of larger changes on the convention business. Javits convention and tradeshow attendance had fallen by 22.5 percent from 2007 to 2009. The "oversupply of convention center space" was not something that would go away after 2011 or 2012. A number of cities—Philadelphia and Indianapolis, for example—were about to complete major expansions at the time of the Javits presentation. And other cities—Boston, Cleveland, Nashville, San Diego, Seattle, Los Angeles—are building or planning center expansions. That continuing increase in supply acts to provide a counter to whatever attendance rebound might take place in the future.

The View from the Consultants

While terms like "oversupply of space" or "buyer's market" were part of the industry's discourse by 2009 and 2010, they were not part of the analysis by the small group of convention center consultants. Assessing the state of the convention and tradeshow market for Boston's "T5 Partnership" in February 2010, John Kaatz of CSL International "showed the linkage between the economy and the events industry and suggested that in the future meeting planners believe this linkage will stay tightly related." He illustrated that point with a chart of "Convention and Tradeshow Industry Growth Measures" from Tradeshow Week's "200" data, adding a line labeled "Real GDP." The lines for exhibit space use, number of exhibitors, and number of attendees showed steady growth through 2007. For 2008, the exhibitor and attendance counts showed a modest decline. But as if to reassure the partnership members, the chart's line (shown in red) for Real GDP continued beyond 2008, showing strong upward movement in 2010 and 2011. If the "linkage" was indeed "tightly related," the measures of convention demand would no doubt soon be on a similar upward path.[58]

Kaatz also presented charts of the Boston Convention and Exhibition Center current and projected future occupancy. While center occupancy was shown as falling from 63.2 percent in fiscal 2008 to 53.2 percent in fiscal 2009, the chart indicated occupancy rates rising to a steady 70 percent for fiscal 2011, 2012, and 2013. Jim Rooney, CEO of the Massachusetts Convention Center Authority, concluded the February 2010 session with the observation that the "Tradeshow marketplace continues to grow and our competitors are growing physically in size and service offerings to meeting planners."

John Kaatz returned to Boston and the T5 Partnership in late November 2010. By then the scale of the decline in convention demand was demonstrable. Kaatz's presentation to the group did not include the historical chart of the Tradeshow Week "200" performance he had shown earlier. Instead, there was a chart of annual changes in convention demand, including the drop in "200" event space use in 2009 of 11.7 percent with a 9.7 percent drop in attendance. But a subsequent slide added the heading "Recent Indications of a Recovery." Kaatz then included a slide titled "Performance Trends in Similar Markets," indicating that for Philadelphia "Event and attendance levels are down 10 to 15 percent year over year since 2007, starting to see signs of improvement," with "signs of improvement" emphasized in red. Describing San Antonio, the presentation included the information that after a strong 2008, attendance levels "decreased by 10–15 percent in 2009," "Nice rebound in 2010," and "bookings for 2011 and 2012 follow a consistent pattern of growth." Again, "consistent pattern of growth" was emphasized in red. For Houston, the red print emphasized "trend up," and made the point that for San Diego occupancy and attendance "trends are reversing." There was good news from across the country.[59]

The emphasis and conclusions of Kaatz's presentation were clear—growth in demand was just around the corner, and Boston was poised to take advantage of it with a major expansion. Kaatz did not tell the assembled Boston leaders that Philadelphia's convention center had seen its generation of overnight hotel stays plunge from 574,000 room nights in 2002 to 336,000 in 2007, 303,000 in 2009, and 179,000 in 2010. "Signs of improvement" indeed. Nor did Kaatz's description of "continued growth" in San Antonio's convention business for 2011 and 2012 reveal that from 340,425 convention and meeting attendees at the Gonzalez Convention Center in 2010, attendance would drop to an estimated 273,419 for 2011 and 255,658 for 2012.[60]

In presenting information on the state of convention demand to the T5

Partnership group, a group established to assess the need and potential for an expansion of the Boston Convention and Exhibition Center, John Kaatz was at best highly selective, at worst fully misleading. And when the CSL firm was employed by the city of Los Angeles in mid-2011 to assess the potential convention performance of a new enclosed stadium as part of the Los Angeles Convention Center, its sole mention of the larger market realities consisted of the statement, "The national inventory of large, nationally-rotating conventions and tradeshows is relatively stable. Future growth in the segment of events will likely be limited over the next several years."[61]

Much the same positive message was part of CSL's analysis of a potential expansion of the Lexington, Kentucky, Convention Center in August 2011. Using historic data from Tradeshow Week, the annual Center for Exhibition Industry Research Index, and a survey of meeting planners, the firm offered the conclusion, "It is believed that the worst of the economic downturn is behind the exhibition industry." And while the CSL report quoted the CEIR 2011 report that "The exhibition industry, however, could be directly impacted by state and local government expenditure reductions," it did not continue to the following paragraph: "However, on the positive side, the supply of exhibition space exceeds demand. As facilities deteriorate or fail to upgrade, they can no longer compete for national business and the supply-demand imbalance will begin to normalize."[62]

Other consultants offered similar upbeat assessments about the future. The HVS Convention, Sports & Entertainment consulting practice offered its view of convention "Industry Trends" as part of its January 2011 market analysis for a proposed convention center in Cedar Rapids, Iowa. HVS employed, among other data, the information from Tradeshow Week's annual *Data Book* on exhibit space use. The firm's conclusion for Cedar Rapids:

> Over the past few decades, the meeting and convention industry has evolved dramatically from a budding industry to an important driver of the national economy. As a mature industry, the rapid growth of the last four decades is not likely to persist. However, continued evolution and growth can be expected as the economy as a whole changes. . . . With meeting industry trends pointing to demand growth and a slower than normal supply increases, Cedar Rapids should act quickly to reenter the market and regain its position in the industry that it has lost over the last decade.[63]

HVS offered no indication of an "oversupply of convention center space." There was no discussion of a significant drop in both the number of events and the expected exhibit space use reported in the annual *Data Book* for 2010—the last figures in the chart of supply and demand for exhibition space in the HVS report were for 2009. This was despite the fact that the 2010 edition, with its publication date of October 2009, would have been available to the HVS consultants for over a year before the completion of their report for Cedar Rapids. Instead, there was the promise of more growth: "Event planners are reporting a more optimistic outlook in coming years as the U.S. economy continues to recover."[64]

It is impossible to read the CSL work for Boston, Los Angeles, and Lexington or the HVS 2011 report for Cedar Rapids and conclude that either firm was offering a reasonable, complete, or balanced market assessment to their clients. For Boston, CSL offered anecdotes about some individual cities rather than substantive data, pressed "Recent Indications of a Recovery," and concluded that more nearby hotel rooms and more center space would boost the center's occupancy and attendance. For Los Angeles, despite "limited growth," there was the promise of a significant increase in convention business and economic impact. Cedar Rapids, too, was poised to reap the economic rewards of a sizable increase in its convention business with a new center and a city-owned hotel next door. Indeed, HVS argued, "With an increased number of destination choices, it is imperative that the proposed Cedar Rapids Convention Center Complex be a state-of-the-art facility with high quality features in both amenity and operation."[65]

There appeared to be good news for Boston and Los Angeles, Lexington and Cedar Rapids. The promise of success for these cities, of course, followed on the promises of success for cities from Albany to Washington from these same consultants. And those promises and forecasts were much the same as these consultants and their counterparts had offered cities, large and small, since the mid-1980s.

Yet every substantive index of convention center demand and performance indicated that centers had not, by 2007 or 2008, returned to the levels of attendance of a decade earlier. The recession of 2008 brought, by 2009 or 2010, a drop in convention business from Philadelphia and Washington to Chicago and Las Vegas even more striking and dramatic than that after 9-11. This recent performance may herald a new era in convention and tradeshow activity.

It will be some years before it is possible to conclude whether the effects of the 2007–2008 recession are purely short term, or represent a longer-term change in travel spending and behavior. The National Restaurant Association's annual tradeshow at McCormick Place, for example, saw total attendance (including professional attendees and exhibitor personnel) at a peak of 103,946 in 1997. Attendance fell to a low point of 70,287 in 2003, came to a post-2000 high of 73,664 in 2007, and dropped again in 2009 to just 53,319. The "rebound" in 2010 saw attendance at 57,892, followed by 57,782 in 2011. And even in the health-care sector, often cited as a meetings industry success story, the long-term pattern of attendance does not indicate a bright future of growth. RSNA, the Radiological Society of North America, has long met at McCormick Place in Chicago. The 1996 event drew 62,160 attendees, a total not reached again until 2005, when attendance hit 62,251. With the impact of the recession, attendance fell to 56,824 in 2009, before recovering to 59,097 in 2011 and dropping again, to 52,980 in 2012. At best, over this entire span, the attendance might best be described as flat.

These individual events do not reflect the entire convention and tradeshow industry. But they do suggest that a growing U.S. economy in the years ahead will not necessarily lead to parallel levels of growth in convention and tradeshow demand. Private firms and nonprofit and public organizations, having cut back on travel and convention attendance during the recession (much as employment was reduced), may well be slow to return to previous levels of spending and activity, if indeed they ever do.

The larger problem, the oversupply of convention center space that created a "buyer's market" even before 2008, is not going to change in the near future. Cities rarely conclude that they should abandon the quest for convention business. Centers are thus almost never closed, except in those cases like New Orleans and Washington, where an older, smaller center is replaced by a newer venue.

The consultant studies of the late 1990s and 2000s—most particularly those after local CVB directors and center managers recognized the buyer's market in 2006 and 2007—manifestly did not convey the realities of convention and tradeshow demand, and the competition for business. The divergence between the reality of an enormously competitive convention market and the consultants' optimistic assertions about event and attendance growth, and their reassuring conclusions about market feasibility for more space, suggests that the actual purpose of those "expert" analyses was less to assess market potential and guide investment choice than to sell the case for more convention center space to the media and the public.

Chapter 4

They Will Come . . . and Spend

"Economic impact" has long been the central justification for local public investment in new and expanded convention centers; it is the substance of endless consultant studies, mayoral and gubernatorial press conferences, and banner headlines in the local press. Build it, and more convention and tradeshow attendees will come to a city by the tens or hundreds of thousands. Those attendees will stay in local hotels for multiple nights, as well as spending their dollars for meals, entertainment, and retail purchases. The promise of that additional visitor spending is typically measured in the hundreds of millions of dollars. The 2003 forecast for an expansion of Philadelphia's convention center amounted to $133 million more each and every year, from 519,000 additional nonlocal attendees. Those new dollars, in turn, will be respent by local hotel employees, restaurant workers, and cab drivers. That spending, directly by convention attendees and indirectly by those benefited by convention spending, will in turn yield thousands of new jobs, and new development as well. The new-job creation for the Philadelphia center's expansion was put at 2,320. And every new visitor dollar would also generate new revenue for Philadelphia and the state government, primarily in terms of increased hotel taxes, sales taxes, and employee wage taxes.[1]

The argument for convention center "economic impact" has been stated over and over by center consultants and public officials. Take the case of Washington's new convention center. Testifying before the U.S. House of Representatives District Subcommittee in July 1998, Chair Linda Cropp of the District of Columbia City Council proclaimed that the direct spending generated by an expanded Washington Convention Center would amount to $618 million in the center's first year, growing to $776 million by its fifth year. She went on to say, "This is business the city desperately needs to increase local revenues that will help fund the Council's twin priorities of improved service delivery and tax cuts for both our residents and our businesses." Cropp also argued that a far larger new convention center would ultimately generate nearly 10,000 new jobs for District residents.[2]

Five years later, on the eve of the opening of the grand new Washington Convention Center, the consulting firm Conventions, Sports and Leisure International produced a new analysis of the center's finances and economic impact. The January 2003 estimate of annual direct spending came to $328,359,000—about half the figure cited by Cropp. The CSL analysis concluded that at full operation the Washington center would generate 1.14 million annual convention "delegate days" and 654,632 attendee hotel room nights for 2006, and then a stable annual room night total of 729,448 by 2010.[3]

Consultant estimates of convention delegate direct spending and economic impact are usually stated quite precisely, in hundreds of millions of dollars each year. But, as the case of the new Washington Convention Center suggests, those estimates are just that—guesses, often highly variable and uncertain, based on assumptions that may or may not have any real validity. The CSL analysis, however, should have been far more accurate, as it was completed just a few months before the center opened, with full information about its future calendar and the aftermath of 9-11.

The January 2003 CSL study for Washington included estimated attendance figures for individual events, based on pre-opening bookings. For the annual FOSE (Federal Office Systems Expo) show, the center's single largest attendance event, CSL showed consistent annual attendance of 60,000 into the future. But for 2006, the FOSE event attracted just 20,951 attendees. By 2010, FOSE's attendance was down to 13,398. The 2011 edition attracted a mere 8,160. CSL's spending analysis also assumed that each and every convention attendee stayed in the Washington metro area more than three days, with three nights spending on hotel rooms—a total of more than $1,000 in spending for each attendee. But the Washington Convention and Tourism Corporation's data indicate that the 390,000 convention and tradeshow attendees in 2006 used just 455,379 hotel room nights. An average stay of three nights each should have produced more than 1.1 million room nights. For fiscal year 2010, the center housed about 267,000 convention and tradeshow attendees who produced just 274,951 room nights in total, a far cry from an average stay of three or more days. And if the convention center attendees weren't staying overnight in area hotel rooms, they were spending just a fraction of what CSL had assumed.[4]

As the Washington example illustrates, the forecasts of millions of dollars of "economic impact" are estimates based on a string of assumptions. The plausibility and reliability of each of those assumptions can be examined and compared to empirical evidence. The ultimate validity of each consultant forecast is only as good as each of those assumptions.

A Times B Times C . . .

A focus on economic impact and the new dollars ostensibly brought to a community by convention and tradeshow attendees has long been a centerpiece of the public argument for center development. When Cleveland's convention bureau and hospitality leaders began their press for a new convention center in 1956, they argued, "Conventions mean big business to the country," and "Trade show visitors on big expense accounts spend heavily in a town. . . . To get more of this cash other cities are expanding their convention facilities." And the *Cleveland Plain Dealer* would offer the editorial opinion, "If Cleveland wants to go on enjoying this convention pot o' gold, it must act quickly. . . . No one can sneeze lightly at the $22.54 each convention visitor spends here on an average day."[5]

The argument was much the same on the verge of the grand opening of the nation's newest and largest convention center, Chicago's McCormick Place, in November 1960. Harry Kipke, president of the Chicago Convention Bureau and chairman of Coca-Cola Bottling of Chicago told the *Chicago Tribune*, "McCormick Place, with its magnificent trade show facilities, will attract an estimated 32 million dollars in business from out of town visitors." More than 30 years later, as the Illinois state legislature was debating yet another expansion of McCormick Place, the view from the *Tribune* was much the same, with much the same rhetoric: "One can view it as a tremendous economic boost for Chicago and Illinois that would bolster the region's trade industry and provide 11,000 jobs and $80 million a year in tax revenue." The conclusion of the editorial writers: "the expansion would be a boon for Illinois without costing the state. It's time to get this project moving."[6]

The argument that more center space will yield substantial local economic return from visitor spending has been defined by the estimates and forecasts of a small group of consultants. It has been supported by a series of surveys of convention and tradeshow attendee spending conducted by the International Association of Convention and Visitor Bureaus, the professional organization of local convention sales organizations. These surveys, first begun in 1948 but only undertaken systematically since the mid-1980s, provide the basis for translating forecasts about new convention activity into the dollar values of “economic impact.”[7]

In the simplest terms, the consultant who estimates economic impact takes a series of assumptions or estimates, and multiplies one by another. The typical formula is

> Number of convention and tradeshow events X average attendance X average stay (in days) X average daily spending = total direct spending.[8]

By breaking down the estimation process into a series of components, a consultant can create a plausible-sounding result out of a diverse set of individual estimates. The final, multimillion-dollar “impact” derives its apparent legitimacy and reasonableness from the seeming plausibility of the components. But in none of the more than one hundred economic impact analyses and forecasts I have reviewed has there been any evidence of a more sophisticated mathematical or dynamic statistical model. No evidence of how changing levels of competition might affect future center performance or impact. No evidence of how national (or regional or local) economic change—from a national recession to downtown decline and the shuttering of restaurants, entertainment, and retail stores—might affect the attractiveness of a center, its attendance, or attendee spending patterns. Indeed, the estimates of economic impact and attendee spending are almost never stated as variable or uncertain. New or expanded centers are expected to “ramp up” to a full level of performance over three to five years, and then continue at a stable, consistent attendance and spending level for the indefinite future.[9]

But if future economic impact appears fixed and readily predictable, the spending predictions themselves appear malleable and subject to change. Just as in the Washington case, direct spending numbers are subject to change, usually upward.

When PriceWaterhouse analyzed the impact of a 500,000 square foot expansion of Atlanta’s Georgia World Congress Center in January 1993, the firm calculated the direct spending impact from the proposed larger center at $811.5 million, an increase of $174.6 million. Three years later, a subsequent PriceWaterhouse assessment put the total direct spending impact of a similarly expanded center at $1.229 billion, an “incremental” $295 million. The economic gain from an expansion had thus grown by over $100 million, more than 60 percent.

PriceWaterhouse also managed to evolve its economic impact estimate for the expansion of the Jacob Javits Center in New York. In its March 2000, the firm calculated the direct spending from an expansion at $942 million. When it analyzed the prospects of an enlarged Javits again in January 2004, it calculated the direct spending impact of the bigger center at $1,108,650,000.

The ease with which these direct spending numbers can "grow" over successive studies suggests that they represent at best guesses, readily subject to change in the component assumptions. Seemingly modest changes are made in one or two dimensions of the underlying assumptions, and hundreds of millions can be added to the direct spending total.

Beginning With A: The Event Count

The starting point for many, but not all, consultant estimates of economic impact is the count of annual conventions and tradeshows at an existing center. For Washington, D.C.'s new convention center, the first study by Deloitte & Touche in April 1993 began with a description of the performance of the existing center, presumably as a baseline for forecasting the events at a far larger venue. The Deloitte report noted that the existing Washington Convention Center had averaged 31 conventions and tradeshows for fiscal years 1989 through 1992. It forecast that the far larger new center would ultimately (about five years after opening) host 48 annual convention/tradeshow events—a total that would presumably be realized indefinitely.[10]

Some four years later, the prospects of a new center for Washington were assessed anew by Coopers & Lybrand. The December 1997 Coopers report showed the existing center hosting 38 conventions and tradeshows annually during the mid-1990s. Coopers forecast that the planned new center would accommodate 48 conventions and tradeshows by its third year of operation. Deloitte and Coopers, despite differences in method, seemed to be in full agreement that a far bigger new convention center would yield the District a host of new conventions.[11]

By the time the former principals of Coopers & Lybrand revisited the estimated convention and tradeshow count in the January 2003 Convention, Sports and Leisure study, the forecast was rather more modest. CSL projected that the new center would house 39 conventions and tradeshows annually—almost exactly what the older center had done. What had begun as bounteous forecasts of new conventions had dwindled to an estimate of effectively no change whatsoever, based on real information about bookings.

The Washington case illustrates the typical pattern of consultant event forecasts. Recent history (often a single year or the last three years) provides a baseline of convention and tradeshow activity. The consultant concludes that more center exhibit and meeting space will result in more events. For PriceWaterhouseCoopers in its 1999 analysis of Cincinnati's convention center, "Based on an analysis of the Center's history event calendar, the annual number of professional association events has ranged from 10 to 14. Average attendance ranged from 1,800 to 2,900. It is estimated that with an expanded facility the Center could host 20 professional association events with an average attendance of 3,500."[12] The event forecast was simply stated, with no logical connection to an assessment of competition, community desirability, or uncertainty. As in the Washington studies, a bigger center would inevitably yield more convention events.

In cities where there is no existing convention center, or the extant center is not competitive, the forecast of future events is based entirely on the consultant's own guesswork, albeit presumably with some sense of the relationship between overall market demand and the proposed center.

For Baltimore's first foray into pure convention center development, in the mid-1970s, it relied on the work of the Stanford Research Institute. SRI's market analysis did not rely on any independent data on the size or growth of the convention and tradeshow market. Such data, largely from Tradeshow Week, would not be available until the late 1980s. Instead, SRI employed a survey of 105 associations to determine their interest in Baltimore. Based on those results "and the known experiences of other major convention centers," "it is estimated that the new Baltimore Convention Center will host 20 major exhibit-oriented conventions and trade shows in the first normal year of its operation."[13]

By the early 1990s, consultants could seek to tie their predictions of future events at new centers to overall market demand, referencing the numbers and growth of events from Tradeshow Week. Thus David Petersen and his colleagues at PriceWaterhouse could offer the Massachusetts Convention Center Authority in 1993 the assessment that "573 new shows are expected to be launched over the next decade, according to *Tradeshow Week*. It is estimated that these new shows will require 60 million net square feet of exhibition space, draw 185,900 exhibiting companies and attract 6.8 million attendees annually by 2001."[14]

The growth argument, and the Tradeshow Week data, were employed by most consultants during the 1990s and 2000s to make the case that new centers could count on gaining events. Thus KPMG consultants Ronald D. Barton and Susan Sieger could report to officials with Hartford's Capital City Economic Development Authority in January 2000, "Because buyers and sellers find tradeshows to be an efficient marketplace, positive growth in the tradeshow industry has occurred over the last two decades." Their report went on to note, "*Tradeshow Week* predicts demand for exhibit space, the number of exhibiting companies and attendance at tradeshows will average a 4% growth rate annually through 2000."[15]

The KPMG consultants' use of Tradeshow Week's data and predictions is not surprising. KPMG's convention practice director, Ronald D. Barton, had been hired by David C. Petersen of Laventhol & Horwath as a convention center consultant in the late 1980s.

KPMG thus estimated that a new 150,000 square foot facility in Hartford would gradually "ramp up" to a stable level of 36 annual conventions and tradeshows, with additional consumer events, banquets, and meetings. While KPMG did not provide a specific justification for the 36-event forecast, the preceding paragraph did note, "The fact that the proposed center will be built in an MSA [metropolitan statistical area] without an existing and established convention center will positively impact its ability to attract conventions/tradeshows as well as consumer shows and other local events."[16]

For a proposed new 160,000 square foot center in Omaha, Nebraska, another KPMG study in January 2000 projected a stabilized total of 35 conventions and tradeshows. Again, there was no direct connection to any measure of Omaha's competitiveness or market position, although the preceding paragraph did note, "The fact that the proposed center will be built in a market without an existing and established convention center will positively impact its ability to attract conventions/tradeshows as well as consumer shows and other local events." Omaha and Hartford were thus forecast to deliver essentially the same level of convention business, despite a host of differences in such things as air service volume, area hotel supply, and regional convention center competition.

Times B: Average Convention/Tradeshow Attendance

Local convention centers and convention and visitor bureaus market and promote themselves to individual event organizers and meeting planners. But securing an event is only the first part of the "economic impact" equation. Impact is driven by attendees and their spending, so the type of convention or tradeshow, and its usual attendance, are critical in yielding visitor spending and "impact."

Some consultant studies appear to skip any analysis or forecast of future attendance. The studies for the new Washington Convention Center by Deloitte & Touche in April 1993 and Coopers & Lybrand in 1997 provided no information on average attendance or forecast total attendance. They both presented estimates of future direct attendee spending, with no logical link to anticipated attendance. Without such data, it is clearly impossible to tie visitor dollars to likely attendance, and thus justify the projected economic impact of the new center.

PriceWaterhouse's 1995 study for an expanded facility in Cincinnati did provide full details on events, average attendance, and estimated total attendance, broken down by event type. Professional associations, for example, were forecast to average 3,500 attendees, and average trade association events 6,000. These averages represented significant increases over the center's previous performance, and thus yielded a substantial increase in projected total attendance levels.[17]

PriceWaterhouseCoopers used much the same approach in a second study of an expanded convention center in Cincinnati in 1999. PWC argued that the Cincinnati center should be expanded from 162,000 square feet of exhibit space to 400,000—more than doubling the center's size. That expansion was forecast to double the numbers in some categories of events, notably trade association conventions and wholesale shows. At the same time, average attendance at professional association conventions would grow from 2,500 to 3,500, and for trade association events from 3,500 to 6,000. The *product* of the combined growth in number of events and average attendance would increase Cincinnati's convention and tradeshow attendance from 141,000 to 302,500—more than doubling attendance.[18]

For the entirely new Connecticut Convention Center in Hartford, the 2000 KPMG market analysis employed the standard "a times b" logic. The firm argued that just as the number of annual conventions and tradeshows would grow from 32 in the opening year of 2004 to 36 by 2008, average attendance would grow as well. KPMG put average convention and tradeshow attendance at 1,800 in 2004, reaching 2,200 by 2008. The product of more events and increasing average size would be a total of 79,200 attendees for Hartford in 2008.[19]

In its December 1990 feasibility study (subsequently updated in January 1993) for Baltimore and the Maryland Stadium Authority, Economics Research Associates (ERA), argued, "An expanded Baltimore Convention Center will draw significantly more visitors to the City and the State, increasing demand for hotel facilities, and bring more business to retail, restaurant, entertainment and cultural activities in the area." The ERA analysis put "net new visitor expenditures" at "nearly $175 million annually," with the single largest portion for overnight lodging. In justifying an expansion that would double the center's exhibit space, ERA forecast that the number of conventions and tradeshows would increase from 41 without expansion to 70. Average attendance would grow from 3,939 to 4,714, primarily by almost doubling average tradeshow attendance. The product of more events and larger average size would be an increase in convention and tradeshow attendance from 161,501 to 330,000.[20]

ERA's attendance forecast was apparently too "conservative" for the Stadium Authority's predecessor organization, the Baltimore Convention Center Authority. Facing a questioning state legislature in the summer of 1991, the authority updated ERA's baseline data with more recent figures, boosting the average convention count from 48 to 56 and average convention attendance from 180,000 to 207,000. The authority then went on to argue, "In the real world, even though ERA has utilized an after expansion of 183% [percent increase], it is likely that actual post expansion delegate convention and tradeshow attendance may be 200%, 225% or even 250% of the base year attendance." With that sleight of hand, the ERA forecast of 330,000 annual attendees became 452,000, 508,500, or even 565,000.[21]

The PriceWaterhouse October 1996 assessment of a potential expansion of Atlanta's Georgia World Congress Center also concluded that an expanded center would see increased convention and tradeshow attendance, and hence greater economic impact. But while the PriceWaterhouse consultants, led by David Petersen, set out forecast attendance and impact, they did not individually specify or differentiate the number of events or the average attendance. As with the ERA study of Baltimore, they set out the logic of multiple simultaneous events at a larger center, noting, "Thus, it is the desire of Center management to accommodate 2 to 3 shows simultaneously." Toward that end, the expanded center could "Host more mid-size events which generate proportionately more room nights per occupied square foot day (OSFD) than the larger events."[22]

The really big shows in Atlanta, such as the Bobbin Show for the textile industry or the International Poultry Exhibition, took a number of days to set up and take down. Those "move in/move out" days "occupied" the center, but there were no attendees to fill downtown Atlanta hotel rooms. Focusing on "mid-size" events would yield a more steady and predictable stream of out-of-town attendees.

The logic of going after multiple small and medium-size events was not limited to ERA and PriceWaterhouse, Baltimore and Atlanta. Consultant C. H. Johnson had set out a similar logic and forecast in his January 1990 marketing study for Chicago's McCormick Place. Johnson argued, "the key area where Chicago is not penetrating demand is medium and large conventions, an area where, perhaps 15 years ago, the City was very successful." The KPMG report then set out a goal for McCormick Place to "Become dominant in the large and medium sized convention and convention with exhibit market." The analysis concluded that an expanded McCormick could attract 13 new conventions each year, averaging 15,000 attendees each, "Capturing events from Midwest regional and national competition."[23]

McCormick Place officials reiterated the KPMG strategy in the 1992 bond issue statement that provided the financing for the expansion project: "Additionally, the Authority has proposed to provide additional meeting facilities in response to the changing requirements of the trade show segment and to attract a larger share of the medium and large convention segment of the meetings market." McCormick Place increased its investment in the "mid size" convention strategy with bond financing for a new 800-room hotel, bearing the Hyatt brand, as part of the complex. The central argument for a new "headquarters hotel," set out by consultant Coopers & Lybrand, was that "The Hotel will be especially important in attracting the mid-market shows that the MPEA has targeted as an important sector for potential growth in MPCC [McCormick Place Convention Center] demand." The analysis forecast that the addition of the hotel would increase the number of large "200" events, which produced an average of over 25,000 hotel room nights each, by three. The number of mid-sized conventions, averaging about 8,200 room nights, would grow 50 percent—from 18 to 27.[24]

With the completion of the expansion funded by the 1992 bonds as well as the new Hyatt hotel, McCormick Place and Chicago tourism officials did not alter their efforts to attract mid-sized events. Seeking state financing for yet another expansion in 2000, the Chicago Convention and Tourism Board argued that more space meant that "Our largest events would have more flexibility to expand beyond the current 2.2 million square feet. . . . More mid-sized trade shows and meetings could be hosted simultaneously."[25]

The nation's largest center, McCormick Place, a mid-sized center in Baltimore (post-expansion circa 1997 it ranked 41st), and Atlanta's major Georgia World Congress Center were all thus pursuing essentially the same strategy of expanding to attract multiple simultaneous mid-sized events. There was a certain logic to that. The universe of U.S. conventions and tradeshows has been essentially shaped like a pyramid, with a very small number of large events in terms of exhibit space use at the top, and a far larger array of small and medium-sized shows at the middle and bottom. Convention centers like Chicago's McCormick Place and the Georgia World Congress Center might be able to accommodate the very largest events. But there were only a few of those to compete for. The "multiple events" strategy focused on where the majority of conventions and tradeshows actually were. Still, in competing "down market" for the middle of the universe, these big centers and their communities were necessarily competing against cities with mid-sized centers for the same business. And there was no real limit to the big centers that too envisioned competing for mid-sized events.[26]

Conventions, Sports and Leisure International completed a market analysis for a potential expansion of New Orleans's Morial Convention Center in June 2000. The Morial's last expansion had opened just over a year earlier, at the beginning of 1999. Yet CSL felt confident in predicting that more space would yield substantial new attendance and economic impact, putting annual "incremental direct spending" at $355,545,000. The consultants described "increasing market demand . . . and continued development within competitive cities, particularly Orlando, Atlanta and Las Vegas." But the focus of a Morial expansion would not be large events. "We do not envision single events requiring space in excess of the 1.1 million square feet currently offered at the Morial Center. Rather the 500,000 to 600,000 square foot addition to the New Orleans convention center inventory will target added multiple events in the 200,000 to 600,000 gross square foot range."[27]

In its January 2003 feasibility study for an expansion of Philadelphia's Pennsylvania Convention Center, CSL also stressed the potential for accommodating multiple simultaneous events. The firm's report noted that a larger ballroom at the center would "allow for concurrent event usage of such space."

And the CSL's focus on multiple events was regularly repeated in the Philadelphia media. With the funding for the expansion seemingly assured in mid-2004, the *Philadelphia Inquirer* reported, "The larger center will be able to attract bigger groups or hold multiple events, such as a trade show and annual flower show." And with the center "Halfway to its Big Rebirth" in November 2009, the *Inquirer* quoted Ahmeenah Young, CEO of the Pennsylvania Convention Center Authority, as saying the expansion "means attracting larger national conventions, especially health and medical groups, and accommodating multiple conventions at the same time."[28]

The consultant argument that a bigger center could succeed by attracting a larger number of small or mid-sized groups became quite common during the latter part of the 1990s and through the 2000s, seemingly applicable to a wide variety of cities and convention centers of dramatically different sizes. Even where a consulting firm had applied it—without success—to one study for one community, it could easily be contended again, somewhere else.

PriceWaterhouse had argued in 1996 that an expansion of the Georgia World Congress Center could accommodate simultaneous multiple events. And PriceWaterhouseCoopers argued in 2008 that an expansion of the San Diego Convention Center would bring 35 new convention and tradeshow events. "It is estimated that many of these events will be held concurrently at the facility (an active event, an event moving in/out, etc.), *and some conventions and trade shows will be smaller in terms of attendance than the average size event held at the facility historically*" (italics mine). Thus the PWC study showed the average attendance of national/state conventions and tradeshows at the San Diego center in fiscal year 2007 at 9,209. But with the major expansion, the average size would fall to 8,260.[29]

Repeated by "expert" consultants in city after city, the concurrent or simultaneous event argument had a seeming plausibility. Yet it depended upon the assumption that the *number of conventions and tradeshows* in the U.S. would be consistently growing. Otherwise, Baltimore and Atlanta and New Orleans and Philadelphia and San Diego would be competing against one another for a larger slice of a fixed pie. That would pit Baltimore's Inner Harbor against Atlanta's Georgia Aquarium and abundant hotels, New Orleans's visitor attractions, entertainment, and food against Philadelphia's history, and all against San Diego's weather, bayfront, and "Gaslamp Quarter." They would in turn also compete with Washington, Orlando, Anaheim, San Francisco, and Chicago. That was a battle not everyone likely would win.

Times C: Average Attendee Spending

With a forecast of future convention and tradeshow attendance, the final piece of the calculation of direct spending "economic impact" is an assumption about the average or typical spending of those attendees. All other economic impact figures, from "multiplied" local spending (both direct and induced) to job creation and new tax revenues, are effectively a product of that direct spending.

For decades, center consultants relied upon estimates of per-delegate spending produced by the International Association of Convention and Visitors Bureaus (IACVB), now the Destination Marketing Association International (DMAI). The IACVB Convention Income Survey, updated every few years, would in turn base its estimates on national surveys it sponsored of convention and tradeshow attendees. In its 1988 economic impact analysis for the proposed Pennsylvania Convention Center, PKF used data from the IACVB 1986 "Convention Income Survey" that indicated, "convention delegates spend approximately $477.49 in total, or $125.66 per day, while attending a convention." The biggest single part of that spending, 51 percent, would be for a hotel room over the three-plus day stay.[30]

Economics Research Associates also employed the IACVB spending estimates (for 1988) in its 1993 study of an expansion of the Baltimore Convention Center. ERA put total per-delegate spending at $522.89, including $267.91 for lodging. KPMG's Susan Sieger (now with Crossroads Consulting) employed the IACVB Convention Income Survey (from 1998) to estimate economic impact from a new convention center in Hartford. Convention delegate daily spending was estimated at $237.93, with additional spending (per delegate) from associations (presumably sponsoring the event) of $18.54 and exhibitors ($85.49 per delegate). The KPMG analysis assumed each delegate spent just about three days in Hartford. And when CSL conducted the market demand analysis for an enhanced Morial Center in New Orleans, it too employed IACVB data, from the 2004 ExPact Convention Expenditure and Impact Study. That gave, "adjusted to 2009 dollars and for cost levels in the New Orleans area," a daily spending figure of $335.00 for association and corporate events. The New Orleans study did not indicate the average length of stay for association convention attendees. But IACVB/DMAI had put the figure at 3.56 nights.[31]

The CSL firm used the ExPact spending numbers from 2004, "adjusted to 2008 dollars and for cost levels in the San Antonio area," in its July 2008 analysis of an expanded Henry B. Gonzalez Convention Center. The firm also relied on the 2004 ExPact spending estimates in its March 2010 study of an expanded convention center in Boise, Idaho, noting that the figures were "adjusted to 2010 dollars and for cost levels in the Boise area" and "vary by event type and range from approximately $150 to $260 per person, per day."[32]

The IACVB/DMAI survey results, updated every few years and sometimes adjusted for local hotel rates or inflation, have been a constant, central part of the economic impact calculation. They neatly provide "average" figures for convention attendee spending and length of stay that seemingly represent a reasonable benchmark for all sorts of conventions and tradeshows across a broad array of cities. They have become the norm for consultant after consultant in study after study. Yet occasionally a consultant study adds its own additional, perhaps complicating, information about attendees.

In its January 1993 economic impact analysis for an expansion of Atlanta's Georgia World Congress Center, PriceWaterhouse described two very different types of convention and tradeshow attendees: overnight attendees and "day-trippers." Overnight attendees represent the typically assumed convention visitors from out of town who stay at an event for multiple days. PriceWaterhouse reported that the "Average length of convention/trade show delegate stay for overnight visitors is assumed to be 4.25 days," and that "Overnight attendees are assumed to comprise approximately 45 percent of total convention/trade show attendance (based on historic percentages)." And what of the other half of convention attendees?[33]

PriceWaterhouse reported, "The 55 percent of delegates which are day trippers are assumed to spend an average of one day at GWCC." The day trippers represented attendees who drove or flew into downtown Atlanta for just the day or days of the event. The overnighters and day trippers thus had radically different spending patterns. Overnight visitors were estimated to spend a total of $710.59 during their visit—comparable to the figures used by ERA in its Baltimore study and KPMG in its Connecticut Convention Center analysis. Day tripper spending, which did not involve a hotel stay, was estimated at just $55.22. Day trippers were effectively just spending for parking, a meal, and incidentals. The consultants added in spending by exhibitors, associations, and contractors (about $474 per delegate) to get a "weighted average" per delegate of $821.81. Armed with the estimate that convention and tradeshow attendees in Atlanta were about equally divided between overnighters and day trippers, PriceWaterhouse estimated that an expansion would yield 212,000 new annual attendees with an added $174.6 million in direct spending.

PriceWaterhouse revisited its assessment of the potential economic impact of an expanded Georgia World Congress Center in October 1996. This second time, for about the same sized expansion, the consultants pegged the number of added convention and tradeshow attendees at 350,000, with 296,100 "New to State." But where they had previously described a 45–55 percent breakdown of overnight stayers versus day trippers, that fraction appeared sharply (perhaps magically) changed: "Based on IACVB survey results, other spending survey results, [Atlanta Convention and Visitors Bureau] room night information and GWCC event data, it is estimated that approximately 95 percent of incremental professional association, 85 percent of trade association and 90 percent of SMERF [Social, Military, Educational, Religious, and Fraternal organizations] delegates are overnighters while the remainder are day-trippers."[34]

At the same time as the passage of three years had sharply boosted the apparent attendance of overnighters, the PriceWaterhouse spending estimates also increased. Overnight delegates were now assumed to spend $893.42 each (exclusive of association or exhibitor spending), and day trippers' $166.13. Combined with the modest increase in estimated post-expansion attendance, the new forecast of added direct spending came to $295,000,000—almost twice the $174.6 million of the previous report.

The two successive PriceWaterhouse reports for the World Congress Center put in high relief the ease with which estimates of attendee spending and economic impact—and the assumptions on which those estimates were built—can be manipulated at the discretion of the consultant, or perhaps the preference of a client. It appears unlikely that the business of the Georgia World Congress Center had shifted so dramatically from 1993 to 1996 as to all but eliminate attendance by day trippers. But that shift, and the change in assumed spending, could produce a far more impressive "impact" result.

The Atlanta reports also introduced a factor that has largely been ignored, before and since, in estimating economic impact. Some not insignificant fraction of event attendees are likely to live in the metropolitan area or region of the convention center. They may well choose to drive to the event, paying for parking even for multiple days, rather than for an expensive hotel room. Indeed, events like Boston's Yankee Dental Congress, put on at the Boston Convention and Exhibition Center by the Massachusetts Dental Society, or the annual BookExpo (often held in New York City) put on by Reed Exhibitions for the publishing industry, are likely to draw many, if not most, of their attendees from the immediate environs—dentists, dental assistants, and dental students from the Boston area; publishing personnel, literary agents, librarians, and booksellers from greater New York and nearby cities. For the 2011 edition of BookExpo at New York's Javits Center, fully 50.2 percent of attendees came from New York, New Jersey, or Pennsylvania. The 2010 Yankee Dental Congress, with attendance of some 28,000, was pegged at generating just 13,500 hotel room nights—far less than an assumed "average stay" of three nights for each attendee.[35]

Even for professional association conventions that regularly rotate from city to city, much of the attendance will be drawn from the immediate region. Consider the annual convention of the American Institute of Architects (AIA). The 2006 AIA meeting took place in Los Angeles, and drew 46 percent of its attendees from California. The 2007 convention in San Antonio gained 32 percent of its attendees from Texas, and just 9.8 percent from California. And when the AIA met in Boston in 2008, 25 percent of attendees came from Massachusetts, with just 8.6 percent from California.[36]

With rare exceptions, such as the 1993 PriceWaterhouse analysis of the Georgia World Congress Center, consultants simply assume that each and every convention and tradeshow attendee will manage the "average" length of stay on the order of 3.5 days at a convention destination, seemingly ignoring the reality that even for national association events, some portion of the attendees will be "locals" who simply drive to the event for a day or two.

Multiplying A Times B Times C—Or Not

The consultant calculation of aggregate or incremental direct spending, the central element of "economic impact," is thus a remarkably simple product of a forecast and a forecast and an assumption. The two forecasts, for future events and future average attendance, each have a certain surface plausibility. It seems reasonable that a bigger convention center could accommodate more groups, even by hosting simultaneous small or mid-sized events. And it appears equally reasonable that a larger exhibit space could also house larger groups and events with greater attendance than previously would have fit in the space of a convention facility.

The consultant forecasts of both future events and attendance are still just guesses. Consultant studies, and responses to government requests for proposals to do studies, often list previous clients and studies. But they effectively never provide evidence of a firm's track record or accuracy in forecasting, or an explicit model by which the forecasts are derived. With rare exceptions, the study forecasts for number of events and attendance are also stated, seemingly precisely, as single numbers. There are no ranges, no "best" or "worst" case results, no apparent uncertainty depending on outside factors such as the national economy or competition from other cities. Despite that seeming certainty, sometimes the guesses don't work out.

When Jeff Sachs of Ernst & Young completed the firm's "Long-Range Strategic Plan" for Orlando's Orange County Convention Center in mid-1998, the OCCC was hosting 115 convention and tradeshow events that year. Sachs and his colleagues were not explicit about the forecast count of added events with a major expansion, but they promised that a 62 percent increase in space would yield about a 61 percent increase in attendee direct spending. The far grander expansion completed in 2003 doubled the center's space. Yet even in a year when the national economy was strong, 2007, the event count was just 107. It had hit 111 in 2006. In the wake of recession, it managed just 95 in 2010 and then 89 in 2012. For one of the nation's largest and historically most successful centers, more space did not translate into more events. And without more conventions and tradeshows, the Orange County center would need to have seen a massive increase in average attendance to reach the 100, 60, or even 50 percent increase in attendance forecast by Ernst & Young.

The "A times B times C" string of multiplications that estimated direct spending "impact" depends on would appear to yield a substantial product when number of events and average attendance both grow. Yet, as the Orlando example indicates, a modest difference in any one of the elements can yield sharply different results. Take the theoretical case of a large center with 100 annual conventions, each averaging 10,000 attendees. A 20 percent increase in event count would generate 120 conventions, while a 20 percent increase in average attendance would bring that figure to 12,000. Multiplied, they would yield total attendance of 1.44 million. But if, as in the Orlando case, there is no growth in total conventions and tradeshows, the larger average attendance produces just 1.2 million attendees.

Just as slight changes in number of events or average convention and tradeshow attendance substantially reduce the actual spending impact, modest changes in the "C" component—average attendee spending—will yield significant differences in the "economic impact" centers produce and cities actually see. And it is important to understand that these amounts are simply *assumptions*—based most commonly on national average spending figures derived from regular surveys conducted for the Destination Marketing

Association International (DMAI, the former International Association of Convention and Visitors Bureaus).

The DMAI spending estimates in turn assume that the average convention and tradeshow attendee stays in excess of three days. That "average" must necessarily include some fraction of attendees who are day trippers, as Price-Waterhouse found for Atlanta. Those attendees would average under a one day stay, as they are not staying overnight and spending for a hotel room. When, as PriceWaterhouse found, the proportion of attendees who attend for the day amounts to half total annual center attendance, the overall spending will be a fraction of that produced by the assumed three and half day average stay.[37]

Specific analysis of spending by day trippers versus overnighters was a part of some PriceWaterhouse studies in the mid- and late 1990s. But it has not been a part of all the firm's studies in the years since, nor does it appear in the work of other firms. PWC did differentiate between day trippers and overnighters in its March 2000 assessment of an expansion of New York's Javits Convention Center, noting:

> Overnight convention and trade show attendees (or those requiring hotel rooms) generate the highest level of impact. Day-trippers, or attendees who drive or fly to New York City to attend an event for the day and do not require hotel rooms, also generate economic impact, albeit to a lesser degree. Many of these day-trippers are likely to be from neighboring states (e.g., New Jersey, Pennsylvania, Connecticut, Massachusetts, etc.) or other parts of the State of New York.[38]

The 2000 study went on to put average daily spending per delegate at $384 for overnighters, compared to $69 for day trippers.

Although PWC did not specify the number or proportion of overnighters to day trippers, the 2000 study did contain a striking and highly relevant figure on the ability of the Javits to produce overnight hotel stays. The consulting firm estimated a "no build" alternative of no expansion, where the Javits would draw 1,114,000 annual convention and tradeshow attendees (not including attendees at local public shows). But for that "no build" scenario, it put the annual number of hotel room nights produced at just 664,000. That implied that on average convention attendees at the Javits were spending *less than one night each in New York City hotels.*

PWC was somewhat more explicit about the split between overnight and day tripper convention and tradeshow attendees in its subsequent Javits study, dated January 2004. Again, the firm found striking differences in daily spending patterns: $362 for overnighters compared to $75 for day trippers. For the "no expansion" scenario of the Javits, it estimated a total of 1,113,000 convention and tradeshow attendees: 445,000 overnighters, 409,000 day trippers, and 259,000 "other local attendance." That would put overnighters as 40 percent of convention and tradeshow attendees. Clearly PWC assessed the majority of Javits convention attendees as not staying overnight and using hotel rooms.[39]

The 2004 report also noted the hotel demand generated by the Javits Center at "668,000 estimated room nights." The Javits had seen about 955,000 convention and tradeshow attendees in 2003, and some 934,000 the previous year. Over 900,000 annual attendees appeared to produce just 668,000 hotel stays—a clear measure of the reality that convention and tradeshow attendees in New York City were simply not staying and spending in accord with the IACVB/DMAI survey numbers. And when PWC reviewed the economic impact of the Javits Center for 2009, it concluded that just 43 percent of convention and tradeshow attendance that year was from overnighters. But was this phenomenon of a substantial share of local or day tripper attendees unique to just New York, or perhaps Atlanta?[40]

The most direct answer is "no." Take the case of Hartford's Connecticut Convention Center. The 2000 feasibility study by KPMG's Susan Sieger estimated that by 2008 the center would accommodate 36 annual conventions and tradeshows with a total attendance of 79,200. The typical convention/tradeshow event would last three days, yielding 216,000 total "delegate-days." Assuming each delegate spent in excess of $200 per day (together with added spending by associations and exhibitors), total "direct spending" in 2008 was put at $67,480,000. Once again, the assumption was that every convention and tradeshow delegate would stay overnight in the Hartford area for a total of three days.[41]

The KPMG assumptions about convention attendance and length of stay would also suggest overnight hotel stays well over 100,000 each year, perhaps as many as 200,000. But the actual number of hotel room nights produced by the Connecticut Convention Center came to just 38,600 in 2008, 21,600 in 2009, and 28,400 in 2010. For 2011, the reported 330,366 total attendees produced 35,108 room nights. The new Hartford center was drawing well over 200,000 total attendees each year, but most of them came for public shows, meetings, and banquets. And the bulk of attendees at the few actual conventions and tradeshows—23 in 2007—largely came from Connecticut or nearby.

It is of course possible that New York's Javits Center, Hartford's Connecticut Convention Center, or the Georgia World Congress Center are somehow unique in drawing a substantial volume of local attendees or day trippers. The Javits, for example, regularly hosts tradeshows like BookExpo and the International Toy Fair that draw from industries and firms largely located in Manhattan. But systematic comparisons of convention and tradeshow attendance and hotel room night generation at other major centers and destination cities suggest that the "three day plus average stay" routinely used in predicting "economic impact" is a fiction.

The 2009 CSL International "Strategic Plan" for the Boston Convention and Exhibition Center contained data on both convention and tradeshow attendance and hotel room night generation. In fiscal year 2007, the BCEC accommodated 253,200 convention and tradeshow attendees. Yet the room night generation only came to 303,998—a ratio of 1.2 room nights per attendee (other events added 47,435 nights). The ratio works out to 1.14 for fiscal 2008, with 295,814 attendees, and 1.05 for fiscal 2009.[42]

The results for Boston's new convention center, showing slightly more than one room night per attendee, are the product of a series of factors common to all centers. As PriceWaterhouse documented, a fraction of convention and tradeshow attendees come from the metropolitan area or region and day trip. Others stay with family or friends. Some portion "double up" on hotel rooms, particularly in expensive destinations. Add all those factors, and the "average" overnight stay becomes far less than three nights, the average spending (particularly on the largest category, lodging) a fraction of the total IACVB/DMAI figure.

The phenomenon of a ratio of convention center room nights to attendees of about one to one can be seen in a number of other cities, and over time. Take the case of a prime visitor destination, the nation's capital. In fiscal year 2008, the Washington Convention Center saw 352,776 convention and tradeshow attendees. According to the authority responsible for the center, it produced 376,296 hotel room nights that year, a ratio of 1.07. Fiscal 2009 saw 331,766 attendees and 280,478 room nights, a ratio of 0.85. Or look at the performance of Charlotte, North Carolina's Charlotte Convention Center. In 2007, the center's 164,435 convention and tradeshow attendees produced a total of 183,715 room nights, a ratio of 1.12. The following year attendance fell to 152,043 and a room night ratio of 1.23. From 2001 to 2010, the annual room night ratio varied from 0.78 to 1.23, and averaged 1.05. These ratios were right in line with those of Washington and Boston, and somewhat higher than New York's. In no case did they approximate the 3.5 night average stay assumed by the DMAI survey.[43]

Where convention centers and local convention bureaus have produced and made available annual data on both convention and tradeshow attendance and room nights, the ratio regularly averages to 1.1 room night per attendee. Some cities and centers, like New York's Javits, which have a large volume of tradeshows with a local audience, see ratios a bit lower. For Chicago's McCormick Place, which routinely tracked actual hotel room use for center convention and tradeshows, the ratio came to 0.63 in 1999 and 0.71 for 2000. And when San Francisco's Moscone Center reported on convention attendance and room nights during the late 1990s, the ratio worked out to 1.21 for fiscal 1999 and 1.31 for 2000. For the San Diego Convention Center in fiscal 2007, 641,000 convention and tradeshow attendees produced 729,300 room nights, a ratio of 1.14. For 2005–2007, the room night ratio averaged 1.24.

Chicago's McCormick Place provides an additional data point for viewing the relationship between event attendance, hotel room night generation, and economic impact. C. H. Johnson Consulting conducted a detailed analysis of the June 2009 International Plastics Expo at McCormick, as part of the state's effort to reform union work rules and keep McCormick Place competitive. The five-day 2009 Plastics Expo drew 43,102 attendees. Under the Expo's room block agreement with the Chicago Convention and Tourism Board, the "Plastics Show occupied 28,322 room nights. . . . However, McCormick Place also stated that many attendees did not go through the room block for their accommodation, and it can reasonably be assumed that approximately 50 percent, or 14,161 additional room nights should be added."[44]

Even with the generous "assumption" that there were 50 percent more hotel room nights used than accounted for by the formal room block, the room night to attendee ratio for the Plastics Show came to 0.99—just under one room night produced per attendee.[45]

The IACVB/DMAI convention spending surveys have long contended each attendee stays and spends in excess of three days. The 2005 "ExPact" expenditure figures assumed an average 3.56 night stay for every convention attendee, with daily spending put at $290, 47 percent of total spending for lodging. Yet where the actual ratio of room night generation to attendance is about one to one, the DMAI figures substantially overstate estimated direct spending impact. Actual hotel use—DMAI's 47 percent of total spending—is thus less than half, more likely a third, of the spending estimates. And with a sharp drop in estimated overnight stays, spending on other items—meals, retail, local transportation—is also going to be sharply less, reflecting a greater proportion of convention attendees who are day trippers or stay overnight with friends or relatives.

The assumed daily or per event spending by convention and tradeshow attendees, regularly repeated by consultants, local convention and visitor bureaus, and convention center proponents, cannot be validated by real world performance of convention centers and individual events. The "C" piece of the direct spending multiplication that produces "economic impact" is most likely far smaller than the assumption built into estimates of impact. But what of the two guesses—the "A" and "B" pieces of the consultant forecasts—that reflect the knowledge and forecasting skill of the consultants and, necessarily, the uncertainties inherent in market competition and the larger national (and global) economy?

"Objective and Accurate Information . . . To Gain Community Support and Interest"

The consultant market and feasibility studies of the 1960s, 1970s, and early 1980s appear to be very much "seat of the pants" efforts, based on relatively limited data and without any consistent base of information on national convention and tradeshow demand or attendee spending. But by the late 1980s consultant studies had gained the appearance of scientific rigor, presenting analyses of national demand trends based on data from Tradeshow Week and an image of predictive and analytical certainty. That image of rigor and quantitative analysis was exemplified by the work of David Petersen and his colleagues, first at Laventhol & Horwath and later at PriceWaterhouse and other firms.

Speaking to convention center managers in November 1984, Petersen argued that "realistic market analysis is a necessity these days." He then added, "A traditional (but inadequate) method of predicting market support has been based on size. An analyst might say, 'Because the number of square feet in my facility is 2% of all the exhibition space in the U.S., I'll get 2% of all the meetings.'" Petersen proposed "several more reliable methods," including comparing facilities in other cities, surveys of meeting planners, and measuring such things as nearby hotel rooms, retail facilities, and direct air access.[46]

When Petersen and his Laventhol & Horwath colleagues presented a proposal for a study of a new convention/civic center to Homestead, Florida in 1989, they could assure city officials, "The Convention Facilities Advisory Group is uniquely qualified to conduct this work given our prior experience in virtually every other convention market in the State, the national recognition of our work and, most importantly, our commitment to specialize in providing these services."[47]

The Laventhol proposal included a copy of the 1989 edition of the firm's "Convention Center Annual Report," with its summary data on center performance and economic impact. The report described Laventhol's research and analysis capabilities, including its "Predictive Attendance Model": "Using a computer based regression analysis, relevant criteria/resources have been identified which predict over 70 percent of the change in attendance at conventions in those cities included in the model." The Laventhol estimates of attendance at a new or expanded facility were thus ostensibly based on a formal statistical model, not mere guesswork.

Laventhol's claim for rigor was stated even more directly in the glossy promotional brochure for its convention and sports consulting services:

> And since we are part of a public accounting firm, our clients are assured of a rigorous review process. Our analytical techniques and reports are subject to a review that is comparable to the firm's tax and auditing services. This relationship also allows us special insights into engagements involving bond offerings and other financing methods under the jurisdiction of the Securities and Exchange Commission (SEC).[48]

David Petersen's argument for Laventhol's consulting services went beyond a computer model and a claim for rigor. The firm's brochure told local officials and potential clients precisely why forecasts of new economic impact were so important and relevant. The firm's services included "Estimates of economic impact generated by your project so decisions can be evaluated on the fiscal and employment benefits to the community. In addition, impact can be used to gain community support and interest." The forecasts of economic impact and job creation that Laventhol, and subsequently PriceWaterhouse, were providing were not numbers, guesses that stayed within the bulk of a thick consultant report. They were vehicles, based on a "Predictive Attendance Model," for gaining "community support and interest." They were, in short, central elements in selling convention center development.[49]

Laventhol was not the only firm seeking Homestead's business in late 1989. KPMG Peat Marwick offered a proposal as well, promising a "comprehensive market analysis." The KPMG team would be led and directed by Charles H. Johnson, IV. The firm could boast of Charlie Johnson's work "on over 100 related facility consulting assignments" and his "extensive experience." And without noting that Johnson had earlier been hired and trained by David Petersen at Laventhol, KPMG too could make its own claim for analytical rigor:

> Mr. Johnson was largely responsible for development of a computerized market position model which enables the client to isolate characteristics within a community and adjust them in order to determine the effect of improved facilities, more hotel rooms, modified marketing efforts, etc. . . .
>
> With his previous firm, he was partially responsible for the development of a convention center trend report, and assisted in the writing of the Urban Land Institute's new publication entitled *Convention Centers, Stadiums and Arenas.*

Just as Laventhol & Horwath's materials had stressed the role of "economic impact" as a sales tool in building community support, KPMG portrayed its own "economic and fiscal impact analysis" in the same vein. The Homestead proposal noted, "This reporting will allow you to document the economic and fiscal benefits associated with the project at each level [City, County, and State] for use when approaching each jurisdiction for funding support."[50]

From the late 1980s to the present, consulting firms such as PriceWaterhouseCoopers, C. H. Johnson Consulting, CSL International, HVS, KPMG, and Strategic Advisory Group consistently stressed their experience in convention center feasibility studies and the rigor of their analysis. They also pointed to the importance of economic impact assessment, much as KPMG did in their 2006 proposal to Las Cruces, New Mexico:

> One of the primary reasons convention centers are expanded or developed is because of the economic impacts the project can generate in terms of spending, employment and tax revenues to local and state governments. When soliciting funding from various governmental units or when evaluating the merits of pursuing a project of this

> magnitude, clients often present the benefits the governmental entities could receive as a result of the project. Benefits generated by operations of the proposed center are estimated based on direct spending by various users.[51]

Yet while all these firms, and others, dealt in the business of forecasting and predicting future convention center performance and promised economic impact, what they almost *never did*—indeed, still never do—is document how actual center performance compares to their predictions, or what their track record for forecast accuracy has been.

The "benefits the governmental entities could receive" noted by KPMG were and continue to be a vital element in promoting center investment and in appealing to state and local officials. With new visitor dollars will presumably come new tax revenues: hotel tax dollars, sales tax dollars, property taxes from new private development, income or wage taxes from new employment. That promise of public revenues distinguishes convention center building from other local capital investments or basic services. And it was and is a central theme in securing the public dollars for center development.

Seeking a commitment from the Maryland General Assembly for state dollars for a major expansion of the Baltimore Convention Center, attorney Robert S. Hillman argued in July 1991: "The conference, convention and trade show business taxes generated since the opening of the Center . . . demonstrates [sic] that the State of Maryland has already turned a large profit on its original $35 million investment in the original Baltimore Convention Center." He then argued, "The Convention Center Authority and its consultants have concluded in their detailed report and reiterate their belief that the increased State tax collections which will be generated from new and additional convention business from an expanded convention center will more than pay for the amortization costs of the required expansion bond issue over the life of the bonds."[52]

The notion that an expanded Baltimore Convention Center would literally pay for itself, through the new state taxes generated by a flood of new convention visitors—ERA had forecast an additional 150,000 a year, Hillman had promised 200,000 or 300,000 more—ultimately proved successful. The state agreed to $100 million, two-thirds of the cost, and to bear two-thirds of the center's annual operating loss.

The reality of forecasts of economic impact, and the estimates of related revenue benefits to state and local governments, is that they are an amalgam of guesses, estimates, and assumptions, only a portion of which have any real grounding in the reality of convention and tradeshow attendance and visitor activity. They nonetheless are the crucial, foundational element in the mayoral press conferences, newspaper headlines, and legislative deals that "sell" and seal convention center projects. Yet things like growing demand, increased event counts, and substantial visitor spending do not always work out the way the consultants forecast and state and local officials assume. The relationship between the consultant guesses and estimates, and the real world of convention center performance, is the subject of Chapter 5.

Chapter 5

Missing Impact

June Arney's front page article in the June 2, 2002, *Baltimore Sun*, under the title "Baltimore Built It—They Didn't Come," brought home the striking gap between the predictions of a consulting firm, the promises of city and state officials, and the reality of convention center performance in a competitive market. Arney narrated the promises surrounding the expansion project: "bigger conventions than ever before, more people than ever before, more spending and tax revenue than ever before. In April 1997, the transformed center, with three times the exhibit space, opened. Officials waited for the people to come."

What of the throngs of promised new convention visitors? "They haven't." When Robert Hillman had pressed the case for the expansion in 1991, he and the Convention Center Authority he chaired had sought to base the post-expansion forecasts on updated attendance numbers rather than those used by consultant Economics Research Associates: 217,884 convention and trade-show attendees in fiscal year 1990, 233,461 for fiscal 1991. But the *Sun* reported that the larger center had only drawn "234,394 last fiscal year—only 1,000 more than a decade earlier." Not only had the expansion failed to produce the likely 452,000 or even 508,500 attendees promised by Hillman in 1991, it was far short of ERA's 330,000 forecast. Arney quoted Hillman that "it hasn't been up for that many years. The story isn't over."

But the "story" wasn't substantially different fiscal year 2004, when the center drew 221,586 convention attendees, or in fiscal 2010, when attendance came to just 218,603. The response of Baltimore officials and business leaders? First, city officials undertook the financing and ownership of a new 757-room hotel next door to the center. Then, in May 2011, local business leaders called for another expansion of the center, justified by yet another consultant study and the promise of greater attendance and economic impact.[1]

The business and political leaders of Baltimore who had promoted public investment in a major center expansion were wrong. Yet their failure did not lead to a call for greater accountability, or serious reconsideration of the city's commitment to tourism and the visitor economy. It simply led to more public investment, justified by more promises. The experience was just the same in Boston, where a new convention center failed to perform anywhere close to consultant forecasts and official promises. Underperformance was just followed by the call to make Boston a "Top 5" city in convention business, with more center space and a new hotel. And in Washington, D.C., a brand new center, opened in 2003, produced no more convention business than its far smaller predecessor, and a fraction of that forecast by a series of consultants.

The experience of Baltimore, Boston, and Washington is by no means unique. Over and over, from Chicago and Milwaukee to Philadelphia and Orlando, to San Antonio and Seattle, the actual performance of new and expanded convention centers has fallen far short of consultant projections. That disparity is not limited to the work of a single consultant or firm. Forecasts from Laventhol, PriceWaterhouse, and Coopers & Lybrand in the 1980s and 1990s have proved effectively as faulty as more recent products of PKF, HVS, and CSL. It is possible to argue, as officials at the Massachusetts Convention Center Authority have done, that one particular analysis or one individual firm was overly optimistic. But the pervasive reality is that actual performance, indexed by convention and tradeshow attendance or hotel room night generation, is often half or less that in feasibility report predictions. Expanded centers in places like Dallas, Austin, Minneapolis, Pittsburgh, and Seattle have generally yielded no more business than their smaller predecessors.

This chapter reviews the history of consultant analyses and forecasts for an array of cities of varying sizes and regions, major visitor destinations and new contenders, for both new convention centers and expansions. It focuses on the central factors that drive economic impact—the volume of annual convention and tradeshows attendees and the hotel room nights they produce. And it tells a remarkably consistent tale of consultant misestimates and overpromising, little serious analysis or review, and the result—not a questioning of consultants, state and local officials, and public accountability, but rather a call for more public investment in order to "compete."

Atlanta

From its opening in 1976, Atlanta's Georgia World Congress Center has been expanded again and again, to a total of 950,000 square feet of exhibit space in the early 1990s. The center's successive expansions have been fueled by the willingness of Georgia governors and state legislators to take on debt, and by arguments that each addition would bring real economic returns in the form of more conventions and tradeshows with more attendees and a boost in visitor spending. Writing in 1989, David Petersen of PriceWaterhouse described the city's evolution "into a convention and trade show mecca," boasting the "premier facility of its kind in the southeastern United States." Indeed, as the center grew from its original 350,000 square feet of space, Atlanta's downtown hotel stock grew apace, from 7,700 rooms circa 1970 to over 11,500 by 2008.[2]

Each successive expansion effort saw the repeated contention that Atlanta would lose out to competitive cities if the state failed to fund an expansion, coupled with pleas from event organizers such as Harold Ford of the Southeastern Poultry and Egg Association in September 1990: "Give us a little more space so those of who want to stay here can, and those who want to come here can."[3] At almost the same time as the "Phase III" expansion opened in August 1992, World Congress Center Authority officials commissioned a study of a further expansion from PriceWaterhouse.

The January 1993 PriceWaterhouse report described the city's "success in attracting conventions and trade shows," noting that "Since its opening and with every expansion, GWCC has consistently achieved convention/trade show occupancies which are above averages of facilities in markets of similar size." Looking forward, the assessment stressed the benefits from the city's hosting of the 1996 Olympic Games, "giving Atlanta additional exposure through media coverage." World Congress Center officials were calling for a major expansion of some 525,000 square feet, presumably needed to "accommodate simultaneous events and retain major conventions and trade shows which are outgrowing GWCC's existing space."[4]

Atlanta's record of success paralleled that of the overall industry, with tradeshows growing "approximately 6-8 percent [annually] over the past two decades." The PriceWaterhouse report stated that "there is currently no persuasive evidence that exhibition space demand for either trade shows or conventions will abate in the foreseeable future." That growing demand would boost annual attendance at the existing World Congress Center from about 625,000 to the range of 750,000 to 800,000 by 2001. But a major expansion boosting the center's exhibit space by 55 percent would yield even more convention business, to some 950,000-1,025,000 by 2001.

With Georgia state officials focused on the run-up to the 1996 Olympics, the expansion of the GWCC was given a low priority in the wake of the 1993 study. Just months after the close of the Games, in October 1996, the Congress Center Authority released another study from PriceWaterhouse. David Petersen, longtime adviser to the authority and the report's principal author, recommended an expansion even larger than that proposed in 1993, adding 700,000 square feet of exhibit space to the center's stock. Petersen stressed the need to keep up with competing cities, and authority executive director Dan Graveline added, "The report makes it obvious that we need to move forward in order to keep our competitive position."[5]

The October 1996 PriceWaterhouse report differed from its predecessor in a number of respects. First, the new analysis stressed the idea that the large industry tradeshows that had long dominated the center's schedule had created a "feast or famine cyclical impact" with long move-in and move-out periods not filling hotel rooms. An expansion would be targeted to accommodate "2 to 3 shows simultaneously . . . [allowing the center to] host more mid-size events which draw proportionately more room nights." And although the adjacent Georgia Dome stadium had added more potential space, it was only serving about four shows a year that also used the Congress Center.[6]

The 1996 report paralleled the 1993 edition in stressing the increasing competition for conventions and continuing growth of the industry and demand. Using figures from Tradeshow Week's annual "200" listing, PriceWaterhouse noted that annual attendance growth over the previous decade had averaged 4 percent and that "the more popular destinations for trade associations [such as Atlanta] are capturing a greater proportion of the growing demand than less popular destinations." Based on that assessment of continuing growth for major events, the report described two expansion alternatives, of 500,000 and 700,000 new square feet.

PriceWaterhouse argued that the larger 700,000 square foot expansion would be "most beneficial for preparing Atlanta and the GWCC for the next decade." Without expansion, the report predicted the center would host 1.1 to 1.2 million annual convention and tradeshow attendees. The larger expansion would boost that to between 1.5 and 1.7 million. Even the more modest 500,000 square foot expansion—the alternative actually built—would generate 1.4 to 1.5 million annual attendees.

The 1996 report argued that expansion would yield far more new attendees than the previous analysis. And where the 1993 PriceWaterhouse effort predicted that expansion would boost annual delegate spending by $174.6 million, the later assessment increased that added spending (for the 500,000 square foot option) to $295 million.

Despite the enthusiastic recommendation from PriceWaterhouse, state commitment to more money for the World Congress Center was not automatic. Expansion efforts stalled during the 1997 legislative session, and local newspaper accounts regularly reported the possible loss of major events like the sporting goods industry's annual Super Show if the center was not expanded. Finally in early 1999 the state legislature approved, and the governor signed, a state budget including $220 million for the World Congress Center.

The expanded Georgia World Congress Center, with 1.4 million square feet of space, opened in time to accommodate the annual SuperComm show for the telecommunications industry in June 2002. But the convention world the center faced was far different from that of 1996. The SuperComm show that inaugurated the expansion in 2002 held its last Atlanta meeting in 2003 before moving to Chicago. The summer Comdex computer show had also moved to Chicago's McCormick Place. And the Super Show for the sporting goods industry, with its roughly 100,000 annual attendees, had left Atlanta for Las Vegas after the 2000 event. The PriceWaterhouse forecasts had assumed that the center could house two or three simultaneous events. But while the convention and tradeshow counts fluctuated from year to year, there was no consistent increase after the expansion opened. The Center had hosted 50 conventions and tradeshows in fiscal 1995; it managed just 56 in fiscal 2006 and 57 in 2007.

PriceWaterhouse had confidently predicted attendance of 1.4-1.5 million. In fiscal 2005, the World Congress Center managed a mere 452,258 attendees. Boosted by events relocated from New Orleans after Hurricane Katrina, the convention attendance hit 806,672 in fiscal year 2007. Yet that total was still below the pre-expansion peak year, 1995, with 879,036 convention and tradeshow attendees, and not much better than the 724,677 in 2001 on the eve of the expansion's opening.

After fiscal year 2007, with the impact of a recession and a sharp drop in business travel, the convention and tradeshow attendance at the World Congress Center plummeted. For fiscal 2008, the center accommodated 65 convention events with 697,578 attendees. The figures for fiscal 2009 were far worse—just 53 conventions and tradeshows with attendance of 548,603.

Fiscal 2010 was down even more, to 45 conventions and tradeshows with 473,448 attendees—even lower than the GWCC saw in 1989. The center's performance improved slightly in 2011, to 49 conventions and tradeshows with 539,680 attendees, and then dropped to 462,267 attendees in 2012.

The center's actual fiscal 2008 convention attendance came to less than half that forecast by PWC. The fiscal 2009 total, and those for 2010, 2011, and 2012 amounted to about one-third or less of the forecast. Apparently assuming that convention demand would inevitably grow year after year, and that the Georgia World Congress Center would be unaffected by the boom in convention center space that a host of PriceWaterhouse analyses had helped sustain, David Petersen and his colleagues thoroughly missed the larger forces at work on convention activity.

Austin

Austin's quest for a place in the national convention market began in the mid-1980s with a scheme for a new downtown center. The city commissioned a consultant study from Coopers & Lybrand, which was completed in May 1988. Describing a national convention market capable of persistent, sustained future growth, the Coopers study forecast that a new convention center could draw 26 events in its first year of operation (fiscal year 1993), rapidly increasing to 55 by fiscal 2000. Fully 18 of the initial 25 first-year events would be national or regional conventions, with the balance made up of state events that Austin, the state capital, had long attracted. By 2000, the national/regional meetings would make up 68 percent of the center's events.[7] The center was forecast to see 117,300 convention and tradeshow attendees in its first year, growing to 204,500 by 1997. By 2000, the new Austin center would attract 298,000 attendees, primarily from national and regional events.

The opening of the new convention center in July 1992 brought a reality somewhat different from the Coopers & Lybrand predictions. Despite a program of offering "discounts on facility rental for conventions and trade shows during the first 18 months of operation," the initial reports indicated that the center was filling with state events.[8]

The *Austin American-Statesman* on July 2 reported that the center's first major convention would be a meeting of the State Bar of Texas, and "The majority of bookings are from state associations, many of which are conveniently headquartered in Austin." Indeed, among the center's early bookings were the Texas Hotel-Motel Association, the Texas Bankers Association, and the Texas Medical Association. The largest booked event, the Government Technology Conference, neatly illustrated the issue. The event was on the center's books for every year from 1993 through 1999. But while the tech conference had projected attendance of 18,000 each year, it was forecast to use just 2,377 annual hotel room nights. And it had been held in Austin in previous years, at the old Palmer Auditorium which the new convention center replaced. This event, and other state meetings, might fill the center but they would largely draw local and drive-in attendees.[9]

The news on the center's performance was no less problematic a year later, with the release of a May 1993 report from the city auditor's office. The report stated, "the Center is struggling to book the number of national and regional conventions and tradeshows projected by C. & L. . . . with state bookings almost doubling the number of national/regional bookings." Despite the rental discounting program, much of the new center's business (like the Government Technology Conference) had simply moved from the Palmer Auditorium—"the transfer of old business . . . would seem to overstate the Center's accomplishment of attracting new money and visitors."[10]

The center's seemingly modest accomplishments did not long defer the call for even more space. Just two years after the scathing audit report, the *American-Statesman* brought the news that the center "couldn't serve all the groups that wanted to come," thus losing some $2.7 million in just 1995. The article went on to note that the city had circulated a request for proposals for a consultant study of a potential expansion, although city and CVB officials also bemoaned the lack of sufficient downtown hotel rooms to accommodate the growing demand.[11]

The city chose to employ consultant Charles H. Johnson, then with Stein & Company, to carry out the market analysis of the convention center and the city's performing arts facilities. Johnson's November 1995 report described the meetings market as "consistently growing," and argued, "It is quite conceivable that the city will experience [convention] growth to a point over the next twenty years whereby it rivals San Antonio and other strong second tier cities in terms of market penetration, desirability and level of business." Johnson went on to note the city's "bright future in the convention, trade and consumer show markets," with a table that showed the center's 1995 convention and tradeshow attendance at 137,565, and predicting that by 2000 attendance would reach 314,000.[12]

"With an expansion," the Johnson report stated, "the center will more than double its current volume of exhibit hall based attendance from conventions, trade and consumer shows . . . [that] will allow the city to gain market share in state demand, which the city can not accommodate, more annual repeat trade show demand and more national association demand." Johnson also promised that more space "will also allow the center to host back to back and simultaneous events of the size the center currently attracts."[13]

Charlie Johnson was no less enthusiastic about Austin's convention future to a broader audience. An *American-Statesman* story on December 3, 1995, that described the center as "half empty" quoted Johnson as saying it was time to expand—"The point is this: Austin's going to be a big city and you need to set the framework for that today."[14]

Johnson returned to Austin in 1997, this time with his eponymous consulting firm (in collaboration with Dave O'Neal of Conventional Wisdom Inc.), and firmly reiterated his advice to double the size of the convention center. Johnson counted the center as having hosted "over 135,000 high-impact attendees, those that come from out-of-town and stay in hotels, annually." He put the center's convention and tradeshow performance in 1996 at 47 events and 150,000 attendees, for a total of 150,500 annual hotel room nights.[15]

Charlie Johnson forecast that by doubling the size of the existing center, the city would more than double its convention business, to a total of 98 annual conventions and tradeshows, with 329,000 attendees generating "approximately 332,600 room nights in Austin." That increase in business would in turn boost the direct spending impact in overlying Travis County from $47 to $104.2 million a year, creating 2,464 new jobs.

Johnson's conclusion and forecast were headlined on the front page of the *American-Statesman*'s Metro section on July 26. The immediate reaction of some city council members, faced with a price tag of some $84 million, was less enthusiastic. But the project was pressed by Mayor Kirk Watson with the statement, "We need to create a great downtown . . . . Having sufficient convention capacity is a part of that—if we can afford to do it."[16]

Austin voters approved a hotel tax increase and the center expansion in a May 1998 bond vote, persuaded by repeated claims that "A larger center would bring $86 million more in annual spending to Austin and provide 1,800 additional jobs." Yet even as the center expansion was beginning, the city was obliged to tackle another recommendation of consultant Charlie Johnson. While Johnson had argued that the expansion would more than double the hotel room nights produced by the center, he also called for the development of new hotel rooms downtown. His 1997 report argued, "An 800-room plus hotel would be the most appropriate for accommodating Austin's increasing meeting-related demand."[17]

Austin city officials began soliciting hotel development proposals shortly after the approval of the center expansion, and by October 1998 had some seven bids for a new 800-room hotel. But the deal with chosen developer Landmark Organization quickly proved more complex and expensive than promised. Landmark proposed that the city finance the hotel with tax-exempt bonds, effectively owning the property. Yet even that public financing arrangement ultimately required an additional direct city investment of $15 million.[18]

Austin issued $109.7 million in bonds for the new Austin Hilton in June 2001. The bond issue was supported by a study from the HVS consulting firm that projected the performance of the new hotel, contending, "The expanded Center, with the support of the headquarters [Hilton] hotel, is estimated to induce approximately 158,00 new room nights in the market as a whole," bringing the center's room night generation to 314,000 by 2005.[19]

The expanded Austin Convention Center fully opened in June 2002. The city-financed Hilton hotel officially opened on January 1, 2004. Prior to the expansion, the Austin CVB reported that the center had generated a total of 141,788 room nights in 2000, followed by 142,896 for 2001. In the first full year of operation of the expanded center, it produced a total of 147,648 hotel room nights. With the addition of the headquarters hotel, the convention center's room night performance increased to a total of 190,220 room nights for 2004. The following year, room night activity fell back to 149,253. The 2006 room night total showed a slight increase to 161,776, followed by 144,570 in 2007.

The June 2011 report of the Austin Convention and Visitors Bureau shows 142,161 convention and tradeshow attendees using 165,029 room nights in 2009, with the room night total hitting 189,681 for 2010.

The doubled-in-size Austin Convention Center has consistently failed to come even close to the 332,600 total room nights forecast by Johnson in 1997, or the 314,000 projected by HVS in 2001. Rather, the overall performance of the expanded center, supported by the new city-financed Hilton hotel, has been only modestly (and inconsistently) above the 150,500 room nights Johnson described in his 1997 report on the pre-expansion center, or the 142,896 generated in 2001.

Faced with an expansion and city-financed hotel that were yielding far less convention business than the consultant forecasts and local expectations had hoped for, Austin officials and the Austin CVB argued that the failure was due to a lack of a sufficiently large hotel to support the Hilton. The CVB's 2008-2009 marketing plan noted the development of new thousand-room headquarters hotels in San Antonio, Dallas, Orlando, and Indianapolis, and argued, "It is imperative to the future health of the [Austin] convention center and the convention and meetings industry that the development of a new convention hotel happens immediately." Yet even with that, the CVB also announced a "new pricing model . . . [that] has allowed us to become more competitive in the marketplace as center rental remains the key buying deciding factor." Austin thus joined a host of other cities in offering convention center rental incentives, including discounts and even free rent, in an effort to be "more competitive."[20]

Boston

Boston's effort to develop a new convention center to replace or supplement its Hynes Convention Center extended over almost a decade, beginning with an effort in the early 1990s to build a "Megaplex" combining a stadium and a convention facility. The result was an impressive stack of consultant studies, each of which endorsed the need for a new, large convention facility.[21]

Coopers & Lybrand, led by consultant John Kaatz, completed a study of the stadium/convention center project in late 1992, narrowing the site selection to two sites in Boston and one in Cambridge. That work was followed by a more extensive study of a new convention center and sports stadium by PriceWaterhouse and David Petersen in July 1993 for the Massachusetts Convention Center Authority. The PriceWaterhouse report argued, "Boston has far too little convention/exhibit space to meet the present and projected market demand. . . . A major, well located expansion is virtually assured to attract large numbers of out-of-town delegates." Describing the existing Hynes Center as "too small to meet today's demand," the consultants predicted that "Failure to undertake a major expansion of convention space in Boston would result in large and growing losses to the Commonwealth resulting from lost convention business."[22]

The PriceWaterhouse report noted that the Hynes Center had averaged convention and tradeshow attendance of 330,000 from fiscal 1990 through 1993. Combined with Boston's strong amenities as a visitor destination and the continued growth of the largest 200 conventions and tradeshows tracked by Tradeshow Week, Boston would see strong demand for a new facility. The 1993 analysis then laid out a variety of expansion options, with likely future performance. With no expansion, the existing Hynes would continue to draw 320,000 to 350,000 annual convention attendees. With the Hynes continuing to operate and a new center offering 450,000 square feet of exhibit space—the closest alternative to what was actually developed—the two centers would combine for 720,000 to 780,000 attendees. That meant the new center itself would generate, assuming no loss at the Hynes, 400,000 to 430,000 new attendees to the city.

The PriceWaterhouse consultants did not directly predict the hotel room nights the new convention center would generate. But in estimating that total annual direct spending by attendees at both the Hynes and the new center would total $686.9 million, they laid out their logic for estimating overnight stays. They first asserted, based on a survey of delegates at four Boston events, that "Approximately 70-75 percent of convention/trade show attendees are estimated to stay overnight." Only a "small percentage" of those attendees were assumed to not use hotel rooms. And these overnight attendees "were assumed to spend 4.1 nights in Boston." Multiplying out 400,000 new attendees, with 70 percent staying overnight some four nights, yields a total of more than 1.1 million annual room nights.

The debate over a "Megaplex" was joined by Boston city officials with their own study in October 1994, produced by the Boston Redevelopment Authority (BRA). The BRA assessment largely focused on the potential of an "exposition center," as "spending by exposition center attendees is substantially greater than that of football or other sports patrons." The BRA study reviewed alternative sites, and then set out potential economic and fiscal impacts from a new convention facility with 550,000 square feet of exhibit space. The number of new center attendees in 2010 was forecast to be 371,622 per year, producing $209.4 million in annual direct spending. The BRA's work assumed that 70 percent of the attendees would be from out of town, each of those staying "an average of 3.2 nights in hotels." That would produce 832,433 hotel room nights in the Boston area each year.[23]

As Boston and Massachusetts officials argued over the merits of a standalone convention venue versus the "Megaplex," the Convention Center Authority commissioned a second study from PriceWaterhouse's Petersen in 1995, to "reevaluate the costs and benefits associated with two building program options." The May 1995 PriceWaterhouse study assumed a somewhat larger convention center—650,000 square feet versus the earlier 450,000—and focused on the potential for dual sports and exhibit use for the stadium plan.

PriceWaterhouse reiterated its previous finding that Boston suffered due to the small size of the Hynes Center, and that "without additional exhibition facilities, Boston's losses in terms of convention/trade show business will increase over the next ten years." And the Megaplex option, designed for sports events and blocked out during the fall for football games, was not as cost-effective as a pure convention facility. The consultants concluded that a large new center would complement, rather than compete with, the existing Hynes, and thus add 575,000 to 625,000 new convention and tradeshow attendees each year.[24]

Neither PriceWaterhouse study laid out a methodology for estimating future convention attendance. Instead, the analysts assumed a roughly proportional relationship between exhibit space and attendance, with the 450,000 square foot facility of 1993 producing a bit over 400,000 attendees and the 650,000 square foot center of 1995 producing some 600,000. The new Boston Convention and Exhibition Center as built, with 516,000 square feet of space, would thus likely yield some 480,000 to 500,000 annual attendees.

In calculating economic impact, the 1995 study differed from the earlier one by assuming that fully half of the new convention and tradeshow attendees would be "day-trippers" from Massachusetts or neighboring states, rather than overnight visitors. For the half who would likely stay overnight, the new estimated length of stay was 3.48 days. That would yield a room night total of about 900,000—somewhat less than the previous calculation.

The 1995 PriceWaterhouse analysis played a role in derailing the Megaplex scheme, but it did not make a new convention center politically or fiscally viable. Boston lacked the financial resources to build a new center itself, so the politics and deal-making were focused on the state government and a state legislature that had previously proven not necessarily interested in financing a center that solely benefited Boston. The legislative session ended in early August 1996 with no movement on the center plan. But one major backer, Governor William Weld, proposed that the state finance a new study of the costs and benefits of a major new convention center. The *Boston Globe* immediately endorsed the proposal in an editorial, arguing, "Speaker Thomas Finneran needs to be convinced that the project is fiscally sound." New numbers on "the economic ripple effects of luring large conventions" from an independent source would cinch the city's case.[25]

The new study would be managed under the aegis of a special committee, including representatives of the governor, the mayor of Boston, the House speaker, and the State Senate president. The committee in turn chose a large team of consultants to examine everything from the center's financing, design, and planning, to community involvement and market feasibility and likely performance. The lead consultants, focused on the center's potential market, were ZHA Inc. (represented by Dave O'Neal of Conventional Wisdom Inc.) and C. H. Johnson Consulting of Chicago. In announcing the consultants in mid-November 1996, Marisa Lago, Mayor Menino's appointee and Boston's chief economic development officer, described the ZHA/Johnson team's "absolutely sterling reputation specifically in convention centers," adding, "These folks are pros."[26]

It didn't take the consultants long to provide the first assessment of the proposed center's results. A bold headline in the *Boston Globe* on January 7, 1997, announced that the consultant team "enthusiastically endorses construction" of the center, with the promise it would generate an annual $436 million in new direct visitor spending and support the creation of 6,800 new jobs in Massachusetts. The *Globe* went on to quote consultant David O'Neal on the city's convention prospects—"Boston is an incredibly appealing destination for national conventions, especially for large, top-tier groups like medical and educational conventions."[27]

The formal consultant study was finally released at the end of March 1997. It endorsed a $695 million project to construct a new convention center in South Boston with 600,000 square feet of exhibit space, with the promise (again) of $436 million in annual new visitor spending. C. H. Johnson's report described the rate of convention center supply growth as slowing, "Now that most major metropolitan areas have a convention center." At the same time, using data from the annual Tradeshow Week *Data Book*, the report described demand as having "increased dramatically," from 4,400 events in 1996 to a forecast 4,791 in 2000. Attendance was predicted to grow from 101 million in 1996 to 140 million in 2000, because "overall growth is expected to be strong."[28]

With Boston's strong appeal as a visitor and meeting destination, the new convention center was forecast to house 38 conventions and tradeshows in its first year, 2003, rising to 64 by 2012. Those events would bring 302,800 attendees to Boston in 2003, 470,600 by 2007, and 537,600 by 2012. Those attendees would consume 398,135 room nights in the center's first year, 675,000 in 2007, and 794,000 in 2012. And all these events and attendees would be new, rather than coming at the expense of the existing center—"The Hynes will be able to replace these larger events with smaller events that are currently turned away to other cities because of space and schedule conflicts."[29]

The analysis by C. H. Johnson and ZHA proved the final study in the run-up to the actual development of the new Boston Convention and Exhibition Center. The state legislature passed chapter 152, authorizing construction of the new Boston center, in November 1997, overriding the veto of acting governor Paul Cellucci. The act anticipated an immediate start on building, with the center planned to open in 2002. It also contained language requiring an additional marketability study of the center's need, and a requirement that some 2,800 new hotel rooms be added to the city's hotel supply by the end of 2000.

An updated marketability study, completed by the Massachusetts Convention Center Authority in November 1998, was yet another product of C. H. Johnson Consulting. Much as its predecessor had done, it described a convention market where "the rate of growth in demand for exhibit space appears to be double the rate of growth in the supply of space." And given Boston's appeal, the new BCEC would see solid and steadily increasing success in luring events and visitors. The new center was now forecast to generate 398,135 hotel room nights in 2004, its likely first year of operation, growing to 654,000 by 2008, and ultimately 789,000 room nights by 2013—just slightly reduced and shifted back from the 1997 forecasts.

But as construction of the new center was beginning, it faced two signal changes. First, the available financing could not support the planned 600,000 square feet of exhibit space. The center was thus redesigned and downscaled, to a total of 516,000 square feet. And second, the recession of 2000 impacted both travel behavior and the short-term prospects of the meetings industry. Facing questions about marketing the new center, the Greater Boston Convention and Visitors Bureau commissioned yet another consultant study in June 2001, turning once again to PriceWaterhouseCoopers.[30]

The new PriceWaterhouseCoopers analysis, completed in early 2002 and overseen by Rob Canton after David Petersen's retirement, was quite upbeat about the prospects of the new center, noting that "unmet demand does exist in Boston" and that while there was a recent decline in convention industry growth, the previous declines in the early 1990s had been "followed by six to seven years of strong growth in demand during the latter part of the 1990s."[31]

The PriceWaterhouseCoopers analysts recognized that the larger economic factors would have some impact on the performance of the new BCEC, particularly in its early years. They concluded that a "stabilized" level of performance would come somewhat later than previously assumed, and "The first few years following opening, the BCEC will achieve lower performance levels than desired." But by its fifth to seventh year of operation the center was now predicted to achieve convention and tradeshow attendance on the order of 360,000 to 410,000. Unlike the firm's work for Atlanta a few years earlier, there was no distinction between out-of-town attendees and day trippers.

The PriceWaterhouseCoopers report then translated the forecast of convention attendance into a total of likely hotel room nights. Assuming, based on the performance of the Hynes and other convention centers, a ratio of room nights to attendees of 1.7 to one, PWC provided an estimate of annual room nights ranging from 612,000 to 697,000. These figures were lower than those of C. H. Johnson, and well below the previous PriceWaterhouse estimates of the 1990s. But the PWC consultants continued to argue that the new BCEC could achieve this level of performance without affecting business at the Hynes.

As the construction of the BCEC proceeded toward a June 2004 opening, it was becoming increasingly obvious that the initial convention bookings at the center would be well below all of the consultant projections. The authority's fiscal year 2004 budget noted that industry observers were now describing the supply of convention center space as exceeding demand. The budget document reported a total of 16 definite and tentative conventions for fiscal 2005, with only 14 for fiscal 2006. A strategic plan for the Convention Center Authority, developed by business faculty at Northeastern University and presented in July 2003, included a new set of demand and performance projections for the center (deemed "reasonable, plausible, and conservative"), showing a total of 40 conventions and tradeshows by 2010, with 467,000 attendees and just 481,000 room nights. And the authority's budget analysis laid out a new "official" assessment of the Johnson projections of a few years earlier: "In the mid to late 1990s, during the project development phase of the BCEC, consultants made what have turned out to be unrealistic and overly ambitious market share and booking projections for the new convention center, particularly during the initial ramp-up period."[32]

Faced with the prospect of a substantially empty convention hall in the first few years, the authority mounted a marketing blitz seeking to lure events to Boston. The annual Macworld computer event, which had decamped to New York some years earlier, was induced to return to Boston with the promise of substantial incentives, including free banner advertising on city streetlamps, use of the Boston Public Library courtyard for receptions, guaranteed reduced hotel rates, and free rent at the new BCEC for two years.[33]

The deal for Macworld was just one instance of the city and Convention Center Authority's effort to attract business to the new hall. Deals became the norm. The authority's fiscal 2005 budget proposal noted that rental revenue would be only a small proportion of BCEC revenues, "due to initial penetration pricing efforts to gain customers."[34]

The Macworld event also proved symbolic of the larger issues facing the authority and the new center. Macworld returned to Boston in 2004. But instead of the more than 50,000 attendees it had drawn in its last Boston outing in 1997, attendance came to just over 8,000. Since Macworld didn't need the large spaces of the BCEC, the event moved to the older Hynes Convention Center in 2005. And that would be its last year in Boston or the East Coast.

In the years after its 2004 opening, the Boston Convention and Exhibition Center demonstrated the "ramping up" phenomenon C. H. Johnson and PriceWaterhouseCoopers had anticipated. From only 22 conventions and tradeshows in fiscal year 2005, the new center managed to attract 25 in fiscal 2006 and 31 in fiscal 2007. Attendance rose in parallel, from just over 159,000 convention and tradeshow attendees in fiscal 2006 to 253,200 for fiscal 2007.

The scale of consultant misestimation (and corollary overstatement by local officials) is even more dramatic when looking at individual events. Each and every consultant had reassured the public that the new center would not cannibalize business at the Hynes Center. They were wrong.

Either from individual event organizers seeking more exhibit space to sell or from a concerted effort on the part of the Convention Center Authority, a number of the largest events at the Hynes gradually relocated to the BCEC. For fiscal 2008, former "Top Ten" Hynes events, the International Boston Seafood Show (18,000 attendees; 15,075 room nights), Yankee Dental Congress (28,047 attendees; 13,500 room nights), and New England Grows (15,500 attendees; 2,831 room nights) had all moved to the new venue. And as large events relocated, the Hynes proved unable to make up the loss with other, smaller events. Where the older center had accommodated events representing a total of 333,349 room nights in 1999 and 411,535 in 2000, the total was 237,535 in 2007 and 239,982 in 2008. For fiscal year 2010, the room night generation was about 217,000. Overall, the Hynes had lost perhaps 100,000 or more annual room nights. And while some of that loss reflected broader national trends, it was clear that a significant fraction had simply moved to the new center and not been replaced.

Even with the addition of events and hotel room nights simply shifted from the Hynes, the BCEC's performance in terms of room nights has proved remarkably modest. The 1997 C. H. Johnson study had estimated 675,000 room nights in 2007, growing to 794,000 in 2012, albeit for the somewhat larger proposed center. PriceWaterhouseCoopers had pegged annual room nights at 612,000 to 697,000. But for fiscal 2006 the new center yielded just 141,668 room nights from conventions and tradeshows, rising to 303,998 in fiscal 2007 and 337,932 for 2008 ("other events" brought the room night totals to 202,200 in fiscal 2006, 351,400 in 2007, and 389,600 in 2008). The overall room night generation by the BCEC for fiscal 2009 was just 313,200, with 286,531 from conventions and tradeshows. For 2012, the room night total was estimated to be 324,588. These totals, boosted by the shift and consequent decline at the Hynes, were half or less of the consultant estimates. And they can also be put in the larger context of Boston's overall hotel demand. In 2006, a strong hotel demand year with 76 percent occupancy, the total occupied room nights for Boston came to 4.4 million. The BCEC, with some 367,000 room nights, was responsible for just over 8 percent of this demand. Relative to the larger metropolitan Boston area, the BCEC's room night generation amounted to only 2.1 percent. Lots of folks were visiting the Boston area circa 2006 and 2007 and staying in hotel rooms. But they weren't there for conventions at the BCEC.[35]

The new Boston Convention and Exhibition Center was born on a sea of consultant studies. Over and over, those consultants appear to have assumed that Boston's appeal and the consistent growth of the convention business would inevitably fill a major new facility and Boston hotel rooms. They were perhaps half right. The consultant forecasts were commonly twice the actual results a few years later.

For James Rooney, executive director of the Massachusetts Convention Center Authority, perhaps the context of the consultant studies provides a clue to why they "missed"—"they were generated around the question of should we build. . . . There was a lot of criticism at the time. . . . It wouldn't surprise me if [the reports] were produced to generate some level of support." Asked about the competitive prospects of other cities with other consultant studies, Rooney responded, "When I talk to people from other cities about making a public investment in a convention center, I'm equally blunt with all of them about the feasibility studies these consultants use to justify [such] investments. . . . Some of these guys ought to be taken out and shot."[36]

The firing squad apparently does not extend to all consultants. With the argument that Boston could be among the nation's "top five" convention cities, the Massachusetts Convention Center Authority employed Conventions, Sports and Leisure International (CSL) in 2009 to provide a "strategic development plan" for the future of the BCEC. And perhaps not surprisingly, CSL's John Kaatz and an associated team of architects and planners laid out the need for more proximate hotel rooms, an additional large ballroom, a 5,000 seat auditorium, and "added exhibit and corresponding meeting space as BCEC occupancy percentages continue to increase towards practical maximum capacity."[37]

That was of course much the same advice as the CSL firm had provided to Miami Beach, Kansas City, Washington, San Antonio, and Philadelphia in recent years.

Denver

The new Colorado Convention Center in downtown Denver opened in March 1990, after more than a decade of political squabbling and conflict over location and financing. Yet just a few years after its opening, while the center was still not drawing the number of conventions and convention attendees that consultants had promised, the Denver Convention and Visitors Bureau commissioned a consultant study of a potential expansion.

The report that Coopers & Lybrand delivered in January 1997 told city leaders that Denver faced losing $182 million in annual delegate spending if it failed to expand the convention center and add a thousand-room headquarters hotel. Coopers proposed that the city double the size of the center's exhibit space to 600,000 square feet, boosting the center to fifteenth largest in the nation. That expansion would in turn draw substantially more conventions, tradeshows, and attendees, boosting the center's annual economic impact from $122.5 to $214.5 million. That 75 percent increase in economic impact would be the product of an equivalent boost in the annual count of convention and tradeshow attendees from circa 166,000 in 1996 or 172,000 the following year. And it would see a parallel boost to the center's generation of hotel room nights, then 247,714 in 1996 and 245,135 for 1997. Eugene Dilbeck of the Denver CVB argued, "We have a tremendous growth potential here."[38]

Dilbeck's enthusiasm for more convention center space did not guarantee either public approval or financing. Faced with poll results that indicated little citizen enthusiasm for paying for a bigger center, Denver Mayor Wellington Webb chose to appoint an "independent" task force of local residents and city officials to "explore" development and financing issues in July 1998. The mayor's task force reported back in February 1999, urging the expansion and development of a large new hotel. The task force recommended paying for the expansion (Dilbeck would term it "completion" of the center) with taxes on hotel rooms and car rentals. But while the task force report devoted substantial space to financing alternatives, architecture, and urban design issues, it simply embraced the findings of the earlier Coopers & Lybrand report. The report concluded, "In summary, the Task Force finds that there is a market and an economic justification to expand the Colorado Convention Center, including the development of a headquarters hotel."[39]

Mayor Webb and the city council embraced the task force recommendation and placed the proposal for the $268 million expansion, and the tax increases needed to finance it, on the ballot in November 1999, together with proposals for light rail, the zoo, and the Denver Art Museum. Backed by a concerted public relations campaign and little organized opposition, bolstered by repeated claims of millions in new economic impact from added convention delegates, the convention center financing passed with the lowest level of voter support among all the proposals, 55 to 45 percent.[40]

The promises surrounding the convention center vote proved decidedly questionable rather quickly. The developer who had promised before the vote to build the "needed" headquarters hotel ultimately failed to secure financing, and the city broke off negotiations in early 2002. The alternative proved to be a fully publicly financed and owned hotel, developed with a $354.8 million bond issue, sold in mid-2003.

The city's investment in the 1,100-room hotel had been justified by the work of the Mayor's Task Force and the recommendations of Coopers & Lybrand. It was also supported by the work of the HVS consulting firm, in an April 2003 report to the city and potential bond purchasers. HVS reported that the city would be competing for convention business against Atlanta, New Orleans, Boston, and Orlando following the expansion. Yet even in the face of that competition, the consultants forecast that the number of annual hotel room nights produced by the convention center would increase from a "base" without the expansion or new hotel of 365,100 to a total of 628,500 in 2009 and 658,000 in 2010, neatly filling the new city-owned Hyatt-branded adjacent hotel.[41]

Coopers & Lybrand had promised that the expansion would boost the attendance and direct spending impact of the Colorado Convention Center by some 75 percent. A few years later, even after the impact of 9-11 on travel and convention activity, HVS forecast both continuing growth in convention center-related hotel activity *absent the expansion and hotel* and a significant surge in total room nights with the combination of expansion and a major new hotel, reaching over 600,000 annual room nights.

From 1996 through 2000, the original Colorado Convention Center had averaged 161,770 annual convention and tradeshow attendees. After the expansion, from 2005 through 2010, that attendance averaged 225,795—about a 40 percent increase. That was of course rather less than Coopers had predicted, although obviously affected by the national recession. The room night totals forecast by HVS in 2003 proved even more dramatically wide of the mark. The expanded center and Hyatt hotel complex produced 351,778 room nights in 2007, a bit less than the "base" figure cited by HVS, but somewhat more than the approximately 246,000 room nights the smaller center had yielded in the mid-1990s. The total for 2009 came to 315,820 rather than 628,000. And room night bookings for 2010 were put by the Denver CVB at 408,107, still well short of the forecast 650,000.[42]

Unlike a number of its competitors, the Colorado Convention Center actually gained some added convention business after a major expansion, albeit less than the consultants promised. But that limited success had come at a price. Denver had put the convention center on sale. As early as 2003, before the expansion was open, the Seattle CVB had noted that "Denver has been offering free convention center rental to promote its new convention center expansion." Two years later, Seattle's marketing analysis noted, "Denver frequently offers complimentary or discounted convention center rent and more economical hotel rates than Seattle."[43]

Indianapolis

Indianapolis has often been cited by both academic observers and consultants as an example of successful downtown revitalization sustained by public investment. Much of the public investment behind the city and state revitalization effort has been centered on new sports facilities: the RCA Dome, the new Lucas Oil Dome, Market Square Arena, Conseco Fieldhouse, and Victory Field. The city and state have also collaborated on major public investments in tourism and conventions, financing a series of expansions of the Indiana Convention Center and subsidies for new hotel development.[44]

The Indiana Convention Center opened in 1972 with 124,000 square feet of exhibit hall space. An expansion in 1984 brought the center to 206,000 square feet. A further $43 million expansion was completed in September 1993, adding a new ballroom, entrance lobby, and meeting space. Discussion of yet another expansion initiative began in 1994, and the consulting firm of KPMG Peat Marwick produced a formal feasibility and market analysis in early 1995. Contemporary press accounts of the consultant study reported it found that "Indianapolis will soon need more exhibition space unless it wishes to lose out in the scramble for lucrative convention business," and recommended an expansion of the center to add some 130,000 square feet of exhibit space.[45]

The city began to move ahead on a $45 million expansion effort in 1997, designed to add 100,000 square feet of exhibit hall space, with the argument that more space would allow the city both to keep its existing convention business, and to accommodate "more simultaneous, back-to-back, and overlapping conventions." A January 1998 story in the *Indianapolis Star* quoted the KPMG Peat Marwick study as predicting that the expansion would yield "about 147,000 additional hotel room nights a year," beyond the more than 450,000 annually the city was then attracting.[46] Indianapolis Convention and Visitors Association head Rick Hughes forecast that with the expansion "the city should see the equivalent of an additional two-day convention of about 5,000 to 6,000 people a month," or a total of 72,000 new attendees each year.[47]

The $45 million expansion project, largely financed by the Lily Endowment, formally opened in July 2000. An article in the *Indianapolis Star* on the eve of the opening reported that local officials said it would "put Indianapolis in competition for bigger and more frequent conventions," repeating the argument that the larger center would allow "two, three or more medium-sized conventions to be held at once."[48]

At the same time as the expansion was under construction, the city was also following a policy of subsidizing new downtown hotel development in order to accommodate the anticipated new convention attendees. The city provided $23 million in infrastructure improvements to support development of a new 616-room Marriott hotel, and financed the asbestos abatement of the former Blue Cross-Blue Shield building for conversion to a 285-room Adam's Mark hotel.[49]

The fundamental promise of the expansion, from the 1995 KPMG study and local officials, was that it would boost the overall convention and tradeshow attendance at the Indiana Convention Center, and increase total annual room nights from circa 450,000 to about 600,000.

The circa 450,000 annual hotel room night figure described by the Indianapolis Convention and Visitors Association actually counted meetings and sports events well beyond those hosted by the Indiana Convention Center and the Hoosier/later RCA Dome. For example, the city hosted 421,583 room nights at 417 individual events in 1998. From 1995 (following the earlier expansion) through 1999, the city garnered an annual average of 439,622 room nights. Its peak year during that period was 1995, with a total of 493,078. In the wake of the expansion, avoiding the years possibly impacted by the recession and 9-11, average room night activity from 2004 through 2007 came to 489,834. Compared to the pre-expansion figure, that amounted to a gain of about 50,000 room nights. Relative to the 450,000 figure claimed as the "baseline" in 1998, the increase comes to less than 40,000 room nights. That represented a great deal less than the 147,000 added room nights predicted in the KPMG report, well short of the promised 600,000. And the room night totals, based on a wide array of meetings and events, don't actually represent the performance of the convention center itself.

The Indianapolis Convention and Visitors Association also compiles an annual total of convention delegates, including all area meeting events—those that solely use hotels or other venues, as well as the convention center. The peak years for the overall delegate count were 1995 and 1996, with 1.074 million and 1.090 million delegates respectively. From 1995 through 1999, the average annual delegate count was 955,499. In the wake of the 2000 expansion, the best year for delegate attendance was 2008 with 855,460. The annual average from 2004 through 2008 (excluding the years immediately after 9-11 with reduced delegate counts) amounted to 800,462. The convention delegate counts thus actually show a decline in the years after the completion of the 2000 expansion. But those figures are far more expansive than the performance of the convention center and dome facility itself.[50]

The Indiana Convention Center/Dome staff maintain their own records on events and attendance, classifying conventions as "national" or "state/regional" in scope, and differentiating them from tradeshows, public shows, sports events, and business meetings. In 1998, for example, a year the Convention and Visitors Association counted room nights at 417 individual events, the convention center hosted 49 national conventions, 75 "state/regional" events, and 10 non-public tradeshows. The national events are the most clearly and consistently defined, and the most desirable events for both the city and the convention and visitors association.

In 1995, following an expansion, the Indiana Convention Center saw

351,113 attendees at "national" conventions, followed by 426,178 in 1996. The center's peak year in the 1990s for national convention business was 1999, with 530,010 attendees. The center averaged 382,477 national attendees from 1995 through 1999.

After the 2000 expansion, the center managed 354,487 national convention attendees for 2001. The total came to 372,568 for 2004, and with 2005 data unavailable, 298,994 in 2006. Overall, averaging the national convention attendance for 2004 and 2006 through 2008, annual national convention attendance was 320,840. Rather than gaining national convention attendees, the Indiana center actually saw its attendance drop after the expansion. For 2009, the center managed 333,576 national attendees. But the 2010 total fell sharply, to 303,882. The national event attendance peak of 1999—over 530,000—has not been matched in the decade since.

State and regional convention attendance is more difficult to track due to possible inconsistency in definition and inclusion. But in 1999, prior to the expansion, the center saw 68 events with 98,663 attendees. For 2003, the state/regional total came to 59 events with 76,204 attendees. And in 2007 the comparable figure was 64 events with 92,685 attendees. Only in 2009—72 state/regional conventions with 126,368 attendees—did state and regional convention attendance equal or exceed the 1999 figure. And that total promptly fell in 2010, to 85,331. The 2000 expansion does not appear to have boosted attendance at state/regional conventions, nor has there been any noticeable increase in attendance at the handful of nonpublic tradeshows (9 in 1998, 10 in 2007). Rather than growing with each successive expansion, the convention attendance at the Indiana Center has been sliding since the late 1990s, a slide that mirrors the increased competition for national events and changing attendance trends.

The actual performance of the expanded Indiana Convention Center appears to have had little import to local officials interested in boosting downtown and increasing tourism. The Indianapolis/Marion County Capital Improvement Board commissioned a market demand study for a further expansion from PWC's Rob Canton in late 2003. The report Canton delivered in March 2004 contained no figures on the historic attendance of the convention center, no data on its recent performance, and no annual room night numbers—an unusual omission for a PWC market study. The 2004 report did examine the occupancy rate for the center's exhibit hall space, noting an occupancy of 69 percent in 2001 and 66 percent in 2002 and concluding that, despite the "difficult times experienced industry-wide," the Indianapolis center's "occupancy has remained strong, repeatedly bordering on practical maximum occupancy." That strong occupancy performance led the consultants to the conclusion that an expansion adding 275,000 square feet of exhibit space and more meeting room space was justified. PWC concluded that another expansion would boost the center's business by 18 to 23 new conventions and tradeshows each year, increasing attendance from 400,000 to between 508,000 and 538,000.[51]

The prospect of yet more space was eagerly promoted by Bob Bedell, head of the convention and visitors association. Bedell also argued there would be a need for a major new hotel of 1,000 or more rooms, much as he had a few years earlier in St. Louis: "If our Convention Center is almost doubled in size, then we're going after business that is bigger than most of the business that we currently have. We would need to have a bigger hotel than what we currently have."[52]

Indianapolis city officials sought and found a developer, White Lodging, that promised a new 1,000-room J. W. Marriott hotel and other Marriott-branded properties, albeit with the requirement of some $50 million in city investment to pay for meeting space, parking, and supporting infrastructure. The expanded center was opened in January 2011, followed by the new Marriott hotel in February.

PWC's case for an expanded convention center was largely made in terms of the strong occupancy rate of the exhibit halls, with the center "consistently operated at or very close to practical maximum operating levels." Yet even as the firm was completing its report, that occupancy rate was slipping. PWC had described a 69 percent occupancy rate in 2001. But by 2006, that rate had fallen to just 58 percent, followed by 60 percent in 2007. At a time when the convention and tradeshow business was ostensibly rebounding from the impact of 9-11, Indianapolis was losing ground, not gaining. And in the current economic environment, the center's performance has proven even worse in terms of the utilization of its exhibit halls. Hall "F," one of two added in 2000, had a 65 percent occupancy rate in 2002. That fell to 58 percent in 2007, 41 percent in 2008, and just 39 percent for 2009. Other halls showed a parallel pattern of decline. The image of a "full" convention center depicted by PWC no longer appears entirely accurate, and the failure of the previous expansion to boost the center's convention business necessarily raises questions about the likely results of even more space.[53]

The PWC forecasts for an expanded Indiana Convention Center had assumed that the "strong destination package" offered by Indianapolis and the growth in overall convention and tradeshow demand would inevitably bring more convention attendees to the center and city. But in the years between the 2004 report and opening of the expansion in early 2011, center attendance steadily slipped, with a sharp drop in 2010. And of course it faces increasing competition from other new or expanded centers that PWC had provided with equally positive market studies.

New Orleans

Convention center consultant David C. Petersen, writing in 1996, described the New Orleans Ernest Morial Convention Center as an "extraordinary success through its unusual ability to attract both major trade shows and major conventions." The center had originally opened in 1984 as the main building of the city's World Exposition. It began operation as a convention center in January 1985, with 327,300 square feet of exhibit space. Louisiana and New Orleans leaders had long viewed the initial building as "Phase I" of a larger convention facility, and rather quickly they commissioned an analysis of the market for an expansion from Coopers & Lybrand.[54]

The September 1987 Coopers report argued that New Orleans was "viewed very favorably by major users of convention and exhibition space," concluding, "Current and future market demand warrants an expansion of the existing New Orleans Convention Center at this time." The Coopers consultants, using data from Tradeshow Week, noted that exhibition space use "has increased 9.2 percent annually between the years 1972 and 1981, and by over 7 percent during the years 1982 to 1986." They then recommended that the center be doubled in size, to 700,000 square feet.[55]

The "Phase II" expansion of the New Orleans center was completed in July 1991. But even before the expansion opened, the New Orleans Exhibition Hall Authority turned once again to Coopers & Lybrand. The November 1990 Coopers report once again concluded there was sufficient market demand to sustain a "Phase III" expansion, adding 200,000 to 300,000 square feet of exhibit space by 1996. Phase III ultimately grew to an addition of 400,000 square feet.[56]

As state officials debated the expansion proposal, Morial Center management produced a report in April 1994 that deemed the center "one of the greatest economic assets of the City of New Orleans and the State of Louisiana," one that put New Orleans "in the major league of convention cities in the United States." Arguing that the center had already lost "millions of dollars in bookings," the report pressed yet another expansion with the contention that more space would boost attendance, economic impact, and overall tax revenues by over 70 percent. For a city substantially dependent on tourism, the potential for more convention business appeared both crucial and all but assured.[57]

The 1994 report included the information that the Morial had attracted 405,334 convention delegates the previous year. The Exhibition Hall Authority's more broadly defined convention attendance figure for 1993, including guests and spouses, was later shown as 567,497, with 723,651 reported for 1992. For the broader attendance measure, the forecast 70 percent increase in convention business post-expansion would bring the Morial to some 965,000 annual convention delegates. Using the larger 1992 attendance as a baseline, the expansion should have consistently yielded 1.23 million annual attendees.

When the expansion opened in late 1998, bringing the Morial Center to a total of 1.1 million square feet of exhibit space and putting it in fifth place among U.S. centers, it was supposed to be on the verge of even more success in an expanding convention market. Convention and tradeshow attendance hit 885,997 for 1999, at a total of 111 events. But in the wake of 9-11 and economic slowdown, attendance fell to 692,522 in 2001 and 523,761 in 2004—back to where the center's performance had been in the late 1980s. Then came Hurricane Katrina in August 2005.

The hurricane both devastated New Orleans and darkened the center's reputation. Further expansion plans were put on hold, and the building was gradually renovated through 2006. For 2007, convention attendance came to 330,255. But in the face of a national recession, the Morial's comeback slowed, hitting just 437,956 at 106 conventions and tradeshows in 2009, with attendance increases to 463,371 in 2010, 472,840 for 2011, and 549,474 for 2012.

New Orleans had planned on an even more expansive bet on the convention business in 2003, selling bonds for a planned $455 million expansion of the Morial—"Phase IV"—that would add 525,000 square feet of exhibit hall space by the fall of 2006. The expansion project was backed by a study from Conventions, Sports & Leisure International (CSL), completed in June 2000, that argued of the ten major convention centers, "only three facilities, those in Orlando, San Francisco and New Orleans, have experienced continuous growth in market share." The consultant, John Kaatz of CSL, who had led earlier expansion studies by Coopers & Lybrand, used data on Tradeshow

Week's "200" to argue, "Going forward, it appears that key measures of the industry (attendance, events, space) will likely continue to increase modestly and steadily." Kaatz then recommended that the Morial Authority seek to "target added multiple events in the 200,000 to 600,000 gross square foot range," and forecast that the added space would bring $355,545,000 in added annual convention attendee spending. Kaatz updated his 2000 effort in late 2004. His recommendation once again was "Build it": "Everything we've done indicates the industry is on solid ground," Kaatz told New Orleanians. In the end, Morial officials canceled the expansion effort in 2007, investing instead in renovation of the existing facility.[58]

David Petersen of PriceWaterhouseCoopers had described New Orleans as a great tourist destination and the Morial Center as a stellar performer in the mid-1990s. Over and over through the 1990s and into the 2000s, consultant John Kaatz told local officials and center managers that growing convention demand would fill a repeated series of center expansions. The city certainly had an impressive history as a visitor and meeting destination, with more than 34,000 hotel rooms in its metro area. Yet little more than a decade after Petersen's comments, the convention center was yielding about as many attendees as in its first year of business, or about two-thirds of what it had drawn in 1995 *before a $247 million expansion*. The Greater New Orleans Convention and Visitors Bureau had begun an aggressive program of incentives and discounts on center rent in early 2008, "offering whatever it takes" to lure business, according to bureau president Stephen Perry. But faced with what Perry termed a "proliferation of center construction combined with a second element—the continuing expansion of mega-hotels," New Orleans was in "a competitive environment that has changed the nature of our game."[59]

Two years later, in late 2010, the Morial Center Authority president forecast an operating deficit of $9.8 million for the coming year, and argued that the center was obliged to act as a "loss leader" to fill local hotels. President Bob Johnson told the *Times-Picayune*, "The economics of the situation are such that the clients expect concessions when they pick a market. That's industry wide."[60]

New York

When New York City mayor John Lindsay unveiled plans for a new convention center on the city's West Side in March 1970, he no doubt had little sense of the depth of conflict and division that would result, or that it would be another 16 years, until April 1986, before the center would open its doors. Yet while issues of site, financing, environmental impact, and construction quality would regularly imperil and delay the project, there was never any real debate or question about its presumed economic import or results for the city.

The *New York Times* article that announced Lindsay's convention center initiative said "Hopefully the new center would put New York back in the running for major trade shows and even national political conventions now being lost to halls in Chicago and other large cities," and that one consulting firm had estimated it would yield $70 million in new visitor spending in its first year.[61]

The Arthur D. Little consulting firm produced one of the first formal market and economic impact studies of the proposed new center in 1973. Noting that "New York has the attributes required to make it the leading convention city in the United States," they concluded that a new center would eventually house some 41 events annually, drawing some 634,000 convention and tradeshow attendees. Based on the estimate that attendees would stay an average of three to four nights in the city, Little forecast a total of 2 million added hotel room nights and a total direct spending by convention and tradeshow attendees of $246 million annually.[62]

As local interests debated the location for the center—West Side, Times Square, Battery Park City—there were more studies and more seeming certainty about the need for a major new center. A lengthy May 1977 editorial in the *New York Times*, "Build the Convention Center," argued, "New York needs a new convention and exposition facility as the cornerstone of its future economy and it needs it quickly." That assessment was bolstered by a 1978 analysis by the New York City Planning Commission that concluded a new convention facility would house 56 to 64 convention and tradeshow events per year, with a total of 598,000 to 712,000 attendees. The estimate of hotel room stays was now based on an average stay of two days for local delegates and four and a half for out of town visitors (511,000 to 618,000 per year), or at least 2 million total room nights, and direct spending was assumed to reach some $347 million a year.[63]

The final word on the center's anticipated performance came in a 1980 environmental impact study prepared by the New York Convention Center Authority. Noting that the existing New York Coliseum was drawing some 492,000 people to 24 convention and tradeshow events each year, the impact study projected a total of 62 to 71 events and a total of between 920,000 and

1.17 million attendees. Assuming an average stay of 3.25 nights—the figure used in earlier studies—yielded a projected 3.4 million hotel room nights to be generated by the Javits, and an estimated total of $485 million in annual direct spending.[64]

"Barely four years after its completion," the *New York Times* reported in July 1990, Javits officials were arguing that the center needed to expand "to remain attractive and to attract the nation's largest trade shows." Although one industry analyst was quoted as suggesting that growth in events and attendance was flattening, Javits officials contended "there were many shows that routinely bypassed New York because of the need for large spaces."[65] Still, it was not until 1997 that the Javits Operating Corporation released a formal consultant study of a major expansion.

The report produced by Coopers & Lybrand in April 1997 brought good news about the performance of the Javits Center, and its prospects. Based on activity and attendance for the previous three years, the Coopers study stressed that the Javits "appears to have reached its practical maximum capacity," while hosting an average of 1.15 million convention and tradeshow attendees from 1995 through 1997. "Given past success," Coopers & Lybrand concluded, "there appears to be a significant opportunity for New York to solidify and enhance its standing as a major trade event destination."[66]

The attendance numbers presented in the Coopers analysis compared quite favorably to the earlier consultant forecasts. An average convention and tradeshow attendance in excess of one million was at the high end of the estimate in the 1980 environmental assessment and well above the 1973 and 1978 forecasts. Yet by isolating attendance figures for three years—a standard methodology for Coopers & Lybrand—the consultants missed the larger and more complex performance history of the Javits Center.

In 1988, the newly opened Javits had accommodated over 1.5 million convention and tradeshow attendees. That total grew to 1.87 million in 1989 and 1.92 million in 1990, followed by 1.42 million in 1991. Compared to these earlier figures, the 1.15 million average annual attendance noted by Coopers & Lybrand in 1997 represented a clear and substantial decrease. And mentioned just briefly in the 1997 analysis was another, far more troubling performance measure.[67]

All the analyses of the Javits's likely performance made in the 1970s had stressed that convention delegates would routinely stay overnight in New York City for two, three, or even four nights. The forecasts for annual room night use were all in the realm of two to three million. But Coopers &

Lybrand didn't find that figure, or even one million room nights. The Coopers report said the Javits had generated a total (including from public shows) of 312,700 hotel room nights in fiscal year 1996 and 306,700 in fiscal 1997. And performance in those years was actually better than in fiscal 1995, where room night generation came to just 201,600.[68]

For all the volume of attendees who walked through the doors of the Javits Center each year, the facility seemed to be failing at its primary purpose of bringing out-of-town attendees to New York. And the findings of the Coopers analysis for the mid-1990s did not appear to be a fluke or error. With Mayor Rudy Giuliani pressing for development of a new stadium as part of an expansion of the Javits, the basic idea of expanding the convention center became stalled in city politics. The Javits Operating Corporation commissioned another consultant analysis of expansion, this time from PriceWaterhouseCoopers.

Rob Canton of PWC delivered the expansion study in March 2000, and effectively echoed the Coopers conclusions: "JKJCC will lose existing business if it does not expand," and "JKJCC will attract new events if it is expanded." PWC stressed that "New York City is a destination where many shows must have a presence" and described the existing center as "reaching or exceeding practical maximum occupancy limiting the possibility for growth in occupancy or attendance."[69]

Unlike the 1997 analysis, PWC provided convention and tradeshow data back to 1993, and noted that the center had averaged 1.2 million attendees a year. Notably, PWC did not go back to the far higher figures in 1988, 1989, 1990, or 1991. The 2000 report did not follow Coopers & Lybrand and directly present a figure on hotel room night performance. But it did present a "no expansion" option to indicate the incremental impact of the proposed expansion. Under the "no expansion" alternative, PWC calculated total convention and tradeshow attendance at 1.14 million—about equal to historical performance. It then said, "under no expansion, JKJCC generates approximately 664,000 hotel room nights."[70]

The PriceWaterhouseCoopers estimate of 664,000 annual room nights was decidedly higher than the Coopers total. But it was still a fraction of the two to three million room nights assumed in the pre-opening forecasts. The remarkably modest volume of hotel stays produced by the Javits Center was further reinforced in a second PWC expansion analysis, completed in January 2004.

The 2004 PWC study, again directed by Rob Canton, repeated and reinforced the case for expansion, describing the existing Javits as at "practical maximum occupancy," arguing, "If the Javits Center does not add substantially to its prime contiguous exhibit space, as well as to the number of conference and meeting rooms, it is likely that its market share will continue to erode." The analysts did not stress the more recent attendance performance of the center. The figures in the report's chart of annual attendance for 1999-2002 are shown as "estimated." The actual numbers should have been available to PWC. They tell a striking story.[71]

The Javits had accommodated 1,277,000 convention and tradeshow attendees in 1999, and 1.25 million the next year. With the impact of the economic downturn in 2000, that dropped to 977,600 for 2001, and after 9-11 to 931,850. The Javits was clearly affected by the larger changes to the national economy and travel. The real question was whether it would see a quick return to previous levels. On that, the PWC consultants were reassuring: "Increases and declines in exhibit space demand and attendance at Gateway Centers have been consistent with periods of national economic growth and decline—a trend that is expected to continue in the future." With national economic recovery, the performance of the Javits Center would presumably rebound.

The 2004 PWC report did not provide a detailed analysis of the room night performance of the Javits. But buried on page 127, in an analysis of the Manhattan hotel market, was the mention of "the 668,000 estimated room nights generated by the Javits." That 668,000 figure was almost exactly the same as the 664,000 noted for the "no build" option in the 2000 report, and thus likely a plausible estimate of the actual performance of the center. Strikingly, it was not anywhere near two million. And with a 2000 total hotel room demand in Manhattan of 17,336,463, the Javits Center was producing on the order of 3.9 percent of total demand.

The decline in convention and tradeshow attendance to 2002 that PWC had assured would rebound in fact did not. Attendance came to 961,600 in 2004, and increased somewhat to 1,026,730 for 2006. But 2007 convention and tradeshow attendance was just 817,100, falling to 708,200 in 2008, followed by 633,600 for 2009. The 2007 total amounted to just 65 percent of the 1.25 million attendees the center had managed in 2000 and much less than half of the center's attendance in 1989 and 1990. In the wake of the 2008 recession, the Javits saw a further decline, to 548,800 convention and tradeshow attendees in 2011 and 533,700 for 2012.[72]

Over a long time period, the convention and tradeshow attendance at the

Javits had simply plunged. Notable as that is, it is quite easy to understand. Both the attendance decline and the modest yield of hotel room nights are products of the same forces, rooted in the central business at the Javits.

The Javits Center's event calendar has long been dominated by a number of recurring annual major tradeshows. These events include such things as the American International Toy Fair, the International Hotel/Motel & Restaurant Show, the National Stationery Show, and the two annual New York International Gift Fairs. BookExpo, the publishing industry's annual tradeshow, rotates some years but is regularly held in New York at the Javits Center.[73]

These trade events have seen a dramatic change in attendance in recent years. The Toy Fair attracted 17,000 buyers in 1999 and 19,901 in 2000. It was down to 13,050 in 2005, and 11,650 in 2007, 10,321 in 2009, and 10,592 in 2012. The Hotel/Motel Show boasted 29,440 attendees in 1998 and over 27,000 the next year. Attendance was 19,200 in 2007, followed by 21,948 in 2008. By 2011, the show's attendance was at 23,953—still well below the late 1990s level. And the Stationery Show fell from 17,700 in 1998 to 13,362 in 2007, 13,319 for 2008, and 10,880 in 2009.[74]

BookExpo's audited attendance total for the 2005 edition at the Javits came to 28,953. But attendance was just 21,028 in 2010, followed by 20,430 in 2012 and 20,641 in 2013. These substantial long-term attendance declines for major Javits-based tradeshows reflect more than just short-term economic cycles or changes in a particular industry or sector. The attendance declines at the BookExpo, Gift Fairs, Toy Fair, and Hotel/Motel Show point to a far broader and more systematic change in the role and appeal of major trade events, particularly evident in New York City but probably at work in a host of other cities and convention centers. The Javits Convention Center has seen a marked decline in its business, not because events are leaving New York or migrating to Las Vegas (it hosted 78 events in 1990 and the same number in 2006), but largely because the events that "built" the Javits have themselves seen a dramatic change in role and relevance.

Just as the major trade events that dominate the Javits' calendar have changed, it is increasingly obvious that they are serving a different attendee population from what has often been assumed. Simply put, the reason the Javits could both host a million or more attendees yet produce a far smaller (circa 660,000) number of hotel room nights is that the majority of attendees at these large tradeshows come from the New York metropolitan area and its immediate environs.

Recent attendance audit reports for some events, produced by independent third-party firms, provide data not only on the number of attendees, but also on where they live. Take the case of the publishing industry's BookExpo, held at the Javits Center in 2007. Over 5,000 of the 15,634 meeting attendees came from New York State. Nearby New Jersey, Pennsylvania, and Connecticut added another 2,758—51 percent of the total attendance. The 2011 BookExpo saw 55 percent of its attendance from New York, New Jersey, Connecticut, and Pennsylvania. For the 2008 InterOp mobile business show, New York attendees made up 42 percent, and nearby states brought the total to 69 percent. And for the 2008 International Restaurant and Food Service Show, residents of New York and nearby states made up 92 percent of the 13,203 attendees.

A very large fraction of the attendees from New York, New Jersey, and nearby states are day-trippers. That phenomenon is especially pronounced when an industry—toys, publishing, advertising—is headquartered in Manhattan and its employees live in commuting distance.

The results in terms of out-of-town attendance are indicated in the most recent economic impact analysis of the Javits Center by PriceWaterhouse-Coopers, covering 2009. The center accommodated 66 convention and tradeshow events that year, bringing 633,600 attendees. But PWC classified just 275,000 attendees as "overnighters"—less than half the total. The remainder were termed "day-trippers" or "other local attendance," presumably primarily from the New York metropolitan area.[75]

For years, the Javits Convention Center succeeded because it served events and industries that were centered in or oriented to the New York region. But those events, much like the industries and activities they served and supported, have changed dramatically. Even at its peak in the late 1980s, the Javits Center was a New York-serving facility, not a center that drew the large volumes of distant visitors editorial writers and consultants had invariably assumed. Perhaps the most direct and telling commentary on the Javits success in generating overnight visitor activity can be found on the ground, in the center's immediate environs. Within a couple of blocks, there is still just one hotel near the Javits, a quite modest 83-room Best Western. The large hotels that have developed near other major centers have simply not appeared by the Javits Center. The big convention-oriented hotels in Manhattan are clustered around Times Square and in midtown, near shops, restaurants, entertainment, and office concentrations. And recent efforts by the city and state to promote a large, new adjacent "headquarters hotel" have not succeeded.

Orlando/Orange County

Supported by the stream of revenues from a countywide tax on hotel rooms filled by its theme park visitors, Orange County has been able to expand its convention center over and over. In 1997, county officials turned to Jeff Sachs of Ernst & Young to assess the county's future as a convention locale and to plan its future expansions.

Sachs delivered his "Long Range Strategic Plan" in late 1997, providing an answer to the question posed by county leaders, "What is the next step?" He and his colleagues mapped out a broad assessment of trends in technology, society, and business that would affect travel and meeting activity into the future, concluding, "More demand for meetings worldwide," and "Businesses should thrive. . . . And it is business that creates demand for conventions and trade shows."[76]

The Ernst & Young report described Orlando as an "Up and Comer in Hosting the Large Events" and added that "large shows"—the ones the Orange County Convention Center sought to lure—"are likely to experience the highest growth as they fold in smaller shows and learn through experience how to grow their shows." And although Ernst & Young saw new convention centers and more exhibit space coming, they concluded that these developments simply sufficed to "meet the pressures of demand by adding more space." As for Orange County, its only competition would be the "top cities." Indeed, "These top destinations should have full buildings for the foreseeable future."[77]

After describing the competitive advantages and expansion plans of a number of cities, the Ernst & Young analysis focused on two: Chicago and Las Vegas. Both were then expanding their centers to attract "medium-sized events." And for Sachs and his colleagues, "*Orlando is the only other destination that can compete on this level—these three cities have what it takes to pull away from the pack.*"[78]

There were issues Orange County had to address in serving the convention market. Meeting planners wanted large hotels adjacent to the center. And in leisure travel-oriented Orlando, local hotels were often not very interested in convention business. Indeed, the Ernst & Young report noted, "the OCCC generates approximately 5 to 10% of the hotel room nights in Orange County." There was also the issue of transportation, most notably the traffic in spread-out Orlando. But the report argued that these issues could be resolved by systematic planning for a major convention district—"a dense and cohesive, pedestrian-friendly environment."

The centerpiece of the "OCCC 2025" envisioned in the report would be a very much larger convention center. Ernst & Young told county officials they "should master plan for a total of three million square feet of prime exhibit space (the existing OCCC with two million additional) over the next 30 years . . . brought on line over three phases as demand dictates."

Sachs and the Ernst & Young group moved ahead with detailed planning for possible sites and financing in early 1998 and delivered a "Volume II" report to the county in June 1998. They reiterated the potential for the Orange County Center to "maintain a leadership position in the industry" with the addition of two million square feet of exhibit space "over the next two to three decades." But the Ernst & Young report stressed the need for the county to decide about at least the first phase of expansion quickly—"The sooner the project opens, the sooner the County reaps the economic benefits."[79]

The final part of the Ernst & Young analysis focused on a cost-benefit assessment. The authors were clear about the present—"The operation of the OCCC has a significant impact on Orange County and the State of Florida in terms of spending, employment, and tax revenue generation." They reported that the center was attracting convention and tradeshow delegates from around the nation and the world, and had hosted 250 events, generating 4.2 million attendee days and over three million hotel room nights in 1997, with a total direct spending impact of $1.05 billion.

The report then forecast the economic benefits from a "clean site" expansion (as actually occurred) with a first phase of 680,000 square feet, or about a 66 percent increase. Attendee days would increase by 2.6 million—a 62 percent increase—and annual hotel room nights would grow by 1.9 million—a 63 percent increase. Direct spending would also grow proportionately, by $646 million, boosting private development around the convention center and providing the county with an 11 percent return on its investment.

Orange County ultimately went beyond the Ernst & Young recommendation, adding some 950,000 square feet in an expansion that opened in September 2003. Based on the forecasts in the 1998 report, the expanded center should have boosted convention and tradeshow attendance by almost 100 percent, with comparable increases in hotel use and spending.

The Ernst & Young analysis was not entirely accurate in how it described the center's performance in the late 1990s, before expansion. Where the report cited 250 *events* in 1997, only 121 of those were actually conventions and tradeshows, with a total of 760,000 attendees. The 1997 performance was not entirely representative, as the previous year had seen 848,911 attendees, and the attendance total would actually hit a peak of 921,247 in 2000, before the expanded facility opened. The convention attendance from 1996 through 2000 thus averaged about 852,000. Had convention attendance followed the Ernst & Young forecasts, the total should have roughly doubled, to almost 1.7 million convention attendees. Unfortunately, it didn't work out as Ernst & Young had forecast and the county government had planned.

Following the expansion, the Orange County Convention Center garnered 1,060,960 attendees in 2004, and reached 1,089,844 in 2007. Those were real increases from the 852,000 average of the last half of the 1990s and the peak of 921,247. But even the 2007 figure represented just an 18.3 percent increase from the 2000 peak—far, far below 1.7 million anticipated based on the Ernst & Young analysis. And even Orlando was not immune to the impact of the larger national and global economy, with convention attendance dropping to 993,998 in 2008, and 781,740 for 2009. The 2009 attendance figure effectively put the Orange County Convention Center back to where its attendance had been in 1997 and 1998—when the center had half the space it now has.

The Orange County Center did gain back some of the ground it lost from the recession, reaching attendance of 912,235 in 2010, 1,004,128 in 2011, and 1,079,883 in 2012. But that rebound still put the center's attendance not much greater than what the smaller center had seen in 2000.

Even more striking than the modest return on a massive expansion has been the center's capacity to produce overnight hotel stays. The Ernst & Young study had pegged the center as producing over three million hotel room nights in 1997. In recent years, the Orlando CVB has regularly produced a "Convention Center Housing Summary" for its members, listing individual events and their estimated attendance and requested hotel room nights. For 2009, the summary compiled in July 2009 estimated total attendance for the year at 872,163, slightly higher than actual. But those estimated 872,000 attendees were shown as "requesting" just 992,099 hotel room nights—a ratio of nights to attendees of 1.14. That ratio is in line with most other major centers. But it represents a fraction of the three million described by Ernst & Young.[80]

The June 2010 housing summary showed 91 convention and tradeshow events with 926,490 attendees for 2010, compared to an actual 912,000. But the estimated 926,000 attendees were shown as requesting 1.19 million room nights. That was a slightly better room night ratio—1.29—but it still meant that the Orange County Convention Center attendees weren't staying in area hotels two, or three, or four nights each. And they certainly were not yielding the more than 4.9 million hotel room nights promised by Jeff Sachs and his Ernst & Young colleagues in 1998.[81]

For all the obvious advantages of Orlando and Orange County as a meeting destination—winter weather, abundant hotels, excellent air service, a remarkable collection of visitor attractions, and a vast convention center—the payoff from doubling the center's exhibit space at a cost of $750 million proved remarkably modest. The approximately 1.1 million convention attendees the center attracted in its recent peak years can be contrasted with the 45.5 million total visitors to Orange County in 2008, and the 10.2 million business visitors that year.

The public investment in building, subsidizing, and marketing the two million square foot center has not yielded the county a great deal in terms of attendees and visitors in recent years, and the course of its future performance remains open to serious question. In retrospect, Jeff Sachs's 1997 assessment of the state and future of the convention business, one he would repeat word for word through 2001 in studies for Albany, New York; Schaumburg, Illinois; and Wilmington, North Carolina, among other clients, appears rather ill-founded: "In summary, the industry is healthy and growing, and is expected to continue to grow for at least a decade. No real threats appear to be on the horizon."[82]

Portland

The new Oregon Convention Center opened in 1990 with 150,000 square feet of exhibit space. The center was the centerpiece of an effort by the city and the Portland Development Commission to renew and upgrade the Lloyd District, on the east side of the Willamette River across from the city's downtown core. Other public investments in the area, including the new MAX light rail line and the Rose Garden arena, were intended to spur new private development and investment.

Planning and analysis for the new convention center had begun in the 1970s, with a market study by Gladstone Associates completed in June 1978, followed by a site analysis by Skidmore, Owings and Merrill and a financial and economic impact report by Gladstone, both finished in November 1978. Gladstone stated their conclusion quite directly—"A convention center could be a significant stimulant to economic, urban and job development in

Portland." The consultants termed a new center "a significant new 'basic industry' for Portland," and recommended that the city move ahead with a new facility offering at least 100,000 square feet of exhibit space.[83]

The 1978 Gladstone report set out a series of alternative development possibilities for the planned center, ranging in size from 75,000 to 125,000 square feet. For a center with 100,000 square feet of exhibit space, Gladstone forecast that "Twenty new events would likely result in an additional 80,000 delegates to the city annually . . . . Many of these would stay overnight in the city, adding nearly 140,000 additional 'delegate nights' in city hotels." For a larger 125,000 square foot venue, Gladstone projected 100,000 new delegates. The city ultimately built the new Oregon Convention Center with a total of 150,000 square feet of exhibit space. Based on the Gladstone forecasts, the larger facility would be expected to draw 120,000 new convention delegates. At the same ratio of room nights to delegates as the somewhat smaller facility, that would produce 210,000 annual room nights.[84]

City officials had long assumed that the stream of visitors and event attendees at the new convention center would support a host of new developments—hotels, restaurants, retail shops—on the largely underdeveloped blocks surrounding the center. But in the years after the center's 1990 opening, very little new development had actually occurred. City officials had planned for at least one new headquarters hotel on the blocks adjacent to the convention center. But while downtown Portland saw a spate of new hotel developments in the 1990s, no developer appeared particularly interested in a large Eastside/Lloyd District hotel.[85]

The failure of that anticipated development to materialize partly reflected the choice of site, one which Gladstone had specifically recommended against in 1978 as too far from the downtown core. It also reflected the failure of the center to generate the business that Gladstone Associates had forecast. Where the Gladstone analysis yielded a projection that a 150,000 square foot center would produce 210,000 room nights a year, the actual performance of the center averaged just 134,956 room nights over the 1993 to 1999 period.[86]

The first public calls for an expansion of the convention center came in early 1995, with Patrick LaCrosse of the Metropolitan Exposition-Recreation Commission contending the center was effectively full: "We are at the point where we're starting to turn away business." Convention center director Jeff Blosser repeated the call for more space in early 1997, arguing the center "is essentially running at capacity" and calling for an increase to 250,000 square feet. In February 1998, Portland's Metro government, owner of the center, approved a ballot measure for an $82 million bond issue to expand the center. Although there was no reference to a formal feasibility study, project backers argued that conventions were being turned away, and that an expansion would allow for larger conventions, or for multiple smaller events.[87]

Portland area voters apparently were not particularly moved by the arguments for a larger convention center and promises of more jobs and spending. The bond proposal was overwhelmingly defeated in November 1998. City and Metro officials then succeeded in gaining the backing of local hotel interests for an increase in the hotel tax, and added an increased tax on car rentals. With these revenue streams committed, it was possible to finance and build an expansion without voter approval, increasing the center's exhibit space from 150,000 to 255,000 square feet.[88]

With construction of the expansion under way, the Portland Development Commission and the convention center commissioned a formal analysis of the potential for a convention center hotel from Economics Research Associates (ERA). The January 2001 ERA analysis went into some detail on the center's historic performance, noting that from 1993 to 1999 it had drawn an average of 135,000 annual hotel room nights. The expansion would, however, provide a significant boost in the center's performance, more than doubling annual room nights, in ERA's forecast, to between 280,000 and 290,000.[89] They were wrong.

The expansion was completed in April 2003. The Development Commission and the area convention and visitors bureau continued to fund a series of studies and initiatives aimed at producing an adjacent headquarters hotel. One of these studies, completed by the PKF consulting firm in May 2006, included specific data on the center's annual room night generation. In 2003, the year the expansion opened, the Oregon Convention Center generated 139,527 room nights—slightly above the 135,000 average of the late 1990s. But rather than growing, room night activity slipped to 104,097 in 2004 and 118,076 for 2005. Instead of a substantial increase, the larger center was performing decidedly worse than years earlier.[90]

The convention center's declining performance is equally evident with data on annual convention and tradeshow attendance. Center attendance was 248,359 in 1998 and 286,410 in 1999. With the expansion in 2003, convention and tradeshow attendance came to 249,357. Yet that total dropped to 215,060 for 2005 and 161,791 for 2006. The center then shifted its reporting to a fiscal year, with convention and tradeshow attendance total reported as 171,154 in fiscal 2008, and 176,016 in 2010. For fiscal 2011, attendance fell even more, to 126,853—less than half the center's pre-expansion business in 1999.[91]

Through the 1990s, the Oregon Convention Center failed to reach the level of room night activity projected by Gladstone Associates. An expansion that substantially increased its size failed to yield any new business. Indeed, the 118,000 room nights the center produced in 2005 were just about half of what Gladstone had projected 27 years before. And in comparison to the 1.52 million room nights actually used in Portland in 2005, the convention center's production amounted to just 7.8 percent.

Portland city and Metro government officials regularly contended that the failure of the center to produce new private development or increased convention activity after the expansion was due solely to the lack of a sufficiently large headquarters hotel adjacent to the center. The Portland Development Commission, the city's urban renewal agency, sought to lure a private hotel developer, but ultimately failed. The city and the Metro government then floated a scheme for a publicly financed and owned headquarters hotel. But in the face of concerted opposition from Portland hotel owners and the unwillingness of elected officials to bear the risk of supporting a public hotel development with tax dollars, the public hotel scheme was abandoned in September 2009. But a new effort for a privately financed but publicly subsidized hotel rose again, in late 2012, endorsed by a market study from the Strategic Advisory Group, the same firm that had produced studies for Portland in 2003 and 2007, with the promise that it would boost the convention center's lagging business.[92]

San Antonio

The expanded Henry B. Gonzalez Convention Center opened in June 2001, providing San Antonio with 440,000 square feet of exhibit hall space. The process of implementing, financing, and building the expansion had stretched out over more than a decade, beginning with a market and feasibility study commissioned by the city in 1990.

The November 1990 "Expansion Feasibility Analysis" prepared by Arthur Andersen & Company examined the history of previous convention center additions, the center's performance, and the nature of the national demand for convention center space. A January 1987 expansion had boosted the center from 111,000 square feet to 240,000, yet by 1990 Arthur Andersen could describe it as "effectively operating at near full capacity." For 1989, the center hosted 76 convention events and a total of 336,966 attendees. Over the 1987 to 1990 period, it averaged 251,000 delegates a year. The study also estimated the performance of the center in terms of hotel room nights, estimating that downtown hotels "will have accommodated approximately 361,200 room nights of demand directly related to convention activity at the HBG Center."[93]

The Arthur Andersen analysts then sought to forecast the performance of an expanded center, focusing on the growth in national demand and the overall number of convention attendees. They first projected the 1989 total for the center, 336,966 convention delegates, at annual growth rates of 4, 7, and 10 percent. They concluded that the "number of potential delegates that may attend the HBG center by 2000 could range between 500,000 and 874,000," with 660,000 a "reasonable solution." The firm then used an alternative model in which attendance declined while expansion construction was underway, and then increased following completion. This second approach yielded a total attendance for 2000 of 586,000. Based on those projections, the report called for an expansion of between 176,000 and 230,000 square feet, bringing the center to about 440,000 square feet of exhibit space. The firm's final conclusion was that "historic market trends, current market conditions, and the ability of the City to attract future tourism and convention business warrant expansion of the HBG Center."[94]

Arthur Andersen followed the November 1990 report with a second, in December 1991, outlining the economic impact of an expansion and financing alternatives. For the same expansion described a year earlier, Andersen now forecast projected annual convention attendance at 728,000. They then added another 108,000 annual spouses or companions, based on assumptions from the San Antonio Convention and Visitors Bureau. Finally, based on local surveys, they estimated that each attendee generated 2.1 hotel room nights. Multiplied out, those assumptions yielded some $594 million in new direct attendee (plus spouse) spending each year. And with over 286,000 *new* convention delegates would come increased hotel demand—an added 601,230 annual room nights, bringing the center to over 900,000 annual room nights.[95]

Arthur Andersen's final conclusion, one the report labeled "conservative," was that "expansion of the HBGCC facility would bring $18.4 billion in new economic activity and 5,960 new jobs to the San Antonio area over the period 1994-2016." That impact would in turn yield the city government millions in additional tax revenues. And once again using the language "particularly conservative," the report also argued that new convention business would actually sustain "twice the justified number of [hotel] rooms" added to the local market, with an "actual increase in hotel employment . . . twice as large as this analysis estimates."[96]

The expansion did not move ahead immediately, as city officials had to seek state legislative approval for increasing the city's hotel tax rate. There was also division within the downtown business community, as some favored a new stand-alone center on a different site rather than an expansion of the existing center. Debate over the expansion plans continued into 1994, when Mayor Howard Peak invited a panel of experts from the Urban Land Institute to assess the convention center expansion and related development issues. The ULI panel, a group that included PriceWaterhouse consultant David Petersen, noted the city's "several competitive advantages in attracting convention business," but stressed that the city needed a larger facility in order "to continue to compete effectively in the convention market, retain its enviable convention market share, maximize the potential of the convention visitors market and maintain its strong economic base." If there was to be more space, it had to be "fully contiguous with the current facility." And the panel emphasized the importance of the expansion to the city's future, with the conclusion "that a strong, economically sound convention and tourism market is critical to the overall success of the San Antonio economy."[97]

The 2001 expansion should have propelled the city to a new level of convention performance. But a new consultant study of a potential expansion told a very different story. The CSL International consulting firm delivered a report in July 2008 on the feasibility of a further expansion. That report noted the center's high occupancy, concluding, "The relatively high occupancy levels experienced in recent years may be an indication that the HBGCC is turning away significant business." And a CSL survey of meeting event planners ranked the city on a par with Las Vegas and San Diego—"These survey results begin to demonstrate the status of San Antonio as an emerging Tier 1 destination."[98]

The report's figures on convention and tradeshow attendance suggested a somewhat more nuanced conclusion. Although attendance fluctuated from year to year, from 2002 through 2006 attendance averaged 278,234. Ignoring a lower total for 2007 which the report said reflected inadequate data, convention attendance for 2008 came to about 310,000, followed by 250,000 in 2009. A 2012 report by HVS put "convention center demand," a more broadly defined measure, with attendance at 277,022 in 2009, 341,392 in 2010, and 273,284 in 2011.[99]

Recall that for the three complete years covered in the Arthur Andersen report, 1987 through 1990, convention and tradeshow attendance averaged 251,000, with 337,000 in 1989. Even the more broadly defined attendance figures from HVS were only modestly above the late 1980s level. The center's performance post-2001 expansion was thus about the same as it had managed some twenty years earlier, at half its current size.

The numbers on hotel room night generation tell much the same story. In 1990, Arthur Andersen had counted a total of 361,200 room nights. In 2008, CSL reported that the center's room night bookings over the period from 2001 through 2010 averaged out to 290,000. HVS reported 370,000 in 2010 and 310,000 in 2011.

Arthur Andersen had forecast that an expanded center would see annual convention and tradeshow attendance of more than 700,000, with total hotel room nights on the order of 800,000 to 900,000. The actual performance amounted to less than half the predicted totals. Indeed, the center has been doing effectively the same business circa 2008 and 2010 as it had years before.

The failure of the 2001 expansion to yield anything close to the promised increase in convention business did not deter San Antonio leaders from seeking to boost the city's convention activity through more public investment. In May 2005 the city sold $205 million in federal empowerment zone bonds to finance the construction of a thousand-room headquarters hotel adjacent to the center, backing those with a combination of direct hotel revenues and citywide hotel occupancy taxes. Then, in 2008 and 2010, the city turned to CSL and John Kaatz for feasibility analyses of a potential expansion. Buffeted by a sharp downturn in hotel tax revenues in fiscal 2009 and 2010, the city restructured the expansion planning, proposing instead to reconfigure the center by demolishing its oldest wing and replacing it with a new addition to the east, without adding a significant volume of new exhibit hall space.

In late 2011, Kaatz and his CSL colleagues concluded a detailed assessment of San Antonio's convention and tourism business in their "Destination SA" report. They noted the city's success as a convention destination, due to the "concentration of convention center, hotels, and entertainment in one area," as well as the city's walkability. But they also stressed that the city could not afford to stand still: "Destinations including Dallas, Phoenix, Oklahoma City, Indianapolis, Chicago, New Orleans and others are investing in convention and visitor industry product. Over time, with no investment in the San Antonio visitor product, new visitor levels and repeat visitation will decrease."[100] Of course, Kaatz and CSL had also previously advised Oklahoma

City and New Orleans, as well as Boston, Philadelphia, and Miami Beach, that they too needed to invest in new, improved, or expanded convention facilities to improve their "visitor product."

San Francisco

San Francisco's Moscone Convention Center opened in December 1981 with a 270,000 square foot exhibit hall, as the centerpiece of the city's Yerba Buena urban renewal project. Just over a decade later, in May 1992, the Moscone Center North expansion opened, boosting the center to 442,000 square feet of exhibit space, with the expectation it would secure the city's place in the convention market.[101]

The next year, in July 1993, with the city's hotel business "booming," San Francisco's chief administrative officer proposed funding a consultant study of the need for more space and potential sites. The study, completed by Economic Research Associates in September 1994, supported the idea of expanding the Moscone Center with the addition of up to 250,000 square feet of exhibit space, arguing, "the market will still respond positively to additional facilities in San Francisco." But the ERA analysts were relatively conservative in assessing the state of the convention business, arguing, "while the major meeting industry as a whole has been fairly flat, the largest trade shows have shown consistent growth." The report estimated the performance of the existing center at 690,000 annual room nights based on national data—a total that did not fully account for the results of the expansion completed in mid-1992. In actuality, the San Francisco Convention and Visitors Bureau put the 1994 room night performance at 769,000.[102]

The ERA consultants forecast that an expanded Moscone would increase its volume of events, and generate an additional 270,000 room nights each year. From the estimated baseline of 690,000 the consultants reported, that would put the expanded Moscone at 960,000 annual room nights. From the higher 1994 benchmark, it would yield 1,039,000 room nights.

The ERA report also laid out an alternative view, assuming San Francisco was an "extremely attractive" destination and outdrawing other destinations. That alternative put the estimated baseline for room night activity at 869,500, and pegged the gain from expansion at an added 337,500 room nights. Based on the center's actual 1994 performance, that meant an expanded Moscone would see some 1.2 million room nights each year.

The *San Francisco Chronicle* heralded the findings of the study with an article that began, "If we build it, they will come," and quoted John Marks, president of the San Francisco Convention and Visitors Bureau estimating that an expansion would bring 450,000 more people a year, and an added $135 million in spending.[103]

With the endorsement and forecasts of the ERA study, San Francisco city officials moved ahead on a plan to add 300,000 square feet in a new stand-alone building, Moscone West, with a final construction price tag of $187 million. The proposal to issue $157.5 million in bonds to pay for the new facility, with an increase in the local hotel tax, was on the ballot in March 1996, enthusiastically endorsed by the *Chronicle* with the headline "Expanded Moscone Would Enrich S.F." The editorial promised thousands of new permanent jobs. And while recognizing the growing competition for conventions, it argued, "Meanwhile, Moscone Center is booked through the turn of the century and is being forced to turn away business for lack of space—resulting in about $871 million a year in convention business being diverted to other cities." With Mayor Willie Brown terming it a "referendum on Willie," the voters provided a 66.4 percent "yes" vote for the bond issue.[104]

The passage of a statewide tax limitation measure in November 1996 necessitated a second referendum on the hotel tax increase, on the ballot in November 1998. The second vote was overwhelmingly positive as well, with "yes" ballots from 84 percent of the voters.

The official statement for the city's 1998 hotel tax revenue bonds contained an analysis of future hotel tax revenues by PKF Consulting that provides a formal benchmark for assessing the Moscone's pre-expansion performance. PKF put the center's room night activity at "approximately 769,000 in 1994," increasing to "approximately 843,000 room nights estimated in 1997." The PKF analysis concluded, "Essentially, the convention center is running at capacity at approximately 825,000 room nights generated annually and only minor fluctuations are expected from year-to-year until the new expansion is completed by the beginning of 2003."[105]

Moscone Center's own annual reports also provide a set of performance measures prior to the completion of the new West Building expansion. During the period PKF described, the center averaged 662,716 annual convention and tradeshow attendees, with a peak of 705,358 in fiscal year 1997. For a somewhat later period prior to the completion of the new West facility, from fiscal year 1996 through 2001, the center averaged just over 694,000 convention and tradeshow attendees. Moscone Center's own annual reports contain data on hotel room night generation for a limited period in the 1990s. From the 1996 fiscal year through 2001, the center averaged 819,833 hotel room nights annually. The gain from the expanded space at the new West Building, based on the ERA forecast, should thus have increased the total room nights produced by the Moscone complex to at least 1.1 million each year.

The Moscone West venue opened in June 2003 in time to host a major convention of Meeting Professionals International. John Marks, head of the San Francisco Convention and Visitors Bureau, told the *Chronicle*, "in the next couple of years we should approach 1 million room nights a year generated as a result of our convention facilities . . . .That's huge."[106]

The Moscone Center's annual reports contain detailed data on hall occupancy, events, and attendance. But the attendance at the original Moscone North and South facility and the new West Building are counted separately. For large events like the Pacific Coast Builders Conference and Semicon that use the entire facility, that means attendees are double-counted. It is, however, easy to track the attendance of the pre-expansion North/South facility over time. While the original Moscone Center averaged 694,000 convention and tradeshow attendees during the late 1990s, the figure began to slide after the expansion, to 540,660 in fiscal 2004 and 482,035 the next year. There was a modest jump in fiscal 2008, to 588,735—still well below the 1990s average. The economic distress of the following year dropped attendance to just 458,968 for fiscal 2009. The convention and tradeshow attendance came to 436,595 in fiscal 2010, and 416,495 in 2011—Moscone's lowest attendance count since 1992.[107]

The expectation for the new building, on the part of everyone from ERA and PKF to Mayor Willie Brown and John Marks, was that the city would see a substantial gain in overnight hotel stays, to a million room nights and more. That didn't happen either. In its first full year of operation, the expanded Moscone Center attracted events producing 848,874 hotel room nights. The 2005 figure was down, to 780,859. The larger Moscone did manage to generate 992,843 room nights in 2008, according to the San Francisco CVB, but that represented its post-expansion peak to date. From 2004 through 2007, the center averaged 807,507 room nights. Extending the period to 2004 through 2009, the annual average came to 846,145. The most recent figure reported by PKF, for 2010, was 778,004.[108]

The performance of Moscone after the opening of the new West building can be compared to the 825,000 room night figure noted by the 1998 PKF study, or the average of 820,000 based on the center's reports for the late 1990s. The major expansion produced no real increase in room night generation. Even the 2008 peak year performance of almost 993,000 room nights can be compared to pre-expansion totals of 955,000 in fiscal 1999 and 962,000 in 2001.

San Francisco has long been described as a prime visitor and convention destination, with its strong array of hotels and amenities. It also has substantial appeal to two important sectors, medical and technology, that should have provided a boost in attendance and room night demand in the years after 2003. Yet in the larger context of overall hotel demand, the contribution of the Moscone has been relatively modest. In 2007, the city's total occupied room nights came to 9,332,443. The 755,898 room nights counted for the Moscone thus amounted to just 8 percent of total demand. The roughly 844,000 room nights produced by the center in 2006 constituted 9.2 percent of the occupied room night total that year.

The relatively modest recent performance of Moscone Center—and the lack of any sustained growth in the wake of the expansion—did not lead to any serious public discussion about the place and prospects of the city's convention business. Instead, decrying the age and physical deficiencies of the complex, the CVB promoted an increase in the city hotel tax in a special "tourism improvement district" that could be used for both Moscone improvements and a more expansive marketing campaign. The new improvement district, and its higher hotel taxes, were adopted in December 2008 and expected to produce some $27 million the first year.

Yet even as the San Francisco CVB ramped up its marketing efforts, its head was making the case for even more exhibit space. Convention bureau president Joe D'Alessandro argued that the center was losing prime business due to its size, and that a contiguous underground expansion of the original facility would redeem the city's competitive position. D'Alessandro told the *San Francisco Business Times* in March 2010, "Long term, conventions have always been a growing industry . . . . Since Moscone was first built, and after it expanded twice, it has again outgrown its space. . . . Since tourism is San Francisco's No. 1 industry, we have to find a way to keep up."[109]

D'Alessandro and the city's visitor industry interests apparently succeeded in persuading one San Francisco elected official. In June 2012, Mayor Ed Lee announced the start of development on a 25-year expansion plan for Moscone, arguing, "Tourism is our City's number one industry and bringing Moscone into the 21st Century will boost our City's economy." Lee was joined by Joe

D'Alessandro, who added, "Other competing cities have either recently expanded their convention centers or are planning expansions. We can't sit back and let other cities around the world take our business away."[110]

Washington, D.C.

The Washington Convention Center opened in January 1983, with 380,000 square feet of exhibit hall space. The "new" Washington Convention Center (since renamed for former Mayor Walter Washington) opened in April 2003, with an $850 million price tag and 703,000 square feet of exhibit space. The old center was demolished in December 2004.

The relatively brief life of the "old" Washington Convention Center neatly illustrates the constant quest for bigger centers, with more space intended to yield more business, that typifies cities. The effort to develop a true public convention center for the nation's capital dated back to the 1950s, and became a more pressing issue for the city's business leaders during the 1960s, as retail activity left the traditional downtown core, most notably in the aftermath of the 1968 riots. The development of a center was justified by a number of consultant studies, including a penultimate analysis by Gladstone Associates in 1977 that forecast the center would attract an average of 305,000 annual convention attendees who would stay for an average of 4.4 days.

Just four years after the "old" center opened, calls for a new, larger facility began. The argument was that the center was so successful it was running out of space. District government officials cited the impact of the center in promoting development of new hotels and in attracting some 286,840 out-of-town attendees in 1996. But if the center was full in terms of space, the convention attendees it was attracting did not appear to be staying over four nights each.[111]

In 1988, when the center housed more than 330,000 attendees at 23 conventions and tradeshows, the center produced just 311,825 hotel room nights. Two years later, the *Washington Post* reported a total of 29 conventions with 498,830 out-of-town attendees for 1989, and the Washington Convention and Visitors Association totaled 316,540 room nights. And in 1990, 33 convention and tradeshow events brought 333,915 attendees and 355,511 hotel room nights. From 1988 through 1993, the center room night generation averaged 375,657, although it began to slip somewhat in 1994 and 1995.[112]

Even as the Washington Convention Center was producing far less hotel demand than forecast, the calls for a larger new center began. Four years after the center's opening, an article in the *Washington Post*, headlined "Center Needs Room to Grow," reported that consulting firm GA/Partners had prepared a presentation on a possible site for a new facility. It went on to quote Luther Hodges, chairman of the National Bank of Washington and a member of the center's board: "Our principal industry is tourism, and the best thing we can do for city employment is to continue to promote that. It is logical we should have the best convention center in the country."[113]

The move for an entirely new and far larger center gained momentum in late 1988, with a proposal from the Washington Convention and Visitors Association for a new hall with at least 750,000 square feet of exhibit space—double the existing center's size—on a site just a block or two north. Dubbed by *Post* columnist Rudolph Pyatt a "trial balloon," the visitors group plan was justified as needed to keep Washington among the front rank of convention destinations, and with the promise that a larger facility would "double or triple" convention activity by bringing in larger groups.[114]

By 1992, the local political environment was sufficiently favorable that the Washington Hotel Association and the Visitors Association commissioned a formal consultant study on the need for a new center and the suitability of the nearby site, which had originally been cleared for the University of the District of Columbia. The report that arrived in April 1993 from consultants Deloitte & Touche argued there was a need for a larger center, as the overall convention industry had grown since 1983, and the largest shows (represented by the Tradeshow Week "200") had grown over 30 percent between 1985 and 1991. Saying, "the District has lost its competitive position vis-à-vis other convention cities," the Deloitte report called for a new center with 750,000 to one million square feet of exhibit space, that would in turn "produce more than twice the economic output of the current center." The Deloitte consultants forecast that the larger facility would boost the number of national and international events from the 33 of fiscal year 1992 to 48 a year, and that convention visitor spending would more than double, presumably as the direct product of a roughly doubled count of convention and tradeshow attendees.[115]

The District government moved ahead through the mid-1990s to arrange financing for the proposed center, creating a new convention center authority and refining the size and design of the building. The city and the new Convention Center Authority (created in 1994) also sought to refine the potential economic impact and fiscal benefits from the facility, and commissioned another formal consultant study in 1997.

The assessment, delivered by Coopers & Lybrand in December 1997, focused on a center with 730,000 square feet of exhibit space, somewhat smaller than the one described by Deloitte in 1993. The Coopers analysts also predicted 48 annual convention events, but a more modest growth of new visitor spending, about 72 percent more than the existing center. The report stressed that the center would enable the city not only "to host larger conventions and trade shows, but simultaneous events as well, thereby allowing Washington to realize its market demand potential." And its ultimate benefits would include "enhanced economic growth and ancillary private development spurred by the operations and activities associated with the proposed convention center."[116]

The 1997 Coopers report did not contain any data, either historical or forecast, on convention center attendance. But an appendix on the Washington hotel market did contain historical data on convention center bookings and room nights, including the fact that the center had drawn 284,376 room nights in 1997. The Coopers consultants then argued, "the proposed convention center is estimated to generate approximately 176,000 incremental room nights in the first full year of operation, increasing to over 200,000 room nights in future years." That addition of 200,000 room nights would amount to a 70 percent increase from the 1997 figure—fully in keeping with the firm's forecast of about a 72 percent increase in visitor spending.[117]

The Washington Convention Center Authority began construction on the new center in October 1998. In late 2002, months before the planned April 2003 opening, the authority commissioned a new consultant analysis, from the former Coopers & Lybrand analysts now at CSL International, focused on the center's likely operating performance. With substantial information on the bookings for the center's first years, the January 2003 CSL study was intended to provide guidance in estimating near-term costs and revenues. Its projections were now based on real data, and its figures were decidedly different from the earlier consultant work.

The CSL analysis, led by Bill Krueger, projected that the center would attract 39 annual conventions and tradeshows as a "base case" (with an "aggressive case" forecast of 44), compared to the 48 previously forecast. And with a smaller number of events would come an even smaller number of attendees. Coopers & Lybrand had pegged the level of new "direct spending" in the metropolitan Washington area from convention center attendees in 2006 at $630.4 million. The updated estimate from CSL for a comparable year, 2007, was now projected at just $328.4 million—a little better than half the previous estimate by the same consultants.[118]

Perhaps the most telling figures in the 2003 CSL report, buried on page 37, were the updated estimates of total hotel room nights. If the new center was to double the business of its predecessor, as Coopers & Lybrand had projected, it would have to generate total convention and tradeshow attendance on the order of 600,000 or more attendees a year. The *Washington Post* in May 1998 had cited a consultant estimate of 500,000 attendees. The 1997 Coopers spending estimates had assumed an average stay of three days or more. Those figures would have implied a total number of room nights on the order of 1.5 to almost two million.

Now, the CSL 2003 report put the projected room night total for 2004 at 664,914, growing consistently by 2007 to 761,907, with the same total room nights forecast each year out to 2013. With real information on future bookings, the future performance of the big new center appeared far more modest to CSL than the guesses of a few years earlier. The reality would be even more different.

In 2004, its first full year of operation, the new convention center generated 460,221 hotel room nights, according to DestinationDC, the city's convention and visitors organization. The following year, room night activity hit a total of 614,552—the center's peak year to date. But the room night total fell to 473,037 in 2006, and 433,427 in 2007. Overall from 2004 through 2009, the new Washington Convention Center averaged 478,904 room nights annually, based on data from DestinationDC. That figure represents a modest increase from what the far smaller old center yielded from 1988 through 1993, an average of 375,657 a year. But the new center's performance is well below the 760,000 forecast by CSL in 2003. And compared to the earlier Deloitte report that forecast a doubling of convention visitor activity, or the 2007 Coopers & Lybrand report that predicted growth of more than 70 percent, the 479,000 annual room night performance is well below the circa 650,000 to 750,000 that should have occurred.[119]

The 479,000 hotel room night average represented something of a high water mark. For fiscal year 2008, the center reported 352,776 attendees at conventions, tradeshows, and corporate events, for a total of 376,296 hotel room nights. Those figures fell to 331,766 attendees and 280,478 room nights in fiscal 2009. And for fiscal year 2010, the Washington Convention Center hosted just 267,008 convention and tradeshow attendees, producing only 274,951 room nights. The room night total for fiscal 2011 came to 294,475, followed by 288,281 for fiscal 2012—well below the performance of the old center during the mid-1990s.[120]

The convention center's room night performance can also be assessed in the larger context of District of Columbia overall hotel demand. With over 27,000 hotel rooms in the city, total occupied room nights came to about 7.4 million in 2011. The convention center's 294,475 room nights that year thus amounted to about 4 percent of the District's recent hotel demand.

District government and Washington Convention Center Authority officials did not wait to assess the performance of the new center. In 2004, recognizing that the center was not performing as expected, they attributed its failings to the lack of a large, adjacent headquarters hotel, and commissioned yet another consultant study. Once again, they turned to CSL, headed by the former Coopers & Lybrand consultants.

The August 2004 CSL analysis focused on the capacity of the center to accommodate overlapping multiple events. The consulting firm called for the immediate addition of 75,000 square feet of meeting and ballroom space to handle those multiple events. But it went on to stress that the addition of 1,200 to 1,500 new hotel rooms "would offer significant market support for attracting large and overlapping multiple events." The CSL consultants forecast that a new 1,220-room hotel would produce an added 173,000 hotel room nights from the center each year. That new convention business would, according to CSL, boost the center's annual direct spending economic impact by $103.6 million from the current $432 million—24 percent. It would also position the center to consider an expansion, to accommodate "events that over time will outgrow the WCC inventory of space."[121]

The new convention center that was supposed to bring new private development and more hotel rooms had not done so. And in order to get those hotel rooms, the Convention Center Authority was finally obliged in late 2010 to commit $206 million in public funds toward the $516.2 million cost of the 1,180-room new Marriott hotel. The consultant study by HVS that accompanied the authority's bond issue now estimated that the new hotel would yield ("induce") 72,000 additional hotel room nights for the convention center—less than half of CSL's 2004 estimate. But as the count of convention and tradeshow attendees and their room nights fell from 2008 to 2009 and stayed down through 2012, it was unclear that the new hotel would be able even to help return the center's business to where it had been.[122]

And Beyond

The story of consultant misestimates and flawed forecasts, of new centers that see half the promised business (or less), of expansions that produce the same attendance or room nights as their smaller predecessors, is not limited to these larger centers in major cities. It is effectively the norm.

Anaheim, California, embarked on a major expansion of its convention center, completed at the end of 2000, supported by a 1995 report from Coopers & Lybrand. In 1996, the center drew 679,465 convention and tradeshow attendees. After expansion, it saw a peak of 666,796 attendees in 2001. Attendance fell to 583,197 in 2008, 513,314 in 2010, and then to 328,425 in 2012.

ERA forecast that an expanded Baltimore Convention Center would see annual convention attendance grow from 180,000 to 330,000. The Baltimore Convention Center Authority was more expansive, promising at least 452,000 annual attendees, up to as many as 565,000. After the 1997 expansion opened, Baltimore's convention attendance never came close to those estimates, hitting a peak of 286,784 in fiscal 2007 before dropping to 218,603 in 2010—less than in 1991.[123]

Charlotte built an entirely new center in 1995, justified by consultant studies from both Laventhol & Horwath and, later, KPMG consultants Charlie Johnson and Jeff Sachs. The 1991 KPMG economic impact analysis forecast that the center would produce 528,800 hotel room nights each year. When Sachs returned to Charlotte in 1997 to assess the center's actual performance, he put the actual room night generation for 1996 at just 170,300. He and consultant Tom Hazinski of C. H. Johnson Consulting recommended development of an adjacent headquarters hotel. Even with the addition of the new Charlotte Westin, the Charlotte Convention Center produced only 152,043 room nights in 2008, and 142,000 in fiscal 2011.[124]

Johnson did little better in forecasting the performance of a new center in St. Charles, Missouri, a St. Louis suburb. The C. H. Johnson firm produced a study of a proposed center in St. Charles in October 2003. Johnson put the annual room nights at 43,000 in 2008, rising to 50,100 by 2011, largely from new conventions and tradeshows, as well as some consumer shows. But the center's management, Global Spectrum, reported that 2008 room night generation came to just 19,904, with 2011's total at 20,064. Johnson was about half right.[125]

The new Pennsylvania Convention Center was justified in part by a 1988 PKF report that forecast a total of 346,000 convention attendees and 664,800 room nights by 2001. The center's best year in room night generation was 2002, with 573,875. But that was the unusual year. By 2007, the room night total was 336,000. And with the opening of its major expansion in early 2011, that year's total came to just 311,810—less than half the PKF forecast decades earlier.[126]

Seattle too undertook a major expansion of the Washington State Convention and Trade Center in 2001, with the endorsement of a December 1994 market and economic impact analysis from Coopers & Lybrand with the promise that more space would boost the annual convention event count from 37 to 64. In fiscal year 1997, before the expansion, the center hosted 183,875 out-of-state attendees. It post-expansion peak was 182,406 in fiscal 2007, a total that fell to 147,345 in fiscal 2011.[127]

Even Las Vegas, where the Las Vegas Convention Center had seen its attendance grow from 744,968 in 1990 to 1,267,482 in 2000, was not immune. Promoting a doubling of the center's space in July 1998, Manny Cortez, president of the Las Vegas Convention and Visitors Authority argued "We've got people standing in line. We just don't have the space." Three years later, just weeks before the opening of the expansion that would bring the center to almost two million square feet of exhibit space, CSL's John Kaatz said "You've got a lot of potential out there . . . big users . . . who want to come to Las Vegas but couldn't get Las Vegas into their rotation." In 2011, the expanded Las Vegas Convention Center accommodated 1,279,383 convention and tradeshow attendees, and then 1,212,038 in 2012—fewer than it had seen in 2000, at half the size.[128]

Missing Attendees, Missing Room Nights, Missing Impact, Missing Accountability

Over the last two or three decades, the pattern or "script" of local convention center development would play out in a remarkably similar, patterned fashion. A local business organization such as the chamber of commerce, or the city convention and visitors bureau, or on occasion a local elected official, would proclaim that the community was falling behind other cities in competing for convention business, that its facilities were outdated, that one or another group would no longer return.

One of the small group of convention center consultants—first Laventhol & Horwath or ERA in the 1980s, then PriceWaterhouse, Coopers & Lybrand, or KPMG in the 1990s, more recently C. H. Johnson, HVS, Strategic Advisory Group, PWC, or CSL—would be commissioned to produce a market and feasibility study. Those studies too followed a common pattern, with a description of the community and its economy, a broad assessment of the national and regional convention and tradeshow market and its future, and then a recommendation on the size, attributes, and on occasion siting of a new or expanded convention center.

Perhaps most important for local citizens and center promoters, there would be an "analysis" of future center performance and ultimately "economic impact," with the implicit promise that the public investment in more center space would bring a concrete, measurable, and predictable return in new direct spending by convention attendees. That projected spending, in turn, would be pumped into a regional economic model that would produce estimates of new job creation, indirect spending, and added local tax revenues. Almost invariably, the consultant would rely on the convention delegate spending and stay estimates produced by IACVB and its successor, the DMAI, with little or no alteration for local circumstances and realities.

With those concrete and highly specific estimates of new spending and employment, the consultant findings would be unveiled to the local media and public. As Phyllis Kaniss has described in the case of Philadelphia's new convention center, local journalists would respond to the announcements by local officials and claims of the consultant reports "unquestioningly . . . . No impartial sources were sought to verify the accuracy of the estimates." The result, as described by the editorial editor of the *Philadelphia Daily News*, was "They fooled me. . . . They made it an issue of civic need. We were too unsophisticated about our sources."[129]

That lack of questioning and absence of sophistication Kaniss observed in 1985 Philadelphia appeared just as evident in the media coverage of the 2005 center expansion effort. And it appears almost pervasive in local media coverage of convention center proposals, whether in San Diego or Cedar Rapids.

Yet for all the seeming "scientific" authority and substance of the consultant studies, for all the bulk of numbers and detailed forecasts, the work of the consultants is at best guess work, based on a set of assumptions—most notably those about growth in convention demand and the average length of stay by convention and tradeshow attendees and thus about average spending—that appear unjustifiable if not misleading.

In city after city, from Anaheim and Atlanta to Seattle and Washington,

D.C., the consultant forecasts simply are not realized, the actual center performance in terms of new convention and tradeshow attendees and hotel room nights often half or a third of what the consultants promised. Still, there is no real evidence such "errors" are recognized or acknowledged by the small group of convention center consultants, and employed either in a systematic record—a "scorecard"—of accuracy, or as a means of refining and improving their future forecasts.

That issue was addressed directly by long-time consultant Charlie Johnson, in his 2005 legal deposition in a case involving a proposed publicly financed hotel in Erie, Pennsylvania. The lawyer representing Erie hotel owners who were opposing the new hotel asked Johnson, "Do you have any system whereby you go back and gauge the accuracy of the projections that you make from time to time?"

Johnson replied, "Once the deal is done, if we're not engaged, we wish them good luck, give them our report, our final invoice, and wish them luck. . . . I am unaware of the specifics of any hotel deals after the fact. I have not gone back and analyzed them."[130]

Johnson was directly addressing the issue of convention center hotels. But his reply indicates that he and his firm made little or no systematic effort to assess the accuracy of his projections or the longer-term performance of the projects for which he conducted market and feasibility studies. There is certainly little evidence, from his forecasts of the performance of the expanded Cervantes Center and dome in St. Louis in the 1980s, through his work on McCormick Place expansion in 1990 and a new center in Charlotte a few years later, Boston in 1997, to studies of new or expanded centers in Peoria, Rockford, Springfield, St. Charles, and Nashville in the 2000s, that his methodology or model for predicting convention center performance has evolved and improved.[131]

Johnson's forecasting acumen apparently was not relevant to places like Nashville and San Jose that have employed him and his firm in more recent years. And the comments by Jim Rooney, CEO of the Massachusetts Convention Center Authority, appear to be equally irrelevant to consultant employment: "When I talk to people from other cities about making a public investment in a convention center, I'm equally blunt with all of them about the feasibility studies these consultants use to justify [such] investments. Some of these guys ought to be taken out and shot."[132]

In similar fashion, the forecasting track record of CSL and its predecessor Coopers & Lybrand in places like Anaheim, Fort Worth, and Minneapolis during the 1990s was apparently no impediment to the firm being hired in more recent years by Miami Beach, Oklahoma City, San Antonio, and Boston. Nor did CSL's recommendation that Kansas City and Miami Beach add more ballroom space lead to a questioning of the firm's later advice to Boston and Detroit that their centers too needed more ballroom space.[133]

When seeking consulting contracts from state and local governments, these consulting firms would regularly tout their experience and document their previous clients. Thus, in successfully competing for the contract to advise the Miami Beach government on the development of the convention center "campus" through a public-private partnership, the principals of the Strategic Advisory Group noted Jeff Sachs's "management and practice leadership positions with Ernst & Young and KPMG Peat Marwick." The consultants also described such previous experience as their 1997 work with Orange County, Florida, in developing a strategic plan for the "$750 million Phase V of the convention center," and an "ongoing relationship with the center." They didn't bother to mention how the expanded Orange County Convention Center had actually performed. And while SAG described its work in Charlotte, in "outlining public-private partnership options [and] creating an industry-leading hotel room block agreement," the firm did not bother to mention that Sachs had touted a new hotel as a solution to the problem of an underperforming center, and that while the public-private partnership had brought the new Westin hotel into being, the hotel project had never succeeded in improving the convention business produced by the center.[134]

For an economist or thoughtful observer who believes in the power of markets and market discipline, the consultants and their prediction records pose something of a problem. Presumably, consultants who consistently "miss" on their forecasts would be impelled to improve, lest they be replaced by consultants who are more consistently accurate or reliable. Yet the same small group of convention center consultants has succeeded in gaining new business year after year, decade after decade. The absence of any sort of market "penalty" for regularly overestimating attendance and economic impact suggests another possibility, one that focuses not on the work or accuracy of the consultants but on the decisions and choices of the government officials and local business leaders who employ them.

For journalist Victoria Murphy, writing for *Forbes* magazine in 2005, Jeff Sachs of the Strategic Advisory Group had some explanations for the misestimates and poor forecasts: "We have to make a lot of assumptions. This industry isn't tracked very well." But his most telling comment was, "You lose clients if you shoot down projects. They've already made up their minds by the time they come to us."[135]

Sachs's observation probably does indeed reflect the reality of the business of convention center consulting. By the time local officials hire a consultant, they likely already *know they want to build or expand a convention center*. In that context, the bulky consultant report is not really an assessment of true market feasibility, it's part of the public sales job, icing on the cake of a project and deal already done. If consultant accuracy, or even substantive analysis, really plays no part in the decision by state and local government officials to invest in a convention center, then what does? If new and expanded convention centers regularly fail to meet consultant projections—even in prime visitor destinations such as Orlando, San Francisco, and Washington—and often produce little or no new visitor demand and overnight hotel stays, why has convention center development boomed across American cities over the last two decades? Why have cities like Cleveland, Philadelphia, St. Louis, and Atlanta, facing downtown decline, serious economic issues, and fiscal pressures, chosen to invest hundreds of millions of public dollars in investments that generate such limited and uncertain returns?

The answers to those questions cannot be found in reams of consultant studies, or piles of glowing newspaper stories and booster editorials about a flood of new visitors and millions in economic impact. Nor are those answers to be found in the visible public record of public officials, usually mayors, council members, and city managers, who embrace convention center building and deliver the rhetoric of consultant forecasts and economic impact. Rather, the answers lie with those at the locus of decisions about downtown revitalization and public investment, the leaders of the local business community and the organized downtown interests.

The historical record makes clear that in cities like Chicago, Atlanta, and St. Louis, it is the organized local business community that presses the need for convention centers and sells the vision of new convention visitors and development efforts to both elected officials and the larger public. Although the original *idea* for a new center may lie with a local architect, planner, or civic leader, it is the local business leadership that has had the capacity to sustain and propel convention center development forward.

The interests of that business leadership are not necessarily focused primarily on the promise of economic impact and convention success that is the public face and rhetoric of convention center development. Rather, as the case studies that follow make evident, the business leadership in these cities has had other purposes and goals in mind. The language of business leaders in St. Louis dealt with "property values" and "erosion." Chicago's business leaders sought an "anchor," a means of serving the "obvious need to bolster the downtown business district." And for the business leadership of Atlanta, the proper location for a new civic center offered both the opportunity to clear and erase a "deteriorating Negro residential section" and "protection" for nearby white neighborhoods.

Where many of the convention center projects of the 1960s and 1970s were tied to downtown-oriented urban renewal efforts—Baltimore's Civic Center, Atlanta's Civic Center, San Antonio's Henry B. Gonzalez Convention Center, and St. Louis's Cervantes Center are examples—more recent center developments have been no less tied to visions of reshaped land values and development opportunity. Baltimore's new convention center that superseded the Civic Center was an anchor for the renewed Inner Harbor. Houston's George R. Brown Convention Center was very much a bridgehead for new development on the east side of downtown, just as New York's Javits Center was intended to spur new building and development on the west side of Manhattan's midtown, and Boston's new Boston Convention and Exhibition Center was intentionally sited to "anchor new related development in the Fort Point Channel District" while providing "Accessibility from downtown [that] allows for natural integration in [the] future."[136]

The case studies in Part II review the history and politics of convention center development in a group of cities that have longstanding commitments to both downtown revitalization and a development strategy focused on visitors and conventions. Informed by the records and conversations of city business leaders and political decision makers, they offer a unique platform to observe the longtime goals of downtown revival and land reshaping that have both defined and evidenced business power in major cities over the last five or six decades.

PART II

From Economics to Politics

The contemporary boom in convention center building has its roots in the post-World War II efforts by cities to redevelop, renew, and revitalize their downtown cores and inner cities. Some cities sought to build a civic auditorium or convention hall that had long been blocked by political conflict or voter disapproval. Others sought to burnish their economic competitiveness or central role. For others, the initiative to construct a new convention facility began as an effort to reposition an underused railroad station or boost the prospects for new private development and investment.

The case studies that follow, of Chicago, Atlanta, and St. Louis, all share the reality that local organized business interests played the central role in developing, promoting, and ultimately realizing a new or expanded convention center. They also share a common focus on the most central business purpose—shaping, reshaping, and defining land values and development potential. That common focus in turn reflected two specific objectives. First, *restructuring* the role and value of specific downtown or downtown fringe locations, either through eliminating an undesirable use or population, or by "anchoring" a particular development project. Second, *shaping the expectations* about land use and locational potential. Business leaders regularly described the imperative for "momentum," providing investors "with a better feeling," and giving "our place of business a major shot in the arm." The fundamental goal of these businessmen was, in the words of St. Louisan Howard F. Baer, a longtime member of the Civic Progress Inc. group, "a determination that downtown shall not disappear."[1]

For all the public rhetoric about the convention "pot o' gold" and the presumed economic boon of greater visitor spending, the detailed case histories that follow describe a persistent pattern of conflict and division. In some cities, such as Chicago, that conflict was quite evident to the regular newspaper reader or interested citizen. In others, the conflict that played out over center development—primarily around the question of location—was largely hidden from public view, discussed only in the meetings of senior business leaders or in communications with local elected officials. It has been the capacity to manage that conflict and division *within the business community* that has been critical to the realization of convention center financing and development. It has been in turn the maintenance and exchange needs *within local business organizations* that have sustained ever more convention center and related development, even in the face of market failure.

Chapter 6

Chicago: Bolstering the Business District

When Chicago's McCormick Place convention center opened in November 1960 as the "world's greatest meeting place," it represented a triumph over some 50 years of debate, conflict, and public failure. Chicago business and civic leaders had begun to promote a major new auditorium or convention hall in the 1910s, as other cities began to build their own impressive new facilities. In the 1920s, Col. Robert McCormick's *Chicago Tribune* had embraced the quest, with the regular editorial call to "Build Chicago the best convention hall in America."[1]

With a location on a prominent lakefront site some three miles from the heart of the downtown "Loop," the *Tribune* editorial writers could gush that the massive new hall "was a tribute to the foresight and drive of Col. Robert McCormick, late editor and publisher of *The Chicago Tribune* . . . [and] his campaign for an exposition center that would give to the city the facilities for perpetual maintenance of the title of convention city of the world."[2]

Yet despite the enthusiasm of the *Tribune* and a host of civic leaders, the convention hall effort met repeated failure. Part of this failure reflected the unwillingness of city voters to pay for an impressive new hall, and a lawsuit that derailed one positive vote. But the effort to build a major convention hall was also stymied by the division and conflict within the city's business community. Different and distinct geographic interests sought the new venue on their turf, for their benefit. Planner Daniel Burnham, in his 1909 *Plan of Chicago*, emphasized the potential of a major public improvement to reshape development prospects: "To the West Side especially the development of a civic center along the lines indicated is a matter of prime importance, for it will give to that portion of the city the needed impetus towards higher standards than now prevail."[3]

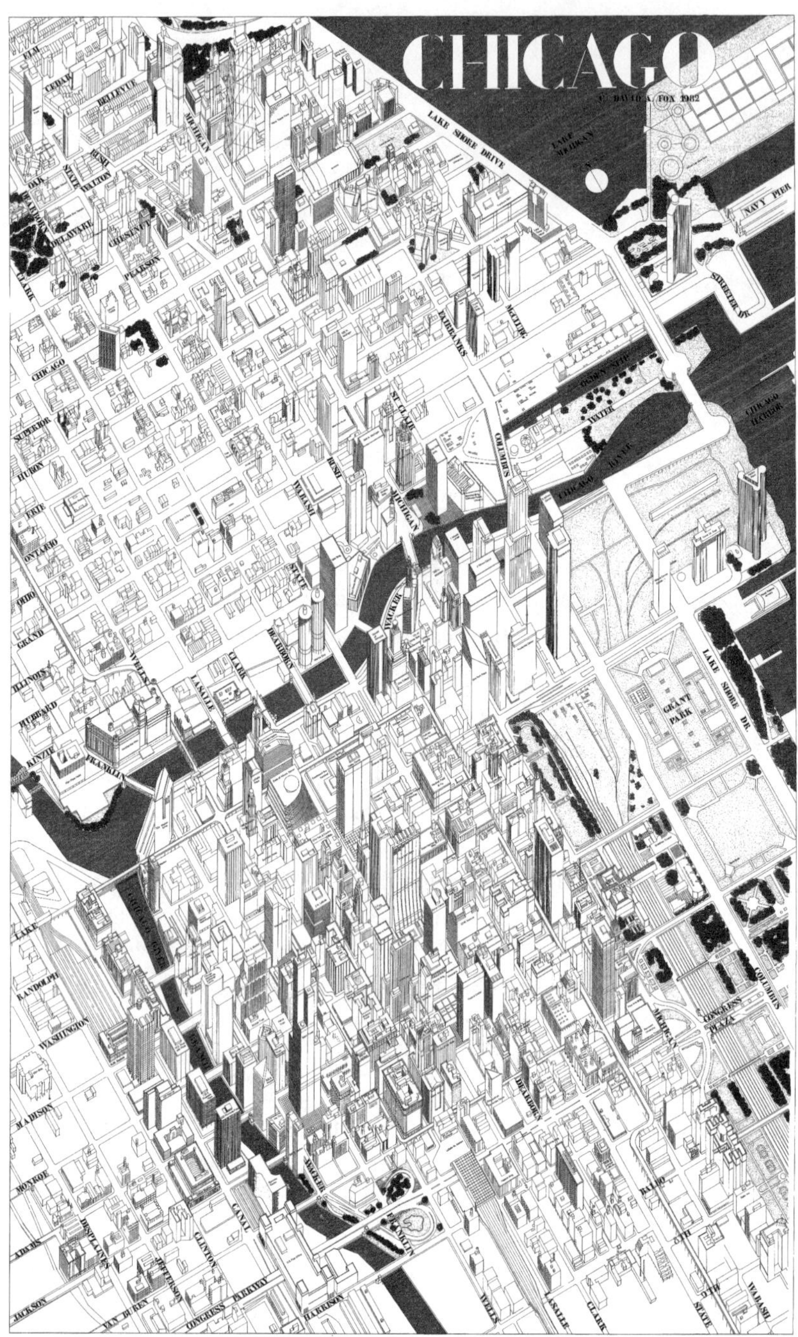
CHICAGO
© DAVID A. FOX 1982
LAKE SHORE DRIVE
LAKE MICHIGAN
NAVY PIER
ELM
CEDAR
BELLEVUE
MICHIGAN
RUSH
STATE
OAK
WALTON
DELAWARE
CHESTNUT
PEARSON
CLARK
CHICAGO
SUPERIOR
HURON
ERIE
ONTARIO
OHIO
GRAND
ILLINOIS
HUBBARD
KINZIE
FRANKLIN
WELLS
LASALLE
CLARK
DEARBORN
STATE
WABASH
RUSH
ST. CLAIR
MICHIGAN
FAIRBANKS
MCCLURG
COLUMBUS
CHICAGO RIVER
WACKER
LAKE SHORE DR.
GRANT PARK
LAKE
RANDOLPH
WASHINGTON
MADISON
MONROE
ADAMS
JACKSON
VAN BUREN
CONGRESS PARKWAY
HARRISON
DESPLAINES
JEFFERSON
CLINTON
CANAL
WACKER
DEARBORN
WELLS
LASALLE
CLARK
STATE
WABASH
CONGRESS PLAZA
COLUMBUS
MICHIGAN

Figure 1.

What Burnham viewed as providing an "impetus" for the West Side was viewed of equal import and value by interests in the Loop, on the North Side, and on the South Side. Business leaders in each area wanted their own major public improvements as a boost to land values and development prospects, in the 1950s as in the 1920s. It would ultimately take the political clout of the *Tribune*, and a shift to the political environment of the state capital in Springfield, to make the "best convention hall in America" a reality.

By shifting the locus of both politics and public finance to the state government, the *Tribune* succeeded in avoiding both the desires of the city's voters and the needs of the city's and county's elected officials. The *Tribune*'s efforts put the new convention hall in the hands of an "independent" public authority created by the state. The newspaper also put the new hall in a *location* that the *Tribune* wanted on the lakefront, rather than on a site sought by the city's business and planning leaders, one intended to boost the land values and development prospects of the central area. The "loss" of the new convention hall to the lakefront, together with the failure of a proposed civic center development scheme on the Chicago River north of the Loop, propelled the city's major business leaders—Holman Pettibone of Chicago Title and Trust, Hughston McBain of Marshall Field's, Joseph Block of Inland Steel, Fairfax Cone of Foote, Cone & Belding—to establish a new organization, the Chicago Central Area Committee, that could move forward a unified set of public improvements and investments.

The name "McCormick Place" for Chicago's new convention hall was a singular testimony to the role of the *Chicago Tribune* in making it a reality. For political scientist Edward Banfield, the center's name properly reflected both the initiative of Col. Robert McCormick, publisher of the *Tribune*, in promoting a major exhibition facility and the political force of the newspaper in making it happen. Yet the larger history of Chicago's convention hall shows that conflict over location and development promise was the central reality over some forty years. From the initial proposals in the early twentieth century until its ultimate completion, a new public convention venue was seen by a host of different individuals and interests as the key to realizing one or another development scheme. The success of the *Tribune* in securing the new convention center on the lakefront site it had long favored was the product of both its own political manipulations and a continuing conflict over siting that effectively divided the business community.[4]

Chicago had long hosted national political conventions and major business gatherings. But well into the twentieth century, the venues for these events, including the Chicago Coliseum, the Stadium, and the International Amphitheater (opened in 1934), were privately owned and managed. The first effort for a major *public* convention or exhibition hall came in 1915, with the city's major business organization, the Association of Commerce, proposing the development of "The Town Hall of the Nation," capable of seating 32,000 and providing 100,000 square feet of floor space. The association's promotional materials argued, "Many large conventions requiring space for heavy exhibits never come to Chicago" and that "In no other way can public money bring greater return to the public." The business group's preference for building a new meeting hall as part of the Municipal Pier No. 2 (later renamed Navy Pier) then under construction proved abortive. But the pressure for a massive gathering place financed by the public sector continued. By April 1919, the Chicago Association of Commerce was proposing state legislation to enable the city to issue debt for a new convention hall in order to compete with Cleveland, Kansas City, and Denver, which have "constructed mammoth convention halls." Yet at the same time, the Northwest Side Business Men's Association was promoting its own convention venue bill, for its part of the city. The state legislation passed in June 1919 authorized the city to issue bonds for a new convention hall, but stipulated that it be built on the north or northwest side, rather than the lakefront location by Navy Pier the Association of Commerce had earlier endorsed.[5]

With state authorization in hand, the city's business leaders and the Association of Commerce in early 1920 resumed their call for a new convention hall, this time in the form of a $5 million bond issue proposed by Chicago mayor William Hale Thompson as part of a package with bonds for parks, bridges, and streetlights. The Commerce Association's president contended, "We are being outbuilt now by other cities, and it is only a question of months before we shall be seriously challenged as the convention city of the United States."[6]

The plea from the Association of Commerce came at a time when the city's finances were already strained, and passage of the bond package would exceed the city's debt limit. The result was a flurry of opposition from civic organizations and the city's leading newspapers, much of it directed at the fiscal policies of Mayor Thompson. The convention hall proposal ultimately fared the worst at the polls, with just 40 percent of the voters saying "yes."[7]

Another scheme for a new convention facility appeared from the South Park District (an independent district later combined into the Chicago Park District) in 1924, as that public body sought a new use for the grand Palace of

Fine Arts that had been a centerpiece of the 1893 World's Columbian Exposition at Jackson Park. The park commission proposed rebuilding the palace as a convention hall seating some 25,000 with the proceeds of a $5 million bond issue, promising that the South Side structure would bring half a million people to Chicago each year. The vote for this convention hall effort was limited to South Side voters and proved more successful than the one four years earlier. But despite the promise of a new convention hall, the palace was ultimately the beneficiary of a $3 million gift from Julius Rosenwald that financed its rebuilding as what is now the Museum of Science and Industry.[8]

The business community's commitment to a public convention hall continued through the 1920s. By early 1927, the goal had been embraced by Anton Cermak, then the president of the Cook County board. Cermak offered Chicago Mayor William Dever the use of the county government's credit for development of a major assembly hall, repeating the Commerce Association's vision of the "Town Hall of the nation."[9] Cermak also offered an available site, the location of the criminal courts and county jail on the Near North Side, about to be vacated for new facilities. The reception by the *Tribune* and the city's civic organizations was rather different from the response to Mayor Thompson's 1920 proposal. The *Tribune* editorialized that the city needed "a hall like the civic auditorium in Cleveland," one capable of "clinching Chicago's position as the nation's meeting place, the unofficial capital of industry, trade, agriculture, and transportation."[10]

The route to the convention hall bond vote in June 1927, pressed by the possibility of luring the Democratic or Republican national convention in 1928, required approval of the proposed county bond issue by the state legislature and governor, and then a rapid vote by the county board. With no serious opposition, the prospect for voter approval of the $15 million convention hall/auditorium bond plan appeared good. But even as the plan moved through the levels of governmental review, there was clear division over a site for the new facility. At one point, in May, the *Tribune* reported general agreement that the new hall "must be built within a few minutes' walking distance of the loop."[11]

Cermak had initially proposed a Near North Side site that would be free and readily available. South Park District commissioner (later mayor) Edward J. Kelly called for the new building to be located on the lakefront south of the downtown core, as part of a proposed world's fair. Kelly argued that a lakefront site would be both economical and dramatic. Architect and planner Edward Bennett and the West Central Association argued for a West Side location, the site the 1909 Chicago Plan had decreed for a new civic center. Each interest tied to a specific locale sought the new convention auditorium as a potential boost to its own area land values and development prospects.[12]

Anton Cermak and the county board sought to mediate the division over location by deferring the ultimate choice to a citizens' commission that would render its decision only *after* the passage of the bond issue. Indeed, Cermak promised that "politics and politicians will have nothing to do with the building of this auditorium."[13] The commission, in turn, concluded that the hall should be located within a few minutes' walking distance of the downtown loop, close to the concentration of major hotels and stores. The division over a site presaged the central conflict that would accompany the development of the new McCormick Place convention center in the 1950s. Each of the sites suggested in 1927 would in fact reemerge in the 1950s. The conflict persisted because the 1927 bond scheme never yielded the city a new convention center.[14]

The voter support for the convention hall bond issue in June 1927 was an overwhelming 62 percent, and citizens' commission chair William Dawes promised an immediate decision on the site and a nationwide architectural competition for the design of the new structure. The new convention hall, however, would never be built. In the wake of a suit contesting the capacity of the county government to undertake a "private" function, the Illinois Supreme Court found in April 1928 that the rush to place the bond proposal on the ballot had afforded insufficient public notice, invalidating the election.[15]

With no "Town Hall of the nation," the difficult issue of a potential site was never resolved, although the essential geographic divisions between the North, West, and South Sides and the business interests of the Loop persisted. Any proposal for a new convention hall was fated to set off a debate about who and where would benefit. There was little prospect of reviving convention hall or auditorium plans, given the city's fiscal straits during the Depression. But during the 1940s, the Chicago Plan Commission began to consider the city's needs for the postwar period. The future of the central area was of major concern to the planners, as the growth of suburban areas and the spread of office and retail buildings appeared to threaten the viability and property values of the Loop. The commission's planners announced a tentative scheme for the central core in December 1942, combining new superhighway access with a network of parking garages. The scheme also included a plan for a new civic center, including a civic auditorium, to be located at the western edge of the Loop (and crossing the Chicago River to Clinton Street) between Jackson Boulevard and Washington Street, that would serve to clear a section of "outmoded" buildings.

The focus of the Plan Commission's effort was clearly to revitalize the Loop, with a combination of improved automobile access and a concentration of new public structures. The aim was to promote new investment "so that once more its [the Loop's] buildings will put adequate taxes into the City Treasury."[16] The Plan Commission, chaired by architect Nathaniel Owings of Skidmore, Owings and Merrill, formally unveiled a model of the "Downtown Civic Center" scheme in March 1949. Owings termed the project "a necessity in the city's redevelopment." Yet while the planning body's focus was on the western edge of the Loop, there were other interests in the city that viewed a collection of new civic buildings—and in particularly the long-sought convention hall—as the vital element in sustaining their own development plans.[17]

With the end of the Second World War, a host of development plans that had been stymied by the Depression and the war began to be announced. The air rights over Illinois Central's rail yards, in a prime location just east of Michigan Avenue, and the office concentration of the Loop, were a central focus. The air rights had been proposed as the site of the world's tallest building in 1929. And in early 1951, the city's first new office structure since 1934, the Prudential Insurance building, was announced for the site. But a few years previously, in April 1946, the rail yard air rights were promoted as the site for a 70-acre new development that would combine offices, hotels, and a new consolidated rail terminal with a convention hall/auditorium that would serve as a war memorial. The new development was proposed by the North Central Association, the group of property owners first organized in 1917 to promote the development of North Michigan Avenue ("making it the most attractive high grade shopping street in the world") and the Near North Side, and quickly endorsed by the city's convention bureau. The convention bureau had long pressed for a major new convention hall; the convenience of such a facility adjacent to a new rail terminal and hotel was viewed as providing Chicago with a competitive advantage. For the North Central Association, although it spoke of the "aesthetic beauty" of the lakefront site and public convenience, the strategic interest was in boosting the attractiveness and development fortunes of the Near North Side. Just as a civic center or convention hall on the western edge of the Loop would tend to pull development there, the Illinois Central site would serve to tug the central area to the north.[18]

The next year would see a more dramatic promotional and development plan for North Michigan Avenue, with realtor and developer Arthur Rubloff's announcement in April 1947 of a $200 million effort to create "the most magnificent mile in the world." Rubloff, who had started a real-estate career in Chicago in 1919 at age seventeen, announced a new office building to be developed by William Zeckendorf of New York, and new stores for Saks Fifth Avenue and Bonwit Teller. But to make his vision of a new "magnificent" office and retail corridor a reality, Rubloff needed public investment, both to attract potential shoppers and to accommodate the automobiles they would use. Rubloff's prepared speech called for a public esplanade to the east of the existing Water Tower (replacing "an old mid-Victorian pumping station"), to include a park and skating rink, "similar to that in Rockefeller Plaza, New York." Under the esplanade he envisioned a parking garage for 2000 cars.[19]

On a grander scale, Rubloff proposed construction of "a much needed civic auditorium" east of the Water Tower esplanade, with adjacent property "that could be given over to construction of other civic buildings which might be associated with the Auditorium—thus creating a 'Civic Center' similar to the development in San Francisco."[20]

Arthur Rubloff's vision for the "Magnificent Mile" proved quite effective in promotional terms, generating both national and local publicity and helping to spur a continuing stream of new private development. In a "personal and confidential" letter to Col. Robert McCormick, the publisher of the *Chicago Tribune*, he announced, "the Avenue has had more inquiry since this promotion . . . than at any other time I know of." The public scheme—of auditorium, civic center, and underground parking—never came to fruition. But it made evident the tie between the development of a new civic auditorium/convention hall and the potential for private investment. Rubloff saw the *possibility* of major public investment as key to changing the expectations of landowners and developers, and to making plans into reality. As he began working on a grander development scheme for the Near North Side, initially dubbed "Project X," he turned again to the potential impact of major new public facilities.[21]

Arthur Rubloff's "Project X" was a scheme to clear and rebuild most of the 150 acres of the Near North Side of Chicago—an area just north of the Chicago River and immediately west of Rubloff's "Magnificent Mile" on North Michigan Avenue. Much of the planning for Rubloff's scheme was carried out by architect Nathaniel Owings of Skidmore, Owings and Merrill. Owings had devised the Chicago Plan Commission's scheme for a West Side civic center just a few years earlier. Now, with the SOM staff, he planned yet another civic center complex, this time on the north bank of the Chicago River and west of Michigan Avenue, as the anchor and magnet for Rubloff's larger scheme for new housing offices in Project X.[22]

Together with a new county courts building, state and federal government offices, and a new campus for the University of Illinois, Rubloff and Owings considered a new convention hall as part of the "anchor" complex for Project X. Rubloff employee Lou Capron reported back in January 1952 on a conversation he had with Convention Bureau executive Sam Anoff on the city's convention hall facilities. Anoff recommended a new structure with a "minimum gross display area of 150,000 sq. ft." with added space for storage and restaurant facilities. Anoff also described the requirement that such a building "must be extremely flexible to serve its purpose well."[23]

Rubloff's papers include a "Project X Building Program" dated November 25, 1953—a few months before the public unveiling of the redevelopment scheme—that included a "Trade Fair Bldg." of undetermined size. A new convention hall must still have been a possibility at this point for Rubloff and Owings. But when Project X was announced as the "Fort Dearborn Project" in March 1954, with a front-page headline in the *Tribune* proclaiming "Outline Vast Civic Center!" a convention hall was no longer a part. Rubloff's "trade fair" development had been overtaken by events, largely led by the *Tribune* itself.[24]

A Fair for the Colonel

The *Tribune* was a Chicago booster, and it embraced plans for a Railroad Fair on the lakefront in the summer of 1948 enthusiastically. Deeming the planned fair the inheritor of the 1933 Century of Progress exhibition at the same locale, the paper backed the lease of Park District land for the site and promoted the rail event to its Midwestern readers. The paper went on to promote the idea of using the site for a permanent exposition or trade fair, organized and managed by a nonprofit corporation. The trade fair notion appeared to receive strong backing from Chicago hotel owners and business leaders, and the *Tribune* continued to back the site's use for expositions, with the railroad fair extended for a second year in 1949 and another fair mounted in 1950. Despite a rainy summer the 1950 fair was touted as a great success, attracting a total of 1.7 million visitors. The fiscal constraints of the Korean War stopped a continuation in the summer of 1951. Yet by then the *Tribune* had already mounted a sustained push at the state capital to secure annual funding for a permanent lakefront fair, using a part of the state's share of racetrack revenues.[25]

As former *Tribune* reporter George Tagge recounted in a 1984 memoir, Major Lenox Lohr, who had headed both the Century of Progress and the subsequent railroad fairs, reported to *Tribune* editor and publisher Robert R. McCormick in 1951 that "the buildings are just falling apart, with the kind of weather than Chicago has in the winters, that it's a wonder they could have been used a second year, and they couldn't be used any longer." With this prodding from Lohr, McCormick called a meeting of "some of the people from the Chicago Association of Commerce and Industry and State Street merchants, people who would benefit from any kind of major activity in the nature of a fair."[26]

George Tagge of the *Tribune* played a fascinating dual role in the quest for state support for a Chicago fair, both reporting from the state capital in Springfield and managing the political bargaining to make the state government's financial backing a reality. As Tagge recalled, "I stopped at the desk of Paul Powell, then the Democratic majority leader. . . . I said, 'Well, we've got this problem up in Chicago. We had this lakefront fair and [*Tribune* editor Don] Maxwell has been out with his hat in his hand just. . . . With the help of a lot of nighttime and post midnight persuasion collecting money and all, but that's gone and the thing is flat. Why couldn't something—couldn't there be a bill that would put on—I don't want to touch your dole or the county fairs, but the parallel of that for Cook County which would be used for lakefront fair building?' And Paul, a man of action, said 'Well, what the hell. That sounds square to me.'"[27]

With an assured, albeit modest, source of state financing, the *Tribune* continued to press for creation of a nonprofit corporation that could support a permanent fair at the lakefront site. The newspaper editorialized in January 1952 that the call for a permanent fair "should be heeded on the twin grounds of civic spirit and intelligent self-interest," noting the millions of visitors the earlier fairs had lured to the city.[28] At some point, probably in early 1953, the focus of Col. McCormick and the *Tribune* shifted, from a fair like the Century of Progress or the Railroad Fairs to the construction of a permanent building for trade fairs and conventions.

Edward Banfield's case study of the "Exhibition Hall" ascribes the shift from an open-air fair to a new convention hall to department store chief executive James L. Palmer and a visit to Toronto's exhibition facilities some time in 1952. George Tagge recalled that the trip to the Canadian National Exposition in Toronto involved the *Tribune*'s airplane and included *Tribune* editor Don Maxwell, Mayor Martin Kennelly, former Senator C. Wayland Brooks, businessman Henry Crown, engineering consultant Ralph Burke, and himself.[29]

The visible push for a new convention hall began in January 1953 with a public warning from Otto Eitel, owner of the Bismarck Hotel and president of the Chicago Convention Bureau, that the city was on the verge of losing convention business to other communities. At the bureau's annual luncheon, a visiting convention consultant compared the city's performance to others, and said, "Chicago is missing a big bet in delaying construction of an exposition hall like those in Atlantic City, Cleveland, and Philadelphia." Also echoing the argument was the bureau's executive director, Chester Wilkins, who argued, "the convention dollar does much to bolster the otherwise fading volume of downtown business because virtually all buying by convention guests is done in the central district."[30]

The Convention Bureau's initiative was followed up at the end of March, with a meeting called by Eitel "to discuss a movement to acquire a Chicago fair and exposition building." Again, the arguments for a new convention hall focused on the city's competitive position, with new exhibition facilities under development in both Detroit and New York City. By the end of April, the *Tribune* was headlining "Big Exhibit Hall for City Pushed by Civic Groups," and announcing that James Palmer of Marshall Field's would chair a new civic committee to develop a convention building. Palmer's committee drew backing from an array of organizations, including the hotel association, the retail merchants, and the numerous business groups representing the sections of the central area, including the Greater North Michigan Avenue Association, the Michigan Boulevard Association, the State Street Council, the Wabash Avenue Association, and the West Central Association.[31]

The *Tribune*'s commitment to a convention hall plan, not solely a fair, was evident in a May 1 editorial that compared Chicago's stasis and loss of convention business with the new buildings under way in Detroit, New York, Los Angeles, Cleveland, St. Louis, and San Francisco. Arguing that racetrack revenues, not general taxes, would pay for a new hall, the editorial concluded, "Better convention facilities would bring to the city business worth 50 million dollars a year."[32]

The image portrayed by the *Tribune* and Palmer's new civic committee was of broad unanimity and interest group support for an effectively private initiative focused on state legislation and financing, thereby neatly avoiding the perversities of Chicago city government and politics and the weak leadership (Arnold Hirsch has termed it "political ineptitude") of Mayor Martin Kennelly.[33] But even as the *Tribune* announced the push for a convention hall, it portrayed obvious conflict over the *location* of the structure, much the same conflict that had plagued efforts dating back to the 1920s.

Six possible sites were discussed at the April meeting, including the lakefront fair site at Twenty-Third Street that had housed the railroad fairs, one that the *Tribune* obviously endorsed. The other possible locations were on the West Side at Halsted Street, the railroad tracks and yards south of the Loop near Roosevelt Avenue, the Illinois Central air rights site east of Michigan Avenue that had long attracted developers and the North Central Association (later renamed the Greater North Michigan Avenue Association), Navy Pier, and the site of the existing privately owned Chicago Stadium on Madison Street west of the Loop.

Otto Eitel of the Bismarck Hotel and Convention Bureau sought to downplay the potential conflict over the site by arguing, "Differences in views about the location . . . should be set aside until funds are assured."[34] But the political reality was that most of the sites were backed and promoted by specific interests that were focused on geographic and development opportunities. The West Side location, at Congress and Halsted, was the favored site of the West Central Association and Aldermen Sain and Lancaster, who sought to realize Daniel Burnham's vision from the 1909 plan of a major civic center on the West Side and its potential for spurring new office and commercial development. Interests on the south side of the Loop, including the Conrad Hilton Hotel and some of the State Street department stores, saw a convention hall on the near south rail yards as key to rebuilding the decaying South Loop, with its collection of what Frederick Aschman, the city's planning director, would term "obsolete office and loft buildings, burlesque houses and a Skid Row, and the rail terminals."[35]

The Illinois Central air rights site east of Michigan Avenue had long been promoted by North Side interests for major public and private development. In November 1953, Nelson Forrest, executive director of the Greater North Michigan Avenue Association, reported, "The Association remains hopeful that this needed municipal structure (the Convention Hall) will be located adjacent to the Central Business District on the Illinois Central and Michigan Central air rights along the River or in some other location convenient to the central district hotels and shopping areas." Forrest went on to note, "This position apparently will be supported by the other central business district associations, whose influence together with that of your Association should be substantial."[36]

The North Michigan Avenue Association would continue to argue that the air rights site would put a new convention hall within walking distance of the concentration of hotels and shops of the Loop. The group also recognized, as did Arthur Rubloff, that a location just across the Chicago River from the *Tribune* Building and the "Magnificent Mile" would be a boost to the development of the Near North Side.

The array of possible sites, and interests committed to the selection of their own preferred site, did not end with the list of six presented by the *Tribune* in April. On November 18, 1953, the South Side Planning Board, a private body founded by Michael Reese Hospital and a group of major South Side institutions and focused on the redevelopment of their environs, presented its own scheme for a new convention hall, together with a dramatic architectural model of a structure designed by Mies van der Rohe and his students. Mies's vast column-free convention hall would be widely reprinted in the architectural press. But the planning group's real focus was to add a new potential location, west of Michigan Avenue on the city's South Side, between Cermak Road and Twenty-Fifth Street, one intended to clear a swath of the South Side then in the early stages of renewal and "sow seeds" for future investment and development.[37] This site would eventually become the location of a major expansion of McCormick Place, McCormick West, which opened in mid-2008.

The Carson Pirie Scott department store chain would add yet another alternate location in 1954. As part of the store's hundredth anniversary, top executives of the store sponsored a national contest to design a plan for Chicago's Loop for 2054. The winning design, by students from New York's Pratt Institute, envisioned the Loop expanding to the west, with a civic center developed on the Illinois Central air rights east of Michigan Avenue. To the immediate south of the Loop, below Harrison Street, the plan proposed "a permanent trade fair site encircled by hotels." The second-place team, largely staff members of the Philadelphia City Planning Commission, proposed a new consolidated passenger terminal to the west of the Loop, including rail terminals and a heliport, with a new civic center at the Loop's northern edge and a convention center anchoring the Loop south of Congress Street.[38]

The winning plans in the Carson's competition thus placed a convention center or trade fair not at the lakefront/Twenty-Third Street site that the *Tribune* had long been promoting, but at the immediate southern edge of the Loop, quite close to the existing concentration of hotels and State Street department stores (including Carson Pirie Scott). That outcome of the plan competition certainly should have pleased the firm's president at the time, John T. Pirie. Pirie had not been among the visible supporters of Arthur Rubloff's Fort Dearborn project, announced a few months earlier and backed by the leadership of the competing Marshall Field's department store and a number of other Chicago business leaders. Pirie's outlook on Fort Dearborn, and his own preference for new public development, was summarized by Earl Kribben, the full-time director of the Fort Dearborn effort and a Field's vice president: "Basically, John is too good a citizen to oppose anything that is good for Chicago. In the past he has said that he was for Fort Dearborn if a similar project to improve and stabilize the south side of the Loop could also be devised, and sooner or later I am sure that some such project will materialize."[39] A convention hall anchoring the south side of the Loop rather than on the lakefront may well have been the "project" John Pirie sought.

Despite the apparent array of competing locations for the planned convention hall, the *Tribune* gave the impression that the site issue was fully resolved in early June 1954. A front-page article announced that "Chicago's new convention and exhibition building will be on the lake front from 16th st. to beyond 23rd st., according to plans approved yesterday by the Chicago park district board." The article went on to report that a formal study of 18 possible sites conducted by two local engineering firms had yielded "scores" ranging from 16 to 85 percent—"the winning tally for the lake front location selected."[40]

The Park District and the new nonprofit organization charged with building the hall had sought to resolve the location issue with a "scientific" study by consultants. The 92-page analysis by Chicago architects Holabird and Root and Burgee, joined by the Ralph H. Burke engineering firm, had evaluated each of the potential sites on some 18 individual variables, each weighted in terms of measures seen as relevant. Yet for all the seeming "science" of a quantitative evaluation, the consultants neatly overweighted the items that tapped the size, "expandability," and "setting" of the site. Not surprisingly, the large, open lakefront site received the highest score for "adequacy," while close to the Loop, built-up, or smaller locations managed far lower scores. Then the consultants included a measure of "extraordinary cost," ostensibly just five percent of the overall total. But they devised a scheme for a "negative deduction" for land acquisition costs that yielded a minus 60 (on a scale of 100 overall) for the South Side site, and minus 72 for the Illinois Central air rights location. Only a big, undeveloped site with lots of adjacent property could gain a reasonable "score," and that only fit the lakefront location. The outcome was thoroughly predetermined.[41]

Two days after the Park District announcement, the chair of the city's official planning body, the Chicago Plan Commission, made his own statement in a letter to the president of the park board. William Spencer of the Plan Commission criticized the lakefront site, arguing "that a site closer to the central business district would have more advantages." Spencer laid out a set of reasons for denying the "mathematical" scores of the Park District's consultants, citing the "need to redevelop deteriorating areas on the borders of the Loop, the advantages of a hall within walking distance of the Loop's facilities, the transportation advantages of a close-in site, and the preference for preserving the lakefront for recreation and cultural facilities."[42]

Spencer's position appeared to reflect the larger judgment of most Plan Commission members and certainly that of its professional staff. Frederick T. Aschman, the city's planning director, had often expressed concern about the immediate circumstances and future of the Loop, as office and retail activities continued to move to the Near North Side and decentralize to the suburbs. Aschman had played an advisory role in shaping the implementation of the Fort Dearborn scheme, meeting with Arthur Rubloff, mayoral advisor James Downs, Earl Kribben, and others. He was particularly sensitive to the political realities that might stymie the development of the North Side civic center plan, including the "problems likely to be created by the West Side group" and the need for "mollifying the principal people in the Greater North Michigan Avenue Association, who were miffed because the Fort Dearborn Project had been conceived and announced without their advance knowledge or cooperation."[43]

Aschman laid out his vision for the rebuilding of the Loop's larger environs in a memo prepared for the Chicago Central Area Committee (the new organization of Loop business leaders initiated in 1955) in early 1957, and those views and outlook no doubt were behind his (and the Plan Commission's) position on the convention hall site in 1954. Noting that the Near North and Near South Sides surrounding the Loop were "severely blighted," and the tendency of business districts was to "spread out over a period of time," Aschman promoted the idea of "a combined program" for "rebuilding of the two areas [Near North and Near South] with uses that complement those in the Central Area" and would serve as "'anchors' to the North and to the South."[44]

Aschman identified such possible "anchor" uses as new residential development, a new campus for the University of Illinois, other government buildings, a research center, and a "civic auditorium." The Aschman memo also noted aesthetic advantages of improving the entryways to the Loop and increasing accessibility, providing an environment that would "encourage new construction from Jackson Boulevard south" and help conserve such "existing properties as the Monadnock, Board of Trade, and Insurance Exchange Buildings."

The anchor strategy laid out by Aschman reflected his assessment of both development and political imperatives. By coordinating the rebuilding of the northern and southern fringes of the Loop, he sought to contain the locus of development and boost land values. But the strategy also reflected a larger political reality, one made evident in both the conflict over the Fort Dearborn project and the division over a site for the new convention hall. Aschman's memo noted, "It is almost universally true that there is an unhealthy rivalry in major commercial districts between property interests in different sections whenever there is noticeable shifting of values or when major projects are proposed affecting one 'side' or another." Such a "rivalry" was certainly the case in mid-1950s Chicago, with the tension between the north and south sides of the Loop exemplified by John Pirie's position. Aschman then went on to argue, "In Chicago the combined planning of the 'anchor projects' would tend to dissipate any real or potential rivalry of this kind by offering a program which reflected the comprehensive objective of overall stabilization of values." In essence, Aschman was proposing to deal with anchor projects like new government buildings, an auditorium/convention hall, or a new university campus as *distributive goods* to be spread around the central core with the goal of both broadly sustaining land values and dissipating political conflict *among property and development interests.*

Ted Aschman's views of both downtown planning and urban politics might simply be a peculiar footnote were it not for his personal history. After serving as the city's planning director, he went on to form a leading planning consulting firm, Barton-Aschman Associates. The firm developed plans for a large number of major cities, such as Syracuse and Minneapolis. But, far more important, Aschman served as the principal planner and consultant for the new Chicago Central Area Committee, created in 1955. The committee was the moving force behind the development of the plan for the Central Area promulgated by the city in 1958. And Aschman's strategic and political approach to distributing major public goods and benefits was the essential strategic basis of the plan.

The opposition of the Plan Commission to the lakefront site was rooted in Ted Aschman's perspective and that of the professional planning staff. Aschman's immediate successor at the Plan Commission, John Cordwell, would recall some years later: "we developed a proposal to put the convention hall on the south end of the Loop to be an anchor for developing the south end of the Loop, which was eroding away like mad and lots of buildings were already dying of attrition."[45]

Aschman, Cordwell, and the Plan Commission were not the only major players in the city's development and planning circles focused on the potential of a new convention hall on the south side of the Loop. James Downs was the founder of the Real Estate Research Corporation in Chicago, and in the 1950s was the principal adviser on land use and development issues to Mayor Martin Kennelly and subsequently Mayor Richard J. Daley (one of Daley's "most trusted advisers").[46]

Speaking in May 1954 at a meeting of the board members and staff of the city's Land Clearance Commission with the business leaders—Holman Pettibone of Chicago Title and Trust, Hughston McBain of Marshall Field's, Willis Gale of Commonwealth Edison, Arthur Leonard of the Association of Commerce—sponsoring the Fort Dearborn plan, Downs "called attention to the plan to locate the Convention Hall and other suggested improvements at the south end of the Loop." That was, of course, the site proposed by the Plan Commission and necessarily opposed by the *Tribune*. Downs "noted some advantages of this [south Loop] site over the one at 23rd Street and the Lake. He felt that a large scale redevelopment in this site would tend to balance Fort Dearborn and anchor the Loop securely."[47]

The public opposition of William Spencer and the Plan Commission to the lakefront site, and the concern of James Downs to "anchor" the Loop, ultimately did not stop the efforts of the *Tribune* or dictate the final outcome. It did have the effect of emboldening and strengthening the opposition to a site distant from the Loop.

Days after the Plan Commission announcement, the *Chicago American* printed an editorial opposing the lakefront location for the convention hall. In a letter to Arthur Rubloff on July 1, the *American*'s publisher, Stuart List, said his paper "is taking a strong stand that the right place for the new convention hall is in the area from Congress to Polk Sts., from State to Clark Sts."

List went on to outline his reasons: "We feel that this location will help strengthen our downtown business area; aid in vital slum clearance and increase real estate values . . . just to mention a few."[48]

The combination of the Plan Commission's argument and the newspaper endorsement of a south Loop site appeared to provide a political opportunity for organizing the opposition and promoting a site that would serve the goal of supporting development *somewhere* in the Loop. For the Greater North Michigan Avenue Association and its commitment to the Illinois Central air rights location, it provided an opening to take the case to the state legislature in Springfield. Nelson Forrest reported to the association membership in August 1954, "The Chicago Park District, Chicago Fair Board, and Plan Commission have agreed to reconsider the most logical site for the proposed large Convention Hall." The August progress report for the North Side group noted, "Legislation may be introduced in the 1957 legislature to provide 'eminent domain' right of land acquisition to the Fair Board."[49]

In his oral history memoir, George Tagge of the *Tribune*, who shepherded the project through the state capital through this entire period, termed the fight over siting "a controversy of major size." He took particular note of the role of the Greater North Michigan Avenue Association, "a bitter experience for me," where the "top hired man insisted that the thing be built in his backyard, or very convenient to his chief subscribers, and they had no idea where the many additional millions of dollars for the purchase of a site would be obtained. "[50]

The legislation for the Fair Board and convention hall project at this point required the use of a publicly owned site. By providing the board (or a new public authority envisioned by convention hall backers) with the capacity to acquire land by eminent domain, the opponents—despite their division on the exact site to be an alternative to the lakefront locale—could enable the Fair Board to use a different site, particularly one already developed, at a reasonable cost.

The effort to pass new state legislation creating a Metropolitan Fair and Exposition Authority, with the legal authority to issue bonds for a convention center and governed by a board jointly appointed by the governor and the mayor of Chicago, was announced by the *Tribune* (under George Tagge's byline) on April 12, 1955 with the bold headline "Tell Exposition Hall Plan" and the subhead "Action Urged on Center at Lake, 23d St." [51] The newspaper's editorial the following day was no less expansive: "The institution as it is now planned will be the finest facility of its sort in the world, and it is possible to start it before the year end."[52]

The *Tribune*'s coverage of the convention facility declared the seemingly unanimous support of the city's business and civic leadership, proclaiming, "Business and civic leaders of Chicago voiced warm praise yesterday of the plan to construct the world's greatest exposition on the lake front at 23d St." The paper's coverage, in Tagge's dispatches from Springfield, its Chicago "news," and its editorials, stressed the broad support for the hall and its location, while belittling and dismissing opponents' "big lie campaign." Yet about the same time, the Greater North Michigan Avenue Association was informing its members that the Merchants Council had passed a resolution opposing the lakefront location on April 13, and that the GNMAA had sent a delegation to the state capital in Springfield in support of the eminent domain amendment.[53]

The efforts by those opposed to the lakefront site ultimately failed, with the legislature passing, and Governor William Stratton signing, a bill creating a new fair authority but without the eminent domain authority vital for securing a close-in site. The *Tribune*'s editorial writer acknowledged the concerns of the North Michigan group—an organization that included the newspaper among its members—but argued that their plan was "not feasible" and that "the added cost would be fatal if delay were not. . . . If the dream is to be realized, the site must be the one where the hall can be built most quickly and economically."[54]

Tribune publisher Col. Robert McCormick did not live to see his vision of a new convention hall built. He died in April 1955, just before the formal signing of the authority legislation. But the paper could still declare in July that "Col. McCormick's dream is now about to be realized," and herald the promise from the director of the Chicago Convention Bureau that "he can book the facility solid for five years."[55]

The *Tribune*'s assessment that the "dream" of a new convention hall was "coming true" was not entirely accurate. The state legislation that created the Fair and Exposition Authority did not give the new entity a sufficient source of cash to finance the new building or resolve the longstanding debate over a site. But the authority moved in early 1956 to request a formal lease of the Twenty-Third Street location from the Chicago Park District. A parade of witnesses at the March 12 hearing argued the immediate need for a large convention center and the wisdom of the lakefront location as "the one place near the center of Chicago where large crowds of people can be handled," and "To build anywhere else would be unthinkable." Others, including realtor Ferd Kramer, representing the Metropolitan Housing and Planning Council, and restaurant owner Marion Isbell, argued for a location closer to the Loop.[56]

The Park District hearing was to have been the sole opportunity for the public to comment on the convention hall plan and the location, with a final vote on the site lease at the end of March. But the *Tribune* noted the "noisy attack on the site during the last few days" and retorted in an editorial that "the 23rd st. site is the only feasible one."[57] The increased "noisy" opposition at this juncture was largely the result of the new involvement by the Metropolitan Housing and Planning Council, a nonprofit organization that had long promoted urban redevelopment, public housing, and public planning in the Chicago region and included a number of leading businessmen, realtors, and architects on its board. MHPC president Joseph Pois led a delegation that met with Mayor Daley at the end of March to "protest against the selection of the 23rd Street site," arguing that public hearings on the convention hall location should have been held by the Fair Authority, as the Park Board could only consider potential park sites.

With Mayor Daley's acquiescence to new hearings, the Metropolitan Housing and Planning Council initiated an effort "to join with various technical societies to suggest various alternate sites. "[58] The intervention of a respected "good government" group—the MHPC was at the same time opposing the city's "concentration of high rise public housing on the near South Side . . . creating a low income, social and racial ghetto"—added legitimacy to an opposition the *Tribune* had long tagged as parochial and self-interested. When Joseph Pois did testify with others for MHPC at a formal hearing on July 2, he made clear that the organization backed the planned convention hall and did not advocate any particular site. But Pois argued that such a major project needed to meet "the needs of the City as a whole and reflect sound planning." The MHPC position was that the hall's location "should be confined to a belt extending around the periphery of the Central Business District," with "strong consideration . . . given to the redevelopment needs" of the downtown area, such as "the stabilization of declining areas." The group called for "a searching study" of both alternative sites and the "economics of the proposed project."[59]

Pois was joined at the authority hearing by department store president John Pirie (sponsor of the Carson, Pirie, Scott Loop competition), who contended that for a convention hall "the obvious location should be in the central commercial district reasonably close to transportation, hotels, entertainment and shops." Graham Aldis, representing the Building Managers' Association, argued the imperative for a location "approximately adjacent to the loop area." Pirie and Aldis had both been joined in opposing the Fort

Dearborn project earlier, and Aldis had been a member of the team that placed third in Carson's Loop planning competition.

Among the opponents of the lakefront site was restaurateur Marion Isbell, effectively speaking on behalf of the Greater North Michigan Avenue Association. A few days earlier, Nelson Forrest of the association had written to Arthur Rubloff of the "sensitive question" of the convention hall hearing. Forrest noted "A very strong civic protest against the 23rd St. site by top people" and a presentation of an alternative site just west of the Loop on the Union Station air rights. Recognizing Rubloff's desire to "avoid the matter if possible presently, in view of the *Tribune* relationships, etc.," he suggested Isbell as "our spokesman in favor of a downtown site"—the Illinois Central air rights the Michigan Avenue Association had long promoted.[60]

The central political dilemma faced by Pois, the Metropolitan Planning and Housing Council, and the array of opponents was clear at the July hearing. The Twenty-Third Street site so singularly promoted by the *Tribune* would do little to spur the revitalization of the Loop and secure the larger development and planning goals sought by the council, as well as south Loop merchants such as Pirie. But allied as all these groups and interests might be in opposition to the lakefront location, there was no agreement in the least on a preferable site. A few days before the hearing, Pois had confided to the MHPC board that "he felt as though in the front line without an army behind him." He noted the "passivity of Major Lohr (Fair Authority director), who avows no concern for the location of the Hall, and the Booz Allen Hamilton economic study which assumes that the site is satisfactory present us with the problem of deciding how much of an issue we want to raise."[61]

The Booz Allen & Hamilton study, commissioned by the Fair Authority and delivered in August 1956, posed yet another problem, for both proponents and opponents. The construction of the convention hall had been premised on financing from both the state racetrack tax revenues and revenues generated by the hall itself. But Booz Allen found that the development cost would be higher than first estimated, and that revenues would likely be about $365,000 a year—far too little to support the anticipated debt. These fiscal constraints effectively ruled out any site that was not publicly owned and therefore free. Pois reported to the MHPC board that a reduction in the cost of new convention building "will probably rule out consideration of other sites."[62]

The Booz Allen report was also the first independent assessment of the likely *performance* of a new convention hall, and its findings were sobering for convention hall boosters. The report concluded "that the exposition center, alone, will not bring about a significant increase in the number of large conventions which choose Chicago as the site of their meetings." It went on, "While the center will undoubtedly be a prestige location, there are factors present which will limit the ability of the city to realize a substantial increase over its present volume of convention business." And while it assured the Fair Authority, "The proposed exposition center is an ambitious undertaking, worthy of the great traditions of the City of Chicago," it offered the prescient judgment that "Because of facilities being built or planned by other cities, the competition for the country's major conventions will increase markedly."[63]

The Fair Authority sought to deal with the Booz Allen study and its forecast of very limited revenues through a piece of sleight-of-hand. The group commissioned a new revenue study from the Chicago Convention Bureau. Not surprisingly, the Bureau reported that the hall's annual net revenue would be far higher than the Booz Allen estimate—a total of $1,713,550. Based on that remarkably precise total, plus racetrack tax revenues of $1.5 million, there would be sufficient coverage to make the revenue bonds for the convention hall salable. The authority appeared unconcerned about the report's conclusion that Chicago was unlikely to see a significant increase in its convention business.[64]

The Metropolitan Housing and Planning Council's principled stand against the lakefront site could be backed by a variety of interests. But there was no agreement among the opponents on an alternative site, and a mechanism for generating the revenues needed to support either a major rebuilding of the Loop's fringe or the far greater cost of an air rights site. Pois and the MHPC recognized the link between the project's financing and the site alternative, noting, "The fight for the park site is liable to become bitter since the reduction in the estimated cost of the Hall itself makes free land more necessary." In particular, the MHPC looked to the support of the official Chicago Planning Commission in making a case for a near-Loop location. Pois told his colleagues, "There appears to be considerable confusion in the Plan Commission offices about the project and no report is expected from that quarter in the near future."[65]

The absence of the Plan Commission from the debate over an appropriate site for the new convention hall was not happenstance. Instead, it represented a measure of the kind of pressure the *Tribune* management was capable of applying to assure the Twenty-Third Street location.

Architect and planner John Cordwell had succeeded Frederick Aschman as the city's planning director in early 1956, and shared his predecessor's preference for a convention center location that would anchor and renew the south side of the Loop. And the Plan Commission accepted that recommendation. As Cordwell would later recall,

> One afternoon with my commissioners—these milkmen and bankers—they accepted and approved my scheme to build the convention hall at the south end of the Loop. . . .
>
> It was all approved and they were just about to go. Then Joel Goldblatt of Goldblatt's Department Store was one of my commissioners. He came in one day, and he looked like fluorescent yellow. I've never told this story to anyone, and I don't know whether I should tell it now, but it's how the convention center got to be on the lakefront at 23rd Street. It happened because Joel Goldblatt persuaded the commissioners. He told a story of people leaning on him heavily, politically, influenced by the Chicago *Tribune*. . . .
>
> Well, the guy who was the publisher of the *Tribune* at the time [Don Maxwell]. But they picked up Joel Goldblatt one Saturday morning and took him for a ride—literally a ride. . . .
>
> They took him for a ride in this extended vehicle—this limousine. They took him for a ride up to Lake Forest [a Chicago suburb], where he lived. Don Maxwell, who the publisher of the Trib was at that time, picked up Goldblatt at his department store on State Street, and whatever they threatened Goldblatt with, Joel Goldblatt capitulated. A judge was one of those who was with public officials in the car. . . .
>
> These men went for a ride, according to Joel Goldblatt, and they took him for a ride up to his house, and then the rest of the group were all there, waiting for him—the *Tribune* people, I think. Whether they threatened to cut off his advertising or whatever it was, it was something heavy like that that stopped it. When Joel Goldblatt came back, and I was there and I saw him come into the meeting. But he came back and they went into executive session with the plan commissioners, and when they came out the site had moved to 23rd Street.[66]

John Cordwell left the Chicago Plan Commission in 1956. Mayor Daley reorganized the body later that year to make it a city department under the mayor's control, with an appointed commission that was purely advisory. Without any formal support for an alternative location, the MHPC's fight against the lakefront convention center became lonely and thoroughly ineffective. Meeting with Ira Bach, the new head of the planning department, in October 1957, the Housing and Planning Council board "expressed disapproval" of the Twenty-Third Street site. In response, the new head of the Plan Commission, Clare Roddewig, told the group, "that this matter has been decided and the best that can be done is to learn to live with it."[67]

The MHPC, joined by representatives of Carson Pirie Scott, the American Institute of Architects Chicago Chapter, the local chapter of the American Institute of Planners, and the South Side Planning Board, issued a statement in late October 1957, expressing concerns with the lakefront site over questions of cost, traffic, and access. But that last ditch appeal was notable for the absence of any broad business support. On November 1, Joseph Pois informed the MHPC board that "there is not active support of any wide spread opposition to the project." He went on to say, "Every conceivable approach has been tried by the MHPC. The present coalition between [Governor] Stratton and [Mayor] Daley make any opposition difficult."[68]

Aftermath

The McCormick Place convention center opened in November 1960 and immediately placed Chicago at the front of cities competing for major national conventions and tradeshows. In its first year, the new center hosted meetings of the National Association of Home Builders, the National Housewares Manufacturers Association, the National Restaurant Association, and the National Supermarket Institute. And it spurred immediate efforts on the part of a number of other cities, including New York, Las Vegas, Atlanta, and Washington, to build new or expanded convention facilities. In turn, Chicagoans quickly began to speak of a need for even more exhibit space. Gerald Sanderson, executive director of the Chicago Convention Bureau, contended in 1966, "We could use another 200,000 square feet at McCormick Place," noting the increased competition from other cities.[69]

When a fire totally destroyed the convention hall in 1967, it was rebuilt at the same site with a larger total exhibit space, bringing it to over 500,000 square feet. Further expansions in 1986, 1996, and 2007 brought the McCormick Place complex to a total of 2.7 million square feet of exhibit space.

Yet, even as each successive expansion of McCormick Place was hailed in the local and national press as a boon to Chicago's economy and the key to gaining future national political conventions, its actual performance has been rather more modest. Local officials reported a total of 3,444,859 attendees at both conventions and public shows in 1965, a figure that included a large fraction of Chicago-area residents. Thirty years later, in 1995, the same attendance total came to 3,217,434. Convention and public show attendance came to just 2.22 million a decade later in 2005, 2.27 million in 2007, and 2.05 million in 2011. Despite some nine times the exhibit space at its 1960 opening, McCormick Place had effectively flat total attendance from the 1960s into the 1990s and is currently attracting smaller aggregate attendance than in the mid-1960s.

For at least some backers of the new Chicago hall, the expectation was that it would act as a spur to new private investment and development on the Near South Side, particularly of facilities to house convention visitors. The South Side Planning Board in 1956 had described an anticipated $228 million program of new development adjacent to the convention hall, including a 1,500-room hotel, a smaller motel, a 40-story office building, and new apartment towers. When McCormick Place opened in November 1960, a local development group promised a 750-room hotel, complete with heliport, to open in January 1962. Nothing more was seen of the promised development until the announcement in January 1967 that the first phase of a planned "McCormick City" development on the railroad air rights adjacent to McCormick Place would begin in a few months with construction of a 750-room hotel. The promised development was ultimately to include 2,000 new hotel rooms, 1,200 apartments, and six office towers. Yet again, in March 1971, the same development interests, Martin Gecht and Eugene Heytow of Aristocrat Inns, promised to begin work on a 640-room hotel, while still promising that a far larger project would eventually rise next to the convention center.[70]

Finally, in April 1973, the long-delayed, 625-room McCormick Inn opened next to McCormick Place. For all the promise of new development, it took more than 12 years to see any new hotel tied to McCormick Place. But the larger "McCormick City" development has never occurred, and the McCormick Inn remained isolated as the only new private investment near the massive convention center. Even with the presumably captive next-door convention market, the *Chicago Tribune* in July 1976 termed the hotel "a financial flop since it opened in April 1973."[71] The McCormick Inn closed in 1993, as the Metropolitan Pier and Exposition Authority took the property for another expansion of the convention center.

Despite long being the nation's largest convention center, McCormick Place has yielded very little development impact. Only the modest-sized

McCormick Inn was developed by private capital, and the promised "McCormick City" never materialized. When the MPEA sought private investment in a new hotel to replace the inn, it was unable to secure a developer. The MPEA itself ultimately financed and developed a new hotel, the 800-room Hyatt McCormick Place, in 1996, using tax exempt revenue bonds.

For all of its vast exhibit hall space and over one million convention and tradeshow attendees in 1995, McCormick Place's calendar was dominated by major tradeshows. And those shows pulled in a great many attendees who did not stay overnight in Chicago hotel rooms. The one million convention attendees in 1995 generated just 585,926 hotel room nights, according to data from the Chicago Convention and Tourism Bureau. That was far from the assumed three-night stay that consultants and local officials often touted. With the expansion in 1997, more space got McCormick Place up to 55 conventions and tradeshows in 1999 with 1.24 million attendees. But they still yielded the Chicago area just 786,329 hotel room nights.

McCormick Place also was obliged to deal with the legacy of its peculiar lakefront location. While the *Tribune* had enthused about the site's unique attributes and "scenic beauty," the reality was that it was both isolated and quite distant from existing concentrations of hotels, restaurants, and stores in the Loop. When new hotels were built in the 1970s and 1980s, they rose within walking distance of the Loop or North Michigan Avenue.

When PriceWaterhouse assessed the development impacts of a number of large convention facilities in 1995 for the Massachusetts Convention Center Authority, the verdict on McCormick was dramatic. The consulting firm noted that the "McCormick Inn was financially unsuccessful, since its location required it to rely, almost completely, on convention groups from McCormick Place." The consultant assessment went on to conclude, "Since the opening of McCormick Place in 1960, retail, restaurant, and residential development has not taken place in its vicinity."[72]

Paying and Planning

McCormick Place was a pathbreaking development in terms of public investment and financing. Chicago's previous convention and meeting facilities, like those in a number of other cities, were privately developed and financed. The commitment of millions of public dollars was a notable shift, albeit one that had been attempted in Chicago since the 1920s.

Even more remarkable was the source of McCormick's financing. Cities such as St. Louis, Cleveland, and Detroit had financed their convention centers with general obligation bonds that required a public vote. The efforts by the city of Chicago and Cook County to develop a convention hall through the 1920s had also involved the need for public approval at the polls. But in turning to the state government for financing, McCormick Place was never subject to a direct public vote. The only requisite was approval by the state legislature and the governor. By avoiding both a public vote and the vagaries of Chicago city politics, the *Tribune* could operate in a political environment that was both more certain and more controllable. Such "deals" as had to be made, including packaging the Chicago hall funding with monies for downstate county fairs, could be made in Springfield, the state capital.

The innovative character of McCormick Place was also visible in its actual governance structure. The convention center was built and overseen by an independent public authority, governed by board members jointly appointed by the mayor of Chicago and the governor of Illinois. The public authority vehicle neatly insulated the Metropolitan Fair and Exposition Authority from public visibility, while its appointed board provided the image of "good government" citizen oversight, even as its membership too was initially dictated by the *Tribune*.

The *Tribune* promoted Maj. Lenox Lohr as chairman of the new authority. Lohr had run the 1933 Century of Progress Fair and the subsequent Railroad Fairs, and served 28 years as head of Chicago's Museum of Science and Industry. Lohr was joined on the initial Fair Authority board by such civic notables as former U.S. senator C. Wayland Brooks, Henry Crown of the Materials Service Corporation, and George Halas, president of the Chicago Bears. This group was intended to lend substantial credibility to the development of the convention hall and convey the sense that the project was being managed outside the rough world of Chicago and Illinois politics.[73]

The notion that McCormick Place could be managed and developed fully outside the state and city political environment was far from reality. McCormick Place has generated far more than its share of corruption scandals and convictions over contracts, labor agreements, and personnel. But in the mid-1950s, with overt conflict over the location of the new convention hall, a board composed of respected public figures helped convey the image that the site selection was made outside narrow, parochial considerations.

The case that the lakefront site was the most sensible choice was also justified by a formal analysis. The *Tribune* regularly referred to the rigorous technical assessment of alternative sites conducted by Ralph Burke and the Holabird and Roche architectural firm in 1955. An April 1956 editorial in the paper argued, "In spite of some of the irresponsible statements made in recent days, the 23d st. site was not picked by whimsy. On the contrary, it has been under discussion three years. Eleven proposed sites were subjected to a technical analysis that took eight months' work. The lake front location is not only the best site, it is the only feasible one."[74] The Burke/Holabird and Roche analysis is indeed an impressive, oversize, multicolor document. But even a cursory examination makes clear that the "technical analysis" of location alternatives was remarkably loaded and effectively preordained.

The "technical" aspect of the Burke/Holabird assessment consisted of a set of broad factors, each assigned a relative weight or value. The site factors included *adequacy* (with a weight of 30 percent), composed of measures of area required (including parking for a minimum of 4,000 cars), expandability, and setting ("natural prominence of the improvements"); *accessibility* (30 percent), made up of measures of access from the city center and the greater city; *availability of service* (30 percent), based on service by rail, truck, air, and water; and *extraordinary costs* (10 percent), estimates of land acquisition and construction costs.

Overall, the Twenty-Third Street location long promoted by the *Tribune* came in at a total of 84.5 percent, well above two other lakefront sites (at 73.7 and 70 percent), and far better than the close-in sites proposed by other groups. The South Side Planning Board's preferred site at Twenty-Second Street and Michigan Avenue garnered a total score of 18 percent. The West Side location at Union Station managed a total of 29 percent. The Illinois Central air rights site backed by the Greater North Michigan Avenue Association came in at a total of −7 percent. And a close-in site at Harrison and Dearborn Streets, "suggested as part of a composite plan to clear the south side of the central business district of obsolete structures," was dismissed as "deficient for immediate needs" and not even given a formal score.

The study effectively weighted its criteria and scoring to favor large, undeveloped sites with ample open area over developed locales. But the actual scoring was neatly rigged. While the "extraordinary cost" dimension was ostensibly only 10 percent, the actual calculation gave negative values based on land and foundation costs. On that one modest measure alone, the Burke/Holabird study assigned the Planning Board preference a score of −55 percent, the Union Station location a −26 percent, and the Illinois Central air rights a whopping −82 percent.

The work of Ralph Burke and the Holabird firm was far from a serious analysis of locational alternatives or a substantial planning effort. But a serious analysis was not at all what the Park Fair group that commissioned the study sought. As Edward Banfield describes it, "The directors knew, however, that there was bound to be a long public argument over the site. . . . Anticipating trouble, the directors provided for it." And Ralph Burke, formerly the chief engineer of the Chicago Park District and the city, was apparently fully capable of providing the technical legitimacy the group sought.[75]

Politics, Interests, and Coalitions

From the 1920s through the 1950s, there was no shortage of plans and proposals for a new convention hall to serve the city. In parallel, there was manifestly no shortage of specific geographic interests promoting sites for a convention hall that would serve their own ends and development plans. The Chicago Convention Bureau and Loop hotel owners, as well as the Association of Commerce, could back a convention hall scheme at any reasonably convenient site. For almost everyone else, including the Chicago Plan Commission, planner Ted Aschman, and mayoral adviser James Downs, the real value of a new convention facility lay not in the ability to attract convention delegates or maintain the city's place as a major meeting destination. A convention hall was instead a mechanism for shaping and altering land values and development prospects.

The Greater North Michigan Avenue Association backed the Illinois Central air rights site for the convention hall because they saw in it both a lure for new hotel development on Michigan Avenue north of the Chicago River and a magnet for new shoppers and retail activity along the avenue. In a similar fashion, the GNMAA promoted a new civic center on the Near North Side (as part of the Fort Dearborn scheme) because it "will add *considerable impetus* to the redevelopment of the Chicago River north bank and near northside." The group also backed and succeeded in implementing an urban renewal project, the North Clark-LaSalle project, west of Michigan Avenue, designed to "eliminate blight and protect the residential section to the east" while bolstering the security of Michigan Avenue property owners. This project, built as Carl Sandburg Village, ultimately brought almost 3,200 new middle and upper-income housing units to the Near North Side.[76]

The focus of the Greater North Michigan Avenue Association during this period was resolutely on employing public projects, from the prospect of a civic center or convention center to the reality of urban redevelopment, to bolster land values and spur private investment.

It was much the same for the host of geographic interests and organizations in and around the Loop. The goals of the West Central Association—dating back to the 1909 Burnham plan—were much the same for its locale, albeit with far less success. The South Side Planning Board sought a new convention hall on the south side between Cermak Avenue and Twenty-Fifth Street, where it would "sow seeds" for the area's redevelopment. The focus of Loop property managers and owners such as Graham Aldis and Carroll Sudler was just as resolutely on their turf, the financial and office core of the Loop, and on assuring that new public investment would support and reinforce their private investment. They promoted a near West Side location on air rights over Union Station for the convention center, with the argument, "we should not try to attract the people to a remote location."[77]

For developer Arthur Rubloff, a major public investment project served a dual role as both symbolic assurance of the future viability of a new private development and as a magnet or anchor for that development. Thus Rubloff promoted a new civic center (and originally a new campus for the University of Illinois) as part of the Fort Dearborn project, and the convention hall on the Illinois Central Railroad air rights where it would serve North Michigan Avenue. But as a developer, Rubloff could gain from any number of different public investments and development opportunities. When the GNMAA secured city backing for the North Clark-LaSalle redevelopment project, Arthur Rubloff was the major investor in the development syndicate that built new apartments and townhouses. And after promoting Fort Dearborn's civic center as the location for a new courts building, Rubloff could still gain when Mayor Daley chose to build the new structure, the Chicago Civic Center, adjacent to the existing City-County Building.

Once the new Civic Center was announced, Rubloff began to develop a new office tower, the Brunswick Building, immediately across the street, seeking to capitalize on the increased demand for law offices convenient to the courtrooms in the Civic Center. A developer like Rubloff could and did promote a variety of projects and development schemes for a number of different locales. His own fortunes were not necessarily tied to the choice or success of a single location. Rather, his interests and those of other developers were best served by a number of distinct new public projects and development initiatives, which promised increased value in specific locations and demonstrated the city and state government commitment to the Loop.

The situation of the Metropolitan Housing and Planning Council—the focus of Edward Banfield's case study in *Political Influence*—was somewhat different from that of the geographically defined business organizations or a developer like Rubloff. The MHPC viewed itself as a proponent of "good planning" and appropriate urban development and redevelopment. Its opposition to the lakefront site for McCormick Place was based on its support for the redevelopment of inner city slum neighborhoods and the enhancement of the Loop. It sought a close-in site for the convention hall, preferably on the decayed south side of the Loop, because this both served larger planning aims and demonstrated the openness of the planning process. But if the MHPC and Joseph Pois "lost" the fight over the location of McCormick Place, the reality was that there were other means to achieve these same larger land use goals.

Both for the Metropolitan Housing and Planning Council, and for Loop interests and the city's business leaders, there was the possibility that another major public development project could serve much the role of "stabilization of declining areas" that had been envisioned for the new convention hall. When the possibility of a Near South Side location for a new University of Illinois campus arose, the MHPC both allied itself with Mayor Daley in support (after having decried his lack of activity on McCormick Place) and took the initiative to "rally civic support for the near south side location," with the aim of "strengthening the whole philosophy of supporting city planning generally as well as . . . influencing the site selection of the University branch." One MHPC board member suggested moving to establish "a joint committee consisting of members from other civic organizations to rally support for the south side site."[78]

The MHPC ultimately called "an extraordinary meeting" in May 1959 of organizations backing the South Side site for the new university campus, including the State Street Council, the West Central Association, the Federation of Labor, the Association of Commerce and Industry, the Building Managers Association, the Chicago Real Estate Board, the South Side Planning Board, and the Central Area Committee, creating a "Joint Action Committee of Civic Organizations." Notably, the list of organizations willing to band together in support of the south Loop site for the campus included almost every one of the entities that had been divided on the new convention hall, each then backing its own preferred site for what became McCormick Place.

Where two or three years earlier the landscape of spatial interests in and around the Loop area of Chicago had been one of thoroughgoing conflict and division—what Edward Banfield had termed "fundamental conflicts of interest and opinion among the business leaders"—there now emerged a remarkable degree of agreement among those same leaders in support of a single, specific site for the University of Illinois campus. For the MHPC and a host of other interests, a new university campus and a convention center were much the same.[79]

Planning consultant Frederick "Ted" Aschman's 1957 memo on rebuilding the environs of the central area called for "complementary uses" to the north and south of the Loop, arguing that "rebuilding to residential use would make new high-level purchasing power highly accessible to Central Area stores," and that other such uses might include "the projected University of Illinois in Chicago, other government buildings, a civic auditorium, an institutional office campus for non-profit organizations, or a research center." Aschman's views when the memo was drafted in mid-April 1957 were particularly relevant, because of both his position and the evolution of Loop business interests.

Aschman, having left the position of director of the Chicago Plan Commission, had begun to work as the chief planning adviser for a new group, the Central Area Committee. This was a new organization of the city's business leaders focused on the downtown core, in many ways a direct outgrowth of the conflict over sites surrounding the two major development projects of the 1950s, the new convention hall and the Fort Dearborn redevelopment scheme.

In March 1955, Harold Moore, senior vice president of the Chicago Title and Trust Co. and a close associate of Holman Pettibone, wrote to Patrick Hoy of the Hotel Sherman about a luncheon where they had "discussed some of the problems of the Central Business District" and the "need for some more active program than had existed in the past." Moore went on to note the suggestion of Graham Aldis—one of the major opponents of the Fort Dearborn plan sponsored by Pettibone and colleagues—"for a Downtown Commission to represent more effectively the overall interests of the Central Business District." Moore's notion was obviously a single broad-based organization that could unite the very different groups then warring over Fort Dearborn and the convention hall in a single entity that could promote some concerted action of mutual benefit.[80]

Holman Pettibone had worked his way up at Chicago Title and Trust, and was elected president in 1931. He had long promoted the value of real estate investment in Chicago, helping to initiate Homer Hoyt's landmark study, *One Hundred Years of Land Values in Chicago*. Pettibone had also played a central role as a business and civic leader, as a member of the senior council and later president of the Chicago Association of Commerce, a trustee of Northwestern University, and a director of the U.S. Chamber of Commerce. He had also collaborated with Hughston McBain of Marshall Field's in developing and implementing Illinois state redevelopment legislation in the 1940s.[81]

Pettibone subsequently explained his role in the genesis of the new Central Area Committee to his fellow Fort Dearborn sponsors by noting, "there had been opposition on the part of some of his friends and associates to his sponsorship of the Fort Dearborn plan," and that "as Chairman of the Central Area Committee he thinks it is important to preserve a proper balance between the conflicting claims of various Central Area interests to insure maximum accomplishment."[82] He later expanded those remarks to describe his belief "that it is possible to achieve a proper balance between rival claims of different portions of the Central area and periphery," noting that "the very expression of these rival claims is an encouraging symptom, as contrasted with the relative lethargy of the past twenty-five or more years in these same areas."[83]

By late 1955, Pettibone and his colleagues had sketched out a design for the "Central Area Committee" with the goal of "strengthening and improvement" of the central area under the direction of a small executive committee. In an exchange with Pettibone, planner Ted Aschman described a work program for the new organization, including an inventory of major problems and "preparation of a concrete program of action" including "specific projects . . . as exemplified by the Fort Dearborn Project." The anticipated structure of the central area group included committees (two of which were chaired respectively by Patrick Hoy and Harold Moore) and an executive committee made up of a small number of Chicago's most prominent business leaders, including Joseph L. Block, president of Inland Steel; Fairfax M. Cone, president of Foote, Cone and Belding advertising; realtor Newton Farr; architect Charles Murphy; Wayne Johnston, president of the Illinois Central Railroad; Kenneth Zwiener, president of Harris Trust and Savings; and Homer Livingston, president of the First National Bank, the city's largest bank.[84]

Perhaps the most unlikely pair of proposed (and subsequently actual) members of the Central Area Committee were Hughston McBain and John T. Pirie. McBain, chairman of Marshall Field and Company, was a prime mover behind the Fort Dearborn development effort. John Pirie, head of the Carson, Pirie, Scott department store chain, was an overt opponent of Fort Dearborn and prime backer of the effort to boost the fortunes of the south Loop.

In describing the relationship between the two, one Chicago business leader at the time said, "Pirie is against anything that Field's is for. Hell, if Field's was against syphilis, Pirie would be for it. And this is true of all the merchants on State Street. They hate each other."[85] The involvement of both in the efforts and decisions of the new Central Area Committee was something of a triumph for Pettibone. But it also symbolized the role and intent of the new organization in seeking to find common purpose and direction in a program or set of projects that could broadly benefit the Loop, its firms, and property owners. A broad array of business leaders (with widely varying locational interests) could support improved highway access to the Loop, better and more accessible parking, and general promotion. Yet, just as the organization could bring McBain and Pirie together, it could also define a set of development projects that could be distributed both to the north of the Loop—as with Fort Dearborn—and to the south as well. Aschman, in arguing for "the combined planning of the 'anchor projects' [that] would tend to dissipate any real or potential rivalry," was effectively calling for a scheme of logrolling in the leadership group of the city's major business leaders. If Pirie and McBain were naturally opposed over the potential benefit from a *single project*, their interests could well be joined with the combination of two or more projects, placed where each would gain or be advantaged.

Holman Pettibone sought to unify the downtown interests divided over the Fort Dearborn project's planned civic center by supporting new public buildings *both for the north Loop/Fort Dearborn locale and for existing Loop locations.* According to Peter Clark, who was the principal author of the Fort Dearborn case in Edward Banfield's *Political Influence* volume,

> Both as [Fort Dearborn] project sponsor and as Central Area Committee chairman, Pettibone worked to placate the various factions on Fort Dearborn, so that civic leaders might present a united front to the politicians . . . . But as they continued to voice their objections to it, Pettibone looked for more tangible ways to get their agreement. A new Chicago Federal building had long been anticipated. . . . Pettibone, however, suggested that it be built in the south of the central area near properties controlled by some members of one of the opposing committees. . . . In other words, Pettibone supported the interests

of some of the Fort Dearborn opponents. In 1959, the Federal government announced that it would build in the south central area.[86]

In the case of both the Fort Dearborn plan and the new convention hall, a *single project conceived and promoted alone* inevitably generated opposition over its location and concentrated spatial impact and benefit. But two or more such projects, whether university campus, government office building, or convention center, could be "packaged" and promoted in a fashion that could sustain a larger coalition. Such projects need not necessarily be "paired" in any public way. Much as Pettibone worked with the Central Area Committee leadership to gain broad support *within the business and property owning community*, the *promise* that one public investment project would follow upon another could well suffice to maintain the support of disparate interests.

Relatively early in the history of the Central Area Committee, it faced just such a situation over the issue of a new University of Illinois campus. Following the end of World War II, the university had begun to offer classes at Chicago's Navy Pier, near the Loop. The possibility of a new close-in campus was appealing to a number of interests, and Nat Owings and Arthur Rubloff had considered including a new campus site as part of the Fort Dearborn scheme. Pressure from students and faculty began to build for a permanent four-year branch campus in Chicago, and in 1954 the trustees commissioned an analysis of potential campus sites in the Chicago area. By 1956, the university appeared committed to a large, undeveloped site in the western suburbs, owned by the Cook County Forest Preserve District. Much as with the convention hall, that location appeared to provide a large open site at relatively low cost. The Central Area Committee chose to intervene in early 1957, making the case for an alternative location close to the Loop.[87]

Ted Aschman first set out the issues surrounding a "Central Area location for the U. of I. in Chicago" in a February 16, 1957, memo to Holman Pettibone. Aschman noted the university's preference for a site in the western suburbs, and one proposal for a site on Lake Michigan. Then Aschman went on to describe the advantages of a "peripheral Central Area Site," including the support of downtown restaurants and hotels, and the idea that "The campus development would be a major physical improvement for the Central Area and could contribute substantially to the beautification program through coordinated planning."[88]

Following a set of meetings in February 1957, Holman Pettibone wrote to university president David Henry, stating a case for "possible sites in or adjacent to the central business district of Chicago." Pettibone and the CAC had already consulted with James Downs of the Real Estate Research Corporation, who had conducted the original site assessments for the university. The Central Area Committee letter identified three potential campus sites: the Fort Dearborn project on a plaza fronting the Chicago River, offering about 60 acres; the air rights over the Illinois Central Railroad yards east of Michigan Ave. with about 45 acres; and 65 acres south of the Loop and Congress Parkway, occupied by railroad terminals. The letter went on to establish the logic of the committee's recommendation, noting the importance (clearly from Aschman) of maintaining the compactness of the central area and the benefits of "additional business through patronage of stores, hotels, restaurants, banks, and other business houses" from a nearby student population. But the letter was much more a statement of the Central Area Committee's spatial and political interests than an assessment of the value of an institution of higher education.[89]

The Central Area Committee's communication neatly reiterated three potential sites that had previously been promoted as locations for the new convention hall. In doing so, it presumably balanced and assuaged the various locational interests that had split over both Fort Dearborn and McCormick Place. But the letter (and the CAC position) devoted the greatest attention to the south Loop site. The two others had previously been considered and rejected by both university adviser James Downs and the Board of Trustees. The south Loop/railroad terminal site was new. It also neatly fit what John Pirie and the south Loop merchants had long sought to "balance" the proposed Fort Dearborn project and reshape the trend of land values—a major public investment on the south.

The university's response to the south Loop site was not particularly positive. Indeed, the rail terminal consolidation ultimately proved too expensive and infeasible, and the new Chicago campus was instead sited in a close-in urban renewal project area on the near West Side not far from the Loop. But in pressing for the south Loop site, the Central Area Committee had taken a major step in forging a workable and continuing coalition of business interests by embracing an array of public projects that could distributed to different sections of the Loop and its environs. That distributive strategy took a more formalized shape with the beginnings of an overall downtown plan in 1958.[90]

Ted Aschman set out the background of what would become the

Development Plan for the Central Area in a January 1958 presentation, noting, "the Central Area Committee's planning and research committee examined carefully the plans and proposals made in other cities, those which had been made for Chicago in the Carson Pirie Scott competition, and in other city planning work; this being followed by a set of principles and objectives which were then recommended to the proper city planning authorities."[91]

The first major principle Aschman enunciated was that the Central Area must be the most accessible in the metropolitan area. Yet he then added that "accessibility" also meant "that the surrounding areas, the slum belt around the heart of the city, should be transformed into new communities."

Aschman's second principle called for compactness: "It is the objective of this theory to contain as much as possible of our future commercial development within the confines of the Chicago River and Congress Street." That in turn called for "strong anchors at the north and the south . . . . It was this objective that motivated the Central Area Committee in proposing to the University of Illinois that they seek to develop their new Chicago campus on land that possibly will be released through railroad terminal consolidation." Aschman's presentation went on to describe additional principles dealing with parking and pedestrian access. But his penultimate principle, dealing with "timing," called for advancing a series of coordinated activities and projects year by year, with the goal that "the city's plans themselves, would offer some guidance to the *private developer* so that he may adjust his plans to fit long term goals that will *make the Central Area a better place for his investment* as well as for the overall welfare" (italics mine).

Aschman was voicing the larger imperative that defined the new Central Area Plan as well the greater purpose of the Central Area Committee—to make the core area safe and profitable for new private investment, as well as bolstering the environment for the big State Street department stores. And as the formal planning process, directed by Ira Bach (appointed by Mayor Daley to head the Department of Planning after its reorganization) and the Department of City Planning, moved ahead, the Central Area Committee defined the planning program, financed and oversaw studies of the retail area and the housing market, and "furnish[ed] the services of its staff and consultants." The final Development Plan for the Central Area was published by the city's Department of City Planning and addressed to Mayor Richard J. Daley. But it was in most ways the product of the Central Area Committee, Frederick Aschman, and John Cordwell.

Edward Banfield referred to the August 1958 Central Area Plan as "the

List and Prediction," noting that the document was both a list of decisions already reached and "partly a prediction of the outcomes expected in various controversies then underway."[92] It was that, of course, as it dealt with issues and projects like the Fort Dearborn scheme and the location of new federal government buildings that had been going on for some time. But in stating and endorsing locations for an array of public buildings, it was fundamentally a political document, less a "plan" than a "deal." The plan contained requisite calls for a distributor roadway system around the core, more parking, and improved rapid transit. Its most vital contribution was Section II—"Proposals for Specific Development."

The conflict over the location of major public buildings, from the division over the Fort Dearborn scheme to the debate over the convention hall and the issue of a new University of Illinois campus, had fundamentally involved location. Loop property interests did not want to see neighboring federal offices (where their tenants did business) shifted blocks to the north. South Loop merchants and property owners wanted a buffer or total clearance of the declining area to their south. The Central Area Plan sought to accommodate all these different spatial interests by proposing major public projects located to serve each.

Instead of the single concentration of public offices in the new civic center envisioned by the Fort Dearborn plan, the Central Area scheme called for "new government buildings on both the north and south sides of the Loop. . . . [where] the location of buildings in the proposals will contribute to conservation measures in the downtown area." The first new structure, the Civic Courts building, would go on the block adjacent to the existing City-County Building—just where Mayor Daley wanted it. The plan also envisioned a new state office building nearby, with a new federal government building on the northern edge of the core along Wacker Drive.[93]

The other half of the federal government's space needs was to be accommodated in the south Loop, including a new courts building on the site of the existing federal building. That was exactly where Graham Aldis and Carroll Sudler wanted to keep the federal government presence. By proposing to keep government buildings in the Loop area, there would be no civic center for Fort Dearborn. But the city plan provided for a plaza and park on the north bank of the river instead, complemented by a new office area for institutional uses (as envisioned by the Fort Dearborn sponsors), and redevelopment for new residential use.

The southern edge of the Loop, where the railroad terminals "have contributed to the growth of blight and decreased land values in adjacent areas," the plan proposed as the site for the new four-year campus of the University of Illinois. The plan recognized the potential problems of timing due to land acquisition and cost. But in language clearly shaped by Frederick Aschman, it argued that the south Loop site "will act as an anchor to contain further southward commercial expansion," and "would also greatly assist the Near South Side in reaching its highest level of potential development."[94]

In seeking to "anchor" the Loop on the south side, Aschman was neatly repeating and reiterating the approach and language James Downs had set out in May 1954, describing the planned convention hall: "a large scale redevelopment in this [south Loop] site would tend to balance Fort Dearborn and anchor the Loop securely."

The Central Area Plan also contained a project aimed at the West Side interests that had promoted the Union Station air rights as a site for the convention hall. There the plan envisioned a "transportation center" combining a new railroad station, an airlines terminal providing for airport limousines and future rapid transit to Midway and O'Hare airports, and a heliport linking downtown to the airports and suburban areas.

The plan thus offered a full set of public building projects, both inside the Loop's core and at its fringe, distributed north, west, and south. Each of the different locational interests that had emerged in the debates over the Fort Dearborn and convention hall locations was thus promised a project—and a specific benefit—of its own. As Peter Clark observed, "negotiators try to alter the form of the issue by suggesting the simple expedient of giving something to the opponents . . . they proposed that a Federal building be built in the south Loop, but that *some* of the Fort Dearborn ideas should be included in the Plan."[95] The Central Area Plan succeeded in unifying the various Loop interests behind a single vision and set of projects. It thus embodied one of the signal goals of Holman Pettibone and his colleagues in creating the Central Area Committee. It also placed the imprimatur of the city government behind a broad set of planning and development principles for the core area first set out by Ted Aschman.

Aschman authored a "review" of the formal Central Area Plan for the Central Area Committee in September 1958. He noted that the committee's "objective of 'compactness,' considered by the Committee as of prime importance . . . is succinctly advocated in the Development Plan." The review also noted the committee's recommendation of "anchors . . . to the north and south of the existing commercial core." That goal too was endorsed by the city's plan, with the plans for a residential Fort Dearborn and the new university campus on the south side of the Loop, "on land now occupied by railroads and blighted sections immediately south of Congress Street." With the city's apparent support for such projects as a downtown university campus, a West Side transportation terminal, and new street and parking improvements, Aschman argued that planning needed to continue, coupled with "Decisions concerning the specifics of the proposals . . . i.e., the financial, administrative, and physical details of such projects as the government centers, the rail terminal consolidations, transportation center, etc."[96]

The new Central Area Plan did not fully eliminate the locational and "turf" conflicts that had earlier divided the business interests in the central area. When Ted Aschman, in a speech in February 1958, described the westward expansion of new Loop office development, the leadership of the Greater North Michigan Avenue Association took serious exception. Nelson Forrest of the GNMAA wrote Central Area Committee members Fairfax Cone and Newton Farr, "since each of you has large investments in the near northside," complaining that Aschman's observation "indicates an unfair, negative attitude to the near northside." Representatives of the two groups met the following June, ultimately deciding "there should be exchanges of view from time to time between the Association and Committee to the end that we work together for the benefit of both areas and of the City as a whole."[97]

The Central Area Plan thus appeased and reduced much of the division within the central area, and city, business leadership that had stymied Fort Dearborn and other public projects. But it did not guarantee the successful realization of those projects. The West Side Transportation Center was never built; the railroad consolidation remained unrealized for years. And the plan for the new university campus on the south Loop site proved to be a victim of both the development cost and the opposition of the railroads, although the new campus was constructed during the 1960s on a close-in site, cleared under the federal urban renewal program, just west of the Loop.

What the plan, and the resolution of siting issues for the new federal building and the courts, did do was provide the framework for a shift by the Central Area Committee from planning to action. The group began in December 1958 to "translate this necessary but now virtually completed fact-finding task into a program of action." CAC executive director Randall Cooper set out a program for 1959 that included the new governmental buildings, a traffic program, improvements to Grant Park and parking, attraction of new offices, and a start on new residential development. The Central

Area Committee was fundamentally dependent upon public decisions and public action for the investments, improvements, and transportation access improvements the Loop needed in order to attract new private investment and development. Mayor Daley thus occupied a critical position for the business group, and was the focus of much of their interest and concern.

But while Daley occupied a vital position in deciding upon and allocating public resources, he was also loath to intervene where the business community was divided. As Edward Banfield concluded, "The political head, therefore, neither fights for a program of his own making nor endeavors to find a 'solution' to the conflicts that are brought before him."[98]

The *Tribune*'s George Tagge was rather more direct in describing Daley's role and performance on the convention hall issue:

> I think I was probably double-crossed more often by Richard J. Daley than anybody else. More often . . .
>
> . . .when we got into the years of the more bitter battling, and it went on for years and years, over the exposition center, you'll find Mayor Daley on one side today one day and leaning the other side the next day and back again the next day and back and forth and back and forth. . . . They [the *Sun-Times* and *Daily News*] didn't have the power but he still naturally wanted to avoid as much trouble as possible. And that's why he kept bouncing around.[99]

With the new-found unity within the business leadership and the broad backing of the city's newspapers, the CAC executive committee members sought to cultivate a relationship with Mayor Daley, and to point up the potential mutual advantage of cooperation. Thus, advertising executive Fairfax Cone wrote the mayor in mid-June 1957, noting Daley's meeting with Holman Pettibone and Randall Cooper of the CAC on the group's beautification report and arguing that "this is one of the finest things that has come out of your desire to make all of Chicago more attractive." Cone emphasized that the proposals "could become a feature for coverage by the national magazines and newspapers. . . . If you could present this to the Chicago newspapers I believe they would embrace everything about it with enthusiasm."[100]

In the wake of a relatively narrow general election victory (55 percent) in 1955, Mayor Daley had his own political concerns, particularly after the Democratic organization faltered in the 1956 state and national elections. As historian John M. Allswang has argued, Daley "began his successful campaign to win over the social and economic elite of Chicago and to support business and his ambitious building program." The support, indeed enthusiastic backing, from the Central Area Committee's leadership and of the city's newspapers was thus of real import for the mayor.[101]

The relationship (and mutuality of interest) between the mayor and the Central Area Committee was described by CAC director Hughston McBain of Marshall Field's in a February 1959 memo to the group's board. McBain reviewed his January lunch with Daley, "to give the Mayor a succinct and comprehensive report on at least the major projects in which the Committee is interested and on which it has done a great deal of work." McBain noted "that communications between the Committee and the Mayor have been most infrequent and impersonal," leaving "some distortion in the Mayor's ideas and impressions of the actual program, accomplishments and objectives of the committee." But, McBain reported, "The Mayor listened intently and without interruption . . . . I believe that his attention to my remarks showed unusual interest, absorption and respect for the Committee."[102]

The Central Area Committee had been formed in response to the failure to secure major projects such as Fort Dearborn and the new convention hall. Holman Pettibone and his colleagues sought in large part to build an enduring consensus within the city's business community over the structure and location of a variety of public projects, such as the Civic Center and planned federal office buildings. The mayor was key to the realization of many of those. But Daley made clear to McBain that his interest also lay in seeing the business community's own investment effort: "The Mayor indicated his belief that the Committee was concerning itself too much with projects and plans properly in the province of public organizations and too little with projects and plans properly in the province of private organizations. . . . He asked for more private initiative on such matters, and consequently, the investment of more private capital."[103]

Daley sought to remake the Loop with a new skyline—the development of new office buildings and hotels that would both signal the commitment of the major firms that the CAC's leadership directed, and boost the city's tax base. Inland Steel, headed by CAC board member Joseph Block, had begun the development effort with a new headquarters, announced in 1955. It was joined by a new building for Harris Trust and a new office building for Hartford Insurance. By the time the CAC published a six-year report in April 1962, the group could boast of $250 million in new construction completed or begun since 1958, and "The confidence of investors in the Central Area's future has been clearly re-established."[104]

The "anchors," "compactness," and "accessibility" that were the focus of Ted Aschman's interest and the key to creating an environment for sustained new private investment were not necessarily all realized. But Daley's commitment to an array of public initiatives, including the Civic Center and new University of Illinois Chicago campus, brought the political backing of the business leaders.[105]

A month after McBain's January 1958 meeting with Daley, "a bipartisan group of businessmen and labor bosses held a joint press conference at the Palmer House [hotel] to endorse [Daley] and laud not only his 'progressive program, but also his major accomplishment in making Chicago a better place in which to live and work.'" Among the businessmen backing Richard J. Daley in his bid for re-election were CAC directors William A. Patterson, president of United Airlines, and Fairfax M. Cone of Foote, Cone & Belding advertising.[106]

Conclusion

Chicago planning director Ira Bach met with the Metropolitan Housing and Planning Council leadership in September 1960. He told the group directly that the new downtown plan was less a long-term vision than a way of dividing new public investments, saying "that the Central Area Plan was actually brought out in order to fix the locations of certain projects." He went on to note, "The City is still firmly in favor of the South Loop Site for the University of Illinois, but must have a second choice if railroad consolidation fails." Bach proposed "an alternative use for the railroad terminal site if the University usage does not work out . . . residential, with some commercial."[107]

Bach's statement reflected a political reality that had changed dramatically from the time in 1954 when the Fort Dearborn plan was first announced. Mayor Richard J. Daley was now firmly allied with the city's dominant business leaders in a development strategy intended to bolster and enhance the central area. And a unified business leadership, largely embodied in the Central Area Committee, was in a position to realize the planning principles and goals that Ted Aschman had laid out in 1956 and 1957.

With the completion and publication of the Development Plan for the Central Area of Chicago in August 1958, Holman Pettibone realized his goal of creating a united business leadership, in marked contrast to the factional conflict that had become visible in the wake of Fort Dearborn. He had done so in large part by following Aschman's political and development strategy, laid out in his "Rebuilding the Near-North and Near-South Side" memo of 1957.

Ted Aschman had argued that "the combined planning of the 'anchor projects' would tend to dissipate any real or potential rivalry [between property interests in different sections] of this kind by offering a program which reflected the comprehensive objective of overall stabilization of values. . . . This would enhance the unity of the Central Area Committee in general while offering the best of possibilities for mustering all-out civic leadership and support for the specific program." By giving something (in terms of promised public investment) to each of the various geographic subsections of the central area, Pettibone could maintain a unified committee.

Edward Banfield had enunciated in *Political Influence* the central problem faced by Pettibone, or perhaps any business leader: "There exist fundamental conflicts of interest and opinion among the business leaders . . . e.g., what is good for the owners of the downtown hotels is not good for the owners of the amphitheatre; and what is good for the owners of real estate on the north side of Chicago River is not good for the owners of real estate in the Loop. . . . To suppose that these conflicts would be resolved if the 'top leaders' met at lunch is naïve."[108]

As he had conducted in-depth case studies of the Fort Dearborn project, the development of McCormick Place, and the development of a new Chicago campus for the University of Illinois, it is not surprising that Banfield saw a business community riven by conflict, disagreement, and dissent. But what Banfield did not observe were the issues and projects—downtown transportation and parking improvements, the construction of multiple new public buildings, the completion of a new downtown university campus—on which a great range of business leaders could indeed sit down together (as the Central Area Committee's executive committee members did monthly) and find agreement.

When describing for his colleagues a future program and projects for the CAC in July 1959, Holman Pettibone of Chicago Title and Trust could "submit that transportation takes first place," adding other activities, including to "eliminate unsightly, uneconomic structures in the loop" and "improve the loop's periphery including near-in privately owned housing." Faced with the same issue of the group's future, Joseph Block of Inland Steel could place first priority on "The question of the rail terminal consolidation and the location of the University of Illinois campus at the south end of the Loop." And Wayne

Johnston, president of the Illinois Central Railroad and a trustee of the University of Illinois, stressed "the mass transportation problem of the City of Chicago [as] the number one problem that ought to be handled by the Central Area Committee," adding rail terminal consolidation and a central area location for the new university campus as the second and third most important projects.[109]

These Chicago business leaders, each with his own immediate business concerns, showed remarkable unanimity in their assessment of larger problems. They all knew that the functioning of the Loop depended upon an adequate transportation system, and that a downtown campus (particularly sited where it would "anchor" and bolster the south side of the Loop, long a concern of CAC directors John Pirie and Robert Williford of Hilton Hotels), would be both to their mutual advantage and of larger benefit to Loop firms and the city. The Central Area Committee operated in precisely the fashion that Banfield labeled "naïve," by meeting and defining areas of agreement and by structuring programs that served their interests, narrow or broad, whether they were located on the north side of the Chicago River (as was Fairfax Cone and his firm) or well within the confines of the Loop, as were Pettibone, Homer Livingstone of the First National Bank, and department store heads McBain and Pirie.

It was planner Ted Aschman who had defined the essential *political strategy* behind the internal agreement within the new Central Area Committee—a "combined" set of projects that would serve to dissipate "rivalry." It worked fully, indeed magnificently. But the full impact of the Central Area Committee lay in its continuity and persistence. The group was not focused on a single project. Once established, it maintained an ongoing focus on the intersection of public policy and investment and the needs of the private business community. When the CAC published its six-year report in 1962, a number of the projects it had endorsed and promoted as part of the 1958 plan were still unrealized. Railroad consolidation and the decline of the south Loop remained "unsolved, in spite of several attempts." The CAC argued that "urban renewal . . . should be utilized more fully in providing sites for new Central Area development," and the report still portrayed the need for a consolidated "Transportation Center immediately west of the Chicago River."[110]

The capacity of the Central Area Committee to maintain a focus on the broad array of development needs and public investments framed by the 1958 Central Area Plan was largely the product of a remarkable continuity in leadership. Of the 13 founding board members of the CAC in January 1956, seven were still on the board in 1962. When Hughston McBain of Marshall Field's had left the group in June 1959, he termed it "fitting and proper" that his place be taken by the new chief executive of Marshall Field and Co., James L. Palmer. And when Randall Cooper, who had served as the group's executive director from the outset, circulated a listing of board members in January 1968, it still included four of the original board members (Cone, Livingston, Pirie, and Zwiener), and five other individuals (such as Field's James Palmer) who represented firms—Chicago Title and Trust, Inland Steel, and the Illinois Central Railroad—from which the original board had been drawn. Two other 1968 board members had literally been present at the creation. James C. Downs of the Real Estate Research Corporation had long advised both Mayor Daley and the Central Area Committee (and contributed to the 1958 plan), and architect William Hartmann of Skidmore, Owings, and Merrill, who had been involved in the planning for Fort Dearborn and then as a consultant on the 1958 plan, not only had joined the CAC board in the mid-1960s but would go on to lead the planning effort that resulted in the 1973 "Chicago 21 Plan" for the central area produced jointly by the city and the Central Area Committee.

With this continuity in both individual and interest membership, the Central Area Committee could take the "long view" of the prospects of the Loop and its immediate environs. When railroad consolidation proved "unsolved" for some two decades, the 1973 Chicago 21 plan could propose a "South Loop New Town . . . on the railyards site," and ultimately see it realized in the late 1970s as "Dearborn Park," a new residential community. And while the plan for a transportation terminal just west of the Chicago River adjacent to Union Station (once a potential site for the convention hall) proved abortive, the area attracted the attention of a consortium of New York and London builders, who proposed developing a series of skyscraper office buildings. And when that scheme too proved infeasible, Tishman Realty stepped in to develop the Gateway Center complex of offices.[111]

In parallel fashion, a developer like Arthur Rubloff could profit from a variety of initiatives and proposals, whether realized or not. The Fort Dearborn scheme proved unworkable and unrealized. But Rubloff still managed to redevelop a large area just west of North Michigan Ave., the North-LaSalle urban renewal project, as the Carl Sandburg Village residential development. When it proved impossible to build a new civic center complex north of the river at Fort Dearborn, Rubloff could switch to an office development adjacent to the realized Civic Center, now the Richard J. Daley Center. And then, in 1973, Rubloff could unveil a grand scheme to clear and rebuild the "North Loop" with a complex of an enclosed shopping mall, office buildings, and a hotel, using a new public library as an "anchor" for the development.[112]

Throughout this period, there was an intimate tie of mutual self-interest between the Central Area Committee and the city government. The plans for the central area were formally done by the city, but actually carried out by Skidmore, Owings, and Merrill under the guidance of the Central Area Committee. And the downtown businessmen were careful to maintain and burnish their connections to the city. Before a meeting with John Duba, the commissioner of the city's new Department of Development and Planning, in September 1965, the CAC president, Kenneth Zwiener, could tell Fairfax "Fax" Cone, "*we should be prepared* to ask specific questions about the City's capital improvements projects for the Central Area, such as those on the attached list." Zwiener's "Confidential" memo went on,

> Our relationship with John should be as close and compatible as possible. However, if we just listen to Duba and [deputy commissioner] Wetmore and don't avail ourselves of the opportunity to question them and let them know how important these items are to the Central Area, they will leave the meeting with the feeling that we are content with things as they are. This is our opportunity to impress upon Duba how important the Central Area is to the City and its continued economic growth and the need for stepping up his capital improvement projects in the area.
>
> From all indications, capital improvement money will not be as plentiful as it has been. So unless we present our case in a positive manner we can expect little help.[113]

Coda

Meeting with Hughston McBain of Marshall Field's in April 1945, Holman Pettibone shared a concern over the blighted areas "near the central business district." McBain offered his view that the department store firm has "a very vital interest in trying to remedy conditions in this nearby area." They jointly commissioned an analysis from housing expert Miles Colean that recommended two redevelopment projects, one on the west side of the Loop, the other on the south, that would "anchor" the Loop and generate new investment and development.[114]

By early 1954, as the Fort Dearborn proposal was unveiled, Pettibone had come to recognize the need for a larger effort to aid the Loop and boost private investment. At a meeting with senior city officials, he told Mayor Kennelly, Ted Aschman, Jim Downs, and a group of the city's planning leaders of his belief that "it was a mistake to confine major redevelopment to only one part of the city, such as the south side." He then went on "that there was obvious need to bolster the downtown business district by such a project as the one under discussion [Fort Dearborn]." Pettibone was not wedded to the idea of a concentration of new public buildings at Fort Dearborn—the centerpiece of Arthur Rubloff's vision and Nat Owings's plan. For Pettibone, Hughston McBain, and the businessmen behind Fort Dearborn, "the idea related to an appropriate redevelopment of a rundown area on the north river bank, whether or not it included a civic center."[115]

It was Pettibone's quest to "bolster the downtown business district" and attract new private investment that underlay the creation of the Central Area Committee, and the new organization's focus on planning for the Loop and immediate environs. Thus when Aschman set out the overarching vision for rebuilding the Near North and Near South Sides in April 1957, he began with the purpose "to stabilize and strengthen the Central Area," and concluded with the appeal for new "anchor projects" that would serve the "comprehensive objective of stabilization of values."

Pettibone's central purpose never varied, from the 1930s through the 1940s and 1950s until his death in 1962. That purpose was to "bolster," to "anchor," to "stabilize," and ultimately to boost the property values of the Loop. Yet one project or proposal would not suffice to realize that purpose. Indeed, it proved remarkably difficult in the early 1950s to bring even a single development project, such as the new convention hall or Fort Dearborn, to completion, and in the right place. It would take a comprehensive set of projects, shaped by a grander planning strategy, to sustain the central area.

The Central Area Committee's ultimate planning and political strategy owed its greatest debt to Aschman and his view of "anchor" projects. But Aschman's larger contribution and impact lay well beyond the Loop and its environs that were his and the CAC's focus. As a consultant with the planning firm of Barton-Aschman, Ted Aschman played a major role in shaping the downtown planning and development efforts of a number of cities, including Milwaukee, Minneapolis, Cincinnati, and Boston. His ideas on the importance of compactness for the core, of constraining the tendency of business districts to "spread out," and of using systematic rebuilding of the downtown fringe, together with the development of "anchors," as a means of supporting new private investment and reducing the "unhealthy rivalry . . . between property owners in different sections" would help define planning practice and development initiatives throughout the country. And while Chicago's McCormick Place was built well away from the central area, new convention centers in other cities would neatly serve as precisely the sort of "anchor projects" that Aschman had envisioned in 1957.[116]

In a parallel fashion, Aschman's judgment that "combined planning of the 'anchor projects' would tend to dissipate any real or potential rivalry . . . while offering the best of possibilities for mustering all-out civic leadership and support for the specific program" would be the political touchstone for a host of other business groups and their cities. A single project, in one location, would simply not suffice to ensure business unity. A larger package, broadly distributed and planned, would prove the political solution. And, Aschman argued, those "complementary" public projects might be a university campus, an institutional office campus, a research center, or a civic auditorium. That may have been much of the reason why Holman Pettibone, reflecting on the CAC's accomplishments and its future program in July 1959, termed Ted Aschman "our star."[117]

Chapter 7

Atlanta: Enhancing Property Values

Atlanta's development of a modern convention facility in the 1960s came at the political intersection of two broad development efforts. The first initiative sought to boost the city's hotel and hospitality business and cement the city's role as a regional center by attracting a growing volume of convention and meeting activity, with a focus on the development of the downtown core. The second was overtly spatial—intended to alter land use patterns and reshape private development opportunities in and around the downtown core. In seeking to shape development patterns, the city's business and civic leaders were acutely aware of the diversity of interests and sub-areas of the city. They therefore sought not just a single project but a combination of major initiatives that could serve a variety of interests and factions.[1]

Beginning in the early 1950s, the city's quest for an auditorium/convention center—and ultimately a broader set of public development projects—came to involve both the city and state governments and to extend over a period of some 25 years. That quest and commitment provided a demonstration of the capacity of local development and business interests to shape public investment politics in a manner that effectively assured that big things got done, despite competing interests and policy priorities.

Gearing Up

As Atlanta entered the 1950s, the city's major public convention venue was the Municipal Auditorium. Originally constructed in 1909, it had been substantially rebuilt in 1943 after a serious fire. Yet, as Atlanta's business leaders sought to promote their community as the dominant regional center in the South, it

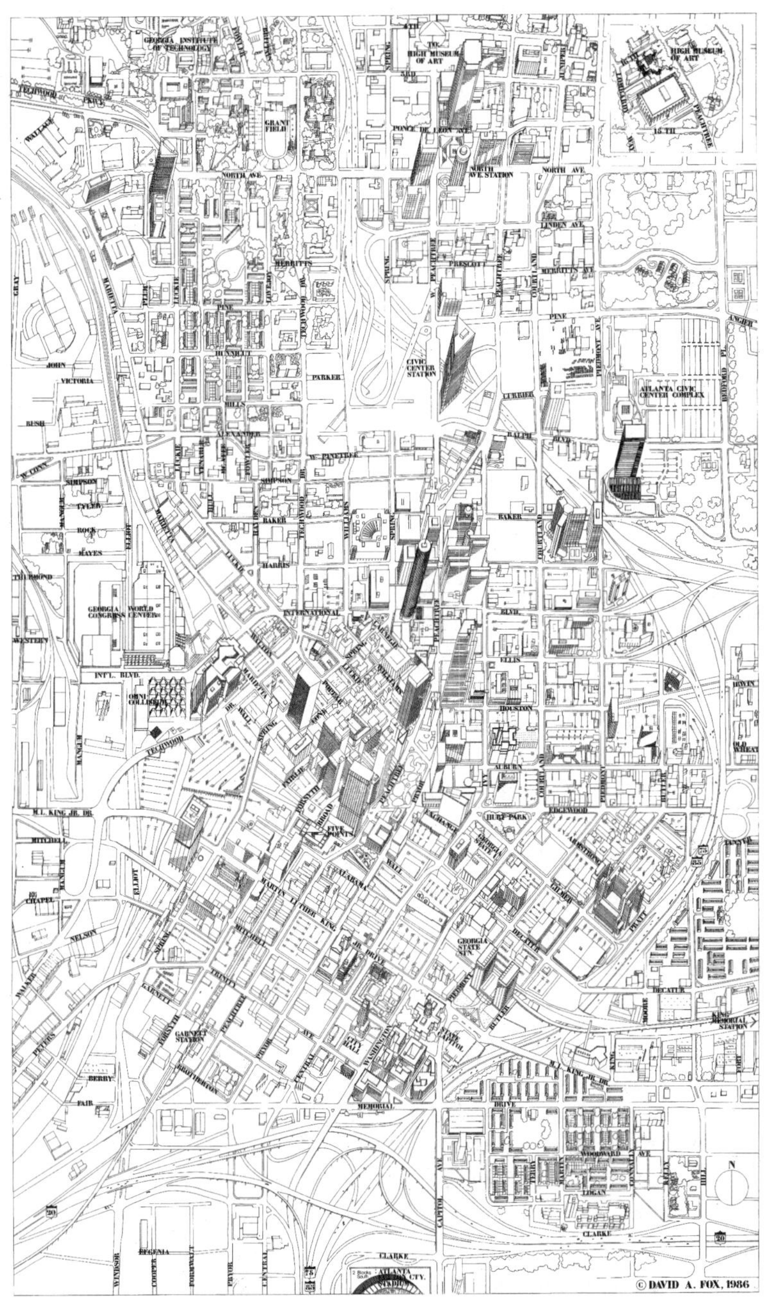

ATLANTA

Figure 2.

was far smaller and less functional than more recently built centers, and lagged well behind the plans of cities like Chicago and Detroit. A new convention center was, however, just one piece of a larger focus on major, catalytic public investment in the downtown core. But before Atlanta's business leaders and public officials could mount a program of new public facilities, they had to tackle the band of slum housing that surrounded the downtown core.[2]

The 1950 Census of Housing had classified some 65 percent of Atlanta's nonwhite-occupied housing units as lacking a private bath or dilapidated. To the east of the downtown core, in longtime African American neighborhoods such as "Darktown" and "Buttermilk Bottom," poorly built shacks with outdoor privies were the norm.[3] These neighborhoods became the natural focus of the city's development efforts, including highway construction and urban redevelopment. The 1946 Highway and Transportation Plan for Atlanta (the "Lochner Plan") specifically focused the routes for planned new expressways on neighborhoods "so depreciated that much of the improvement could aptly be classed as slum clearance," and included a full page of photos of "substandard areas which would be razed by the expressways."[4]

A focus on clearing the African American neighborhoods bordering the central business district was made explicit in early 1952 with the Atlanta Metropolitan Planning Commission's regional land use plan, "Up Ahead." The "Up Ahead" document described the close-in "badly-blighted sub-areas" as made up of "the small shack-like structures that were inadequate to start with, and the larger, older homes that have seen better days." It went on to link the blight of these neighborhoods to the larger problems of the downtown core, calling for action to "be taken as soon as possible" to provide both for "new facilities to make it possible for the downtown district to carry on its legitimate central functions" and for "Redevelopment of substandard and slum areas which blight and choke the downtown district."[5]

The plan's initial proposal for clearance and rebuilding focused on the Auburn Avenue district (the "Black Bottom"), just east of the downtown business district and the heart of the African American business area. Noting that "This area now contains one of Atlanta's worst slums," and "it is a definite menace to the future of the downtown area," the "Up Ahead" report argued, "It could be converted into a large civic center to contain an art museum, library, *large convention auditorium*, recreational facilities and downtown park areas." The plan went on to propose that this cleared site could be used "for the proposed 'world's fair' now being considered by local leaders," a development that "would wipe out slums and leave permanent civic improvements."[6]

To the north of the Auburn Avenue district, from Highland Avenue on the south to North Avenue on the north and east of the planned expressway, the plan showed a zone of "downtown housing." This was "Buttermilk Bottom," which the plan showed as among "Other Blighted Housing Areas" planned for clearance and rebuilding. The plan recognized that the capacity to reconstruct this area depended in large part on the future of Auburn Avenue. The redevelopment of "Sweet Auburn" as a "permanent park and civic center of great beauty and usefulness" would in turn "make possible new downtown housing and hotel development in sections," including Buttermilk Bottom.[7]

The "Up Ahead" plan thus joined a spatial focus—the clearance of the east side "Black Bottom" slum—with the creation of a civic complex that would serve as a development magnet that "would make possible new downtown housing and hotel construction in adjacent sections." The plan also endorsed the clearance and rebuilding of a swath of slums south of the downtown core, on either side of the south leg of the planned expressway, providing for "white and colored housing" as well as a new industrial district. And to the west of the core, in the area known as "Railroad Gulch," the plan proposed the development of a "large central transportation terminal," including facilities for buses and trains, with a "helicopter landing field" on the roof.[8]

The "Up Ahead" report laid out a dramatic vision for reshaping Atlanta's downtown "Golden Heart" and its immediate surroundings. It was in many ways the product of a single individual—Philip Hammer, the director of the Metropolitan Planning Commission. Hammer, educated at the University of North Carolina and Harvard University, came to Atlanta in the late 1940s after having worked at the Federal Farm Security Administration and as an assistant to former New York governor Herbert Lehman at the United Nations. Prior to directing the Metropolitan Planning Commission, he had served as project director of the Fulton County Local Government Commission, and authored the "Plan of Improvement" published in January 1950. The "Plan of Improvement" had proposed both a rearrangement of governmental functions between the city and Fulton County and a large-scale annexation program for unincorporated territory surrounding the city that, when implemented, would assure a stable revenue base for the city and a continuing (for a time) white population majority and political control.[9]

Phil Hammer was thus an unusually capable administrator and technician at the central juncture of local public policy in Atlanta in the 1950s, responsible for both analyzing the broader forces affecting the city and its development and providing guidance to Atlanta's business and civic leadership. He also shaped the Metropolitan Planning Commission's production of a more detailed development plan, "Now . . . For Tomorrow," published in 1954.

The "Now . . . For Tomorrow" document followed its predecessor in laying out a long-term development vision for the Atlanta region, with a notable focus on the downtown core. For the city's "'Golden Heart' of the future," the "Now . . . For Tomorrow" plan presented a full-page aerial view of the core, with drawings indicating proposed new buildings and the completion of the downtown expressway loop. On the eastern side of the downtown area, the plan proposed a "university-cultural center," combining a campus for the Atlanta division of the University of Georgia with a fine arts center and a "new public auditorium," including both an arena-auditorium for large groups and conventions and a music hall for concerts and plays. The plan noted, "convention facilities for regional and national conferences of all types will be required as metropolitan Atlanta continues its prominent role in the Southeast." The development of the convention hall would in turn lead to the development of a large hotel "between the conference facilities and the Five Points business district."[10]

"Now . . . For Tomorrow" also expanded on the vision for the railroad gulch at the western edge of the downtown. It proposed the construction of two new viaducts to improve circulation, and a new street route that would make possible the development of parking below the viaducts. With streets and parking, the air rights above the rail lines "would become in effect a regional shopping center right at the heart of the downtown . . . [that] would have an immediate favorable influence on private investment throughout the central business district." The plan's vision for the air rights site included a new department store, several office buildings, a transportation center, and "an 800–1,000 room hotel in conjunction with a new convention auditorium."

The 1954 plan thus neatly linked the university-cultural center on the eastern edge of the core with the development potential of the air rights to the west. A new auditorium-convention center not only would bolster the appeal of the central area and clear undesirable land uses, but was viewed as spurring major new hotel development and cementing Atlanta's role as a convention destination for the region. The spatial goals—of clearance and buffering the central core—thus combined with functional objectives of gaining convention business and spurring new hotel development.

Both the "Up Ahead" and the "Now . . . For Tomorrow" plans reflected

Phil Hammer's concern with bolstering the future of Atlanta and supporting the central business district. He had long bemoaned the absence of any sustained commitment to the planning and support of private development initiatives downtown. In 1954, he chose to leave the public sector and open a new planning and economic consulting firm focused on the city. Among his first clients was Richard Rich, owner of the Rich's Department Store chain, long a major fixture in downtown Atlanta. Rich sought a continuing source of reliable information on the city's economy and urban growth, and Hammer proposed to develop a base map and supporting data on new subdivisions, commercial development, and public projects intended to "keep you abreast of the most important things that are happening." All of this would be "undertaken in complete confidence . . . available only to Rich's, Inc."[11] Over the next few years, Phil Hammer prepared a series of reports for the department store chain on Atlanta's growth and development, and on the potential for new suburban stores.

Beyond advising Rich's and other clients, Hammer continued to play a central role in advising Atlanta's business leaders and shaping urban development policy. One of his first products as a consultant was a study of the air rights site over the railroad gulch for a group headed by attorney Robert Troutman, Jr., and including realtor John O. Chiles and engineering firm Robert and Company. In both the "Up Ahead" and the "Now . . . for Tomorrow" plans, Hammer had emphasized the development potential of these air rights. In his December 1954 analysis of "Air Rights Plaza," Phil Hammer emphasized the relationship between the air rights site and Rich's department store, just a block away. The study portrayed Rich's as a major "draw" for millions of shoppers a year, and the potential synergies between Rich's and a major national department store such as May Company or Gimbel's. The "Air Rights Plaza" report envisioned a large new commercial complex that could both build on the existing magnet of Rich's and offer the opportunity for new commercial development that would in turn spur new private investment in downtown Atlanta. The emphasis on development magnets and on the air rights site would be a constant in Phil Hammer's work, and in public investment policy, for the next 40 years.[12]

Beyond work as a private planning consultant, Hammer served as a member of the Atlanta Chamber of Commerce's board of directors from 1955 to 1958, and chaired the chamber study committee that in 1957 made the central decisions on the city's bond and capital investment program. It was thus not surprising that in 1959, when Richard Rich and a small coterie of the city's business leaders sought to jumpstart the city's downtown development efforts, they turned to Hammer to develop both a plan and a program of action.

Writing to Atlanta telephone company executive Fred J. Turner in March 1959, Hammer outlined "the assignment which you and Mr. Rich very kindly gave me last Saturday . . . regarding the formation of an Action Organization of business and professional leadership in Atlanta to promote the large-scale physical development of the city, with particular emphasis upon the Central Area." Hammer proceeded to sketch out the "Urgency of downtown problems" as well as the "Inadequacies of local civic organizations to organize action programs." Richard Rich and Fred Turner were likely frustrated with the inability of the Chamber of Commerce and the Central Atlanta Improvement Association to press a vigorous public improvement effort, as well as the resistance of Mayor William Hartsfield to a major spending effort. Political scientist M. Kent Jennings quoted one of the leader's of the city's 1957 bond program as saying, "Hartsfield definitely dragged his feet all the way until he was really pushed into it by the Chamber [of Commerce] . . . . As I said, Hartsfield was definitely against talking about a bond issue because he saw an election coming up, and he did not want to stick his neck out and talk about huge public expenditures."[13]

The program Hammer proposed for the new "action organization" was obviously built on the work and direction of the 1952 and 1954 metropolitan plans. Hammer recommended the proposed group take up promoting and expediting large-scale development projects in the Central Area, to be undertaken jointly by private interests and public agencies.[14] Fred Turner and Richard Rich immediately turned to a more senior and crucial member of Atlanta's business elite for his review and approval of Phil Hammer's proposal.

Attorney Hughes Spalding occupied a crucial position among Atlanta's business and civic leaders. A partner in the prominent law firm of King & Spalding, he served on the boards of both the Coca-Cola Company and the Trust Company of Georgia, and was effectively the principal advisor to Robert Woodruff, the chief executive of Coca-Cola and the wealthiest man in Georgia. Spalding was also sociologist Floyd Hunter's guide to the power structure of Atlanta. In an interview with Hunter, he averred, "I know I'm a 'stooge' for the Coca Cola Company and the Trust Company. I guess I'm a top stooge, but I don't mind admitting it. When Mr. Woodruff wants something done, and if I can possibly do it, I do it!"[15]

Hughes Spalding wrote back to Fred Turner and Richard Rich within a few days, noting of Hammer's proposal, "I think well of what he has to say and of the plan in general . . . we must have a long range plan which would take many years to complete." But Spalding went on to argue, "It would seem advisable and practical that we select some definite objective to start on now . . . and I for one would like to see one, possibly two, worthwhile projects started, let us say, during this year." Spalding was quite direct and specific about the project he favored: "a real, bang-up, first class auditorium." His reasoning was impassioned:

> It has always seemed a howling shame to me that cities like Jacksonville and Miami and New Orleans and Dallas have great stadiums for athletic and other events and we here in Atlanta have nothing. If I were running this show, the first thing I would go after would be a large tract of land where we could have a stadium seating from 75,000 to 100,000 people, along with accommodations for basketball, ice skating, hockey, and so forth. . . . Great sporting events such as professional football, ice hockey, championship Bowl games, et cetera, would means millions of dollars in the course of a year in Atlanta to the hotel and motel people and the merchants, not to mention the liquor stores . . . it is one that would appeal to the imagination of the whole community and one which I think, if we had the right people behind it, could be financed by revenue bonds.[16]

The report Phil Hammer produced for Richard Rich and Fred Turner in June 1959, "Action at the Core," laid out an argument for a downtown plan "to stimulate private investment and guide public and private development efforts," and a new civic organization to "get action on specific improvement and development projects." Hammer began with a striking depiction of the "plight of Downtown," marked by declining retail sales, dropping tax values, mounting office vacancies, and increasing competition within the metropolitan region. But Hammer also saw an array of development opportunities and private investment projects on the horizon, including a planned new merchandise mart, "a central plaza over the railroad air rights," and new apartment buildings and downtown office buildings and motels. In his judgment, Atlanta and downtown were at something of a crossroads. Hammer viewed a downtown plan as a "realistic framework for specific project development." There would be a central, perhaps catalytic role for new public investment efforts. Indeed, Hammer's assessment singled out the city's urban renewal program as the means "to remove the ring of slums around the neck of the core—an essential element in any Downtown improvement program, but only indirectly effective in meeting problems within the core itself."[17]

What Philip Hammer ultimately sought for both the plan and the new private organization outlined by "Action at the Core" was a dramatic boost in large-scale new private development: "It is the creation of new values through design and drastic restructuring of buildings and space that made Rockefeller Center succeed. This principle is at the heart of numerous other smaller but no less significant central plazas in other cities. In economic terms, the margin of safety is provided for the new investments by the creation of new values where none were before." Yet again, as he had in the "Up Ahead" and "Now . . . for Tomorrow" plans, Phil Hammer pointed to the enormous private development potential to be unlocked in the 1.5 million square feet of new space over the railroad air rights.[18]

Hammer's vision of a new, official downtown plan never reached fulfillment. Nor was any new civic organization created. The locus of business power continued to rest with a small leadership group, largely represented by the Chamber of Commerce and its board of directors. And there were internal divisions within the business community, most notably over which of a number of major private development projects would actually come to fruition, and how (and where) public investment would be deployed in the "creation of new values." Indeed, by the summer of 1959, yet another potential major public investment effort would join the auditorium and stadium projects that had so enthralled Hughes Spalding.[19]

Ivan Allen, Jr., scion of his family's office equipment firm, was part of a "new group of leaders"—"the presidents of five major banks, the heads of the Atlanta-headquartered industries like Coca-Cola, the presidents of the three leading big utilities, the heads of the three or four top retail establishments"—poised to take over Atlanta's civic leadership from Woodruff and an older generation.[20] In mid-1959, Allen was vice-president of the Atlanta Chamber of Commerce, in line to assume the group's presidency and considering how he might position both the chamber's agenda and the city for the new decade. Allen also regularly sought the advice, and approval, of Robert Woodruff. After meeting with Woodruff in late August 1959, Allen wrote him regarding some matters he sought to discuss when Woodruff returned from a visit to Wyoming, among them "a cultural civic center for Atlanta."[21]

Allen told Woodruff that "a small group" was seeking to "secure unofficial approval of the City, the County and a number of prominent citizens" for a cultural center (combining an arts center and concert hall), and to "come up with a definite answer as to what is needed, how it should be financed, who should operate it and what it should do." With Woodruff "paramount in such an effort," Allen sought both his advice and his backing, and perhaps ultimately—as the city's principal philanthropist—his financial commitment was well. And Woodruff replied that he was "especially interested in and think we should have a talk sometime before too long" about that subject.[22]

The cultural center that Allen was discussing with his small group was different from the auditorium and stadium projects that were part of the downtown development program outlined by Phil Hammer. Thus, by the end of 1959, there were three distinct potential public development projects—auditorium-convention hall; stadium; and cultural center—on the city's civic agenda. Yet there was no clear agreement, even within the business community, about where each of these should go. The west side railroad air rights site, long the concern of Phil Hammer, was the focus of the "City Center" development effort by local attorney Robert Troutman, Jr. Architect John Portman was seeking to develop a merchandise mart complex in the northern section of the central business district. And there were other plans, including one for a cultural center on Peachtree Street from architect Cecil Alexander and developer Ben Massell. Each of these developers and his very different locational interests stood to benefit from an adjacent public project that would draw people and attention. And in a parallel fashion, there was no clear means of financing each individual project, let alone all three.

When the Chamber of Commerce had proposed a city bond issue program in 1957, one major concern was the total scale of new debt. The business leaders were reluctant to take on so much debt that it would increase the city's property tax rate. Mayor Hartsfield was also a reluctant participant, facing the need to sell the city's voters on major bond projects.[23]

The chamber leadership thus faced a limited total fiscal scope and a host of needed investments, particularly for highways, street improvements, and urban redevelopment. Despite an interest in replacing the aging Municipal Auditorium, the chamber leadership opposed a modest $500,000 bond issue for the auditorium, with the argument, "Unless this facility is built on the proper scale, we do not believe it should be built at all, and the cost would appear prohibitive in light of other pressing demands for capital funds at this time."[24]

Hughes Spalding had offered Richard Rich one plausible route to fiscal success, using revenue bonds issued through a public authority. Revenue debt would arguably not fall directly on Atlanta property owners and taxpayers.

And it could avoid the problem of the direct public vote required for city or county general obligation bonds. For Atlanta's business leaders, financing the planned stadium with revenue bonds thus offered a combination of attractive fiscal and political benefits. And rather than following Phil Hammer's recommendation for creating a new civic organization, at least some business leaders were willing to use their positions with the Chamber of Commerce to move the chamber itself forward. Ivan Allen, as the vice president of the chamber, was prepared to try to link the stadium and the auditorium-coliseum proposals together as a larger package of public investments.

"All Factions Concerned"

Speaking at the January 13, 1960, regular meeting of the Atlanta chamber's board of directors, secretary Frank Shaw reported that the parks committee of the city's board of aldermen was prepared to ask the local delegation of the Georgia state legislature for legislation "creating an authority in Atlanta and Fulton County for the purpose of selling self-liquidating revenue certificates to build a stadium on city property in Lakewood Park." The aldermen appeared to be moving to get the professional baseball and football teams that a number of Atlantans, including Hughes Spalding, had sought. The initiative also provided the opening for a far larger undertaking.

Shaw's remarks were followed by Ivan Allen (slated to become chamber president in 1961), who "stated that it was generally agreed that the proposed stadium was needed and should probably have a seating capacity of from 60,000 to 75,000." Then Allen expanded on the stadium authority scheme:

> He also stated that there had in recent years developed a substantial sentiment to the establishment of a first-class music hall in Atlanta—probably to seat 3500, and that there had also developed a sentiment for a large indoor coliseum with an approximate searing capacity of 20,000. *He expressed the opinion that there would be some advantage in having the proposed stadium legislation broadened to include these two additional projects without additional legislation when and if it were deemed desirable to build them* (italics mine).[25]

Allen thus joined together the stadium and coliseum that Richard Rich and Fred Turner had described to Hughes Spalding, and that Phil Hammer had long endorsed, along with the music hall-cultural center that he had discussed with Robert Woodruff. By bundling them together as part of the proposed stadium authority legislation, Allen was laying out a solution to the combined fiscal and political problem facing the city in seeking to build three major public projects simultaneously.

Yet Ivan Allen also recognized that he faced a far larger problem in dealing with these three major public investments. There was clear division *even within the city's business leadership* over the relative priority of each, and far more importantly, over location and benefit. Allen's comments to his Chamber of Commerce colleagues continued, "It was pointed out that if all these facilities were included in one joint effort it would bring support for the authority from all factions concerned. . . . [Allen] stated he would like to see the Chamber sponsor a program to include all three projects."[26]

By bundling all three public initiatives together, even in the absence of a clear financing scheme, Ivan Allen saw that he could resolve the political problem that he, Fred Turner, Hughes Spalding, John Portman, Robert Troutman, Ben Massell, and Richard Rich faced of competing "factions"—even if wholly within his own political and social circle. The solution was the most basic of deals, a "logroll" promising everyone a project of his own. It was critical that Atlanta produce not just a single public project, but instead a package of projects that would be broadly beneficial. Those multiple projects could in turn be spread to quite different locations, potentially advantaging different subsections of the downtown area.

Ivan Allen proposed a motion to his chamber board colleagues that the group "seek omnibus legislation" from the state legislature to create an authority that could bring all of these projects to fruition. The motion carried, and the chamber then moved to formally communicate their interest and goal to the mayor and aldermen. But within the month, the apparent broad agreement behind the "joint effort" appeared to fray.

At the February 10 meeting of the chamber board, Allen reported, "all the necessary steps had been taken to secure legislative approval." But he also noted a problem—"due to some opposition on the part of Mr. Portman of the Atlanta Merchandise Mart, who is of the opinion that a coliseum will be competitive with some of the things he is doing, the bill as introduced may be amended to restrict it to a stadium only."[27] For Allen and his colleagues in the chamber and the larger business community, maintaining agreement and consensus was crucial. If architect John Portman was opposed to a coliseum/arena that might compete with his trade mart project, then the arena proposal would be abandoned, or at least deferred. A coliseum/arena to serve a new Atlanta basketball team, the Hawks, would eventually emerge as a public project in the late 1960s, finally to be completed in 1972. But in 1960, Portman's opposition was decisive. The new authority's future role would be restricted to just a stadium.

The chamber's capacity to realize both a new stadium and an auditorium was also constrained by the city's political leadership. William Berry Hartsfield had served as Atlanta mayor—with one brief interruption—since 1937. While he had developed and sustained an interracial electoral coalition, he was reluctant to take on new debt and boost city taxes. If the plans for the stadium, auditorium, cultural center, and a larger urban renewal program were to be realized, it would take a different kind of political leadership and greater effort from the city's business leaders.

As vice president of the Chamber of Commerce in 1959, Ivan Allen sought to develop and then present to his colleagues a program to grapple with "the general malaise the city was in at the time."[28] While Allen's memoir recounts his working on a possible program through 1960, in late October or early November of that year he turned to Philip Hammer. Hammer wrote to Allen on November 3, 1960, with "some rough ideas" for an inaugural speech to the chamber and a possible program for his term.

Hammer's "rough ideas" covered six specific efforts, ranging from dealing with school desegregation to expressway and rapid transit developments and an expanded urban renewal program. But much along the lines he had sketched out for Richard Rich and Fred Turner, Hammer also promoted the effort to "finance, build and support a new auditorium-coliseum and a stadium."[29]

In Hammer's view, there was a "growing need for and interest in" the two proposed public facilities. The auditorium-coliseum was seen as vital for "the city's rapidly-expanding role as a central convention site, meeting place and trade mart for both regional and national participation" and as an investment that "will generate further additions to local hotel and motel space . . . creating a completely new dimension of potential convention business." Phil Hammer went on to argue, "Metropolitan Atlanta is ready for major league professional football, baseball and other spectator sports," and "The key to Atlanta's participation is the availability of a major stadium, and the time is now ripe to build it. . . . The public wants these facilities and there is no time to lose."[30]

Ivan Allen outlined the "six major points of his proposed program" to the chamber board on November 9. At the group's annual meeting on November 28, he formally presented his "Six Point Program." He neatly included each of Hammer's initiatives, quoting (without attribution) Hammer directly on the pressing need for both the auditorium-coliseum and stadium. The chamber's endorsement of the entire program assured the general backing of Atlanta's business community. But it did not solve the problem of how to pay for the proposed facilities, and the cultural center as well. Nor did it resolve the question of where each would be located, and which "faction" among the city's business and development interests would be served. A scheme for resolving the planning and location issues would come from the city's most senior business leaders. And for the technical analysis of sites and alternatives, they turned once again to the most trusted and authoritative planning analyst in the region.

At some point in the fall of 1960, Richard Rich and Robert Woodruff jointly commissioned a study of "locations for key civic projects" from Philip Hammer. Rich's files contain no communication on the specifics of the assignment. But Hammer's report, dated November 11 (just days after his "Six Points" recommendations to Ivan Allen), focused on "the most suitable locations for . . . a Cultural Center, an Auditorium-Coliseum, and a Stadium," prepared "at the request of civic leaders interested in the promotion and development of these projects."[31]

"Atlanta Sites" would eventually make its way to the chamber's board members in mid-1961. In late 1960, it was solely for the use of Rich, Woodruff, and their immediate personal circle. The report itself, totaling 62 pages, was a remarkable document. Phil Hammer built on and elaborated his work in "Action at the Core," as well as his longstanding commitment to the need for a downtown-oriented rail rapid transit system. Yet in recommending alternative sites for each of the major civic projects, "Atlanta Sites" provides a detailed picture of local development interests, contending political pressures, racial and social geography, and a roadmap for the future of central Atlanta.[32]

Hammer's specific locational recommendations were ultimately followed only in part. Hammer, recognized at the time and after his death as a "progressive" white on racial issues, was quite sensitive to the circumstances of the city's African American population and the prospects for rehousing displaced residents. That prompted him to suggest development sites that would minimize the impact of urban renewal and displacement. For the city's business and political leadership, those issues and concerns finally proved of no real import.

"Atlanta Sites" recommended that the cultural center described by Ivan Allen to Robert Woodruff, with its combination of symphony hall, theater, a possible museum, and arts facilities, be built in Piedmont Park, the major public park on the city's north side—"where the major support comes from." For the auditorium, Hammer suggested the site of the "City Center" project over the railroad air rights on the western edge of the downtown core, a development location he had promoted since the 1952 "Up Ahead" plan and his later work for Robert Troutman. And he recommended placing the stadium on city property formerly occupied by the James L. Key golf course in the southeastern part of the city. These locations were either at the edge of the downtown area or somewhat distant, characterized by an absence of existing development and thus presenting no real problems of land acquisition or displacement. Hammer laid out a compelling logic for using public development to support new private investment—"it is better to pay more for a location that supports other developments than to acquire sites elsewhere whose initial cost is less." But "Atlanta Sites" also described and considered a number of other locations, much closer to the heart of the central area and far more problematic in terms of the existing residents and the burden of urban renewal relocation.

For the cultural center, Phil Hammer considered four alternative sites to Piedmont Park. He dismissed the downtown campus of Georgia State College, largely due to land cost and accessibility. The Butler Street urban renewal project, already under way, would also involve high land costs and a congested downtown location more suitable to private development. A site at Baker and Peachtree Streets, in the northern part of the core (a location "set forth a year or so ago by the architectural firm of Finch, Alexander, Barnes Rothschild and Pascal" in cooperation with property owner Ben Massell), would require the clearance of a number of existing commercial buildings at significant cost. Hammer argued, "it would be best suited for creating an outstanding 'showpiece' for Atlanta." But much of his analysis focused on a site also considered for the auditorium—the "Buttermilk Bottom" section bordering the core area on the northeast. Hammer described Buttermilk Bottom as "a highly-congested, deteriorating Negro residential section" for which urban renewal clearance had already been proposed.

Buttermilk Bottom as the site of a major public development project posed both "pros" and "cons." Hammer noted, "clearance of Buttermilk Bottom would displace several thousand Negro families." That displacement would presumably require new housing for the relocated families, and there was "already a serious shortage of land for Negro housing." Hammer argued, "Eventually this problem might be solved, but anyone who has even worked on it at the firing line knows how tough it is—particularly now." Atlanta had seen a number of overt conflicts over renewal clearance and new African American public housing developments. And Hammer also saw a political problem: "Negro leadership—a not inconsiderable force in local politics—is not likely to look with favor on a full-scale conversion of Buttermilk Bottom from colored to white housing."

"Atlanta Sites" also discussed Buttermilk Bottom as a location for the proposed auditorium-coliseum, intended to serve conventions and large meetings. Hammer was particularly interested in a highly accessible site "with easy proximity to the key facilities of Downtown Atlanta." Buttermilk Bottom certainly offered a convenient, close-in location. And Phil Hammer could describe it as "a deteriorating Negro residential section whose clearance is regarded as highly desirable and necessary to the protection of the Uptown area." Indeed, the Buttermilk Bottom site was most appealing for what it cleared and whom it moved away from such a central location.[33]

The "Atlanta Sites" report emphasized the interest of the Uptown Association and its members, representing the area just to the north of the business core, in changing the population and land use in the Bottom. Again, he noted, "the Auditorium-Coliseum project in this area would assist in the clearance of a bad slum and assist in the protection of the Ponce de Leon [Avenue] corridor and the Uptown area." He concluded, "The latter point is of considerable interest to responsible businessmen and property owners."

The interest of the all-white Uptown Association in removing the threat of African American expansion and neighborhood change by bulldozing the neighborhood was quite clear. The organization's board included a number of prominent Atlanta business leaders who were also active in the chamber's leadership, including developer Ben Massell, Arthur Montgomery (who would lead the chamber's stadium committee), Sears executive Lucien Oliver, banker James D. Robinson, and attorney Hughes Spalding. Hammer's larger assessment thus indicates a parallel political imperative, of seeking to maintain the consensus within the business community by providing the Uptown organization (which would ultimately merge with the downtown-oriented Central Atlanta Improvement Association to form what is now known as Central Atlanta Progress) with a project that would serve its goal of "protection of the Ponce de Leon corridor." The auditorium, with its substantial size and need for abundant adjacent parking, could provide a perfect semblance of a wall or buffer zone between Buttermilk Bottom (or what might be left of it after clearance) and nearby white residential neighborhoods and commercial zones.

There was also a more specific development logic for placing the auditorium in Buttermilk Bottom. "Atlanta Sites" noted that the area was "the next major Urban Renewal project to receive local attention," and a major local engineering and architecture firm, Robert and Company, "has extensive plans for the area, which is one of the major blighted sections of the central community." A new convention facility in the area would boost the Robert and Company plans while securing the broader "protection" and "stability" that the Uptown Association sought.

For Phil Hammer, the problems involved in clearing Buttermilk Bottom, including "difficulties of Negro displacement, political pressures and delays in Urban Renewal," together with high land costs, militated against the area as a site for the planned auditorium or the cultural center. This is one of the rare recommendations that he provided the city's business leadership that they chose not to follow.

If Hammer concluded that the auditorium would not work in Buttermilk Bottom, he had a clear preference for its site. Reviewing the proposal from Robert Troutman, Jr., to develop the railroad air rights to build what was termed "City Center"—a "complex of major new private buildings" including office towers, a major hotel, and new retail stores as well as a Transportation Center (which Hammer had proposed for the site in 1952)—Hammer's report cited the "obvious advantages of tying the Auditorium-Coliseum into this air rights development." It would be highly accessible, easily served by rapid transit on the existing rail lines immediately below, with limited land acquisition costs. But perhaps above all, Hammer saw the auditorium as the key to "make the entire City Center project possible through support of necessary public improvements," while spurring the "construction of a large new hotel or motel facility in City Center."

"Atlanta Sites" also laid out the logic of site selection for the proposed sports stadium. For Hammer, the "massive traffic generator" of the stadium required a site with exceptional accessibility and great opportunity for rapid transit service. He immediately ruled out any site that could not be served by rail-based rapid transit, and focused on locations that offered that access and the capacity to "make possible the opening of the Stadium in the reasonably near future," as the city was already negotiating for both baseball and football franchises. Hammer then focused on three alternative sites, some of which overlapped with his assessment for the proposed auditorium.

The Central Air Rights appeared to offer a plausible, close-in and accessible option. But he concluded that there was "relatively small tie-in between Stadium activities and the Downtown population or facilities." That argued for leaving the air rights available for the development of downtown-oriented private projects. A second alternative was the "South Urban Renewal Area," formally designated the Rawson-Washington project, located just south of the downtown core and immediately adjacent to the city's major Interstate highway interchange. The South renewal site offered excellent accessibility, the potential for rail transit service, and the ability to "eliminate a bad slum area, provide a healthy fringe to Downtown Atlanta and make the best possible use of the site." There would also be no need for major city investment in infrastructure to serve the site, given its highway access and terrain.

For all of its advantages in terms of location and access, Phil Hammer saw the same problems of displacement and relocation at the South site that he viewed as problematic in Buttermilk Bottom: "Although there would not be strong opposition from the Negro community to converting this particular area from residential to Stadium use (in light of previous agreement that its best use would be for non-residential purposes), the Negro relocation problem would still pose a serious difficulty." Subsequent federal government figures would show that Rawson-Washington contained some 1,400 housing units and 950 largely African American families. Added to the existing burden of displacement from the Butler Street renewal project and the likely relocation from Buttermilk Bottom, Hammer viewed the impact on the black community and the capacity of the city to rehouse displaced families as unmanageable. He proposed as an alternative the site of the James L. Key golf course. Deeming it as providing excellent access and immediate availability, "Atlanta Sites" backed the golf course site as the best location for a new stadium. Bisected by one leg of the city's expressway system, and owned by the city, it would avoid the relocation problems of the South urban renewal site, while offering the promise of "a stabilizing influence in a section of town which needs an 'anchor.'" And looking ahead to the financing of the stadium "under the new Stadium Authority," Hammer argued "In the long run, the Stadium should become self-supporting (including amortization of capital costs) if its initial outlay is not loaded with too many public improvements such as traffic and parking facilities."

Phil Hammer's assessment of alternative locations for the city's major civic projects demonstrated a substantial understanding of social and racial realities, as well as the political environment of Atlanta circa 1960. He

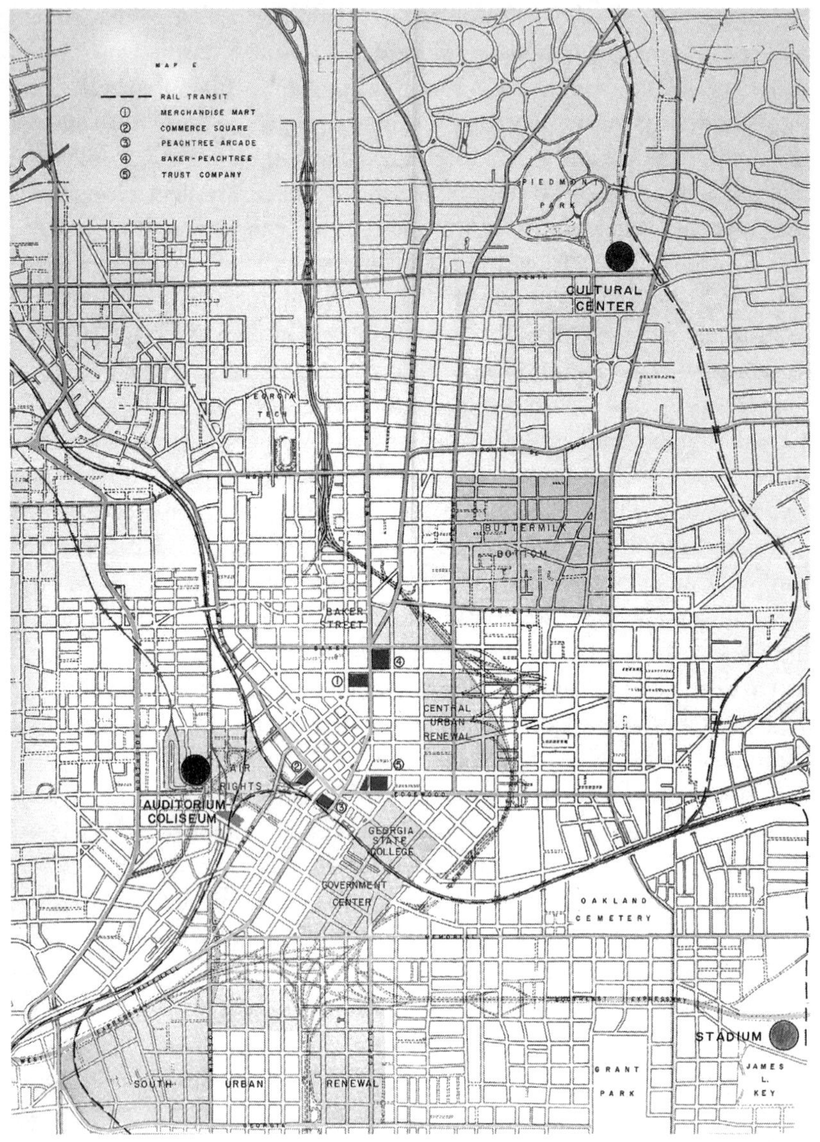

Figure 3. Locations for key civic projects from "Atlanta Sites," November 1960. Courtesy Emory University.

fundamentally understood—as did Ted Aschman in Chicago—the potential of public investment to catalyze private development opportunities. He sought to use both the auditorium and the cultural center to spur new development in prime, underdeveloped sites he had long recognized and championed. Indeed, in the final section of the "Atlanta Sites" report, he stressed the catalytic role of public investment for the air rights project: "As mentioned earlier, the introduction of the Auditorium-Coliseum into the plans might well be the decisive factor in the success of City Center. If this total project becomes the main interest of Atlanta leadership, there is no doubt it could be put across as the main elements of demand could be channeled in to support this outstanding development."[34]

Hammer understood that there was a *distributive imperative* as well. A major investment in the "City Center" air rights might provide the foundation for a Southern Rockefeller Center, and support Rich's department store business and location nearby. But it would do nothing to placate the seemingly insistent demand of the Uptown Association members for "protection." Nor would it aid John Portman's trade mart or the properties controlled by Ben Massell. A neat solution to these competing locational interests was a multitude of projects, or at least the promise of a multitude of separate projects to be realized over time.

In dealing with a package of projects, Hammer was reiterating and reinforcing the deal that Ivan Allen had outlined—garnering "support from all factions concerned." He described the competing development projects on the immediate horizon. And perhaps most importantly, he provided a *planning logic* for placing individual projects on very different sites, with very different political benefits.

The assessments of "Atlanta Sites" were also grounded in a full recognition of the racial issues surrounding housing in Atlanta. Years earlier, Hammer had tried to formally designate "Negro expansion areas" in the "Up Ahead" plan. This had created a furor, such that a mimeographed apology and errata were inserted into the printed copies of the plan volume. Subsequent years had seen serious conflict over new public housing sites. And in October 1960, the sit-in movement had begun in earnest at lunch counters in downtown Atlanta, targeting Rich's among other stores. Phil Hammer's November 28, 1960, letter to Richard Rich requesting payment for the "study of auditorium, stadium and cultural center sites for you and Mr. Woodruff" contained a postscript: "Your evaluation of the irresponsibility of Negro leadership was completely borne out. It's a sad day for Atlanta."[35] But Hammer was acutely aware of the larger social and political problems that would be posed by the large-scale clearance of Buttermilk Bottom, particularly if (as the Uptown group appeared to require) the existing African American neighborhood would be replaced by an auditorium or all-white housing. So for both the auditorium and the stadium, he recommended sites that would minimize displacement and clearance, even as he appeared to understand that the city would move forward with its renewal plans. For all Phil Hammer's sensitivity to race and neighborhood change and the potential for political conflict, the goals of Robert Woodruff, Richard Rich, and their colleagues in Atlanta's business leadership lay in precisely the opposite direction. Hammer's November letter to Rich recognized the vital role Rich and Woodruff could play in moving the major projects ahead. He wrote, referring to Woodruff, "I certainly hope that he finds time to give this matter his attention—if he does, we are one important step further along the way."

Coming on the immediate heels of Ivan Allen's installation as chamber president, "Atlanta Sites" laid out a blueprint for developing a package of projects that would collectively boost the city's fortunes and aid the overall downtown core, while solving the needs of specific subareas and development interests. With the auditorium and stadium officially included in the chamber's "Six Point Program," together with an expanded urban renewal effort and a rapid transit system, the next set of moves lay with Allen and his chamber colleagues and friends.

The Chamber of Commerce began the year of Ivan Allen's presidency with the creation of six new committees, one for each of Allen's "Six Points," and his observation of "these six projects being foremost in the Program of Work." The auditorium-coliseum and stadium committee was chaired by Arthur L. Montgomery, president of the Atlanta Coca-Cola Bottling Company, and included Allen, insurance man Rankin Smith, convention bureau director Walter Crawford, architects James Finch and George Heery, and planning consultant Philip Hammer. It was far from a neutral or disinterested group.

At its first meeting, on January 11, 1961, the committee "was asked to accept full responsibility for seeing that an Auditorium-Coliseum be developed for the Atlanta area in the near future." The group decided that the chamber would be the "catalyst" for leadership and initial funding of what was envisioned as a "joint city-county effort." And perhaps most importantly, in light of Atlanta's fiscal realities and Hammer's "Atlanta Sites" conclusions, that "Federal funds (urban renewal) would be used if available, for preliminary studies and actual construction." The group then held a meeting on

January 13 with the city's urban renewal director, Malcolm Jones, "devoted to the discussion of several site selections that could be available for our projects." In view of Hammer's membership on the committee, it seems most likely that the sites and issues described by Hammer in "Atlanta Sites" were a significant part of that meeting's agenda.[36]

By mid-April, committee chair Arthur Montgomery reported to the chamber board that the committee had already "looked into sites and has some models prepared, but prefers not to say too much openly until the present local political situation clears up regarding the 1961 election." Richard Rich, who had joined the chamber board and the auditorium-stadium committee, noted, "a study by Phil Hammer has recommended three locations for three different structures needed." Rich described Hammer's preferred sites for the concert hall/cultural center and the stadium, while terming the recommended site for the auditorium as "downtown Atlanta." Richard Rich was clearly blurring Phil Hammer's recommendation of the air rights site for the auditorium, perhaps leaving open the question of that location versus a cleared site in Buttermilk Bottom. In any case, Rich's presentation (much like Hammer's report and Ivan Allen's 1960 discussion) dealt with the package of three major projects. Yet, for the first time, the chamber's leadership appeared willing to make some choice of relative priority. Lucien Oliver, vice president of Sears's Southern division (and board member of the Uptown Association), and others "expressed opinions that the Concert Hall and Auditorium are badly needed now and should have priority over the stadium." With no immediate prospect of a professional sports team, the chamber leadership effectively chose to press ahead on two of the three projects.[37]

The choice by Atlanta's business leaders to pursue the auditorium and cultural center first was a product of both fiscal and political realities. The architects, downtown business owners, and convention bureau head on the chamber committee obviously wanted the long-deferred convention facility quickly. The cultural center/concert hall was a priority in large part because of its backing from Woodruff, and the potential for substantial private financial support. The stadium, with no team on the horizon, could be deferred for a time. Arthur Montgomery's comment about "the local political situation . . . regarding the 1961 election" was a thinly veiled reference to the serious possibility that Ivan Allen would run for mayor. Allen's friends in the business community were pressing him to formally seek the mayor's office, using the "Six Points" as the focus of his campaign. By deferring the stadium, Arthur Montgomery was seeking to ensure that an expensive, and potentially divisive, issue could be avoided.

Ivan Allen announced to the chamber's board on June 14, 1961, that he was resigning as chamber president, "stating that he will make his political intentions known officially at a later date." His colleagues praised him for his "handling [the] settlement of the recent Negro "sit-in" troubles for Atlanta merchants," having averted "what could have been a major blow to our economy." Allen's mayoral campaign that fall was a major focus of the chamber leadership, which sought both to promote turnout and to boost Allen's fortunes. Richard Rich told his fellow chamber directors that "the most important thing to do . . . was to 'build up a crescendo' through the press, radio and television," and went on to urge major merchants "to open a half hour later than usual" to boost turnout.[38]

Allen led the field of candidates in the general election in September 1961, and then won the runoff, with support from a biracial coalition. Much of Allen's campaign focused on the same "Six Point Program" that he had laid out for the Chamber of Commerce, and almost immediately after he assumed office in January 1962, he moved ahead with an ambitious development agenda. In early March, Mayor Allen appointed the members of a joint city-county bond commission to review the city's capital needs and propose a bond package. The Atlanta members of the commission largely came from the small circle of business leaders around Allen, including Jack Adair, who had preceded Allen as chamber president and was president of the Central Atlanta Improvement Association, realtor John O. Chiles (a former president of the Central Atlanta Improvement Association), druggist C. R. Yates (described by the *Atlanta Constitution* as "Negro"), and Richard Rich. Longtime auditorium proponent Cecil Alexander congratulated Rich on March 7 on his appointment, pleased that "It looks like the city is in good hands."[39] And on March 13, Rich could send a memo to his store president Frank Neely with the news that at the first organizational meeting of the Bond Commission "'our candidates' won out against rather spirited competition." The Bond Commission was thus poised to deliver on the projects that Rich and the business crowd sought.[40]

Even before the formal City-County Bond Commission began the work of inviting proposals and evaluating alternative public investments, the chamber's board of directors had begun to consider specific dimensions of the auditorium proposal. Arthur Montgomery introduced architect George Heery to the chamber board on February 14, 1962. Heery in turn announced that his firm had been working for the previous eight months on a plan for the complex, and presented a 48-page report to the group. Heery estimated the cost of an auditorium-coliseum complex at between $30 and $35 million. The architect also presented two possible sites—"the same ones recommended in a recent study by Hammer and Company"—over the railroad air rights or at Piedmont and Ivy Streets in Buttermilk Bottom, and said the Heery scheme could be employed at either.[41]

Heery's presentation and its focus on the two principal sites recommended by Hammer were not entirely embraced by the chamber's directors. Alderman John White argued that "strong consideration should be given by the City Government to selection of Piedmont Park as the site . . . because the city already owns the property." White was likely unaware of Hammer's recommendation of the Piedmont Park location for the cultural center sought by Allen and Woodruff. In any event, the chamber's discussion of the Heery report and the focus on Hammer's site selections make clear that it was the chamber—not the newly appointed Bond Commission—that was the locus of decision-making on the auditorium proposal and its location, and that by early 1962 there were only two plausible sites for the planned convention facility.

The City-County Bond Commission began with the difficult charge of relating the city's capital needs, from streets, sewers, and schools to the auditorium and proposed cultural center, to the available public resources. Richard Rich made it clear at the group's first substantive meeting that the city's capital improvement program included $137 million in projects, while the available fiscal capacity came to just $27 million. That would be the effective limit for all the city's needs and plans—with the Heery design for the auditorium/convention center pegged at over $30 million itself. If the longstanding commitment of the business community to at least the auditorium was to be served, Rich and "our candidates" would have to parse the fiscal resources very carefully.

There was little doubt about the commission's recommendation on a new auditorium. The group's Public Buildings Committee was chaired by real estate executive John O. Chiles and included Richard Rich. When the committee held a hearing on Atlanta's building needs, the first to testify was Kelly Mosley of the Convention Bureau, followed by Arthur Montgomery of the chamber's auditorium-stadium committee. Montgomery told the committee that the chamber "saw a great need for an Auditorium-coliseum in Atlanta, that we needed this to make Atlanta a leading Southern city." And, he argued, "if we had a stadium we could get major league ball and this would pay for itself."[42]

Mayor Allen addressed the committee as well, contending that the "pattern has to be cut to fit the pocketbook." The mayor was followed by Robert Troutman, president of City Center Inc., who came to the meeting "to suggest a site." Troutman told the group "that Phil Hammer has made a study about where the Auditorium should be placed and suggested West of Spring Street and Techwood Viaduct or that general location," at Troutman's air rights location. But Troutman went on to estimate the cost of the facility "at probably 20–40 million dollars. . . . A partial package could be put together for possibly $15,000,000."

Troutman had correctly noted Phil Hammer's endorsement of the air rights site. But his estimates of cost, particularly in the wake of Mayor Allen's expressed concern about fitting the "pocketbook," may well have effectively doomed the air rights as the auditorium location. Given the likely cost of access and building above the railroad, the city simply did not have the money to accommodate Troutman's plans.

The Bond Commission's final recommendation included $10 million for a new "multi-purpose convention facility"—the largest single project. The Commission report said, "Our Community is far behind other cities of comparable size in its auditorium colosseum [sic] facilities . . . essential to the continued existence of an element vital to this Community's economic well-being, our annual $30,000,000 convention business." The commission specifically called for a "facility in the downtown area, with full parking and exhibition space to serve it."[43]

The Bond Commission left open the question of a specific site, although the "downtown area" language largely restricted the options to either Phil Hammer's preferred air rights site or the urban renewal site in Buttermilk Bottom. Yet with only $10 million, the appeal of a cleared urban renewal site was evident. The commission members also took concrete steps to assure the highest priority for clearing Buttermilk Bottom.

As the bond review group was beginning its work in mid-March, Alderman G. Everett Millican wrote to his colleague Hamilton Douglas on the city's urban renewal needs. Millican submitted a request for $8 million, "already reduced from an original proposal of $12 million," focused on a group of projects "urgently needed through 1963." Millican's listing of those urgent projects included Buttermilk Bottom as priority "4A," below higher priority projects for Georgia State University, Howard School, and East Atlanta.[44] The following month, the Bond Commission's Urban Renewal Committee heard a different sense of priorities from Richard Forbes of the city's planning department. Forbes pressed a "high priority" for the Cooper-Glenn area south of the downtown core and the Rawson-Washington project (ultimately the site of the stadium), "because of planned city improvements to be placed there plus the fact that it would afford relocation housing facilities in the event plans were made to undertake an Urban Renewal project in Buttermilk Bottoms area."[45]

By April 20, the committee had reached its own conclusions about renewal priorities. Recommending that $6 million be allocated to urban renewal projects, the group gave first priority (and some $4.5 million) to the Buttermilk Bottom project, "the largest remaining blighted area near the heart of Atlanta and . . . Atlanta's No. 1 Urban Renewal opportunity." The Cooper-Glenn area, intended to resolve the city's serious lack of relocation housing, was given second priority.[46] The city's planning department followed up with a memo to the committee's secretary, recommending that "all bond funds" for urban renewal purposes "be utilized for the execution of the proposed 211 acre Buttermilk Bottoms project," as "Proximity to downtown and freeway connector makes this land particularly valuable," and "this was one of the most blighted areas in the city." With the endorsement of the Urban Renewal Committee and the backing of the professional planners, Buttermilk Bottom was now the prime focus of the city's renewal efforts and a viable site for the proposed auditorium. The relative absence of conflict over the auditorium and urban renewal projects did not extend to one other area of public investment, the city's street improvement program.

The commission's Roads, Streets, and Highways Committee, chaired by Rich, faced a plethora of needs to be fitted within the $27 million of city debt capacity. At its April 9 meeting, Ray Nixon, Atlanta's chief of construction, presented a list of projects amounting to $6.95 million. Richard Forbes of the city's planning department added another set of project proposals "which might tie in with urban renewal." Turner McDonald of Fulton County presented a list of $18.6 million of suburban road projects. And Burton Sparer and Tom Roberts of the Metropolitan Planning Commission voiced the concern that the suburban projects should have a greater priority, "since they tie into plans for State and Federal roads and streets." Finally, Bond Commission member C. R. Yates urged the group to include "paving the road on the Washington Street extension," apparently a particular concern of the African American community.[47]

Planners Roberts and Sparer wrote to Rich almost immediately after the April 9 meeting, listing proposed projects which either should not be done immediately, or which do "severe violence to the Plan." Roberts singled out a downtown project on Lower Wall Street as well as a proposed widening of a section of North Avenue. Sparer complained about another downtown project, the widening of Hunter Street.[48]

Richard Rich expressed his own opinion of the judgment of the "technicians" to W. L. Ramsey, who was serving as the committee's secretary: "While I am sure that we all wish to approach our decision with an open mind, it is my opinion that to give too much credence to the 'blue sky' planning for the future, at the expense of some practical downtown immediate relief would be a terrible mistake."[49] Rich was clearly focused on accommodating the "immediate" needs of the downtown, with projects that would aid Rich's as well as the larger core area. And these two projects were also central elements in the viability of the "City Center" air rights development being promoted by Robert Troutman, Jr. Both Hunter Street and Wall Street made it to the final list of the Bond Commission's recommendations.

One other project made evident the larger political process and accommodation within the city's business community. One recommended street project was the widening of North Avenue, east from Boulevard, including a new underpass under the Southern Railway tracks. This was the project planner Thomas Roberts had described as doing "severe violence" and "looks good at first but does not stand up under responsible scrutiny." Roberts's judgment was joined by city planning engineer Wyont Bean, who argued, "I do not think this project is necessary."[50]

Where the "technicians" viewed the North Avenue project as a waste of public resources, there were others who viewed it quite differently. The Uptown Association had focused on widening North Avenue in its January 1962 "Uptown Ideas" report, arguing that Uptown's growth depended upon accessibility and freedom from congestion, and that "Development of North Avenue into a major east-west thoroughfare will help solve both of these problems," thereby stimulating "Increased property values and new development."[51] Atlanta aldermen John White and Everett Millican wrote Rich urging "serious consideration" for North Avenue, as "It would also be of considerable benefit to any and all improvements that might be placed in the 'Buttermilk Bottom' area and, in fact, we feel it is vital to the growth of this section of the City."[52]

North Avenue was viewed as the likely northern boundary for a cleared and redeveloped Buttermilk Bottom, and of direct interest to the Uptown Association. That conclusion was echoed by the city's urban renewal director,

Malcolm Jones, in a June 4 memo that made its way to Richard Rich. Jones noted the "emphasis which the Uptown Association is still applying for Bond Funds for the North Avenue widening project," saying, "This project would tie in perfectly with our proposed Buttermilk Bottoms Urban Renewal Project." He ended, "If the Citizens (Advisory) Committee would . . . go on record and push as hard for Bond Funds for Urban Renewal Projects, as the Uptown Association is doing for its project, we would probably come out better in the overall Bond Issue."[53]

In the end, the interests and pressure of the Uptown Association won out over the "technicians," and the North Avenue widening was included among the $6.5 million of street projects proposed by the Bond Commission. The commission's priorities clearly reflected the collective interest of the business community, primarily focused on aiding both downtown and Uptown. In many ways, Rich and his commission colleagues appeared primarily concerned with maintaining unanimity within the business community. And their interest in securing the support of the Uptown Association probably applied to Buttermilk Bottom and the location of the proposed convention facility.

By 1962, the Chamber of Commerce had settled on either the "City Center" air rights site or Buttermilk Bottom as the location for the auditorium. The Bond Commission offered no specific site in its proposal—only that the center be located "downtown." But as the Commission concluded its work, it appeared quite likely that the city's business leaders, and Ivan Allen, were prepared to move ahead with the Buttermilk Bottom renewal site. The air rights location would have required a substantial expenditure of public funds for new streets and access, and some potential added cost in dealing with the railroads. The Buttermilk Bottom site had the advantage of a low cost, after the site was cleared with federal funds. And the Uptown Association's pressure for the North Avenue widening, and for clearing "Buttermilk Bottom" in order to provide "protection," would likely have led to that site as the city's first priority. But in order to avoid any potential public conflict, or a reaction from the African American community over the issues of clearance and relocation that had long concerned Phil Hammer, the locational question was sidestepped.

The Bond Commission's final report accommodated two major projects in addition to the auditorium. While the group did not provide financing for a new stadium, it did allot "a sufficient sum . . . to prepare a stadium site on land owned by the City at the Southeastern Fair Grounds." Then, after describing the commission's general work as "typical of bond commissions," it acknowledged that the group was "privileged to be a part of something rare and exciting—something off the beaten track of ordinary bond issues . . . something really new under the sun—the beginning of something that can grow into a living memorial to the bright spirit of Atlanta." That "memorial" was to be a new "Community Center in Atlanta which will, in the fullness of time, rival the world-famed Tivoli Gardens of Copenhagen as an international attraction."[54]

The proposed Community Center was the realization of Allen's and Woodruff's vision of a cultural center, to be financed with a $4 million gift from an "anonymous donor"—clearly recognized as Woodruff—and located in Piedmont Park. The Bond Commission allocated $4.1 million to prepare the park for the first stage of the new center, which was intended to contain a country store, stable, boat basin, aviary, lake, bandstand, coffee shop, multiple gardens, concert hall, theater, fine arts gallery, golf course, tennis courts, and an open sports area. And the entire project was termed a "national tourist attraction . . .[that] will focus attention of the entire nation on Atlanta to the end that new business and industry will be even more attracted to the unique advantages this community offers for pleasant, good living."[55]

The Bond Commission's full program was endorsed by Mayor Allen and approved by the Board of Aldermen, then placed on the ballot for an August 2 vote. The response of the chamber was fully predictable. Yet it also fully illustrated the character and operation of Atlanta's business leadership.

Mayor Ivan Allen joined the chamber's board of directors at their June 27, 1962, meeting, presenting the overall bond program. Richard Rich moved adoption of a resolution endorsing the bonds, with a three-man committee to review the final wording of the chamber endorsement. That committee comprised Richard Rich, Charles Thwaite (chair of the Trust Company of Georgia), and architect Cecil Alexander. Thus the chamber charged the man who had chaired the Bond Commission to draft the business group's endorsement of his own handiwork. Finally, Arthur Montgomery, who had led the chamber's stadium and auditorium committee, proposed that the board "offer to serve as a steering committee and coordinating body along with other civic organizations in Atlanta in support of the effort."[56] The chamber and the city's business leadership had thus initiated the bond program with the plans of "Action at the Core" and "Atlanta Sites," and then succeeded in electing Ivan Allen, dominating the City-County Bond Commission, and producing a recommendation for public investment focused on the downtown core and the auditorium and cultural center. They were now poised to implement a campaign to sell the public on the chamber's vision of the city's future.

The bond campaign was pressed by an array of Atlanta's civic organizations, including the Atlanta Labor Council, the Central Atlanta Association, and the Real Estate Board, as well as the Uptown Association and the Retail Merchants Association. The *Atlanta Constitution* provided a blizzard of coverage, with articles headlined, "$80 Million a Bargain to Keep Atlanta Thriving," and "Want Your Share of Sports, Music?" as well as editorials headed, "Let's Remove Brakes on the Future," and "Choice Thursday Involves One Issue: Forward Atlanta or a Backward Step." Yet, despite the seeming civic unanimity, there was some serious division within the city. African American community leaders complained that the allocation of projects had slighted their community in terms of both street improvements and schools. And the Piedmont Park cultural center proposal became the focus of particular opposition, both over potential loss of parkland and the possible creation of a "honky-tonk," as well as a whispering campaign that the "anonymous donor" of the cultural center funds was a "Yankee Philanthropist" and that the center "would attract Negroes into a presently all-white residential district."[57]

The vote outcome proved a crushing defeat for Ivan Allen and the city's business community. All 18 individual bond proposals were defeated, with the Piedmont Park cultural center voted down by almost two to one. The interracial coalition of middle-class white and African American voters that had elected Allen mayor simply failed. In the words of Robert Woodruff confidant and advisor Philip Weltner, "Ivan won, as you know, by a coalition of the Northside and the negro block. Ivan counted on this coalition helping him make good on his campaign promises. The coalition did not work. His opposition did. The figures are surprising as well as enlightening."[58] For Woodruff, the overwhelming defeat of the Piedmont Park proposal and the character of the opposition were telling. Weltner had spent years developing the plan for the cultural center and building the needed support in the city's arts and cultural communities. The vote outcome halted the plan.

Ivan Allen, however, did not back off from the vision of a major bond program. Almost immediately after the vote, he appointed a "Bond Study Commission" to analyze the reasons for the defeat and propose a new, alternative program. The Study Commission initiated a survey research program, directed by Georgia State psychology professor Cameron Fincher, to determine the causes of the bond issue defeat.

The report from Fincher concluded that "Voters rejected the bond proposals . . . because they were unwilling to sustain the expected increase in property taxes and because they did not feel they had enough information about the proposed projects or enough time to consider the issues properly." While an overwhelming majority of the survey respondents wanted to see another bond vote held, their preferences for individual projects must have come as a shock to Allen and the business leadership. Some 40 percent of those surveyed believed that schools should be part of a new issue, followed by 29 percent for streets and 17 percent for sewers. Among the "big projects" that had long occupied Allen, Rich, Woodruff, and the top business leaders, the auditorium won the backing of just 10 percent, with a fine arts center at 8 percent, and a new sports arena or stadium endorsed by just 7 percent. And when queried about why they had voted "no" in August, the bond issues that drew the greatest opposition were led by the Piedmont Park cultural center, at 86 percent opposed, and the auditorium and convention hall at 51 percent.[59]

If there was to be a second bond election, the individual projects would have to be chosen very carefully, and the overall size limited, to avoid the prospect of a property tax increase. The report the Bond Study Commission presented to Allen in early January 1963 pared some $25 million from the previous package. Where the 1962 program had included a dozen city street and road projects, the new list was down to just six. Strikingly, the streets projects that had been rejected by the "technicians" and insisted upon by Rich for the downtown core—Hunter Street and Wall Street—remained in the new bond proposal. And the key focus of the Uptown Association, the widening of North Avenue at the edge of Buttermilk Bottom, was also included.

The Piedmont Park cultural center was eliminated from the commission's recommendations, presumably due to Woodruff's unwillingness to support the project and the specter of continuing voter opposition. The auditorium-convention hall, however, was recommended for the same funding as in the original 1962 proposal, $10 million.

The Study Commission's report argued that while a "sports arena and a stadium are desirable . . . the cost of such facilities is at this time prohibitive." But, "It is the opinion of this commission that Atlanta's first responsibility is in the area of convention facilities." A new auditorium, the group argued, would enable Atlanta to "serve at least 80% of all of the conventions in America now and in the foreseeable future" and compete with other communities across the South. Ultimately Mayor Allen and the aldermen trimmed some of the commission's recommendations, settling on a final allocation for the auditorium of just $9 million.[60]

The revised bond program quickly won the endorsement of the Chamber of Commerce, and chamber members were encouraged to contribute to a $12,000 "public information campaign," while the "front line" of the publicity effort would be the city and county Parent-Teacher Associations. Both bond proponents and the *Atlanta Constitution* emphasized that this was a "rock-bottom, bare bones" package with "No Tax Increase." The *Constitution* editorialized that Atlanta's "national reputation as a forward-looking city" would be on the line with the bond vote, drawing a comparison between the racial strife in nearby Birmingham and Atlanta's relative peace and progressivism.[61]

In contrast to the outcome the previous year, Atlanta voters on May 15, 1963, approved all 13 bond propositions, including the auditorium proposition. Ivan Allen interpreted the result as a personal triumph. The following day, the mayor announced that he would pursue a stadium —"it's next on the list . . . . I intend to address the same energy toward getting a stadium."[62]

The successful passage of the auditorium bonds was a coup for both Allen and the business leadership. But it came at a price. With the funding for the auditorium reduced, the *Atlanta Constitution* had assured readers that "the new auditorium will be built downtown," with a "precise site . . . selected by a commission appointed by the mayor," it was evident that the air rights location was simply too expensive, particularly in terms of preparation and required street improvements. Buttermilk Bottom, cleared with federal urban renewal dollars, offered a far more financially attractive site, one that also served to maintain unanimity in the business community by aiding the Uptown Association. Just as Philip Hammer had forecast, there would be serious conflict involving relocation, replacement housing, and racial change. Yet the city would persist in ultimately building the new Atlanta Civic Center in Buttermilk Bottom.[63]

The 1963 bond vote also held another lesson for Ivan Allen and the chamber. Although Allen would succeed in winning re-election in 1965, he never again proposed a bond issue on the ballot. The city's capital needs, and the other major civic projects, would be financed without a vote. And just as he had promised, the next of those projects was a stadium.

Furman Bisher, sports editor of the *Atlanta Journal*, had arranged a visit to Atlanta by Charles O. Finley, owner of the Kansas City Athletics, in late April 1963. Showing Finley some potential sites for a new stadium, most of them analyzed by Phil Hammer in "Atlanta Sites," Finley had not found anything of real interest. According to Ivan Allen's memoir,

> I happened to be facing a map on my office wall that outlined the urban-renewal areas in Atlanta, and my eyes fell on a large acreage adjoining the expressway interchange: what was referred to as Washington-Rawson area, which was being cleared of its decaying slum houses and had no immediate plans for use. "I've got the greatest location in the world," I told Bisher (in pure desperation, since I wasn't sure what we could do with the area and knew little about how much land would be required for a stadium).[64]

Allen's description of the site selection would appear somewhat disingenuous.

The Rawson-Washington renewal area had been considered by Phil Hammer as a potential stadium site in 1960, with findings that were widely known (and circulated) to Allen and his colleagues on the Chamber of Commerce board. Hammer's assessment of the site was largely colored by his concerns over relocation housing and potential political conflict. Yet just as in the case of the Buttermilk Bottom location for the auditorium, Allen and the city's business and political leadership were apparently willing to deal with that conflict, and ignore the potential negative impacts of displacement and relocation on adjacent neighborhoods and housing problems.

The location south of the Atlanta's central core, adjacent to a massive freeway interchange—"'Thirty-two lanes,' [Allen] said . . . 'Biggest in the South'"—obviously "impressed" Charlie Finley. And the Rawson-Washington site had the advantages that Phil Hammer had laid out, notably creating the "healthy fringe for Downtown." The exact site of the proposed stadium had already been cleared. But parking and access would require additional clearance, and Allen immediately faced the issue of purchasing the stadium site and financing a new public facility.

Mayor Allen turned first to Robert W. Woodruff. Writing to Woodruff on May 22, in a letter headed "Confidential," Allen wrote, "The City of Atlanta now has nine million dollars for an auditorium and one extremely valuable piece of land." Listing four "major needs of the city"—an auditorium and exhibit hall, a "coliseum for athletics," a cultural center, and a "municipal stadium," Allen proposed acquiring a site of forty acres (unidentified in the letter itself, but most likely part of the Rawson-Washington urban renewal area), appointing "an auditorium committee to recommend the architect, design and site for the new auditorium," reactivating the stadium authority the legislature had authorized in 1960, and having the authority to issue revenue bonds backed by both stadium revenues and an annual commitment of city parks revenues. Describing this as "a sound plan, which, of course is encumbered with numerous complications," Allen sought Woodruff's "full support and confirmation" and asked that he "would consider buying this land from the Atlanta Housing Authority and giving it to the City for the above purposes." Allen's letter also asked "for the Coca-Cola Company to consider some assistance in the deficit financing of the municipal stadium, if this is feasible." He also noted this was the "second time I have come to you for major assistance to the city"—the first was the Piedmont Park cultural center—and that this was "a personal request."[65]

Allen's plea to Woodruff neatly illustrates the limitations and constraints faced by Atlanta's business leadership. For all of their social interaction and coherence, for all of their capacity to define the city's investment and development agenda, for all their political manipulation of the Bond Commission process and outcomes, the business group was ultimately dependent upon voter approval of its plans and projects. And Atlanta's voters, in 1962 and 1963 and again and again in subsequent years, could restrain their efforts and defeat their pet projects.

Faced with the prospect of a new baseball team filling a city stadium and the limited resources available for constructing the planned auditorium, Ivan Allen was apparently willing to consider building both on the Rawson-Washington site, if he could get the funds he needed from Woodruff. And while Woodruff's reply is not among his papers, he evidently had little interest in backing a stadium or paying for the site Allen had in mind. With a "no" from Woodruff, Allen moved ahead with reactivating the Atlanta-Fulton County Stadium Authority and appointing Arthur Montgomery of Atlanta Coca-Cola Bottling and head of the chamber's stadium committee as chair.

Without private funds from Woodruff, Ivan Allen, Montgomery and the Stadium Authority turned to banker Mills Lane, a longtime friend of the mayor's, to lend the initial funding for the planned stadium. And in accord with his personality and ties to Allen, Lane took on the risk of the stadium financing and advanced the funds to pay architects Heery and Heery and FABRAP (in a "shotgun marriage" of the two firms arranged by Ivan Allen).[66]

While the initial overtures to Charles Finley and the Kansas City A's proved fruitless, Allen, Lane, Montgomery and the stadium backers continued to pursue a major league team, eventually reaching an agreement with the Milwaukee Braves to relocate to Atlanta. The stadium financing scheme eventually came to involve a combination of governments, with Arthur Montgomery reporting to the chamber board in February 1964 that stadium revenues would provide $600,000 per year, Fulton County would commit $100,000 annually, and the city would shift $200,000 in annual tax revenues from Grant Park to the new stadium.[67] With that backing in place and the ability to avoid both a public vote and any form of city tax increase, the "deal" was presented to the public and Atlanta's Board of Aldermen in March. With a positive vote from the aldermen ten days after the hearing, and agreement from the county commission, the Stadium Authority held a groundbreaking ceremony on April 15, overlooking the Rawson-Washington site that Charlie Finley had embraced just a year earlier.

As the city's stadium effort was advancing, some questions began to be raised from within the business community about the plans for auditorium/convention hall. When Arthur Montgomery briefed his Chamber of Commerce colleagues on the status of the stadium in August 1964, noting construction was "on schedule," he "expressed concern over plans for the $9,000,000 auditorium complex." There was no issue of the site. Mayor Allen had continued to support the Buttermilk Bottom location, and urban renewal efforts had begun in April 1964. But what Montgomery argued was "that the city needs a coliseum-type-multi-purpose facility instead of the permanently-fixed auditorium of 4,500 seats and 30,000-plus square foot exhibition space." Montgomery was apparently joined in that sentiment by "Several Board members," and Richard Rich made the suggestion that the group confer "with the Mayor for the purpose of expressing the chamber's concern."[68]

The chamber group met with Mayor Allen and expressed concern over the scale of the auditorium project, and Arthur Montgomery could report back to his colleagues in early September that the mayor "assured the Chamber group that the exhibition space will contain at least 70,000 square feet, or enough to seat 10,000 persons, even if the city has to put up additional money." Montgomery then noted that this position "partly satisfied the Chamber's concern."[69]

The concerns of the chamber leadership reflected two fundamental aspects of the intertwined political and fiscal issues facing the city. First, the $9 million allocation for what would ultimately be termed the Atlanta Civic Center was a quite limited, bare bones sum. The business leadership would eventually see the entire Buttermilk Bottom area cleared and rebuilt, although not without an extended conflict over the character of clearance and new development. But any more extensive convention or coliseum facility would have to wait until there was more money available. That was the second reality. Ivan Allen appeared to have little interest in another bond package.

Indeed, the city would not propose a general bond issue program on the ballot until 1975, under Mayor Maynard Jackson. With no substantial source of capital funds, the $9 million approved in 1963 was effectively the limit of what could be spent, and thus what the city could build.

Construction of the new Atlanta Civic Center began in January 1965, with the new auditorium followed by the 70,000 square foot exhibit hall. The city's community facilities plan in 1965 promised that these would just be the start, the "first stage," of a much larger complex. Anticipated for a second stage was an expansion of the exhibit hall to a total of 140,000 square feet. A third stage, proposed for 1970, was to be a 15,000-seat coliseum—the final element in the set of major public projects planned by Phil Hammer in 1960—to accommodate an NBA basketball team as well as hockey, wrestling, and other sports events. The final piece of the Civic Center was to be a "restaurant and service center," with shops and services for center users, coupled with new private development on adjacent streets.[70]

The Civic Center would ultimately never progress beyond the first stage. Atlanta would see a new coliseum/arena. But that facility, built to house the new Atlanta Hawks NBA team, would have its location decided by the developer who purchased the basketball team to bring to Atlanta, Tom Cousins. And Cousins's goal in buying an NBA team had less to do with basketball than with his need for a prime tenant to anchor the arena that would serve, in turn, as the anchor and draw for a new mixed-use complex on the air rights over the railroad gulch.

When Robert Troutman had secured the development rights for the Westside gulch from the state in 1956, he faced a ten-year deadline to invest a minimum of $5 million in developing the site. With the deadline approaching in 1966, Troutman joined with Atlanta developer Tom Cousins to construct a parking garage, "The Decks," to meet the state's requirement. But to reach the development potential of the air rights, Troutman and Cousins needed a magnet or anchor to draw people and new activity.

When Phil Hammer had studied the development possibilities for the "Air Rights Plaza" in 1954, he had seen its future as "the best possible site in the Atlanta area for the development of a large, regional shopping center now or within the reasonably near future." Hammer had envisioned 700,000 square feet of air-conditioned retail space, anchored by a major department store—the "key tenant" on which the success of the larger development depended. But Troutman's efforts to secure an anchor department store failed. And the other major lure that the air rights development had hoped to capitalize on, the appeal and business volume of the nearby Rich's department store, had obviously weakened during the 1960s as new suburban department stores were opened.[71]

Faced with the need for an alternative magnet or draw, Cousins commissioned a market study (apparently from Phil Hammer's firm, Hammer, Greene, Siler Associates) that recommended an arena and basketball team. He then joined Georgia Governor Carl Sanders in purchasing the St. Louis Hawks and moving the team to Atlanta, playing initially at Georgia Tech's Alexander Memorial Coliseum. But what Cousins ultimately needed was a new arena built on the air rights.

An arena was key to creating development potential for the air rights. With a host of activities beyond just basketball games—a March 1970 study by Hammer for Cousins Properties forecast a total of 217 annual events ranging from NHL hockey to circuses and conventions, with total attendance of 1.6 million people—the coliseum would provide the magnet pulling activity to the barren air rights. At the same time, the bulk of the new structure "will serve as a barrier against the warehousing and industrial area to the west . . . [while] generating large numbers of local and out-of-town people to the Air Rights Development and to the downtown." What Tom Cousins planned was a grand megastructure that would provide a "super-concentration of urban activities," with office buildings, hotels, and retail stores together with a unique adult entertainment complex "similar in some respects to . . . Larimer Square in Denver, Ghiradelli Square in San Francisco, and Old Towne in Chicago."[72]

What Phil Hammer envisioned for the air rights and Tom Cousins now proposed to develop was a literally interconnected complex, with the proposed coliseum funneling Atlantans and visitors to the development, who would then patronize the stores, entertainment, and restaurants, stay overnight in the proposed hotel, and provide the activity and demand required to make the project work. But first Cousins needed to have a coliseum built at the air rights site, rather than (as long anticipated) as part of the Civic Center complex.

Cousins appears to have made the initial overtures about his coliseum plans to Arthur Montgomery, then still chair of the Atlanta-Fulton County Recreation Authority that had built the stadium. The first backing for Cousins's plans had to come from within the business community, and Cousins and Montgomery turned to the Central Atlanta Progress, Inc., organization. In early 1969, CAP formally examined three possible locations "known to be under active consideration" for a new coliseum/sports arena—adjacent to Atlanta Stadium, adjacent to the existing Civic Center's exhibition hall, and the air rights location at Hunter Street.[73]

The downtown group backed Cousins's site, arguing that the "sports arena will do more for the City in this location that in any other one proposed." CAP's planning assessment concluded that the air rights site offered the advantages that "Land is readily available without displacing people," "Would be served by Rapid Transit," and "Because of its proximity to downtown Atlanta and because of the available space for private development . . . tremendous tax-producing private development would be stimulated by such a facility." With much the same analysis and language employed by Phil Hammer in "Atlanta Sites," and the concurrence of the city's planning department, Cousins had the technical justification for a new arena on his site. The CAP review and the acquiescence of the city's professional planners also forestalled any overt conflict over location, bolstered by the argument that the city had invested street improvement bond funds since 1957 "to serve and stimulate this type of development in this area." To get it built, he needed access to public financing and the city's formal approval.

With backing from newly elected Mayor Sam Massell, Cousins pressed a scheme for the city to issue the debt for the coliseum project. In a memo to Mayor Massell on February 17, 1970, city finance director Charles Davis laid out a series of fiscal alternatives. Two possible approaches, involving a commitment of city debt and funds, Davis concluded, "could be possibly damaging to our bond rating."[74] Another possibility, funding the project with general obligation bonds, would be the cheapest but would require voter approval. Clearly the most plausible avenue was a revenue bond issue by the stadium authority, backed by revenues from the authority and "Cousins Properties and/or others."[75] Davis also reported a willingness by Cousins Properties officials to back a change in state law that would allow the city to impose a hotel and motel tax "for athletic improvements, recreation improvements, parks and the like."[76]

Cousins and his staff negotiated with city staff through the summer and fall of 1970. The central issue revolved around the fiscal exposure of the city versus the revenue commitment of Cousins. The feasibility and financial studies indicated that an arena with both basketball and hockey teams could generate almost enough revenue to pay off the thirty-year bonds. Cousins eventually agreed to further cover any deficits in coliseum revenues with a commitment of parking revenues from The Decks garage over the air rights.

At one negotiating session, Alderman Joel C. Stokes argued that the city "should plan to try to work out a long range contract and retain the right to put the Cousin's [sic] people out of the Coliseum with our option. . . . We don't want to give the impression to the public that we are giving the Coliseum to the Cousins' people."[77]

By promising to back the bonds with coliseum revenues and the additional security of parking income, Cousins effectively relieved the city of any financial exposure. And by using revenue bonds, Massell and the aldermen would avoid the need for a public vote. The financial arrangement was also backed by Fulton County, with county commissioner Walter M. Mitchell arguing that the project would be "self-supporting" and that "A study made sometime ago comparing three different possible sites . . . showed without question that the Air Rights location is the proper one."[78]

Tom Cousins and developer Lloyd Whitaker presented the final coliseum deal to the Chamber of Commerce board on December 11, promising a 17,000 seat venue to be built at a fixed price of $17 million, using revenue bonds issued by the Atlanta-Fulton County Recreation Authority and guaranteed by the city. Cousins told the group, "It was anticipated that no costs would be incurred by the taxpayers."[79] The chamber board then passed two resolutions calling on the city, county, and Recreation Authority to approve the agreement and praising Mayor Massell for his "diligence." In a measure of the intimacy of Atlanta's business leadership, chamber vice president Allen S. Hardin abstained from voting—his construction firm was already contracted to build the planned coliseum.

The next few days saw a media blitz by Cousins, with an editorial in the *Atlanta Journal* praising "such a fine deal for the city and the county," and arguing that "This coliseum will be another great asset to this community, bringing in more visitors, creating new jobs and otherwise boosting the economy." One local sports columnist termed Tom Cousins "Santa Claus."[80] Lost in the upbeat coverage were some of the details. The project would clearly be of enormous benefit to Cousins, and its public status would relieve him of any tax burden. It would also require a number of street improvements the city would have to pay for. But the newspaper coverage was consistently upbeat, calling on city and county officials to endorse the deal and move ahead quickly.

The city's Board of Aldermen and the Fulton County commissioners quickly approved the project in principle on December 16. But concerns over the financing dragged the political negotiations into early January. The final hurdle to public approval came from a group of black aldermen. Led by alderman Marvin Arrington, the group presented a set of demands that could kill the project. They sought a commitment from the coliseum project's general contractor and Cousins that local construction unions would pledge to hire black workers for the project: "Only after 20 minutes of fist pounding, shouting and bickering back and forth were the black aldermen appeased . . . . At the time of the final vote, black Alderman Joel Stokes rose and said that as a result of the unions' concessions, Tuesday will be remembered as a milestone for Atlanta in terms of minority employment."[81]

Atlanta Builds for the World

By the end of 1970, Atlanta had built a new stadium, completed an auditorium/convention hall, and committed to a new coliseum. The cultural center—Atlanta's planned "Tivoli Gardens"—had been halted by a failure at the polls in 1962. But a new arts center arose not very far away, on Peachtree Street, built as a memorial to the 106 Atlantans killed in the crash of an Air France flight in 1962 and financed with Robert Woodruff's backing. In just over a decade from Ivan Allen's argument for a package of major projects in January 1960, the city had effectively realized each of the projects he and his compatriots in the city's business leadership had planned and envisioned. In short, the city had managed a dramatic, substantial success in public investment.[82]

Ivan Allen, Richard Rich, Robert Woodruff, and their friends and colleagues had managed politically by building and sustaining a broad coalition *within* the business community. They had developed that coalition in classic logrolling fashion, promising an array of public projects that could be spread around the downtown core to solve a multitude of problems and aid a diverse group of spatial interests. Indeed, the "all factions concerned" that Ivan Allen had identified in his 1960 remarks to the chamber board, ranging from Bobby Troutman and John O. Chiles with their interest in the air rights site, to the Uptown Association's concern with the possible northward expansion of Buttermilk Bottom, to John Portman's desire not to compete with a publicly financed coliseum, were neatly accommodated over time. Allen, Rich, and others recognized the diversity of interests within the business leadership group and effectively provided some locationally specific benefit to each. Yet the "logroll" approach to maintaining business unity came at a price. The city was obliged to move on a number of projects almost simultaneously, despite the broader conflict and division involved in an urban renewal effort that would displace thousands of low-income families in a brief period of time.

Although the stadium, auditorium, and coliseum obviously served larger community purposes and (as Hughes Spalding had argued) helped position Atlanta as the dominant center for the Southeast, each was vitally necessary in a different role. As Phil Hammer fundamentally understood (and argued in his various studies), these projects were necessary to shape and define the development prospects of specific zones of the downtown core. The stadium location at Rawson-Washington served to protect and reinforce the southern sector of the downtown. The auditorium/civic center at Buttermilk Bottom resolved the "threat" to Uptown while reinforcing the hotel and Merchandise Mart complex developed by John Portman on Peachtree Street. And the ultimate location of the coliseum on the air rights site long studied and promoted by Hammer provided the kind of development anchor that Tom Cousins and that underdeveloped site required, and also promised increased traffic for the nearby Rich's.

The spatial interests that these projects supported were quite specific, and linked to specific individuals. In some cases, like Troutman, Cousins, and Portman, those individuals were developers. In other cases, such as Richard Rich or Ben Massell, the persons involved owned business firms or property that stood to benefit from public investment. Finally, others like Hughes Spalding or Robert Woodruff had broader interests and concerns that meshed with the spatial interests of their friends and colleagues. Those like Rich and Spalding *needed* developers such as Portman and Troutman to initiate the projects, assemble the capital, and take the risks that shaped the future downtown. Their locational interests were quite distinct, but their larger purpose was common. They were fundamentally dependent upon public investment to shape the future of downtown Atlanta and provide a foundation (and security) for their own investment.

For all the obvious success of Atlanta's business leadership in realizing public projects and new investment, the results of their efforts in the convention field were quite modest. When, after years of effort, the Atlanta Civic Center finally opened in 1968, it boasted just 70,000 square feet of exhibit hall space. That volume of exhibit space was far exceeded by other competitive cities, including Chicago with 600,000 square feet, the New York Coliseum's 300,000, or Philadelphia's 357,000. And a host of other cities, including Washington, D.C., and regional competitors Birmingham and Charlotte, were planning or building larger new convention facilities. Each of the latter two would provide more exhibit space than Atlanta.

City officials and Atlanta business leaders had planned on a larger, more expansive convention complex. But they were constrained by the fiscal limits on the city government, as well as the need to secure voter support for any major bond project. There was simply no political or fiscal capacity to add to the Civic Center in the late 1960s.

The problems of the new Civic Center went beyond its limited space. In his "Atlanta Sites" analysis, Phil Hammer had noted the disadvantages of the Buttermilk Bottom site. He recognized that the area suffered a "basic disadvantage" because it could not be served by a future rapid transit system. His argument was "To fail to put the Auditorium-Coliseum at a location which might take advantage of these rapid transit facilities would be poor planning." For the city's business leaders, the clearance of Buttermilk Bottom and the interests of the Uptown Association outweighed the limitations of a site that was rather distant from the center of downtown's hotels, restaurants, and stores, to say nothing of protests from the African American community. But there were others who fully understood the limitations of the Civic Center's location.[83]

Collier Gladin, head of Atlanta's Planning Department, laid out the problems with the Civic Center's site in a January 1968 memo to alderman Rodney Cook. Noting that adding about 200,000 square feet of exhibit hall space would make Atlanta's facility "competitive with all but the major convention cities such as New York, Chicago and Los Angeles," Gladin noted that the existing facility has

> problems such as
>
> —in a hole
> —poor vehicular access from expressways
> —too far from rapid transit
> —too far from downtown
> —inadequate parking,

and he asked, "then why add to the mistakes?"

Gladin, like Hammer before him, argued that the additional facilities such as a museum or arena should be "easily accessible . . . with direct access to a rapid transit station." He then went on to list three possible sites for new facilities, starting with "Air rights south of Hunter Street Viaduct." That was, of course, the air rights site that Hammer had long promoted and Tom Cousins would seek to develop with the new coliseum. But Gladin had one central criterion that he shared with Rodney Cook—"that these facilities should be used to bolster the downtown."[84]

Even as the Civic Center was opening, it was obvious that it was too small, and too poorly located, to properly compete in the national market. For the city's business leaders, there was no question Atlanta needed a bigger convention center. The real issues were where it would go, and how to pay for it.

Writing to alderman Rodney Cook in late 1967, Oby Brewer, the president of the city's Convention Bureau, argued, "We are on the threshold of making Atlanta one of the top ten competing cities in the United States. . . . It is therefore apparent that our exhibit hall will have to be expanded if we are going to be competitive."[85] Three months later, Convention Bureau executive vice president James Hurst wrote Cook and the Atlanta Housing Authority about recent discussions on "adding 100,000 square feet to the present 70,000 square feet on the same level."[86]

The officials of the Convention Bureau regularly pointed to the limited space at the Civic Center compared to other major convention cities. They planned on a significant expansion of the existing center, adding at least 100,000 or perhaps 200,000 square feet of exhibit space. Yet their plans and interest never took hold, as both Ivan Allen and his successor Sam Massell shied away from the political problems posed by the need for majority approval at the polls for any major bond issue.

The impetus for an expanded meeting facility actually came from the private sector, in the form of an initiative by downtown building owner and slum clearance veteran Charles F. Palmer, who had led the city's early public housing efforts in the 1930s. Palmer envisioned a facility capable of hosting major international meetings that would propel Atlanta's vision of developing as an "international city." In early 1970, he assembled an "ad hoc committee" for an "intercontinental congress center." The group included Opie Shelton, executive vice president of the Chamber of Commerce, and James Hurst of the Convention Bureau, as well as chamber leaders Pollard Turman and John C. Wilson, and Louis Truman, the commissioner of the state's Department of Industry and Trade.

John Wilson reported to the Chamber of Commerce board in early February 1970 that chamber officials had "reviewed a plan to expand the Civic Center into an international center, with facilities for holding international meetings." The committee's initial goal was to commission a formal study of the feasibility of an international center, and with the commitment of $17,000 from the chamber and the Atlanta Convention Bureau, Palmer and the business leaders turned to Phil Hammer and his firm of Hammer, Greene, Siler and Associates to "determine the practicality and potentials of such a center."[87]

Thus from the outset, the quest for an international center was focused on an addition to the existing Civic Center and its site. There was no serious consideration by the business community or the Convention Bureau of an entirely new facility at a different location. Indeed, architect and developer John Portman prepared a study and architectural plan at about this time for developing a new "international" convention hall just across Piedmont Avenue from the Civic Center, edging the complex close to his Peachtree Center development to the west.

Phil Hammer would thus reprise a role he had played for Atlanta business leaders since the early 1950s, assessing and shaping major public projects that would in turn define private development opportunities and prospects. Those leaders, in turn, regarded his analyses and conclusions as near gospel.

Hammer and his colleagues began to investigate the market potential for an international meeting center, with Hammer traveling to London and Amsterdam to examine the work and performance of their conference centers. Finally, in early August 1970, Hammer could write Palmer that the report was in the final stages, and proposed a meeting with the ad hoc committee in Atlanta at the end of the month. The Hammer firm's feasibility study ran to over a hundred pages. But its central conclusion was likely not what Palmer had hoped.[88]

The Hammer, Greene, Siler analysis described a growing international conference activity. But it also concluded that European conference centers were largely reliant on trade fairs, community events, and national meetings—"In short, there are no truly 'international conference centers' catering exclusively or even predominantly to international meetings." In terms of competing for international events, that market in the U. S. was dominated (for obvious reasons) by New York City, Washington, and Chicago. Those cities had the existing infrastructure and, most importantly, the international air service, to handle international conferences. Atlanta was well behind, particularly in terms of international air routes. And at that time, routes were allocated by a federal government agency, so the city would likely have to wait some time for a boost in its international connections.[89]

But if Hammer concluded that "A specialized facility built exclusively for the international conference market in Atlanta is not justified by the potential market," he did offer the guidance that the city was in an "excellent position" to meet international conference needs by adding certain features to the Civic Center and new private developments still in the proposal stage.

The far more relevant finding from Hammer's study dealt with the city's existing convention facilities. Just three years from the opening of the long-planned Civic Center, the Hammer study argued that the city's meeting facilities "had clearly not kept pace with the growing need and demand or with the development of private support facilities." Simply put, "Atlanta's Civic Center is inadequate as to both meeting space and exhibition area." The city was "clearly being outdistanced" by others, including Detroit, Dallas, New Orleans, Denver, and Cleveland. That demanded an expansion of the existing Civic Center "to 200,000 square feet, which would make it competitive with other major facilities throughout the U.S." What Atlanta really needed was "the expansion of existing facilities to provide a major facilities complex capable of accommodating the largest domestic events plus international events."[90]

But Hammer clearly recognized the larger political and fiscal limits the city government faced. Stating that "The major problem is in financing the development," the report stated quite directly, "At present, Atlanta has no funds for carrying out the expansion," and, "in the order of priorities facing the city, an expansion of the Civic Center, including special facilities for potential foreign visitors, admittedly is near the bottom of a long list."[91]

Hammer's report went on, in a section headed "Statewide Benefits," to describe how Georgia as a whole benefited from the "inflow of dollars resulting from convention activities in Atlanta." He then went on to argue that these larger benefits provided a logic for state financing for an Atlanta convention facility. Noting that state governments had been involved in financing centers in Philadelphia, Indianapolis, and Birmingham, he suggested either a direct state appropriation or a "Georgia Convention Authority" that could carry out the project.

If Palmer and his committee members may have been disappointed in the Hammer conclusion that there was little immediate international market for Atlanta, what they actually received was a roadmap for convention center development that shifted away from the politically and fiscally constrained city of Atlanta to the state government and its greater financial resources. It was that shift that altered the politics of convention center building in Atlanta, and that alternative route that Palmer began to follow.

The Hammer feasibility study did contain one small, but ultimately prescient, suggestion about an interim step for serving international meetings. He argued that a modestly sized international facility could be developed—and located—separately from the planned Civic Center expansion. That facility might be "incorporated into a new hotel adjacent to or in one or another of the major private developments in downtown Atlanta," listing the Cousins air rights project, the existing Peachtree Center developed by John Portman, or a planned mixed-use project in the southeastern corner of the core near the State Capitol by Ray Nasher of Dallas.

The Hammer study thus opened the possibility of perhaps two separate convention facilities, building on the Civic Center while also aiding (and supporting) one of the three major new private developments in the core. Notwithstanding the consistent assumption that an "international congress center" would be an addition to the Civic Center, Hammer suggested that it might instead be a prize for one or another major developer.

Palmer and the ad hoc committee followed Hammer's guidance, and began to develop the idea of a major new international congress facility linked to the Civic Center, but financed and developed by the state government. The group approached state auditor Ernest Davis and House Appropriations Committee chair James H. Floyd with the notion that statewide benefits (most notably the sales tax yielded by visitors) justified state financial assistance. With initial backing from the state's legislative leaders, John C. Wilson reported to the chamber executive committee in May 1971 that the state and city "have gotten together on a $175,000 study for expansion of the Atlanta Civic Center, the study to be financed by the state." What was envisioned was an "international center at the Civic Center site," supervised by a new entity called Georgia International Congress Center, Inc., with financing from a statewide one percent tax on hotel rooms.[92]

The switch to the state government neatly avoided the prospect of a likely failure at the polls as a city bond proposal. It still carried its own political difficulties, requiring selling rural legislators on an expensive project that would directly benefit Atlanta. And the case for the new convention facility was made almost exclusively by Palmer, John Wilson, and the business leadership. Mayor Massell, city aldermen, and even the local legislative delegation were rarely in evidence. But, even as the Congress Center backers changed the fiscal politics and pressed the state legislature, they remained committed to the Civic Center location.

The first problematic issue was paying for the new center. Backers had initially proposed a statewide "sales tax" on hotels. In January, John C. Wilson told the chamber leadership that the Congress Center plans called for a $35 million project with 274,000 square feet of exhibit space and facilities for simultaneous language translation. The group was also told that the planned center would "draw 200 international conventions to Georgia by 1980," and be paid for with a statewide tax on hotels and restaurants, with receipts divided between the new center and local tourism promotion.[93] Opposition from some state legislators killed the hotel tax part of the proposal, but it moved ahead with the promise of a state government-backed bond issue. Yet even as prospects for actually financing the Congress Center moved forward and a formal oversight board was appointed, an entirely new political problem arose.

At the end of August, Tom Cousins upended the plans for building the center as part of the existing Civic Center by offering the state—free—a six-acre site adjacent to the Omni coliseum as part of his planned air rights megastructure development. A site selection committee, headed by state auditor Ernest Davis and including a number of state legislators, was charged with choosing the Congress Center's location, effectively refereeing the contest between John Portman (and his preferred Civic Center location) and Cousins. It was now a state-level, not just Atlanta, issue, and it quickly landed before Governor Jimmy Carter.[94]

Carter, in a handwritten memo to Ernest Davis on October 27, noted, "There has developed a great deal of concern about the site selection of the World Congress Center." He went on to say that both Portman and Cousins "have been to me to request an *objective* professional analysis of the factors involved with the understanding that the Congress Center Board would make the final recommendation." Carter urged that the study be "done quickly" and that he would "furnish the funds."[95] Louis Truman, the head of the state's Department of Industry and Trade, who had been a member of Charles Palmer's original ad hoc committee, replied to the governor that a majority of the Congress Center Executive Board was willing to "go along with the outside study," and the group would hire Chicago consultant Martin Dwyer "as soon as possible."[96] At least one board member, state representative Michael Egan of Atlanta, protested that while Portman and Cousins were "fine men [and] good friends of mine," the interest of the people would best be served "if we would quit dillydallying around . . . and move immediately to make decisions . . . [on] the selection of an architect and the selection of a site."[97]

Dwyer delivered his "objective" site assessment in a December 7, 1972, report. Dwyer's findings were "overwhelmingly in favor of the Civic Center site on almost every factor listed by him . . . [including] hotel room availability, adequacy of acreage, appearance, character and safety of the area . . .availability to restaurants, shopping and entertainment facilities . . . and visibility."[98] But for their own reasons, the majority of the site selection committee endorsed Tom Cousins's air rights site over Portman's.

The choice of Tom Cousins's air rights site did not quiet the conflict over the Congress Center's location. Four members of the site selection committee, including representative Michael Egan and Charles Palmer, issued their own minority report, blasting the majority for violating the committee's own requirements for convenience to downtown hotels and a site "dramatic enough to generate its own world wide publicity."[99] The minority report emphasized the objective findings of Martin Dwyer and "noted that a fair reading of every report done on this project either at the request and expense of this Board or of the predecessor Board [including one by Phil Hammer's firm], either strongly recommends the Civic Center site or contains information pointing inexorably to that conclusion." But in the retelling of Ernest Davis and at least one member of the site selection committee, John Portman had been so insistent and demanding on both the Civic Center location and his own selection as architect that he had succeeded in alienating a number of committee members. In the words of one unnamed committee member, "what he said was that any damn fool could see that the Civic Center site was the best, and if you couldn't see that without a whole lot of details and explanation, then you really didn't have sense enough to be talked to by an intelligent man."[100]

Portman's outburst may have played a significant role in the site choice, but it was also relevant that the state government-dominated committee and board were looking for a location *different and distinctive* from Atlanta's Buttermilk Bottom, with its history of insensitivity and racial conflict. Even the majority vote of the site selection committee in December 1972 did not resolve the conflict. Developer Ewell Pope, then building a massive new Hilton hotel adjacent to Portman's Peachtree Center complex, offered to donate land at the Civic Center location. Jimmy Carter for a time backed a private development plan offered by a favored developer. Finally, in February 1974, the Cousins site was reaffirmed and the Congress Center moved ahead.[101]

The Georgia World Congress Center opened in September 1976, boasting 350,000 square feet of exhibit hall space, an auditorium seating 2,000, and the promise of vaulting Atlanta into the top rank of convention cities. James

Hurst, who had long promoted a new convention hall as executive vice president of Atlanta's Convention and Visitors Bureau, termed it "the finest I've seen in this country—at any cost," and said the city's goal was "to be Number 1," challenging Chicago and New York as the nation's leading convention city.[102]

The new GWCC did bring a boost to the city's convention business as the center ramped up its activity. By fiscal year 1978, it claimed a total of 302,114 out-of-town attendees, with almost 394,000 the following year. Yet calls for a bigger center and more exhibit space began almost immediately. The state commissioned a feasibility study in 1979 for an expansion that found "expansion would be warranted," and that any delay would cost the state in lost convention business. The first Georgia World Congress Center expansion was completed in 1984, followed by further expansions in 1992 and 2002, each justified by a consultant feasibility study and bringing the Congress Center to a total of 1.4 million square feet of exhibit space.[103]

Promotion, Space, and Business Coalitions

Atlanta's business leaders needed, and sought, more than just the concrete physical improvements represented by a new civic center, stadium, and coliseum. They also needed new *private investment*, investment that they sought to lure to their city.

Thus when Phil Hammer drafted the program for Ivan Allen's year as Chamber of Commerce president, he began with those physical improvements, including completion of local expressways, a rapid transit system, and urban renewal. But point number six was different—a call for the chamber to "develop and carry out an aggressive 'Forward Atlanta' Campaign of national advertising and salesmanship."[104]

Hammer's recommendation was rooted in the belief that an earlier "Forward Atlanta" campaign in the 1920s had, according to Hammer, "brought the city to the attention of the world." Business leaders such as Richard Rich and Robert Woodruff had long been committed to selling the virtues of Atlanta and Georgia to a larger national (ultimately international) audience and luring new business. Hughes Spalding had recounted to Floyd Hunter how Woodruff, who was "also a director of the Southern Railroad. . . . Worked the Ford and General Motors project through the railroads," bringing new plants for both automakers to Atlanta in 1947. Spalding also boasted how "we have been able to get all of the Coates [Clark Company] thread works into Georgia out of New England. I have been rather proud of that."[105]

The "Forward Atlanta" education and advertising effort the chamber began in 1961 had a clear intent, to draw to the city "the new business and industry that such a campaign would generate." Investing in major public projects like the stadium and auditorium served to portray Atlanta as a city on the move, while providing leverage for the kind of new private investment and development, such as John Portman's trade mart or Robert Troutman's "air rights plaza," that Phil Hammer had envisioned in "Action at the Core." They thus validated specific sites or areas as suitable for new private investment, while also building the public foundations for private initiatives. When Hammer assessed the city's progress in a letter to the chamber in May 1964, he stressed how the city had added 38,000 new jobs. But, he argued, "I think Forward Atlanta is needed to keep the momentum going, not to obviate real or potential competition." That sense of momentum, of big things happening and even bigger things in prospect (Atlanta as a "national city"), was crucial to the business leadership's vision of the city.[106]

Looking back on the city's development accomplishments over the previous decade as part of an assessment of the air rights project for Tom Cousins, Hammer concluded: "The Downtown Connector served a function perhaps more important than improving traffic flow, because it formed a physical and psychological boundary for the east side of the downtown area."[107]

Public investment thus reshaped both land value and the *perception of development opportunity.* That vital role for public projects continued well after the civic center, stadium, and expressways were under way or completed. In 1967, Central Atlanta Progress staffer Robert Bivens and Atlanta city planner Collier Gladin contemplated a broad planning agenda, involving the city government and the metropolitan planning agency setting long-range goals for the downtown core. The business leaders themselves had a more narrow and directed focus in mind. A small committee of CAP's leaders, including Richard Rich, banker Mills Lane, Lucien Oliver of Sears, newspaper publisher Jack Tarver, and developer John Portman instead recommended that the downtown organization pursue "an alternate approach . . . with emphasis on developing a list of short-range projects to which priorities will be assigned." What Rich and his colleagues sought was not some grand plan, but a set of projects—projects which could serve to promote downtown, projects which could aid specific new private developments, and projects which could benefit a broad array of downtown interests.[108]

John Portman, Richard Rich, and their CAP colleagues wanted a means of leveraging city, state, and federal investment in the projects they needed to bolster the prospects of downtown. Their interests—and objective—were evident in a discussion of the Central Atlanta Study at CAP's March 1970 board meeting. CAP president Robert Wood told his colleagues, "We will, through this work, get the facts and figures which will give us 'leverage' for helping influence vital decisions for the accomplishment of the potentials of our central core. . . . Public improvements don't just happen, except via the planning process, and we need the same tools that the public agencies use if we are to exert any influence on what materializes." John Portman, just elected as the new president at the end of the meeting, added, "he will be organizing special task forces to develop and implement projects vital to the Central Core and the City."[109]

The "plan" that finally emerged from the joint effort of CAP and the city government in December 1971, the Central Atlanta Study, was indeed rather more a list of projects than a grand design. It began with a clarion call for the provision of public goods: "The necessary public steps must be taken to respond to the private investment potentials which Central Atlanta's highly specialized functions will generate." Then, looking back on the "spectacular development" in Atlanta's downtown, the study contended it "has not been accidental," pointing to "one of the nation's first urban renewal programs," and "Substantial public projects such as the Civic Center, Stadium, Grady Memorial Hospital, and Georgia State University [that] were carefully planned as to location to provide the maximum development leverage."[110]

The historical narrative of the 1971 Central Atlanta Study thus established that developments such as John Portman's Merchandise Mart and Peachtree Center and Tom Cousins's Omni were direct products of the farsighted public investment and development decisions made by a generation of Atlanta's business leaders. Looking forward, the study called for even more public spending. All told, the "grand total" cost came to $326.7 million. Although the planners anticipated substantial fiscal aid from the state and federal governments, the total for the city of Atlanta alone came to $183.1 million.

Yet, much as Central Atlanta Progress needed and desired hundreds of millions of dollars in public capital investment, the city was becoming an increasingly unreliable fiscal and political partner for the business community. Philip Hammer completed one of his regular assessments of Atlanta's economy for the Chamber of Commerce—he had done them throughout the 1960s—in November 1970. In "Prospects for the '70's," Hammer summarized how far the city and its metropolitan region had come over the decade of "Forward Atlanta."[111]

But as Phil Hammer looked ahead, he argued, "The No. 1 item of everybody's priority list . . . should be the restructuring of local government." As he saw it, the region's critical problem lay with racial division, and "the sharply growing polarization of political leadership, with the blacks in a position to exert increasingly decisive leverage in the city and the whites coalescing their strength in the suburbs."[112]

With the election of Maynard Jackson, the city's first African American mayor, in October 1973, the gap between Atlanta's business leadership and the city's political leadership began to widen, and Central Atlanta Progress soon made that gap publicly obvious. Maynard Jackson took office in early January 1974. By August, a group of downtown property owners and the leaders of Central Atlanta Progress had met "to discuss the status of the Central city and certain trends which are of concern to the downtown." That meeting culminated in a letter addressed to Mayor Jackson in mid-September, over the signature of Harold Brockey, the president of CAP and the chief executive of Rich's. While Brockey averred, "there is no discernible trend to indicate any business movement from the downtown to warrant major concern," he did describe a consensus in the downtown business community of the "need to reforge the progressive partnership between business and City Hall on commitment to the viability of Downtown."[113]

The "reforging" that Brockey and CAP sought went beyond mere interaction with and rhetoric from the mayor. The downtown group sought a number of specific public investments and projects to support the core, many of them laid out in the 1971 Central Atlanta Study. Indeed, the September "Brockey letter" had appended a quite lengthy listing of downtown problems and needed public actions, including the use of tax increment financing to rebuild parts of the core and provide parking, development of new housing in the Bedford-Pine/Buttermilk Bottom renewal area, and a renewed call to develop a "secondary distribution system/people mover [transit system] in stages to fit downtown needs." CAP's focus was, much as the city's business leadership's focus had long been, on downtown public investment projects.

What Central Atlanta Progress really sought was not a dialogue but "priority actions which must take place if we are to sustain the very healthy and desirable growth we have enjoyed in the past." In a follow-up letter to the mayor on December 11, 1974, Brockey described the downtown business leadership as "encouraged and pleased at the positive and personal interest" shown by the mayor in the wake of the September letter. But Brockey went on in his four-page missive to note "four key areas of concern which we believe must be given the highest and most immediate priority." What CAP wanted was not conversation but the city's commitment to major projects.[114]

Brockey's letter called on the mayor for "immediate action" on the one-way pairing of Spring and West Peachtree Streets at the northern end of the central area, city support for housing development in the Bedford-Pine [Buttermilk Bottom] renewal area, and the use of tax increment financing to redevelop the "Triangle Area" at the south end of the downtown core. Finally, it also stressed that the "City should seriously consider proposals to move toward planning and construction of a people mover joining the Civic Center with the World Congress Center and connecting a great number of the convention hotel rooms." As a major public initiative and investment the planned—if never actually realized—people mover offered some signal advantages for Central Atlanta Progress. It would serve as a promotional vehicle, indeed as a "tourist attraction" itself, while providing a concrete benefit for the disparate geographic interests of the downtown area, literally linking the investments of Portman and Cousins.

The promise of the people mover, and the rhetoric of CAP and Brockey in the December letter, were that the new World Congress Center and the wave of new convention business the city would see justified (more properly, necessitated) even more public investment. One project—stadium, Civic Center, coliseum—was not an end in itself. Each reshaped the development prospects of a specific area while adding to the city's image. Each neatly provided a justification for yet more public projects.

By mid-1975, with little change to the continuing division between business and City Hall, increasing national attention to the city's crime problem, and a growing office vacancy rate, the leadership of Central Atlanta Progress recognized the need to reassure major downtown real estate investors, "for the purposes of being updated on key Downtown issues and receiving feedback as to investors' concerns about downtown Atlanta."[115] What builder and CAP president Larry Gellerstedt sought was to "make these people feel intimately part of the Atlanta community." More implicitly, it was to assure a continuing flow of funds from firms like Prudential Insurance, Metropolitan Life, and New York Life into downtown projects. Atlanta's downtown core was dependent on outside private investment capital. The November daylong session for the investors, whose collective investment in downtown totaled more than $1 billion, was to describe the major private developments under way, including Portman's Peachtree Plaza and Tom Cousins's Omni complex.

But the major focus of the CAP presentation was on the new *public* projects on the books, including the soon-to-open World Congress Center, the expansion of Hartsfield Airport, and the region's new rapid transit system. These efforts would, the CAP leaders argued, "affect this city and the entire region economically like nothing in the past and perhaps nothing in the future." The new World Congress Center would generate "direct expenditures of $402 million" in its first four years of operation. And there was the promise of even more substantial public investment, notably a "People Mover system to distribute workers and visitors to major points throughout the downtown."[116]

Just as the successive "Forward Atlanta" campaigns had sought to bring Northern firms, investment, and jobs to Atlanta, the CAP leadership sought to reassure "these people" of the promising future of the city and the core, and of CAP's capacity to promote and realize major public projects like the long-discussed people mover. By the November 1975 date of the investor conference, the people mover had been under discussion for more than four years. Yet there was now a signal change in the message the city's business leaders were selling. CAP officials told the investor group that the transit system was being studied and planned by the "Georgia Department of Transportation, with the encouragement and support of Governor Busbee." The decisions on the transit system would thus not be in the hands of Mayor Jackson or even the Metropolitan Atlanta Rapid Transit Authority, but instead would rest with the state government. In turning to the state government, CAP was neatly following the political path laid out by Phil Hammer a few years earlier for financing and building the World Congress Center.

The focus of Atlanta's business leadership on the state, rather than the city or county governments, was particularly overt in the November 1975 investor session. While the formal presentation on the city and downtown involved Mayor Jackson and CAP during a morning and afternoon session, the investor group had met with Georgia Governor George Busbee for dinner the previous evening. The CAP staff instructed the governor's press secretary that he would be meeting the "big 'hosses' . . . who make the final decisions on whether or not to invest millions of dollars in real estate development." And Dan Sweat of Central Atlanta Progress went on to say in his memo that "the impression we want to leave our guests with is that we have a solid intelligent Governor who understands the importance of business and the importance of Atlanta to the economy of the state and region." Sweat's memo noted such major state government investments in downtown as the Capitol complex, Georgia State University, and the soon-to-open World Congress Center, emphasizing that the "Governor [should] cite the economic impact of the $35 million State [Congress Center] Construction money on the Atlanta and State economy."[117]

The message that CAP wanted Governor Busbee to convey—neatly underlined in Sweat's text for the press secretary—"The point is that if these private investors can see that the State is committed to Atlanta and is putting dollars into real economic generators, they will leave with a better feeling." Both the downtown business community and these major real estate investors needed—more realistically, demanded—public dollars put "into real economic generators" like the Georgia World Congress Center. Those "generators" were what supported new private investment, and reduced the sense of market risk and uncertainty about the direction and future of downtown Atlanta. The state would not easily walk away from major investments like the Georgia State University campus or the World Congress Center. And the prospect of even more investment and public dollars could be the driver of demand for new hotel rooms, new retail space and restaurants, and new office space development.

The November 1975 investor meeting and the dinner with Governor Busbee also marked a turning point for city business leaders. It was the state government that CAP's leaders sought to portray as "committed to Atlanta." The city government under Maynard Jackson was no longer the focus of business interest, as it had been under Ivan Allen or even Sam Massell. If there were to be major public investments, they would most likely have to be financed and managed by the state, rather than the city. The city government, independent of the conflict evidenced by the Brockey letter or the repeated efforts by CAP to get what it saw as its proper piece of new federal dollars allocated to the city, was increasingly a threadbare fiscal partner.

The successful 1963 bond program pushed by Mayor Allen and the Chamber of Commerce was something of a high water mark. With the aid of state legislation that enabled a small regular annual bond program (without a public vote) starting in 1969, the city's net general obligation debt grew from $77 million in 1960 to $160 million in 1970. But with no bond proposals on the ballot after 1963, debt issues stalled. CAP began to press the city for a new bond program in late 1974 and 1975, and the city council finally proposed a $48.92 million funding package in November 1975. The new bond program included $10 million for sorely needed storm sewer projects, $10 million for the Atlanta Zoo and parks, $10 million for street improvements, and $18.9 million for a new downtown central library. The street improvement funding was particularly critical for downtown interests, as it included funds for at least one project needed to serve the new World Congress Center and Omni complex.

Despite a campaign fueled by CAP member firms with some $75,000 in contributions, the library bond issue was the only one to gain the needed majority. After a dozen years of no city bond votes or major public improvements, Atlanta had again proven itself an unreliable source of public dollars for "real economic generators," or even modest dollars for needed street improvements. And that political and fiscal reality would prove remarkably persistent. Following the 1975 bond program defeat, city officials did not propose another general bond program until May 1988. The 1988 bond package, a total of $308 million in needed city and school improvements, was entirely defeated by the city's voters. The first successful voted city bond effort after Ivan Allen's much reduced 1963 program would not come until 1994.[118]

Just three years after its 1976 opening, the management of the Georgia World Congress Center had begun to call for an expansion, arguing that the facility was rapidly being booked to capacity and that groups too large to fit in the existing center "had expressed interest" in coming to a larger facility in Atlanta. Again, the fiscal focus was on the state government.[119]

A bigger World Congress Center was clearly a priority for CAP, and the group's officers noted in January 1980 "great concern over the likelihood of the State government's moving ahead with the proposed funding." The sentiment of the business leaders was that "three hotel expansions and one new 1500 room hotel were waiting in the wings and were dependent upon the decision with respect to expansion." The group also noted that the governor "had been favorable to aiding the passage of such legislation."[120]

What drove CAP's focus on expansion was less an understanding of the larger market realities of the convention business and city competition, than the imperative to support new private investment and development with the *expectation* of increased hotel demand. A substantial increase in exhibit space—the "Phase II Expansion" would almost double the exhibit space to 650,000 square feet—brought with it the *promise* of a significant increase in convention business and a real boost in hotel demand. A 1982 analysis of the city's convention industry by a business-supported research organization argued that an expanded center "will be able to house more than one convention at the same time, providing a major thrust for an increased amount of convention traffic into Atlanta," while also enabling the center "to accommodate the 'super shows' that require more than 500,000 square feet of space."[121]

The ultimate performance of an expanded Georgia World Congress Center was in many ways less relevant to the needs of Atlanta's business leaders (or hotel developers) than the prospect and potential of greater business and increased hotel stays. The Phase II expansion, with a price tag of $103 million, that the Georgia state legislature finally authorized in 1981 partially opened in November 1983, with the full building program completed in January 1985. But within a very few months—in late April 1985 to be precise—World Congress Center director Dan Graveline told the *Atlanta Journal* that the center was "already 85 to 90 percent booked for the next 10 years," and "there is no question we could justify larger expansion, especially of exhibit space." With an immediate judgment that the expansion was a success, Graveline and the business leadership followed up with a formal proposal for expansion to 960,000 square feet of exhibit space in March 1987.[122]

Just as the "Phase II" expansion of the World Congress Center was being assured with the state legislature in 1981, yet another issue arose that appeared to threaten the viability and future of the city's convention business and downtown's visitor appeal. Beginning in 1969, a group of private entrepreneurs had revived a group of turn-of-the-century storefronts beneath the "surface" streets carried by viaducts above the downtown rail lines as "Underground Atlanta." With a collection of restaurants, nightclubs, and tourist retail, Underground offered a concentrated entertainment district located conveniently to the World Congress Center and downtown hotels. But a series of events, including a growing crime problem and construction for MARTA, the region's new rail transit system, resulted in a dramatic decline in business and a gradual loss of tenants. In September 1981, the "Dante's Down the Hatch" restaurant, long a mainstay of the district, was shuttered, and Underground finally closed in early 1982.[123]

The failure of Underground Atlanta reflected the larger market pressures on downtown. But with the expansion of the World Congress Center moving ahead and a substantial investment in hotels and businesses geared to the meeting and convention business, the failure of the city's prime downtown entertainment locale was viewed by the business community as a serious threat. One effort to keep Underground afloat with a new developer and a modest infusion of city dollars failed. It would obviously take a major initiative to revive the area, and CAP and the city's business leaders were unwilling to abandon it. And almost no one had a greater stake in the future of Underground than developer Tom Cousins.

Cousins had bet that the new transit system, with a station at the Omni and adjacent arena, would "draw them in from the suburbs by the tens of thousands, filling the empty office space with workers and the boutiques with well-heeled shoppers." But, as Frederick Allen recounts, "Cousins guessed wrong," and by late 1980 "the lone viable role for the Omni International, it seemed, was to service the convention traffic that continued to pour into the nearby World Congress Center."[124]

In fiscal year 1981, the World Congress Center had accommodated about 369,500 out-of-town visitors, and the expansion was promised to substantially increase that number. But with a host of other cities building more convention center space, that business was dependent on maintaining Atlanta's appeal as a destination.

The solution to reviving Underground, in the eyes of the CAP leadership, lay in bringing in a major national developer who could in turn lure national tenants as well as local firms. Circa 1980 there was no more visible downtown developer than James Rouse. Rouse's reuse of Boston's Faneuil Hall market was an acclaimed success, and Baltimore's Harborplace would open in July 1980. In June 1981, with Underground on the verge of closure, CAP President Dan Sweat wrote to James Rouse, congratulating him on his new "Enterprise Development Corporation" and adding, "By the way, you are missing a great opportunity by not coming on down to Atlanta and doing the Underground project like it should be done!" Rouse's involvement could garner the kind of national visibility and promotional reward that would in turn boost the prospects of the downtown core and aid the Omni.[125]

Jim Rouse's June 25 reply to Sweat was both pleasant and direct. He said, "We have tried on several occasions, as you know, to work with Atlanta on 'Underground'—and the 'overground' above it—but something has always intervened." He concluded, "The two must be integrated to have any real meaning for Atlanta and to be successful."[126]

Rouse's brief reply did not offer any more details on his views of the city government or the development prospects for Underground. But it did suggest a need to conceive of the project in larger, and thus more expensive, terms. Rouse was not racing to do a festival marketplace on the order of Boston's Faneuil Hall or Baltimore's Harborplace in Atlanta. The CAP leaders, most notably Tom Cousins, were unwilling to wait or to find someone else.

With the election of Andrew Young as mayor in 1981, CAP faced a new city chief executive far more friendly to business and willing to tackle major projects than Maynard Jackson had been. One of Young's first actions after taking office in January 1982 was to seek the rebuilding of Underground. Tom Cousins wrote to Dan Sweat in February on what he saw as the issues and prospects for a new Underground. In Cousins's view, Rouse's involvement—despite the project's cost—was a necessity to leverage local officials and public spending: "there will be many millions of dollars of both city and county funds required to pull it off. I think the only chance of getting those funds is by way of a foreign developer such as Rouse Company."

He also recognized that the promise of Rouse's involvement was the means of selling the project's financial potential: "A good case can be made to prove that an investment of these millions on the part of the city and county will provide dramatic returns. I clearly recall, however, how difficult it was to convince the state legislature on the World Congress Center."[127]

The new Underground Atlanta opened in June 1989, after a tortured series of financial machinations and political deals. Tom Cousins proved entirely correct about the role of the local public sector. A 1981 analysis of the project by the Urban Land Institute termed it "unusual in the degree to which it is leveraged," with less than $18 million in equity used to raise $111 million in debt. Most of the project's financing was provided by the Atlanta Downtown Development Authority through a bond issue, backed by the city's promise to make up any gap in annual debt service after revenues from rents and parking revenue. The Development Authority mechanism allowed the $85 million bond issue to proceed without a public vote, supplemented by a $10 million federal grant, $12 million in city "windfall" sales tax revenues, and an $8.5 million loan from Community Development Block Grant funds. Rouse appeared to disagree with Cousins on the "tremendous opportunity" afforded by Underground, putting only $1 million of equity in the project.[128]

The Underground project was floated and developed on the same sea of promotion and grand expectations that had carried a host of public development projects before it. Days before its opening, the *Journal-Constitution* ran an article headlined "From Dream to Reality." Maria Saporta reported that local civic leaders "see it as a chance to transform Atlanta from a place where the sidewalks roll up at 5 p.m. into a lively place for both locals and visitors—not just a rosy vision, but a necessity to maintain growth of the city's convention industry." Her article went on to quote the president of the Atlanta

Convention and Visitors Bureau—"There's too much at stake for Atlanta to let Underground fail. . . . If it does fail, Atlanta will be an also-ran city."[129]

The premise that Underground would succeed, both itself and in securing the city's place as a convention mecca, proved not fulfilled. The June 1989 *Journal* article had noted that the project was 90 percent leased and was "expected to cost the city $2 to $3 million a year for the first few years." But when the project's ownership changed hands in 2000, it was only 60 percent occupied. And when the Development Authority refinanced the project's bonds in 2002, it reported that the project was 71 percent occupied, and that the city "has not derived sufficient revenues from the Project in the past and does not expect to derive sufficient revenues from the Project in the foreseeable future to make the payments required by the Contract and the Lease." In a more recent assessment, as part of the city's budget review in May 2010, one council member suggested trying to sell Underground, as it "costs the city $16 million each year, with no return on the investment."[130]

The renewed Underground Atlanta proved no salvation for the city's downtown, and no persistent boon to Atlanta's convention business. What it did demonstrate was the process through which Central Atlanta Progress regularly pressed for major development projects, at great public cost, to boost the image and investment prospects of the core. Yet even as CAP and the city were working out the details of the financing and development of Underground, they were faced with another threat and development opportunity.

Stadium Interregnum

The Atlanta-Fulton County Stadium Ivan Allen and Mills Lane had brought into being in 1965 was, twenty years later, accommodating both major league baseball and the NFL Atlanta Falcons. Falcons owner Rankin Smith was not entirely happy with what the stadium offered his team as a venue, complaining in 1983 about the playing field and drainage issues and arguing that the stadium was now obsolete. While behind-the-scenes discussions had gone on through 1984 involving Smith, Braves owner Ted Turner, and the Recreation Authority, the pressure for a new stadium (or two) surfaced publicly in early 1985.

Georgia House speaker Tom Murphy, who had been closely involved in the construction and expansion of the World Congress Center, broached the idea of a new sports complex combined with state offices, located in the suburbs south or east of Atlanta. Murphy had played a critical role in moving the original development of the World Congress Center through the state legislature, and as his biographer Richard Hyatt noted, "For decades, the road to getting something done in Georgia has had an exit ramp to Tom Murphy's inner office."[131]

Faced with the possible loss of the Falcons and the economic advantage of professional football adjacent to downtown, the Central Atlanta Progress leadership drafted a letter to Murphy. Although there were distinct spatial interests among the downtown business leaders, exemplified by the split between Cousins and Portman, CAP could be united in insisting that any major public facility be located in the downtown core.

CAP's January 1985 letter expressed support for Murphy's goal of "improved athletic facilities," but argued that the state and city governments should study "the potential benefits of utilizing properties surrounding the [existing] Atlanta-Fulton County Stadium for the sports and office complex you envision." CAP contended that the stadium parking lots offered a readily available building site, and that new parking garages could serve both state workers and football fans. But the prospect of a new stadium enabled the downtown business group to resurrect an unrealized dream of yet another grand project—"And a people-mover system connecting MARTA and Capitol Hill to the stadium could be mutually beneficial as well, for office patrons and for spectators."[132]

For Rankin Smith and the Falcons, a new stadium offered an opportunity to sell an improved product and boost the team's revenues. For CAP, the Chamber of Commerce, and Atlanta's business leadership, it was an opportunity to reinforce existing downtown activity levels, provide yet another source of development momentum, and realize the vision of a people mover connecting the core area's disparate sub-areas. The immediate problem for Smith (and the business leadership) was that neither the city government nor the Recreation Authority had the fiscal resources to develop an entirely new stadium. The obvious fiscal solution, barring the intervention of Speaker Murphy, was the state government.

When the push for a new stadium surfaced publicly in the *Atlanta Journal* in mid-February, it featured the role of John Aderhold, president of a local auto parts firm and chair of the World Congress Center Authority, in organizing a group to meet with Governor Joe Frank Harris to secure funding. Quite soon thereafter, the Chamber of Commerce, obviously working with the management of the World Congress Center, proposed that the domed stadium would be a natural addition to the convention facility. The chamber's sports task force promoted the idea that as part of the GWCC/Omni Coliseum complex, a domed stadium "would be able to host the NFL Super Bowl, the NCAA basketball finals, a national political convention or a convention whose exhibits cannot be accommodated in the Georgia World Congress Center."[133]

A special study committee chaired by John Aderhold, including representatives of the state, city, and county governments, as well as the Chamber of Commerce, the Falcons, and the Braves, began a formal study of stadium options in early 1985. The committee's initial recommendation was that the existing stadium could not be renovated to suitably serve both baseball and football. Finally, in late June 1986, it reported its endorsement of a new domed stadium. Briefing the CAP leadership in July, Aderhold noted that the plan included "a new domed stadium for football to be located next to the Omni; and a new baseball stadium to be located next to the existing stadium." The dome would be finished by 1991, with the baseball facility completed by 1995. The plan was to be financed with revenues from club boxes and seats, with the World Congress Center location also serving "overflow" convention and meeting activity. Just as with the Congress Center itself, the *state government* provided a fiscal and political vehicle that made major public projects possible, despite the disinterest and potential opposition of Atlanta voters, and offered a *pair* of projects rather than just one.

It would take another four years before the financing for the domed stadium was finally worked out, with public dollars from Atlanta's hotel and motel tax supplementing the revenues to be generated by seat sales and the Falcons. But that deal once again fit the pattern established in the 1960s. The Georgia World Congress Center Authority, rather than the city or county governments, issued the $200 million in bonds for the stadium. Hotel tax dollars, amounting to $15 million or more per year, provided about 40 percent of the backing for the stadium debt. But the critical element of the deal was that it required no public vote. Atlanta got a domed stadium downtown, and the promise of a new home for the baseball Braves (eventually realized after the 1996 Olympics), together with the expectation that the city would play host to the Super Bowl and a variety of other national events. It was exactly the kind of promotion, a major public project seemingly enhancing the city's national image as a "can-do" community, that the chamber leadership and Ivan Allen had envisioned in 1960.

Perhaps the most telling comment on the Georgia Dome and its larger role was made by Larry Gellerstedt, Jr., former president of the Chamber of Commerce and CAP, and head of Beers Construction, the firm that would build the dome, to his Central Atlanta Progress colleagues: "Additionally, Mr. Gellerstedt stressed the crucial importance of the completion of Underground Atlanta, the passage of the upcoming bond referendum, the construction of the Georgia Dome (stadium), and hosting the Democratic [national] convention to the continued success and viability of the city."[134]

What CAP wanted, and downtown needed, was not one public project, but a series of projects intended to draw Atlantans, suburbanites, visitors, and ultimately private investment dollars downtown. In order to sustain that imagery and development momentum, it needed a series of major events—a Super Bowl, an NCAA Final Four, and ultimately an Olympic Games—as a means of promoting and selling the city and the downtown core. And when projects, public or private, failed to either prosper or sustain the expectations and promise on which further investment depended, the answer was more public investment.

Space

Urban space is never static, with its use and value fixed. It can be shaped and defined, altered and redefined. The thriving retail corner marked by major department stores can lose its appeal, the neighborhood of once-grand homes near the core abandoned and left to other uses or decline. And new centers of gravity can exert their own pull, pulling in people and attracting investment that seeks to capitalize on the flow of economic activity.

Phil Hammer understood what it took to shape and alter urban space and development opportunities. From his first assessment of the underused railroad air rights of the "gulch" in the 1952 "Up Ahead" plan and call for a new "central transportation terminal," to the plan's scheme for a civic center on an urban renewal clearance site on the eastern edge of the core, Hammer recognized how the space in and around the central area could be reshaped and redefined through public action and investment. Then, and later through a series of reports and studies for an ever-expanding list of public agencies and officials, business leaders, and developers, Hammer laid out a series of crucial roles that public decisions and investments could, and ultimately did, play in Atlanta. For developer Tom Cousins, who ultimately bought the Hammer,

Siler consulting firm, Hammer's analysis was invaluable. "Anything Phil did, I listened to," said Cousins in a recent interview.[135]

The first place to be reshaped was the band of low-income, largely African American neighborhoods to the east and south of the central core. Hammer had argued to Ivan Allen in his draft "Six Point Program" that the city should "encourage private capital to take advantage of the unprecedented development opportunities in urban renewal projects." The clearance of Buttermilk Bottom for the new Civic Center and the Rawson-Washington area for the stadium neatly served what Hammer foretold: "redevelopment will substantially improve the environment of Downtown Atlanta."[136]

The purpose was the same for developer Tom Cousins in 1970, with Hammer arguing that a planned coliseum "will serve as a barrier against the warehousing and industrial area to the west."[137] And much of the appeal of what became the Georgia World Congress Center, adjacent to the Coliseum and the Omni complex, also lay in its capacity to differentiate the air rights from the area of decline to the west.

The Coliseum, and later the Congress Center as well, were enormously valuable to Tom Cousins in their potential role as *anchors* and *magnets*. Shopping center and mall developers have long understood the vital role of anchor department stores in demonstrating the financial viability of a proposed center, and in making the entire project salable to potential tenants. That was why, having envisioned the air rights as the "best possible site in the Atlanta area for the development of a large, regional shopping center now or within the reasonably near future," Phil Hammer sought to induce a major department store to commit to the project. His initial prospects were major national stores that would be new to Atlanta: New York's Gimbel's or the St. Louis-based May Company. Absent that "anchor," Robert Troutman struggled for a decade to find sufficient tenants for a real development opportunity.[138]

When Tom Cousins entered the picture, he too needed an anchor, and again turned to Phil Hammer. Cousins needed a new kind of anchor, one that could provide a focal point for his planned development, and also serve as a *magnet*, pulling people to the air rights site. New basketball and hockey teams would serve as the magnets, and the Coliseum would be the anchor, with the forecast from Hammer that sports and other events would draw 1.6 million annual attendees. The commitment of local government to the project, evidenced by the construction of the Coliseum (and its 30-year bonds issued by the Atlanta-Fulton County Recreation Authority), also served to "enhance the image" of the air rights project.

The "magnet" of the Coliseum would be bolstered by the "entertainment complex" envisioned by Hammer, providing "both the intown and out-of-town visitors with distinctive entertainment options to appeal to nearly all tastes and pocketbooks," with a variety of retail outlets and "common and uncommon food and beverage establishments." The "anchors" for the air rights were the Coliseum and entertainment complex themselves. They in turn would presumably generate the activity and business volume to support retail stores, the new hotel planned by Cousins, and ultimately the new office buildings that would provide the real financial return on the development.

Cousins had to take a financial risk on the Coliseum, pledging the revenues from the adjacent parking complex to back the Recreation Authority's bond issue. But that risk was obviously "worth it" in boosting the development prospects for the air rights by literally guaranteeing a stream of visitors for games and events. Yet even with the prospect of millions of attendees at the Coliseum, Phil Hammer's 1970 hotel analysis supported the development of just 350 new hotel rooms. A larger hotel, and indeed a larger and more impressive complex, would require a bigger and more substantial magnet. That magnet, the proposed International Congress Center, thus became the great prize for Cousins.

The Georgia World Congress Center plan neatly fit into Cousins's and Hammer's vision of a development complex oriented to visitors, with its combination of hotel, restaurants, entertainment, and retail stores—directly served by the new rapid transit system. Such a potentially enormous activity generator at the air rights would do much to boost the confidence of both potential investors and tenants in the economic viability and returns from the entire project. Cousins's enthusiasm for the Congress Center was demonstrated by his willingness to donate six acres of the required 13-acre site. But Cousins's offer of free land also came with a "string"—the condition that the Congress Center build a pedestrian connection between the new convention facility and the planned Omni International hotel complex. Cousins needed the two fully connected.

While Tom Cousins sought the "magnet" of the Congress Center to boost the prospects of the air rights development, developer John Portman had long backed it—on a site adjacent to the existing Civic Center—as a natural complement to his nearby Peachtree Center development and its growing supply of hotel rooms. The prospect of a far larger convention facility as part of the Civic Center was also a motivator for realtor Ewell Pope, who joined with Dallas developer Trammell Crow in proposing a new complex, including the city's largest hotel, a 1,250-room Hilton. The Pope, Crow, and Land firm proposed joining the major new hotel with a 20-story office tower, 100,000 square feet of new retail space, and a 1,200-car garage. On the large block to the northwest of Pope's project, New York developer Harry Helmsley, together with American Realty Trust, proposed another hotel/retail/office complex with a projected value of $250 million.[139]

Both the Pope and Helmsley projects were based on the development of the new Congress Center at the Civic Center site, with its ability to draw more convention and event attendees. Indeed, the "loss" of the Civic Center site prompted Pope to offer to buy a site near the Civic Center and donate it to the state. With the final choice of Cousins's air rights site, the Pope and Crow project shrank to just the new Hilton hotel—no offices or retail. And the Helmsley project, without a "magnet," never came to fruition.

For developers like Cousins, Portman, and Pope, the real value of the proposed center lay in its promise as an anchor and magnet for their own development schemes. With the commitment of both the Coliseum and the GWCC, Tom Cousins could move ahead with his plans for the air rights. Without a magnet, Ewell Pope's effort and the Helmsley plans simply couldn't be realized in their planned form.

For all of these Atlanta developers (and the broader set of land-based interests), and others before and since, large-scale public investment in civic center, coliseum, or convention hall (or indeed a new rapid transit station, entertainment complex, or stadium) offered the potential of a people-attracting magnet and anchor. Build one next door, or even nearby, and potential land values were enhanced and development prospects seemingly assured. Build it blocks away, and someone or something else would reap the benefits in speculative land value and development prospects.

A significant feature of these public investments is the way they are "stuck"—fixed in place over years and decades. Paid for with long-term debt over 20 or 30 years, they are not readily replaced or abandoned. In Atlanta's case, the World Congress Center remains the focal point of the city's convention activity, regularly expanded and supported by new public investment, including a domed stadium and Centennial Olympic Park.

In shaping major public investments to serve the needs of particular development interests, from the Uptown Association, to John Portman, and Tom Cousins, the city and state created a set of quite disparate and widely separated centers. The locational choices for both the Civic Center and the stadium were shaped almost entirely by the business community's desire to eliminate the slum neighborhoods bordering the core. They succeeded in that goal, but at a cost. City planner Collier Gladin quite appropriately wrote in 1968 that the Civic Center was "too far from rapid transit . . . [and] too far from downtown." And the stadium, with its 4,000 adjacent parking spaces, offered a potential solution to the parking woes of the downtown core, but it too was too far to serve commuters.

Assessing the spatial issues downtown in 1976, a joint city and state transportation proposal described "isolated activity areas in the inner core . . . the functional isolation created between areas encourages a disaggregate environment in the downtown, and discourages the intensification of economic activity which could otherwise result from adequate circulation and interaction between functional areas." In more direct language, the "activity areas" were simply too spread out.[140]

The solution, earnestly promoted by Central Atlanta Progress and enunciated in the 1976 proposal to the federal government, was a people mover system. The formal system plan was designed to link the Civic Center with the Hilton and Portman's hotels, serve the Omni and the World Congress Center, and tie into Georgia State University and the state government complex. It also offered the prospect of a spur serving the stadium and its parking spaces. And to make clear how vital CAP considered the need for a publicly financed linkage mechanism, the proposal argued, "Increasing circulation in the CBD . . . is critical to the success of the new megastructure developments and to the promotion of the convention and tourist trade important to the city."[141]

Despite the failure of the 1970s people mover plan, successive efforts to better link the separate activity centers of downtown Atlanta have been a regular part of both public plans and private development initiatives. Central Atlanta Progress never fully abandoned the hope for fixed-line transit to supplement the MARTA system in the core. The 1988 Central Atlanta Study II included a call for "possible enhancements . . . such as exclusive guideway transit facilities, to enhance the MARTA rail system." And in 2007 and 2008, a proposal emerged from a city-created committee calling for a streetcar line on Peachtree Street, linking the fast-growing Buckhead and Midtown sections with the activity centers downtown. After one failed attempt to gain federal grant funds, a more modest application for an east-west streetcar loop linking Centennial Olympic Park on the west, past the Portman-developed Trade Mart and Marriott and Westin hotels, to Auburn Avenue and the Martin Luther King National Historic Site to the east, was submitted by the city in August 2010 and ultimately approved for federal financing.[142]

If the Georgia World Congress Center, the Georgia Dome, and the Omni Coliseum and later Philips Arena were effectively "fixed" in the space of downtown Atlanta, the efforts to expand, improve, build upon, and connect them to other places and zones of potential development and investment were seemingly unending. The World Congress Center was expanded in 1985, again in 1992, and again in 2002. And if the proposed people mover and successor guideway scheme never were realized, there was always the possibility of a new streetcar line. And for the adjacent zones of the southern section of the downtown core, the focus of the 1973 Triangle Action Plan and an area that had long frustrated a succession of city planners and developers, Central Atlanta Progress would propose in 2007 a "Green Line" of new public plazas and open space, in the expectation that it would create an "iconic destination" capable of "stitch[ing] the city together through public space, transit and daily life" and fostering new "public and private investment." CAP proposed to anchor the "Green Line" by a new multimodal transportation terminal to be financed with a combination of state and federal dollars, as well as a new headquarters building for MARTA.[143]

A transportation center by the "gulch" would represent the realization of a dream of Phil Hammer's from 1952 and a goal of Central Atlanta Progress since at least the early 1990s. While there were no immediate prospects for financing and building the scheme, once again major public investment was seen as the key to spur investment and reshape land value and development potential.[144]

Coalitions

When Ivan Allen addressed his friends and colleagues on the Chamber of Commerce Board in January 1960, he spoke of the agreement and "substantial sentiment" for building a new stadium, a new music hall or auditorium, and a "large indoor coliseum." But he went on to stress that a "joint effort" for all these projects would "bring support . . . from all factions concerned."

Allen was not speaking for public consumption. His observation about "all factions" made it clear that even within the leadership of Atlanta's business community, there were indeed "factions." It was not merely that Allen saw factional divisions. He was fully conscious of the need to appease and accommodate them in order to secure all of the major public investments that he—and others—were proposing.

The need for and manifestation of that accommodation was obvious within a month, when architect and developer John Portman objected to the inclusion of a new coliseum as part of Allen's (and the chamber's) planned package. Speaking to the chamber leadership, Allen noted the "opposition on the part of Mr. Portman of the Atlanta Merchandise Mart" to the coliseum proposal, which was then dropped.

That Allen and his friends perceived "factions" was striking but not surprising. Factions or "crowds" had long characterized Atlanta's business and civic elite. When sociologist Floyd Hunter sought to describe the city's "power structure" in 1950, he deemed one of his first interviews "with one of the big wheels" as "the most revealing of the lot." That interview, with attorney Hughes Spalding, introduced Hunter to both the character of the city's leadership, and its "crowds."[145]

Spalding told Hunter, "Simply that there are several 'crowds' in Atlanta that pretty well make all the big decisions." He placed himself in the "Coca-Cola-Trust Company crowd," and then noted the "Georgia Power crowd; the C&S [Bank] crowd; the Rich's crowd; the 1st National bank crowd; and the like." Spalding deemed Robert Woodruff "the biggest man of them all . . . in the Trust Company group." Then there was the C&S crowd that included Mills Lane, contractor L. L. Gellerstedt, and R. W. Courts of Atlanta Realty. The First National Bank crowd included bank chair Robert F. Maddox, financier Lee Ashcraft, and Albert Thornton.[146]

Hughes Spalding saw clear differences in the performance and attitudes of the different crowds. The C&S Bank crowd he described as "dry rotted" and "satisfied"—"they let things go that others are after." The First National crowd was "pretty aggressive yet." And the city's major institutions were tied to one "crowd" or another, with Emory University linked to Woodruff and the Coca-Cola crowd, while Georgia Tech was linked to the Rich's crowd.

Spalding described how the various crowds could cooperate on a community project, providing the example of seeking to bring the headquarters of the National Safety Council to Atlanta. But Spalding's comments emphasized the divisions and distinctiveness of the city's crowds. What is perhaps most relevant about Spalding's vision of crowds is how it parallels Ivan Allen's observations of "factions," as well as Phil Hammer's observations in his 1959 "Action at the Core" plan of different interests in the downtown core and Uptown areas. Spalding saw the crowds as organized around the city's dominant financial and business institutions, and those institutions in turn had very particular spatial concerns.

The Rich's crowd, for example, centered around Richard Rich and Rich's company president Frank Neely. While the Spalding interview describes the group's ties to Georgia Tech, Richard Rich had a particular interest in the main store's downtown locale. He pressed Phil Hammer in the early 1950s, while he then headed the Metropolitan Planning Commission, for a "West-side Connector" highway that would bring highway traffic and access to the western edge of the core, near the department store.[147]

The C&S crowd, in turn, sought public improvements and investment as part of its interest in developing "Commerce Square," including a new headquarters for First Federal Savings in the downtown Five Points area. The First National Bank group, in contrast, was willing to hedge its bets on the future of Five Points and the downtown core, constructing a new office building in the Uptown area at Peachtree and North Avenues in 1959.

Faced with a diversity of "crowds" and spatial interests, the Atlanta Chamber of Commerce was obliged to avoid difficult (and divisive) policy or locational issues that affected the city's future development. In 1959, as developer John Portman was promoting his plans for a new Merchandise Mart on Peachtree Street downtown, developer and builder Robert Holder proposed a competing mart as part of his Peachtree Industrial Boulevard development in suburban Gwinnett County. Atlanta's Board of Aldermen adopted a resolution calling on local organizations and the chamber to promote a "centrally located" facility rather than the suburban one. The chamber, faced with the choice between backing a city project or a suburban one, noted that it had "studiously avoided any favoritism and had accorded both of the competitive private enterprise groups the same assurance and courtesies," and declined to go along with the Atlanta aldermen.[148]

Projects were no less problematic when they were located entirely within the city. There had long been a division within the downtown retail sector between Rich's department store at Five Points and Davison's/Macy's to the north on Peachtree Street. The north-south division was exacerbated as new development moved to the north. In his 1955 report on Atlanta's economy to Richard Rich, Phil Hammer noted, "The amount of commercial building along Peachtree, West Peachtree and Spring Streets since the end of the war has been almost phenomenal . . . .Virtually all of this activity has taken place north of North Avenue."

The split between the uptown and downtown (Five Points) business interests became evident with the formation of the Uptown Association in 1960. The new Uptown group included on its board a number of mainstays of the chamber's leadership, such as George Brodnax of Georgia Power, Buick dealer Hix Green, Lucien Oliver of Sears, and Coca-Cola bottler Arthur Montgomery. It also included a number of very prominent business and civic figures, such as Hughes Spalding and property owner (and John Portman ally) Ben Massell.

The divide between the Uptown Association and the downtown-oriented Central Atlanta Improvement Association was fully evident in the development of the 1962 bond program. The Uptown interests were committed to—insistent on—immediate clearance of Buttermilk Bottom and improvements on the North Avenue corridor, while the CAIA was focused on the traditional heart of the core area at Five Points. And the Uptown group was ultimately accommodated, while the CAIA received its long-sought street improvements.

In proposing his package of improvements to unite all "factions," Ivan Allen was both recognizing the diversity of interests *within the business community*, and structuring a compromise solution. By joining three disparate public projects, Allen could spread out their impact and benefits. And by deferring the coliseum in deference to Portman, he could avoid any visible, public conflict over the city's goals and public investments.

What is perhaps most central about Allen's effort to accommodate the diverse factions and interests was that effort was limited to the leadership of the city's business community. The "package," enunciated by Allen and effectively reinforced by Robert Woodruff's and Richard Rich's reliance on Phil Hammer to consider the locations of all of the proposed projects, was defined and moved forward *privately*. There was no public review or planning effort, either of the individual projects or the package of public investments as a whole. There was no substantive city staff input on the priorities or locations. And the public, most notably the African American community to be affected by the renewal projects for both the auditorium and the stadium, was uninvolved. It was only when the one project that required tax revenues, the auditorium, was obliged to be voted on that there was any real public involvement.

The very existence of a "package" of projects to be financed and implemented over a period of a decade was not necessarily visible to the Atlanta public. Even the historical accounts of the clearance of Buttermilk Bottom for the new Civic Center, the development of the new stadium, and the construction of the Omni Coliseum portray them as quite distinct undertakings with their own seemingly unique political and financial arrangements. Yet the independent authority that Ivan Allen embraced in 1960 as the vehicle for financing the stadium would also be used to finance the bonds for the coliseum. And repeatedly through the decade of the 1960s, Allen and the chamber leadership operated on the basis that there was indeed a *standing commitment* to realization of the full package of projects.

Ivan Allen reiterated the notion of package of major public investments when, immediately following the approval of the auditorium bonds, he sought financial help from Robert Woodruff in building a new stadium. Allen's May 22, 1963, letter began with the statement that

> The major needs of the city in the area of public entertainment and development are
>
> 1. An auditorium and exhibition hall
> 2. A coliseum for athletics
> 3. A cultural center
> 4. A municipal stadium.[149]

Despite the voters' rejection of public funds for the proposed Piedmont Park cultural center, Allen knew Woodruff was still committed to its realization. And notwithstanding Allen's willingness to defer to John Portman on the coliseum three years earlier, that project too was still included among the "major needs." And if Mayor Allen later appeared to be uncomfortable in delivering all of the projects in the 1960 package, the chamber leadership was willing to remind him.

In August 1964, as the construction of the new Civic Center was under way, Arthur Montgomery expressed his "concern" to the Chamber of Commerce board about the need for a "coliseum-type-multi-purpose facility," and found agreement among his colleagues to press the mayor on the issue. The continuing pressure for a coliseum came, not from the mayor or the general public, but rather from the business leadership.

The initiative for a coliseum continued from Cousins and the business community, with Central Atlanta Progress both endorsing the idea of a new coliseum and providing a "very strong recommendation" of the air rights site desired by Cousins. And just as Ivan Allen had planned in January 1960, the bonds for the coliseum—although backed by Cousins and parking garage revenues—were issued by the city-county Recreation Authority in a move that avoided a public vote.

With the commitment to the coliseum, Atlanta's business leaders effectively realized the full package of major public projects described by Ivan Allen and analyzed by Phil Hammer in 1960. The key to successfully realizing all of these projects was the capacity to forge agreement within the business community that all were necessary public investments, and that support for each would ultimately redound to the benefit of the entire business leadership. The Uptown Association, the Five Points interests, those focused on a convention facility, those who sought to develop the west side air rights, those interested in clearing slums and creating buffer zones, and those excited about the potential of major league sports with a stadium were all eventually accommodated.

The continuing pressure for the final elements of the deal and package sketched out by Allen and embraced by the chamber and the larger business community did not come from Allen as mayor, or indeed from other local elected officials. It was the business leadership, backed by Phil Hammer's continuing studies and analyses, that pressed for development of the coliseum and then an enlarged convention facility.

The capacity of the Chamber of Commerce and parallel organizations such as Central Atlanta Progress was rooted in their long-term continuity and their leadership. Richard C. Rich, for example, had served as chamber president in 1950 and developed a "31 Point-10 Year Program" for the group. A decade later, Rich could confidently present an accounting of the business community's success in achieving almost all of these goals. It was the capacity of both the chamber as an organization and of individual business leaders such as Richard Rich to maintain a focus on a public agenda year after year and decade after decade, as mayors and governors came and went, that provided much of its capacity to realize business goals.

A listing of the directors of the chamber in 1972 included architect Cecil Alexander, who had served as head of the advisory committee on urban renewal in the late 1950s and had promoted the renewal of Buttermilk Bottom; former mayor Ivan Allen, Jr., and his son, Ivan Allen III; Larry Gellerstedt, who followed his father's involvement in chamber affairs; and Richard Rich. Yet another form of continuity came from institutional affiliation, with the chamber's leadership regularly including the chief executives of major Atlanta banks, such as the Trust Company of Georgia and First National Bank, and a senior executive of Georgia Power.

The product of this leadership continuity was a long-term focus on major projects and plans. Phil Hammer had decried the lack of a substantial downtown plan in 1959, and even with the success of both the stadium and auditorium projects, in 1965 the chamber's Long Range Planning Committee (headed by Cecil Alexander) said, "First, we need an effective plan for the Central Business District . . . [noting] there has never been an official policy." A joint city-private sector downtown plan was one of the first goals of the new Central Atlanta Progress organization in 1967. And finally in late 1971, CAP and the city were able to produce "Central Atlanta: Opportunities" as the first "Central Area Study."[150]

The Central Area Study contained both an assessment of the state of the core area and a set of forecasts. But its central recommendations focused on transportation and street improvements, and new parks and pedestrian linkages. And those improvements took a distinct form. The downtown group's plan neatly offered public improvements to all major interests in the central area.

The study and its scheme for an automated people mover system established both a planning pattern and a political reality. With the hotels, convention center, stadium, entertainment complex (Underground Atlanta), and visitor attractions widely dispersed, much of the subsequent effort of Central Atlanta Progress was oriented to linking and reinforcing these centers in the face of market and social pressures.

The strategy of employing new public investment, from a people mover to parks and promenades, as a means of linking together the disparate centers of downtown also offered potential benefits to each of the varied interests, from Cousins to Portman, from Five Points to Uptown and beyond, represented in Central Atlanta Progress. These public projects were distributive goods, spread broadly in a way that could keep a set of varied and geographically distinct interests and developers united in a common purpose. The central goal, as it had been for Ivan Allen in 1960 in securing the support of "all factions," was—and remains—to assure the coherence of purpose and support within Atlanta's business leaders. So, in the wake of the conflict between John Portman and Tom Cousins over the site of the World Congress Center, both could sit on the board of Central Atlanta Progress in 1975 and endorse a broad package of city bond projects that would serve both of them and the larger downtown business community.

The "victory" of Tom Cousins in securing the World Congress Center was not the end of their conflict over the development space of downtown Atlanta. A 1988 *Atlanta Journal* story, headed "Dueling Developers," described "two decades of pulling and tugging downtown development in different directions," and noted the fight over the Congress Center, their competing efforts to lure Rich's to support separate new retail developments, division over locating an entertainment complex, rival 1984 efforts to develop a technology mart, and competing plans for office skyscrapers in 1988.[151]

But while the competition between Cousins and Portman continued from the 1970s, through the 1980s into the 1990s, it *was possible* for them to agree on and support a set of plans and proposals for the downtown core. And for Central Atlanta Progress as an organization, the key to maintaining its membership and effectiveness was replicating the strategy that Ivan Allen had employed in 1960—providing something for all "factions" and differing spatial interests.

One part of the strategy of inclusion followed Allen's model, backing multiple projects that offered advantages to different sub-areas downtown and to different development interests. When John Portman assumed the CAP presidency in March 1970, he called for "special task forces to develop and implement projects vital to the Central Core and the City." His goal, and that of the organization, was not a single grand project, but plural "projects" that could serve multiple interests and spaces. Thus the 1971 Central Atlanta Study called for the development of a new "Peachtree Promenade" from Baker Street to Margaret Mitchell Square, aiding Portman's properties on Peachtree, together with a new "Five Points Park" for the heart of the core.[152]

Much the same calculus and strategy of multiple projects serving disparate interests appeared in the wake of the 1974 "Brockey letter," when CAP and Harold Brockey listed their "key areas of concern" to Mayor Jackson. The use of the plural was notable. CAP did not have one preferred project or concern. Instead, the organization listed improvements in the northern portion of the core together with implementation of the redevelopment plan for the "South CBD Triangle Area."

The Brockey letter exemplified the persistent strategy of Atlanta's business leaders in seeking a package of public projects serving varied interests. So although the group regularly expressed concern over crime and panhandling in the core from the 1970s into the mid-1990s, it was unwilling to focus solely on public safety.

In February 1990, CAP president Joseph Martin told the group's executive committee about meeting with Mayor Jackson "and representatives of major business organizations," resulting in an agreement "to join with the City in a 'partnership' to address crime, drugs, and homelessness," and the prospect of a 25 percent increase in police personnel. After a discussion about the "ambitiousness of the agenda," covering the needs of the mentally ill as well as criminals and the homeless, newspaper publisher Jay Smith "asked if CAP shouldn't drop all its other major projects to concentrate on public safety." Sam Williams, a partner of John Portman's and later CAP president, added "that CAP should focus on public safety and try to establish almost a contractual relationship with the City."[153]

Yet in a rare instance of internal disagreement, CAP president Joseph Martin responded "that certain CAP efforts, such as the Peachtree Street Design Competition and Bedford-Pine [housing development] could not be dropped, but that reinforcements might be needed in certain areas."

Central Atlanta Progress, like most comparable business organizations, faced a continuing need to maintain the support of a variety of individuals and entities. That was particularly the case in downtown Atlanta, with potential (and often overt) tension between different sub-areas and development interests. Even an issue as persistent and politically difficult as public safety could not be the organization's sole concern. CAP simply could not "drop all its other major projects," to concentrate solely on one. Issues of space, physical development, and public improvements were far too central to the organization's maintenance, a reality that was clear within months of Jay Smith's call for a singular focus on public safety.

Despite the reopening of Underground Atlanta in mid-1989 and the prospect of a major expansion of the World Congress Center to be completed in 1992, the nearby center of downtown at Five Points was suffering. After Richard Rich's death in May 1975, the fortunes of the downtown store continued to decline. Rich's put its downtown retail properties on sale in April 1991, ultimately closing the store in July. The initial reaction of CAP's leadership was to support Rich's and its immediate environs, with executive committee member Sam Williams suggesting "encouraging state and local government occupancy of the Rich's building." But once Rich's closed the store, city officials began to promote the idea of converting the store into a new federal government office center.[154]

By July 1992, the proposed new "Federal Center" scheme had emerged as an entirely new 40-story structure with a price tag of over $400 million. The plan would consolidate some 8,000 federal employees scattered largely through downtown at the new building. And as the scale of the proposed new building emerged, so too did its implications for downtown property owners. In a market with a 30 percent vacancy rate, the division among downtown interests and the CAP leadership became public.[155]

For some, the plans for the new Federal Center were just one piece of the ongoing effort to bolster downtown in advance of the 1996 Olympic Games. Yet the promise of a new federal center on the Rich's site would come with some larger costs, draining government tenants from other buildings. Commercial realtor and CAP executive committee member James B. Carson took his concerns and objections public in an opinion piece in the *Journal Constitution* on August 23, arguing, "housing the workers in a new office tower is bad news for a Downtown area that is struggling to fill vacant space." He called for revitalizing the Five Points area by having the federal government support existing structures, concluding that "Atlanta isn't likely to see another opportunity as good as this one to bring renewed vitality to its former commercial heart."[156]

When CAP's executive committee took up the federal building plan at its August 27, 1992, meeting, the result was a stalemate. The meeting minutes recorded that "Opinions are mixed as to the best approach" to meet the government's needs, and the group "agreed to endorse the location of federal workers in Downtown without endorsing a specific development or redevelopment scenario."[157]

The solution to CAP's internal conflict over the Federal Center came in the form of another real estate deal. James Carson and his firm, Carter and Co., had been representing the owners of the First Atlanta building, near the Rich's site and largely vacant with the loss of its prime tenant, Wachovia Bank. In December 1992 the state government announced that it would purchase the First Atlanta tower and consolidate state offices there. The state's use of the First Atlanta building would take the structure's 925,000 square feet of vacant space off the market, solving the problem stressed by Carson and other downtown property owners. And its timing was far from coincidental.

The state government had considered purchasing the First Atlanta building, but demurred, in part due to concerns over cost. With the intervention of the Woodruff Foundation and a small group of business leaders, the price was reduced to $14 million, to be paid by a grant from the foundation to the state. With the First Atlanta building's sale resolved, and perhaps some other accommodation as well, Carson and his colleagues were willing to back the Federal Center plans.[158]

Addressing CAP's executive committee in mid-July 1993, vice president Paul Kelman reviewed a "fact finding" meeting with federal officials, city officials, and local architectural firms to "help determine the general degree of support or opposition to the project within the Downtown business community." Kelman noted, "GSA's [federal General Services Administration] position was that it will eventually consolidate its offices somewhere, whether it be Downtown in the near future or elsewhere at a later time."[159]

CAP chair Patrick Flinn asked the committee to "discuss the question of whether CAP should take a public position on the project, and if so, what that position should be." The response from committee members was clear. Sam Williams argued "that the question would be moot if GSA were a relocating corporation. . . .They should be thought of as a client interested in filling space that needs to be filled in the South CBD." Williams also reminded his colleagues of the support of representative John Lewis, who "would be an important ally in the effort to obtain federal funding and approval of the proposed multimodal passenger terminal. . . . To oppose the Atlanta Federal Center would be politically unwise." James Carson, once the most outspoken opponent, added, "given CAP's mission of promoting central Atlanta, and particularly Downtown, CAP should enthusiastically support the project." With a motion to support the project, the CAP executive committee "unanimously endorsed" the new federal center project.

Just as Ivan Allen had sought to unite "all factions" with a set of public projects realized over time, the successive Central Atlanta Studies and the "deal" for the Federal Center and First Atlanta tower neatly demonstrated how a *combination of projects* and investments could resolve the predictable conflicts from different downtown interests. The Federal Center deal was also not conceived and realized in a vacuum. The CAP leadership, as well as city officials, viewed it as a key part in sustaining the investment in Underground. And the CAP endorsement of the Federal Center was also part of a larger strategy to secure federal financial support for the proposed multimodal transportation center. Like the pieces of a real estate jigsaw puzzle, each of these projects combined to enhance the development prospects of an ailing central core.

The downtown business leadership faced serious problems in grappling with the city's larger office and development market, where aging and aged downtown buildings no longer commanded the value and demand they once did. But CAP could leverage a host of resources, from building purchases by an expanding Georgia State University to funding from the Woodruff Foundation to induce nonprofit organizations to move to Five Points, in order to respond to those market pressures. And it could sustain that agenda over years, if not decades, despite the apparent failure of individual projects.

Conclusion

> [Central Atlanta Progress] Chairman Flinn introduced Mayor Campbell, who arrived late due to traffic problems. Mayor Campbell stated he is looking forward to working with CAP to revitalize Downtown. In his opinion, the key to that revitalization is public safety, and he is working with Chief Bell to implement more walking beat patrols and other community policing initiatives. He is also concerned about the proposed multimodal terminal project and the City's relationship with the State. He said that he will work to improve that relationship and thereby improve the chances that the terminal will receive the necessary legislative support. He pledged to be proactive on other issues of importance to CAP. He supports the panhandling ordinance and the parking lot ordinance, but could not support the arrest of people who "slouch" on the benches in public parks. He will work to run the government more like a business and to institute a more accessible management style. The City will continue to manage the Airport. Finally, he encouraged CAP and the business community to improve relationships with the Fulton County delegation, in particular, and the State Legislature, in general, so that Atlanta will get the positive attention needed during the next session.[160]

Big public investment projects have long been the lifeblood of Atlanta's business leadership. From Phil Hammer's 1952 vision to "protect and improve" the "Golden Heart" of downtown Atlanta in the "Up Ahead" plan, through "Atlanta Sites," to the Intercontinental Congress Center, the Georgia Dome, the rebuilding of Underground, and the successive expansions of the World Congress Center, to the contemporary plans for a streetcar line and multimodal transportation center, public projects have been the means to protect private investment and property values, and to enhance the prospects and possibilities for future development. Decade after decade, the potential for future public investment was the key to sustaining and unlocking private development.

During the 1950s and 1960s, fortified by national programs for urban renewal and highway building, the focus of Atlanta's business leadership was on reshaping the racial landscape surrounding the downtown core. From the 1970s through the 1980s, Central Atlanta Progress sought catalytic public projects—the coliseum, the World Congress Center, a people mover, the revitalization of Underground Atlanta—that could both promote private development opportunities *within the core* and support a new kind of visitor-oriented downtown. In more recent years, Atlanta's business leaders have embraced the Olympic Games, new sports facilities, an aquarium, and the conversion of private buildings to public use as a necessary means of sustaining property values and investment prospects downtown.

Central Atlanta Progress and the business leadership generally have by no means been uniformly successful. A host of proposed and planned projects, from the people mover of the 1970s and plans to expand the Civic Center, through successive aquarium schemes, attractions such as the Grammy Hall of Fame and the NASCAR Hall of Fame, and the multimodal transportation center have eluded the city and downtown. Yet these policy failures are rarely viewed as permanent or decisive. A people mover could be replaced by a streetcar scheme after two or three decades and a shift in national policy. The unwillingness of the Georgia state legislature to finance a multimodal center in the 1990s might well be different in 2010. Project initiatives fail, only to rise phoenix-like, as part of subsequent plans or development schemes.

Indeed, the failure of public investments to produce the sought-after outcome did not result in any serious reconsideration of investment policy or larger goals. Despite the enormous effort committed by Richard Rich and his colleagues to realizing a rail transit system focused on Five Points and the downtown core, Rich's downtown department store proved economically unviable. A host of plans and studies by Phil Hammer never did yield the regional shopping center he anticipated for Troutman's gulch property. The grand expectations of Tom Cousins for the development of the railroad gulch and the Omni International complex were never realized, despite the investment of hundreds of millions in the Omni coliseum, then the World Congress Center, and later the Georgia Dome. And even John Portman ultimately faced the realities of a recession and overbuilt downtown office market as well as growing competition, losing control of most of his most valuable developments in the 1990s. Yet failure—both of public projects themselves and of the larger downtown office and retail market—simply prompted greater efforts to direct public resources to support property values and reshape development opportunities.

From the early efforts of Richard Rich, Robert Woodruff, Ivan Allen, and the chamber leadership to the contemporary initiatives of Central Atlanta Progress, there has been a striking consistency in goal and focus. The focus on "protecting and improving" the core has changed remarkably little from what Phil Hammer outlined in 1952. What has changed is the governmental vehicle for realizing those ends. As early as 1960, Ivan Allen and his chamber colleagues recognized the limits of the city's fiscal and political circumstances, and the growing issue of the rise of the African American population and its electoral power. The effort to create an independent authority that could finance and build a new stadium was based solidly on that recognition. But in the wake of the bond votes of the early 1960s, Atlanta's business leaders sought an alternative fiscal vehicle for the public projects they needed.

The state government proved to be that fiscal alternative, first and most directly in the case of the World Congress Center, and then over and over for projects like the Georgia Dome, street improvements, the expansion of Georgia State, and the purchase of the First Atlanta tower. The initial argument for state investment in the World Congress Center was the flood of new state sales tax revenue that would be generated by hundreds of thousands of out-of-state convention attendees. Subsequent expansion efforts were in turn justified by the significance of the state's investment in Atlanta as a convention mecca. In early 1991, for example, Georgia Governor Zell Miller termed expansion vital, arguing, "This is a money generator for the entire state and—especially at this time—we cannot afford the economic loss in state revenue that would take place if we do not do this, do it now." And a few years later, with an expansion just completed, the *Journal Constitution* editorialized that "legislators should reflect on what a boon the World Congress Center has been to the state. On the subject of expansion, they need to think B-I-G."[161]

The image of the World Congress Center, and Atlanta's overall visitor industry, as a "money generator," combined with the political acumen and generosity of the city's business leaders to make them—and their development agenda—a powerful force in Georgia state politics. The cultivation of a succession of governors, as well as longtime House speaker Tom Murphy, enabled Atlanta's business leaders to secure a series of major public investments, even as the city government became less functional and relevant. Governor Zell Miller said of speaker Murphy, who served in that role from 1973 to 2003, "this man from rural Georgia . . . knows that you have to have this economic engine that is Atlanta in order to have the revenue that is needed to run the state . . . . he has often times been the champion of these projects in Atlanta."[162]

When Mayor-elect Bill Campbell implored CAP for its help with the Fulton County legislative delegation and the entire state legislature, he was reflecting the political reality that had developed over some thirty or more years. The fiscal resources, and the political action, had moved to the state government. The city of Atlanta, and its mayors, needed CAP in many ways more than the business community needed them.

Chapter 8

St. Louis: Protection from Erosion

Writing to St. Louis Mayor A. J. Cervantes in March 1966, architect Arthur Schwarz announced, "our studies in connection with Union Station were looking 'mighty good.'" Schwarz told Cervantes that his firm was making "a reasonably comprehensive study of convention centers, sports centers, merchandise marts and convention hotels throughout the country," and that "I am convinced more than ever that St. Louis has to move forward in these areas in a large way if we are to take advantage of the potentials of tourism and convention business. As I see it, there is no reason why St. Louis cannot attain the number one spot in the country in this regard."[1]

Schwarz headed one of the most prominent architectural firms in the city, and had been involved in a number of major development projects, including the design of Busch Stadium. His interest and focus was on a particular client and a specific site—the city's grand Union Station. But his vision was shared more broadly within the local business community.[2]

Writing to Schwarz in July 1966, Gordon Hopper, executive director of Downtown St. Louis Inc., quoted *Amusement Business* magazine on San Diego's new center, saying, "But San Diego has no Arch and convention spending has doubled to $40 million in that city since its Community Concourse convention center opened a year ago January"—and adding, "Powerful statement to sell the economic impact of a convention and exhibit center."[3]

The proposal that Arthur Schwarz presented to the Terminal Railroad Association in June 1966 described the declining fortunes of a rail station that had accommodated some 280 daily trains in 1929, but by 1965 was serving less than 75.[4] But if its future as a passenger facility appeared grim, its location and scale offered a particularly attractive development opportunity—as the site for a convention center, hotel, merchandise mart, and possible

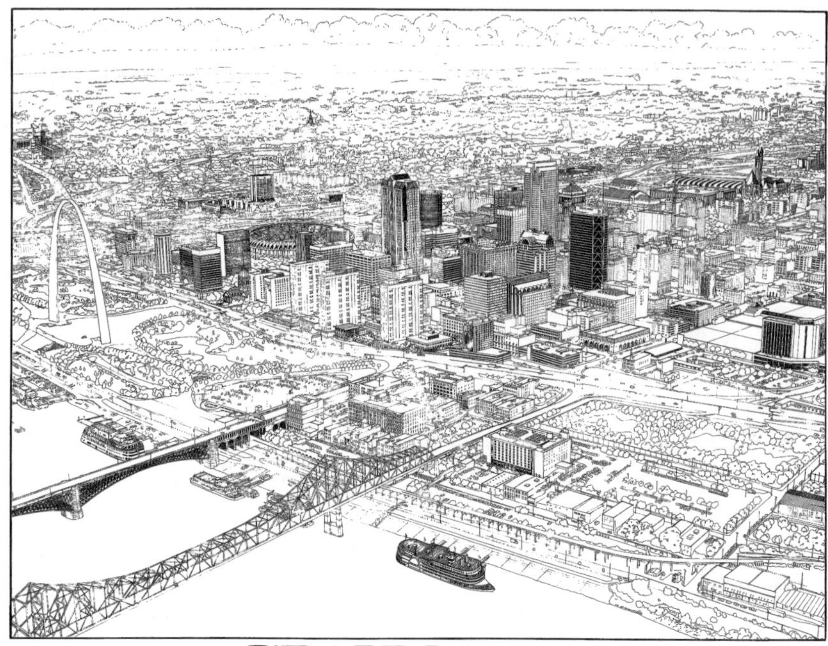

Figure 4.

entertainment center. Architect Schwarz was notably enthusiastic about the city's convention potential, noting that "the revival of downtown St. Louis is in itself creating a new exciting environment," with the Gateway Arch itself expected to "attract three to six million visitors a year." He concluded, "Therefore if St. Louis while currently developing related convention assets such as the Arch, Stadium, Spanish Pavilion and the Gateway Mall does not move forward with new convention facilities it will not only lessen its convention potential but will minimize the importance of these newer assets."[5]

Arthur Schwarz's scheme for a multiuse project built around a new convention center came at a time—mid-1966—when St. Louis and its top business leaders were focused on the possibilities of developing the city and its downtown core as a major visitor destination. That business leadership was well organized, and fully focused on using the city government as a means of sustaining downtown as the economic heart of the region. That business commitment to downtown and the use of public dollars to support and "develop" it has continued for almost five decades.

Organizing Business

The formal organization of top business leaders in St. Louis began in 1952, when a small group of them visited Pittsburgh to see the work of Richard King Mellon, heir to the Mellon fortune, and that city's business leadership group, the Allegheny Conference on Community Development. Their reaction was that St. Louis needed a similar organization, to address the city's problems and begin a program of major public investment. Mayor Joseph Darst formally appointed a "sponsoring committee" in January 1953, including Sidney Baer, vice-chair of the Stix, Baer and Fuller department store chain, Arthur Blumeyer of the Bank of St. Louis, Powell McHaney of General American Life Insurance, David Calhoun, president of St. Louis Union Trust Company, and former Mayor Aloys Kaufmann. The group's initial foray involved backing a 1953 urban renewal bond issue to rebuild a section of downtown.[6]

The failure of the March 1953 urban renewal bond vote and the election of a new mayor, Washington University professor and political reformer Raymond Tucker, in April 1953 led to the recommitment of the business leadership, and the expansion of the "sponsoring committee." With the addition of August Busch of Anheuser-Busch, Edwin Clark of Southwestern Bell Telephone, Donald Danforth of Ralston-Purina, Sidney Mastre of Mercantile Trust, Edgar Queeny of Monsanto, and Morton May of Famous-Barr department stores, the group was named Civic Progress Inc. The group included the heads of the dominant firms in the St. Louis region, the area's principal financial institutions, local utilities, and major downtown department stores. Its first task was to back a new campaign for the failed urban renewal bond proposal.[7]

The September 1953 vote on the Plaza renewal bonds proved a success, the opening gun in an ongoing effort to improve the city's finances, mount a major capital improvements program, and reform city government. Civic Progress could provide the financial backing and the imprimatur of the city's leading businesses to a program of civic improvement. But the group and its members were clear about their focus. Life insurance executive Powell McHaney summarized that outlook at the group's monthly meeting in November 1953: "the basic theory in Pittsburgh is that you must take care of the 'core' of the city first, keep industry and its payrolls from deserting the downtown, and let the workers live wherever they want."[8]

McHaney went on to note the problems he saw downtown, including the development of new office buildings in suburban St. Louis County luring firms to leave the city—"If we continue to do that . . . we are going to let this city disintegrate." His suggested course of action was "that there must be more and better parking facilities downtown."

The Civic Progress group struggled with the proper approach to downtown problems and turned to a group of outside experts, the Urban Land Institute and its advisory panel of developers, realtors, and planners. The Institute had been founded in 1936 as a research entity for real-estate professionals, and was dominated by major developers and realtors. The Urban Land Institute panel that visited St. Louis in October 1954 included commercial realtors Newton Farr of Chicago, Joseph Lund of Boston, and Henry S. Miller of Dallas, as well as Ernest Fisher of Columbia University and planning consultant Larry Smith. Their 145-page report effectively shaped the agenda of Civic Progress and the city for the next decade.[9]

The first words of the ULI report were, "St. Louis must be a more convenient city in which to live and work." The group pressed the city to move ahead on the expressway system, compressing a 16-year plan into five years. They urged the improvement of transit and new downtown parking. And in assaying the future of the downtown, they urged that "evidences of blight which now exist should be removed and a dynamic program of modernization encouraged."[10]

The ULI recommendations were far from unusual, and could well have been applied to dozens of Eastern and Midwestern cities. But one of their observations would prove telling. The panel noted an "unusual feature" of the city, "in that the amusement, restaurant and so-called glamour area, which in most cities is adjoining the office and financial section, is here located about twenty blocks to the west," in what is today termed the "Grand Center" district. The panel argued, "This unfortunately gives to the casual observer the impression that the downtown area is lacking in life and activity especially in the evening . . . . We see no immediate way of improving this situation."[11]

The need to attract "life and activity" to the downtown core would prove a focal point of Civic Progress's efforts over the next years, and ultimately decades. The organization of business leaders came to play a central role in the city's civic life, filling the committees that selected projects for a major bond program in 1955, backing and financing charter change efforts, and grappling with broader issues involving the United Way, the St. Louis Symphony, and area cultural institutions. Yet the focus of Civic Progress remained firmly on downtown. Meeting in November 1958, the group agreed to support further city charter changes, to work to attract new industry, and to foster new downtown promotion efforts. One dimension of that downtown concern involved local public housing policy—promoting the development of new housing projects "near the central downtown area—because of their value as a means of eliminating slum districts that now run right up to the edges of the downtown office and retail district and have a damaging effect on downtown property values." Indeed, preserving property values and "eliminating" slums would remain a focus during the 1960s and well beyond.[12]

The Stadium

A single project that would serve those goals simultaneously emerged in late 1958, from the head of the city's urban redevelopment agency: a new downtown stadium that "would help draw the people needed to revitalize the area."[13]

Charles Farris, director of the Housing Authority and the Land Clearance Authority, presented his idea for a downtown stadium to the Civic Progress group in late 1958. His initial presentation stressed two points. First, the proposed site on the south side of the core was an area where "the majority of the buildings are blighted"; the site (including the city's Chinatown), "only six blocks from the heart of downtown St. Louis," would be inexpensive to acquire and redevelop.[14]

Farris then went on to argue that the stadium area would serve a dual purpose. His plan called for 12,500 new parking spaces in garages to serve the stadium. The planned parking "would have a dual purpose—it could be used by downtown workers and shoppers as well as by spectators for the sports attractions in the stadium." And, Farris told the business leaders, the addition of a removable roof would give St. Louis "an exposition center, enabling the city to obtain shows and conventions it is now losing because of lack of this kind of space."

The immediate response of the city's business leaders was highly supportive. Brewery magnate August Busch, owner of the team that would be the stadium's prime tenant, "said the stadium would re-make downtown St. Louis," and "should have the strongest possible support all the way down the line." A new home for the baseball Cardinals would not add a team to St. Louis. But a stadium fed by the city's new freeway system immediately adjacent to the "heart" of the core was viewed by the Civic Progress leaders as a boon, particularly in terms of clearing "blight" and adding abundant new parking for downtown shoppers.

Within days of Farris's presentation, bank president James Hickok and his colleagues had arranged for local engineering consulting firm Sverdrup & Parcel to investigate the feasibility of the stadium scheme. Leif "Jack" Sverdrup wrote to Hickok in early January 1959 that the stadium idea "should contribute tremendously to the development of St. Louis," and that "Mr. Farris has come forth with the best idea we have ever heard of for the development of Downtown St. Louis, and that it is worthy of every possible support." The business leaders thus saw the stadium primarily as a redevelopment and revitalization vehicle—its merits defined in terms of the "development of Downtown St. Louis."[15]

The Sverdrup feasibility study was completed by September 1, 1959. Writing to banker Hickok the following day, Sverdrup proffered a report "flexible enough so that it provides a framework wherein ideas and thoughts of various groups will fit in." That idea of a broad framework of multiple appeals to "various groups" seemed to recognize the diversity of interests—business and political, geographic and economic—concerned in the city and the central business district.[16]

Sverdrup's interest went beyond the steel and concrete of the stadium itself. He sought a "shot in the arm" for downtown—a major project that could convey excitement and forward momentum beyond the city's urban renewal efforts. His focus was beyond mere development symbolism. It involved protecting and enhancing the existing property investment—including Sverdrup & Parcel's investment in a headquarters building—in downtown St. Louis. He argued, "Just as surely as there is a major investment in Downtown St. Louis, we at this time must do something to protect and enhance this investment. I believe and know that this will do the job."

The actual report argued, "It must generate in the minds of all persons a zealous enthusiasm for the program, an honest belief that an outstanding and committed effort is being made, and an abounding faith in the future of St. Louis and, particularly, in its downtown area as the key to the entire city." The study then concluded, "Its prosecution to completion more or less concurrently with the Jefferson National Expansion Memorial [Gateway Arch] . . . *should attract the favorable attention of the entire country*" (emphasis mine).[17]

Leif Sverdrup and Civic Progress sought "favorable attention," both to draw new investment capital and opportunity to St. Louis, and to lure the new visitors and activity that could support and revitalize the downtown. National newspaper coverage of the city efforts was highly favorable, with a lengthy July 1963 article in the *New York Times*, headlined "St. Louis to Have Nation's Tallest Monument." This described the three million annual visitors expected at the Arch, noting, "This prospect is stimulating a face-lifting in the adjacent downtown business district, a program that may match the turnaround on the rundown riverfront."[18]

In January 1964, the *Times* again ballyhooed St. Louis, with the announcement that 1964 would see "more than hope and prayers. . . . The city has plans," describing the Gateway Arch and the new stadium and related redevelopment efforts. It also briefly mentioned an adjacent "block-long entertainment area," adding, "Walt Disney has been asked to develop it."[19]

Disney had been contacted by St. Louis business leaders in early 1963 to serve as a consultant on a film about the city's upcoming bicentennial. A delegation from the city then met with Disney in late March to interest him in a scheme for an entertainment attraction—"Riverfront Square"—to be developed as part of the stadium-area rebuilding.[20]

To assess the project's potential, Disney turned to Harrison "Buzz" Price, the analyst who had completed the original feasibility studies for Disneyland and who would later assess the planned Disney World in Orlando. Price completed his analysis of the planned dining and entertainment complex in August 1963.

The "Economic Potentials of Riverfront Square" report set out the goal that the Disney project "should support and enhance existing downtown activities" and "serve as a traffic generator and provide a commercial anchor in the southeast portion of the downtown area." Price focused in large part on the potential of the Arch—the Jefferson National Expansion Memorial—to draw new visitors to St. Louis, and estimated "a 1965 attendance of 2,047,000 persons per year" for the Riverfront Square venue, placing its annual attendance above that of the Washington Monument.[21]

The Disney organization was not particularly sanguine about the financial prospects of the proposal. One senior executive concluded, "it is not one which necessarily requires our association or which seems to offer the kind of creation opportunity and economic incentives which we seek." But Walt Disney himself remained interested in the project. He came to St. Louis in March 1964 for a formal press conference setting out the project's design. The *Wall Street Journal* reported in mid-June 1964 that the Disney organization was then negotiating with "community interests" in St. Louis for a planned "large amusement center" of 2.5 acres to open in 1966 or 1967. But the report made clear that while Disney would own and operate the St. Louis attraction, it would involve "outside financing."[22]

There proved to be no one in St. Louis willing to assume that financial obligation. Reporting the story in July 1965, the *Wall Street Journal* quoted a Disney officer as saying, "I'm inclined to think it's cold now, maybe for good and all. . . . The main problem is that no way has been found to make a unique entertainment center like that economically feasible for that kind (urban renewal) of a market."[23] And yet the failure of the Disney venture did little to curb the enthusiasm of Civic Progress and city officials for more visitor and tourist-oriented development. The flirtation with the Disney organization appeared to reinforce the belief among the Civic Progress leaders that the city was uniquely positioned to see a flood of visitors and their dollars. With the stadium pegged to open in the spring of 1966, the business leaders were obviously interested in another project that could capitalize on and further the sense of development momentum and the promise of tourist benefits. That project appeared on the scene in the fall of 1965, just months after the failure of St. Louis's Disneyland.

In October 1965, Mayor Alfonso Cervantes announced that the city would seek to purchase the Spanish Pavilion at the New York World's Fair, and move it to St. Louis. The pavilion had been a popular hit at the World's Fair, and Cervantes envisioned it as a new cultural and culinary landmark downtown. But the move would require funds the city did not have. So Cervantes turned to Civic Progress and its members.[24]

Civic Progress formally endorsed the idea of moving the pavilion in a January 1966 press release, praising the mayor for acting "boldly and imaginatively." But, the group noted, "some important details remain to be worked out," dependent upon an "economic feasibility study now underway." And for that feasibility study, Civic Progress turned (not surprisingly) to Buzz Price and his firm, Economics Research Associates (ERA).[25]

The report that ERA delivered in March 1966 described the Spanish Pavilion as "a culinary, cultural, exhibit-merchandising facility serving residents of the St. Louis area and the millions of tourists visiting the area each year." It assured the Civic Progress group that, combined with the Gateway Arch and the new Busch Stadium, it would constitute "one of the most impressive recreation complexes assembled in any Midwestern city."[26]

Buzz Price and project manager Fred Cochrane concluded that the reconstruction of the pavilion building next to the new Busch Stadium "appears to be economically viable and in the cultural and recreation interests of the entire community," with the prediction that it would attract over two million annual visitors and operate at a profit. Price and his colleagues also performed a "break-even" analysis, calculating that "the project can cover all costs of operation and capital investment at an attendance of 1.1 million, less than 50 percent of that projected."[27]

With Price's conclusion in hand, Civic Progress members agreed to have their firms contribute to the cost of the pavilion and to lead a public fund drive, as they "know that the Pavilion will be self-sustaining and economically sound."[28]

Armed with Buzz Price's numbers and the mayor's vision that "St. Louis will have the greatest tourist triangle in the United States with the Pavilion, the Arch, and the Stadium," the city's business leadership financed the move and reconstruction of the fair pavilion. This time, Buzz Price's analysis and the development expectations proved faulty. Within a year after its May 1969 opening, the Spanish Pavilion closed. It had attracted just 450,000 people, far short of the ERA prediction of 2.25 million, and the *New York Times* headlined, "New York World's Fair Hit Turns Into St. Louis Fiasco."[29]

By mid-1966, the ULI panel report, the stadium project and associated redevelopment scheme, the Arch, the Disney venture, and the Spanish Pavilion had created a policy environment, coupled with the strong Civic Progress role in leadership, financing, and civic promotion, which set the stage for yet another visitor-oriented public investment. There appeared to be no question that the city would see a flood of new visitors and downtown activity, ran the logic of business leaders. It was the *promise* and *prospect* of all of these efforts, on the heels of the Disney negotiations and well before the failure of the Spanish Pavilion, together with the ongoing concern for the future of downtown St. Louis, that were uppermost in the minds of both Mayor Cervantes and the Civic Progress leadership when Arthur Schwarz began to set out his vision for a new downtown convention center to be built as part of Union Station and the adjacent rail yards.

There was another dimension to the perception of these projects within Civic Progress. The Jefferson National Expansion Memorial was far more than Saarinen's Arch. The project had involved the clearance of some 62 acres of riverfront warehouses and buildings at the eastern edge of the business core, relocating rail lines into a tunnel. The stadium project included the clearance of some 59 additional "blighted" acres on the southern flank. The Plaza Square renewal project—the effort that had led to the formation of Civic Progress—demolished another 16 acres near Union Station and the previously cleared Memorial Plaza area. And the Mill Creek Valley urban renewal effort, begun in 1958, cleared 454 acres immediately west of Union Station. The city had largely succeeded in "eliminating slum districts that now run right up to the edges of the downtown office and retail district." Yet there was one major exception.

Blight and Erosion

St. Louis's city planners had long been committed to dealing with the "slums" and "blight" that surrounded the office and retail core and the crowded slum housing immediately outside the doors of the magnificent Union Station. In 1919, the City Plan Commission had argued, "St. Louis is probably criticized more because of the surroundings of its Union Station than for any other reason," and proposed the area as a possible site for new public buildings. The Plan Commission's program for *Saint Louis After World War II*, authored by planning chief Harland Bartholomew, included a series of maps depicting a U-shaped zone of blighted slum housing surrounding the central business district, arguing, "Central areas must be reconstructed if eventual municipal bankruptcy is to be avoided."[30]

First public housing, and then the federal urban renewal program, provided the city with the means to clear and rebuild the zone ringing the downtown core to the north, west, and south with modern structures. That effort had long been a central commitment of the leaders of Civic Progress and local newspapers. For them, the stadium effort, with its full-scale demolition of a site Charles Farris had termed "blighted," was a success even before the new Busch Stadium opened or the Spanish Pavilion was reconstructed. As Leif Sverdrup had promised, the project's very beginning had served to "protect and enhance" the value of downtown property investment.[31]

While the stadium project provided the impetus for rebuilding the south side of downtown, the north side of downtown had long been a focus of clearance and rebuilding efforts, with the Carr Square Village public housing project in 1942, Cochran Gardens public housing in 1953, and the infamous Pruitt-Igoe housing project in 1955. That north side area, DeSoto-Carr, had been described as an "obsolete area [that] must be cleared and reconstructed" in the city's 1947 Comprehensive Plan. And the Plan Commission's 1953 analysis of potential clearance areas for commercial and industrial renewal had laid out a scheme for redeveloping the larger DeSoto-Carr area surrounding the public housing complexes with a mix of new highways, parks, and industrial areas. But while DeSoto-Carr was formally declared an urban renewal area in 1959, the city was unable to finance the redevelopment effort. A bond issue for renewal funds had failed in 1962 (even as the stadium bonds passed), and a 1966 scheme to clear and rebuild part of the area as an entertainment complex modeled on Copenhagen's Tivoli Gardens also failed to win voter approval.[32]

Thus by 1967, the southern and western flanks of the downtown business core had already been substantially cleared and partially rebuilt. The north side of the core, the flank adjacent to the DeSoto-Carr renewal area, the locus of the city's downtown department stores, still awaited large-scale public action. One structure in that northern sector had long been a source of concern to Civic Progress.

The Old Post Office, designed by Alfred Mullett and built in the late 1870s, sat at the very center of the downtown core and had long dismayed business leaders. Longtime Civic Progress member Howard F. Baer termed the building "a pigeon roost" and "a cancer in the heart of the town."[33] By 1959, there was a plan to demolish the Old Post Office and construct a new federal building on the site. But the *St. Louis Post-Dispatch* and local preservationists opposed the demolition, and the new federal office plan was withdrawn.

Nevertheless, the interest of the city's business leaders in replacing the Old Post Office remained undiminished through the 1960s. In 1967, the members of Civic Progress were still pressing for its replacement with modern federal government offices, and trying to remove the *Post-Dispatch* as an impediment. The June 26, 1967, monthly meeting of Civic Progress began with a discussion of membership and the campaign to raise funds for the Spanish Pavilion. Then Frederic Peirce, president of General American Life Insurance, reported on a meeting with Joseph Pulitzer, Jr., publisher of the *Post-Dispatch*, on "the controversy between the Post-Dispatch and Globe-Democrat over whether to save the Old Post Office or tear it down." Pulitzer proved unmoved, contending that new legislation made possible federal funding for preservation. But the focus on the Old Post Office reflected an immediate concern about the northern side of the downtown.[34]

"Cubby" Baer, president of the Stix, Baer and Fuller department store—perhaps the city's premier downtown department store—addressed his concerns to his colleagues: "He said there is an increasing amount of property decay in the downtown area north of St. Charles Street. His point was that the downtown area needs the kind of protection from erosion on the north side which it is receiving on the south side from the Stadium complex." Baer's comments provide a vital insight into the perceptions of the city's business leadership and those invested in downtown.[35]

First, the Stadium complex was described not as simply a sports venue, but as a means of "protection from erosion" of property values. In both clearing out a decayed section of buildings (including Chinatown) and providing a buffer zone on the south, it served a far larger purpose related to "property decay." And, having concluded that the recently completed Stadium "worked," Baer (and likely his colleagues) felt that the north side merited the same attention. The long-deferred DeSoto-Carr renewal project could provide a land clearance effort parallel to the stadium redevelopment area. But what Baer sought in June 1967 was some sort of public project that could replicate the success on the south side.

The larger point of the Civic Progress discussion of the Old Post Office and "property decay" on the north side of the downtown was that a project such as the stadium really aided just one "side" of the downtown. The north side was seen *at least within the business community* as meriting its own clearance project, as the north side firms and their chief executives had united with their Civic Progress colleagues behind the stadium, the Arch, and even the new Spanish Pavilion. By mid-1967, the time for a project dealing with "property decay" on the northern flank had come. And within a few months, the leadership for that north side effort would come from Leif Sverdrup, the chief planner of the stadium and now a new member of Civic Progress, whose firm's headquarters were on the north side of downtown.

With the groundbreaking for the Spanish Pavilion reconstruction in late June 1967, Mayor Cervantes was ready to turn to another grand project—the prospect of a new convention center. For a formal market assessment, the mayor sought—as had Disney and Civic Progress earlier—Harrison "Buzz" Price and his firm, Economics Research Associates. Writing to Price in July 1967, Cervantes said, "We of St. Louis are considering the creation of a major convention center. Further, we are considering having your firm make the feasibility study for such a center." Cervantes secured backing and partial financing from both the Terminal Railroad Association and the Convention and Tourist Board, and engaged ERA.[36]

It was clear that Cervantes, like Arthur Schwarz, favored a development on the south side of the downtown area, most likely at the Union Station site. The mayor briefly reported to the business leaders of Civic Progress in October 1967 that he had contracted with Economics Research Associates for "a feasibility study concerning a new Civic and Convention Center for St. Louis," and that the firm had three sites in mind, including the area near Busch Stadium, the existing Kiel Auditorium, and "the Terminal Railroad area around the Union Station." The mayor continued, "it might be possible to begin working out ways of financing the building of this center by sometime next year if the city receives a favorable report on its feasibility." The mayor's plans for a convention center neatly followed Arthur Schwarz's lead in including the Union Station area, with all three possible sites on the southern side of the downtown. He failed to mention any sites on the north side.[37]

The bulky study that ERA delivered to the city in May 1968 concluded, "the addition of a modern convention center is both appropriate and economical," attracting annual attendance of 518,000 (including 386,000 at conventions and tradeshows) and generating 192,000 new hotel room nights in the city every year.[38]

Yet where the ERA assessment was quite positive about the promise of a new convention center, it also argued that the site of the proposed facility would be critical to its achieving its potential. The ERA analysis was quite direct (and prescient) in arguing that, while "a convention center can play an important role in stimulating nearby commercial development . . . construction of a single building regardless of its ancillary economic benefits, seldom stimulates downtown revitalization to any great extent."[39]

The study examined three possible sites. A civic center location, with proximity to hotels, ample parking, and an excellent environment would yield a net annual income of $71,000. A Union Station location, at a greater distance from the center of the core, would generate a net income of $20,000. The third site, the north side, was far and away the most problematic. While the location was convenient to existing hotels, the ERA conclusion was that a center built there "would operate at a serious disadvantage." The problem was that the location was a "marginal environment," filled with "one-, two-, and three-story retail stores in a generally deteriorated condition." With greater likelihood of traffic congestion, the "North Side location would seriously curtail convention center use by local residents and by conventions." A center there would attract half the annual convention and local events of an alternative site, generating far less attendance and an annual loss.[40]

Mayor Cervantes received a draft version of the report some time in the spring of 1968. Yet, months earlier, he began to contemplate a larger and somewhat different development around the Union Station, one that harked back to Walt Disney's earlier vision for the city. The mayor embraced the possibility of developing the rail yards with a theme park, moving the St. Louis Museum of Transport from the suburbs to downtown for a new "transportation theme park."

In early April, Cervantes wrote to ERA's Fred Cochrane, asking him to "give some very preliminary consideration to impact [sic] of an even broader project . . . not only a convention center but also an incorporation of a large new hotel facility and what we might call the Village of Transport which would, of course, be an amusement-oriented area which would have as one of its focal points the displays of the Saint Louis Museum of Transport."[41]

By early May the mayor had begun to consider an even grander potential development. Mayor Cervantes met with the executive committee of the Terminal Railroad Association (Union Station's owners) on May 6, to investigate the potential for expanding the proposed development to cover an additional 39 acres owned by the association west of the station. J. H. Sharp of the Terminal Railroad wrote the mayor that the property "can be made available for development," and that the railroad "would share equally in [paying for] a study to be conducted by the Economics Research Associates group."[42]

The early May lunch meeting also included Harold McKenzie, president of the St. Louis Southwestern Railway (the "Cotton Belt"), one of the owners of the Terminal Railway Association and thus Union Station, who offered a possible Texas connection. McKenzie wrote to the mayor on May 15 that he "promised to contact Angus Wynne, as well as Judge Hofheinz, in regard to architectural and industrial engineers that could prepare drawing and make feasibility studies such as you have in mind for the St. Louis Union Station property." Angus Wynne and his Great Southwest Corporation were the developers of the Six Flags over Texas and Six Flags over Georgia theme parks. Roy Hofheinz was the builder of Houston's Astrodome and the adjacent AstroWorld theme park, which was to open the next month. With that connection to Wynne, Cervantes began to seriously pursue development of a Six Flags theme park on the Union Station property.[43]

ERA's Fred Cochrane visited St. Louis in June, and on June 12 gave the mayor a formal proposal for "economic and preliminary physical planning for the proposed convention center complex in St. Louis." The ERA analysis was now solely focused on the Terminal Railroad Association property and its potential for a "convention center, hotel, and a theme recreational center."[44]

ERA produced its formal analysis on the convention center/theme park proposal in October 1968, concluding that the 110-acre complex "could become one of the most popular and highly publicized civic developments in the nation." It went on to state that a similar set of facilities could be found in only two other cities in the nation—Anaheim, with the Disneyland complex and the Anaheim Convention Center; and Houston, with the Astrodome, Astrohall, and AstroWorld theme park. The firm then recommended that "the city proceed with development of the project as rapidly as possible."[45]

Having lost Walt Disney's Riverfront Square not long before, St. Louis and Mayor Cervantes were positioned in mid-1968 to refashion the city's downtown core (and presumably much of its local economy) as a major visitor destination. It was a direction neatly laid out, researched, and supported by Buzz Price and his firm, the most highly regarded consulting firm in the theme park business, in a whole series of studies. And with the involvement of Civic Progress in the stadium, the Disney effort, and the Spanish Pavilion, it appeared to have the full support of the city's business leadership.

Protection from Erosion

By the fall of 1968, the efforts by St. Louis business leaders to revive the north side of the downtown core had stalled. The defeat of the 1966 urban renewal bond proposal had blocked the city funds for clearing and rebuilding the DeSoto-Carr renewal area and stopped the Tivoli Gardens scheme. The situation of the downtown core itself was no better. A December 1963 analysis of the north side of downtown by Larry Smith & Company described "a continuing decline in importance as the commercial focus of the region," and called for a new project "large in scope and dramatic in concept" that would "exert a significant impact upon the shopping and business habits of area residents." The Larry Smith study recommended a new "integrated downtown shopping center development," adding a new major department store, and the potential development of a new convention center. But downtown business owners appeared reluctant to take on a major *private* investment effort without some new public anchor or catalyst.[46]

The long-sought effort to demolish the Old Post Office and spur new private development had proven equally unsuccessful. A September 1968 Civic Progress report on the group's accomplishments over the previous year noted it had "Explored ways of breaking the stalemate which had kept a new office building from going up. . . . However, the opposition of the *Post-Dispatch* and others to tearing down the old building continues to stymie the project."[47]

The initiative and direction for a new north side rebuilding push would come from Leif "Jack" Sverdrup, principal of the Sverdrup & Parcel engineering firm headquartered on the north side of downtown adjacent to the Desoto-Carr renewal area, Civic Progress member, and major force in the development of Busch Stadium and its surroundings. Sverdrup's efforts in 1968 first focused on the prospect of a new federal government building that could anchor the start of renewal in Desoto-Carr.

Sverdrup's senior staff had joined commercial realtor Myron Moss in September 1968 in an effort to formulate a proposal for the General Services Administration, the federal government landlord. Moss was apparently "unable to come up with a satisfactory site . . . in the DeSoto-Carr area," believing land acquisition would be difficult and that "for the Government to be interested the whole area would have to be developed with a financing group similar to the [Civic Center Redevelopment Corporation] as they did on the Stadium Project." Just as ERA had recognized, Moss and the Sverdrup staff acknowledged that renewal would require a large-scale project.[48]

In October, Sverdrup personally tried to persuade the GSA regional director of the potential of the site, arguing, "A G.S.A. facility for 4,000 people would put the DeSoto-Carr renewal a long way toward success . . . . [it] would give the Federal Government an opportunity to assist in revitalizing the north side of our downtown area." But just a week after sending that letter to GSA's Earl Lund, the Sverdrup staff came up with an alternative, far bolder development scheme that put Sverdrup directly in conflict with Mayor Cervantes's efforts at Union Station.[49]

In an October 16, 1968, internal memo, Sverdrup vice president Brice R. Smith laid out a renewal project "keyed around a convention center which would be attractive for the development of this 30-acre tract." Having obtained a copy of the May 1968 ERA center study, Sverdrup chief planner Elliott Chamberlain proposed a scheme including the new convention center, a 500-room hotel, a new department store, a shopping center, a medical arts building, a merchandise mart, and a possible bank building. Chamberlain's plan would connect these together with a second-story plaza "unhindered by vehicle traffic . . . [offering] many ideal possibilities for generation of an aura of excitement and interest."[50]

The memo to Sverdrup made clear that the convention center was the vital element in the whole project—"The key to the economic feasibility of this project is the people generation of a convention center." The center would presumably attract activity and support a new hotel, while a new department store would link the larger project to the Famous-Barr and Stix, Baer and Fuller department stores of the nearby retail core, very much along the lines of the 1963 Larry Smith recommendation. And Chamberlain also recognized the need to win the support of community leaders in adjacent neighborhoods, with a new school and commercial development adjacent to the Cochran Gardens public housing project, in order "To make this possible project viable to the near north side community."

The Sverdrup memo contained no stirring descriptions of a center's economic impact on the city or the region. It had no assessment of the city's prospects as a convention or meeting destination. There was no mention of ERA's concerns with the north side location. The entire plan was focused on just the "protection from erosion" that the Civic Progress leadership had discussed a year earlier.[51]

Brice Smith and the Sverdrup staff saw that their convention center proposal would stand in direct conflict with Mayor Cervantes's own plan to build a center at St. Louis's Union Station. They went on to narrate General Sverdrup's efforts to work around the mayor and garner his own political support. A day earlier Sverdrup had met with the leadership of the city's urban renewal agency and the head of the Civic Center Redevelopment Corporation (the entity responsible for the stadium project and its environs), and gained "enthusiastic support" from both. He had also met with James Hickok, chairman of the First National Bank and fellow Civic Progress member, as well as the leadership of Sears in Chicago about a possible new department store. And where Mayor Cervantes's efforts were joined with and dependent upon the owners of Union Station, the Terminal Railroad Association, "General Sverdrup is going to contact them [Terminal Railroad] tomorrow (October 17) to discuss this possible project." Well before going public or confronting Cervantes, then, Sverdrup obviously sought an effectively unified front from the city's business leadership—"He is not interested in promoting such a project unless all of the business community is in whole-hearted support."

Sverdrup apparently received the reassurances he needed from both Union Station's owners and major business leaders. A few days later he joined Edwin Jones of the Chamber of Commerce in meeting with the mayor and presenting the Sverdrup plan for redevelopment of the area immediately north of downtown as a new convention center-hotel complex.

Mayor Cervantes's response, addressed to Jones on October 30, praised Sverdrup's interest and concurred with the need to address the "northern flank of the downtown area." But the mayor remained committed to his version of a convention center scheme at Union Station, which, he argued, "could provide a unique convention-amusement center which would not be matched anywhere else in the nation and probably in the world." Cervantes was clear—"I feel that we are obligated to pursue our plans."[52]

Sverdrup's efforts were not at all slowed by the mayor's lack of support. The firm's planning effort continued, with chief planner Elliott Chamberlain reporting in late November on the details of design and the logic behind the inclusion of the convention center. Chamberlain's memo described a complex of exhibition hall and convention center with a 500-room hotel, a merchandise mart, department store, office building, and parking for 7,000 cars, providing "a counter-balance to Busch Stadium and its support facilities . . . establish[ing] a firm anchor upon which new investment can be based."[53]

Chamberlain's focus on land use and future value was paramount—"The location of the new convention center in conjunction with the existing CBD facilities rather than one-half to one mile outside the area [as would be the case with a Union Station site] is of great significance in establishing faith in the future of the center city." The Chamberlain memo concluded with language that mirrored the 1967 observations of Civic Progress member Baer. "Without a project of this scale, the north side of the CBD will continue in its state of creeping paralysis which will continue to influence more and more CBD enterprises."

Armed with Chamberlain's planning logic and design, Leif Sverdrup and Brice Smith took their case to the executive committee of the Chamber of Commerce on November 27, 1968. Sverdrup told the chamber leaders that he was "hopeful" that his plans and the mayor's "could be reconciled," suggesting that the Union Station area be used for a short take-off and landing airstrip. But "It was his belief that the proposed convention center would provide an effective 'anchor' to the north side of the downtown area and prevent further deterioration."[54]

Sverdrup told the eight chamber leaders that his planned center would be closer to downtown hotels, and that it "would be financed principally with private capital, with perhaps a city bond issue for the convention hall." The chamber group took no vote or formal position on Sverdrup's plan. But it was obvious that in seeking the backing of the chamber, Sverdrup was attempting to limit the support for both Mayor Cervantes and the original promoter of a convention center, architect Arthur Schwarz.

The promotion effort for the Sverdrup convention center scheme ramped up through the first of the year, as the firm's staff prepared an elaborate model of the north side redevelopment area with the convention center and adjacent high-rise buildings, together with architectural renderings of individual new structures. Sverdrup made a formal presentation of the plan to local leaders and reporters on January 28, 1969, garnering newspaper headlines and an editorial in the *Post-Dispatch* that argued the scheme would "solve a number of pressing metropolitan problems."[55]

The *Globe-Democrat* editorial, "Bold Twin-Plan for Downtown," termed the north side scheme "the logical site" for a new convention center, as "the northern section of downtown has been largely neglected, continuing to decay and die." It concluded, "Let's hope that the men who will make the decisions will have the vision and the wisdom to carry them to fruition."[56]

The "Convention Plaza Redevelopment Proposal" distributed by Sverdrup & Parcel stressed the land use implications of the project, noting that "the Civic Center Redevelopment Corporation's efforts, Busch Stadium, Stouffer's Riverfront Inn, the stadium garages, the Spanish Pavilion, and the First National Bank have assured a firm future for the south edge of the area . . . . Equal attention should now be given to establishing firm potential for the north edge of the area. . . . By ringing downtown with new activity, further redevelopment of the core will evolve as a natural process of business activity promoting other supporting businesses." The proposal argued, "A major convention facility as a dominant unit of the proposed northside redevelopment would establish two 'activity poles' on the boundaries of the CBD—Busch Stadium complex (south) and Convention Center (north)—which would be complementary in operating characteristics."[57]

The formal announcement of the Sverdrup north side plan made public the conflict between the mayor and the business leaders. There was no debate over the merits of a new convention center or the city's potential as a destination. It was simply a matter of who stood to gain the benefits of a bold public initiative. Thus Irving Edison, chairman of the Edison Brothers Stores chain, wrote the mayor on January 30, telling "Al," "Those of us who have stayed with the Northern end of our downtown retail area feel strongly that dramatic new projects that will benefit that portion of the central retail area should be considered." Civic Progress member Edison argued that new firms "will come to the Northern portion of the central business area just as they did around the Stadium project."[58]

Cervantes's reply "heartily" agreed with the need to provide the northern part of downtown "the same kind of treatment" as the stadium area enjoyed. But he "cautioned against the use of the northern area of downtown for a convention center," and concluded, "I do believe that the Union Station area is the better of the two sites for a convention center." Edison, in his response a day later, demurred by noting, "We have an honest difference of opinion." Edison then made clear his expectations for the Sverdrup initiative in language that surely represented the views of many of his colleagues—"I feel the Sverdrup Plan will be better for the building up of the downtown retail section and will start a chain of new activities around the lower downtown section on the North."[59]

Edison's arguments did not focus on the benefits to St. Louis of competing for conventions, or the city's prospects as a major visitor center. Like his counterparts on the north side of downtown, Edison was focused on the promise of new investment and revival *for his immediate environs*.

Despite the pressure from Irving Edison and other business leaders, and the public embrace by the city's newspapers, Cervantes still appeared unwilling to abandon his vision for Union Station. Indeed, the mayor contracted with ERA in late March 1969 for yet another "study of Union Station property as a convention and theme park development," presumably to aid in negotiating the addition of a theme park to his plan.[60]

As Mayor Cervantes was seeking the leverage of an ERA study that would support a theme park development, Sverdrup and his firm's staff were pursuing their own plans. Brice Smith met with representatives of Chicago's Marshall Field's department store in late January in an effort to secure a commitment for a new store as part of the convention center development. And at the end of February, Sverdrup made a presentation on the "Convention Plaza" plan to the Downtown St. Louis organization, gaining that organization's formal backing.[61]

Finally, with a press release on April 1, Sverdrup announced that a newly formed "Convention Plaza Redevelopment Group" had submitted a formal proposal to the city's urban renewal authority to redevelop 16 blocks of the DeSoto-Carr area. The release pointedly noted that, in addition to Sverdrup & Parcel, the group included Mercantile Trust Company, the First National Bank, the Bank of St. Louis, Edison Brothers Stores, the Stix, Baer and Fuller department store chain, Interco, and Myron Moss Real Estate. Sverdrup had assembled the city's leading financial institutions and north side property owners. He had effectively put in front of the mayor a unified combine of business leaders, prepared to invest in the Sverdrup convention center plan.[62]

The implication of the announcement was obvious to the *Post-Dispatch*, at the very least. A lengthy editorial on April 3 called on the mayor (who had just won a new four-year term) to "profitably begin his second term . . . committing himself firmly to at least one project that promises hope for additional stability in the city's core." That one project was the Sverdrup effort, and the editorial noted that the firms supporting it "are deeply interested in preventing the encroachment of blight from the north; the core is amply protected on the south by new and planned construction." The paper went on to describe the linkage between a new center and Busch Stadium and the Spanish Pavilion to the south, arguing that "The logical north-south axis would pass the Old Post Office which, it is hoped, will be converted into a civic center."[63]

A tidal wave of business backing came next. Downtown St. Louis announced its support of the Sverdrup plan on April 4, followed by a formal report from the Chamber of Commerce on April 9, embracing the north side scheme over the Union Station plan. The chamber assessment noted that architect Arthur Schwarz had presented the Union Station scheme, complete with a theme park "along the lines of Disneyland and Six Flags Over Texas, but in abbreviated form" to the group. The chamber committee also toured the DeSoto-Carr area and viewed a presentation by General Sverdrup. Noting that the increased tax revenues from the redeveloped area could pay off the debt from the convention center, the committee averred, "There is no doubt in the collective minds of the committee that a convention facility is needed and would generate a considerable amount of business and economic benefit for our metropolitan community. . . . St. Louis could and should become one of the most attractive and desirable convention cities in the United States." The chamber committee report went on to argue that the "convention and commercial complex envisioned for this area would serve as an effective barrier against further deterioration of the north side business district."[64]

With the formal backing of the area's major business firms and organizations and a string of endorsements from the local daily newspapers, Sverdrup moved ahead in early April 1969 with the formation of an investment group to organize and support the "Convention Plaza" redevelopment scheme. Brice Smith proposed that the group meet by the first of May, with the goal of establishing a "promotional fund of say $100,000" to manage the scheme through the city's urban renewal agency, Plan Commission, and the Board of Aldermen, and setting a schedule of priorities "necessary to successfully promote the project."[65]

The group that convened at the May 1 luncheon represented many of the leading local business institutions, each with a direct interest in the renewal of the core's north side. It included a number of Civic Progress mainstays: Donald Lasater, president of Mercantile Trust, who had worked with

Sverdrup on the stadium project; Preston Estep of the Bank of St. Louis; Charles Edison, brother of Irving Edison, representing Edison Brothers Stores; the Interco Inc. shoe manufacturing firm's president M. R. Chambers (yet another longtime Civic Progress member); and J. A. Baer II, president of the Stix, Baer and Fuller department store chain. It was Baer who had remarked two years earlier about the need for "protection from erosion on the north side." Leif Sverdrup had achieved his goal of garnering unified, "wholehearted" business community backing for his convention center plan, and the direct financial commitment of a group of St. Louis's leading financial firms.[66]

The unified business support for Sverdrup did not sway Mayor Cervantes. He continued his efforts to bring a theme park to downtown St. Louis, now seeking to attract Sea World. But in late June 1969, Sea World president George Millay formally wrote ERA's Fred Cochrane that "I honestly don't believe we have any sincere interest in a downtown location in St. Louis and, therefore, will not waste any more of your time, or ours, responding to your request."[67]

Mayor Cervantes's commitment to Union Station as a convention center location was increasingly unsustainable by mid-1969. The final blow came in mid-July when Great Southwest announced that the planned "Six Flags over Mid-America" would be built on a suburban site in west St. Louis County. With no possibility of a theme park, Cervantes was left with no real options for Union Station.

A *Globe-Democrat* story on July 18 announced the inevitable with the headline, "Mayor Favors Near North Side Convention Site." It reported that Cervantes had switched his support to the Sverdrup site in the wake of the previous day's loss of Six Flags. The mayor was quoted as saying the Union Station plan "looks at this point like it is dead," and that "maybe in the long run the north side is best," with a new convention center to be financed by a city bond issue. Charles Edison wrote the mayor a few days later, complimenting him on his announcement: "Your backing for the rejuvenation of the North Side of Downtown St. Louis is, I think, a most important step in the direction of progress, and your remarks were those of an astute chief executive and do you honor."[68]

It was a victory for Sverdrup's plan, with "protection from erosion" on the north side apparently near at hand.

With Mayor Cervantes's apparent acquiescence to the Sverdrup plan and the north side site—he would later waver—the location for a new convention center appeared resolved. The conflict over the convention center had never involved any serious question of need, cost, or likely public benefit beyond the initial ERA study. There were no stirring editorials on the relative merits of investment in a convention center versus more basic public improvement needs, or on St. Louis's capacity to compete for major convention events. Nor, at a time when the business leaders who made up Civic Progress were also concerned with issues of civil rights, potential urban disturbances, and the city's racial divide, was there any extended consideration of alternative investments or development strategies.

The Convention Plaza effort was the direct inheritor of the business focus on rebuilding the Old Post Office site, clearing the near north side and its "erosion," and building a development magnet—be it a Tivoli Gardens or a convention center—that could spur and sustain the "chain of new activities" sought by Irving Edison and his colleagues. It was simply too critical to downtown businesses, for too long, to allow Cervantes's vision of Union Station as a tourist mecca to be realized.

There was also a larger factor at work in shaping the commitment of Civic Progress to the north side location. The two major downtown department stores, Stix, Baer and Fuller and Famous-Barr (a division of the May Company), had long faced a declining market and the difficult environment of the near north side just a handful of blocks away. The solution to these problems, their executives concluded, lay in creating a new retail environment modeled on successful suburban shopping malls. And both Morton May, the chairman of the board of May Department Stores, and J. A. Baer, II, president of Stix, Baer, were members of Civic Progress, together with Leif Sverdrup. By the summer of 1969, with the prospect of Sverdrup's Convention Plaza plan and the clearance of the larger DeSoto-Carr area seemingly assured, developer Raymond Wittcoff could tell his colleagues on the Downtown St. Louis Inc. board in August the shopping mall "had been discussed for many years," expressing the hope that "this would become the No. 1 priority" for the downtown organization.[69]

May, Baer, and Mercantile Trust jointly announced in October 1970 a $95.3 million "Development Plan" that included a proposal for adding a third department store, joining the three together with a 835,000 square foot, climate-controlled mall, linked to a new Mercantile Trust office tower on the western edge of the site. The plan noted that the area north of the Stix, Baer store "has deteriorated," but that a new development for the area included "a new Convention Center, stores, hotel, parking facilities and public open space." Without the promise of the convention center and the clearance of the "deteriorated" north side, the grand mall scheme simply would not be viable.[70]

Paying and Selling

From Arthur Schwarz's designs for a convention center complex at Union Station through the Sverdrup & Parcel planning process, there appears to have been almost no real concern about how a new convention center could be financed. The ERA studies had viewed a larger project, including a theme park that would draw large volumes of paying customers, as effectively self-financing. But by itself, a convention facility was unlikely to yield much of an operating profit, let alone pay for its debt service.

The initial Sverdrup assessment of the convention center in October 1968 had largely dismissed financing issues, noting that the "actual cost of such a development for the City would be minimum," assuming that the project would yield increased tax revenue, and projected that the center itself would operate on a "break-even basis." The firm suggested both internally and externally that the convention facility could be financed by the city on a lease basis, with regular annual payments. The Chamber of Commerce's April 1969 endorsement of the Sverdrup scheme had seconded that, noting, "plans call for leasing the convention center building to the City for debt service and having it revert to City ownership after the $10 million obligation has been discharged."[71]

When Leif Sverdrup laid out the path to implementing the convention center in October 1969, he noted that the "legal authority for City to lease Convention Center facilities" and to commit "general funds for a lease program" had yet to be resolved. A lease had a number of obvious advantages for Sverdrup & Parcel. For one, it would allow the firm to actually design and build the center quickly without the problems of city bidding requirements. But the most important result of lease financing was political—it would avoid a bond issue, and the needed public vote with its required two-thirds majority.[72]

The recent history of St. Louis bond issue proposals was not entirely positive, and the city's business leaders were not entirely comfortable with Cervantes's performance and his commitment to the north side convention center. The city had crafted a major package of bond issue proposals for a November 1966 vote, including 16 general obligation issues, for a total of over

$79 million. Only five of the 16 received the required two-thirds majority, and the worst performers included urban renewal bonds and two downtown projects—expansion of the Gateway Mall and expansion of the existing Kiel Auditorium. Much of the reason for the defeat lay with the city's largely African-American wards. In previous bond elections they had sustained massive majorities, such as an 80 percent "yes" vote for the 1962 stadium bonds in one ward. But in 1966, black voter support was far less, often below the two-thirds majority.

Mayor Cervantes and civic leaders chose to try a second proposal for just one of the 11 defeated issues. A $2 million bond for the Jefferson National Expansion Memorial Arch and its grounds was placed on the ballot for March 7, 1967. While the modest Arch bond issue passed, the leadership of Civic Progress recognized that the city faced a serious problem in garnering political support. Discussing the Arch bond vote in its February 1967 meeting, the Civic Progress leadership was "disturbed at the development of opposition among some few Negro leaders," focusing on Fred Weathers, committeeman of the 18th ward, "who usually produces substantial majorities in favor of bond issue proposals." Civic Progress secretary Harry Wilson said Weathers was opposing the bonds "because he is afraid if this single issue is passed the white community may lose interest in future passage of other bond issue programs of more direct interest to the Negro community." Preston Estep of the Bank of St. Louis added, "residents of the outlying parts of the City, whether white or Negro, think downtown has already gotten too big a share of bond issue funds."[73]

Although the modest Arch bond issue did pass in 1967, the message understood by the city's business leaders was that support for future large downtown projects, particularly from African American voters, was uncertain at best. Fred Weathers chose to openly oppose the Arch bond proposal, together with another ward leader (later Congressman), William L. Clay. Their wards generated "yes" votes of just 45 and 42 percent, far less than historic African American support for bond proposals and well below the needed two-thirds majority. Coupled with the fact that the project was part of a major clearance effort on the largely African American north side, the prospects of any convention center bond issue at the polls appeared dim.

The quest for a politically viable financing scheme grew more complicated in January 1970, when Mayor Cervantes wrote to Sverdrup about an informal legal opinion from the city counselor's office on the leasing alternative. The opinion stated clearly—in wording likely underlined by Sverdrup—that "it is quite evident that the City can not enter a long term lease." There was a possible mechanism for leasing an off-street parking facility. But a lease could not be used to finance the convention center.[74]

The Sverdrup firm considered a host of options in early 1970 while it employed consultant Herman Penn to analyze the center's likely revenue and expenses. Penn's conclusions confirmed Sverdrup's "suspicions that as a practical matter the construction of a Convention Center for St. Louis must be supported by tax funds in some manner." That left Sverdrup and the Convention Plaza group little alternative to reaching some sort of accommodation with Mayor Cervantes that could provide a politically and legally viable form of public financing.[75]

As the negotiations with the mayor and the city's renewal agency dragged, the convention center's price tag continued to grow. Brice Smith's October 1968 cost estimate had been $9 million, and subsequent discussions had involved a $10 million estimate. When Sverdrup officials met with representatives of the mayor, the renewal agency, and the Convention and Tourist Board at the end of June 1970, the cost of land and construction had risen to $15 million, and meeting notes summarized, "Financing is biggest hurdle."[76]

By July, when Sverdrup met with the mayor, the city's finance director, the city controller, and bankers from the Bank of St. Louis, the total cost had risen to between $22 and $25 million. It was agreed "that the only feasible method of financing the Center was through a General Obligation bond issue." There was no way around the city's voters. But there were some possibilities, indeed political necessities, to make a bond issue more saleable to the voters.[77]

City Controller (later mayor) John Poelker proposed a special benefit district covering downtown as a means of repaying a portion of the center's cost, largely to "show the voters that these [downtown] interests were willing to carry a fair share of the costs." With the potential for spreading the debt service cost of the center, Mayor Cervantes ventured that a bond campaign would require at least $125,000 for advertising and promotion. Sverdrup and Mercantile Trust CEO John Fox agreed, and Cervantes offered a statement of his hope to make an announcement of center plans in late September, well in advance of the city election in the spring of 1971, with an "educational campaign . . . to sell the idea of more jobs" and that the "various neighborhood groups" would have to be involved.

The July 1970 meeting fixed the basic structure and politics of the convention center. There was no alternative to a voted general obligation bond issue with its requirement for a two-thirds majority, as Controller Poelker's scheme for splitting the costs proved unworkable. The convention center proposal would stand alone on the ballot. Unlike most earlier bond efforts, there would be no package of projects and benefits. And Cervantes insisted on shaping and defining the bond campaign himself.

The mayor announced the plans for the convention center and its financing in October, and insisted on being the public face of the campaign effort. Earlier city bond issue campaigns had been organized and run by the Fleishman-Hillard public relations firm, which provided the public relations and staff arm of Civic Progress. But for what would be termed the "Smile!" campaign, Cervantes insisted on employing Sam Weintraub, a longtime political ally who had handled his mayoral campaigns, with the bulk of the campaign financing from Civic Progress and the business leadership.[78]

In appealing to his fellow Civic Progress members for financial backing, Leif Sverdrup repeated both the logic and almost precisely the same language as J. A. Baer had employed three and a half years earlier—"the Convention Center and Convention Plaza development could shut off the north side of downtown from erosion and decay the same way the Stadium complex and other developments in the area have shut off the south side."[79]

The Sverdrup & Parcel firm's efforts went well beyond a simple financial contribution, pressing employees to canvass for votes. In a statement to his employees, Leif Sverdrup (the "Old Man") stressed the importance of the convention center to the firm—"We foresee the construction of the Convention Center as the trigger for additional construction projects reaching a figure of $100,000,000 and more. We certainly intend to have a large share of that business."[80]

The bond campaign faced a number of obstacles, including the fact that the issue stood alone and required property tax revenues. Too, Cervantes's tourism promotion efforts had literally collapsed. The Spanish Pavilion had closed on April 30, 1970, after drawing only a fraction of the forecast patronage. The mayor had sent Leif Sverdrup a copy of one letter soliciting funds for the bond campaign with the note, "Just like the Spanish Pavilion," scrawled on the bottom. Cervantes had written at the top, "Jack, we are getting this comment frequently." Whether as a function of the property tax question, Cervantes's dropping popularity, or the city's racial divide, the convention center bond flopped with the voters.[81]

The March 1971 vote yielded just a 36.5 percent "yes" vote. In discussing the failure at a Civic Progress meeting that month, M. R. Chambers of Interco said, "it was surprising to see it beaten so strongly." The mayor said it represented a "revolt against higher taxes" and the public's perception that "someone . . . the downtown business interests and the City Hall . . . was going to make some money off it." Noting that the bonds were defeated "even in traditionally solid Democratic wards . . . and in public housing projects where the vote is normally controlled by the political organizations," the mayor concluded, "there was no chance of passing a bond issue to finance a convention center at this time but there might be other ways to approach the problem."[82]

The bonds did poorly in the largely white south side wards that often voted "no" on spending proposals. In low- and middle-income white wards, the "yes" vote came to just 30 percent. But, as Mayor Cervantes said, they also failed to gain much support in the African American wards of the north side, where the vote was typically guided by ward organizations such as that headed by Fred Weathers. Those largely African American wards produced on average just a 45 percent "yes" vote. The need for super-majority voter support appeared to pose an insurmountable problem for Sverdrup and the business leaders.[83]

A week after the defeat, Brice Smith completed a memo laying out the immediate political reality. First, "There should be no attempt to go back to the voters of the City of St. Louis for either a general obligation or a revenue bond proposal." There was a need for tax revenues behind the project, but Smith argued, "The Downtown business interests should assist in financing the Convention Center and Plaza *to protect their existing investment*" (italics mine). Smith's proposal involved employing the Civic Center Redevelopment Corporation, which had undertaken the stadium project, to raise capital, purchase the land from the urban renewal authority, and develop a smaller, less expensive center. That could provide, he contended, "a further stimulus to Downtown at a much lower land cost basis."[84]

The search for alternatives continued into 1972 under the aegis of a Convention Center Task Force. By the middle of the year, there was some change in the larger environment. Cervantes was facing a mayoral election in April 1973 and was seeking some significant new initiative to bolster his prospects, particularly after the abject failure of the Spanish Pavilion. There was also an increasing possibility that St. Louis could garner some new dollars from the federal government, with the passage of federal revenue sharing legislation by the House of Representatives in June 1972.

A June 20, 1972, memo from Brice Smith to Sverdrup assessed that "the Mayor will be very receptive to any proposal that will help to get a Convention Center built and started before the next Mayoralty election in Spring

1973." Smith laid out a roadmap with "downtown interests" paying for design work for a center built with revenue bonds "backstopped by the Convention & Tourism Tax."[85]

Revenue bonds would still require a public vote, albeit with a smaller required majority. But Smith was candid in his view of the mayor—"The key question is can any bond issue be passed by the current administration, even one structured with no property tax increase, some federal money, and Downtown financial participation?" His conclusion: "With the basic 'no' vote in St. Louis, it might just squeeze by if an independent citizen, say Harold Gibbons [local Teamsters Union vice president] or Gussie Busch, would take the lead. I am advised Cervantes has been told by the other half of the Task Force that the Center doesn't have a chance if he is identified with it personally." Smith reported the mayor "did not react to the statement in any way."

The proposal that emerged in August was crafted by urban renewal chief Charles Farris to neatly avoid the use of the property tax by reallocating existing taxes on businesses, hotels, and restaurants. They would be bolstered by the argument that a flood of convention visitors would boost city tax revenues. The new scheme would still require a vote on a $25 million bond issue, scheduled for November 1972. That timing would serve the mayor's interests and also take advantage of the boost in turnout for a presidential election. But the issue of the center's location again emerged as a sticking point.

Banker Donald Lasater informed his Civic Progress colleagues in September that "some consideration has been given to a site on the south side of downtown as well as to the near north side location—in the DeSoto-Carr area—developed by the first Convention Center bond issue election by Sverdrup & Parcel and Associates, Inc." Members were also concerned about the timing of a November 7 vote, although the group was "united in saying the Convention Center is a must . . . the Number One community need." Donald Lasater finally proposed that the north side site be specified on the ballot, and only then would Civic Progress back the bond campaign. Lasater's proposed resolution passed on a vote of 13 to 8—an unusual divided vote among the Civic Progress leaders—with real displeasure over the timing of the vote.[86]

For the 1972 effort, the Civic Progress role went well beyond its endorsement, unwilling to leave the bond campaign to the mayor. The actual campaign was placed in the hands of the Fleishman-Hillard firm, under the direction of Donald Lasater and longtime Civic Progress secretary (and Fleishman executive) Harry Wilson. Lasater organized the fundraising, "appealing to each of you [Civic Progress members] for your personal evaluation of what a Convention Center can mean to the future of our total community." The campaign material headlined "Make St. Louis a Really Great City. . . . The Entire City Benefits and with NO TAX INCREASE." The promise was that a "yes" vote would "Bring $43,000,000 More Tourist Dollars a Year to St. Louis Create More than 5,000 New Jobs in the City," support the "third largest business in the City," and reverse the steady loss of conventions to "cities like Detroit and Dallas, Pittsburgh and Indianapolis, Milwaukee and Minneapolis."[87]

Mayor Cervantes made the same point about new visitors and jobs in an October 6 address to the city's Board of Aldermen. The mayor said,"We must avoid discussions which appear to pit neighborhoods against downtown," concluding, "I don't think there is any question of where we will spend the money we will receive under federal revenue sharing. . . . Our emphasis has been and will continue to be in the neighborhoods."[88]

The second attempt proved a success, with the bonds passed with a comfortable 75 percent majority, 90,185 to 29,819. With Cervantes largely invisible, the bonds actually managed an 82 percent "yes" vote in the majority African-American wards. An internal memo to Civic Progress members after the election victory said it "helped create new hopes for the future of the downtown business district." Donald Lasater reported to the Civic Progress group at the end of November, "Mayor A. J. Cervantes stayed in the background, as agreed . . . and was very cooperative in expediting campaign matters and persuading the neighborhood groups in the City to support the bond issue proposal." M. R. Chambers then added, "the members of Civic Progress owed a vote of thanks to Don Lasater for putting his money where his mouth is and providing great leadership in the city . . . . [The] public relations for the Convention Center bond issue campaign had been handled without charge by Fleishman-Hillard, Inc."[89]

By November 1972, Civic Progress had succeeded in resolving the "Number One community need." The business community had defined a new convention center as the single most vital community investment, found a way to finance it based on a flood of new tax revenues from convention attendees, and engineered broad community support. They had done so despite the initial opposition of the mayor, the limitations on the city's finances, and the city's larger problems of population loss, racial division, and crime.

Aftermath

Voter approval was just the first step in developing the center itself and the Convention Plaza redevelopment effort. Faced with increased construction costs, the city was obliged to boost the funding beyond the $25 million approved in November 1972. The Land Clearance Authority added some $3 million to the project. And for the balance, Mayor John Poelker (who had defeated A. J. Cervantes in the 1973 election) turned to Civic Progress, saying, "he hopes the companies represented on Civic Progress will contribute about $1,500,000." The Civic Progress firms ultimately donated an additional $2 million for construction costs, and the new Cervantes Convention Center opened in July 1977.[90]

With the convention center funding committed, Sverdrup & Parcel was in a position to move ahead with the larger renewal effort. The firm commissioned a formal feasibility study of the potential for new hotel development in January 1973 from Laventhol Krekstein Horwath & Horwath. The Laventhol report concluded that the local meetings market "will enjoy a high annual growth rate after the proposed convention center is completed, adding an additional 860,000 annual room nights."[91] Bolstered by the consultant findings, the first major private development was a new 620-room Sheraton hotel, developed and designed by the Sverdrup firm. The Sheraton was joined by a second, smaller Radisson hotel, a parking garage, and a new office building housing Sverdrup & Parcel offices. Brice Smith reported to a Civic Progress meeting in late 1978 that "St. Louis has moved ahead of Dallas and other cities in its size range in attracting conventions since the new Center opened. Its success has exceeded expectations."[92]

Even before the convention center was completed, the prospect of "protection from erosion" sought by J. A. Baer and the "building up of the downtown retail section" envisioned by Irving Edison were under way. A revised plan for joining the two downtown department stores was finally announced in October 1972—on the verge of the second convention center bond vote—by Mercantile Trust and its chairman, Donald Lasater, together with Dallas developer Trammell Crow. The "Mercantile Center" scheme would connect the department stores with a two-level enclosed mall, four major high-rise office buildings, an 800-room hotel, restaurants, and entertainment, just two blocks from the Convention Plaza redevelopment. The timing of the announcement was no doubt intended to bolster the electoral fortunes of the convention center bonds. It also made evident that Donald Lasater's "putting his money where his mouth is" went well beyond a civic commitment to tourism and the convention business. The convention center and Convention Plaza were critical to making the office and retail development economically viable.

The new 35-story Mercantile Trust tower opened in 1976 as Missouri's tallest building. The new shopping mall proved rather more difficult. The May Company, owners of the Famous-Barr department store, took over the project in the late 1970s and eventually brought in mall developer Melvin Simon in 1980. The new "St. Louis Centre" mall finally opened in early 1985, aided by substantial city and federal government subsidies, albeit without the promised hotel. The "glittering" new mall was described at the time as the nation's largest downtown shopping center, and in December 1985 *Fortune* headlined, "Downtown Is Vibrant Once Again."[93]

The promise of hordes of new convention attendees also played a major role in yet another downtown renewal project, the reuse of Union Station. James Levi, president of Oppenheimer Properties of New York, was grounded in St. Louis by a snowstorm in 1979. Discovering Union Station, he envisioned a combination of hotel and shopping mall under the vast train shed, aided by federal Urban Development Action Grant funds and historic preservation tax credits. The new Union Station complex, combining an Omni hotel and a retail and entertainment "festival marketplace," opened in August 1985.[94]

The potential of a new convention center was no less important to Civic Progress. At the same November 1972 meeting where the business leaders congratulated Don Lasater for the successful campaign, the organization also laid out its future direction. A "study and action committee" including Lasater, W. R. Persons of Emerson Electric, Harold Thayer of Mallinckrodt Chemical, Hadley Griffin of Brown Shoe, and Edwin Jones of the First National Bank recommended that the "mission of Civic Progress needed to be re-defined in relation to problems of today." That meant the group should "deal with big, long-range projects and, especially, those which would help revive the central city," emphasizing the new convention center and Mercantile Trust's building as well as rehabilitation of the "downtown north side area" and redevelopment of midtown, near St. Louis University's campus. The group's future focus was clearly to be on real estate and redevelopment, whether through its continuing interest in the downtown core or on the declining neighborhoods surrounding the city's major institutions.[95]

Politics, Planning, and Private Interests

St. Louis's quest to refashion its downtown as a prime visitor destination, peculiar and quixotic as it may appear in retrospect, was built on a foundation of the best available planning expertise and analysis. The focus on clearing the ring of "blighted and obsolete" structures that surrounded the central business district was deeply embedded in the city's planning history. Harland Bartholomew had called for just such an approach in his 1919 plan for a public building group. He had regularly renewed that call as part of city bond programs and subsequent planning studies. His plan for St. Louis after World War II had explicitly focused on the zone of obsolescent and decayed housing, with the call, "It is apparent that these areas must be reconditioned and rebuilt." From a position as a nationally recognized planning expert, Bartholomew had repeated the call for major clearance in the city's 1947 comprehensive plan.[96]

For generations of St. Louis elected officials and business leaders, the expert wisdom was that a massive program of clearance and rebuilding, either through the public housing program or urban redevelopment, was a vital necessity to keep the central business district, and the entire city, economically sound. That land clearance policy in 1950s and 1960s St. Louis was far from unusual—it was built on the dominant planning orthodoxy of the time, exemplified and reinforced by what Civic Progress leaders found in their visit to Pittsburgh. And it was reinforced by yet another set of "expert" conclusions and recommendations from the 1954 Urban Land Institute panel study.

The ULI panel stressed that the city "must tear down decayed and obsolete buildings and redevelop great segments of the close-in city," endorsing the urban renewal scheme for the massive Mill Creek Valley project. The panel also endorsed the demolition of the Old Post Office and its replacement by a new office project. Again, the notion was that eliminating old buildings was key to spurring new investment. It was this focus on "blight" elimination that supported the idea of clearing the southern flank of the core and building both the new Busch Stadium and the larger Civic Center renewal project—the intended home of a new visitor attraction.[97]

Undoubtedly the most "expert" and influential advice in shaping the vision of downtown St. Louis as a visitor mecca came from the association of the Civic Progress leaders with Walt Disney during the 1960s. Disney's own interest in the possibilities of an attraction by the Gateway Arch and the new stadium served to validate the goals and perspective of the city's business leaders. The formal assessment by Disney's "numbers man," Buzz Price, that one downtown official termed "very optimistic," amply sustained the notion that millions of visitors and attendees would flock to downtown. Price's imprimatur on the Riverfront Square project thus neatly validated the judgment of Sverdrup and the Civic Progress leadership—St. Louis was on the verge of becoming a major visitor destination. When Mayor Cervantes's Spanish Pavilion plan was hatched, it neatly followed both the model of Riverfront Square and its location. And the premise of the 1966 ERA study of the pavilion was that "Millions of local residents and tourists will be attracted" to the Arch, and that the new stadium would draw "Hundreds of thousands of persons . . . many of them from 100 to 200 miles away."[98]

Buzz Price's positive assessment of the Spanish Pavilion was reinforced by the Disney connection. In turn, the forecast numbers from Price and Economics Research Associates for the Pavilion's attendance and revenues bulwarked the sense *among the Civic Progress members* that the downtown would see a flood of new people and economic activity. When the possibility of developing a major new convention facility surfaced in 1966, the experience of Chicago, Boston, and San Diego appeared to validate the potential of a center. And once again, the assessment by ERA provided a seemingly expert and reliable forecast of the likely performance and attendance of a new convention center.

ERA's estimates of the performance of a new center were indeed viewed as so reliable by the St. Louis business leadership that Sverdrup and his firm's staff simply appropriated them—verbatim—for their own analyses and for the formal presentation of the Convention Plaza redevelopment plan. It was the seeming credibility of ERA, Buzz Price, and project manager Fred Cochrane, as well as the firm's connections and reputation within the theme park industry, that sustained Mayor Cervantes's extended commitment to the Union Station site.

St. Louis's downtown revitalization plans were thus based on the expert judgments of the "best and the brightest" in the planning and economic analysis world. Yet the city's business leaders were not entirely devoted to following the consultants' recommendations. When Fred Cochrane of ERA repeatedly warned against building a convention center on a north side site, the interests and goals of a unified business leadership simply overrode his conclusion. For the members of Civic Progress and their colleagues, the interests and concerns of "Cubby" Baer, Donald Lasater, Leif Sverdrup, and the Edison brothers fully trumped outside expert advice. The new convention center was far more about "protection from erosion" than potential as a meeting venue.

Leif Sverdrup, Gussie Busch, Irving Edison, Morton May, John Fox, Don Lasater, and their colleagues did not cast votes in St. Louis. They did not control mayoral or aldermanic elections, or determine the outcomes of bond issue votes. Civic Progress members appeared to enjoy a close relationship with Mayor Tucker, a Washington University engineering professor seen as a non-politician. With his successor, Mayor Cervantes, who had owned a cab company, there was clearly a more distant relationship. Some sense of that distance was provided by the mayor's remarks at the annual Civic Progress dinner meeting in June 1968: "I don't know if you all are aware of the new order of the day—check your guns at the door. . . . I'm getting a lot of opposition to the proposed Downtown Amusement Park. . . . A lot of people are telling me they get all of the amusement they need from City Hall."[99] There was no pervasive regime or business capacity to pick candidates or determine electoral outcomes. Indeed, the repeated failures of bond issues for urban renewal and downtown projects made evident how little *direct* sway Civic Progress had over St. Louis voters.

What Civic Progress could and did control were the resources and financial capital upon which major public initiatives were dependent. Mayor Cervantes needed private dollars to make the Spanish Pavilion relocation a reality. He turned to the business leaders again when he needed the funds to purchase a replica of Christopher Columbus's flagship, the *Santa Maria*. The campaigns for city bond issues and tax increases also required private funds, and Civic Progress firms had historically played the major role in providing those tens and hundreds of thousands of campaign dollars.

Perhaps more important than dollars was the backing for projects from the region's business and civic leaders. The leadership of Civic Progress could and did appear to stand for a broad view of the area's needs. They could appeal to the public, newspaper publishers, writers, and editorialists for things that represented their vision of community good. And they could do so in a way that partisan politicians and political officeholders could not.

Civic Progress in the late 1960s could build on a fifteen-year history of promoting city bond issues, "good government," arts and cultural improvements, the United Fund, and a "public interest" vision for the city and the suburbs. That afforded the organization and its individual members a level of "civic legitimacy" that was vital to public acceptance of any mayoral initiative. The connections and sway of Civic Progress also went well beyond the city limits. Just as the mayor of St. Louis was an ex officio member of the group, so too was the elected supervisor of suburban St. Louis County. And just as the organization played the vital role in financing and supporting bond issue campaigns for both the city and county, it also backed and financed statewide votes on bonds, tax increases, and development proposals. The organization could and did aid the city in gaining state support for a number of projects.[100]

The combination of civic legitimacy, appeal to the larger public interest, and campaign financing gave Civic Progress an effective veto over bond and tax proposals where voter approval was needed. When only five of the 16 bond proposals on the city's November 1966 ballot garnered the required majority, the mayor and Civic Progress chose to try again with just one proposal—financing improvements to the environs of the Gateway Arch. With a singular focus on the Arch, the bonds passed on the March 7, 1967, ballot, with a 69 percent "yes" vote. The focus on downtown and visitor-oriented projects, to the exclusion of other city needs, would continue with the two serial votes on the convention center bonds, in 1971 and 1972. Once again, it was a major downtown project—and only a downtown project—that was placed before the city's voters.

The ability of Civic Progress and its members to shape the city's public investment policy and focus on downtown also reflected the *internal politics* of the group. Civic Progress members stayed with the organization for years, occasionally decades. That assured continuity in both knowledge and strategic focus, together with an organizational infrastructure managed by the Fleishman-Hillard public relations firm. And while individual members might retire or move, the major institutions they represented—the downtown department stores, the dominant financial institutions, the utility companies, Monsanto, Ralston-Purina, Anheuser-Busch, St. Louis University, and Washington University—continued to exert a presence over the years.

In its internal decision-making, Civic Progress operated with a great deal of collegiality and mutual deference. Decisions were only very rarely divided. Rather, members tended to defer to the initiatives and policy interests of their peers and colleagues.

During the 1960s, there was perhaps no better example of this mutuality and deference than the commitment to a major public initiative on the north side of downtown. Civic Progress had supported clearance of the DeSoto-Carr area throughout the 1950s and 1960s, and its members had pressed for the inclusion of Howard Ohlendorf's Tivoli Gardens scheme in the city's 1966 bond program. Group members who had supported public projects on the southern flank, including the stadium redevelopment, the Spanish Pavilion, and the Gateway Mall project, viewed the development of the convention center on the north side as part of that mutual accommodation, balancing the group's (and the city's) commitment to the "protection from erosion" on the south side.

The commitment of Sverdrup, the Edisons, John Fox, and Cubby Baer to a north side convention center also meant that Mayor Cervantes would encounter a fully unified and coherent business community in opposition to his Union Station plan. Indeed, the members of Civic Progress regularly addressed a north side project as their natural "due" in light of the stadium, a bulwark that both improved the environment of downtown and secured the necessary "erosion protection." Effectively, St. Louis's business leaders had decided for the city that its most pressing public investment need was a $25 million convention center in the location they chose—and then managed the political process to assure its realization.

The proposed new convention center was sold, as was almost every project before and after, in terms of broad gauge community benefit. There were promises, seemingly verified in a study by the nonprofit Governmental Research Institute, of thousands of new jobs, a flood of new visitor spending, and millions of dollars each year in new city tax revenues. The campaign line in the 1972 effort was "The Entire City Benefits," coupled with the argument that "conventions are a growth industry and a modern Civic-Convention Center can make St. Louis a leader once more."[101]

The campaign rhetoric was matched by the editorial pages of the city's daily newspapers. The day after the successful 1972 vote, the *Post-Dispatch* editorialized that the city's voters had been "attracted by the prospect of economic revival that the center would spark, and spark into the neighborhoods well beyond downtown."[102]

Yet whatever promises of economic boon and revival that were part of the center bond effort were manifestly not the focus of Leif Sverdrup, the members of the Convention Plaza Redevelopment Corporation, or the full membership of Civic Progress. Their focus in 1972—much as it was in 1954 and 1967—was on downtown land value and its "protection." The convention center development was all about land: slum clearance, new private investment, property values, and "protection from erosion." Those concerns were entirely location specific. What Svedrup and his colleagues wanted was a public facility—a source of "people generation" in the words of Sverdrup's chief planner Chamberlain—on the northern flank of downtown *and nowhere else.*

The focus of Civic Progress on the downtown core had not changed from that point in late 1953 when Powell McHaney had observed, "the basic theory in Pittsburgh is that you must take care of the 'core' of the city first, keep industry and its payrolls from deserting the downtown, and let the workers live wherever they want."[103]

What Sverdrup and his colleagues sought was a major public project—the counterpart to the new Busch Stadium to the south—that could serve as both an *anchor* and a *wall*, while also providing the financial backing for the larger urban renewal project. For Sverdrup and for Civic Progress, the new Busch Stadium and the proposed convention center served purposes far beyond baseball games or association meetings. Both major public projects were viewed as changing the physical environment of the core area's fringe, and as spurs to new private investment.

As a wall, the bulk of a massive convention center could literally shut off the business district and the big department stores from the public housing projects and "cancerous" slums to the immediate north. The entrance to the new center would face south, focused on the downtown core, bringing convention attendees from nearby hotels and restaurants. To the north would be blank walls and loading docks facing the land cleared with federal urban renewal funds.

As an anchor, the convention center was expected to serve as a focus for new investment and development. The hundreds of thousands of new convention attendees presumably drawn to the facility would both fill existing hotel rooms and support the new hotels envisioned by Sverdrup and the firm's planners. Those visitor dollars would flow into the new retail establishments envisioned by Sverdrup & Parcel, as well as into the existing department stores run by J. A. Baer and Morton May. Planner E. A. Chamberlain had set out just these arguments to Sverdrup in late 1968, with the center establishing "a firm anchor upon which new investment can be based."

The removal of the "blight" on the north side was no less critical to making the Mercantile Center scheme work and to securing investment capital. Just as with Sverdrup and his firm, the interests of Stix, Baer and Fuller (and Civic Progress member Cubby Baer) and Famous-Barr (and its parent, May Department Stores, represented on Civic Progress by Morton May) were entirely location-specific, fixed to their existing department stores. So too with Mercantile Trust, headquartered on an adjacent block (and represented on

Civic Progress by Don Lasater and John Fox), and First National Bank (and Edwin Jones), just to the south of the planned new retail mall. Although it would takc until 1981 before these St. Louis interests could finalize their plans, find a developer, and gain development financing for the retail mall project, the *promise* of the new convention center was critical in reassuring potential investors and retail tenants of the project's viability.

The conflict with Mayor Cervantes over the convention center site was thus so protracted and important because a center a few blocks, let alone a few miles, from the north side location of Stix, Baer, Sverdrup & Parcel, and the major downtown financial institutions would do little to anchor or spur the north side. Had Sverdrup and his Civic Progress colleagues been seeking to serve the broader public interest, the ERA report with its dismissal of the north side location would have held some sway. Had their goal been the optimal location, with a facility and larger project to maximize the city's appeal as a convention destination, they might well have sought an independent assessment of the center's feasibility and location alternatives. Civic Progress had done just that before financing Cervantes's purchase of the Spanish Pavilion. They did not for the convention center. Instead, the Civic Progress organization, Downtown St. Louis, Inc., and the local newspapers fell in line behind Leif Sverdrup.

A New Mayor and Expansion

The convention center that had been planned and sold to the public when Alfonso J. Cervantes was mayor finally opened in 1981, and it was Vincent Schoemehl who inherited the city-owned facility and its promise. With the slogan, "Every working day Jim Conway's been mayor, one more taxpaying business left St. Louis," Alderman Schoemehl succeeded in defeating Conway in the March 1981 primary and going on to win the general election. Schoemehl took office in a city that was experiencing a host of problems: population loss, including a drop of 27 percent from 1970 to 1980; a dependence on federal funds; and a continuing economic decline. For Schoemehl, the new convention center and the new hotel rooms at Union Station and other downtown projects promised some realizable economic return and job creation.[104]

Speaking to the business leadership of Civic Progress in August 1981, just a few months after assuming office, Mayor Schoemehl said the city "must have more economic growth to provide more jobs for which to train the unemployed." He said, "city government is *encouraging a buildup of the tourism industry to create a large number of new, entry level jobs in a short time*" (italics mine). But as Schoemehl sought to boost the city's tourism and convention activity in the early 1980s, he faced a serious problem. The Cervantes Convention Center, then just a few years old, was failing as a convention venue.[105]

The *prospect* of a huge boost in visitor and meeting activity from the new Cervantes Center had played a clear role in setting off the "chain of new activities" that Irving Edison had sought in fighting for a center on the north side. The $10 million Federal Urban Development Action Grant for the renewed Union Station and its hotel had been announced in 1980, followed by the $18 million grant for the new St. Louis Centre shopping mall in 1981. Just two or three blocks from the new convention center, the old nineteenth-century warehouse and manufacturing buildings along Washington Avenue were being converted to use as offices and apartments. The "protection from erosion" sought by Civic Progress members appeared to have been realized by the early 1980s.[106]

The Cervantes Convention Center itself was having problems. When Economics Research Associates had done their initial analysis in 1968, they forecast that a new center at the Union Station site would draw some 386,000 annual convention and tradeshow attendees, with a total of attendance of 518,000 at all events. That 518,000 figure was used by Sverdrup & Parcel planner E. A. Chamberlain in his justification of building at the DeSoto-Carr location. But ERA had concluded that a north side of downtown site would draw only half its forecast attendance—"a marginal environment . . . . [the] North Side location would seriously curtail convention center use by local residents and by conventions."

The ERA conclusions were neatly verified by the center's actual performance. Where the consulting firm had predicted an annual total of almost 400,000 attendees at Union Station, the Cervantes Center saw convention attendance in fiscal year 1978 of just 215,100—about what ERA had concluded for the "marginal" north side site. When consultants Laventhol & Horwath examined the center's operation in mid-1984, they reported convention attendance the prior year at only 148,235. Laventhol's conclusion was that convention activity in St. Louis "is not nearly up to potential," with the "poor success" in part the result of a facility that was "inadequately operated" and a "local environment surrounding the center [that] has historically been perceived as poor."[107]

If newly elected Mayor Schoemehl was intent on building up tourism and convention business, he had to boost the center's performance, and that of the city's Convention and Visitors Bureau as well. At about the same period in August 1981 that Schoemehl laid out his tourism focus to Civic Progress, he met with the center's governing body, the Convention Center Commission. Schoemehl's blistering talk began with the statement "that we have all the facilities here necessary to basically double the tourism trade overnight . . . . All we need is business." The mayor's assessment did not focus on the center itself. Instead, he portrayed "a series of disjointed efforts" on the part of the convention and visitors bureau, the ("asleep") hotel/motel industry, and a "virtually disorganized" restaurant industry. The mayor concluded, "I would ask you to remember most of all the fact that this is a critical industry to the City and it holds the greatest short term potential for putting people back to work. We have six (6) hotels on the drawing board for downtown St. Louis and those six (6) hotels are going to have a significant impact on the development of downtown St. Louis as a whole."[108]

But beyond reshaping the management of the center and the CVB, Schoemehl also had a larger goal in mind—the expansion of Cervantes Convention Center. As part of the city's annual budget and performance review in November 1981, mayoral aide Marie Jeffries noted (in language underlined by either Schoemehl or his chief of staff), "The possibility of expanding the Cervantes Center must be considered. The present and future development in the downtown area will certainly attract larger conventions which require more exhibit space than is presently available." Her memo went on to note the problem of available land, and, "a few long-shot possibilities which do exist and these areas need to be discussed as soon as possible with the Mayor and his staff."[109]

The expectation on Mayor Schoemehl's part was that convention center expansion would happen. It was simply a matter of when it would be best to surface the issue in public. Serious public discussion of the expansion would not occur until 1986, and the vote on financing an expansion would not take place until November 1987. Yet it is clear that early in his first year in office, Vincent Schoemehl was intent on making the convention center a central priority, and its expansion his ultimate goal. This initiative was purely Schoemehl's. The business leaders of Civic Progress at this time were focused on other goals, ranging from the cost of health insurance to the financial health of the symphony and the clearance of a number of downtown blocks for the planned Gateway Mall. The performance of the convention center was not a particular concern of the corporate leaders, once they secured its development on the north side of downtown.

Nor was the logic of center expansion rooted in some formal examination of need, market feasibility, or cost-benefit analysis at this stage. There would be formal consultant studies of expansion in 1985 and later. Yet these were obviously done *after* the mayor and his staff were committed to the expansion effort. The studies provided evidence on the scale and growth of the convention and tradeshow industry, and forecasts of post-expansion attendance and economic impact. These estimates and forecasts were vital in justifying and selling the expansion. They did not, however, provide any real foundation for the initial commitment on the part of the mayor and the city.

Schoemehl's focus on tourism and the convention center was clearly rooted in his own political interests and goals. The mayor and his staff regularly referred, as he had in his August presentation to the Convention Center Commission, to the need to support planned new hotel development. Efforts like the reuse of Union Station and the development of St. Louis Centre mall were dependent on the promise of growing convention attendance in promoting new private investment. Schoemehl also had longstanding political ties to prominent members of the hospitality industry, including restaurateurs John Ferrara of The Pasta House and Vincent Bommarito of Tony's, perhaps the city's most renowned restaurant. They had the mayor's ear, and were intent on boosting the city's convention trade.

For a mayor interested in big development projects, convention center expansion was a natural focus, one that he could control and that held the promise of more new private investment. But Schoemehl's early and continuing commitment to a larger Cervantes Center did not directly translate into public action. There remained critical and unresolved questions of where the expansion should go and how it could be financed. In the immediate term, in 1982 and 1983, Schoemehl was faced with the pressure to make good on a campaign promise to reopen the Homer G. Phillips Hospital, which primarily served the city's African American community, and to boost city taxes and general revenues.[110]

The opportunity to press his tourism agenda came in late 1983 with a scandal surrounding the director of the convention center. Schoemehl succeeded in replacing the director with a longtime political ally, alderman Bruce Sommer. Even before Sommer took office in January 1984, the mayor sought a formal study of the management and operation of both the older Kiel Auditorium and the Cervantes Center, saying, "Financial operations should be looked at," and "suggested utilization of both Kiel and the Convention Center."[111]

The Convention Center Commission, now chaired by restaurateur Vincent Bommarito, began to look for an outside consultant in the fall of 1983. The proposal formally submitted by Laventhol & Horwath in early November 1983 and accepted the following January acknowledged the city's concern with the "apparent under-utilization" of both facilities and the capacity of the two facilities "to compete . . . with the new and expanding facilities of other major cities for hospitality industry demand."[112]

The L&H proposal did not specify a focus on center expansion. But an assessment of the study plans by the city's new budget director, Stephen Mullin, made clear the larger purpose of engaging the consulting firm. Mullin wrote mayoral aide Jill McGuire on October 27, 1983, that he was familiar with their products, and "while they look good, they are of little substance and the meat of their analyses rest on assumptions that we could just as easily make here." But if Mullin appeared unimpressed by the analytical substance of the likely product, he recognized a larger political imperative—"I understand that the finished report carries a lot of weight because of its pretty format and 'great-looking' recommendations, so I agree that we should hire them, just scale it down in time."[113]

The analysis presented by the Laventhol consultant team (including David C. Petersen and Charles H. Johnson) in mid-June 1984 focused on the problems of both the Cervantes Center and the city. The center itself was described as "not meeting its potential as a convention destination." When it came to the question of expansion, the L&H presentation was direct. The center "presently has excess capacity," and while an expansion could potentially capitalize on the growth of conventions and accommodate simultaneous multiple events, their recommendation was that "Expansion is not recommended in the immediate future." The L&H analysis did suggest some "ground work" for future expansion by preserving land for possible added space. It was far from a surprising analysis of what was clearly an underperforming center in a poor location. The Laventhol consultants repeated much the same findings in a final draft dated July 27, 1984. Their analysis concluded that the center "is appropriately sized for the market it should be serving," but that the city should preserve space for a future expansion.[114]

The L&H report did not provide the justification for the expansion effort sought by the mayor. Yet neither did it deter his quest for a bigger convention center. At some point in late 1984, Vincent Schoemehl clearly committed to pressing for an expanded convention center. An October meeting (later canceled) was set for the mayor with center director Bruce Sommer and restaurant owners John Ferrara and Vincent Bommarito to "Insure they were on the same wave length with you or [sic] to what is to be done at Convention Center and Kiel." And Bommarito would write mayoral aide Tom Mangogna in early January 1985, "We can rightfully take our place in the multi-billion dollar Hospitality Industry—the competition is 'out there.' We need 100% cooperation. Please do all you can to keep our programs on line for Kiel and the Convention Center. . . . We can't do it all, but can sure as heck get a share of that big pie if we work at it. Please show this letter and article [on Dallas] to Vince [Schoemehl]."[115]

Whether pressed by Ferrara, Bommarito, and center director Bruce Sommer, or motivated by the upcoming mayoral election in April 1985, the mayor began to assemble the case for a bigger convention center early in 1985.[116]

On February 12, Schoemehl sent director Sommer a note setting out the need for a memo "outlining your thoughts on expansion of the Convention Center." The mayor said, "I need a fairly detailed narrative explaining why expansion of the Convention Center is necessary, the type of facility you envision, and your initial thoughts on the physical configuration of such an expansion." Schoemehl's request was clearly not for an analysis of the *possibilities* for expansion or a weighing of the pluses and minuses of more convention space. What he sought was an argument for a "necessary" public investment, even as he acknowledged no real sense of its possible cost. Just as was evident in 1981 and after, the mayor wanted an expansion. He just needed the evidence to make that case.[117]

Bruce Sommer's 19-page response in early March is a remarkable document, not only for its length. Sommer laid out detailed replies to each of the questions posed by the mayor, noting that it was prepared "without the benefit of a great deal of research and investigation," but that "the potential benefits to the City in terms of jobs, tax revenues and all the rest is awesome and this could be one of the most exciting things this City has ever done."[118]

His assessment of the need for expansion laid out themes and data that would be the currency of consultant reports and public discourse in city after city for the next 25 years. First, there was the competition—"In 1977, *when St. Louis first opened its modern convention doors, we were the 10th largest in the country. Today we are the 32nd largest in the United States.*" He went on to argue another central theme, that of ongoing convention and tradeshow growth—"*the industry's top 150 trade shows required 26 million net square feet of exhibit space in 1981 and will require 47 million square feet by 1991 and that the number of companies participating will increase from 97,316 to 145,192 and the number of their attendees from 2.87 million to 4.9 million*" (emphasis in original).[119]

Sommer recommended roughly doubling the center's space to 500,000 square feet. Yet, he contended, "Our greatest current marketing problem is our inability to attract events in the winter due to not being connected to hotels, shopping, etc." Laying out a corollary need to improve the Kiel Auditorium, Sommer proceeded to give the mayor "A Civic Center Proposal." "We must attract much more business in the next several years or the upcoming new hotel rooms will remain vacant," Sommer contended, repeating a theme long voiced by the mayor and his staff. But in arguing that the city and the mayor needed to "lay the ground work for the start of the 21st century," the center director called for a "different use" for the existing Cervantes Convention Center and the development of an entirely new convention center in a different location—"connecting Kiel Auditorium to St. Louis [Union] Station/Omni Hotel"—allowing "another possible 500,000 square feet for future development."

In short, Sommer was calling for a return to the site that ERA had backed 17 years earlier, and for many of the same reasons. Sommer wrote, "the existing center does not have room for expansion," and it was surrounded by office and residential developments "which do not compliment [sic] a convention center." In contrast, the Union Station site with the Kiel Auditorium "has the potential of becoming a center far more attractive, though not necessarily larger, than any in the world," a project "potentially very beneficial to the entire region and certainly exciting enough to create the required interest to get the job done." Sommer's memo went on to assess the broader political context of the city and convention center expansion. The timing, he wrote, "is as good or better than it will ever be." The civic center concept could have a major impact on development in the surrounding area. And ultimately, "the combination of the [Union] Station and hotel with a major exhibition center with large useable outdoor space and a potentially nationally famous opera house, a major auditorium and ample parking . . . make this a world-class development . . . [that] could be put together in a way that all major interests benefit." Bruce Sommer also argued that he could be of "great assistance" in a campaign for the project and the required tax increases, and that help from "John Ferrara and Kim Tucci [co-owners of The Pasta House chain] should be a natural for this concept."

Eight years after the opening of the Cervantes Center, its director was portraying a poorly built, inefficient, and ultimately quite limited facility. The pressure to build something on the north side and the fiscal constraints faced by the city had yielded far less of an economic generator than any of its analysts or proponents had anticipated. Sommer was proposing to wipe the slate clean with a scheme that looked back to Arthur Schwarz's 1966 plan for a "Union Station Convention Center."

There is no evidence of a formal response from Mayor Schoemehl to Sommer's memo and his grand "Civic Center" scheme. A few weeks later, the mayor would dismiss the Union Station site in an exchange with an aide, saying work should start on a study of "An expansion of the Convention Center free standing of a stadium."[120]

By the end of March, Sommer's "need" for more convention center space was the focus of a press conference and abundant coverage in the local press about how what had once been the nation's tenth largest convention center had fallen to the middle of the pack. Sommer called on other city officials to finance a further consultant study of expansion need and cost, once again contracting with Laventhol & Horwath. Lest anyone question how Laventhol could reasonably assess center expansion just months after saying there was no need for added space, the firm addressed a letter to Bruce Sommer, signed by consultant Charles H. Johnson IV, who would go on to a series of other consulting firms and eventually head his own eponymous convention center consultancy.[121]

Charlie Johnson's March 25, 1985, letter expressed his surprise "to hear that our study has been interpreted as saying that an expansion for Cervantes is not warranted." Johnson stated. "Increasingly, St. Louis and Cervantes Convention Center are being talked about as being a favorable convention destination," and "Additional space would give you a competitive advantage, plus the ability to host multiple events." Johnson's letter made clear that the latest analysis would provide a favorable picture of St. Louis's potential and the need for expansion. Bruce Sommer, budget director Stephen Mullin, and Mayor Schoemehl did not want a real market study at this point. They sought a justification for a project that they had long embraced and promoted. Apparently, the Laventhol firm was willing to deliver.[122]

On the same day in early April as Sommer sought mayoral approval to fund the Laventhol & Horwath contract, the mayor's office also presented a proposed contract with Public Financial Management (PFM) to assess the city's capital finance resources. When PFM's David Paul met with Mullin the following month, the subject was rather more specific—"the financing of the proposed convention center expansion, and the financing of a new downtown stadium." Paul set out a set of fiscal alternatives for St. Louis in "pursuing an expansion of the Cervantes Convention Center . . . [due] to the inability of the existing facility . . . to compete for the type of conventions that the City feels it should be able to attract." The expansion deal was effectively done. The remaining questions involved financing and design, and the potential for economic impact and local revenue generation (to be documented by Laventhol) that might be used to pay for the expansion.[123]

A Place for Football

The city's NFL team, the Cardinals, had shared downtown Busch Stadium with the baseball Cardinals since 1966. By early 1985, football team owner Bill Bidwell was making clear his dissatisfaction with the size of the stadium and his position as tenant. The February 9 *New York Times* carried the story that Bidwell and the Cardinals were being courted by New York City officials, who were looking for a team to replace the Jets in Shea Stadium.[124]

It was at just that time that Vincent Schoemehl began to talk about the need for a new football stadium in St. Louis. In a February 5, 1985, memo to mayoral chief of staff Tom Mangogna, Schoemehl started out with, "As we pursue the idea of developing a new stadium for the football Cardinals," and sought a variety of information on stadium projects and financing in other cities. Just as groundwork for the convention center expansion was beginning, Schoemehl added a new stadium to the mix. For a time, the stadium and convention center efforts operated on parallel but distinct tracks, involving very different pressures, financing alternatives, and politics. But questions of location and public investment were necessarily intertwined, particularly as the leadership of the business community and Civic Progress made it clear they did not want to lose the city's NFL team. And there was the possibility of combining a new domed stadium with the existing convention center, yielding an even grander facility.[125]

"A lot has happened on this matter in the past two weeks and, quite frankly, I'm confused myself as to exactly what is going on," wrote Schoemehl to new development director Deb Patterson, in an April 22, 1985, memo headed "New Stadium." The mayor laid out a two-week history of meetings on the stadium issue, focused on exchanges with the city's business leaders.

On Thursday, April 4, Schoemehl reported, "I showed the concept plan of the Convention Center stadium to Brice Smith and Fred Kummer in separate meetings." Brice Smith had directed the planning and development of Convention Plaza and was now the chief executive of Sverdrup & Parcel, while Fred Kummer was the developer of the Adam's Mark hotel, the 911-room hostelry that would serve as the city's convention headquarters hotel after opening in 1986. "Both reacted favorably" to the convention center/stadium plan, the mayor reported, and the mayor continued to meet with Kummer, executives of Anheuser-Busch, Civic Progress head Charles Knight, the Cardinals' Bidwell, and Bidwell's attorney.[126]

The mayor's list of breakfast, lunch, and dinner meetings on the football stadium issue demonstrated the focus of the city's business leadership on keeping the Cardinals. Schoemehl averred that the "facts support the construction of any new stadium in downtown," rather than in suburban St. Louis County. But, for Patterson, "we still have need to seriously study an expansion of the Convention Center with or without a stadium." As Anheuser-Busch was preparing its own study of a stadium alone, Schoemehl proposed a series of city studies, covering a convention center alone, one paired with a stadium, or a stadium by itself.

In laying out the direction of the convention center expansion study to be undertaken by the Laventhol firm, the mayor directly addressed the location issue raised by Bruce Sommer and his call for a new "Civic Center." Schoemehl wrote, the study "should center on expansion of the current facility *because the Union Station location will simply arouse too much political opposition*" (italics mine).[127]

An expanded facility at Union Station made sense to Sommer as a convention venue, adjacent to the new retail development and hotel and with room for future expansion, much the same logic set out by Mayor Cervantes some twenty years before. The central problem was the mayor's perception of "political opposition." That opposition could not involve his re-election prospects, as Schoemehl had just been re-elected to a new four-year term. In view of his round-robin set of meetings with business leaders over the previous two weeks, it appears most likely that the source of "political opposition" lay with just those leaders.

Opposition to a move from the north side of downtown would come from some obvious sources. Robert C. West, president and chair of the Sverdrup firm, had served as a member of Civic Progress since the 1970s. He and the firm had an obvious interest in maintaining the current convention center site and expanding there. West had been replaced as chairman of Sverdrup by Brice Smith, who had played the central role in developing Convention Plaza in the late 1960s. Brice Smith formally joined Civic Progress in January 1986. Fred Kummer, with a major convention-oriented hotel under construction, was unlikely to view favorably the prospect of a shift to a site blocks away from his property. The leadership of Civic Progress, critical to the development of the Cervantes Center itself and vital to the mayor, still included the proponents of the original center, notably Donald Lasater and Bernard Edison, among its members. Clarence "Cedge" Barksdale of Centerre Bancorporation had played a crucial role in providing the financing for the Sverdrup-developed Sheraton Hotel in 1975. Any or all of these business leaders would be in a position to oppose abandoning the existing north side convention facility, and to ensure the vocal opposition of Civic Progress. Just as a unified business leadership had blocked Mayor Cervantes's plans for Union Station, much the same business leadership two decades later was capable of deterring any shift in the convention center's location. If St. Louis were to get a bigger center, it would have to be where Leif Sverdrup, Donald Lasater, and their Civic Progress colleagues had insisted that it be—on the north side of downtown.[128]

The stadium represented a quite distinct effort from the center expansion at that point. Anheuser-Busch had initiated its own elaborate analysis of county or city sites and development costs in early 1985. The results, made public in July, showed that any stadium, downtown or suburban, would inevitably require substantial public funding. But the Anheuser-Busch study had focused only on a downtown site adjacent to the existing Busch Stadium, quite separate from the convention center.[129]

The Laventhol & Horwath convention center study proceeded during the fall of 1985, with a work session including the consultants and St. Louis city staff in early October. The L&H preliminary report highlighted the fact that the center "has not been able to attract a competitive level of larger, high impact tradeshows and conventions." But instead of focusing on failings of the building or its management, the center's weak performance was attributed to "increased competition" and events "outgrowing space capacity at Cervantes." The consultants contended, "St. Louis is a more attractive destination than it was only two years ago," and forecast that by 1995 the existing building could host 25 to 27 major conventions and tradeshows with attendance of 353,600, an increase of almost 200,000. A modest addition of 120,000 square feet would provide for more events, and boost total convention attendance to

485,100. And a final option, doubling the center's exhibit space to 480,000 square feet, would place St. Louis among the ten largest centers in the nation and would generate a total of 531,300 annual convention delegates, "more than tripling the City's current level of convention and tradeshow delegates." Each of those delegates (and spouses and family members) "will stay in St. Louis for 4.5 days," yielding the city more than $300 million in annual spending.[130]

The expanded convention center would, of course, not succeed in tripling business after an expansion to some 500,000 square feet of exhibit space in the mid-1990s. It would not succeed in even doubling its level of business circa 1984. The city's "America's Center" complex would draw 201,100 convention and tradeshow attendees in 2000 and 208,400 for 2001. The expanded center was thus performing only slightly better than it had when Laventhol & Horwath conducted their analysis fifteen years before.

In 1985, the predicted tripling of the convention center's business was a notably appealing prospect for Schoemehl, Sommer, Mullin, and those around the mayor. The final Laventhol & Horwath report, dated November 1985, argued that St. Louis needed to keep up with a constantly growing industry. The consultants stated, "We expect the convention and tradeshow market to expand at a rate of three to four percent annually in terms of events, average event attendance to grow at four to six percent, and exhibit space needs to expand at four to six percent." The study then repeated the earlier forecasts and went on to offer a buoyant vision of the city's convention future.[131]

St. Louis was described as in "an ideal position to capitalize on the expansion of the convention and tradeshow market," in a "unique position to complement" ongoing revitalization. The Laventhol consultants promised that "expansion of the Convention Center could serve as a cornerstone project for development of a master plan for the downtown area" and that expansion would "have a net positive fiscal impact."[132]

These upbeat conclusions came as the mayor was seeking to build on the apparent successes of new development in the city and to project a larger national image for himself and the city. In February 1985, the *New York Times* had headlined an article touting the new Union Station and St. Louis Centre mall projects, "Rebound from Long Decline Seen in St. Louis." At the end of the year, *Fortune* magazine would chime in with "How St. Louis Turned Less into More," describing "new commercial megaprojects."[133]

Mayoral counselor Frank Hamsher laid out such a plan in a September 5 memo to Schoemehl—"I wholly agree that we need to build on the momentum of the spectaculars at St. Louis Centre and Union Station during the fall . . . we need to reinforce community perception that things like this are a launching pad for the city and community . . . . Success breeds success, and we need to take advantage of that." Hamsher's missive also warned the mayor about some "sizeable potential pitfalls." Noting the flood of new hotel rooms about to open and that media "will inevitably carry stories about low occupancy and problems of hotels" during the winter, he advised, "It would be desirable to find some ways to be ahead of the curve on this issue, so that it does not play as a major revelation when that happens."[134]

Schoemehl pressed his staff to move ahead on the center expansion (independent of the possible stadium) on January 20, 1986, telling Tom Mangogna, "I think we should prepare to announce our intended expansion of the Convention Center, for a variety of reasons, as soon as possible . . . . I'd like to aim for Friday, January 30." Schoemehl's memo laid out the basics of developing the project, with a refinancing of the existing center debt, use of a nonprofit commission to handle both the center and the Kiel Auditorium, and a committee "to determine the best way to pay for it and suggest final design." The mayor set out 11 potential committee members, including banker and Civic Progress mainstay Don Lasater, hotelier Fred Kummer, restaurant owners (and expansion promoters) John Ferrara and Vince Bommarito, Ed Ruesing of Downtown St. Louis, and mayoral staffers Steve Mullin and Deb Patterson.[135]

The mayor's decision to move ahead on just the center expansion neatly (if temporarily) separated the question of more convention center space from the contentious debate over whether and where a new football stadium should go. The final eight-member Revenue Committee he created was neatly stacked, with the general managers of the Adam's Mark and Marriott hotels, a representative of the Union Station developer, Ed Ruesing of Downtown St. Louis, Mullin, and Bommarito, in a fashion that assured support of the hotel and restaurant tax scheme needed to pay the center project.

The mayor's move—and his public announcement of the expansion effort on February 7—may also have been shaped by the progress of the county government's plans for its own domed stadium at a suburban site. Donald Brandin, the CEO of Boatmen's Bank then serving as president of Civic Progress, informed the group that he had met with county executive Gene McNary on the preceding Friday. Brandin "conveyed the sense of the [Civic Progress] Executive Committee . . . concerning the need for public disclosure."

McNary promised to "put enough together to report to Civic Progress." But for the business organization, the conflict between city and county plans and sites generated an internal division.[136]

A great many Civic Progress members, most notably August Busch III of Anheuser-Busch, favored a downtown site for any new stadium. But the county's preferred site had been purchased from Sverdrup Corporation and was adjacent to the firm's "Riverport" planned development. Robert West and Brice Smith of Sverdrup had an obvious interest in a domed stadium as part of their suburban scheme. Much as the Cervantes Convention Center had served as anchor and "magnet" for the larger Convention Plaza, a new stadium would spur new development opportunities and help fill the adjacent Sverdrup-developed Holiday Inn. The split between Sverdrup and the downtown-oriented Civic Progress members left the organization divided, and the group concluded it was "premature" in early 1986 to take a stand on the stadium issue.

Schoemehl, by pressing ahead with an expansion of the Cervantes Center, would in turn make it much more difficult for a domed stadium in the county to compete for events beyond football games and thereby make it less likely to happen. That calculus was, no doubt, among the mayor's "variety of reasons" for moving quickly.

The revenue committee's recommendation, delivered at the end of April, proposed an increase of 1 percent in the city's restaurant tax and a $2.00 per night hotel occupancy fee. In addition, use of the city's existing amusement or ticket tax was suggested, yielding a total of $7.4 million in annual revenue. The endorsement by leading hotel managers and restaurant owner Bommarito provided some assurance of the backing of affected interests, along with the promise that the center expansion "will create thousands of new jobs and generate millions of dollars in new City revenues."[137]

While the finance effort was focused solely on an expansion of the convention center, the possibility of combining the expansion with an adjacent domed stadium began to emerge in the spring of 1986. Civic Progress provided an opening when it put out a press release in April, indicating that 21 of the 25 members had "serious reservations about the economic feasibility" of a stadium in suburban St. Louis County. The group's majority expressed concern about the "effect the project might have on downtown St. Louis" and the need for more public funding.[138]

For an organization with a history of mutual deference and decision-making by consensus, the public release of a poll indicating a lack of business unanimity was unusual, perhaps unprecedented. It perhaps was intended as a cue to Schoemehl and county executive McNary that there was substantial business support for a downtown stadium, and that the city should move to prepare its own proposal.

In late April or early May, as Schoemehl would later acknowledge, he was "urged by local business leaders to reevaluate the possibility of developing a new domed stadium as part of the expansion of the Cervantes Convention Center in the downtown area." A *domed stadium* changed the game for the mayor, Civic Progress, and the county. A city dome plan would effectively preempt a county effort. Built next to the Cervantes Center, it could create a larger convention center. A dome might also be paid for, in part or whole, by private dollars raised from the local business community. Here, support from individual Civic Progress companies and particularly Anheuser-Busch was key.[139]

The Civic Progress leaders were adamant about keeping major league sports in St. Louis. Discussing the city's National Hockey League team, the Blues, a few months later, Donald Brandin would report to his colleagues that the Civic Progress executive committee had concluded, "keeping St. Louis Hockey Blues in St. Louis was essential to the success of any future efforts to strengthen this area's position as a center for major league sports." Brandin noted, "it would take about $2 million from those Civic Progress companies . . . to complete the purchase of the Blues." The loss of an NHL team would, in the eyes of the mayor and business leadership, weaken the capacity of the city to retain the football Cardinals.[140]

Schoemehl's handwritten notes that appear to be from early May 1986 suggest the variety of elements vital to making a dome proposal actually work, and how those intersected with the various local venues. The notes begin with a section on "Stadium" and indicate the need to have Laventhol & Horwath "re-examine the whole dome concept—will a dome work in concert with the Convention Center?" A marginal note says, "proposal is on its way." The mayor then wrote "Civic Progress" and posed a series of questions:

> What role are they willing to play? How public?
> Will they spend money on a study?
> Where is August Busch?
> Is private ownership possible? Partial?

Schoemehl then noted with respect to the "City," "we should continue on the track we're on with the Convention Center transfer [to the Land Clearance

Authority]. . . . Tax election put off 'til November." The notes go on to pose a series of questions about [Blues owner] Harry Ornest, the Blues, and the Arena and to ask, "Is there room in the market for the Dome, the Arena and the Kiel [Auditorium]?"[141]

The Laventhol & Horwath proposal the mayor sought arrived, dated May 9, and outlined a study "regarding a proposed domed football stadium adjacent and attached to Cervantes Convention Center . . . included as part of the planned 240,000 square foot expansion of the center." Consultants David C. Petersen and Charles H. Johnson (who had both been involved in the two earlier Laventhol studies) assured the mayor's staff that they had recently examined domed stadium options for other cities, describing the "potential *net benefit* to the team and the public sector (county and state) from enclosing the stadium and using it for other public assembly activities."

A dome opened up the possibility for major events in the city (more importantly, downtown), while providing added exhibit space beyond what the city could finance on its own. A statement of the mayor's interest came just three days later with a memo to chief of staff Al Fulvio, titled "Dome Development."

Writing on May 12, 1986, Schoemehl said, "The possibility of developing a dome should be view skeptically, right now. There has been little thought on anyone's part as to how or why we should do this project but there is growing interest. You should know that I'd like to see us do it if it's possible but we must approach it carefully." The mayor's concern obviously focused on the combination of construction cost and needed operating subsidy, asking Fulvio to get a "rough financial picture." He went on, "This exercise will give us some order of magnitude answers so we can begin talking seriously with the Civic Progress guys about how they can either help plug the gap or help reduce up-front capital needs (through box purchases, preferred seating, etc)."[142]

Civic Progress would have a critical role in the development of any domed stadium downtown. Beyond the need to halt the competing county effort, the city could not manage the stadium financing on its own. But the business leadership could reshape the situation in two ways. First, much as Anheuser-Busch had arranged private financing for Busch Stadium 25 years earlier, the Civic Progress companies could assist Bidwell and the Cardinals in limiting the cost to the team. Second, if there was to be substantial public financing (or full public development) of a stadium, the clout of Civic Progress would be crucial to gaining both political support and dollars from suburban governments or the state.

Making the possibility of a domed stadium public on May 12, Schoemehl put out a press release announcing that he was holding a series of meetings with aldermen, business, and community leaders "to see whether there is a consensus that the City should further explore the possibilities of building a domed stadium." He described the stadium concept as a 70,000-seat venue forming the eastern end of the expanded convention center, and promised that the scheme would only be pursued "if there is general agreement among City and community leaders," as well as receiving "some form of voter approval"—"The residents of St. Louis will ultimately decide whether we should construct a new stadium."[143]

With the Laventhol study under way and a preliminary effort to assess cost and business commitment, the mayor's staff continued to plan for a November vote on just the convention center expansion. But the schedule for a November vote on tax increases to finance the expansion was deferred. The July draft report from Laventhol opened a far grander vision of St. Louis's potential.

The consultants laid out a scheme for a 72,000-seat football stadium joined to the convention center, one that could also offer an arena configuration. With the stadium floor used for exhibit space, Laventhol contended the facility would "become the fourth largest convention hall in the country," providing a total of 580,000 square feet of exhibit space. This grand new venue would potentially draw some 1.8 million attendees for sports (football and hockey), concerts, and family events, adding an additional 49,700 annual convention delegates "associated with the larger shows which could not have been accommodated in the original expansion." That would boost the center's convention and tradeshow attendance from 157,800 in 1985 by some 3.7 times, to a total of 581,000.[144]

Laventhol & Horwath provided one other potential boon—the combined convention center/stadium could attract the Super Bowl to St. Louis "once every 10 to 15 years," and the NCAA Final Four "once every 8 years."

The possibility of 50,000 more convention attendees every year could both boost the appeal of the combined venue to local hotel and restaurant owners and help sell the stadium as an economic generator well beyond the small number of NFL games each year. But for a mayor and business leadership seriously concerned about national image and civic momentum, the prospect of major sporting events was a vital selling point. The consultants concluded, "The non-resident fiscal benefits generated by the Cervantes Convention Center and the stadium/arena are substantial, and could also be a source of funding for facility operations and construction. The extent of fiscal participation would depend upon cooperation between the respective municipalities."

Laventhol & Horwath thus portrayed the combined convention center and stadium as a huge fiscal boon for city, suburbs, and state. With an estimated $180 million construction cost, the stadium simply could not be managed by the city alone. The debt service and annual operating losses, in excess of $3 million, would require some sort of larger intergovernmental solution. But Schoemehl now had figures for "net new economic impact" that supported the involvement of other governments. And the appeal of "fourth largest" was enormous, particularly for the Civic Progress leadership.[145]

The Civic Progress corporate chiefs had long been focused on major league sports as a measure of the community and region's status and attractiveness. As 1986 ended, Civic Progress president Donald Brandin, CEO of Boatmen's Bank, reported to his colleagues on the hockey Blues, arguing, "The issue, in my opinion, was not simply that of keeping a sports team in St. Louis—it was whether we, as community leaders, were sufficiently committed to the continued development of the St. Louis region as one of the major metropolitan complexes in the United States to take the initiative to retain such an important activity."[146]

Brandin then went on to lay out a parallel logic in dealing with the football Cardinals and the stadium issue: "For essentially the same reasons, I believe we must make a decision in the near future as to whether we will support a major new or expanded sports-convention complex. This has been a divisive issue that has jeopardized City-County relationships, may result in the loss of the Cardinals, and threatens to block progress on other major issues requiring cooperation between the two political entities." He also reminded his colleagues of St. Louis's failed effort to bring the 1988 Republican national convention to the city, doomed "apparently because of shortcomings in the Arena as compared with more modern convention hall facilities in the two finalist cities, Kansas City and New Orleans."

For Civic Progress and thus for Schoemehl, keeping the Cardinals and Blues in St. Louis, having a competitive, modern convention hall, and demonstrating a commitment to the region's development all came together in the imperative to build a domed stadium downtown.

Vince Schoemehl offered Donald Brandin a route to a new stadium in a five-page memo dated December 2, 1986, outlining "how our people propose we pursue the goal of building the proposed stadium in connection with

Cervantes Convention Center." Schoemehl proposed to reconstitute the existing Regional Convention and Visitors Commission to enable it to own and operate the existing convention center, the Blues Arena, and a new stadium. To appease the county, the commission would be comprised of an equal number of members appointed by the mayor and the county executive, and a chair appointed by the governor. The mayor's plan put the construction cost of the convention center expansion at $59 million, with another $125 million for the stadium portion. With those estimates, he argued, the project could be paid for with a hotel fee and restaurant tax in the city, a county hotel tax, and some $6.5 million in annual state hotel sales taxes.[147]

The city would effectively be shifting much of the fiscal burden to suburban St. Louis County and the state, a move Schoemehl justified with the Laventhol finding that the state government would gain some $140 million in annual sales activity and $25 million in new state revenues, presumably more than justifying the state's investment. "I'm not suggesting the sale will be easy," Schoemehl argued, but "with the right support I believe it's possible."

But if the mayor was optimistic about selling the scheme to the governor and the legislature, county executive "McNary will be another story!" Describing the suburban official as "angry and resistant," Schoemehl concluded, "Gene is becoming increasingly isolated on this issue and will soon have to choose between 'a way out' or simply oppose everyone else in the community." The mayor then laid out three options: "(A) give up, (B) go around him, or, (C) run over him."

Schoemehl's stadium plan depended upon "three key groups," in his view: business leadership, organized labor, and the hotel industry. He concluded that he could gain the support of the hotel owners, and that Fred Kummer of the Adam's Mark "is highly enthusiastic." Labor too would be "enthusiastic supporters," vital to gaining the support of critical legislators. As for the business community, its support "and especially Civic Progress will be essential . . . most importantly from a leadership role. If this approach is to work it must be aggressively adopted by Civic Progress and tailored to meet their needs in order to become their plan." In Schoemehl's view, "It's clear that the Governor, McNary, and the General Assembly are not going to adopt 'Schoemehl's Plan' and if this gets known as such it's done for." He then concluded, "I have taken this thing as far as I can take it. If it's going to go anywhere from here, Don, Civic Progress is going to have to take the lead. I can be an effective supporter of this but someone else has got to take the lead. I hope it can be you."

The missive to Brandin neatly stated the larger political situation and assumptions behind the stadium/convention center quest. Schoemehl was wrong about the stadium's cost—it would be more than twice the $125 million that he estimated—and the political difficulties. But the central elements of his proposal, shifting the project's financing to the county and state and working out a power- and governance-sharing arrangement, would define the ultimate form of the project. Yet for the deal to work, it had to gain far broader backing, notably from those involved in paying for it, such as the restaurants and hotels. It also required the full backing and embrace of Civic Progress to garner the support of the governor, the legislature, and the St. Louis County executive and to have the imprimatur of being in the public interest of the region.

The stadium itself could yield only limited economic impact from convention business. Yet by joining the domed stadium to the expansion project, Schoemehl and the stadium backers could sell the notion of added visitor spending, no matter how small and unpredictable it might be.

The larger logic of the stadium project was set out by budget director Steve Mullin in a "CONFIDENTIAL" memo to the mayor three days later. Mullin, trained at the graduate level in economics and public finance at the University of Pennsylvania's Wharton School and intimately familiar with the city's budgetary problems, might well have raised questions about the benefits from the massive public investment a stadium would require. Instead, noting that he had read the memo to Brandin and concluded the "project and concept are excellent," his message was that "I am in full support of the full [Cervantes Convention Center] expansion and the sports facility project, even if the City has to cover a greater portion of the cost."[148]

Mullin's assessment of the stadium plan recognized "the criticism based on 'it's not worth it logic' and I'm well-versed in the normative economics of optimal public finance. But my problem is that I am familiar with the City budget, and therefore don't take too seriously all talk about whether expenses are 'worth it'!" Mullin argued,

> I think there are *tremendous* advantages:
>
> (1)The project, as planned is an exciting world-class building project. We don't often get this type of opportunity to make an international impact, like the Astrodome.
>
> (2)We don't have many (any?) spectacular items on the drawing

boards to continue the city's incredible momentum. We don't want a pause to [look] like a let-down.

(3)This project could be a slingshot for further development and movement into the 1990s.

(4)Foreign investors, industry, etc. are interested in this project, opening a whole new source of potential development funding and job creation.

(5)It solidifies the *Regional metropolitan*-wide effort to promote tourism, conventions and entertainment. Once this is done, we *should* be able to start distributing pieces *throughout the Metropolitan area*, with the *base* downtown.

(6)It could help efforts to locate a race track in St. Louis County rather than farther away. I *still* believe we should push to help this effort.

(7)It would help to get an NBA franchise.

(8)etc. etc.

The rhetoric of Mullin's analysis is striking in retrospect. While some of the hyperbole may reflect a desire to support and please the mayor about a plan that he had already committed to, Mullin specifically avoided any assessment of the actual performance, fiscal or economic, of a potential new dome and center expansion. His enthusiasm was cast in language remarkably parallel to that employed by Leif Sverdrup and the Civic Progress leadership 25 years earlier in supporting the construction of Busch Stadium, the Disney riverfront project, and the Spanish Pavilion. All of the references were to image ("world class" and "international impact"), the sense of civic movement and momentum that Schoemehl had earlier linked to Union Station and St. Louis Centre, and the future opportunities for private investment and development. Nowhere was there any portrayal of the competition for national convention business, an attempt to validate the Laventhol forecasts, or an assessment of St. Louis's competitive position. It appeared more than enough to seek "incredible momentum" at a public cost of more than $200 million.

Mayor Schoemehl's joint city/county/state stadium proposal was unveiled in a *Post-Dispatch* article on December 19, 1986. But the article quickly noted the opposition of St. Louis County executive Gene McNary, who called the scheme "foolish" as well as impractical. And when the mayor's staff met a few days later to review the "Status of Project," the "financing alternatives" were the paramount concern. Without financial participation by *both* suburban St. Louis County and the state government, the stadium project wasn't viable. A simple, and far less expensive, expansion of the Cervantes Convention Center was rather different: the city presumably could go it alone.[149]

The overt conflict between Schoemehl and McNary also posed a political problem for Civic Progress. Both were ex officio members of the group, and a battle between city and county governments threatened a host of Civic Progress initiatives, including improved air service at Lambert Airport, the development of a new light rail transit system, and the attraction of new firms. Addressing the Civic Progress members at the January 1987 monthly meeting, president Donald Brandin stated, "if St. Louis is to continue as a major city, we should be prepared to support the construction of *a new or expanded convention center/sports complex*." However, he went on, "the whole thing is complicated at this time and should be allowed to calm down before a decision is reached."[150]

Brandin and Civic Progress embraced the notion of a joint sports and convention facility, and believed that a new stadium/convention center was vital to St. Louis's future as a "major city." But Cardinals' owner Bidwell was a political liability—the following month he announced he would ban beer sales at any new stadium, in an obvious slap at Anheuser-Busch. And the conflict between city and county made a plan for a downtown stadium difficult to manage. So as Civic Progress chose to wait and allow the issue to "calm down," Mayor Schoemehl considered having the city move ahead on its own.[151]

Schoemehl decided in early March to put the downtown stadium project on hold. At about the same time, Cardinals' owner Bidwell announced he would focus on moving the football team to the planned Riverport stadium in suburban St. Louis County, the location backed by McNary.

With an apparent stalemate on the stadium plans in the spring of 1987 and estimates that showed the city could manage to pay for just a center expansion by itself, Schoemehl began to focus on a purely city effort, pressed by staff arguments that "The need to make a convention center expansion decision is becoming increasingly important. " The real question came down to what the city's voters might be induced to support, and the mayor commissioned a survey by the Prell Organization in May 1987 "to assess the chances of passing a ballot issue in the Fall of 1987 concerning either the stadium or the convention center."[152]

Prell's report on the survey results showed that 46 percent of voters viewed the current center as "large enough to attract major conventions." The report concluded, "no matter how painless a tax is proposed, it may face some difficulty if the appropriate groundwork (showing a need for the project) is not laid first." The most plausible tax mechanism for the surveyed voters was some combination of hotel and restaurant taxes. But on the issue of a new stadium, the sentiment was clearly against—"There is little perceived need for a new indoor sports stadium at the moment. . . . By a 3:1 margin, the voters reject this idea."[153]

The survey results effectively resolved the immediate prospects for a downtown stadium, and Schoemehl decided in June to press solely for an expansion of the convention center, financed with hotel and restaurant taxes. The mayor held a press conference in late June, describing the lack of voter support for a stadium and announcing a push for solely an expansion of the Cervantes Center. The *Post-Dispatch* editorial, headlined "Onward with the Convention Center," the following day endorsed the mayor's plan with the argument that more convention center space was "essential to the vitality of the downtown, and hence the area."[154]

Mayor Schoemehl elaborated on his decision a few days later, in a widely distributed letter to his supporters. Reiterating the survey results, the mayor argued that while a "consensus about building a sports complex" might develop over a few years, "the convention industry in the St. Louis area must get on with its business." Arguing that the proposed taxes for the expansion represent "the limits of investment that can reasonably be expected to be borne by the hotel and restaurant industry at this time," he called on the state government to contribute to any further expansion.[155]

The mayor's staff immediately began the process of lining up a schedule and political support, looking to a vote on the November ballot. The financing arrangement was structured to have the bonds issued by the Land Clearance Authority, rather than the city itself. That would avoid the need for a two-thirds majority required (as had been the case with the original center bonds) and just require a simple majority for the hotel and restaurant tax increases.

But a June 29 memo from Bruce Sommer also acknowledged that the projected costs of the expansion were growing, as center plans were still evolving. By the time the expansion bonds were sold in 1988, the amount was up from about \$59 million to \$78 million. When the expansion actually opened in May 1993, the total cost had reached \$128 million. But in late June 1987, the immediate focus was on the need to sell the project and the required taxes to the Board of Aldermen and ultimately the city's voters.[156]

Nancy Rice, Schoemehl's political director, joined with Harry Wilson of Fleishman-Hillard (who also served as the secretary and principal staffer of Civic Progress) to "recommend we focus our campaign in July on the Board of Aldermen and use August to plan the public campaign to begin mid-September." "Harry and Nancy" were also at work "developing an initial list of potential industry campaign members."[157]

Harry Wilson's involvement brought the full public relations skills of Fleishman-Hillard to bear in selling the center expansion to St. Louis voters. The Fleishman firm began a series of focus groups with likely voters in August. These revealed that most voters "believe [the center] needs expansion and endorse the measure as necessary to keep St. Louis competitive with other convention cities." But, in a telling conclusion, "the campaign needs to recognize that voters north and south are at least beginning to be irritated by what they perceive as too much focus of City resources on the revitalization and further expansion of Downtown at the expense of the neighborhoods."[158]

Schoemehl then turned—as had most of his recent predecessors—to Civic Progress. On August 24, the mayor reviewed the campaign plans with the board of the Civic Progress Action Committee. Schoemehl told the group, a "voter education campaign to pass the two tax proposals . . . will cost $200,000 or slightly more." He asked Civic Progress for half that amount, with the balance to "come from the hotel and restaurant industry, organized labor, and other groups." And in a nod to the Sverdrup-owned Sheraton hotel, the mayor promised that "everyone involved in planning for the expansion understands the importance of not isolating the Sheraton from the rest of downtown." Civic Progress agreed to commit $100,000 for the campaign.[159]

The campaign emphasized the promise of thousands of new visitors and almost $200 million in new visitor spending, with Mayor Schoemehl contending, "we now have everything it takes to be a major convention city, we just don't have the (convention) space."[160]

The political calculus of seeking tax increases, with a simple majority vote requirement, rather than the two-thirds needed for a city bond issue, proved remarkably prescient. The hotel tax increase passed with a 60 percent "yes" vote. But the restaurant tax boost squeaked by with just a 337-vote majority. That was, however, enough public support to boost the taxes and (largely) support the bonds for what was supposed to secure St. Louis a place among the nation's top convention destinations.

On to a Stadium

The successful passage of the expansion taxes assured more space for the Cervantes Center. But the issue of an attached domed stadium was still unresolved at the end of 1987, as was the future of the Cardinals football team. In late October Bill Bidwell had announced plans to move from St. Louis, and had begun to flirt with city officials in Phoenix, Baltimore, and Columbus. In a last-ditch effort to keep the team in St. Louis, Governor John Ashcroft and Charles Knight, representing Civic Progress, made a final offer to Bidwell, including a new 70,000-seat domed stadium adjacent to the convention center (to be jointly financed by the city, county, and state) and a guarantee of $5 million a year in additional income to the team from Civic Progress companies. Despite the promises, Bidwell announced in mid-January 1988 that he was moving the team to Phoenix.[161]

The loss of the team was termed by an editorial in the *Post-Dispatch* as "a blow to the area's economy as well as its pride." If so, it was a blow the Civic Progress leaders were entirely unwilling to accept. The business leaders continued to press for state legislation creating a Regional Convention and Sports Complex Authority to finance construction of a domed stadium adjacent to the convention center, with the hope that passage could persuade the National Football League to intervene and halt the proposed move to Phoenix. When that gambit failed—the NFL owners voted 26-0 with two abstentions to approve Bidwell's move—Civic Progress remained unwilling to accept the loss of an NFL team. The organization continued to pursue the development of a new stadium as the necessary first step in securing a team.[162]

Charles Knight of Emerson Electric told his Civic Progress colleagues in late March, with the loss of the Cardinals inescapable, that he "had devoted a tremendous amount of effort, as a representative of Civic Progress, in trying to line up a professional football team franchise for St. Louis." Knight went on, "we do not have a football team and we do not have a consensus among our political leaders regarding the construction of a new stadium." Absent some form of agreement between the city and county, and a fiscal commitment from the state government, there was little likelihood of actually building a new stadium.[163]

Charles Knight told the group, "If St. Louis had a stadium, we could get an NFL team. Built as part of the Cervantes Convention Center, a new domed stadium would give St. Louis the fourth largest convention center in the United States. Additional convention business would bring more new money to St. Louis than the revenues from professional football. However, St. Louis will not be perceived as a big league city until it has a modern football stadium and an NFL team."

Civic Progress was fully committed to keeping St. Louis an NFL city. The group was equally committed to seeing a new stadium downtown, built and operated as a part of a larger convention complex. So too was Vince Schoemehl. But for County Executive McNary, the prospect of a downtown stadium offered nothing to the suburban county, except as a bargaining chip. McNary continued to promote the idea of a less expensive, open air stadium at the suburban Riverport site. He addressed a letter to St. Louis leaders in May 1988, saying, "I find it amazing that the same Mayor who drove the football Cardinals to Phoenix can continue to undermine our efforts to move this community into the next century." And he continued his fight with Schoemehl in public, arguing in a June 1988 newspaper article, "Downtown is a very important part of St. Louis but not all of St. Louis."[164]

As McNary was promoting his stadium, Vince Schoemehl was moving ahead with the plans for the expanded Cervantes Convention Center. Denny Coleman, the city's economic development head, outlined the effort to Civic Progress in July, stressing (in language underlined in the meeting minutes), "The southern expansion provides additional room for a stadium, should one be built." But Coleman emphasized that the expanded center "should have a positive impact on Washington Avenue," where efforts to renew the old warehouses and industrial lofts had "slowed in recent months . . . . However, the announcement of plans to expand the center to the south has already created a renewed interest in investing in this area."[165]

Just as Leif Svedrup and the Civic Progress leadership had pressed for the north side site for the convention center originally, Coleman and Schoemehl considered its expansion as a crucial element in bolstering the renewal of the Washington Avenue corridor, and supporting the nearby St. Louis Centre mall as well.

Yet the larger commitment of the Civic Progress leaders was evident in a question from William Cornelius of Union Electric, asking about the possibility of an adjacent stadium. In response (again underlined), "Mayor Schoemehl said that if such a stadium is ever constructed it would make the St. Louis Convention Center the fourth largest facility in the nation. When present plans are implemented, it will be the 10th largest."

Neither Civic Progress nor Mayor Schoemehl was willing to abandon plans for a domed stadium attached to the convention center. For County

Executive McNary, the lack of a football tenant made any form of private stadium financing effectively impossible. Public financing meant that he had to secure approval from the state legislature to raise the county's hotel tax. There, the opposition of the Civic Progress business leaders could make all the difference.

Gene McNary admitted defeat at the January 23, 1989, Civic Progress meeting, and more publicly the following month. After bowing out of the stadium fight, McNary shortly bowed out of St. Louis, with a presidential appointment as commissioner of the Immigration and Naturalization Service, announced in May 1989.[166]

New state legislation for a regional sports facility authority, backed by city, county, and state financing, moved quickly through the legislature in the first months of 1989, greased by the inclusion of language providing state funding for a convention center expansion in Kansas City. But it ran into a political problem with Governor John Ashcroft. The governor took a dim view of the lack of a revenue source for the state debt and the argument that the stadium would generate a "net fiscal benefit," primarily by attracting larger conventions to St. Louis. Still, faced with what the *Post-Dispatch* would later term "intense lobbying from business and civic leaders from the state's three metropolitan areas. . . . some very important people wanted this, no matter what," Ashcroft signed the bill, providing state funds for half the cost of the new St. Louis stadium, in mid-July.[167]

The balance of the roughly $120 million cost for the new downtown dome was to be divided evenly between the city and county governments. With the departure of Gene McNary, H. C. Milford was appointed county executive, and he quickly moved to reassure the Civic Progress leaders of his commitment to the downtown stadium, telling the group in November that the new football stadium was among his "first priorities."[168]

Milford's active support was vital to the stadium project, even with the commitment from the state. The county's one-quarter share of the project needed a new revenue source, and that hotel tax increase had to be approved by a majority of the county voters. Civic Progress made victory in the April 1990 tax vote a central priority, backing the campaign with a contribution of over $400,000. The result was a 65 to 35 percent success.

The *city government* chose a very different fiscal path from the county's. Schoemehl had already succeeded—barely—in boosting hotel and restaurant taxes to pay for the expansion of the Cervantes Center. Local hoteliers and restaurateurs were notably cool to the idea of more taxes. In advance of the county tax vote, the lawyer for the local hotel association sought some assurance about the city's hotel tax. Chief of staff Milton Svetanics wrote a memo to Schoemehl in December 1989, outlining the association's concerns and his response that "our position had not changed. . . . We expect the new fiscal benefit to be sufficient to meet the needs of the bonds. . . . We do not intend to seek a hotel tax, since we don't think we'll need it."[169]

City comptroller Virvus Jones pressed Schoemehl to commit to a new or increased tax for the stadium bonds, a conflict that played out in public through 1991 and into 1992. But, faced with continuing opposition from hotel and restaurant owners, city officials ultimately chose to avoid the voters and assume that the "fiscal benefit" from the stadium and convention center would suffice to repay the bonds.[170]

The expanded Cervantes Convention Center opened for business in May 1993. Center director Bruce Sommer boasted, "we can now go after bigger groups. . . . But the more important reason for the expansion was to allow us to have simultaneous, mid-sized shows." And the general manager of the St. Louis Centre mall just to the south said, "We're expecting a 15 to 20 percent increase in traffic . . . and a large increase in business."[171]

The expanded center was joined by the new stadium, dubbed the Trans World Dome, in November 1995; the full complex offered a total of 502,000 square feet of exhibit space. In 1988, Mayor Schoemehl had told Civic Progress that the total convention complex would place St. Louis fourth in the ranking of centers. Relying on the Laventhol consultants, he was wrong.

Over the decade it took Schoemehl to realize an expanded center, other cities had been planning and building their own new and expanded convention facilities. Laventhol consultants David Petersen and Charlie Johnson had gone on to other cities—San Diego, Atlanta, and Cincinnati for Petersen; Chicago, Charlotte, and Austin for Johnson—and recommended more convention center space there as well.

When the center/stadium fully opened in late 1995, Tradeshow Week ranked it twentieth among U.S. convention centers. That put it below such cities as Detroit, Dallas, and San Diego, and roughly equal to Kansas City, Houston, and Tulsa. Far from being in the lead as a major meeting destination, St.Louis was competing with a host of other cities. Indeed, the expanded convention complex yielded far fewer convention attendees than the Laventhol consultants had predicted.

There were other competitive problems as well. In 1989, another Laventhol study had argued that the expanded center required a major adjacent headquarters hotel with circa 1,100 rooms. But despite repeated efforts over almost a decade, the city could not find a private developer to invest in a hotel. Finally, in 1999, city officials came up with a financing scheme that involved pairing $98 million in federal Empowerment Zone bonds and other public funds with a small amount of private capital to turn two historic buildings into the new headquarters hotel.[172]

The new Renaissance Grand hotel opened in February 2003. But with the America's Center underperforming, the new hotel struggled (and usually failed) to earn an operating profit and pay its debts. In February 2009, the bondholders foreclosed on the hotel. Still, with the America's Center drawing even more poorly in the wake of the recession, the hotel managed an occupancy rate of just 52 percent in 2010, with an operating loss—before debt service—of $420,000.

Vince Schoemehl's vision of conventions as an economic engine boosting the city's overall economy and creating a flood of new jobs proved an abject failure. And many of the downtown projects that had pressed Schoemehl to fill their new hotel rooms and boost their business were proving failures as well. Fred Kummer's Adam's Mark hotel, originally supported by a federal Urban Development Action Grant and intended to be the city's convention headquarters hotel before the Renaissance, saw dropping occupancy after 2000 and was finally sold, cheaply, in early 2008. The St. Louis Centre mall, where managers had pinned their hopes on the prospect of new conventioneers, struggled through the 1990s as major national retailers left and vacancies grew, and was bought out of foreclosure in 2004 "for the bargain basement price of $5.4 million." Two years later, it was empty and was poised for rebuilding as apartments and a parking garage, and yet another hotel.[173]

Civic Progress had neatly succeeded in getting both the new stadium and the NFL football team (the Rams from Los Angeles) that it so wanted, along with other projects aimed at redeeming downtown. Whether those "successes" had indeed succeeded in keeping St. Louis—the city's population having fallen from 453,085 in 1980 to 319,294 in 2010—a "big league city" is open to question.

Plans, Places, and "Experts"

The convention center expansion was not the product of some broad gauge research or analysis, or a studied consideration of the city's economic development alternatives. Instead, it emerged, almost full blown, with Vince Schoemehl's election as mayor in 1981, and his promotion of tourism as a cornerstone of city policy. When in February 1985 he sought information on the market for a bigger center from Bruce Sommer, his purpose was to justify a policy position he had long embraced—"explaining why expansion of the Convention Center is necessary."

There was no pressure for more center space from Civic Progress, no evidence of the Downtown St. Louis, Inc. organization pressing for a bigger Cervantes Center. There was clear interest in expanding the city's tourism business from restaurant owners such as Vincent Bommarito and John Ferrara, and from at least one hotel owner, Fred Kummer. But the real policy initiative came from the mayor, much as it had with Cervantes and the Union Station plan in 1968.

Schoemehl's push for an expanded center was not based on any substantial market assessment. The Laventhol & Horwath consultants had specifically recommended *against* expansion in June 1984, saying the center "has excess capacity to accomodate [sic] additional conventions and trade shows." Under "Recommendations" the Laventhol comments stated,"1. Expansion is not recommended in the immediate future." There was no stirring case for a larger center, just the opposite.

When Mayor Schoemehl continued with an expansion effort and sought information supporting it, Bruce Sommer recommended a new location. Yet just as the mayor had pressed an expansion despite the recommendation of Laventhol and in the face of the obvious deficiencies of the Cervantes Center's site, there was no consideration of any alternative.

The north side site had been a singular victory for Leif Sverdrup and Civic Progress in the 1960s. There was simply no *political* alternative, despite the problems of the center's physical environment. Indeed, a May 1986 mayor's office outline of "AJCCC Expansion Team Plans" listing "Major Actors" included "Washington Avenue Redevelopment," residential developer Pantheon Corporation, Sverdrup & Parcel, Mercantile Bank, Laclede's Landing Redevelopment, St. Louis Centre, and developer Donn Lipton—all with properties or interests in the immediate vicinity of the center. With major new development plans near the Cervantes Center, sponsored by or linked to some of the city's major business and development interests, it was simply politically impossible to shift the convention center and its role as an anchor.[174]

For a mayor interested in major downtown projects—particularly projects that promised a boon in city revenue and development—the convention center expansion was a "natural." The center was owned by the city, and an expansion could be managed within city fiscal resources. Unlike the domed stadium project, which required substantial outside financial assistance and thus a far more complex political deal, the city could (and did) go it alone in search of more convention business.

Circa 1985, the promise of conventions appeared enormous. Bruce Sommer's February 1985 memo to Schoemehl argued the "bottom line on all that follows is that it holds more potential for you and the City than any other development decision you will make this second term. The potential benefits to the City in terms of jobs, tax revenues, and all the rest is awesome and could be one of the most exciting things this City has ever done."[175]

Sommer's vision was echoed and enlarged by budget director Mullin. Disdaining the potential cost of the expansion plus dome, Mullin promoted the "*tremendous* advantages" of a "world-class building project . . . [with] opportunity to make an international impact. . . . This project could be a slingshot for further development and movement into the 1990s."[176]

Mayor Schoemehl did not hear questions or demurrals, but stirring endorsements. In turn, he and his staff repeated the expectations of "advantages" and fiscal benefit. The city's 1988 presentation to the bond rating agencies and investment banks for the expansion bonds included the statement that the "City of St. Louis [is] *highly* committed to the convention and tourism business, and to this project—key to our economy; essential to [a] strong downtown."[177]

The vision of center expansion and stadium went beyond the promise of visitor activity and city revenue increases. Schoemehl and his development advisor Christopher Grace portrayed the expanded center as the new anchor of a significant new district in the downtown core. The *Post-Dispatch* reported in August 1989 that "Grace envisions a convention district attractive and interesting enough to put St. Louis in competition with New Orleans, San Francisco and San Antonio," with city plans for a "convention zone with four new hotels and stores and places of entertainment with one leg ending at Laclede's Landing and the other at St. Louis Centre to capture conventioneers' dollars now being spent in Clayton and the vicinity of the airport."[178]

Two years later, with the bonds for the new domed stadium approved, budget director JoAnne LaSala prepared a memo of "key points" for the mayor to make to the stadium bond banker. Among the "key points" the mayor was to stress: "We are committed to the tourism industry; this facility is a key part of our economic development plan. . . . The project is essential to keeping us competitive in this industry. . . . The project will generate substantial benefits, in excess of its costs; we knew it and proved it to ourselves with the Coopers [Coopers & Lybrand] study . . . clear to us project is key to future of the City."[179]

Vincent Schoemehl first embraced and promoted a major expansion of the Cervantes Convention Center well before there was any real plan or market analysis. Subsequently the city commissioned an impressive series of consultant market and feasibility studies to assess the prospects for a bigger center. David Petersen and Laventhol & Horwath first reported on the performance of an expanded center in 1985, added the stadium to the expansion analysis in August 1986, then updated their work in 1987.

Laventhol & Horwath also produced a market analysis for a convention headquarters hotel in September 1989. And when the potential NFL team owners needed to justify the "net fiscal benefit" to the city from the domed stadium, they and the city turned to Coopers & Lybrand in early 1991 for a study—the one noted by Mayor Schoemehl to the stadium bankers—written by John Kaatz. Finally, in April 1991, the St. Louis Convention and Visitors Commission got yet another study, this time on the future performance and finances of the expanded stadium complex, from former Laventhol consultant Charles H. Johnson, then at KPMG.

Laventhol's first "operational analysis" of the Cervantes Center painted a rather grim picture of an underperforming facility, in an undistinguished, if not undesirable, part of the downtown. Their conclusion in mid-1984 was direct: "Expansion is not recommended in the immediate future." But as the mayor sought to boost downtown development—he would write chief of staff Tom Mangogna in early February 1985, "As I look at the 1985 there are not two major construction projects downtown and with the near collapse of the Near Northside project we are very near lossing our momentum"—the expansion took on increased import. And the Laventhol consultants were apparently willing to reconsider their advice.[180]

Charlie Johnson's letter of March 25, 1985, touted the potential of St. Louis and the promise that "Additional space would give you a competitive advantage." With the commissioning of a new report from Laventhol, the prospects for more convention business appeared far brighter. The November 1985 Laventhol report forecast that the addition of some 120,000 to 140,000 square feet would more than triple the center's annual convention delegate total, from 157,800 to 531,300.[181]

A companion design study by the Campbell Design Group (advised by the Laventhol consultants) proposed that an expansion to the south could provide that "The Radisson, the Sheraton, the proposed hotel above Dillards [department store], a new hotel, parking garages, an office tower, and St. Louis Centre all become linked in a network of enclosed pedestrian connections," creating "an exciting and dynamic intervention on the north side of downtown."[182]

Laventhol received an expanded brief in 1986, adding the domed stadium. Their revised figures in August 1986 boosted the average size of new conventions and tradeshows, and pegged attendance at 581,000 annual convention delegates. That would amount to more than four times the 136,300 convention attendees counted for the existing Cervantes.

The September 1989 Laventhol market analysis for the proposed convention center hotel was aimed squarely at a potential developer. The hotel analysis used previous reports to estimate "approximately 300,000 additional delegates . . . due to the center expansion and development of the 70,000-seat domed stadium." Added to the roughly 140,000 to 150,000 delegates already accommodated, the 1989 estimate would produce a somewhat smaller boost in convention business than Laventhol had previously estimated. The new hotel analysis then went on to estimate added hotel demand, putting it at incremental 409,000 hotel room nights. Applying the same assumptions to the existing attendee total would produce an estimate of some 614,000 total hotel room nights each year from the expanded center. That was smaller than the previous Laventhol work. But it still represented a substantial boost in the city's convention business, yielding more than enough "demand for a new headquarters hotel containing approximately 1,100 rooms . . . positioned at the high end of the St. Louis CBD hotel market in terms of both the overall quality of the property and rate structure."[183]

The 1991 consultant study, by John Kaatz of Coopers & Lybrand, was designed to demonstrate the fiscal benefit to the city from the influx of new convention visitors. The Coopers study, couched in terms of "attendee days" rather than attendees or hotel room nights, does not have figures that are directly comparable to the earlier Laventhol work. But in terms of total visitor spending, the Coopers study projected an increase of 3.45 times. Applied to the circa 150,000 convention delegates described by Laventhol in 1985, that would yield some 518,000 annual convention attendees—just about what the Laventhol consultants had forecast without the new stadium.[184]

Former Laventhol consultant Charles H. Johnson returned to St. Louis in

1991 for yet another assessment of the expanded center and stadium. He estimated possible high, medium, and low performance scenarios, that produced an increase in convention attendance ranging from 4.7 times (the high) to 2.1 times (the low), with a midpoint of 3.4 times. Total annual hotel room nights were presumed to grow from a 1990 total of 225,000 to between 438,000 and 908,000.[185]

St. Louis officials commissioned analyses from respected consultants with track records in other cities. While there was some variation in what those consultants forecast, they were uniform in predicting a substantial boost in the city's convention business—at the very least, a doubling or tripling—that would yield a bonanza of visitor spending and fill new hotel rooms. Mayor Schoemehl and his staff were fully confident that the "key" industry of tourism would provide a sound foundation for the kind of continuing new downtown development that the mayor sought.

Unfortunately, the consultants were wrong.

The first phase of the expansion, the new convention center space, opened in mid-1993. The new dome opened in fall 1995. The first full year of operation for the full facility, 1996, saw attendance of about 219,000. For the 1996 through 2000 period, convention and tradeshow attendance averaged 229,000. Those "after" totals represented a modest increase from the 157,800 reported by Laventhol in 1986. But it was far from a tripling or even doubling.

Even more striking was the expanded center's performance in terms of hotel room nights. The 1996 room night total came to 263,892—a little greater than one room night per attendee. That was a far cry from the assumption of an average three- or four-day stay. And over the 1996 through 2000 period, room night generation averaged just 210,000 per year.

With far fewer attendees than the expert consultants had predicted, the city's effort to develop a new 1,000-room headquarters hotel repeatedly stalled. It was not until 2000, more than a decade after the Laventhol hotel report, that the city was able to finance a new hotel, largely by itself. As the convention attendance remained stalled after 2000—the convention center produced 211,008 room nights in 2005—the new St. Louis Renaissance Grand hotel began to fail as well, failing to meet its debt service and falling into foreclosure in January 2009—after a year when the center generated just 214,825 room nights.

Schoemehl and the city's development staff had linked much of the future of downtown to the traffic generated by the larger convention center, anticipating the conversion of the upper floors of the Dillard's department store to new hotel rooms and a boost for the St. Louis Centre mall. By 2010, the new hotel rooms had failed to appear and the Dillard's itself was closed. Indeed, St. Louis Centre itself was shuttered.

The "expert" advice that Mayor Schoemehl commissioned and endorsed proved anything but. Part of the problem was assuming that bigger—in terms of convention center exhibit space—inevitably meant more business. It was not at all clear, for example, that the flat space on the floor of a domed stadium was of particular appeal to meeting planners, or that downtown St. Louis could really compete with Chicago, New Orleans, or Las Vegas. For the succession of consultants, providing "expert" advice to cities on building and expanding convention centers was their business. And the advice they provided to cities beyond St. Louis—Petersen via PriceWaterhouse to such cities as Atlanta, San Diego, and Boston; Johnson via C. H. Johnson Consulting to Chicago, Boston, Austin, and Tucson; Kaatz via CSL International to Minneapolis, Washington, Philadelphia, and Boston—consistently carried the message that those places too would gain new business when they added space.

In relying upon the advice and forecasts of these consultants, Schoemehl and his staff placed a bet on the success of a convention and tourism development strategy that carried at the very least substantial uncertainty, and actually substantial opportunity and fiscal costs. They, most notably budget director Stephen Mullin, assumed that the "big thing" of convention center and dome would yield a flood of new revenues for the city as well as new private investment. That flood of new revenue did not come. But the annual cost to pay the debt on the convention center expansion, the stadium, and the Renaissance hotel was a certainty, and continues.

Leif Sverdrup and Civic Progress had pressed for, and gotten, a convention center on the north side of downtown, boosting the development prospects of the surrounding "Convention Plaza" redevelopment area and bolstering property values from "erosion." The same interests that had effectively determined the center's location in the late 1960s were still in place two decades later as Mayor Schoemehl and Bruce Sommer considered an expanded center. From Sverdrup to Mercantile Bank and the May Company's (later Federated) department store in St. Louis Centre (then Famous-Barr, now Macy's), those interests and institutions were still represented on Civic Progress and still carried considerable clout. Indeed, with the opening of the St. Louis Centre mall in March 1985, the convention trade was even more important with the promise of bringing more visitor dollars.

If the Cervantes Center was "fixed" spatially and politically, it was not the only major public development effort Vincent Schoemehl was interested in during the mid-1980s. In early February 1985, at about the same time as he sought a justification for a larger convention center, Schoemehl wrote a brief memo to chief of staff Tom Mangogna, headed "Performing Arts Center." The mayor said, "The development of a city performing arts center in the city central area is a top priority for my second administration and I would like you to take the lead in getting this done." Schoemehl told him to arrange a trip to Minneapolis to see "the recently completed Ordway Music Hall," and to discuss the possibilities for a St. Louis center with local developer Leon Strauss and Richard Gaddes, director of the Opera Theatre.[186]

Schoemehl recognized that "Financing such a center in St. Louis will be an enormously difficult task," and pressed Mangogna to develop "any information that you can" on fiscal potentials. At the time, there was little or no city money for a new performing arts center. But Schoemehl was unwilling to let the possibility of a complex of arts institutions disappear. And his memo to Mangogna was intriguing on the issue of location. The mayor explicitly mentioned "central area," not downtown.

The mayor's interest in developing a performing arts center took some time to evolve, but in November 1987 he joined opera director Richard Gaddes in making a formal presentation on "The New Performing Arts Center" proposal to the Civic Progress executive committee. The mayor's vision was built around the St. Louis Symphony's home at Powell Hall. He described "bring[ing] together the area's major performing arts organizations in the "Grand Center" district between Powell Hall and the Fox Theatre." The mayor told the Civic Progress group, "creation of the proposed regional center for the performing arts would strengthen the arts organizations involved and help rejuvenate midtown St. Louis."[187]

The midtown "Grand Center" district is some two and a half miles from downtown, and immediately adjacent to St. Louis University, from which Mayor Schoemehl had graduated. There had been earlier efforts to stabilize and revive the area in the face of ongoing neighborhood change. But those had failed to halt the district's slide. What Schoemehl first sought in late 1987 was initial funding for a feasibility study, and to purchase adjacent land, as "property values would tend to increase as news of the plan got around."

While the arts district plan was pitched as an aid to the symphony and area arts groups, it was largely intended to stabilize midtown: "The purpose behind the creation of a performing arts center is to bring enough activity into this part of midtown St. Louis to stabilize it, thereby protecting and supporting the St. Louis Symphony and Fox Theatre . . . [and to] create a large enough business potential to attract art galleries and other arts-related businesses as well shops and restaurants to an area now largely deserted."[188]

Much as Edison, Sverdrup, and Lasater had sought to protect the north side of downtown from "erosion" with a convention center, Schoemehl's intent was to protect and boost the midtown area and adjacent St. Louis University (the president of the university, then the Rev. Lawrence Biondi, was an ex officio member of Civic Progress). In order to do that, he needed the backing (and financial resources) of Civic Progress members, both in that role and as leaders of the region's arts organizations. Civic Progress member Edwin Trusheim, the CEO of General American Life Insurance, was then serving as president of the St. Louis Symphony. And the mayor wanted backing for a performing arts district not anywhere in metropolitan St. Louis, but in the midtown location. Indeed, when the full Civic Progress group considered the proposal in late November 1987, St. Louis County executive Gene McNary, still jousting with the mayor over the stadium location, said, "more could be accomplished by building such a center in a better neighborhood rather than trying to attract audiences to an area they don't want to go to."[189]

McNary's comments in late 1987 obviously reflected the continuing conflict between him and the mayor over the question of stadium location and the future of the downtown core. By mid-1988, it was clear to Schoemehl that he had to reach an accommodation with McNary that got the city *some form* of major new development. The mayor set out the essential elements of a bargain with the county in an August 1988 memo to lawyer Walter Metcalfe, who was spearheading the effort to organize an NFL ownership group and develop a stadium. Under the heading "*What do we get*" the mayor listed "Support for Murray/Clinton group" (the prospective NFL team ownership group); "Support for Grand Avenue" (the proposed midtown performing arts center); and "Support for private Arena." Last came, "A return to normalcy (maybe impossible).[190]

Schoemehl sought a triad of major development projects: the stadium adjacent to the Cervantes Center, the midtown performing arts center at Grand Ave., and a third—a new arena for the St. Louis Blues hockey team. The mayor wanted multiple development projects, not just because of his enthusiasm for the arts or hockey. He rather recognized that they could service very distinct, disparate spatial interests.

Civic Progress had led the effort to keep the Blues in St. Louis with new ownership. Schoemehl had originally considered the possibility of a joint stadium and arena as part of the Cervantes expansion, housing an NBA team in additional to football. But by late 1987 and early 1988, Schoemehl was envisioning an entirely new arena to replace the Blues' former home.

The mayor first approached the Civic Center Corporation, the Anheuser-Busch subsidiary responsible for operating Busch Stadium, about the prospects for a new privately financed arena adjacent to the stadium. On May 9, 1988, budget staffers Mullin and LaSala, together with Bruce Sommer, met with Mark Sauer, president of the Civic Center organization, on the arena plan. Sauer stressed that Anheuser-Busch wanted it "presented as a community effort, not an A-B project," with the main objective "to save the Blues, and prevent damage to the community that would result if the Blues were lost." Much as Sverdrup had wanted full backing for his convention center proposal, Sauer and Anheuser-Busch wanted the assurance that "The Post[-Dispatch] has to be fully supportive, they have to buy a box and be a player." And for the mayor, the city staffers asked about the "Role of Civic Progress—Will Chuck Knight and Civic Progress take this on and sell the boxes?"[191]

The plan for a new arena had a decidedly *spatial* dimension. Schoemehl was effectively offering the mirror image of the original relationship between Busch Stadium and the convention center, where the case for the latter was built around balancing "erosion protection" on both the north and south sides of downtown. Now, Schoemehl could pair an arena on the south with the center expansion and potential new stadium to the north, neatly maintaining both a development and a political balance. And just as in the case of business interest in a north side magnet in the 1960s, there was an increasing interest in a new development magnet on the south.

The revitalized Union Station on the south side of the core had opened in August 1985, at almost the same time as the new St. Louis Centre mall on the north side. By 1988, Union Station owner Oppenheimer Properties was considering developing a new "draw" for their project that would make use of the city's former convention center, the nearby Kiel Auditorium. On May 6, the *Post-Dispatch* carried the news that Oppenheimer was proposing a redevelopment plan for the Kiel.[192]

Oppenheimer officials would end up proposing a scheme in the fall for a combined arena and equestrian center as a reuse for the Kiel and adjacent land. But in May 1988, the prospect of a competing project led to the public surfacing of the mayor's plan for an entirely new arena in combination with Anheuser-Busch and its Civic Center Corporation. There were thus two competing visions for a new arena to house the Blues hockey team. Oppenheimer sought a redevelopment of the Kiel that could increase the attraction and volume at Union Station. The redeveloped station was not generating the level of business that Oppenheimer and the Rouse Company had anticipated, with the *Post-Dispatch* reporting "Union Station—Still Short of—Making Profit" in February 1989.[193]

The Anheuser-Busch/Civic Center plan would put an entirely new arena next to Busch stadium. But the brewery wanted to replace the parking it would lose at the proposed arena site by razing a number of the nineteenth-century warehouse structures that made up the adjacent Cupples Station area. And as the plans firmed up in early 1989, with the serious possibility of razing the Cupples warehouses, there was a substantial reaction from preservationists.

As he faced pressure to at least reconsider the demolition of the warehouses, the mayor wrote a seven-page letter to Fred Kuhlmann of Civic Center on June 19. He argued to Kuhlmann that "The vast amounts of available land detract from the creation of land value in the core of downtown which leads to further deadening of interest. . . . Strong urban economies demand density, not surface parking lots."[194]

Schoemehl reinforced his argument to Kuhlmann with language remarkably parallel to what Ted Aschman had argued about Chicago's central area thirty years earlier: "The key to success of other urban economies is their ability to shape and pace the natural growth in their downtowns in such a way as to create more growth. Creating a 16-acre vacuum in and around the Cupples site would defeat this effort in St. Louis. It would create competitive land availability at a time when we should be focusing on the core of our downtown." Schoemehl ended his letter noting, "I know you're ready to walk away from this project." Just four days after the mayor's letter, they announced that they were abandoning the project.

In response to the Civic Center decision, the mayor announced a national search for a private developer to take on the arena project, to be somewhere downtown. But newspaper reports suggested that the mayor really wanted the arena and the hockey Blues at the Kiel Auditorium site, where Oppenheimer Properties had proposed an equestrian center.

The final result, a plan for a new arena at the back side of the Kiel, became public in late 1990. And while the first newspaper report described the arena developers as "some of the area's top business leaders," it was once again Civic Progress that took on the responsibility of financing a major development project. Reviewing the arena plans at the November 1989 monthly meeting, Andrew Craig III of Boatmen's Bank described the pressing need to issue bonds for the project before December 30. At that point, 19 of the 28 Civic Progress member companies had written checks for their partnership investments, and Craig anticipated a commitment from a least one more.[195]

The member firms of Civic Progress ultimately committed about $135 million to the arena, with the city contributing another $34.5 million for a new parking garage and partial demolition of the Kiel Auditorium. And while the new arena provided some aid to Union Station, the redeveloped complex continued to face economic difficulties. Still, the Kiel Center arena continued the historic pattern of public-private cooperation in "balancing" the development and land use imperatives of the north and south sides of the downtown core.

Each new grand private development project thus provided an imperative to boost the city's convention business anew, and to "save" its immediate environs with yet another public investment or incentive scheme. As one mall or entertainment complex after another failed to thrive, the city's business and political leadership would somehow find another grand project or vision that would represent the kind of "world-class building project . . . to continue the City's incredible momentum" that budget director Stephen Mullin had so emphatically and enthusiastically embraced in 1986.

Politics and Business

When Mayor Vincent Schoemehl attended the Civic Progress monthly meeting in March 1984, it was to report on the city's increasingly dire fiscal situation, and to ask—perhaps beg—for help from the region's preeminent business leaders. Schoemehl told the group that "he has done everything possible to reduce the size and cost of City government since he took office almost three years ago." But for fiscal year 1985, he said, the city had only two options: "Cutting the fiscal 1985 budget by up to $20 million by laying off 525 more employees," or "Maintaining services and employment at present levels by increasing taxes."[196]

What Schoemehl sought was Civic Progress backing for his plan to a business tax per employee and an increase in the sales tax, on the ballot in June. He needed the backing of the business leaders. Far more importantly, he needed their dollars to finance a campaign to sell the taxes to voters. The mayor's plan provoked an unusual dissenting vote on the Civic Progress

Action Committee, with most of the members committing to provide $100,000 to finance the campaign. Supermarket chain owner Donald O. Schnuck offered the rare objection, agreeing with the need for a tax increase, but saying, "the Mayor's proposal placed too heavy a burden on labor-intensive employers."

The mayor reported the electoral success of both tax increases to the group in late June. But, thanking them for their financial support, he said, "he decided to engage in a last-minute television advertising and direct mail campaign blitz in response to adverse developments as the election drew close." That raised the cost to $137,000, and the mayor needed more money. Banker Clarence Barksdale moved that the group provide Schoemehl with an additional $20,000, and that funding was approved. But William Stiritz, CEO of Ralston-Purina, pressed the mayor to improve the city's long-range budgeting and "thus, avoid sudden calls for a tax increase to avoid a deficit," stressing, "Without long-range budget analysis . . . the police, firemen, and other institutional sources of city expenditures have a big advantage over the elected Mayor and other officials who often are new to their jobs."[197]

Schoemehl's appeal to Civic Progress to finance a tax campaign in 1984 was not the mayor's first request for help from the business group. Civic Progress had given the mayor $121,300 for the development of a financial planning system for the city (in collaboration with the University of Pennsylvania) in 1982 and 1983. It had backed the new neighborhood cleanup program called Operation Brightside with $75,000 in early 1982. Over and over in subsequent years, the mayor turned to Civic Progress. At times it was to finance tax campaigns. On other occasions, as with the battles with the county over the stadium and the financing of the Kiel Center arena, he needed some combination of business clout and investment dollars. There was simply no way that Schoemehl—indeed any St. Louis mayor—could promote and realize major development projects, implement new initiatives, and manage the city's fragile finances without the interventions and blessings of Civic Progress.[198]

For St. Louis and its mayors, Civic Progress served three crucial roles: as gatekeeper, legitimizer, and financier. As a gatekeeper, the initiatives the mayor spun off could easily be stalled or killed by Civic Progress. Just as his predecessors had followed Civic Progress choices for bond proposals, Schoemehl was substantially dependent upon corporate donations that could supplement the city's limited funds and avoid fights with the Board of Aldermen. Civic Progress effectively controlled access to those contributions, by choosing when and how to back mayoral initiatives.

Schoemehl set out a broad array of development plans during his mayoralty: the Cervantes Center expansion, "Kiel deal," the domed stadium, the reuse of the Cupples Station warehouses, a "Technopolis" technology zone in midtown, an aquarium.[199]

A great many fizzled, while *some* were ultimately realized. Much of the difference lay with the interest and backing of Civic Progress. When a project like the new arena, the performing arts center, and the stadium gained "traction" with some Civic Progress member CEO, there was a strong possibility that it could receive the initial seed capital and resources to manage political conflict and competing commitments. When something like the aquarium and the proposed "Cousteau Center" did not interest or excite the business leadership, it rarely happened.

As legitimizer, Civic Progress continued to play much the same civic role that it had in the 1950s and 1960s. The group only rarely initiated major projects such as the convention center, stadium, performing arts center, or new arena. But backing from the region's corporate leadership generally assured a positive reception by local newspapers and their editorial staffs. And Civic Progress, working through Fleishman-Hillard, could define what was important to the city and region's future in a fashion that appeared "above politics." They structured what were central issues in St. Louis (and indeed, in the state of Missouri), particularly in the realms of economic growth, employment, and public policy.

The extended effort to deal with the possible loss of Bidwell's Cardinals, followed by the development of the downtown dome and the relocation of the NFL Rams, could only have been managed by the business leadership, operating in spite of the continuing conflict between city and county governments, and mobilizing the resources of the state government and potential private investors behind a new team. Vincent Schoemehl could not produce a new football stadium by himself, either politically or with the limited resources of the city government. Civic Progress could. And perhaps most importantly, it could conclude that an NFL team was crucial to the image and place of the St. Louis metropolitan area and make that a major public issue.

Civic Progress thus played a critical role in providing Vince Schoemehl with a host of political advantages and fiscal opportunities But the mayor's agenda and interests were not necessarily precisely coincident with those of the business group.

When Mayor Schoemehl sought Civic Progress backing and campaign financing for a sales tax increase campaign in early 1989, mayoral aide Bill

Kuehling conveyed a clear message from Civic Progress secretary Al Kerth. Kuehling told the mayor he was on the group's February meeting agenda. But he also told Schoemehl that Kerth said, "the mood is not great for putting money into this campaign or a lot of other items at this time. Therefore, he feels you need to be very prepared as to stressing why this tax is important to the City and why you believe this campaign is winnable." Despite the apparent reluctance of Civic Progress, Schoemehl pressed ahead with the tax increase vote, which was defeated in April.[200]

The Civic Progress leadership also made evident to Schoemehl that his programs were not necessarily entitled to permanent funding. Operation Brightside, Schoemehl's initiative to brighten neighborhoods, while employing at-risk youth, was initiated with Civic Progress funding in 1982. But in December 1989, when the mayor was seeking additional year-round funding for the program, the business group's Community Affairs Committee was unmoved. The committee recommended that "Civic Progress *not* increase funding," arguing that the program should seek to generate more revenue "*rather than seeking so much of its funding from the private sector*." While Civic Progress agreed to continue the same funding as a year earlier, it made clear that Operation Brightside would receive no more funding after 1993.[201]

Civic Progress, and financing from its corporate members, enabled Schoemehl to support an array of new programs outside the limits of the city's fiscal resources or the purview of the Board of Aldermen. But if cleanup efforts like Operation Brightside were made feasible with the commitment of Civic Progress backing, the group's role was far more critical to major public and private development projects. When, in July 1989, Schoemehl was simultaneously trying to develop both a new domed stadium and a new arena for the hockey Blues, budget director JoAnne LaSala described the role of Civic Progress's dollars and commitment to those two projects. In a "Confidential" memo to other mayoral aides, she noted that "Football: Civic Progress has committed to guaranteeing the sale of at least 63 luxury boxes at Busch Stadium . . . and at least 65 luxury boxes at the Gateway Dome." As for the proposed arena, Al Kerth of Civic Progress "went on to say that it would be fair to say that in some form or another Civic Progress companies would participate."[202]

With the mayor's plans for a performing arts center at Grand Center, the new arena, and the stadium, it was only Civic Progress that could mobilize the necessary private capital, provide the imprimatur of business endorsement, and resolve the political conflicts at the regional and state level to make them possible. Absent that collective engagement and commitment, Vincent Schoemehl (and his successors) would be presiding over a very different city.

The View from the Bogey Club

When Vincent Schoemehl brought his appeal for financing for a tax increase campaign to the March 1984 Civic Progress meeting, his was only one item of a five-item agenda. When Civic Progress came into being in the early 1950s, its efforts were focused on the city—largely in terms of needed bond issues and political reform. By the early 1980s, the monthly meetings at the all-white, all-male Bogey Club (in suburban Ladue) or the University Club (in suburban Richmond Heights) covered a far broader array of goals and interests.[203]

The January 9, 1984, annual planning meeting began with Donald Lasater reviewing the group's "Number One Priority," economic development, "because of the St. Louis area's declining rate of economic growth and job losses." Charles Knight reported on the new state legislation to focus on regional economic development, and the need to press candidates for governor on the importance of economic development.[204]

The group then discussed the efforts of the Business Health Coalition to deal with the adequacy and cost of medical services. That was followed by a report from Bernard Edison on the efforts to assist the St. Louis public school system. Edison noted he had been meeting monthly with the city school superintendent, describing him as "well organized, tough minded, and has high standards." Then came a report from Clarence Barksdale on an effort to review the long-term financial needs of the state of Missouri, including plans for a meeting with Governor Christopher Bond the following month, to be held jointly with a Kansas City business group.

The January planning effort also covered a number of perennial issues for Civic Progress. The St. Louis Symphony had found itself $2 million short of its annual budget needs, with Civic Progress member Lee Liberman arguing "that the orchestra has been responsible for more positive public relations for St. Louis than any other attraction except the baseball Cardinals."

The concerns of Civic Progress were thus dominated by major state and regional level issues, some of which—the St. Louis Symphony was an example—were of particular concern to one or two members. The purely *city* concerns which had once preoccupied the business leadership were, by the

1980s, just one relatively modest focus. Still, the business of development in downtown St. Louis remained an ongoing concern.

Near the end of the January 1984 planning session, the group considered the proposal for a new light rail transit system to run through downtown, to midtown St. Louis (and the region's two major medical centers), and then to Lambert-St. Louis International Airport. The rail transit effort had been a focus of Civic Progress since the mid-1960s, ultimately not realized until 1993. But in early 1984, a downtown-oriented transit plan was seen as key to the future of the core.

Civic Progress member Robert C. West, successor to Leif Sverdrup as chairman of the Sverdrup Corporation, told his colleagues, "new downtown activity centers like Laclede's Landing and St. Louis Centre shopping complex will need this service to generate traffic." West continued, "The light rail line would stimulate substantial economic development." Then David C. Farrell, chairman of May Department Stores, pointed out that "the May Company's $55 million downtown store in Washington, D.C., would probably not be under construction if there had not been a new subway station next to the store location." Farrell's May Company had been a prime mover behind the St. Louis Centre downtown mall project since the 1970s, as a means of improving the fortunes of the firm's adjacent Famous-Barr department store. In early 1984, Farrell was looking ahead to the final completion of the mall in mid-1985, and the need to attract new suburban shoppers to downtown.

Some twenty years after the waltz with Walt Disney, the Civic Progress leadership was still seeking some major, catalytic public investment that could support the city's new downtown development efforts. For Civic Progress members like West and Farrell, these public investments neatly served the interests of their own firms and investments while enhancing the prospects of the downtown core.

The commitment of Civic Progress to downtown St. Louis has remained a constant. In 1992, the group outlined its continuing concern with the downtown as part of its annual planning process. Describing the first of "three broad areas" of focus, it noted, "Civic Progress has *maintained the financial viability of the City of St. Louis*; first through support in 1954 for the establishment of an earnings tax, now the dominant source of revenue for city operations; and second, through substantial and continuing investment in downtown St. Louis, thereby sustaining the region's highest concentration of employment."[205]

The report cited the group's work "to strengthen the region's hospitality industry infrastructure, with an emphasis on development in the downtown area . . . . While this segment of the economy is now poised for dramatic growth, employment in automotive and defense-related industries continues to decline."

During the mid-1980s, the major public investment agenda of Civic Progress was shaped by the group's concern over the loss of major league sports, and thus the city's national image and reputation. Summarizing the group's achievements during 1986, the Civic Progress executive committee first noted among "highlights," "The active role taken by Civic Progress in making it possible to retain the Hockey Blues in St. Louis and convert the Arena into a public facility. It represented a strong commitment by the members to the continuing development of the St. Louis region as a major metropolitan complex."[206]

The efforts by Civic Progress to retain the football Cardinals with the development of a new stadium very much paralleled the effort to keep the Blues in the city. The business leaders neatly linked the continuation of major league sports to the very existence of the city and region. As Don Brandin told his colleagues at the January 1987 monthly meeting, "if St. Louis is to continue as a major city, we should be preparing to support the construction of a new or expanded convention center/sports complex."[207]

But with the departure of Bill Bidwell and the football Cardinals, Charles "Chuck" Knight of Emerson Electric provided the clearest statement of the view from the Bogey Club circa 1988: "If St. Louis had a stadium, we could get an NFL team . . . . Additional convention business would bring more money to St. Louis than the revenues from professional football. However, St. Louis will not be perceived as a big-league city until it has a modern football stadium and an NFL team."[208]

The notion that an NFL team was the necessary prerequisite for "big-league city" status was no doubt shared by business leaders in other large cities. But for Civic Progress, the new stadium offered the conjoint benefits of a major public investment boost for downtown (and a continuing enhancement of the north side of the core area) together with the lure of a new professional football team to assure continuing "big league" stature. It was a perfect example of the business group's larger agenda, both bolstering downtown and arguably sustaining the image of the region.

It was only Civic Progress that could marshal the resources and political clout to deliver a $240 million stadium project financed jointly by three separate units of government—city, county, and state. Civic Progress shaped the deal that brought the support of the state legislature and governor. For suburban St. Louis County, where the deal required a public vote on a hotel tax, Civic Progress was equally central.

Well before the April vote, in December 1989, county executive H. C. Milford told the Civic Progress leaders that the area hotel/motel association was raising "some concerns" about the tax, saying "it would be helpful if [Civic Progress] businesses would write to the Hotel Association, expressing their support for the tax proposal and pledging not to move their meetings elsewhere."[209]

With the campaign expertise of Fleishman-Hillard, Milford envisioned a "two-tiered campaign," with sports fans urged to vote yes to "boost St. Louis's chances of securing an NFL expansion franchise," and "non-sports fans . . . asked to support the measure based on the significant economic impact an expanded convention center would have on the region's economy."[210]

Milford reported to the Civic Progress Action Committee in January 1990 that support for the hotel tax was "about evenly divided." William Cornelius, CEO of Union Electric, the area's electric utility, termed the coalition of the city, county, and state "fragile" and urged the support of Civic Progress firms as "critical to the success of this issue." The Action Committee ultimately committed $434,000 to the successful county hotel tax campaign, the organization's largest single campaign financing effort during the 1987 to 1991 period, dwarfing its backing of the city's convention center campaign with $100,000 or the $300,000 backing for a statewide gasoline tax increase proposal.[211]

For the leaders of Civic Progress, the image of the St. Louis area as "big league" and the physical environment of the downtown were effectively one and the same. And when, in the late 1990s, the city began yet another planning effort aimed at boosting the downtown core, the Civic Progress leadership made clear that, whatever the larger set of needs of the city or metropolitan region, downtown occupied a very special place. Speaking to his Civic Progress colleagues in February 2000, David C. Darnell of Bank of America said,

> The goal of Civic Progress is to make the St. Louis region world class. This goal requires that the downtown area thrives, and that the City's financial difficulties be resolved. St. Louis is in tough competition with other cities [such as Charlotte, where Mr. Darnell visited the preceding week] working to strengthen their downtowns.
>
> To be successful, St. Louis must have the collective will to make something happen, and Civic Progress must help lead this effort.[212]

Civic Progress could not dictate the economic or political future of St. Louis. It could not handpick local elected officials, or even resolve the longstanding problems of local government reform and city-county conflict. It manifestly did not "govern" St. Louis or the larger metropolitan region.

What it could do was propel a set of priorities forward, year after year and decade after decade, reflecting the concerns of business leaders and the view from the Bogey Club. Civic Progress ensured the realization of a regional rail transit system, the expansion of the region's airport, the continuing existence of major cultural and arts organizations, the protection of major institutions such as Washington University's Medical Center, St. Louis University, and the midtown performing arts center from the forces of neighborhood change. It promoted and realized the investment of hundreds of millions of public dollars in projects like the convention center, the domed stadium, and the arena.

Yet even as it pressed for major new public investment in the downtown core, Civic Progress operated through mutual deference and accommodation. Just as downtown's north side firms had sought to balance "protection from erosion" in the 1960s, Civic Progress continued to maintain an exquisite spatial balancing act downtown. The massive governmental commitment to convention center expansion and stadium-building on downtown's north side was matched by the commitment by Civic Progress member firms and the organization to Busch Stadium and the new Kiel Center arena on the south.

Discussing the Kiel proposal at an October 1990 Civic Progress meeting, the group noted that in March 1989 they had "endorsed a presentation by Mr. Knight, which called for participation in supporting efforts to win an NFL expansion franchise (and thereby support the construction of the new stadium/convention center expansion) *AND* in supporting the construction of a new arena south of Busch Stadium." The arena presentation argued, "But St. Louis still needs a first-class, multipurpose facility to provide a venue for hockey, basketball, soccer, concerts, family shows, meetings and similar events . . . . This is an important part of the infrastructure of a competitive, modern city and an important part of our strategy to support the downtown economy by concentrating our convention, tourism and entertainment industries there."[213]

For Civic Progress, the stadium and the new Kiel arena were invariably joined by "and." The group viewed them as a pair. By pursuing *both* the Kiel arena and the stadium *at the same time,* Civic Progress could manifest its commitment to the two major downtown subareas. And when the effort for a new downtown development program emerged in the late 1990s, that too was shaped by the same spatial concerns.

The June 1999 "Downtown Development Action Plan" contended that "Downtown St. Louis has many of the basic qualities necessary to regain its rightful position as one of the nation's greatest cities." The plan then laid out a set of "strategies" for achieving that "rightful position." On the south side of downtown, between Union Station, Kiel Center, and Busch Stadium, the plan proposed to "Undertake a complete makeover of the Gateway Mall to realize its extraordinary civic potential." The Mall, long a focus of Civic Progress, had been created by demolishing blocks of old buildings on the southern flank of the downtown core. But the open space of the Mall had actually created an extensive dead space.[214]

For the Civic Progress leaders of the 1960s, the prospect of the new Gateway Arch offered the city and downtown a potential as a major tourist locale. But the Arch and its grounds were isolated by the multiple lanes of an Interstate highway. The 1999 plan proposed to "Cover I-70 between the Gateway Mall and the Arch Grounds to reconnect the Mississippi River and the Arch to the Downtown core," with the aim of drawing Arch visitors to the downtown core.[215]

Finally, on the north side of downtown, the plan proposed to "Revitalize the Old Post Office; the current situation of dereliction and vacancy is completely unacceptable." The Old Post Office was the third leg of the distributive triad of strategic emphases. On the north side of downtown, it anchored the district of the convention center and dome, as well as the St. Louis Centre mall.

The focus on revitalizing the Old Post Office as the focal point of downtown's north side was a striking parallel to the concern voiced by Civic Progress and the ULI panel study in 1954. Then, the hulk of the Old Post Office was viewed as the singular impediment to new private investment downtown. Civic Progress member Howard Baer termed the structure "a pigeon roost" and "a cancer in the heart of the town." While the structure was saved, the Old Post Office still occupied a vital locus in downtown space, one that could be used by Webster University to presumably draw a steady stream of faculty and students.

The triad of new projects and foci in the Downtown Development Action Plan was thus a triumph of distributive politics, neatly serving the major subareas of downtown much as the development of Busch Stadium and then the Cervantes Convention Center had done for the south and north sides of downtown. Yet with each new development initiative, the same spatial division—and the implicit threat of favoring one side over another—arose.

The call for a new baseball stadium to replace the aging Busch emerged publicly in early 2000. The proposal from the Cardinals' management called for a substantial public financial commitment. For St. Louis mayor Clarence Harmon and his staff, then still focused on making a new convention center hotel a reality, it set off precisely that set of interrelated spatial and political concerns that had long defined public investment downtown.

St. Louis Centre mall, the centerpiece of downtown's revitalization in the mid-1980s, was clearly struggling by 2000. Indeed, former mayor Schoemehl had floated his own convention hotel proposal, calling for turning the Dillard's department store at one end of the mall into a 1,050-room Sheraton hotel. While Schoemehl's scheme went nowhere, it did illustrate the fragility of the mall itself and the imperative of boosting the hotel and the convention business at America's Center.

The Cardinals' plan for a new ballpark next door to Busch Stadium, together with promised new office, retail, residential, and entertainment development ("Ballpark Village") on the old stadium site, threatened to unbalance downtown development and shift attention and investment away from America's Center and the mall. Mayor Harmon's staff set out precisely those concerns at a mayoral meeting of April 27, 2000. In notes for the mayor headed "City issues that need to be addressed," they asserted, "Investment in the baseball stadium would effectively split downtown into north and south areas of emphasis. The north area concentrated on Washington Avenue [by America's Center] and the south area consisting of the courthouse, Cupples Station and the stadium."[216]

Despite the mayor's concerns, the new ballpark project moved ahead, ultimately financed with a combination of private financing from the Cardinals ($310 million) and public dollars from St. Louis County ($45 million) and the state (tax credits and infrastructure improvements for $42.5 million). And while it is not clear that the new stadium "split downtown," the collapse of St. Louis Centre continued, the new convention center hotel proved a failure, and initial construction on Ballpark Village would not begin until early 2013.

Just as in the 1960s and 1970s, the expanse of space and sunk private investment that was downtown St. Louis could not be served solely by a single grand public project. The north/south division had never been healed.

Downtown interests and Civic Progress needed multiple public investment efforts that could support *all of downtown and all of those divergent interests.* And as such efforts as America's Center and the convention center hotel failed to produce new convention business or hoped-for revitalization, there would be new plans and new proposals aimed at assuring a "world class" downtown for a "world class" region.

Conclusion

The Cities Business Builds

The contemporary boom in convention center building has been fueled and sustained by two substantive changes in local politics and finance. First, local public investment finance has been reshaped and reformed over the last three decades, structured to avoid any direct public votes or control over the commitment of millions in state and local debt, and tied to largely "invisible" or seemingly free revenue streams, from visitor-based taxes on things like hotel rooms, car rentals, and restaurant meals. State governments have also come to play a central role in financing convention center development and expansions, bypassing the political and fiscal constraints on city and county governments.

The reformation of center finance has been paralleled by a new set of arguments and justifications. The convention venues of the 1950s and 1960s were promoted as grand civic improvements and a means of enhancing a community's standing and reputation. Those arguments have largely been replaced by the seemingly scientific and expert consultant forecasts of new spending, economic impact, and job creation. Contemporary convention center building is regularly described by local officials and the news media as an economic development boon, one certain to generate new visitor spending with the potential to revitalize a downtown and the larger community. But while fiscal reformation and the rhetoric of economic development have eased the path of convention center development, the impetus for center building lies behind the public scene and the grand promises.

From the 1950s through the 2000s, the public investment in convention center building and expansion has been propelled, supported, and sustained by local business leadership. While those business leaders repeatedly employed the rhetoric and promises of "economic impact" and job creation, their language and references *among themselves and their peers* were fundamentally different and thoroughly focused on the downtown business district. In St. Louis, Civic Progress leader and insurance chief Powell McHaney observed in 1953, mirroring the focus of Pittsburgh's business leaders, "the basic theory in Pittsburgh is that you must take care of the 'core' of the city first, keep industry and its payrolls from deserting the downtown, and let the workers live wherever they want."[1]

McHaney and his colleagues in Civic Progress would indeed seek to take care of the core first from the 1950s through the 1960s, with a series of efforts beginning with urban renewal, extending to a new stadium, and culminating in plans for a new convention center designed to provide "protection from erosion."

For Chicago's Holman Pettibone, the purpose was much the same, if the language was slightly different. Speaking at a meeting of a small group of the city's business and political leaders in early 1954, Pettibone "emphasized that proper redevelopment required a bold approach, sufficiently broad to change the complexion of a whole neighborhood . . . there was obvious need to bolster the downtown business district by a [redevelopment] project such as the one under discussion and that public officials must of necessity take the lead in this connection."[2]

For Richard Rich and Fred Turner in Atlanta, the charge to planning consultant Phil Hammer in early 1959 was for an analysis of how to "promote the large-scale physical development of the city, with particular emphasis upon the Central Area." Hammer's subsequent report sought to answer the question, "What kind of physical plans are needed for Downtown Atlanta to stimulate private investment and guide public and private development efforts?" And when the Atlanta Chamber of Commerce's Long Range Planning Committee reported to the larger group in April 1965, its first priority was "an effective plan for the Central Business District." Other issues, including city financing, transportation, and "racial communications," were ranked lower.[3]

The focus of McHaney and Civic Progress, Pettibone, and Richard Rich and his colleagues of the Atlanta Chamber, was consistently on the downtown core—its economic vitality, its property values, its capacity to attract new investment. That focus and concern would be repeated in Cleveland and Baltimore, and echoed in dozens of American cities. That focus would also remain remarkably consistent and persistent over time.

The quest for a new auditorium/convention hall for Atlanta began in the 1950s, survived one defeat at the polls, and was finally realized in the 1960s. But the Civic Center proved not enough for Atlanta's business leaders and developers. The new Georgia World Congress Center was completed in 1976, and then expanded again and again. And with the argument that the city's convention business required a major downtown entertainment complex, the city continued to invest, in Underground Atlanta and a series of new visitor attractions.

The tie between downtown revitalization and convention center development was no less evident—or persistent—in St. Louis. The business leaders of Civic Progress had embraced a new baseball stadium in the late 1950s, not out of love for the national pastime, but out of a calculus that such a sports facility "would re-make downtown St. Louis," and constituted "the best idea we have ever heard of for the development of Downtown St. Louis."[4]

It was the success of that stadium in clearing a blighted district and promoting rebuilding that prompted other Civic Progress leaders to seek "the kind of protection from erosion on the north side [of downtown] which it is receiving on the south side from the Stadium complex." "Protection from erosion" was not a geological concept. It rather reflected the declining property values and lack of new private investment in the north side of the downtown core. A new convention center, with its capacity for "people generation," would be the necessary catalyst for that new investment and development.[5]

Two decades after the formal discussion of "protection from erosion," and a decade after the opening of the St. Louis Cervantes Convention Center that presumably delivered that erosion protection and "people generation," the leaders of Civic Progress would seek an even grander project:

> If St. Louis had a stadium, we could get an NFL team. Built as part of the Cervantes Convention Center, a new domed stadium would give St. Louis the fourth largest convention center in the United States. Additional convention business would bring more new money to St. Louis than the revenues from professional football. However, St. Louis will not be perceived as a big league city until it has a modern football stadium and an NFL team.[6]

The promise of new convention business was crucial in justifying the public investment by city, county, and state governments in a domed stadium, through the "net fiscal benefit" to be provided by new convention attendees. Once again, it was a major public development project that was viewed by the Civic Progress leaders as vital to the future of downtown and the city of St. Louis. Yet even a new stadium was not enough.

Three years before the 1995 opening of the new stadium, the Civic Progress economic development committee identified a new "convention center hotel" as a central priority, arguing that "The new hotel will be an integral part of the city's ability to attract large conventions to the area." And Civic Progress would repeatedly in subsequent years press for that new hotel, as a centerpiece of a revitalized downtown, as crucial to its vision for the city and region. In February 2000, bank executive and Civic Progress member David Darnell would tell the business group:

> The goal of Civic Progress is to make the St. Louis region world class. This goal requires that the downtown area thrives, and that the City's financial difficulties be resolved. St. Louis is in tough competition with other cities [such as Charlotte, where Mr. Darnell visited the preceding week] working to strengthen their downtowns.
>
> To be successful, St. Louis must have the collective will to make something happen, and Civic Progress must help lead this effort.[7]

With Civic Progress pressing for continuing investment and development downtown, the city's elected officials could little afford an alternative view. When Mayor Clarence Harmon came before the group in early 2001 to discuss his "vision and goals for St. Louis" as a candidate for re-election, his prepared remarks stressed that in "courting development" he was "aggressive," citing the realization of the convention center hotel and its "$200 million/year boost," and his view that an "Attractive Downtown [is] vital to attracting tourism, business and talent to region. . . . Downtown is what people remember about a city, as opposed to prosperous suburbs (which are ubiquitous)."[8]

Anchors and Erosion

For real estate expert and mayoral advisor James Downs, a new convention hall was not just about securing Chicago's place as a visitor destination or filling hotel rooms. Downs described for a 1954 meeting of business leaders and the city's planning officials his judgment that a new convention hall, built "at the south end of the Loop," would "anchor the Loop securely." Downs did not elaborate on specifics of the "anchoring" role, but in other discussions he had stressed the need to maintain a compact and intensively developed downtown core. He would, of course, fail to get the convention hall there, as the *Chicago Tribune* determined the final lakefront site.[9]

Downs's view of the role of an "anchor" was seconded by Ted Aschman, Chicago's former planning director and the principal advisor to the Central Area Committee. Setting out the broad planning and development logic for renewing the Loop and its immediate environs, Aschman called for new "anchors"—he noted a new university campus, government buildings, or a civic auditorium—that "would greatly enhance the Central Area's compactness and discourage any tendency of a shifting of commercial values away from the present pattern of concentration."

For Downs and Aschman, and indeed the Chicago Central Area Committee, a new auditorium or convention hall was potentially—in the right place—a means of shaping land values and development prospects. Aschman's statement of "The Anchor Theory" in 1957 emphasized that anchor developments "would tend to confine future commercial development to the existing core." Effectively, the public anchor developments would provide a wall or barrier, separating the downtown core from its blighted and less valuable fringe.

Phil Hammer had much the same sort of wall or barrier in mind when he set out the criteria for siting Atlanta's planned new public development projects in 1960. The new auditorium/convention hall in Buttermilk Bottom offered a means both to eliminate a slum and to "assist in the protection of the Ponce de Leon corridor and the Uptown area beyond." Much the same larger purpose of anchoring and shaping land values was evident in Hammer's recommendation to site the planned new stadium just south of the downtown core, where it would "provide a healthy fringe to Downtown Atlanta."

In 1960s St. Louis, the call by department store owner Cubby Baer for "protection from erosion on the north side of downtown" was explicitly focused on the problem of "property decay" and the reality that the area was filled with stores "in a generally deteriorated condition," and bordered in turn by a predominantly African-American slum district. Baer's language of "protection from erosion" was echoed regularly by other St. Louis business leaders. In 1969, the St. Louis Chamber of Commerce endorsed the plan for a north side convention center, with the argument that it would provide "an effective frame of civic and esthetic facilities which would stabilize values, attract new investment and assure an atmosphere of vitality which would make our central business district one of the most attractive in the United States."

In seeking to reshape the north side of downtown St. Louis, business leaders, led by Leif Sverdrup, sought an "anchor" that could both reshape "property decay" and alter the prospects for new private investment on the north side. Sverdrup's planner, Elliott Chamberlain, stressed to his boss that the proposed convention center would "establish a firm anchor upon which new investment can be based." But in that quest to induce new investment, Sverdrup and his Civic Progress colleagues were fully committed to putting *land and location first*, prior to the potential for community benefit from new convention activity. The city's business leaders fully dismissed the conclusion of Economics Research Associates that the north side site would cost the city substantial visitor activity. And they commissioned no market analysis of their own. What they wanted, first and foremost, was an "anchor" and "protection from erosion."

For business leaders like Cubby Baer and Leif Sverdrup in St. Louis, Richard Rich in Atlanta, or Holman Pettibone in Chicago, the "anchor" notion extended beyond the planning logic set out by Ted Aschman and Phil Hammer. "Protection from erosion" and "stimulate private investment" had a larger *perceptual dimension* as well as a physical one. A major public investment in a convention center represented a tangible public commitment to the vitality of a specific area downtown, one that was fixed for an extended period of time. For the department store considering its economic future in the core, or the developer contemplating potential new investment possibilities, a new center provided long-term assurance of viability, far beyond what a private property owner or profit-maximizing business might be capable of offering.

"Anchors" were thus of enormous import to private developers. Phil Hammer long promoted the use of the air rights over Atlanta's railroad "gulch" for a major urban development. In his 1960 analysis of "Atlanta Sites" for the city's business leaders, he proposed the air rights location for a new convention center/auditorium, with the argument that "Construction of the [auditorium] facility in this area might make the entire City Center project possible through the support of necessary public improvements. Moreover, the immediate proximity could be a major reason for the construction of a large new hotel or motel facility in City Center."[10] Hammer's vision of a major public facility as the anchor or draw of the planned air rights development was reiterated in his proposal in the late 1960s that Tom Cousins use a professional basketball team and a new coliseum to serve that end. And Hammer's view of public "anchors" was the foundation for Cousins's effort to locate the proposed Georgia World Congress Center at his development over the air rights in the early 1970s.

For developers such as John Portman and Tom Cousins, a major public anchor development not only served as leverage for a broad array of public investment and improvements in a zone of new development, but also served as a magnet for people and activity. Brice Smith had made just that argument to Sverdrup in his 1968 analysis of a convention center for downtown St. Louis, arguing that a new center "would be attractive for the development of this 30 acre tract." Smith's point was that "The key to the economic feasibility of this project is the people generation of a convention center."[11]

As a "people generator"—at least *in prospect* if not necessarily in terms of actual performance—a new center held out the promise of an increase in visitor activity that might support a new hotel, or new retail stores. For a developer seeking to build on an undeveloped tract, like Atlanta's air rights, securing a new convention center as an integral part of the development offered a dramatic public commitment and a seeming diminution of risk.

The development role and logic of a new convention center extended well beyond the initial efforts in Atlanta and St. Louis in the 1960s and 1970s. Faced with the stalled development of the Houston Center project in downtown Houston, the Cadillac Fairview development firm sought a new convention center as the anchor and magnet for their project, going so far as to donate the land for the site. "Free" land was also part of Tom Cousins's successful effort to win the development of the new Georgia World Congress Center over the competing proposal from developer John Portman.

Business leaders in Washington, D.C., promoted a new convention center as a means of reviving the downtown core and boosting development on downtown's east side. The Downtown Progress Inc. organization argued, "Consumer expenditures generated from attendance at the multi-purpose facility will have a dramatic effort on Downtown if it were located in the Mount Vernon Square Area . . . [and] would create demand for 3500 additional hotel rooms, 90,000 square feet of retail space and 200,000 square feet of space for restaurants and entertainment facilities." And when New York City business and political leaders concluded that the existing Coliseum at Columbus Circle was too small, they promoted a new convention center at a site that "promises the most effective upgrading of the West Side."[12]

In these cases, and in cities from Boston to Portland, a new convention center was seen as the leading edge of the urban land development process, a means of both boosting private development opportunity and reshaping land values. For a Tom Cousins or Cadillac Fairview, as for Leif Sverdrup or even Arthur Rubloff earlier, a new convention center was a means of reshaping *expectations*—on the part of investors, firms, and tenants—about the development prospects of a piece of downtown turf. The reality of center performance, and the actual results in terms of economic impact, mattered little in the near term. What the developers, and the local business leadership, cared about was land and land value.

Conflict and Division

From the outside, for the interested citizen, journalist, or academic observer, a local business community (particularly in its organized form) appears a unified, monolithic whole. Sociologists John Logan and Harvey Molotch describe how "The desire for growth creates consensus among a wide range of elite groups, no matter how split they may be on other issues." They go on to note, in the case of Chicago's McCormick Place, "An internal quarrel over where a convention center is to be built, Banfield (1961) shows us, becomes the public issue for Chicago, but Banfield didn't notice that there was no question about whether there should be a convention center at all."[13]

For political scientist Clarence Stone, examining the post-World War II pattern of development issues and politics in Atlanta, the success of the city's business leaders reflected "the high degree of business unity." He notes that "the banks, the utilities, the major department stores, the daily newspaper, and Coca-Cola, in particular, have a long history of acting in concert, and they draw other businesses that may be newer to the Atlanta scene into the same pattern of unified public action. . . . In its relations with the external world, it does not divide into factions; hence, no segment of the business elite can be an ally in a coalition against another segment."[14]

Stone stresses how the business community operates through a dense network of interpersonal ties, reinforced by membership in Central Atlanta Progress. Yet he does not fully explore or explain *how* this degree of apparent business unity was achieved. Indeed, the existence of disparate *factions and factional interests* has long characterized Atlanta's business community, in the eyes of that community's central members.

Informing Floyd Hunter about the realities of community power in early 1950s Atlanta, attorney Hughes Spalding described Atlanta's business leaders as a series of "crowds:" "Simply that there are several 'crowds' in Atlanta that pretty well make all the big decisions. . . . There is the crowd I belong to—the Coca Cola-Trust Company crowd; the Georgia Power crowd; the C&S crowd; the Rich's crowd; the 1st National bank crowd, and the like."[15]

Atlanta's different "crowds" had different outlooks (Spalding described one as "dry-rotted," another as "aggressive") and different locational and development interests. And Spalding himself, as a principal adviser to Robert Woodruff and Coca-Cola, had his own interests as well, in seeking the development of both a "first class auditorium" and a "great stadium." But division into distinct crowds and factions had hampered development of the auditorium, and as late as 1959, planner Phil Hammer could describe "the immediate necessity of developing a realistic Downtown Plan"—a plan Atlanta business leaders had been historically unable to agree on.[16]

It took the initiative of leaders such as Robert Woodruff and Richard Rich to join with Ivan Allen in creating a *package of major public projects* that could bring about the unified support of the business community. Indeed, when Allen introduced his plan for combining the efforts for a stadium, auditorium, and coliseum to the Chamber of Commerce leadership in early 1960 (well before his election as mayor), it was with the premise that it would "bring support . . . from all factions concerned." His statement was yet another explicit recognition of the "factions" within the Atlanta business community, a division that needed to be remedied or accommodated in order to achieve the public development projects he and others sought.

Logan and Molotch argue that in 1950s Chicago "there was no question about whether there should be a convention center at all," and conclude that there was no challenge to "the belief in growth itself." Yet the building of a new public convention hall in Chicago was far from a certain, easily achievable product. Calls for a new convention facility on the part of business and civic leaders dated back to the 1920s. A succession of proposals had failed, due in part to repeated conflicts over *where* a new convention hall should go. Plans for a major complex of public buildings—plans which dated back to the Burnham plan of 1909—were just as regularly abortive. The Chicago Planning Commission's 1949 scheme for a new civic center at the western edge of the Loop failed to gain any serious backing. And the 1954 Fort Dearborn proposal for a major civic center complex north of the Chicago River generated a firestorm of opposition from business and real estate interests in the Loop.

Different geographic segments of Chicago businesses were represented by a variety of area associations (the West Central Association, the Greater

North Michigan Avenue Association, the State Street Council, the South Side Planning Board), each favoring its own zone. Conflict was equally pronounced among interests *within the Loop* during the 1950s, with Marshall Field's executives supporting public investment to the north of the Loop, and the Carson Pirie Scott leadership pressing for public attention to the Loop's south side.

The ultimately successful development of the McCormick Place convention center was by no means a product of a unified business community or growth machine. It was rather the singular product of the capacity of the *Tribune* newspaper to shift the politics of development from the city of Chicago to the state government in Springfield, thereby reshaping the fiscal politics of convention center building and trumping the disparate (and divided) business interests of the Loop and the city.

St. Louis, too, was marked by a clear distinction between the firms and development interests favoring the south side of the downtown core and those concerned with the north side. Thus, Mayor Cervantes's proposal for a new convention center and theme park at Union Station generated a wave of criticism (and the Sverdrup counter-proposal) from firms and interests on the north side of the core.

Atlanta too faced a continuing tension over development and investment efforts along the Peachtree spine long dominated by developer John Portman to the uptown area, and the fate of the historic downtown center at Five Points and Underground Atlanta. That spatial division and tension was exemplified by the overt conflict between Portman and Tom Cousins over the location of the new Georgia World Congress Center.

The tensions within downtown business communities were effectively "built into" the very form and character of the city. A major public investment or activity generator—a convention center, new arena, or arts complex—would naturally draw both potential users and new investment dollars—to it and its vicinity. And new high-value and amenity districts, such as New York's Upper East Side, Chicago's North Michigan Avenue, Atlanta's Peachtree Center and Buckhead, or St. Louis's Union Station, would often succeed at the expense of older, less desirable, or less adaptable sections, spurring a call for yet more public investment and revitalization.

Deals

Holman Pettibone of the Chicago Title and Trust Company faced a serious problem in 1954 and 1955. Pettibone had embraced and promoted the Fort Dearborn project and its plans for a new civic center of public buildings north of the Loop, on the north bank of the Chicago River, a project that would, in the words of developer Arthur Rubloff, "surpass the Golden Triangle in Pittsburgh or Rockefeller Center in New York . . . [that] will anchor the Loop and stimulate further development on all sides." Yet the project and Pettibone himself had immediately encountered a wave of criticism and opposition from business and property interests across the Loop, who feared that a shift in location of the county courts, or a move of federal government offices, would harm their occupancies and property values.[17]

Within a week of the formal announcement of the Fort Dearborn plan, mayoral development advisor James Downs had explained to the mayor, Pettibone, and a group of prominent business leaders that the project would impact office buildings in one part of the Loop, and that "certain real estate interests could also be expected to oppose any such plan, particularly those dealing with space which would be created by the vacation of areas presently rented by the various governments participating in a new civic center."[18]

Downs's assessment did not even tap the full level of division among Loop interests. With the head of the Marshall Field's department store backing the Fort Dearborn effort, another State Street merchant, John Pirie, head of the Carson Pirie Scott department store chain, was thoroughly opposed. Pirie promoted an alternative plan that included a new convention center on the south side of the Loop, and a different site for a potential civic center. If Holman Pettibone was to achieve his goal of a major revitalization project that would boost the fortunes of the entire Loop, he needed an approach that could mediate and reconcile these disparate geographic interests.

One potential approach to bridging the split between Marshall Field's and John Pirie, for example, was described by Earl Kribben, a Field's vice president and executive director of the Fort Dearborn project, in a December 1955 letter. Describing John Pirie, Kribben said, "Basically, John is too good a citizen to oppose anything that is good for Chicago. In the past he has said that he was for Fort Dearborn if a similar project to improve and stabilize the south side of the Loop could also be devised, and sooner or later I am sure that such a project will materialize."[19] Earl Kribben's observation contained the foundation for a solution—a political deal—that could reconcile the interests of Field's and Pirie.

One project that threatened to shift the activity and office demand of the Loop to the north threatened a host of locational interests. *Two projects* could satisfy both the north and south sides of the Loop, and thus sustain Pettibone's quest for Loop renewal with a package of distributive goods.

Holman Pettibone moved ahead on two parallel fronts in 1955 and after. He took the principal leadership role in establishing a new business organization that was broadly inclusive of Loop property and development interests, the Central Area Committee. And he and the new CAC hired planner Ted Aschman to set out a formal planning philosophy and design that could sustain consensus among the disparate Loop business interests, as well as guide a new city planning effort for the Loop.

Aschman's memo to the business group, "The Rebuilding of the Near-North and Near-South Sides of the Chicago Central Area," formally set out his "anchor theory" for focusing and containing commercial development. Aschman articulated both the *internal political problem* that Holman Pettibone faced, and a solution. Describing the "unhealthy rivalry in major commercial districts between property interests in different sections" that makes for "dissension and obstruction," Aschman suggested "combined planning of the 'anchor projects.'" He argued that this would "enhance the unity of the Central Area Committee in general while offering the best of possibilities for mustering all-out civic leadership and support for the specific program."[20]

Ted Aschman's joining of planning principles to a political deal was a masterful stroke, in promising the diverse cast of Loop interests a package of projects that they could all support, assuring the "unity" of the Central Area Committee and downtown business. His principles were formally adopted, complete with reference to "anchor projects," by the Central Area Committee and presented to Chicago's Commissioner of Planning as the basis for the new Central Area Plan being prepared by the city in 1958. And when the formal "Development Plan for the Central Area" was unveiled by Mayor Daley in August 1958, it neatly embraced all the projects—broadly distributed across the Loop—that the Central Area Committee and Ted Aschman had sought as "anchors," while promising to keep major new public buildings effectively where they then were.

The efforts of the Central Area Committee to realize those "anchors" and the broader array of public development projects did not stop with the just the city's plan. The CAC adopted a "program of action" beginning in 1959 that included "A new Federal building or buildings for the Central Area," "rail terminal consolidation" for the south Loop, a new "University of Illinois Chicago campus," the "proposed transportation center" over the air rights of Union Station on the near west side, and "Our Grant Park program" at the lakefront. The CAC did not focus on just a single project. Instead, it promised "action" on all of the major public development efforts in all sections of the Loop, a plan that could effectively continue to "unify" Loop interests. Through the vehicle of an "official" city plan document, the organization committed to something for everyone, with the larger goal of avoiding the kind of public conflict that had doomed the Fort Dearborn scheme.

Not all the promised projects in the Central Area Plan were ultimately realized. The transportation center never really emerged, although some version would be proposed again in later years. And the reuse of the south Loop rail lines really only came decades later with the Dearborn Park residential development in the 1980s. But the mere *promise* that all of the diverse locational interests would be served was sufficient to secure business community unity for an extended period. And the basic *political approach* of the CAC, of sustaining a unified façade of Loop interests and representation through an inclusive program of public improvements, was sustained over a period of decades. There would be a succession of "Central Area" plans after 1958, from the "Chicago 21" plan of 1973, to the Central Area Plan of 1983, through the Central Area Plan of 2003, to the Central Area Action Plan of 2009.

Atlanta's factions, much like their counterparts in Chicago, required a broader deal to make major public developments a reality. That deal was effectively engineered and announced by Ivan Allen in January 1960—not to the public at large, or even a broad civic group, but to the small but far more relevant board of directors of the Atlanta Chamber of Commerce. Allen first proposed a joint effort behind a new stadium, a music hall, and a coliseum—an initiative that "would bring support for the authority from all factions concerned." A month later, he amended that to defer the coliseum, at the specific request of developer John Portman. Atlanta's business community could be unified behind an inclusive *package* of development projects only if *everyone*—including Portman—agreed.

The timing of Allen's proposed deal was highly significant. His January 1960 remarks came months before he approached planning consultant Phil Hammer about a platform—the "Six Point Program"—for his term as president of the Chamber of Commerce. And where observers such as Clarence

Stone have described how as Atlanta's mayor "Allen wanted major-league sports brought to town. . . . He also wanted a new civic center," the essential package of projects and even the six-point program were not solely Allen's. They were the product of plans crafted by Phil Hammer, and development projects pressed by Robert Woodruff, Hughes Spalding, Richard Rich, and the leadership of Atlanta's business community, long before Ivan Allen assumed the office of mayor. Business unity came first.[21]

The package of projects outlined by Ivan Allen in January 1960 would ultimately take over a decade to be realized. But the package served to sustain effective business unity over the 1960s, a unity that was capped by the merger of the Central Atlanta Improvement Association and the Uptown Association in 1967. The product of that merger, Central Atlanta Progress, continued to sustain business community unity, in part by developing a series of Central Atlanta Studies that in turn endorsed public investments and improvements neatly spread out through the core, from Five Points and the traditional downtown heart, up Peachtree Street to John Portman's Peachtree Center complex, west to the railroad gulch with Tom Cousins's developments, and east to the Civic Center and North Avenue.

For Atlanta's business leaders, the lessons of the Ivan Allen era have been well learned. There has been a continuing stream of major public development projects beyond the original Civic Center and Atlanta-Fulton County Stadium: the Georgia World Congress Center, the Georgia Dome, the new Philips Arena, a new federal building and state office building, expansion of Georgia State, and with the Olympic Games the development of Centennial Olympic Park, new student housing, and Turner Field. And in perhaps the best learned and most substantial lesson from the failure of Ivan Allen's first bond proposal and his subsequent reluctance to deal with the city's electorate, effectively all of these major projects were managed without the involvement of the city government or a vote of Atlanta's citizens.

St. Louis had a single downtown. But for business leaders and property owners, there was a clear geographic divide between the north side and the south, a division long deeply built into the social fabric of the larger city. Harland Bartholomew's city plans of the 1940s and 1950s envisioned clearing and renewing the rings of "slums" surrounding the downtown core. The Mill Creek Valley renewal project bulldozed the slums to the west, while the Stadium project was designed to "eliminate approximately 50 acres . . . of the cancerous, blighted area of downtown St. Louis."[22]

That left the north side of downtown, the site of the Old Post Office building—a "cancer in the heart of the town"—and the slums of the near north side, designated as the Desoto-Carr redevelopment area. With the new stadium completed and the south side of downtown "protected," the business leaders of the north side—Cubby Baer, Irving and Bernard Edison—sought "their" project. The embrace of the north side convention center plan proposed by Leif Sverdrup on the part of Civic Progress, the Chamber of Commerce, and Downtown St. Louis was not the product of an explicit quid pro quo or package, as in Atlanta or Chicago. But the norm of mutual accommodation and deference within Civic Progress assured that the business leaders of St. Louis would be united behind Sverdrup. And with the business leadership fully unified, it had no concern about an overt, public dispute with the mayor over the center's location.

The spatial accommodation that produced the Cervantes Convention Center and thus balanced Busch Stadium to the south has persisted since the 1960s and 1970s. When Mayor Schoemehl proposed more space at the failing Cervantes Center, center director Bruce Sommer argued the merits of an *entirely new convention facility by Union Station.* The mayor demurred, arguing that a "Union Station location will simply arouse too much political opposition." The north side business interests, now tied to the new convention center, were still too strong for the mayor to tackle.

The leaders of Civic Progress effectively blocked a suburban location for a new football stadium during the 1980s, and assured the development of what is now the Edward Jones Dome where it too would anchor and support the northern flank of downtown. And when the opportunity came to replace the St. Louis Arena with a new venue for hockey, Civic Progress effectively backed and financed the Savvis/Scottrade Center at Kiel Center, neatly supporting the south side of the downtown core and the adjacent Union Station complex.

Unlike the business leadership in Chicago, the leaders of Civic Progress in St. Louis did not rely on a formal, public plan to cement a distributive "deal" for locating and building major new public facilities. Meeting monthly from the early 1950s, Civic Progress provided a forum for bargaining and dealing with the array of public projects tackled by the city government. That assured ultimately that each side of the core would receive its very own "protection from erosion."

Whether as Ted Aschman's "anchors" or Phil Hammer's "protection" and "healthy fringe," or the "protection from erosion" sought by Cubby Baer and Sverdrup, business leaders in Chicago, Atlanta, and St. Louis *needed* major public development projects—convention centers, stadiums, coliseums, and an occasional university campus—to shape and define downtown development and land value. But they, in each of these cities and a great many others, needed more than one.

The internal divisions and often overt conflict that marked the downtown development and renewal efforts of the 1950s and 1960s made clear how vulnerable these development efforts were in the face of business conflict. The management and amelioration of that conflict was managed through the creation of new organizations, like the Chicago Central Area Committee, through new downtown plans like Atlanta's Central Area Study, and through deals that could package and promise a series of public investments, neatly spread across the space of the downtown core.

The management of business division came first, managed and politicked within the business community. Sometimes the larger business deals would emerge in public form, as with the Central Area Plan in Chicago. Sometimes they would simply be explicated and concluded within the confines of a downtown club, as in the case of Atlanta's Chamber of Commerce or Civic Progress in St. Louis. But before the public announcement and the rhetoric of broad community improvement and economic impact, the deal would have been set within and among the local business leadership, inclusive enough to assure support and committed enough to be realized over a decade or more.

From Inside to Outside

The "package deals" of geographically distributed public improvements were shaped privately by business leaders among themselves. The initiatives for convention center development and their place in "deals" were largely private as well. Chicago's McCormick Place came out of the efforts by the *Tribune* and George Tagge at the state capital in Springfield. Atlanta's 1960s Civic Center was long the subject of discussion, but it was Ivan Allen and the Chamber of Commerce that moved it forward in the early policy process. The initiative for the "Intercontinental Congress Center" too came from a select group of business leaders, dissatisfied with the size and market position of the existing Civic Center.

St. Louis was somewhat different. While Busch Stadium began as an idea of a public official, urban renewal chief Charles Farris, it took the initiative and clout of Civic Progress to move it forward. So too began the new convention center. Originally the idea of architect Arthur Schwarz working for the

Terminal Railroad Association, both the proposal and the site were quickly embraced by Mayor Cervantes. But the new convention center plan was neatly appropriated by Sverdrup for his purposes and his preferred site. The insistence of Civic Progress and the organized business community on the north side of downtown for the center came *despite* a consultant analysis that termed it unsuitable. Yet that site was effectively an imperative for business leaders, literally giving north side firms their due in "erosion protection," while "balancing" Busch Stadium.

St. Louis was also different in the genesis of its center expansion in the 1980s. The expansion proposal did not originate with Civic Progress or a private development entrepreneur, planner, or architect. Instead, it began with newly elected Mayor Schoemehl. Schoemehl's interest in more convention center space was prompted by both his interest in economic development and the desires of hospitality industry leaders such as hotelier Fred Kummer and restaurateur Vincent Bommarito, his political allies.

But while the initiative lay with Schoemehl, the center expansion and the grander proposal for an adjacent domed stadium had to pass through the political gatekeepers of Civic Progress. Only they could provide the financial support and backing critical to a bond campaign, or the clout and state-level deal-making capacity required by these major projects. Yet as in the case of Sverdrup's plans in the 1960s, the initiatives for both the expansion and the dome came *before* there was any serious analysis of market feasibility. Indeed, Schoemehl's backing of the convention center expansion came *despite* the harsh critical assessments in the initial work of the Laventhol & Horwath consultants, and *despite* Bruce Sommer's argument for an entirely new center on the south side of downtown. The expansion and domed stadium were, for St. Louis business leaders, about far larger things—the city's image as big league, the stability of downtown—than mere convention business.

Once the distributive deals for centers, arenas, and stadiums were set *within* the business community, there was the matter of "selling" them, first to local elected officials and then to the general public. For a mayor interested in big initiatives and concrete accomplishments—the "opportunity to make an international impact," in the words of St. Louis budget director Stephen Mullin—a project, or set of projects, backed by a unified local business leadership offered an appealing political opportunity. It effectively assured newspaper editorial backing—indeed, in some cities, the newspaper publisher was a member of the business group—and the image of "community good" that came with business endorsement. It also meant there would be an ample business financial contribution for any campaign to sell a bond issue for the proposed facility.

The business community's backing can also change the political calculus around a major project. As St. Louis Mayor Schoemehl shared with a Civic Progress leader regarding the downtown stadium proposal, "It's clear that the Governor, [county executive] McNary, and the General Assembly are not going to adopt 'Schoemehl's Plan' and if this gets known as such it's done for. . . . If it's going to go anywhere from here, Don, Civic Progress is going to have to take the lead."[23]

While there are mayors in some cities who have largely acted as caretakers, focused narrowly on the day-to-day business of running a city government, most of the mayors in these cities, from the 1950s through the 2000s, have had a measure of political ambition and a policy agenda that sought notable accomplishments. At the very least, elected chief executives in Chicago, St. Louis, and Atlanta sought to promote new private investment and sustain a sense of development "momentum."

The argument for "momentum" was stated most directly by St. Louis budget director Stephen Mullin, in his December 1986 memo to Vince Schoemehl about the convention center expansion and stadium project. Contending that the project was "excellent," Mullin averred that he did not "take too seriously all talk about whether expenses are 'worth it'!" Instead, arguing the project's "*tremendous* advantages," Mullin termed it "an exciting world-class building project . . . .We don't often get this type of opportunity to make an international impact. " He went on, "We don't have many (any?) spectacular items on the drawing boards to continue the City's incredible momentum. We don't want a pause to [look] like a let-down."[24]

Mullin's arguments were not far from what architect Arthur Schwarz had told Mayor Cervantes in promoting a new convention center two decades before: "I am convinced more than ever that St. Louis has to move forward in these areas in a large way if we are to take advantage of the potentials of tourism and convention business." For a mayor, county executive, or governor interested in "big things" and "momentum," the agenda and projects promoted by the business community are enormously appealing.[25]

Where a mayor chose to directly *oppose* a business initiative, as St. Louis Mayor Cervantes did on the convention center proposal, there appeared to be no reluctance on the part of the business leadership to mount and sustain a fight. Cervantes was finally forced to back down. In Atlanta, when Mayor Maynard Jackson chose to oppose or merely slow the downtown development agenda of Central Atlanta Progress, the result was the "Brockey letter" of 1974, with its report of "rumors of an increasing exodus of business from the City," and a resulting flurry of negative local and national press reports of "Atlanta's Confidence . . . Faltering." There was little political advantage in an open dispute with the city's business leaders.[26]

The lesson of how to deal with the business community was obviously learned by one of Mayor Jackson's successors as mayor, Bill Campbell. Addressing the board of Central Atlanta Progress in late 1993 as mayor-elect, Campbell said, "he is looking forward to working with CAP to revitalize Downtown . . . [and] he encouraged CAP and the business community to improve relationships with the Fulton County delegation, in particular, and the State Legislature, in general, so that Atlanta will get the positive attention needed during the next session."[27]

The Atlanta case demonstrates one added dimension of the "outside" game in designing and selling convention centers to public officials and the public. When, in the late 1960s, Mayor Ivan Allen proved uninterested in pursuing another bond vote, either to fund an expansion of the Civic Center or for a new coliseum, business leaders could—and did—simply wait him out. His successor, Sam Massell, proved more amenable to Tom Cousins's proposal for a new arena, particularly when it could be financed without a public bond vote. And when the business leaders sought more convention center space, they and Phil Hammer could successfully make that case not to city officials, but to the state legislature and the governor. It was much the same in St. Louis. Civic Progress successfully steered the domed stadium/center expansion scheme through the Missouri state legislature, across the governor's desk, and through the St. Louis County electorate.

Business leaders thus have a broad array of options available to them in promoting convention centers and other public development projects. They can outwait a reluctant mayor, as they did in Nashville and Atlanta, and deal with his or her successors. They can bypass the city government and work with a county government, as with Cleveland's Medical Mart and Convention Center, or they can seek the creation of an independent public authority such as the Greater Richmond Convention Center Authority or the Detroit Regional Convention Facility Authority that can involve suburban governments. And the state government is yet another potential vehicle, either directly, as in the case of Chicago's McCormick Place and Atlanta's Georgia World Congress Center, or by persuading a state legislature or governor to commit special grant funds, as Pennsylvania Governor Ed Rendell did for Erie and

Lancaster, and the state of Arizona did for the Phoenix Convention Center expansion.

Convention center proposals can often involve a decade or more from initial proposal to firm public commitment and financing. Elected officials at a variety of levels will come and go over that period. It may only take the election of a single proponent, or the replacement of one politician more concerned about taxes and finance with another more interested in the promise of economic impact and job creation, to bring a new center to the point of realization. The organized business community need succeed only once.

Who Governs

Five decades ago, Robert Dahl's magisterial study of democracy and power in New Haven, Connecticut, *Who Governs?* was published. Dahl sought to answer the "ancient" question—particularly relevant at the height of the Cold War—"In a political system where nearly every adult may vote but where knowledge, wealth, social position, access to public officials, and other resources are unequally distributed, who actually governs?"[28]

Dahl's answer, based largely on case studies of specific decisions in New Haven during the 1950s, including the redevelopment of much of the inner city, was that policy-making was shaped by an "executive-centered coalition" around Mayor Richard Lee. Given that Lee, and his policies, were assessed by New Haven's voters every two years, the conclusion for Dahl was that its *citizens* govern New Haven, through their capacity to choose elected officials and thereby to make policy and programmatic choices. There are business leaders in Dahl's New Haven analysis, largely on the sidelines of the policy process and generally in symbolic rather than substantive roles. They—the "economic notables"—manifestly did not *govern* New Haven.

Perhaps the most direct and cogent assessment of the role of business interests was offered by Dahl's graduate student and colleague Nelson Polsby, in his companion volume to *Who Governs?*:

> If a man's major life work is banking, the pluralist presumes he will spend his time at the bank, and not in manipulating community decisions. This presumption holds until the banker's activities and participations indicate otherwise. . . .
>
> On the other hand, it is easy to spot the banker who really *does* run

> community affairs when we presume he does not, because his activities will make this fact apparent. In the absence of the requisite activities, we have no grounds for asserting that the banker in fact does run the community.[29]

A review of the monthly meeting minutes of Civic Progress from the early 1950s to 2000, the monthly minutes of the board of directors of first the Atlanta Chamber of Commerce and later Central Atlanta Progress spanning much the same time frame, and the comparable albeit less consistent records of the Fort Dearborn sponsors and the Chicago Central Area Committee makes a few points obvious.

First, in contrast to Polsby's assertion, the bankers in these cities did not solely spend their time at the bank. Nor did the insurance CEOs spend theirs at their firms, or the department store executives at their corporate offices, the utility presidents at theirs, Holman Pettibone at Chicago Title and Trust, or the Buschs at the family brewery. They were, together with their counterparts in a broad range of major local firms, actively involved over a period of years in major business organizations, regularly meeting with, conferring, and writing to their counterparts. Just as regularly, they participated in other civic organizations, and corresponded and met with an array of public officials on issues of concern. They manifestly did not spend their time just "at the bank."

Yet while St. Louisans Gussie Busch, Don Lasater, Howard Baer, Cubby Baer, Irving Edison, Jim McDonnell, and Buster May did not spend their time solely at the bank, department store, or aircraft plant, neither did they (in Polsby's words) "run the community." It was much the same in Baltimore, or Atlanta, Cincinnati, or Chicago. Civic Progress, and its counterparts the Central Area Committee and Central Atlanta Progress, had a wide array of interests and concerns. But these groups, and local business leaders and their successors and counterparts, had *specific concerns and interests consistently focused on downtown*. St. Louis most likely would not have gotten a stadium, convention center, or a dome—certainly not in the places and ways they did—were it not for these business leaders. Atlanta's downtown development history, from the Civic Center and stadium to the World Congress Center, Georgia Dome, to Underground Atlanta and a downtown streetcar, reflects the same continuing force of persistent business interests.

The business leaders of Civic Progress, for example, in late 1987, planning their program for the coming year at the Civic Progress meeting at the Bogey Club, discussed the "Stadium situation," the plans for a "New Performing

Arts Center" in St. Louis's Grand Center district in midtown, city-county consolidation, the St. Louis public schools, health care costs, plans for a rail transit system, and a project to deal with prejudice and bigotry. They thus covered a diverse array of projects and purposes, albeit with a substantial focus on bricks and mortar development projects in the city's core.[30]

What they did not do, that month, the following year, or the years before and after, was seek to "govern" St. Louis or "run the community." They focused on specific projects, often at the behest of an individual member, that they sought to bring to realization. In the case of the stadium, the performing arts center, and the rail transit system they proved eminently successful over time. They fully failed at governmental consolidation, reining in health care costs, or reforming the public schools. But it is equally evident what they did not concern themselves with.

Despite annoyances or occasional outright conflict with local elected officials, they did not pick and choose candidates. Individual business leaders may well have. But the organization did not pick favorites. Civic Progress, and its sister organizations in other cities, did not try to affect the day-to-day business of city or county government. They manifestly did not "run" things. What they did do was define and shape a policy agenda, largely but not entirely focused on downtown, economic development, and major public investments. What they wanted were "anchors," "magnets," and "protection from erosion."

Chicago got McCormick Place, new public buildings, a university campus, expressways, and a revived Loop. St. Louis garnered stadiums, convention centers, an arena, and a performing arts center. And Atlanta managed a succession of convention facilities, arenas, and stadiums, as well as a revived Underground Atlanta. What business did not do—could not do—was fundamentally change major institutions, people, and the far more intractable divisions of race and class. They could build new downtowns. They could not refashion cities and their residents. They succeeded in producing cities that featured grand public investments, with a continuing push for even more public projects, in order that their respective cores might continue as appealing zones for private investment, even as the cities themselves, their governments, their larger economies, and their social fabric, frayed and faltered. For St. Louis, as for a great many other cities, the discourse of the local business leadership circa 2000 sounded very much like the grand schemes they had discussed and promoted thirty or forty years earlier:

> We also heard an excellent presentation from Dick Fleming and Mike Jones, co-chairs of Downtown Now, regarding the short- and

long-term plans for city growth and revitalization. Dick discussed four key areas for development, including the Washington Avenue loft district; the Old Post Office district; Laclede's Landing and Riverside North; and the Arch grounds and Mall. The cost for the entire plan is approximately $1 billion, which is comparable to other cities.

Mike discussed some of the ongoing projects, including the Convention Hotel, which he said was a prerequisite to all economic development. There is an agreement in principle for the hotel, which will cost $210 million. Mike also noted that the Arena demolition is scheduled for February 27 and that talks with developers for that land site are promising. Darste-Webbe [public housing project] demolition is under way, with a $160 million residential project planned. Grand Center residential is another target area for growth.[31]

Note on Sources

Aschman Papers	Frederick T. Aschman Publications, #3500. Division of Rare and Manuscript Collections, Cornell University Library.
Atlanta Bureau of Planning Papers	Atlanta Bureau of Planning Papers, Kenan Research Center at the Atlanta History Center.
Atlanta Chamber of Commerce Records	Records of the Atlanta Chamber of Commerce, at offices of Metro Atlanta Chamber of Commerce.
Calloway Papers	Ernest Calloway Papers, State Historical Society of Missouri-St. Louis.
Carter Gubernatorial Records	Jimmy Carter Gubernatorial Records, Georgia Archives.
Central Atlanta Progress Internal Records	Central Atlanta Progress Internal Records, at offices of Central Atlanta Progress.
Central Atlanta Progress Records	Central Atlanta Progress Records, Kenan Research Center at Atlanta History Center.
Cervantes Papers	Alfonso J. Cervantes Mayoral Papers, University Archives, Washington University, St. Louis.
Citizens Development Committee Records	Citizens Development Committee Records, Cincinnati History Library and Archives, Cincinnati Museum Center.
Cone Papers	Fairfax M. Cone Papers, Special Collections Research Center, University of Chicago Library.

Conway Papers	James Conway Mayoral Papers, University Archives, Washington University, St. Louis.
Cook Papers	Rodney M. Cook Papers, Richard B. Russell Library for Political Research and Studies, University of Georgia Libraries, Athens.
Downtown Progress Inc. Records	Downtown Progress Inc. Records, D.C. Community Archives, D.C. Public Library.
Downtown St. Louis Inc. Records	Downtown St. Louis Inc. Records, State Historical Society of Missouri-St. Louis.
Fort Dearborn Project Records	Fort Dearborn Project Records, Special Collections & University Archives, University of Illinois at Chicago Library.
Greater Kansas City Chamber of Commerce Minutes	Greater Kansas City Chamber of Commerce Minutes, State Historical Society of Missouri Research Center-Kansas City.
Hammer & Company Records	Hammer & Co. Internal Records, Atlanta, provided by Jeff Wingfield.
Hammer Papers	Philip G. Hammer papers #4527, Southern Historical Collection, The Wilson Library, University of North Carolina at Chapel Hill.
Harmon Papers	Clarence Harmon papers/PP06, Special Collections Research Center, Morris Library, Southern Illinois University Carbondale.
Hartsfield Papers	William Berry Hartsfield Papers, Manuscript, Archives, and Rare Book Library, Emory University.
Hunter Papers	Floyd Hunter papers, Manuscript, Archives, and Rare Book Library, Emory University.
Kinsley Papers	Milton Kinsley Papers, University Archives, Washington University, St. Louis.
Massell Papers	Sam Massell, Jr. Papers, Kenan Research Center at the Atlanta History Center.

Metropolitan Housing and Planning Council Records	Metropolitan Planning Council Records, Special Collections & University Archives, University of Illinois at Chicago Library.
Pettibone Papers	Holman Pettibone Papers, Chicago History Museum Research Center.
Poelker Papers	John Poelker Mayoral Papers, University Archives, Washington University, St. Louis.
Rich Papers	Richard H. Rich papers, Manuscript, Archives, and Rare Book Library, Emory University.
Rubloff Papers	Arthur Rubloff Papers, Chicago History Museum Research Center.
San Antonio City Archives	Municipal Archives and Records, Office of the City Clerk, San Antonio.
Schoemehl Papers	Vincent Schoemehl Mayoral Papers, State Historical Society of Missouri-St. Louis.
St. Louis Chamber of Commerce Records	St. Louis Regional Commerce and Growth Association Records, State Historical Society of Missouri-St. Louis.
Sverdrup Papers	Leif Sverdrup Papers, University Archives, Washington University, St. Louis.
Tucker Papers	Raymond R. Tucker Mayoral Papers, University Archives, Washington University, St. Louis.
Wheeler Papers	Charles B. Wheeler Jr. Papers, State Historical Society of Missouri Research Center-Kansas City.
Wilson Papers	A. J. Wilson Papers, University Archives, Washington University, St. Louis.
Woodruff Papers	Robert Winship Woodruff papers, Manuscript, Archives, and Rare Book Library, Emory University.

Notes

Chapter 1. Building Boom

1. Lester B. Knight & Associates, "McCormick Place: Chicago Meeting the Future," November 1982, 21.

2. Ibid., 11, 25.

3. KPMG Peat Marwick, "Long Range Marketing Study," January 1990, II-7, II-14, II-16, CIL-1163, Current Urban Documents Microfiche Collection.

4. Ibid., II-3.

5. Ibid., VII-6.

6. Metropolitan Pier and Exposition Authority, "Official Statement, $868,849,764.60 McCormick Place Expansion Project Bonds, Series 1992A," 35.

7. Coopers & Lybrand, "Market Analysis in Connection with the Proposed Development of an 800-Room Hotel at the McCormick Place Convention Complex," Appendix D in Metropolitan Pier and Exposition Authority (MPEA), "Interim Board Report: Findings and Recommendations," April 2010; "Official Statement, $127,420,000 Hospitality Fee Revenue Bonds, Series 1996A."

8. Gary Washburn, "McCormick May Grow Again—Convention Center Addition Considered," *Chicago Tribune*, March 23, 1999.

9. Matt O'Connor, "Fawell Pleads Guilty, Cooperates with U.S.," *Chicago Tribune*, September 15, 2004.

10. MPEA, 2010. The MPEA-owned Hyatt hotel has become the authority's primary revenue generator. In fiscal 2009, McCormick Place had an operating loss of $22.7 million, while the hotel generated an operating profit of $17.4 million.

11. Governor Andrew M. Cuomo, "2012 State of the State Address," January 4, 2012; Steve Lopez, "Sizing Up the Stadium Deal," *Los Angeles Times*, January 9, 2011; PKF Consulting, "Los Angeles Special Event Center/Convention Center Study," July 2011; Connie Bruck, "The Man Who Owns L.A.," *New Yorker*, January 16, 2012, 46-57.

12. Jim Nichols, "Expectations too High for Medical Mart Complex, Some Experts Say," *Cleveland Plain Dealer*, March 17, 2009.

13. Although there are abundant studies of the economic impact of stadiums and arenas, there is almost no academic literature on the impact of convention centers. See, for example, Roger Noll and Andrew Zimbalist, eds., *Sports, Jobs, and Taxes* (Washington, D.C.: Brookings Institution Press, 1997). The Javits Center figures are from PriceWaterhouseCoopers, "Javits Convention Center

Economic Impact Analysis 2008 and 2009," January 2011. On the PGA Show, see BPA Worldwide, "PGA Merchandise Show 2008 Event Audit," 2008.

14. Edward C. Banfield, *Political Influence* (New York: Free Press, 1961), 264, 314; Clarence N. Stone, *Regime Politics* (Lawrence: University Press of Kansas, 1989), 176, 195; Paul E. Peterson, *City Limits* (Chicago: University of Chicago Press, 1981), 131-32, 148; Dennis R. Judd, "Constructing the Tourist Bubble," in Dennis R. Judd and Susan S. Fainstein, eds., *The Tourist City* (New Haven: Yale University Press, 1999), 35-53; Peter Eisinger, "The Politics of Bread and Circuses," *Urban Affairs Review* 35, 3 (January 2000): 316-31; Alan Altshuler and David Luberoff, *Mega-Projects* (Washington, D.C.: Brookings Institution, 2003), 220, 268.

15. Patricia Gober, *Metropolitan Phoenix: Place Making and Community Building in the Desert* (Philadelphia: University of Pennsylvania Press, 2006), 178. See also Carol Ann Poore, "Downtown Phoenix Rising: A Case Study of Two Organizations Building Social Capital for Urban Core Revitalization," Ph.D. dissertation, Arizona State University, May 2011.

16. Phoenix Community Alliance, "2007-2008 Strategic Plan," 1; Phoenix Community Alliance, "A Third Convention Hotel in Downtown Phoenix," 1; David Krietor to Sheryl Sculley, "Additional Information on Request for Authorization to Extend the Memorandum of Understanding with the Rouse Company to Construct a Hotel in Downtown Phoenix," September 4, 1997, Public Records Web Search, City Clerk, City of Phoenix.

17. David Krietor to Sheryl Sculley, "Request for Authorization. . . . Market Study of the Phoenix Civic Plaza," October 16, 1998, Public Records Web Search, City Clerk, City of Phoenix.

18. The PWC attendance figures are from Maguire Company, "Possible State Financial Support of Expansion of Civic Plaza," 2002, Archives and Public Records, Arizona State Library. Attendee spending estimates were reported in David Schreiner to Sheryl Sculley, "Subject: Phoenix Civic Plaza Market Study," December 7, 1999.

19. Jeremy Voss, "Convention Hysteria," *Phoenix New Times*, August 31, 2000.

20. Minutes of meeting, Ad Hoc Study Committee on Phoenix Civic Plaza Convention Facility, December 6, 2001, Office of the Chief Clerk, Arizona State Legislature.

21. Jahna Berry, "Final Building Opens at Phoenix Convention Center," *Arizona Republic*, December 26, 2008.

22. Patrick Brady to Sheryl Sculley, "Backup Information . . . Concerning 1,000 Room Downtown Hotel," Phoenix City Council, June 16, 2004, Public Records Web Search, City Clerk, City of Phoenix.

23. Patrick Grady to Sheryl Sculley, "Civic Plaza Expansion Status Report," Phoenix City Council, October 9, 2001, Public Records Web Search, City Clerk, City of Phoenix.

24. David Schreiner to Sheryl Sculley, "Phoenix Civic Plaza Market Study," Phoenix City Council, December 7, 1999, Public Records Web Search, City Clerk, City of Phoenix.

25. Editorial, *Arizona Republic*, October 5, 2001.

26. Grady to Sculley, "Backup Information."

27. Richard Warnick to Patrick Grady, "Hotel Vision Statement," Phoenix City Council, May 12, 2005, Public Records Web Search, City Clerk, City of Phoenix.

28. Moody's Investor Service, "Moody's Downgrades Downtown Phoenix Hotel Corporation's $156.71 Million Senior Revenue Bonds to Ba1," December 20, 2010. The A series bonds were reduced to a rating of Ba1, below "investment grade"; Moody's Investor Service, "Rating Update: Downtown Phoenix Convention Hotel Corporation," September 8, 2011.

29. Downtown Phoenix Hotel Corporation, "Material Event Notice," January 2012.

30. PriceWaterhouseCoopers, "San Diego Convention Center Strategic Plan Update," December 2007, 116.

31. CSL, "Updated Planning Analysis for an Expanded/Improved Boston Convention & Exhibition Center," November 30, 2010, slide 24; CSL, "Market Demand Analysis for Enhancements to the New Orleans Morial Convention Center," February 2009.

32. Tradeshow Week, *Major Exhibit Hall Directory*, selected years.

33. "Council Approves Huge Memorial Auditorium," *Los Angeles Times*, June 15, 1920; "Two New Bond Issues Planned," *Los Angeles Times*, October 28, 1939; Editorial, "Tuesday Primary Propositions," *Los Angeles Times*, March 30, 1951; Editorial, "We Need the Auditorium," *Los Angeles Times*, May 20, 1953; "Los Angeles Vote Bars Center," *New York Times*, June 13, 1954; "Convention Hall Opened by Yorty," *New York Times*, July 11, 1971.

34. See Heywood Sanders, "Building the Convention City," *Journal of Urban Affairs* 14, 2 (1992): 144-48.

35. Editorial, "Tarnished Pot o' Gold," *Cleveland Plain Dealer*, February 16, 1956.

36. See Thomas H. O'Connor, *Building a New Boston* (Boston: Northeastern University Press, 1993), 120-23. See also Earl Foell, "Hynes Unveils Plan for Auditorium," *Christian Science Monitor*, August 7, 1958, and Elihu Rubin, *Insuring the City: The Prudential Center and the Postwar Urban Landscape* (New Haven, Conn.: Yale University Press, 2012).

37. Editorial, "We Much Need a Civic Auditorium," *Los Angeles Times*, February 19, 1953; Fort Dearborn Project, Meeting May 6, 1954, Fort Dearborn Project Records. James Downs was then the city's housing and redevelopment coordinator. He would serve as the de facto real estate and development adviser to mayors Martin Kennelly and Richard J. Daley.

38. Richard M. Hurd, *Principles of City Land Values* (New York: Real Estate Record Association, 1924), 67.

39. Atlanta Metropolitan Planning Commission, "Up Ahead," February 1952, 71; Atlanta Metropolitan Planning Commission, "Now . . . For Tomorrow," September 1954, 38.

40. "Council Approves Huge Memorial Auditorium," *Los Angeles Times*, June 15, 1920. On St. Louis, see James Neal Primm, *Lion of the Valley*, 2nd ed. (Boulder: Pruett, 1990), 447-49. On Cleveland, see Eric Johannesen, *Cleveland Architecture 1876-1976* (Cleveland: Western Reserve Historical Society, 1976), 151-52.

41. DMAI and IAAM, "Best Practices," August 2007, 4.

42. Laventhol & Horwath, "L&H Community Facilities Advisory Group" and "Sports and Convention Facilities Services," n.d.

43. Jan Schaffer, "Big Center Is a Must, Study Says," *Philadelphia Inquirer*, January 12, 1983; Jan Schaffer, "With Center, City Hopes to Fix Image," *Inquirer*, January 23, 1983.

44. Editorial, "A New Convention Center: Do It Now and Do It Right," *Inquirer*, January 17, 1983.

45. Phyllis Kaniss, *Making Local News* (Chicago: University of Chicago Press, 1991), 188-219.

46. Jenice Armstrong, "Open for Business: Now Comes the Hard Part," *Philadelphia Daily News*, June 24, 1993.

47. Ibid.

48. Jenice Armstrong, "It's Too Small!," *Daily News*, February 4, 1993; Tom Belden, "Bigger, Better, Wider, Ever More Competitive," *Inquirer*, November 20, 1997.

49. Tom Belden, "Huge Ballroom Seen for Convention Center," *Inquirer*, January 20, 2000.

50. "Center Survey: If You Expand, They Will Come," *Daily News*, October 4, 2002.

51. Marcia Gelbart, "Smaller Return Seen from Center Expansion," *Inquirer*, October 4, 2002.

52. "Only a single 2002 analysis was done of the center's expansion. The study was never made public and was forgotten when the authority's leadership changed soon after it was drafted." Tom Belden, "Center Raises Money, Doubts," *Inquirer*, July 18, 2004. A copy of the CSL study is in the author's possession. See CSL, "Feasibility Study for an Expanded Pennsylvania Convention Center," January 2003, 52-53.

53. See, for example, Suzette Parmley, "An Unconventional View," *Inquirer*, October 24, 2010; Philadelphia Convention and Visitors Bureau, "Press Release: Pennsylvania Convention Center Expansion Underway—First Building Demolished—A Bigger Future Begins," August 15, 2007.

54. Pennsylvania Convention Center Authority, "Convention Center Expansion Operating Plan," November 2006.

55. Crossroads Consulting Services, "Business Plan for the Pennsylvania Convention Center: Final Report," December 2010.

56. In a rare effort to gain an independent view of the actual prospects of center expansion, the Pew Charitable Trusts commissioned a study and analysis of the national convention center market in late 2006, at the request of Governor Rendell's chief of staff. The study was completed in March 2007, although it did not become public until that September. It concluded that center backers "are likely overselling its benefits." The *Daily News* quoted Rendell saying "that he'd seen a summary of the report and still believed expansion was a good investment." David Davies, "Convention Center Expansion Too Rosy?" *Daily News*, September 25, 2007, and Economic Development Research Group, "An Assessment of U.S. Market Conditions Facing Large Convention Facilities: Implications for Philadelphia," March 2007.

57. David W. Chen, "Expansion Advised for Javits Center," *New York Times*, April 23, 1997.

58. Thomas J. Lueck, "Renewed Calls for Expansion of Javits Center," *New York Times*, May 3, 1997.

59. Editorial, "Expand the Javits Center," *New York Times*, June 20, 1998.

60. Coopers & Lybrand, "A Market, Building Program, Financial Operations and Economic Impact Analysis for Potential Expansion of the Jacob K. Javits Convention Center of New York," April 1997.

61. PWC, "Jacob K. Javits Convention Center Expansion Study," March 2000, i.

62. Elisabeth Bumiller, "Jets Circulate Plan for Football Stadium Linked to the Javits Center," *New York Times*, December 8, 2000.

63. PWC, "Market and Economic Impact Analysis for a Proposed Jacob K. Javits Convention Center Expansion and Headquarters Hotel," January 2004, 17.

64. Charles V. Bagli, "Javits Center Expansion Overshadowed by Stadium Debate," *New York Times*, March 2, 2004.

65. PWC, "Market and Economic Impact Analysis," 2.

66. Ibid., 16.

67. See NYC & Co., "Tourism Barometer—December and Full Year 2003," n.d.

68. PWC, "Jacob K. Javits Convention Center Economic Impact Analysis: Executive Summary," June 2013.

69. New York Convention Center Development Corp., "Javits Center General Project Plan," March 2009, 7.

70. During this same time frame, PriceWaterhouseCoopers also produced positive convention center market studies for other cities, including Boston, San Diego, and Irving, Texas.

71. While the Javits expansion appeared to manage widespread support, the proposed Jets stadium next door generated a storm of opposition from the neighborhood and other elected officials.

Chapter 2. Paying for the Box

1. Minutes of the meeting of the Convention Committee, November 22, 1929, Greater Kansas City Chamber of Commerce Minutes.

2. Address by Mr. Mann before the annual meeting of the Chamber of Commerce, November 26, 1929, UMKC. On the history of public improvements in Kansas City, see William H. Wilson, *The City Beautiful Movement* (Baltimore: Johns Hopkins University Press), 1989.

3. See Kansas City Chamber of Commerce, *Where These Rocky Bluffs Meet: The Story of the Kansas City Ten-Year Plan* (Kansas City: Chamber of Commerce, 1928).

4. On the support of the Pendergast organization, see William M. Reddig, *Tom's Town* (New York: Lippincott, 1947), 180–82. See also A. Theodore Brown and Lyle W. Dorsett, *K.C.: A History of Kansas City, Missouri* (Boulder, Colo.: Pruett, 1978).

5. James N. Primm, *Lion of the Valley: St. Louis, Missouri* (Boulder: Pruett, 1981), 447.

6. "How St. Louis . . . Has Become a Leader in City Planning," *St. Louis Post-Dispatch*, May 23, 1920.

7. James Primm notes that with the inclusion of the new hospital "in the heart of the black district," "Not surprisingly, the primarily black wards supported the bond issue by a 4 1/2 to 1 average margin." Primm, *Lion of the Valley*, 448.

8. Robert B. Fairbanks, "Metropolitan Planning and Downtown Redevelopment: The Cincinnati and Dallas Experiences, 1940–1960," *Planning Perspectives* 2, 3 (September 1987): 241–42; Harland Bartholomew and Associates, "A Master Plan for Dallas, Texas: Report Number One," September 1943, 49–50. See also Robert B. Fairbanks, *For the City as a Whole* (Columbus: Ohio State University Press, 1998), chap. 5.

9. Barry Bishop, "Downtown Civic Center Urged with new County, City Halls," *Dallas Morning News*, April 13, 1945. See also Fairbanks, *For the City as a Whole.*

10. Allen Quinn, "Dallas Votes $40,000,000 Bond Issue," *Dallas Morning News*, December 9, 1945.

11. John M. Findlay, *Magic Lands* (Berkeley: University of California Press, 1992), 217.

12. Al Ostrow, "Gateway Loss Spurs New Plan," *Cleveland Press*, November 6, 1957.

13. See William Zeckendorf, *Zeckendorf: The Autobiography of William Zeckendorf* (New York: Holt, Rinehart, 1970).

14. See Edward C. Banfield, *Big City Politics* (New York: Random House, 1965), 35–36.

15. "Center Bonds Lose," *St. Louis Post-Dispatch*, March 10, 1971.

16. Minutes of the Meeting of the Board of Directors, March 20, 1964, Greater Kansas City Chamber of Commerce Minutes.

17. Ibid., May 22, 1964.

18. Ibid., July 21, 1967.

19. Ibid., September 15, 1967.

20. Ibid.

21. Editorial, "The Real Issue Tomorrow," *Kansas City Star*, December 15, 1969.

22. Minutes of the Meeting of the Board of Directors, December 29, 1969, Greater Kansas City Chamber of Commerce Minutes.

23. Ibid.

24. Ibid., April 27, 1970.

25. Ibid.

26. "Convention Center Financing Studied," *Kansas City Star*, June 26, 1971.

27. Gladstone Associates, "Impact of the H. Roe Bartle Center on the Kansas City Central Business District," March 1976.

28. Minutes of the Meeting of the Board of Directors, June 28, 1971, Greater Kansas City Chamber of Commerce Minutes.

29. Ibid.

30. "Firm on Convention Center," *Kansas City Star*, September 22, 1971.

31. Resolution on Convention Center, Minutes of the Meeting of the Board of Directors, October 21, 1971, Greater Kansas City Chamber of Commerce Minutes.

32. "Convention Center Price Tag Rises Sharply," *Kansas City Star*, July 29, 1973.

33. "Convention Center Options Explored," *Kansas City Times*, September 26, 1973.

34. Nathan Stark to Dick Berkley et al., "Capital Improvement Bond Program Meeting, March 29, 1973," Wheeler Papers, folder 52:28.

35. "Convention Center Dividends Paid in Business, Jobs," *Kansas City Star*, December 16, 1973.

36. Jerry Jette to Mayor Wheeler, "Recommendations for the Passage of the Capital Improvement Bond Issue," Wheeler Papers.

37. Jim Mosley and Fred Lindecke, "Ashcroft Oks Bill for Stadium Here," *St. Louis Post-Dispatch*, July 15, 1989.

38. See Dan Hoxworth and John Clayton Thomas, "Economic Development Decisionmaking in a Fragmented Polity," *Journal of Urban Affairs* 15, 3 (1993): 275–92.

39. Edward Kohn, "Kansas City Voters OK Tax Hikes to Enlarge Convention Hall," *St. Louis Post-Dispatch*, February 8, 1990.

40. Eric Adler, "Bartle Hall Basks in the Spotlight of Expansion Opening," *Kansas City Star*, September 24, 1994.

41. Rick Alm, "Upgrade Urged for Bartle Hall," *Kansas City Star*, September 14, 2000.

42. Kevin Collison, "Bartle, Bonds: What's Next?" *Kansas City Star*, November 8, 2002.

43. San Antonio, "Minutes of the Regular Meeting of the City Council, February 24, 1983," San Antonio City Archives.

44. Gladstone Associates/Arthur Andersen & Co., "Henry B. Gonzalez Convention Center Expansion Feasibility Analysis," November 1990.

45. The state legislation also allowed the two percent tax to be used for improvements to the nearby Alamodome stadium and Municipal Auditorium. The tax was also employed as partial backing for the $278 million in bonds used to finance a 1,000-room convention center hotel.

46. Standard & Poor's, "City of San Antonio, Texas," September 12, 2006; San Antonio Chief Financial Officer, "Financial Plan," Convention Center Expansion Plan Presentation to City Council, May 30, 2012, author's possession.

47. Cincinnati City Planning Commission, "Land Use and Building Groups: Part Two of the Cincinnati Business District Plan," December 1957.

48. Interview with John Gilligan, April 11, 1995, author's possession.

49. Interview with Eugene Ruehlmann, August 16, 1995, author's possession.

50. "Minutes of Meeting of Executive Committee, March 23, 1962," Citizens Development Committee Records.

51. Gilligan Interview, April 11, 1995.

52. Interview with Herbert Stevens, March 2, 1995, author's possession.

53. Laventhol & Horwath, "Structuring the Financing of the Proposed Expansion of the Cincinnati Convention-Exhibition Center in Cincinnati, Ohio," August 1981, IV-5.

54. Britt Robson, "Hotel Wars," *Cincinnati Magazine*, July 1984, 43.

55. Sarah Sturman, "Bigger Convention Hall Urged," *Cincinnati Post*, November 15, 1990.

56. PriceWaterhouse, "Sabin Convention Center Expansion Study," June 1995, ES-2.

57. Cliff Peale, "Waiting Will Only Cost More, Officials Say," *Cincinnati Post*, February 23, 1999; Roy Wood, "Sabin Panel: Scale Back Plan," *Cincinnati Post*, November 9, 2001.

58. Todd Portune to Charlie Luken, "Email Subject: convention center," May 3, 2002 and attachments, author's possession.

59. Rick Bird, "Not Your Father's Convention Center," *Cincinnati Post*, June 23, 2006; Alexander Coolidge, "Opening New Doors: Convention Center Upgrade Breeds Confidence," *Cincinnati Enquirer*, June 18, 2006.

60. San Jose Redevelopment Agency, "Memorandum: San Jose McEnery Convention Center Expansion," May 24, 2007; Katherine Conrad, "$120 Million San Jose Convention Center Expansion Bond Planned," *Silicon Valley/San Jose Business Journal*, October 29, 2010.

61. Editorial, "A Convention Hall Needed," *New York Times*, December 19, 1947.

62. "La Guardia Plans City Auditorium," *New York Times*, September 30, 1955; Will Lissner, "Vast Sports Arena in Columbus Circle Mapped by Garden," *New York Times*, November 14, 1946. See also Hilary Ballon and Kenneth T. Jackson, eds., *Robert Moses and the Modern City: The Transformation of New York* (New York: Norton, 2007), 263–67.

63. "Dewey Signs Bill for Huge Garden," *New York Times*, April 13, 1948.

64. Robert Moses, *Public Works: A Dangerous Trade* (New York: McGraw-Hill, 1970), 443. See also Ballon and Jackson, *Robert Moses and the Modern City*, 263–67.

65. "City Offers Land for Music Center," *New York Times*, May 9, 1951; "Plan Abandoned for 'Uptown' Opera," *New York Times*, March 29, 1952.

66. Edward Burks, "New Exhibit Hall Planned Here," *New York Times*, March 25, 1970.

67. See Robert A. M. Stern, Thomas Mellins, and David Fishman, *New York 1960* (New York: Monacelli Press, 1995), 320–23.

68. Edward C. Banfield, *Political Influence* (New York: Free Press, 1961), 191.

69. George Tagge, "Interview and Memoir: Conducted by Cullom Davis," 1984, University of Illinois at Springfield Special Collections, 5–6. Tagge reported much of this history in "The Eight Year Battle for Progress," *Chicago Tribune*, November 13, 1960.

70. John McCarron, "McCormick Place Has Overrun of Politics," *Chicago Tribune*, July 7, 1985.

71. Harvey Berkman, "To Scrub or Not to Scrub: The Deal to Save Illinois Coal," *Illinois Issues* 25 (August/September 1991).

72. Carolyn Teich Adams, "Philadelphia," in Richard M. Bernard ed., *Snowbelt Cities*, (Bloomington: Indiana University Press, 1990), 219.

73. Jan Schaffer, "Big Civic Center is a Must, Study Says," *Philadelphia Inquirer*, January 12, 1983.

74. My account of the politics surrounding the development of the Pennsylvania Convention Center relies on the insider analysis of city lobbyist Joseph McLaughlin. See Joseph McLaughlin, Jr., "The Invisible Politics of Regional Cooperation," Ph.D. dissertation, Temple University, September 1998.

75. Quoted in McLaughlin, "Invisible Politics," 1: 479.

76. Ibid., 507; Jenice Armstrong, "Open for Business," *Philadelphia Daily News*, June 24, 1993; Dan Meyers, "The Pressures That Sold the Convention Center," *Philadelphia Inquirer*, June 19,

1986. See also Roy Lubove, *Twentieth Century Pittsburgh*, vol. 2, *The Post-Steel Era* (Pittsburgh: University of Pittsburgh Press, 1996), 49–50.

77. Eugene P. Moehring, *Resort City in the Sunbelt: Las Vegas 1930–2000* (Reno: University of Nevada Press, 2000), 93–94. Clark County includes the cities of Las Vegas, Laughlin, and Mesquite, as well as the "Strip" hotels in the unincorporated area of the county.

78. K. J. Evans, "George 'Bud' Albright: 1909–1996," *Las Vegas Review-Journal*, May 22, 1999.

79. On the history of the Las Vegas Convention Center, see Moehring, *Resort City*, 93–96.

80. Editorial, "Vote 'NO' Tuesday on County Bond Issue," *Review-Journal*, January 5, 1964. See also Moehring, *Resort City in the Sunbelt*, p. 124.

81. Editorial, "Vote for Bond Issues But Reject the Lottery," *Review-Journal*, November 4, 1968.

82. "'Understanding Lack' Gets Bond Loss Blame," *Review-Journal*, November 6, 1968; "Businessmen 'Bond' on LVCVA Confident," *Review-Journal*, August 26, 1970; "Chamber of Commerce Takes Aim on Convention Center Vote," *Review-Journal*, August 29, 1970.

83. Advertisement, "Without Tourism You Wouldn't Have a Job," *Review-Journal*, November 2, 1974.

84. On Sheldon Adelson, see Monica Caruso, "LVCVA Calls Financing Plan Similar," *Review-Journal*, April 20, 1999. See also M. Gottdiener, Claudia Collins, and David R. Dickens, *Las Vegas: The Social Production of an All-American City* (Malden: Blackwell, 1999), 50–52.

85. See Adam Steinhauer, "Selling Las Vegas," *Review-Journal*, May 4, 1997.

86. Hubble Smith, "Convention Competition Drives Building," *Review-Journal*, July 20, 1998.

87. Monica Caruso, "Tempers Remain Hot over Center Expansion," *Review-Journal*, May 3, 1999.

88. "Critics Question LVCVA Financing Plan," *Las Vegas Sun*, June 10, 1999.

89. Monica Caruso, "LVCVA Studying Next Step," *Review-Journal*, August 9, 1999.

90. Peter O'Connell, "Judge: LVCVA Plan Legal," *Review-Journal*, October 12, 1999; Hubble Smith, "CES First Show for South Hall," *Review-Journal*, January 8, 2002.

91. Laura Carroll, "Convention Authority Plans to Revive $890 Million Expansion," *Review-Journal*, November 15, 2011.

92. Paul E. Peterson, *City Limits* (Chicago: University of Chicago Press), 1981; Helen Ladd and John Yinger, *America's Ailing Cities* (Baltimore: Johns Hopkins University Press, 1991).

93. See David Rusk, *Baltimore Unbound* (Baltimore: Abell Foundation, 1996).

94. See Neal R. Pierce, Curtis Johnson, and John Stuart Hall, *Citistates* (Washington, D.C.: Seven Locks Press, 1993).

95. David Manning, "New Convention Center," in Mayoral Transition Briefing Book, 2007; Nashville and Davidson County, "Rating Presentation: Convention Center Financing," December 2009.

Chapter 3. Promises and Realities

1. KPMG Peat Marwick, "Long Range Marketing Study: Metropolitan Pier and Exposition Authority," January 1990, III-11. Johnson's assessment of convention growth was apparently equally applicable to Richmond, Virginia. In September 1990 he told the Metropolitan Richmond Convention and Visitors Bureau that from 1971 to 1988, "the average number of attendees increased at an annual rate of approximately 6.5%." With that growth and the evaluation that Richmond "could effectively and successfully compete and achieve levels of demand similar to or slightly less than Baltimore, Indianapolis and Cincinnati," Johnson predicted that a larger center would produce a

3.6-fold increase in direct spending impact. KPMG Peat Marwick, "Expansion Feasibility Study Richmond Centre, Final Report," September 1990, II-2, III-8, IX-2.

2. KPMG Peat Marwick, "Long Range Marketing Study," VI-5.

3. C. H. Johnson Consulting, "Boston Convention & Exhibition Center: Technical Appendices, Volume 1," March 1997, 11.

4. Boston Redevelopment Authority, "Boston Convention & Exhibition Center Marketability Study," November 1998, 3, Table 2.

5. C. H. Johnson Consulting, "Jackson Convention Center Implementation Plan," July 2000, Sec. 3, 4 and 16.

6. C. H. Johnson Consulting, "Rockford Public Assembly Facilities Masterplan," July 2003, Sec. 7, 2.

7. C. H. Johnson Consulting, "St. Charles Convention Center Feasibility Study," October 2003, 19, Table 5-1.

8. Ibid., 19 and 26.

9. C. H. Johnson Consulting, "Convention/Conference Center Feasibility, Brazos County, Texas," February 2004, sec. 4, 2 and 16.

10. C. H. Johnson Consulting, "Feasibility Analysis for a New Convention Center and Hotel in Downtown Rockford," January 2010, sec. 3, 13 and sec. 4, 4 and 14.; C. H. Johnson Consulting, "Clemson Convention/Civic Center Conversion," February 2011, 18 and 38. In April 2009, a Johnson Consulting report for Seaside, California, had observed, "Virtually all categories of meeting activities have experienced rapid worldwide growth since the early 1970s." C. H. Johnson Consulting, "Monterey Peninsula Convention Center Feasibility Analysis," April 2009, Sec. 3, 4.

11. Coopers & Lybrand, "Feasibility Analysis Related to the Potential Expansion of the Anaheim Convention Center," August 1995, ES-i, 26, 29. See also Marla Jo Fisher, "Center of the Future," *Orange County Register*, August 21, 1995.

12. Coopers & Lybrand, "A Market, Building Program, Financial Operations and Economic Impact-Analysis for Potential Expansion of the Jacob K. Javits Convention Center of New York," April 1997, ES-i and 2–5.

13. CSL International, "Long Range Market Demand and Feasibility Analysis, Ernest N. Morial New Orleans Exhibition Hall Authority," June 2000, ES-1, ES-6, and 4.

14. CSL International, "Feasibility Study for an Expanded Pennsylvania Convention Center," January 2003, 45–46.

15. CSL International, "Is the Convention and Conference Center Market Saturated?" presentation at the International Economic Development Council's "If You Build It, Will They Come?" conference, May 20, 2007; CSL International, "Feasibility Analysis of a New Convention Center in Jackson, Michigan," October 2007, 56.

16. CSL International, "Feasibility Analysis . . . Jackson, Michigan," ES-1, 56, 61–62.

17. CSL International, "Feasibility Analysis for Potential Development of New Downtown Convention Facilities in Oklahoma City—Executive Summary," March 2009, 5, 6, 14, and 15. Both the same graph of "200" performance and the "will have to be monitored" language also appear in the firm's February 2009 study for the New Orleans Morial Convention Center.

18. CSL International, "Strategic Development Plan for the Boston Convention & Exhibition Center," November 2009, 20–21 and 42–47.

19. CSL International, "Feasibility Analysis for Potential Development of Convention Facilities in Boise," March 2010, 20 and 55.

20. CSL International, "Updated Feasibility Study for an Expanded/Improved Henry B. Gonzalez Convention Center," December 1, 2010, 15–16.

21. CSL International, "Fiscal Analysis of Proposed Downtown Stadium and Convention Center Project," July 2011, 38, 46.

22. CSL International, "Destination SA Update 2011," November 2011, 34.

23. With the demise of Tradeshow Week in 2010, CSL shifted to employing the annual index produced by the Center for Exhibition Industry Research after 2001. The CSL firm remained upbeat about the future of convention and tradeshow demand, reporting that "the worst of the economic downturn is behind the exhibition industry," with future growth "estimated at approximately two to three percent annually between 2012 and 2014." CSL International, "Updated Market, Financial and Economic Analysis of an Expanded Bismarck Civic Center," November 2012, 14.

24. PriceWaterhouse, "Expansion of Boston's Convention Center Facilities, Final Report—Phase I, for the Massachusetts Convention Center Authority," July 1993, 24.

25. PriceWaterhouse, "Market and Economic Impact Analysis of Proposed Phase IV Expansion: Georgia World Congress Center," January 1993, 34–35, 45. Massachusetts officials too heard that "there is currently no persuasive evidence that exhibition space demand growth for either trade shows or conventions will abate in the foreseeable future." PriceWaterhouse, "Expansion of Boston's Convention Center Facilities," Final Report—Phase II, September 1993, 24–25.

26. PriceWaterhouse, "Georgia World Congress Center: Market, Economic & Fiscal Impact Analysis of Proposed Phase IV Expansion," October 1996, 56, 62. See also Marta Saporta and Melissa Turner, "Congress Center: Expansion Urged to Stay Competitive," *Atlanta Journal and Constitution*, October 30, 1996.

27. PriceWaterhouseCoopers, "Jacob K. Javits Convention Center Expansion Study," March 2000, i.

28. Ibid., 67, 73–74. Strikingly, the PWC consultants noted and discussed precisely the drop in "200" total attendance from 1996 that is never visible in any of the CSL presentations of the "200" in terms of a "Growth Index."

29. Ibid., 52, 60.

30. PWC, "Market and Economic Analysis for a Proposed Jacob K. Javits Convention Center Expansion and Headquarters Hotel," January 2004, 1.

31. Ibid., 103–5.

32. Ibid., 107–10.

33. PWC, "Indiana Convention Center & RCA Dome Expansion Study," March 2004, 13.

34. Robert V. Canton, "The Sky Is Falling! Or Is It Just a Little Rain?" *Facility Manager*, April/May 2004.

35. PWC, "City of Irving and Irving Convention & Visitors Bureau: Analyses of a Proposed Convention Center and Other Public Assembly Facilities," May 2006, 217–22.

36. PWC, "Gwinnett Center Study: Strictly Private and Confidential," October 2007, 3, 79, 81–82, 100.

37. PWC, "San Diego Convention Center Strategic Plan Update," December 2007, 131–33.

38. Ibid., 138–40. Consultants Jeff Sachs and Tony Peterman, first at Ernst & Young, later Strategic Advisory Group (SAG), employed the same sources and data in their analyses. Answering the question "Is the industry growing?" in a 1997 report for Orange County, Florida, they provided a chart of both the overall figures from the *Data Book* and for the "200," headed "The Industry has Grown Steadily." They employed the same data for Schaumburg, Illinois, in May 2001, stating, "The

future growth in square footage demand and attendance is expected to be in the 3.5% range over the next several years." See Ernst & Young, "Long Range Strategic Plan for the Orange County Convention Center," 1997, 11; SAG, "Schaumburg Convention Center and Entertainment Complex Feasibility Study," May 2001, 13–14.

39. KPMG Peat Marwick, "Long Range Marketing Study: Metropolitan Pier and Exposition Authority," January 1990, II-10.

40. Editorial, "An Emotional Blow," *Kansas City Star*, September 12, 1996; Chris Lester and Melissa Bedford, "Going, Going, Gone," *Kansas City Star*, September 11, 1996; Don Terry, "Kansas City Looks for the Silver Lining," *New York Times*, October 18, 1996; Editorial, "Grow or Die," *Fort Wayne News-Sentinel*, June 23, 2004.

41. In the Laventhol & Horwath "Convention Center Annual Report" for 1989, David Petersen and his colleagues simply stated, "Attracting out-of-town attendance to convention and trade show events is still the primary purpose for which convention centers are built and their operations subsidized."

42. *Tradeshow Week*, December 3, 1984. While heading the Laventhol convention center practice in the mid-1980s, David Petersen first hired both Charles H. Johnson, who eventually established his own center consulting firm, and Petersen's successor at PWC, Robert Canton.

43. David C. Petersen, *Convention Centers, Stadiums, and Arenas* (Washington, D.C.: Urban Land Institute, 1989), 9; PWC, "Market and Economic Analysis for a Proposed Jacob K. Javits Convention Center Expansion and Headquarters Hotel," 105.

44. Center for Exhibition Industry Research, "From Boom to Bust—And Boom Again," 2004.

45. Tradeshow Week, *Tradeshow Week 200: 28th Annual Edition*, April 2002.

46. PWC, "2004 Convention Center Report," 1.

47. CSL International and John Kaatz, "Comments on Industry Supply, Demand, and other Characteristics of Convention Industry Development: White Paper" (Washington, D.C.: International Association of Convention and Visitors Bureaus, 2004), 3.

48. After 2001, the Center for Exhibition Industry Research shifted from using Tradeshow Week's annual data to its own annual CEIR Index, based on voluntary responses from about 300 events. Based on the reported index values, 2004 was the first year after 2000 where attendance exceeded the 2000 figure. For exhibit space used, the 2000 total was first exceeded in 2003. These index values solely reflect overall demand, not relative to the supply of available space.

49. HVS International, "Convention Centers: Is the Industry Overbuilt?: 2008 Update," February 2008, 8.

50. CSL International, "Market Demand for Enhancements to the New Orleans Morial Convention Center," February 2009, Exhibit IV-1, 21.

51. PWC, "Convention Center Report," annual, selected years.

52. PWC, "San Diego Convention Center Corporation: San Diego Convention Center Strategic Plan Update," December 2007, 136. These figures were extracted from charts in the San Diego report and are thus not exact.

53. PWC, "Cleveland-Cuyahoga County Convention Facilities Authority: Cleveland Convention Center and Headquarters Hotel Analysis," April 2005, 78.

54. C. H. Johnson Consulting, "Updated Feasibility Study of a Convention/Conference Center for Brazos County," September 2005, sec. 4, 26; C. H. Johnson Consulting, "Convention Center Redevelopment Feasibility Analysis," March 2007, sec. 4, 28; Bill Krueger, CSL International, "Is the Convention and Conference Center Market Saturated?" presentation to IEDC If You Build It Conference, May 20, 2007.

55. "CVBs & Convention Centers: Partnership for Better or Worse?," presentations at 92nd annual convention, Destination Marketing Association International, Austin, Texas, June 2006. The February 2005 report of a special Task Force on Baltimore Convention Center Financing provided one example of the incentive wars: "*ZXY group was to consider Baltimore for their April, 2008 North American Annual Conference. This group has met in Baltimore and experienced great attendance and was anxious to return. Our center pricing was competitive but higher than our competition, which was Philadelphia. Working with the Center, we managed to lower the rate to match Philadelphia, but they came back and offered their space complimentary. This group had a total of 10,195 room nights and 4,000 attendees. Direct spending would have been $3.8 million*" ("Task Force report," 7).

56. Michael Hughes, Tradeshow Week, "Venue Outlook '08," presentation at International Convention Center Conference, July 2007; Destination Marketing Association International and International Association of Assembly Managers, "Best Practices Convention Center Sales and Convention Center Operations: A Report from the Joint Study Committee," August 2007, 4.

57. Javits Center Operating Corporation, "Maximizing Economic Impact," December 2010.

58. John Kaatz, "Presentation: Case for Expansion: Boston Convention & Exhibition Center," February 22, 2010; Minutes, February 22, 2010 meeting, Boston Convention Partnership.

59. John Kaatz, "Presentation: Updated Planning Analysis for an Expanded/Improved Boston Convention & Exhibition Center," November 30, 2010.

60. San Antonio Convention and Visitors Bureau, "Monthly Measure, July 2011," July 2011. A revised figure in the May 2013 "Monthly Measure" put the 2012 attendance at 330,126. At the time of Kaatz's Boston presentation, the 2011 and 2012 figures were somewhat smaller. A 2012 report on San Antonio's convention and hotel demand included a 2011 attendance figure of 273,284. HVS, "Hotel Occupancy Tax Forecast," June 2012, figure 17, 25.

61. CSL International, "Fiscal Analysis of Proposed Downtown Stadium and Convention Center Project," July 2011, 36.

62. CSL International, "Feasibility Analysis of a Potential Expansion of the Lexington Convention Center," August 2011, 24–25; Center for Exhibition Industry Research, "CEIR Index Report 2011," 14.

63. HVS Convention, Sports & Entertainment, "Proposed Convention Center, Cedar Rapids, Iowa," January 2011, 1–8.

64. Ibid., 3–10.

65. Ibid., 3–15.

Chapter 4. They Will Come . . . and Spend

1. CSL International, "Feasibility Study for an Expanded Pennsylvania Convention Center," January 2003, ES-14.

2. Linda W. Cropp, Testimony before U.S. House Committee on Government Reform and Oversight, Subcommittee on the District of Columbia, July 15, 1998, www.dcwatch.com/issues/concent4.htm.

3. CSL International, "Financial Operating and Economic Impact Analysis for the New DC Convention Center," January 2003.

4. The CSL estimates were based on figures from the International Association of Convention and Visitors Bureaus that put daily hotel spending as 41 percent of total attendee spending.

5. John Metcalfe, "Pushes Expansion of Convention Facilities," *Cleveland Plain Dealer*, February 12, 1956; Editorial, "Tarnished Pot O' Gold," *Cleveland Plain Dealer*, February 16, 1956.

6. "Convention Bureau Value in 1960 Put at 250 Millions," *Chicago Tribune*, November 13, 1960; Editorial, "Grabbing a Piece of McCormick Place," *Chicago Tribune*, June 24, 1991.

7. See, for example, IACVB, "1988 Convention Income Survey," by Laventhol & Horwath.

8. Consultant studies often provide additional measures of "economic impact" to the calculation of direct spending. "Indirect spending" applies a "multiplier" to the direct spending estimate to calculate how direct spending is in turn re-spent in a community. Direct spending can also be used as an input to a regional economic model to calculate job creation, or can be translated into estimated future government tax revenues.

9. As CSL put it in its 2003 Washington report, "As with all new facilities, it is expected that a modest startup period will ensue at the new Center following its anticipated opening in April 2003. Many event planners tend to be hesitant to book major events in facilities prior to their completion. As such, the fourth full year of operations (2007) is estimated to represent a 'stabilized year' of operations." CSL, "New DC Center," 2.

10. Deloitte & Touche, "Financial Feasibility Study of a New Convention Center in the District of Columbia," April 1993.

11. Coopers & Lybrand, "Analysis for the Proposed Washington Convention Center," December 1997.

12. PWC, "Cincinnati Convention Center Expansion Study," 1999, 58.

13. Stanford Research Institute, "Baltimore Convention Center Study," February 1975, 19, 52.

14. PriceWaterhouse, "Expansion of Boston's Convention Center Facilities, Final Report-Phase I," July 1993, 24.

15. KPMG, "Market and Financial Analysis for a Proposed New Convention Center at Adriaen's Landing: Final Report," January 2000, 20, 23. KPMG's Susan Sieger would tell Nashville officials in 2004, "Due to its successful nature as an efficient marketplace, positive growth occurred in the tradeshow industry over the last two decades through 2000." KPMG, "Advisory Services Related to the Need for Expansion of the Nashville Convention Center or Construction of a Proposed New Convention Center," November 2004, 40.

16. KPMG, "Market and Financial Analysis for a Proposed New Convention Center at Adriaen's Landing: Final Report," January 2000, 41–42.

17. PriceWaterhouse, "Sabin Convention Center Expansion Study," 1995.

18. PWC, "Cincinnati Convention Center Expansion Study," 1999, 60.

19. KPMG, "Market and Financial Analysis for a Proposed New Convention Center at Adriaen's Landing: Final Report," January 2000, 46.

20. Economics Research Associates, "Expansion Feasibility Update for Baltimore Convention Center," January 1993, 2, 48.

21. George A. Piendak to Robert S. Hillman, Baltimore Convention Center Authority, "Reconciliations Required in Estimating Versus Actual Attendance at the Baltimore Convention Center," July 24, 1991.

22. PriceWaterhouse, "Market, Economic & Fiscal Impact Analysis of Proposed Phase IV Expansion, Georgia World Congress Center," October 1996, i–ii.

23. KPMG Peat Marwick, "Long Range Marketing Study: Metropolitan Pier and Exposition Authority," January 1990, II-7, II-14, VII-6, VII-7.

24. Metropolitan Pier and Exposition Authority, "$868,849,764.60 McCormick Place Expansion Project Bonds, Series 1992A Official Statement," June 1992, 35; Coopers & Lybrand, "Market

Analysis in Connection with the Proposed Development of an 800-Room Hotel at the McCormick Place Convention Center," ca. 1996, 65.

25. Chicago Convention and Tourism Board quoted in Illinois Economic and Fiscal Commission, "McCormick Place Expansion and the Illinois Tourism Industry," October 2002, 1.

26. In a 1997 report to Orange County, Florida, Jeff Sachs of Ernst & Young described the efforts by Chicago and Atlanta to gain more "events in the medium-sized range." He also noted that Las Vegas Convention Center was then expanding "to target the medium-sized events that require 200,000 to 350,000 square feet of exhibit space." Ernst & Young, "Long Range Strategic Plan for the Orange County Convention Center," 1997, 15.

27. CSL International, "Long Range Market Demand and Feasibility Analysis, New Orleans Morial Convention Center," June 2000, ES-6.

28. CSL International, "Feasibility Study for an Expanded Pennsylvania Convention Center," January 2003, ES-9; Tom Belden, "Center Raises Money, Doubts," *Philadelphia Inquirer*, July 18, 2004; Suzette Parmley, "Halfway to Its Big Rebirth," *Inquirer*, November 6, 2009.

29. PWC, "San Diego Convention Center Strategic Plan Update," December 2007, 16–17.

30. Pannell Kerr Forster (PKF), "Market Demand and Economic Impact Study for the Proposed Pennsylvania Convention Center, May 1988, IX-13. More recent DMAI spending analyses have been published as the ExPact Convention Expenditure and Impact Study.

31. CSL International, "Market Demand Analysis for Enhancements to the New Orleans Morial Convention Center," February 2009, 83. The ERA Baltimore report did not include a specific figure for average length of stay. But the 1988 IACVB Convention Income Survey put the national average length of stay at 4.1 nights.

32. CSL International, "Feasibility Analysis for Potential Expansion of the Henry B. Gonzalez Convention Center," July 2008, 80; CSL International, "Feasibility Analysis of Potential Development of Convention Facilities in Boise," March 2010, 60.

33. PriceWaterhouse, "Georgia World Congress Center: Market and Economic Impact Analysis of Phase IV Expansion," January 1993, 54–55.

34. PriceWaterhouse, "Georgia World Congress Center: Market, Economic & Fiscal Impact Analysis of Proposed Phase IV Expansion," October 1996, 74.

35. The "locals" phenomenon can be seen in two successive annual editions of BookExpo. In 2007, at the Javits Center in New York, 46 percent of attendees came from New York, New Jersey, and Connecticut. The next year, held in Los Angeles, BookExpo drew 51 percent of its attendance from California, with just 6 percent from New York State.

36. The attendee geographic breakdowns are taken from the annual attendance audits of the AIA National Convention compiled by BPA WorldWide.

37. For its 2005 ExPact spending figures, the DMAI asserts that delegates spend an average of $1,036 per event, or $290 per day. The average length of stay is 3.56 nights.

38. PWC, "Jacob K. Javits Convention Center Expansion Study," March 2000, 112.

39. PWC, "Market and Economic Analysis for a Proposed Jacob K. Javits Convention Center Expansion and Headquarters Hotel," January 2004, 59–60.

40. Ibid., 127; PWC, "Javits Convention Center Economic Impact Analysis 2008 and 2009," January 2011, 7. The comparable proportion for 2008 was 46 percent overnighters.

41. KPMG, "Market and Financial Analysis for a Proposed New Convention Center at Adriaen's Landing: Final Report," January 2000, 47, 51–53. The room night figures were provided by the staff of the Capital City Economic Development Authority, the center's owner.

42. Sasaki/TVS/CSL, "Boston Convention & Exhibition Center: Strategic Development Plan," November 2009, 24–25.

43. Washington, D.C., data were provided by the staff of the Washington Sports and Convention Authority. Charlotte data were provided by the Charlotte Regional Visitors Authority through the staff of the *Charlotte Observer*.

44. C. H. Johnson Consulting, "MPEA Legislative Analysis, Submitted to: Metropolitan Piers & Exposition Authority," April 2010, sec. 6, 9.

45. McCormick Place attendance and room night data provided by the Chicago Convention and Tourism Board for the 2000 Plastics Show validate the relationship described for 2009. The 2000 show had 90,142 attendees and produced 58,019 hotel room nights, for a room night ratio of 0.64. The drop in attendance from 2000 to 2009 also indicates the larger change in attendance patterns facing both tradeshows and convention centers.

46. "News Flashes," *Tradeshow Week*, December 3, 1984.

47. David C. Petersen, Laventhol & Horwath to Marcie A. Hesse, City of Homestead, Florida, November 20, 1989.

48. Laventhol & Horwath, "Sports and Convention Facilities Services," n.d.

49. Ibid.

50. KPMG Peat Marwick, "Request for Proposal: Convention Civic Center Feasibility Study, Prepared for the City of Homestead," November 20, 1989, n.p.

51. KPMG, "Technical Proposal for Financial and Locational Analysis for a Convention/ Events/ Civic Center, Las Cruces," November 3, 2004.

52. Robert S. Hillman, Baltimore Convention Center Authority, "Financial Plan for Expansion of the Baltimore Convention Center," July 1991, 1–2.

Chapter 5. Missing Impact

1. On the center's performance and the case for expansion, see Crossroads Consulting, "Baltimore Convention Center Expansion Market & Economic Analysis," February 2012. See also Edward Gunts, "Details of Convention Center and Arena Proposal Released," *Baltimore Sun*, December 16, 2010.

2. David C. Petersen, *Convention Centers, Stadiums, and Arenas* (Washington, D.C.: Urban Land Institute, 1989), 86.

3. Maria Saporta, "Convention Managers Urge Legislators to Fund Expansion of Congress Center," *Atlanta Journal and Constitution*, September 15, 1990.

4. PriceWaterhouse, "Georgia World Congress Center: Market and Economic Impact Analysis of Proposed Phase IV Expansion," January 1993.

5. Paige Braddock, "Congress Center: Expansion Urged to Stay Competitive," *Atlanta Journal and Constitution*, October 30, 1996.

6. PriceWaterhouse, "Georgia World Congress Center: Market, Economic & Fiscal Impact Analysis of Proposed Phase IV Expansion," October 1996, i-ii.

7. Coopers & Lybrand, "Market, Financial, and Economic Impact Analysis of the Proposed Convention/Civic Center in Austin, Texas," May 12, 1988.

8. City of Austin, "Austin Convention Center Issue Paper," January 1991, 11.

9. Stuart Eskenazi, "Convention Center Looks for an Angle," *Austin American-Statesman*, July 2, 1992.

10. Austin City Auditor, "Convention Center Department Audit," May 1993, 4 and 8.

11. Diana Dworin, "Downtown Dilemma: Austin Convention Center Profits, But Still Misses Business," *Austin American-Statesman*, June 4, 1995.

12. Stein & Company, "Report to the City of Austin: Market and Financial Analysis, Austin's Convention and Performing Arts Facilities," November 29, 1995, Sec. 3-1 and Sec. 6-4.

13. Ibid., Sec. 3-3.

14. Diana Dworin and Jeff South, "Convention Center Often Half-Empty," *Austin American-Statesman*, December 3, 1995.

15. C. H. Johnson Consulting, "A Strategic Plan for Austin's Convention Center Industry: Final Report," July 1997, section 2-6.

16. Scott Greenberger, "Convention Upgrade Plan Gets Price Tag," *Austin American-Statesman*, July 26, 1997.

17. Chuck Lindell, "Proposition 1: Has Austin Outgrown Convention Center?," *Austin American-Statesman*, April 18, 1998; C. H. Johnson, "A Strategic Plan," sec. 2-8.

18. The public financing for Austin's new Hilton was negotiated and managed by bond bankers Robert Swerdling and Peter Phillippi. Swerdling and Phillippi were also involved in negotiating public financing deals for hotels in Bay City, Michigan; Vancouver, Washington; Denver; Omaha; Baltimore; Coralville, Iowa; and Lombard, Illinois.

19. HVS International, "Market Study Update: Proposed Hilton Austin Hotel, Austin, Texas," March 2001.

20. Austin Convention and Visitors Bureau, "Marketing Plan 2008-09," 15.

21. On the background of the Megaplex, see Wilbur C. Rich, "Who Lost the Megaplex?," *Policy Studies Review* 15, 1 (Spring 1998): 103-13.

22. Coopers & Lybrand, "Megaplex, Convention Center, and Stadium Feasibility Analysis," February 1993; PriceWaterhouse, "Expansion of Boston Convention Center Facilities: Final Report-Phase I," July 1993, vii. The Massachusetts Convention Center Authority was created by the state in 1982 to take over the existing Hynes Auditorium from the city of Boston and finance its expansion.

23. Boston Redevelopment Authority, "Boston's New Exposition Center and Stadium: Interim Report," October 1994, 13, 2-5.

24. PriceWaterhouse, "Convention/Exhibition Facility Needs Assessment," May 1995, i, II.27.

25. Editorial, "Convention Center Rebound," *Boston Globe*, August 8, 1996.

26. Ted Bunker, "Convention Center Task Force Selects Consult Team," *Boston Herald*, November 14, 1996.

27. Meg Vaillancourt and Tina Cassidy, "Report: Convention Center Would Produce $436M Yearly, Jobs," *Boston Globe*, January 7, 1997.

28. C. H. Johnson Consulting, "Boston Convention and Exhibition Center: Technical Appendices, Vol. 1," March 1997, 2, 8, 11.

29. C. H. Johnson, "BCEC Report: Operating Finance," 3.

30. Although the new BCEC, together with the Hynes, would be owned and managed by the Massachusetts Convention Center Authority, the Convention and Visitors Bureau was responsible for marketing.

31. PriceWaterhouseCoopers, "Boston Convention and Exhibition Center Marketing Study," February 2002, I-3, I-4.

32. Massachusetts Convention Center Authority, "Fiscal Year 2004 Budget," 26; Massachusetts Convention Center Authority and Northeastern University College of Business Administration, "Phase 1 Report: Developing an Integrated Strategic Plan for MCCA," July 15, 2003.

33. Hiawatha Bray, "It's Official: Macworld Will Return in 2004," *Boston Globe*, October 17, 2002.

34. Massachusetts Convention Center Authority, "Fiscal Year 2005 Budget: Draft," May 24, 2004.

35. Sasaki/TVS/CSL, "Boston Convention & Exhibition Center: Strategic Development Plan," November 2009, 24-25; Boston Redevelopment Authority, "D Street Development: Notice of Project Change," December 2012, 1.

36. Phil Primack, "Meeting Market," *Commonwealth Magazine*, October 2008. Rooney's comments are primarily focused on the C. H. Johnson report of 1997. He largely ignores the earlier and later PriceWaterhouse reports, as well as the work of the Boston Redevelopment Authority, all of which provided room night forecasts close to or greater than Johnson's.

37. Sasaki/TVS/CSL, "Boston Convention & Exhibition Center: Strategic Development Plan," November 2009, 11.

38. Erika Gonzalez, "Convention Conundrum," *Rocky Mountain News*, January 16, 1997.

39. Erika Gonzalez, "Bigger Convention Center Backed," *Rocky Mountain News*, February 26, 1999; Mayor's Convention Center Expansion Task Force, "Report," March 1999.

40. Editorial, "Boosting Convention Trade," *Rocky Mountain News*, August 8, 1999.

41. HVS International, "Updated Market Study Report, Proposed Hyatt Convention Hotel, Denver, Colorado," April 2003, Appendix A in Denver Convention Center Hotel Authority, "Convention Center Hotel Senior Revenue Bonds Series 2003A, June 2003.

42. Denver Convention and Visitors Bureau, "Contracted vs. Actual Attendance and Room Nights," 2011.

43. Seattle's Convention and Visitors Bureau, "Marketing Plan 2003," 15; Seattle's Convention and Visitors Bureau, "2005 Marketing Plan," 17.

44. See Ziona Austrian and Mark Rosentraub, "Cities, Sports, and Economic Change: A Retrospective Assessment," *Journal of Urban Affairs* 24, 5 (2002): 549-63; William H. Hudnut III, *The Hudnut Years in Indianapolis, 1976-1991* (Bloomington: Indiana University Press, 1996); and Mark S. Rosentraub, *Major League Winners* (Boca Raton: CRC Press, 2010), chap. 3. For one consultant's view, see C. H. Johnson Consulting, "Convention Center Maximization Study, City of Charlotte," June 1996, section V.

45. Gerry Lanosga, "Convention Center Expansion Studied," *Indianapolis Star*, February 18, 1995.

46. Greg Andrews, "Room to Improve," *Indianapolis Star*, January 11, 1998.

47. John Strauss, "Tourism Visions Expand with Convention Center," *Indianapolis Star*, June 2, 1998.

48. Doug Sword, "Expanded Convention Center to Open After 2-Year Face Lift," *Indianapolis Star*, July 13, 2000.

49. Steve Goldsmith, "Indianapolis Council Opens Way for $140 Million Slate of TIF Bonds," *Bond Buyer*, September 16, 1998.

50. Indianapolis Downtown Inc., "Downtown Indianapolis 2008 Economic Indicators," April 2009, 21.

51. PriceWaterhouseCoopers, "Indiana Convention Center & RCA Dome Expansion Study," March 2004, 13. Unlike reports for Atlanta and New York's Javits Center, the PWC Indianapolis report contained no breakdown of the proportion of day trippers versus overnighters, although it estimated average daily spending for overnighters of $169 compared to $46 for day trippers.

52. J. K. Wall, "Indianapolis Hoteliers Reach a Crossroads with Convention Center Expansion," *Indianapolis Star*, June 14, 2004.

53. Indiana Convention Center and Lucas Oil Stadium, "Year-End Totals," selected years.

54. David C. Petersen, *Sports, Convention, and Entertainment Facilities*, (Washington, D.C.: Urban Land Institute, 1996), 195.

55. Coopers & Lybrand, "Market Analysis of the Proposed Expansion of the New Orleans Convention Center," September 1987, i and ii.

56. Coopers & Lybrand, "New Orleans Convention Center Expansion Phase III Location Analysis," June 1991.

57. Ernest N. Morial Convention Center, "Economic Impact: Current and Projected with Phase III Expansion," April 1994.

58. Conventions, Sports & Leisure International, "Long Range Market Demand and Feasibility Analysis: New Orleans Morial Convention Center," June 2000, ES-4–ES-8 and 7; Rebecca Mowbray, "Phase IV Still Seen as Good Idea," *New Orleans Times-Picayune*, December 2, 2004.

59. Jaquetta White, "As a Glut of Convention Space Decreases Demand, the Ernest N. Morial Convention Center is Willing to Make a Deal," *New Orleans Times-Picayune*, April 6, 2008.

60. Jaquetta White, "Ernest N. Morial Convention Center Board Approves 2011 Operating Budget," *New Orleans Times-Picayune*, December 15, 2010.

61. Edward Burks, "New Exhibit Hall Planned Here," *New York Times*, March 25, 1970.

62. Deirdre Carmody, "Mayor Calls Convention Center Personal Goal," *New York Times*, October 25, 1973; Arthur D. Little, "Market and Economic Characteristics of New York City Convention and Exhibition Center: Final Report," 1973.

63. Editorial, "Build the Convention Center," *New York Times*, May 27, 1977; Gladstone Associates, "A Convention and Exhibition Center in New York City," April 1978, II-36.

64. Parsons, Brinkerhoff, Quade, and Douglas; "New York Convention and Exhibition Center: Final Environmental Impact Statement," 1980.

65. Martin Gottlieb, "Head of Javits Center Says Major Expansion Is Needed," *New York Times*, July 18, 1990.

66. Coopers & Lybrand, "A Market, Building Program, Financial Operations and Economic Impact Analysis for Potential Expansion of the Jacob K. Javits Convention Center of New York," April 21, 1997, 1-1.

67. "New York City Tourism Barometer: 1992 Report," 1992.

68. Unlike subsequent analyses from PriceWaterhouseCoopers, the Coopers & Lybrand report did not differentiate convention and tradeshow attendees between day trippers and overnighters.

69. PriceWaterhouseCoopers, "Jacob K. Javits Convention Center Expansion Study," March 24, 2000, I, iii.

70. PriceWaterhouseCoopers, "Javits Expansion Study," 104, 113.

71. PriceWaterhouseCoopers, "Market and Economic Analysis for a Proposed Jacob K. Javits Convention Center Expansion and Headquarters Hotel," January 20, 2004, 2.

72. Figures for pre-2007 convention and tradeshow attendance are from NYC & Co., "Tourism Barometer," annual December edition. Figures for 2007, 2008, and 2009 are from PriceWaterhouseCoopers, "Javits Convention Center Economic Impact Analysis," July 2008 and January 2011 editions, provided by the New York Convention Center Operating Corporation. Attendance for 2011 and 2012 from PWC, "Jacob K. Javits Convention Center Economic Impact Analysis: Executive Summary," June 2013.

73. In an April 2007 report, CSL noted that "In 2006, the Javits Center hosted 64 trade events, and 53 of these were recurring events or events that have been held in the Center in years past." CSL International, "Jacob K. Javits Convention Center Expansion: Analysis of Market, Financial, Economic and Program Issues," April 2007, 6.

74. Event attendance figures from Tradeshow Week, "Tradeshow Week 200" for the years indicated. Figures include only attendees, not exhibitors. The 2010 edition, covering 2009, was the last edition published before Tradeshow Week closed.

75. PriceWaterhouseCoopers, "Javits Convention Center Economic Impact Analysis, 2008 and 2009," January 2011. The proportion of "overnighters" was 44.5 percent in 2008.

76. Ernst & Young, "Long Range Strategic Plan for the Orange County Convention Center," December 1997, 2, 8-10.

77. Ibid., 11-12.

78. Ibid., 17.

79. Ernst & Young, "Long Range Strategic Plan for the Orange County Convention Center, Vol. II," 2-4.

80. Orlando Convention and Visitors Bureau, "Convention Center Housing Summary Monthly 2009-2013," revised July 10, 2009.

81. Orlando Convention and Visitors Bureau, "Convention Center Housing Summary Monthly 2010-2014," revised June 4, 2010.

82. Ibid., 13.

83. Gladstone Associates, "A Convention Center for Portland, Oregon: Financial Analysis and Summary Findings, Conclusions and Recommendations," November 1978, 1, 2.

84. Ibid., 1.

85. Steve Suo, "Portland Takes Second Look at Headquarters Hotel," *Oregonian*, June 25, 1995.

86. Economics Research Associates, "Evaluation of Hotel Market Conditions and Impact Analysis of a Convention Hotel," January 2001, Table III-3.

87. R. Gregory Nokes, "Convention Center May Grow Wing, *Oregonian*, January 7, 1995; Jim Hill, "Decision to Build Hotel a Matter of Money," *Oregonian*, March 23, 1997; R. Gregory Nokes, "Voters Will Consider $82 Million for Convention Center," *Oregonian*, February 28, 1998.

88. Courtenay Thompson, "Portland Approves Bonds for Convention Center," *Oregonian*, January 25, 2001.

89. Economics Research Associates, "Evaluation of Hotel Market Conditions and Impact Analysis of a Convention Hotel," January 2001, III-6.

90. PKF, "Presentation to the Portland Development Commission," May 2006, 12.

91. KPMG, "Economic Impact Analysis for the Oregon Convention Center," June 2002; KPMG, "Economic and Fiscal Impacts Update: Oregon Convention Center," July 2007; Crossroads Consulting, "Oregon Convention Center: Fiscal Year 2010-11 Economic and Fiscal Impact Analysis Report," January 2012.

92. "Joint Statement from Metro President David Bragdon, Portland Mayor Sam Adams, and Multnomah County Chair Ted Wheeler," September 18, 2009.

93. Arthur Andersen & Co., "Henry B. Gonzalez Convention Center Expansion Feasibility Analysis," November 1990, 6, 7, 9.

94. Ibid., 32-38.

95. Arthur Andersen, "Henry B. Gonzalez Convention Center Economic Impact Analysis and Financial Plan," December 1991.

96. Ibid., 7, 9, 24-25.

97. Urban Land Institute Advisory Services Panel, "San Antonio Convention Center," September 1995.

98. Conventions, Sports & Leisure International, "Feasibility Analysis for the Potential Expansion of the Henry B. Gonzalez Convention Center," July 2008, ES-6, 17.

99. Attendance figures for 2008 and 2009 from CSL International, "Updated Feasibility Study for an Expanded/Improved Henry B. Gonzalez Convention Center," December 2010, 5; HVS, "Hotel Occupancy Tax Forecast, San Antonio, Texas," June 2012, 25.

100. CSL International, "Destination SA: Update 2011," November 2011, 27, 54.

101. On the history of the Yerba Buena project, see Chester Hartman, *Yerba Buena* (San Francisco: Glide, 1974).

102. Laura Evenson, "S.F. Hotel Business Booming," *San Francisco Chronicle*, July 10, 1993; Economics Research Associates, "San Francisco Needs Assessment for Additional Meeting and/or Exhibit Space," September 1994, ES-3, IV-6, and VII-14.

103. Kenneth Howe, "Study Recommends a Bigger Moscone," *San Francisco Chronicle*, September 2, 1994.

104. Editorial, "Expanded Moscone Would Enrich S. F.," *Chronicle*, February 12, 1996.

105. PKF Consulting, "Study of the Potential Future Transient Occupancy Tax Collections to be Received from Redevelopment Project Area Hotels Within the City and County of San Francisco," March 24, 1998, 4. An article in the *Chronicle* on January 8, 1999, shows room night generation figures of 786,000 for 1995, 848,000 for 1997, 917,000 for 1998, and an estimated 830,000 for 1999.

106. Carolyn Said, "Bay Area Battles for Tourists," *Chronicle*, June 22, 2003.

107. SMG, "Moscone Center Annual Report," for relevant fiscal years.

108. San Francisco Convention and Visitors Bureau, "Business Plan 2009-10," May 2009, 12; PKF Consulting, "San Francisco Lodging Market: Getting Better, Quicker?," presentation, March 2011, 24.

109. Sarah Duxbury, "San Francisco is Losing Major Conventions Because Moscone Can't Accommodate Them," *San Francisco Business Times*, March 15, 2010.

110. San Francisco Office of the Mayor, "Mayor Lee Announces Major Moscone Convention Center Expansion," press release, June 21, 2012. The San Francisco CVB commissioned a study of the proposed expansion from ERA/AECOM. The firm's January 2010 report contained a discussion of the "Nationwide Concerns about Overbuilding." Noting that some centers were "failing to reach performance expectations," the report dismissed any concern about San Francisco's likely success: "The first tier cities on the west coast (i.e. San Francisco, San Diego, Seattle, Vancouver) have been particularly successful in attracting convention business." See ERA/AECOM, "Feasibility and Economic Impact Analysis for the Proposed Moscone East Expansion," January 2010, 35.

111. Elizabeth Tucker, "Convention Center Needs Room to Grow," *Washington Post*, April 6, 1987.

112. Anne Swardson, "Convention Center The Sequel," *Washington Post*, July 2, 1990. Room night figures from Coopers & Lybrand, "Analysis for the Proposed Washington Convention Center: Washington, D.C. Hotel Market Analysis," December 30, 1997, 2.

113. Elizabeth Tucker, "Convention Center Needs Room to Grow," *Washington Post*, April 6, 1987.

114. Rudolph Pyatt, "The District's Unconventional Choices," *Washington Post*, December 19, 1988.

115. Deloitte & Touche, "Financial Feasibility Study of a New Convention Center in the District of Columbia," April 1993, 3-4.

116. Coopers & Lybrand, "Analysis for the Proposed Washington Convention Center," December 30, 1997, ES-iii.

117. Coopers & Lybrand, "Analysis for the Proposed Washington Convention Center: Washington, D.C. Hotel Market Analysis," December 30, 1997, 2, 25.

118. Conventions, Sports & Leisure International, "Financial Operating and Economic Impact Analysis for the New DC Convention Center," January 2003.

119. Downtown DC Business Improvement District, "State of Downtown 2008," April 2009, 30; "State of Downtown 2009," April 2010, p, 34.

120. See District of Columbia Council, "Washington Convention and Sports Authority: Performance Oversight Hearing, FY2010," March 2011; District of Columbia Council, "Washington Convention and Sports Authority: Budget Oversight Hearing FY 2012," April 2012; "Washington Convention and Sports Authority Performance Oversight Hearing FY12/1Q13," February 2013..

121. CSL International, "Volume I: Convention Center Expansion & Headquarters Hotel Feasibility Study for the Washington Convention Center," August 2004, ES-3, 52.

122. HVS, "Market Study, Proposed Marriott Marquis, Washington, District of Columbia," August 2010, 74.

123. Crossroads Consulting, "Baltimore Convention Center Expansion Market & Economic Impact Analysis," February 2012, 41.

124. Steve Harrison, "Selling Charlotte: Convention Business Requires Millions from Taxpayers," *Charlotte Observer*, August 20, 2012.

125. C. H. Johnson Consulting, "St. Charles Convention Center Feasibility Study," October 2003, Table 5-8, 60.

126. Philadelphia Industrial Development Corporation, "Philadelphia: Smart City. Smart Choice for Hotel Investment. 2012," 9.

127. Coopers & Lybrand, "Washington State Convention & Trade Center, Expansion Development Study, Volume I," December 1994.

128. Hubble Smith, "Convention Competition Drives Building," *Las Vegas Review-Journal*, July 20, 1998; Hubble Smith, "Report Examines LV's Ratio of Exhibit vs. Meeting Space," *Las Vegas Review-Journal*, December 12, 2001; Las Vegas Convention and Visitors Authority, "Marketing Bulletin 2012 Year-End Summary," 6.

129. Phyllis Kaniss, *Making Local News* (Chicago: University of Chicago Press, 1991), 195, 217.

130. Videotaped Deposition of Charles H. Johnson, October 15, 2005, in the case of *Avalon Hotel Partners et al. v. County of Erie et al.*, transcript in author's possession.

131. The C. H. Johnson firm did produce an "Accuracy in Projections" document in October 2003. It included a review of the firm's forecasts for convention centers in Charlotte and Milwaukee. The Charlotte discussion erroneously describes the projections for Charlotte, and presents an inaccurate figure for the center's "actual" 1999 convention and tradeshow attendance. For Milwaukee, the "Accuracy" document compares a "1999 Projection" of 158,000 convention and tradeshow attendance to a "1999 Actual" attendance of 126,000. The 158,000 attendance figure was the "Base" attendance reported in 1996. The Johnson forecast, made in January 1996 for 2000, was 193,750 attendees. A January 2002 report by the HVS firm put the center's convention and tradeshow attendance for 2000 at 94,995.

132. Rooney quoted in Phil Primack, "Meeting Market," *CommonWealth*, Fall 2008, 54.

133. On CSL's forecasts, see Casey Ross, "Case for Bigger Convention Hall has Familiar Ring," *Boston Globe*, April 22, 2011.

134. Miami Beach City Commission, "Supplemental Material (1), Meeting of September 14, 2011."

135. Victoria Murphy, "The Answer Is Always Yes," *Forbes*, February 28, 2005.

136. Boston Redevelopment Authority, "Boston's New Exposition Center and Stadium: Interim Report," October 1994, "C Street" 31.

Part II Intro

1. Howard F. Baer, *St. Louis to Me* (St. Louis: Hawthorn, 1978), 260.

Chapter 6. Chicago: Bolstering the Business District

1. Chesly Manly, "McCormick Place: Chicago's Exhibition Center," *Chicago Tribune*, May 21, 196; Editorial, "Chicago Hall," *Tribune*, April 20, 1927.

2. Editorial, "McCormick Place a Memorial to Him," *Tribune*, November 19, 1960.

3. Daniel Burnham and Edward H. Bennett, *Plan of Chicago* (Chicago: Commercial Club, 1909; reprint Princeton Architectural Press, 1993), 123.

4. "McCormick Place Convention Center Opens," *Tribune*, November 18, 1960.

5. "'Town Hall of the Nation' at Pier Planned," *Tribune*, January 13, 1915; "Meet to Hasten Bills to Give City Convention Hall," *Tribune*, April 16, 1919; and "Chicago's Bill for a Convention Hall is Passed," *Tribune*, June 18, 1919.

6. Wylls Baird, president, Chicago Association of Commerce, "Letter: For a New Convention Hall," *Tribune*, April 8, 1920.

7. "Women's Votes Aid Defeat of All Bond Issues," *Tribune*, April 14, 1920.

8. "Plan World's Largest Hall for Conventions," *Tribune*, May 9, 1924.

9. Oscar Hewitt, "City Is Urged to Get Busy on Big Convention Hall," *Tribune*, February 27, 1927.

10. Editorial, "The Civic Auditorium," *Tribune*, March 2, 1927.

11. "Municipal Hall Bonds Get OK in Legislature," *Tribune*, May 26, 1927.

12. Oscar Hewitt, "Asks South Side Civic Hall Site as an Economy," *Tribune*, April 26, 1927; Editorial, "Placing Convention Hall," *Tribune*, June 9, 1927.

13. "Municipal Hall Bonds Get OK in Legislature," *Tribune*, May 26, 1927.

14. Strikingly in light of subsequent history, the *Tribune*, while not advocating any particular site for the new hall, editorialized on the virtues of a lakefront site, noting, "the lake site could hardly be surpassed by any city in the world." "Placing Convention Hall," *Tribune*, June 9, 1927.

15. James Doherty, "Board to Ask New Vote on Chicago Hall," *Tribune*, April 22, 1928.

16. "Revitalizing of Chicago's 'Loop' Enters Draft Stage of Plan," *Christian Science Monitor*, Dec. 9, 1942.

17. "Plan Huge Civic Governmental Office Center," *Tribune*, March 16, 1949. Owings and his firm would continue to play a role in planning and development efforts in the central area over a period of decades.

18. "Lake Site Urged for 100 Million Civic Project," *Tribune*, April 19, 1946. See also Al Chase, "North Michigan Avenue Future Now Assured," *Tribune*, December 7, 1919. The article reported "North Michigan Avenue . . . is going to come into its own as one of the great thoroughfares of the world." In 1922 the *Tribune* announced an international design competition for its new headquarters on North Michigan.

19. "Mr. Toastmaster, Ladies and Gentlemen of the Press . . . ," [text of Rubloff speech], undated, 10, Rubloff Papers. See also John W. Stamper, *Chicago's North Michigan Avenue* (Chicago: University of Chicago Press, 1991), 206–8.

20. Text of Rubloff speech, 10, Rubloff Papers.

21. Arthur Rubloff to Col. Robert R. McCormick, December 6, 1948, Rubloff Papers.

22. Chicago Plan Commission, "Chicago Civic Center," March 1949. See Ross Miller, *Here's the Deal: The Making and Breaking of a Great American City* (Evanston, Ill.: Northwestern University Press, 2003), 61. My thanks to Ross Miller for making much of his research material available to me.

23. Lou Capron to Arthur Rubloff, Memo, January 12, 1952, Rubloff Papers; "Project 'X' Building Program," November 25, 1953, Rubloff Papers.

24. Clayton Kirkpatrick, "Outline Vast Civic Center," *Tribune*, March 17, 1954.

25. Philip Hampson, "Railroad Fair Gets Approval of Civic Group," *Tribune*, February 21, 1948.

26. George Tagge, "George Tagge Memoir: Oral History Interview by Cullom Davis," 1984, Archives/Special Collections, University of Illinois at Springfield, 1–2. Tagge noted that the meeting did not include any public official, as "the State Street leaders" would not have included them—"This was to let down their hair and find out how people felt, find out what kind of cooperation they might give and so on."

27. Tagge, "Memoir," 5.

28. Editorial, "The Permanent Chicago Fair," *Tribune*, January 24, 1952.

29. Edward C. Banfield, *Political Influence* (New York: Free Press, 1961), 192; Tagge, "Memoir," 13.

30. Banfield, *Political Influence*, 190–231; "Warns Chicago Against Losing Conventions," *Tribune*, January 15, 1953.

31. George Tagge, "Civic Leaders Discuss Fair Building Hopes, *Tribune*, March 20, 1953; George Tagge, "Big Exhibit Hall for City Pushed by Civic Groups," *Tribune*, April 28, 1953.

32. Editorial, "The Convention Hall," *Tribune*, May 1, 1953.

33. Arnold Hirsch, "Martin H. Kennelly, The Mugwump and the Machine" in Paul M. Green and Melvin G. Holli, eds., *The Mayor: The Chicago Political Tradition* (Carbondale: Southern Illinois University Press, 1987), 133.

34. Tagge, "Big Exhibit Hall for City Pushed by Civic Groups."

35. Frederick T. Aschman, "The Rebuilding of the Near-North and Near-South Sides of the Chicago Central Area," April 15, 1957, Fort Dearborn Project Records.

36. Nelson Forrest, "The Area Progress Report: November 2, 1953," Greater North Michigan Avenue Association, Rubloff Papers.

37. "South Side Site for Convention Hall Proposed," *Tribune*, November 19, 1953. On the Planning Board, see Michael Carriere, "Chicago, the South Side Planning Board, and the Search for (Further) Order: Toward an Intellectual Lineage of Urban Renewal in Postwar America," *Journal of Urban History* 39, 3 (May 2013): 411–32.

38. Thomas Buck, "Vast Changes for Loop Pictured by 2054," *Tribune*, August 31, 1954.

39. Earl Kribben to Henry Sell, December 21, 1955, Fort Dearborn Project Records.

40. "Pick Fair Site on Lake for Exhibit Hall," *Tribune*, June 9, 1954.

41. Holabird & Root & Burgee and Ralph H. Burke Inc., "Report to Chicago Park Fair on an Exposition Center for Chicago, Illinois," March 1955.

42. "Opposes Site Selected for Fair Building," *Tribune*, June 11, 1954.

43. Minutes of the Technical Meeting, Fort Dearborn Project, July 28, 1954, Fort Dearborn Project Records.

44. Frederick T. Aschman, "The Rebuilding of the Near-North and Near-South Sides of the Chicago Central Area," April 15, 1957, Fort Dearborn Project Records.

45. John Donald Cordwell Oral History, Chicago Architects Oral History Project, Art Institute of Chicago, rev. ed., 2004, 149.

46. Adam Cohen and Elizabeth Taylor, *American Pharaoh* (Boston: Little, Brown, 2000), 112.

47. Meeting in the Board Room of the Chicago Land Clearance Commission, May 6, 1954, Fort Dearborn Project Records.

48. Stuart List to Arthur Rubloff, July 1, 1954, Rubloff Papers.

49. Nelson Forrest, "The Area Progress Report: August 12, 1954," Greater North Michigan Avenue Association, Rubloff Papers.

50. Tagge, "Memoir," 25.

51. George Tagge, "Tell Exposition Hall Plan," *Tribune*, April 12, 1955.

52. Editorial, "An Exposition Hall for Greater Chicago," *Tribune*, April 13, 1955.

53. Clay Gowran, "Civic Leaders Hail Exposition Hall Project," *Tribune*, April 13, 1955; Editorial, "Deliberate Falsehoods," *Tribune*, June 15, 1955.

54. Editorial, "The Convention Hall Makes Progress," *Tribune*, May 12, 1955.

55. Editorial, "A Chicago Dream Is Coming True," *Tribune*, July 11, 1955.

56. George Tagge, "Exhibition Hall on Lake Front to be Studied," *Tribune*, March 13, 1956.

57. Editorial, "Exposition Hall Realities," *Tribune*, March 30, 1956.

58. Minutes of the Meeting of the Board of Governors, Metropolitan Housing and Planning Council, April 6, 1956, Metropolitan Housing and Planning Council Records.

59. Statement of Citizens Committee for a Chicago Exposition Hall, July 2, 1956, Metropolitan Housing and Planning Council Records.

60. Nelson Forrest to Arthur Rubloff, June 27, 1956, Rubloff Papers.

61. Minutes of Meeting of the Board of Governors, Metropolitan Housing and Planning Council, June 22 1956, Metropolitan Housing and Planning Council Records.

62. Ibid., September 14, 1956, Metropolitan Housing and Planning Council Records.

63. Booz, Allen & Hamilton, "Economic Survey, Metropolitan Fair and Exposition Authority, Chicago Illinois," August 1956, xiii, 33.

64. The Booz, Allen Chicago study is an intriguing case in the history of center feasibility studies. Faced with findings that failed to validate its central purpose and goal, the Fair Authority simply ignored its substance and marched ahead, using another study to dismiss the Booz, Allen conclusions.

65. Minutes of the Meeting of the Board of Governors, September 28, 1956, Metropolitan Housing and Planning Council Records.

66. John Donald Cordwell Oral History, 149–51. Cordwell had begun work as Director of Planning for the Plan Commission in 1952. After leaving the commission, he was employed as a consultant by the Central Area Committee. He also worked as a consultant on the city's 1958 Development Plan for the Central Area. Department store head Joel Goldblatt was appointed by Mayor Daley to the board of the Metropolitan Fair and Exposition Authority in June 1963.

67. Minutes of Meeting of the Board of Governors, October 4, 1957, Metropolitan Housing and Planning Council Records.

68. Minutes of Meeting of the Board of Governors, November 1, 1957, Metropolitan Housing and Planning Council Records.

69. "U.S. Business: Convention-Busy Chicago Looks for More," *New York Times*, February 13, 1966.

70. Thomas Buck, "25-Story Hotel," *Tribune*, January 11, 1967; "Begin McCormick Inn," *Tribune*, March 14, 1971.

71. "Teamster Hotel Investment Here Shows Big Losses," *Tribune*, July 31, 1976.

72. PriceWaterhouse, "Massachusetts Convention Center Authority: Convention/Exhibition Facility Needs Assessment," May 1995, Task III, 1–2.

73. George Tagge noted, "[Don] Maxwell [the *Tribune* editor] decided to begin by choosing every member of the exposition authority and he didn't talk to the mayor, the governor. . . . The exposition authority was effectively under our control, or Maxwell's control. Since he named the people, some of them were his personal friends, the likes of George Halas, owner of the Chicago Bears, and, oh, a number of others." Tagge, "Memoir," 24, 26.

74. Editorial, "The Exposition Site Approved," *Tribune*, April 2, 1956.

75. Banfield, *Political Influence*, 202.

76. Nelson Forrest, "The Area Progress Report: February 15, 1954" and "The Area Progress Report: August 12, 1954," Greater North Michigan Avenue Association, Rubloff Papers. In one instance of the interconnections in Chicago's development community, Carl Sandburg Village was developed by a syndicate led by Arthur Rubloff, and designed by Louis Solomon-John D. Cordwell Associates architects.

77. "South Side Site for Convention Hall Proposed," *Tribune*, November 19, 1953; "New Proposal for Exposition Hall Site Made," *Tribune*, November 13, 1956. The McCormick Place West expansion ultimately used much of the Planning Board's suggested site.

78. Minutes of the Executive Committee meeting, March 13, 1959, Metropolitan Housing and Planning Council, Metropolitan Housing and Planning Council Records.

79. Banfield, *Political Influence*, 294.

80. Harold Moore to Patrick Hoy, March 2, 1955, Rubloff Papers.

81. See Arnold Hirsch, *Making the Second Ghetto* (London: Cambridge University Press, 1983), 100–20; "Pettibone's Body Found," *Tribune*, July 26, 1962; Homer Hoyt, *One Hundred Years of Land Values in Chicago* (Chicago: University of Chicago Press, 1933).

82. Minutes of the meeting of the Fort Dearborn sponsors, January 14, 1957, Rubloff Papers.

83. Earl Kribben, Revised minutes of meeting of January 14, 1957, Fort Dearborn Project, Rubloff Papers. For an alternative view of the origin of the Central Area Committee, see Joel Rast, "Creating a Unified Business Elite: The Origins of the Chicago Central Area Committee," *Journal of Urban History* 37, 4 (July 2011): 583–605.

84. Frederick T. Aschman to Holman D Pettibone, "Organization of Central Commercial District Program," November 23, 1955, Pettibone Papers; Press release, Chicago Central Area Committee, January 12, 1956, Cone Papers.

85. Peter B. Clark, "The Chicago Big Businessman as a Civic Leader," Ph.D. dissertation, University of Chicago, 1959, 44.

86. Clark, "Chicago Big Businessman," 172.

87. See Sharon Haar, *The City as Campus* (Minneapolis: University of Minnesota Press, 2011).

88. Frederick T. Aschman to Holman Pettibone, "University of Illinois Campus in Chicago," February 18, 1957, Cone Papers. Central Area Committee members had met with university staff about the site selection on February 7, 1957.

89. Holman Pettibone to David Henry, May 1, 1957, Rubloff Papers.

90. On the background of the site selection for the U of I Chicago campus, see George Rosen, *Decision-Making Chicago Style* (Urbana: University of Illinois Press, 1980). See also Haar, *The City as Campus*. On the Central Area Plan, see Larry Bennett, *The Third City* (Chicago: University of Chicago Press, 2010), 39–41.

91. Frederick Aschman, "Central Area Planning Presentation Text," January 1958, Aschman Papers.

92. Banfield, *Political Influence*, 157.

93. Chicago Department of City Planning, "Development Plan for the Central Area," August 1958, 13.

94. Ibid., 21.

95. Clark, "Chicago Big Businessman," 179–80.

96. Frederick T. Aschman, "A Review for the Chicago Central Area Committee . . . of the City of Chicago Department of City Planning's Development Plan for the Central Area of Chicago," November 1958, 11, 15.

97. Nelson Forrest to Fairfax Cone and Newton C. Farr, February 7, 1958, Cone Papers; "Memorandum Concerning Meeting Between Representatives of the Greater North Michigan Avenue Association and of the Chicago Central Area Committee, June 20, 1958," Cone Papers.

98. Banfield, *Political Influence*, 253. See also Roger Biles, *Richard J. Daley* (DeKalb: Northern Illinois University Press, 1995) and Adam Cohen and Elizabeth Taylor, *American Pharaoh* (Boston: Little, Brown, 2000).

99. George Tagge, "Memoir," 11.

100. Fairfax M. Cone to Richard J. Daley, June 13, 1957, Cone Papers.

101. John M. Allswang, "Richard J. Daley: America's Last Boss," in Paul M. Green and Melvin G. Holli, eds., *The Mayors*, 147.

102. Hughston McBain to Board of Directors, Chicago Central Area Committee, February 18, 1959, 2, Cone Papers.

103. Ibid.

104. Chicago Central Area Committee, "The Chicago Central Area-Today," April 1962, 3, 10, Cone Papers.

105. In financing the development of the new Civic Center building, Daley employed the vehicle of a Public Building Commission, initially designed and promoted by the Fort Dearborn sponsors, allowing the city to avoid a public vote on the bonds. The lead architect for the Civic Center was C. F. Murphy, a confidant of Mayor Daley and a member of the executive committee of the Central Area Committee.

106. Untitled article, *Tribune*, February 13, 1959, quoted in Cohen and Taylor, *American Pharaoh*, 241.

107. Minutes of the meeting of the Planning Committee, Metropolitan Housing and Planning Council, September 29, 1960, Metropolitan Housing and Planning Council Records. By this point, Ira Bach was already privately proposing the Harrison-Halsted urban renewal project location for the university campus—the site where it was ultimately built. See Gene A. Burd, "The Role of the Chicago Daily Newspapers in the Selection of the Chicago Campus for the University of Illinois," Ph.D. dissertation, Northwestern University, 1964, chapter 6.

108. Banfield, *Political Influence*, 294.

109. Holman D. Pettibone to Bill Kahler, July 16, 1959; Joseph L. Block to William Kahler, July 24, 1959; Wayne Johnston to Bill Kahler, July 10, 1959, all Cone Papers.

110. Chicago Central Area Committee, "The Chicago Central Area-Today," 5, 15, Cone Papers.

111. Carl W. Condit, *Chicago 1930–1970* (Chicago: University of Chicago Press, 1974), 90.

112. See Paul Gapp, "Controversy Likely: North Loop Pins Hope on Drastic Surgery," *Tribune*, October 7, 1973.

113. Kenneth Zwiener to Fairfax M. Cone, September 10, 1965, Cone Papers.

114. Hirsch, *Making the Second Ghetto*, 105–6.

115. Meeting at the Chicago Club, March 24, 1954, Fort Dearborn Project, Fort Dearborn Project Records.

116. In a 1957 text, *Real Estate and City Planning* coauthored with Richard Nelson (Prentice-Hall), Aschman set out "four basic approaches in metropolitan downtown planning," including "To improve accessibility," "To build up major visitor attractions, including entertainment and cultural centers, exposition and convention facilities," "To develop the optimum compactness necessary," and "To achieve the greatest possible physical attractiveness" (350).

117. Holman Pettibone to Bill Kahler, July 16, 1959, Cone Papers.

Chapter 7. Atlanta: Enhancing Property Values

1. On the history of Atlanta tourism, see Harvey K. Newman, *Southern Hospitality* (Tuscaloosa: University of Alabama Press, 1999).

2. A 1956 assessment of the city's capital improvement needs called for $500,000 for immediate remodeling of the existing auditorium, and recommended an entirely new auditorium on a different site at a cost of $12 million. Atlanta Finance Study, "Capital Improvement Needs in Atlanta," April 1956, 26.

3. Andrew M. Ambrose, "Redrawing the Color Line: The History and Patterns of Black Housing in Atlanta, 1940–1973," Ph.D. dissertation, Emory University, 1992.

4. H. W. Lochner & Co., "Highway and Transportation Plan for Atlanta, Georgia," January 1946.

5. Atlanta Metropolitan Planning Commission, "Up Ahead: A Regional Land Use Plan for Atlanta," February 1952, 35–36, 69–70.

6. "Up Ahead," 71. On the reaction to the Auburn Avenue proposal, see Ronald H. Bayor, *Race and the Shaping of Twentieth-Century Atlanta* (Chapel Hill: University of North Carolina Press, 1996), 71.

7. "Up Ahead," 68, 92–93.

8. Ibid., 70, 91–93.

9. Notably, when Floyd Hunter polled Atlanta's "top leaders" on the "two major issues or projects before the community today," the Plan of Improvement (identified as the "Plan of Development") ranked first, chosen by 23 of the 26 leaders. Floyd Hunter, *Community Power Structure* (Chapel Hill: University of North Carolina Press, 1953), 214.

10. Atlanta Metropolitan Planning Commission, "Now . . . For Tomorrow," September 1954, 38–40.

11. Summary of letter from Phil Hammer to Frank Neely, April 27, 1954, Rich Papers. In 1959, Hammer wrote, "The politicians (including the mayor) have never supported planning. Behind the politicians, the civic leadership has given only token backing." Hammer and Company Associates, "Action at the Core," June 1959, 16.

12. Hammer and Company, "Air Rights Plaza," December 1954, Rich Papers.

13. M. Kent Jennings, *Community Influentials*, (New York: Free Press, 1964), 114.

14. Philip Hammer to Fred Turner, March 18, 1959, Rich Papers.

15. Process Recording of Interview, Atlanta Power Structure, Hunter Papers. See Hunter, *Community Power Structure*.

16. Hughes Spalding to Fred Turner, March 24, 1959, Rich Papers.

17. Hammer and Company, "Action at the Core: A Blueprint for Atlanta," June 1959, 16–17.

18. Ibid., 29.

19. Division and conflict over major public initiatives were common in 1950s Atlanta. Floyd Hunter noted of the city's expressway plans, "For several years, the Central Business Association blocked this [by-pass highway] plan, clinging to an outgrown idea that all traffic should go through the central business district because it was felt that many through travellers would 'stop and shop.'" Hunter, *Community Power Structure*, 200.

20. Ivan Allen, Jr., *Mayor: Notes on the Sixties* (New York: Simon and Schuster, 1971), 30–31.

21. Ivan Allen to Robert Woodruff, August 25, 1959, Woodruff Papers.

22. Robert Woodruff to Ivan Allen, August 31, 1959, Woodruff Papers.

23. Jennings, *Community Influentials*, 116.

24. Atlanta Chamber of Commerce, "Report to the Board of Directors: Recommended City of Atlanta General Obligation Bond Issue, 1957," December 1956, 20.

25. Minutes of the Board of Directors Meeting, Atlanta Chamber of Commerce, January 13, 1960, Atlanta Chamber of Commerce Records.

26. Ibid.

27. Ibid., February 10, 1960, Atlanta Chamber of Commerce Records.

28. Allen, *Mayor*, 31. Allen mentions "with help from some of the best thinkers in the city."

29. Philip Hammer to Ivan Allen, November 3, 1960 and attachments, Hammer Papers. Hammer had long pressed for a metro area rapid transit system.

30. Allen wrote Hammer ("Dear Phil") on November 7, "I do not know how you put together so much so quickly and in such fine shape. For whatever the method, I am indeed most grateful." Ivan Allen to Philip Hammer, November 7, 1960, Hammer Papers.

31. Hammer and Company, "Atlanta Sites: A Report on Locations for Key Civic Projects in Atlanta, Georgia," November 1960, 1, Rich Papers.

32. "Atlanta Sites" was also circulated to a broader, if still rather exclusive, set of Atlantans. Writing to Hammer in June 1961, Richard Forbes of the Atlanta-Fulton County Joint Planning Board informed him, "I expect that the job he [Del Paige] will ask of you is to talk about the Atlanta sites report, although you may not wish to discuss that report specifically." Del Paige was then president of the Atlanta Arts Alliance. Forbes's letter went on, "As you know, the Mayor [Hartsfield], Mr. Paige and I are in agreement that the performing arts center is the greatest [civic] need." Richard Forbes to Philip Hammer, June 13, 1961, Hammer Papers.

33. On the Egleston controversy over the development of public housing on the site of an abandoned hospital and the context of black displacement, see Ronald H. Bayor, *Race and the Shaping of Twentieth Century Atlanta* (Chapel Hill: University of North Carolina Press, 1996), 72–73.

34. Hammer and Company, "Atlanta Sites," 52. The coliseum would eventually be built as part of the restructured "City Center" scheme on the air rights.

35. Philip Hammer to Richard Rich, November 28, 1960, Rich Papers.

36. "Project Status: Auditorium-Coliseum & Stadium, January 18, 1961," attachment to

minutes, Board of Directors, Atlanta Chamber of Commerce, January 18, 1961, Atlanta Chamber of Commerce Records.

37. Minutes of the meeting of the Board of Directors, Atlanta Chamber of Commerce, April 12, 1961, Atlanta Chamber of Commerce Records.

38. Ibid., June 14, 1961.

39. Cecil Alexander to Richard Rich, March 7, 1962, Rich Papers.

40. Richard Rich to "FHN," March 13, 1962, Rich Papers.

41. Minutes of the meeting of the Board of Directors, Atlanta Chamber of Commerce, February 14, 1962, Atlanta Chamber of Commerce Records.

42. Minutes of Public Hearing, Public Buildings Committee, Joint Bond Commission, April 18, 1962, Rich Papers.

43. Joint Atlanta-Fulton County Bond Commission, "Report to the Mayor and Board of Aldermen," Atlanta, 1962, Rich Papers.

44. Everett Millican to Hamilton Douglas, March 20, 1962, Atlanta Bureau of Planning Papers.

45. Minutes of the Meeting of the Urban Renewal Committee, April 10, 1962, Joint Atlanta-Fulton Bond Commission, Atlanta Bureau of Planning Papers.

46. Ibid., April 20, 1962, Joint Atlanta-Fulton Bond Commission, Atlanta Bureau of Planning Papers.

47. "Minutes of the Meeting of the Roads, Streets and Highways Committee, Joint Atlanta-Fulton Bond Commission," April 9, 1962, Rich Papers.

48. Thomas H. Roberts to Richard H. Rich, April 11, 1962, Rich Papers; Burton Sparer to Richard H. Rich, April 12, 1962, Rich Papers.

49. Richard Rich to W. L. Ramsey (Confidential), April 16, 1962, Rich Papers.

50. Wyont Bean to Richard Rich, April 17, 1962, Rich Papers.

51. Uptown Association of Atlanta, "Uptown Ideas," Atlanta: January 1962, 12.

52. John A. White and G. Everett Millican to Richard Rich, April 16, 1962, Rich Papers.

53. Malcolm Jones to J. Arch Avery, June 4, 1962, Rich Papers.

54. Joint Atlanta-Fulton County Bond Commission, "Report to the Mayor and Board of Aldermen," Atlanta, 1962, Rich Papers.

55. Information on Piedmont Park Redevelopment Proposal, undated, Rich Papers.

56. Minutes of the Special Meeting of the Board of Directors, Atlanta Chamber of Commerce, June 27, 1962, Atlanta Chamber of Commerce Records.

57. Edward Banfield, *Big City Politics* (New York: Random House, 1965), 35.

58. Philip Weltner to Robert Woodruff, "Dear Bob," August 7, 1962, Woodruff Papers.

59. Cameron Fincher, "Atlanta Studies Its Bond Issue," Bureau of Business and Economic Research, Georgia State College, February 1963.

60. Citizens Bond Study Commission, "Report," January 1963, Hartsfield Papers.

61. Editorial, "Atlanta Has Earned Its Reputation, But It'll Be on the Line Wednesday," *Atlanta Constitution*, May 14, 1963.

62. Rod Spicer, "Stadium Next, Mayor Says," *Atlanta Constitution*, May 17, 1963.

63. On the conflict over the Buttermilk Bottom renewal project, see Clarence N. Stone, *Economic Growth and Neighborhood Discontent* (Chapel Hill: University of North Carolina Press, 1976), and Irene Holliman, "From Crackertown to Model City?" *Journal of Urban History* 35, 3 (March 2009): 369–86.

64. Ivan Allen, *Mayor*, p. 155. Furman Bisher provided his own account of the Finley visit and the site selection in *Miracle in Atlanta* (Cleveland: World Publishing, 1966), 15–17. Bisher notes that Finley was unimpressed with one potential site, at Lakewood Park. The following day, Bisher and the mayor drove Finley "past City Hall and the State Capitol . . . [to] the Washington—Rawson—Capitol Avenue area. . . . As it later turned out, Mayor Allen had stumbled on this plot as a likely stadium site only a few days before."

65. Ivan Allen to Robert W. Woodruff, May 22, 1963, Woodruff Papers.

66. The "shotgun marriage" term was used by architect and FABRAP partner Cecil Alexander, personal interview with the author, Atlanta, June 2009. Alexander was a close friend of Mayor Allen and had acted as his co-campaign manager in the 1961 race.

67. Minutes of the Board of Directors Meeting, Atlanta Chamber of Commerce, February 12, 1964, Atlanta Chamber of Commerce Records.

68. Ibid., August 12, 1964.

69. Ibid., September 9, 1964.

70. Atlanta Department of Planning, "Community Facilities, Comprehensive Plan Part 1," 1965.

71. Hammer and Company, "Air Rights Plaza," 1954, Rich Papers.

72. Hammer, Greene, Siler Associates, "Coliseum Hotel: Central Atlanta Air Rights," prepared for Cousins Properties Inc., March 1970, Hammer & Company Records.

73. Robert Bivens to Arthur Montgomery, July 14, 1969 and attachments, Cook Papers. University of Georgia. Central Atlanta Progress was formed in 1967 from the merger of the Central Atlanta Improvement Association and the Uptown Association.

74. Charles L. Davis to Sam Massell, February 17, 1970, Massell Papers.

75. Ibid.

76. Ibid.

77. Norma Day, Office of the Mayor, Notes on Meeting on June 26, 1970, Central Atlanta Progress Records.

78. Walter M. Mitchell Memo, December 10, 1970, Central Atlanta Progress Records.

79. Minutes of the Board of Directors Meeting, Atlanta Chamber of Commerce, December 11, 1970, Atlanta Chamber of Commerce Records.

80. Editorial, "The Coliseum," *Atlanta Journal*, December 15, 1970; and Jim Minter, "The Coliseum," *Atlanta Journal*, December 15, 1970.

81. "Coliseum Survives Racial Job Clash," *Atlanta Journal*, January 27, 1971.

82. On the history of the Atlanta Memorial (now Robert W. Woodruff) Arts Center, see Frederick Allen, *Atlanta Rising* (Atlanta: Longstreet Press, 1996), 8–30.

83. Hammer and Company, "Atlanta Sites," 29.

84. Collier Gladin Memo to Rodney [Cook], January 16, 1968, Cook Papers.

85. Oby T. Brewer to Rodney Cook, November 20, 1967, Cook Papers.

86. James Hurst to Howard Openshaw, February 21, 1968, Cook Papers.

87. Minutes of the executive committee, Atlanta Chamber of Commerce, February 6, 1970, Atlanta Chamber of Commerce Records.

88. Philip Hammer to Charles F. Palmer, August 5, 1970, Hammer Papers.

89. Hammer, Greene, Siler Associates, "Feasibility Study for an Intercontinental Congress Center, Atlanta, Georgia," October 1970, 1.

90. Ibid., 17.

91. Ibid., C-17.

92. Minutes of the executive committee, Atlanta Chamber of Commerce, May 7, 1971, Atlanta Chamber of Commerce Records.

93. Ibid., January 12, 1972.

94. "Site Near Omni Offered for Center," *Atlanta Journal*, August 30, 1972.

95. Jimmy Carter to Ernest Davis memo, October 27, 1972, Carter Gubernatorial Records.

96. Louis W. Truman to Gov. Jimmy Carter, "Study on World Congress Center by Outside Expert," October 31, 1972, Carter Gubernatorial Records.

97. Michael Egan to Charles Palmer and Eugene Holley letter, October 31, 1972, Carter Gubernatorial Records.

98. Dwyer report quoted in Site Selection Committee, Georgia World Congress Center Executive Board, "Minority Report," December 19, 1972, Carter Gubernatorial Records.

99. Ibid.

100. Margaret Shannon, "The Battle over Downtown Atlanta," *Atlanta Journal and Constitution Magazine*, July 22, 1979, 12.

101. On the site selection controversy, see Irene V. Holliman, "From Crackertown to the 'ATL': Race, Urban Renewal, and the Re-Making of Downtown Atlanta, 1945–2000," Ph.D. dissertation, University of Georgia, 2010, 186–204.

102. Bruce Galphin, "Atlanta's $35 Million Salesman," *Atlanta Magazine* 14, 9 (January 1975): 61.

103. David C. Petersen, *Convention Centers, Stadiums, and Arenas* (Washington, D.C.: Urban Land Institute, 1989), 86.

104. Philip Hammer to Ivan Allen, November 3, 1960 and attachments, Hammer Papers.

105. Floyd Hunter to Gordon W. Blackwell, "Re: Atlanta Study, Power Structure," November 27, 1950, Hunter Papers. On the earlier "Forward Atlanta" effort, see Dana F. White and Timothy J. Crimmins, "How Atlanta Grew: Cool Heads, Hot Air, and Hard Work," in Andrew M. Hamer ed., *Urban Atlanta: Redefining the Role of the City* (Atlanta: Georgia State University, 1980), 25–44.

106. Philip Hammer to Opie L. Shelton, executive vice president, Atlanta Chamber of Commerce, May 13, 1964, Hammer & Company Records.

107. Hammer, Greene, Siler Associates, "Coliseum Hotel: Central Atlanta Air Rights," prepared for Cousins Properties Inc., March 1970, Hammer & Company Records.

108. Alex Smith to Board of Directors, Central Atlanta Progress," December 1, 1967, Rich Papers.

109. Minutes, Board of Directors, Central Atlanta Progress, March 10, 1970, Rich Papers.

110. Central Atlanta Progress, "Central Atlanta: Opportunities and Responses," December 1971, 5.

111. Hammer, Greene, Siler Associates, "The Atlanta Economy: Prospects for the '70's," November 1970, 40–42, Hammer & Company Records.

112. Ibid., 44.

113. Harold Brockey to Mayor Maynard Jackson, September 16, 1974, Central Atlanta Progress Records. The Brockey letter mentioned "other business leaders and major downtown property owners," totaling "approximately fifty people," but did not name them.

114. Harold Brockey to Mayor Maynard H. Jackson, December 11, 1974, Central Atlanta Progress Records.

115. L. L. Gellerstedt, Jr., to A. H. Sterne, June 3, 1975, Central Atlanta Progress Records.

116. Presentation to Investor's Meeting, November 1975, Central Atlanta Progress Records.

117. Dan E. Sweat to [Busbee press secretary] Duane Riner, "Governor's Meeting, Thursday, November 6 at 7 p.m. . . . with Major Investors and CAP Executive Committee," November 3, 1975, Central Atlanta Progress Records.

118. Jim Galloway, "City, School Bond Measure is Voted Down, *Atlanta Journal and Constitution*, May 4, 1988; Douglas Blackmon, "Election '94-Bond Referendum," *Atlanta Journal and Constitution*, July 17, 1994.

119. Georgia World Congress Center Authority, Fiscal Year 1978–79 Annual Report.

120. Minutes of the Meeting of the Officers of Central Atlanta Progress, January 25, 1980, Central Atlanta Progress Internal Records.

121. Research Atlanta, "The Convention Industry in Atlanta," September 1982, 10.

122. Tom Walker, "Expanded WCC Needs to Do It Again," *Atlanta Journal and Constitution*, April 26, 1985; Scott Thurston, "2nd Expansion of Convention Hall Proposed," *Atlanta Journal and Constitution*, March 6, 1987.

123. See Jim Auchmutey, "Raising Underground," *Atlanta Journal and Constitution*, June 28, 1987. On the history of Underground, see Newman, *Southern Hospitality*, 177–79.

124. Frederick Allen, *Atlanta Rising*, 217–18.

125. Dan Sweat to James Rouse, June 1981, Central Atlanta Progress Records.

126. James Rouse to Dan Sweat, June 25, 1981 Central Atlanta Progress Records.

127. Thomas Cousins to Dan Sweat, February 22, 1982, Central Atlanta Progress Records.

128. See Urban Land Institute, "Underground Atlanta," *ULI Project Reference File* 21, 12 (July–September 1991), and David L. Sjoquist and Loren Williams, "The Underground Atlanta Project: An Economic Analysis," Research Paper 28, Policy Research Center, College of Business Administration, Georgia State University, July 1992.

129. Maria Saporta, "Underground: From Dream to Reality," *Atlanta Journal and Constitution*, June 11, 1989. See also David Sawicki, "The Festival Marketplace as Public Policy," *Journal of the American Planning Association* 55, 3 (1989): 347–61.

130. Atlanta Downtown Development Authority, "Underground Atlanta Project Variable Rate Refunding Bonds Series 2002, Official Statement," July 2002. "Why Not Sell Underground Atlanta," *Atlanta Sunday Paper*, May 4, 2010. See also "Atlanta Losing Millions on 75-Year Underground Lease," WSB-TV, February 13, 2013.

131. Richard Hyatt, *Mr. Speaker: The Biography of Tom Murphy* (Macon, Ga.: Mercer University Press, 1999), 185.

132. R. W. Scherer to Thomas Murphy, January 16, 1985, Central Atlanta Progress Records.

133. Tom Walker, "WCCC Area Suggested for Domed Stadium," *Atlanta Journal and Constitution*, April 2, 1985.

134. Minutes of the Meeting of the Board of Directors of Central Atlanta Progress, March 24, 1988, Central Atlanta Progress Internal Records.

135. Author's interview with Tom Cousins, July 31, 2009, author's possession.

136. Philip Hammer to Ivan Allen, November 3, 1960, Hammer Papers.

137. Hammer, Greene, Siler Associates, "Coliseum Hotel: Central Atlanta Air Rights," prepared for Cousins Properties Inc., March 1970, 35, Hammer & Company Records.

138. Hammer and Company, "Air Rights Plaza," Rich Papers.

139. Sallye Salter, "Pope & Land Studying Downtown Proposal," *Atlanta Journal and Constitution*, November 18, 1985.

140. State of Georgia and City of Atlanta, "Proposal for the Demonstration of the Atlanta Downtown People Mover," June 1976, 28.

141. Ibid., 51.

142. Ernie Suggs, "Feds Open Up Funding for Atlanta Streetcar Project," *Atlanta Journal and Constitution*, July 15, 2011. Atlanta Mayor Shirley Franklin established a "Peachtree Corridor Task Force" in 2005 with the goal of transforming Peachtree Street, choosing as co-chairs Tom Bell (Chairman & CEO of Cousins Properties) and Egbert Perry (Chairman & CEO of developer The Integral Group). The group's 2007 report called for "investing more than almost $1 billion in the streetcar, streetscape, and other investments for the entire Corridor [that] will generate additional incremental economic growth in the Corridor." Peachtree Corridor Task Force, "Final Report," March 2007, 37.

143. Central Atlanta Progress, "The Green Line/Downtown Atlanta," 2007, 2.

144. Central Atlanta Progress, "Economic Impact Analysis of the Downtown Green Line Vision Plan and Georgia Multi-modal Passenger Terminal: Summary Report," January 2012. The report concluded that the proposed multimodal terminal would "Increase investment in Downtown Atlanta by nearly $3.1 billion," among its impacts.

145. Floyd Hunter to Gordon W. Blackwell, "Re: Atlanta Study, Power Structure," November 27, 1950, Hunter Papers.

146. Floyd Hunter, "Spalding Interview," n.d., 5–6.

147. Philip Hammer to Richard Rich, June 12, 1952, Rich Papers

148. Minutes of Executive Committee Meeting, Atlanta Chamber of Commerce, February 18, 1959, Atlanta Chamber of Commerce Records.

149. Ivan Allen to Robert W. Woodruff, May 22, 1963, Woodruff Papers.

150. Atlanta Chamber of Commerce, "A Report by the Long Range Planning Committee to the Board of Directors, Atlanta Chamber of Commerce," April 1965, 6, Atlanta Chamber of Commerce Records.

151. Sallye Salter, "Dueling Developers Next Battle Will Be On Peachtree Street," *Atlanta Journal and Constitution*, July 17, 1988.

152. Minutes, Board of Directors, Central Atlanta Progress, May 10, 1970, Central Atlanta Progress Records; Central Atlanta Progress Inc., "Central Atlanta Opportunities and Responses," [Central Atlanta Study], December 1971, n.p.

153. Minutes of the Meeting of the Executive Committee of Central Atlanta Progress, Inc., February 24, 1990, Central Atlanta Progress Internal Records.

154. Chris Burritt, "City Officials Push Rich's as Federal Offices," *Atlanta Journal and Constitution*, July 20, 1991.

155. Sallye Salter, "Space for Federal Workers," *Atlanta Journal and Constitution*, July 30, 1992.

156. James B. Carson, Jr., "Will A New Federal Center Save Downtown?—No," *Atlanta Journal and Constitution*, August 23, 1992.

157. Maria Saporta, "Political Moves Could Determine Five Points' Fate," *Atlanta Journal and Constitution*, October 10, 1992; Minutes of the Meeting of the Executive Committee, Central Atlanta Progress, August 27, 1992, Central Atlanta Progress Records Internal Records.

158. Maria Saporta, "Woodruff Grant Breaks Deadlock on Tower Deal," *Atlanta Journal and Constitution*, December 5, 1992.

159. Minutes of the Meeting of the Executive Committee, Central Atlanta Progress, July 15, 1993, Central Atlanta Progress Records Internal Records.

160. Minutes of the Meeting of the Board of Directors, Central Atlanta Progress, December 15, 1993, Central Atlanta Progress Internal Records.

161. Jeanne Cummings, "Preparing for '96 Olympics—Congress Center Expansion Urged," *Atlanta Journal and Constitution*, January 9, 1991, and Editorial, "Make Room for Bigger Conventions," *Atlanta Journal and Constitution*, November 5, 1996.

162. Richard Hyatt, *Mr. Speaker*, 242. In a 1988 oral history interview, Tom Murphy said, "I could never understand why anybody would be against the World Congress Center because everybody conceded to start with that it would generate way more than enough money to pay the debt service. . . . And then, on top of that, I think I said in that debate that Atlanta is not only the capital city of Georgia, it is the economic capital of the entire Southeast." Clifford Kuhn, "Interview with Tom Murphy," Georgia Government Documentation Project, Georgia State University, May 5, 1988, Special Collections, Pullen Library, Georgia State University.

Chapter 8. St. Louis: Protection from Erosion

1. Arthur Schwarz to A. J. Cervantes, March 8, 1966, Cervantes Papers.

2. A consultant study of development opportunities on the north side of the downtown core in December 1963 had suggested "major convention facilities" in the area. Larry Smith & Co., "St. Louis Missouri: North Side Downtown Redevelopment Opportunities," December 1963, vii.

3. Gordon L. Hopper to Arthur F. Schwarz, July 12, 1966, Downtown St. Louis Inc. Records.

4. Schwarz & Van Hoefen Architects, "A Study for a Union Station Convention Center," prepared for the Terminal Railroad Association of St. Louis, June 1966, 4.

5. Ibid., 6-7.

6. "Approval of New $1,500,000 Bond Issue, With No Tax Increase Needed, Would Doom the City's No. 1 Eyesore," *St. Louis Globe-Democrat*, March 8, 1953. On the Allegheny Conference, see Roy Lubove, *Twentieth Century Pittsburgh* (Pittsburgh: University of Pittsburgh Press, 1996), and Sherrie Mershon, "Corporate Social Responsibility and Urban Revitalization: The Allegheny Conference on Community Development," Ph.D. dissertation, Carnegie Mellon University, November 2000.

7. Harry Wilensky, "Civic Progress Inc.: Twenty St. Louisans Leading the Way," *St. Louis Post-Dispatch*, June 19, 1955.

8. Minutes of the meeting of Civic Progress, November 5, 1953, Tucker Papers.

9. Ibid., April 27, 1954, Tucker Papers. Newton Farr was a member of the executive committee of the Chicago Central Area Committee and had been president of the Greater North Michigan Avenue Association. Consultant Larry Smith regularly advised retail and shopping center developers and business groups such as Baltimore's Greater Baltimore Committee.

10. Urban Land Institute, "Downtown St. Louis—A Panel Study, October 11-15, 1954," 9, 31.

11. Ibid., 31.

12. Minutes of the meeting of Civic Progress Inc., November 14, 1958, Tucker Papers.

13. St. Louis Redevelopment Authority, "1974 Annual Report," 7.

14. Minutes of the meeting of Civic Progress Inc., December 22, 1958, Tucker Papers.

15. L. J. Sverdrup to James P. Hickok, First National Bank in St. Louis, January 9, 1959, Sverdrup Papers.

16. Ibid., September 2, 1959, Sverdrup Papers.

17. Sverdrup & Parcel, "Feasibility Report, Proposed Downtown Sports Stadium Project," September 1959, 1, 4, Kinsley Papers.

18. Donald Janson, "St. Louis to Have Nation's Tallest Monument," *New York Times*, July 28, 1963.

19. James Millstone, "Arch Symbolizes Hope in St. Louis," *New York Times*, January 6, 1964.

20. For the history of "Riverfront Square," see Brian Burnes, Robert W. Butler, and Dan Viets, *Walt Disney's Missouri* (Kansas City: Kansas City Star Books, 2002), 140-51.

21. Economics Research Associates, "The Economic Potentials of Riverfront Square," August 1963, 24, 30.

22. Donn B. Tatum to O. O. McCracken, August 30, 1963, attached to O. O. McCracken to Knox Banner, September 11, 1963, Downtown Progress Inc. [Washington, D.C.] Records; Harrison "Buzz" Price, *Walt's Revolution by the Numbers* (Orlando: Ripley Entertainment, 2003), 59; and "Disneyland-Type Center for St. Louis Planned by Disney Productions," *Wall Street Journal*, June 19, 1964.

23. "Plan for a Disneyland in Downtown St. Louis Is Said to be Canceled," *Wall Street Journal*, July 9, 1965.

24. "St. Louis Shows Interest in Fair's Spanish Pavilion," *New York Times*, October 28, 1965.

25. Civic Progress Inc., "For Immediate Release," January 4, 1966, Cervantes Papers.

26. Economics Research Associates, "Economic Parameters of Locating the Spanish Pavilion in St. Louis, Missouri," March 1966, II-1 and III-2.

27. Ibid., I-6.

28. Minutes of the meeting of Civic Progress Inc., April 3, 1967, Cervantes Papers.

29. J. Anthony Lukas, "New York World's Fair Hit Turns Into St. Louis Fiasco," *New York Times*, June 30, 1970. Buzz Price's memoir, *Walt's Revolution by the Numbers*, mentions the Spanish Pavilion and its failure, but fails to note his own study or forecasts.

30. St. Louis City Plan Commission, "A Public Building Group Plan for St. Louis," September 1919, 14, and St. Louis City Plan Commission, "Saint Louis After World War II," December 1942, 29.

31. On the city's urban renewal efforts, see Joseph Heathcott and Máire Agnes Murphy, "Corridors of Flight, Zones of Renewal: Industry, Planning, and Policy in the Making of Metropolitan St. Louis, 1940-1980," *Journal of Urban History* 31, 2 (January 2005): 151-89, and Colin Gordon, *Mapping Decline: St. Louis and the Fate of the American City* (Philadelphia: University of Pennsylvania Press, 2008).

32. St. Louis City Plan Commission, "Comprehensive City Plan," January 1947, 28-30; St. Louis City Plan Commission, "Rebuilding Industry-Commerce in St. Louis," April 1953, n.p.

33. Howard F. Baer, *St. Louis to Me* (St. Louis: Hawthorn, 1978), 79.

34. Minutes of the meeting of Civic Progress, Inc., June 26, 1967, Cervantes Papers. Pulitzer's *Post-Dispatch* had long editorialized against demolition of the Old Post Office.

35. Ibid., 12.

36. Mayor A. J. Cervantes to Harrison Price, ERA, July 11, 1967, Cervantes Papers.

37. Minutes of the meeting of Civic Progress, Inc., October 1967, Cervantes Papers.

38. ERA, "Economic Feasibility of a Convention and Exhibition Center in St. Louis," May 31, 1968, II-2, Cervantes Papers.

39. Ibid., VI-8.

40. Ibid., VII-15.

41. A. J. Cervantes to Fred Cochrane, April 4, 1968, Cervantes Papers.

42. J. H. Sharp to A. J. Cervantes, May 10, 1968, Cervantes Papers.

43. Harold McKenzie to A. J. Cervantes, May 15, 1968, Cervantes Papers.

44. Fred Cochrane to Alfonso J. Cervantes, June 12, 1968, Cervantes Papers.

45. ERA, "Feasibility of a Convention Center Complex in St. Louis," October 10, 1968, II-1 and II-20, Cervantes Papers.

46. Larry Smith & Company, "St. Louis, Missouri North Side Downtown Redevelopment Opportunities," prepared for Downtown St. Louis, Inc., December 1963, iii.

47. Civic Progress Inc., "June 1967 to September 1968," September 23, 1968 attachment to letter from Frederic M. Pierce, Cervantes Papers.

48. "Memorandum for File: Meeting on the Federal Building Requirements," September 24, 1968, Sverdrup Papers.

49. L. J. Sverdrup to Earl Lund, October 1968, Sverdrup Papers.

50. B. R. Smith, "DeSoto-Carr Renewal Project," October 16, 1969, Sverdrup Papers.

51. Smith's memo to Sverdrup noted they had received a copy of the May 1968 ERA report from Gordon Hopper of Downtown St. Louis Inc. The mayor insisted to Sverdrup the report was confidential.

52. Mayor A. J. Cervantes to Edwin S. Jones, October 30, 1968, Sverdrup Papers.

53. E. A. Chamberlain to L. J. Sverdrup, "Subject: Project Description," November 25, 1968, Sverdrup Papers.

54. Minutes of the Meeting of the executive committee, Chamber of Commerce of Metropolitan St. Louis, November 27, 1968, St. Louis Chamber of Commerce Records.

55. "$60,000,000 Downtown Convention Plaza Proposed," *St. Louis Post-Dispatch*, January 28, 1969; Editorial, "New Plan for Downtown," *St. Louis Post-Dispatch*, January 28, 1969.

56. Editorial, "Bold Twin-Plan for Downtown," *St. Louis Globe-Democrat*, January 29, 1969.

57. Sverdrup & Parcel and Associates, "Convention Plaza Redevelopment Proposal," January 1969, 2, 3, and 13, Sverdrup Papers.

58. Irving Edison to A. J. Cervantes, January 30, 1969, Cervantes Papers.

59. Mayor to Irving Edison, February 4, 1969; Irving Edison to A. J. Cervantes, February 5, 1969, Cervantes Papers.

60. Mayor to Fred Cochrane, March 24, 1969, Cervantes Papers.

61. B. R. Smith, "Memorandum for the Record," January 31, 1969, Sverdrup Papers.

62. "Group Formed to Present Convention Center Plan," *St. Louis Post-Dispatch*, April 1, 1969.

63. Editorial, "Convention Plaza," *St. Louis Post-Dispatch*, April 3, 1969.

64. William L. Behan, Convention Facilities Committee, "TO the Executive Committee, Chamber of Commerce of Metropolitan St. Louis," April 9, 1969, St. Louis Chamber of Commerce Records.

65. B. R. Smith to L. J. Sverdrup, "Convention Plaza Redevelopment Group," April 4, 1969, Sverdrup Papers.

66. "Convention Plaza Redevelopment Group Luncheon," May 1, 1969, Sverdrup Papers.

67. George D. Millay to Fred J. Cochrane, June 30, 1969, Cervantes Papers.

68. "Mayor Favors Near North Side Convention Site," *St. Louis Globe-Democrat*, July 18, 1969; Charles B. Edison to The Honorable Alfonso J. Cervantes, July 24, 1969, Cervantes Papers.

69. Minutes of meeting of board of directors, Downtown St. Louis Inc., August 22, 1969, Downtown St. Louis Inc. Records.

70. John Graham and Company, "Development Plan: Retail Core Area, St. Louis Central Business District," July 1970, Cervantes Papers and "St. Louis Group Proposes $95.3 Million Area Renewal," *Wall Street Journal*, October 13, 1970.

71. “TO the Executive Committee, Chamber of Commerce of Metropolitan St. Louis,” April 9, 1969, St. Louis Chamber of Commerce Records.

72. Minutes of the Third Meeting of the Convention Plaza Redevelopment Group, October 17, 1969, Sverdrup Papers.

73. Minutes of the Meeting of Civic Progress Inc., February 27, 1967, Cervantes Papers.

74. Mayor A. J. Cervantes to L. J. Sverdrup, January 27, 1970, Sverdrup Papers.

75. B. R. Smith to Donald Lasater, Mercantile Trust Company, April 29, 1970, Sverdrup Papers.

76. “Notes on Meeting Regarding Convention Center,” June 25, 1970, Cervantes Papers.

77. L. J. Sverdrup, “Memorandum for Record,” July 31, 1970, Sverdrup Papers.

78. Weintraub & Associates, “Convention Center Bond Issue Campaign Outline,” Cervantes Papers.

79. Minutes of the meeting of Civic Progress Inc., December 28, 1970, Cervantes Papers.

80. “Statement in Regard to the ‘Smile’ Campaign (To be made on Thursday, February 25),” Sverdrup Papers

81. Al to LJS, “Jack, we are getting this comment frequently,” February 23, 1971, Sverdrup Papers.

82. Minutes of the meeting of Civic Progress Inc., March 1971, Cervantes Papers.

83. For ward voting data, see Ernest Calloway, “A Political Primer and Voting Behavior of the St. Louis Black Community,” January 1973, Calloway Papers.

84. B. R. Smith, “Memorandum for Record: Financing of the Convention Plaza,” March 17, 1971, Sverdrup Papers.

85. B. R. Smith to L. J. Sverdrup, “Convention Center,” June 20, 1972, Sverdrup Papers.

86. Minutes of the meeting of Civic Progress Inc. (at the Racquet Club), September 25, 1972, Cervantes Papers.

87. Donald Lasater to the Members of Civic Progress, Inc., October 20, 1972, Sverdrup Papers.

88. “Remarks by Mayor Alfonso J. Cervantes,” October 6, 1972, Cervantes Papers.

89. Agenda for the meeting of Civic Progress, November 27, 1972, and minutes of the meeting of Civic Progress Inc., November 27, 1972, Cervantes Papers.

90. Minutes of the meeting of Civic Progress, Inc., November 25, 1974, Poelker Papers.

91. Laventhol Krekstein Horwath & Horwath, “Feasibility Study for Proposed 300-Room Motor Hotel, St. Louis, Missouri,” March 1973, 24, 30.

92. Minutes, Civic Progress Meeting, November 20, 1978 (at the University Club), Conway Papers.

93. Edward Faltermayer, “How St. Louis Turned Less into More,” *Fortune*, December 23, 1985.

94. See Nathan A. Rauh, “Past Conditions for Future Use: The Adaptive Reuse of St. Louis Union Station,” M. Arch. thesis, Texas Tech University, December 1997.

95. Minutes of the meeting of Civic Progress Inc., November 27, 1972, Cervantes Papers.

96. St. Louis City Planning Commission, “A Public Building Group Plan for St. Louis,” 1919; St. Louis City Planning Commission, “St. Louis After World War II,” 1942; St. Louis City Plan Commission, “Comprehensive City Plan,” 1947.

97. Urban Land Institute, “Downtown St. Louis—A Panel Study, October 11-15, 1954,” 9.

98. ERA, “Economic Parameters of Locating the Spanish Pavilion in St. Louis, Missouri,” March 1966, III-1.

99. "Remarks by Mayor Alfonso J. Cervantes, Civic Progress Inc. annual dinner meeting," June 18, 1968, Cervantes Papers.

100. At the same time in mid-1972 as Civic Progress was backing the convention center vote, it was also supporting and financing the campaign for a $730 million statewide transportation bond issue. See minutes of the meeting of Civic Progress Inc., June 26, 1972, Cervantes Papers.

101. Governmental Research Institute, "Economic Benefits to St. Louis of the Proposed Convention Hall and Plaza," January 1971.

102. Editorial, "On with the Center," *St. Louis Post-Dispatch*, November 8, 1972.

103. Minutes of the meeting of Civic Progress, November 5, 1953, Tucker Papers.

104. David S. Jackson and Ellie McGrath, "St. Louis Sings the Blues," *Time*, May 4, 1981. See also James Neal Primm, *Lion of the Valley*, 2nd ed. (Boulder: Pruett, 1990), 531-35.

105. Minutes of the Civic Progress meeting, August 31,1981, Schoemehl Papers.

106. E. R. Shipp, "Rebound from Long Decline is Seen in St. Louis," *New York Times*, February 2, 1985.

107. Laventhol & Horwath, "Operational Analysis, Kiel Auditorium and Cervantes Convention Center, Phase III Progress Meeting," June 11, 1984, Schoemehl Papers.

108. Minutes of the Cervantes Convention Center Commission Meeting, August 12, 1981, Schoemehl Papers.

109. Marie Jeffries to John J. Temporiti, "Convention Center-November 16, 1981," Schoemehl Papers.

110. On the hospital controversy and the larger Schoemehl mayoralty, see Lana Stein, *St. Louis Politics: The Triumph of Tradition* (St. Louis: Missouri Historical Society Press, 2002), chap. 9.

111. Mayor to Jill McGuire, October 26, 1983, Schoemehl Papers; Vincent J. Bommarito to the Honorable Vincent C. Schoemehl, January 13, 1984, Schoemehl Papers.

112. Laventhol & Horwath to Mr. Vincent Bommarito, November 8, 1993, Schoemehl Papers.

113. Stephen P. Mullin, Budget Director to Jill McGuire, Mayor's Office, October 27, 1983, Schoemehl Papers.

114. Laventhol & Horwath, "Operational Analysis, Kiel Auditorium and Cervantes Convention Center, Phase III Progress Meeting," June 11, 1984; Laventhol & Horwath, "Analysis of Operations of Kiel Auditorium and Cervantes Convention Center," July 1984, Schoemehl Papers.

115. TJM to VCS, October 12, 1984; Vincent J. Bommarito to Mr. Tom Mangona [sic], January 2, 1985, Schoemehl Papers.

116. Schoemehl clearly viewed the center expansion as critical in boosting downtown, and downtown as crucial to the city's finances: "I think all of us assume a very significant level of impact from recent downtown development and overall downtown employment on the tax base of the city. I would like to see this quantified." VCS to Susie Roach, "Financial Planning for the City," February 5, 1985, Schoemehl Papers.

117. VCS to Bruce Sommer, February 12, 1985, Schoemehl Papers.

118. Bruce T. Sommer to Mayor Vincent Schoemehl, "Response to Mayor's Request of February 12, 1985," Schoemehl Papers.

119. Sommer's figures for the "150" largest tradeshows can be compared to the actual performance of the successor "200." For 1991, exhibit space use came to 51 million square feet. But attendance was well under his projection, at 3.9 million. The total attendance for 2008 came to just 4.56 million—still below Sommer's 4.9 million forecast. The 2009 total was 3.84 million—the last year the "200" were counted.

120. VCS to Deb Patterson, "New Stadium," April 22, 1985, Schoemehl Papers.

121. Bruce T. Sommer to Members of the Board of Estimate and Apportionment, April 2, 1985, Schoemehl Papers: "The results of this study are needed as soon as possible so the City can consider taking the required steps to keep us in a competitive position and to fully realize the potentials and benefits from the rapidly growing hospitality industry throughout the county."

122. Charles H. Johnson IV to Bruce Sommer, March 25, 1985, Schoemehl Papers.

123. David A. Paul, Public Financial Management to Stephen Mullin, May 16, 1985, Schoemehl Papers.

124. Gerald Eskenazi, "City Reportedly Seeking N.F.L. Cardinals for Shea," *New York Times*, February 9, 1985.

125. VCS to Tom Mangogna, "Performing Arts Center," February 5, 1985, Schoemehl Papers.

126. VCS to Deb Patterson, "New Stadium," April 22, 1985, Schoemehl Papers.

127. Ibid., 3.

128. Reporting to the mayor on a meeting with the Laventhol team, Frank Hamsher said "Brice Smith [of Sverdrup] has apparently told Bruce Sommer and L&H in no uncertain terms that any expansion of the Convention Center should occur within the Convention Center redevelopment area or perhaps north (into Columbus Square), and that he would not support any move south toward the heart of downtown." Hamsher to Mayor, August 14, 1985, Schoemehl Papers.

129. Minutes of the Civic Progress Meeting, July 22, 1985, Schoemehl Papers; "For Immediate Release," Civic Progress Inc., July 22, 1985, Schoemehl Papers.

130. Laventhol & Horwath, "Cervantes Convention Center Expansion Analysis, St. Louis Missouri," October 1985, II-1, V-11, Table V-2.

131. Laventhol & Horwath, "Cervantes Convention Center Expansion Analysis, St. Louis Missouri," November 1985.

132. Ibid., II-11, IX-1, IX-2.

133. Shipp, "Rebound from Long Decline"; Faltermayer, "How St. Louis Turned Less into More."

134. Frank Hamsher to Mayor, "Fall Schedule/Planning," September 5, 1985, Schoemehl Papers.

135. VCS to TJM, Patterson, "RE: Convention Center Expansion," January 20, 1986, Schoemehl Papers.

136. Minutes of Civic Progress Meeting (at the University Club), January 27, 1986, Schoemehl Papers.

137. Revenue Committee for the Cervantes Convention Center Expansion Project to Mayor Vincent C. Schoemehl, Jr., April 24, 1986, Schoemehl Papers.

138. "For Release," Civic Progress Inc., April 18, 1986, Schoemehl Papers.

139. "For Immediate Release, Office of the Mayor, May 12, 1986," Schoemehl Papers.

140. Minutes of the Civic Progress Meeting, (at the Bogey Club), September 22, 1986, Schoemehl Papers.

141. "Stadium," [in Mayor Schoemehl's handwriting], undated, Schoemehl Papers.

142. VCS to Al Fulvio, "Dome Development," May 12, 1986, Schoemehl Papers.

143. "For Immediate Release, Office of the Mayor, May 12, 1986," Schoemehl Papers.

144. Laventhol & Horwath, "Preliminary Market Analysis, Financial Projections, and Estimated Economic Impacts for an Enclosed Football Stadium/Arena," Draft as of July 23, 1986, Schoemehl Papers; Laventhol & Horwath to Al Fulvio, August 15, 1986, and attachment "Summary of Enclosed Stadium Option," Schoemehl Papers.

145. Office of the Mayor, "For Immediate Release," August 29, 1986, Schoemehl Papers.

146. Minutes of the meeting of Civic Progress Executive Committee (at the Bogey Club), December 23, 1986, Schoemehl Papers.

147. Vince Schoemehl to Don Brandin, "RE: Downtown Stadium," December 2, 1986, Schoemehl Papers.

148. "To: Mayor Vincent C. Schoemehl, From: Stephen P. Mullin, Subject: CVC Project," December 5, 1986, Schoemehl Papers.

149. Karen Koman and Margaret Gillerman, "Mayor Wants County, State In on Projects," *St. Louis Post-Dispatch*, December 19, 1986.

150. Minutes, Civic Progress Meeting, January 19, 1987 (at the Bogey Club), Schoemehl Papers.

151. A January 1987 staff memo asked, "What will activate community and galvanize community behind Convention Center/Stadium plan now?" and answered, "Massive public relations effort," Bidwell's "positive endorsement," and "Endorsement by Civic Progress and other leadership." "Football Cardinals Options: Confidential," January 24, 1987, Schoemehl Papers.

152. Alfred J. Fulvio to Vincent C. Schoemehl, "Summary of Stadium/Cervantes Center Expansion Recommendations," April 20, 1987; Prell Organization, "Voter Attitudes Towards Convention Center Expansion and Indoor Stadium Construction, Prepared for Mayor Vincent C. Schoemehl, Jr.," May 1987, 1, Schoemehl Papers.

153. Prell Organization, "Voter Attitudes," 6, 9.

154. Editorial, "Onward with Convention Center," *St. Louis Post-Dispatch*, June 26, 1987.

155. Vincent Schoemehl Letter, July 8, 1987, Schoemehl Papers.

156. Bruce Sommer to Vincent Schoemehl and Alfred Fulvio, "Memorandum, Status of Convention Center Expansion," June 29, 1987, Schoemehl Papers.

157. Ibid.

158. Lisa Richter to Vincent C. Schoemehl, "Analysis of August 20, 1987 Focus Groups on Convention Center Ballot Issues," August 25, 1987, Schoemehl Papers.

159. Minutes of the Meeting of the Civic Progress Action Committee, August 24, 1987, Schoemehl Papers.

160. Vincent Cunnetto, "Commentary," *St. Louis Post-Dispatch*, October 25, 1987; "Two Questions on November 3 Ballot," *St. Louis Post-Dispatch*, October 28, 1987.

161. Mark Schlinkman, "Participants Assess Blame for Loss of Team," *St. Louis Post-Dispatch*, January 17, 1988; William E. Cornelius and Charles F. Knight, Civic Progress to Pete Rozelle, NFL, January 30, 1988, Schoemehl Papers.

162. Editorial, "The Cardinals Leave St. Louis," *St. Louis Post-Dispatch*, January 17, 1988.

163. Minutes, Civic Progress Meeting, March 28, 1988, Schoemehl Papers. For Knight and his business colleagues, keeping St. Louis a "big league city" was the central purpose for investing in a new stadium. But the logic of the stadium's use as a convention venue—the "additional convention business" it would bring—was vital in selling the public funding for a new football stadium to a governor and state legislators less enthralled with St. Louis and the NFL.

164. Gene McNary to "St. Louis Leaders," May 20, 1988, Schoemehl Papers; Margaret Gillerman and Mark Schlinkman, "McNary Renewing Talk of Stadium, Sources Say," *St. Louis Post-Dispatch*, June 29, 1988.

165. Minutes, Civic Progress Meeting, July 25, 1988, Schoemehl Papers.

166. Ibid., January 23, 1989, Schoemehl Papers; "McNary Plan for County Stadium Dead," *St. Louis Post-Dispatch*, February 24, 1989.

167. Mike Reilly, "Governor was Skeptical But Backed Stadium Bill," *St. Louis Post-Dispatch*, June 24, 1990.

168. Minutes, Civic Progress Meeting, November 27, 1989, Schoemehl Papers.

169. Milt to VCS, December 11, 1989, Schoemehl Papers.

170. "City Officials Rule Out April for Vote on Tax for Stadium," *St. Louis Post-Dispatch*, January 20, 1992.

171. Charlene Prost, "Officials Here Reveling in New Center," *St. Louis Post-Dispatch*, May 7, 1993.

172. Laventhol & Horwath, "Market Study for a Proposed Downtown Convention Headquarters Hotel," September 1989.

173. Lisa Brown, "St. Louis Centre: Take 3," *St. Louis Business Journal*, May 7, 2010.

174. "AJCCC Expansion Team Plans," May 28, 1986, Schoemehl Papers.

175. Bruce T. Sommer to Mayor Vincent Schoemehl, "Response to Mayor's Request of February 12, 1985," Schoemehl Papers.

176. "To: Mayor Vincent C. Schoemehl, From: Stephen P. Mullin, Subject: CVC Project," December 5, 1986, Schoemehl Papers.

177. "Cervantes Convention Center Expansion: Going South," 1988, Schoemehl Papers.

178. E. F. Porter, "Schoemehl Confident in Downtown Plan," *St. Louis Post-Dispatch*, August 6, 1989. Laclede's Landing is an area of hotels, restaurants, and night clubs in the nineteenth-century warehouse district along the Mississippi River, just blocks from America's Center.

179. "Memorandum; JoAnne to Mayor, Subject: Tomorrow's Meeting with Stadium Bankers," March 26, 1991, Schoemehl Papers. LaSala referenced Coopers & Lybrand, "Report on the Expansion of the Cervantes Convention Center," February 1991.

180. "VCS to Tom Mangogna, Continuing Construction Activity," February 5, 1985, Schoemehl Papers.

181. Charles H. Johnson to Bruce Sommer, March 25, 1985, Schoemehl Papers.

182. Campbell Design Group, "Convention Center Expansion Study, City of St. Louis," November 1985, 47, Schoemehl Papers.

183. Laventhol & Horwath, "Market Study for a Proposed Downtown Convention Headquarters Hotel, St. Louis, Missouri," September 1989, 49-50, 52.

184. Coopers & Lybrand, "Report on the Expansion of the Cervantes Convention Center," February 1991.

185. KPMG Peat Marwick, "Cervantes Convention Center and Stadium Complex Financial Projection, Final Draft Report," April 1991, Schoemehl Papers.

186. VCS to Tom Mangogna, "Performing Arts Center," February 5, 1985, Schoemehl Papers.

187. Minutes of the Executive Committee Planning and Budget Meeting for 1988, Civic Progress, November 4, 1987, Schoemehl Papers; "The New Performing Arts Center," Schoemehl Papers.

188. Minutes, Executive Committee Planning and Budget Meeting for 1988, Civic Progress, November 4, 1987, 6, Schoemehl Papers.

189. Minutes, Civic Progress Board Meeting, November 23, 1987, Schoemehl Papers.

190. "Vince Schoemehl to Walter Metcalfe, August 2, 1988," with handwritten notes "To VCS From WLM 8/12/88 Response," Schoemehl Papers.

191. "To Mayor Vincent Schoemehl from LaSala, Mullin, Sommer, Subject New Arena, May 10, 1988," Schoemehl Papers.

192. Tim O'Neil, "Union Station Landlord Weighs Overhaul of Kiel," *St. Louis Post-Dispatch*, May 6, 1988.

193. Judith VanderWater, "Union Station—Still Short of—Making Profit," *St. Louis Post-Dispatch*, February 6, 1989.

194. Mayor to Fred Kuhlmann, June 19, 1989, Schoemehl Papers.

195. Tim O'Neil and Charlene Prost, "Plan Calls for Arena at Kiel," *St. Louis Post-Dispatch*, October 30, 1990; Minutes, Civic Progress Meeting (at the Bogey Club), November 26, 1990, Schoemehl Papers. At the same meeting, the group discussed plans for an Olympic Festival in 1994 or 1995, the continuing development of the Midtown cultural and performing arts district, and fundraising for the area's arts council.

196. Minutes, Civic Progress Meeting, March 26, 1984, Schoemehl Papers.

197. Ibid., June 25, 1984, Schoemehl Papers.

198. Civic Progress also provided the principal source of financing for the 1987 campaign to support the convention center expansion taxes. Nancy Rice to Mayor, "Civic Progress," August 10, 1987, Schoemehl Papers.

199. "Development (Grace)," n.d., Schoemehl Papers.

200. Bill Kuehling to Mayor, January 1989, Schoemehl Papers; Agenda, Civic Progress Action Committee Meeting, February 27, 1989. Schoemehl sought $150,000 from Civic Progress for the tax campaign.

201. Minutes, Civic Progress Meeting, December 18, 1989 (At the Bogey Club), Schoemehl Papers.

202. JoAnne LaSala to Milt Svetanics, Chris Grace, Lynn Edwards, "Subject: Civic Progress Support of Gateway Dome/NFL Partnership and Arena," July 13, 1989, Schoemehl Papers.

203. See Jeannette Batz Cooperman, "Dinner at the Club, Darling?," *St. Louis Magazine*, June 2006. Civic Progress elected its first black member in 1997. See Tom Uhlenbrock, "Civic Progress Gets First Black Member," *St. Louis Post-Dispatch*, November 26, 1997.

204. Minutes, Annual Planning Meeting of Civic Progress Executive Committee, January 9, 1984, Schoemehl Papers.

205. "Recommended Priorities," 1992 Annual Planning Meeting, Civic Progress Executive Committee, n.d., Schoemehl Papers.

206. Meeting of Civic Progress Executive Committee, December 23, 1986, Schoemehl Papers.

207. Minutes, Civic Progress Meeting, January 19, 1987, Schoemehl Papers.

208. Ibid., March 28, 1988, Schoemehl Papers.

209. Ibid., December 18, 1989, Schoemehl Papers.

210. Agenda, Civic Progress Action Committee Meeting, January 22, 1990, Schoemehl Papers.

211. Ibid.

212. Minutes, Civic Progress Meeting, February 28, 2000, [at the Bogey Club], Harmon Papers.

213. Minutes, Kiel Center Project Report, Civic Progress Meeting, October 22, 1990, Schoemehl Papers.

214. "St. Louis Downtown Development Action Plan: Executive Summary," June 1999, n.p.

215. As one measure of the persistence of downtown development efforts, the scheme to deck over the highway gained renewed impetus in the mid-2000s, with former Senator John Danforth joining a group of local nonprofit organizations in pressing for reconnecting the Arch grounds to

the downtown. See Danforth Foundation, "Riverfront Development and the Arch Connector: A Report to the Mayor," 2005, and Jake Wagman, "One City Icon Takes on Another," *St. Louis Post-Dispatch*, May 18, 2008. In 2012 the Missouri state legislature approved a plan for a local option sales tax for park purposes that could provide funding for the deck and Arch ground improvements. The tax was approved by both city and county voters in April 2013. David Hunn. "Steady Turnout Pushes Arch-Parks Tax to Win in City and County," *St. Louis Post-Dispatch*, April 3, 2013.

216. "Development Meeting with the Mayor: Proposed Baseball Stadium Discussion," April 27, 2000, Harmon Papers.

Conclusion. The Cities Business Builds

1. Minutes of the meeting of Civic Progress, November 5, 1953, Tucker Papers.

2. Minutes of Meeting at the Chicago Club, Fort Dearborn Project, March 24, 1954, Fort Dearborn Project Records.

3. Hammer and Co., "Action at the Core," June 1959, Foreword; "Report of the Long Range Planning Committee to the Board of Directors, Atlanta Chamber of Commerce," April 1965, Atlanta Chamber of Commerce Records.

4. Minutes of the meeting of Civic Progress Inc., December 22, 1958, Tucker Papers.

5. Minutes, Civic Progress Meeting, June 26, 1967, Cervantes Papers.

6. Ibid., March 28, 1988, Schoemehl Papers

7. Civic Progress Economic Development Committee, "Options for New Action," November 11, 1992; Minutes, Civic Progress Meeting, February 28, 2000, [at the Bogey Club], Harmon Papers.

8. Mayor Clarence Harmon, "Presentation, Civic Progress Regionalism Committee Meeting," February 20, 2001, Harmon Papers.

9. Meeting in the Board Room of the Chicago Land Clearance Commission, May 6, 1954, Fort Dearborn Project Records.

10. Hammer and Company, "Atlanta Sites: A Report on Locations for Key Civic Projects in Atlanta, Georgia," November 1960, 34, Rich Papers.

11. B. R. Smith, "DeSoto-Carr Renewal Project," October 16, 1969, Sverdrup Papers.

12. "Informational Summary, Proposed Convention/Sport Area Complex," n.d., Downtown Progress Inc. Records; Editorial, "Build the Convention Center," *New York Times*, May 27, 1977.

13. John R. Logan and Harvey L. Molotch, *Urban Fortunes* (Berkeley: University of California Press, 1987), 50-51, 65.

14. Clarence N. Stone, *Regime Politics: Governing Atlanta, 1946-1988* (Lawrence: University Press of Kansas, 1989), 169.

15. Floyd Hunter to Gordon W. Blackwell, "Atlanta Study, Power Structure," November 27, 1950, Hunter Papers.

16. Hammer's analysis explicitly compared the absence of a plan or planning effort in Atlanta to "spectacular central developments in New York, Pittsburgh, Chicago, Cleveland, Detroit, St. Louis and Philadelphia." See "A Plan for Downtown Atlanta," 3.

17. Clayton Kirkpatrick, "Outline Vast Civic Center!" *Chicago Tribune*, March 17, 1954.

18. Minutes of the meeting of the Fort Dearborn Project sponsors, March 24, 1954, Fort Dearborn Project Records.

19. Earl Kribben to Henry Sell, December 21, 1955, Fort Dearborn Project Records.

20. Frederick T. Aschman, "The Rebuilding of the Near-North and Near-South Sides of the Chicago Central Area," April 1957, Fort Dearborn Project Records.

21. Stone, *Regime Politics*, 60.

22. Sverdrup and Parcel, "Feasibility Report: Proposed Downtown Sports Stadium Project," 1959, 8, Kinsley Papers.

23. Vince Schoemehl to Don Brandin, "RE: Downtown Stadium," December 2, 1986, Schoemehl Papers.

24. "To: Mayor Vincent C. Schoemehl, From: Stephen P. Mullin, Subject: CVC Project," December 5, 1986, Schoemehl Papers.

25. Arthur Schwarz to A. J. Cervantes, March 8, 1966, Cervantes Papers.

26. Wayne King, "Atlanta's Confident Hope Is Faltering," *New York Times,* October 7, 1974.

27. Minutes of the Meeting of the Board of Directors, Central Atlanta Progress, December 15, 1993, Central Atlanta Progress Internal Records.

28. Robert A. Dahl, *Who Governs? Democracy and Power in an American City* (New Haven, Conn.: Yale University Press, 1961), 1.

29. Nelson W. Polsby, *Community Power and Political Theory* (New Haven: Yale University Press, 1963), 117.

30. Minutes of the Executive Committee Planning and Budget Meeting for 1988, Civic Progress, November 4, 1987, Schoemehl Papers.

31. "Report on the February 22, 1999 Civic Progress Meeting," February 26, 1999, Harmon Papers.

Index

Acknowledgments

This book is the product of a research effort over a great many years involving a large number of communities. Along the way, I have relied on the information, interest, and support of many people, well beyond the small number I can acknowledge and thank here.

My efforts to examine the realities of convention center performance began with the support of Boston's Pioneer Institute in the late 1990s, and Gabriella Mrad and Charlie Chieppo, then of the Pioneer staff. Nathan Glazer encouraged my further work on the topic. Edward "Ned" Hill, now Dean of the Levin College of Urban Affairs at Cleveland State University, provided enormous encouragement and valuable feedback that resulted in the publication of "Space Available: Convention Centers as Economic Development Strategy" by the Brookings Institution in early 2005. My effort to understand the politics of convention center projects was also aided by a number of dedicated local officials willing to question orthodoxy and consultant forecasts, including Emily Evans and Mike Jameson in Nashville, Steve Kozachik in Tucson, and Kiefer Mitchell in Baltimore.

It would not have been possible to study consultant forecasts and actual center performance without the aid of the dedicated interlibrary loan staffs at Trinity University and the University of Texas at San Antonio. Their efforts, and those of countless librarians at university and public libraries around the country, made it possible to review often forgotten public documents.

The case studies of Chicago, Atlanta, and St. Louis that comprise the second part of the book reflect the talents and dedication of a number of archivists. In St. Louis, Carole Prietto then at Washington University introduced me to the wonders of the university's collection of mayoral papers. Sonya Rooney and her staff were also magnificently helpful in making Washington University's resources accessible. At the University of Missouri—St. Louis, Zelli Fischetti, Ken Thomas, and the staff of the Western Historical

Manuscript Collection both made their collections accessible and provided their own unique insights and observations.

The wonderful resources of the Manuscript, Archives, and Rare Book Library at Emory University made is possible for me to understand Atlanta's development in an entirely new way. The staff and resources of the Atlanta History Center were just as accommodating and invaluable. Other librarians and archivists at the Georgia State University, and the Georgia State Archives helped make my research possible, particularly Mary Linnemann at the Hargrett Library of the University of Georgia.

Urban historians have long been reliant on the collections of the Chicago Historical Society and the commitment of their staff, and I join them in my thanks. The archival collections at the University of Illinois at Chicago aided my initial efforts to understand Chicago's business leadership, and the University of Chicago's Special Collections Research Center provided a final, invaluable capstone.

Colleagues Amy Bridges, Bill Domhoff, Cindy Horan, Marc Levine, Harvey Newman, and Bob Whelan read portions of the manuscript and provided their counsel. At Penn Press, Bob Lockhart saw the value in this effort, and shaped it into a far more focused and polished work.